LAW EVERY NURSE SHOULD KNOW FIFTH EDITION

HELEN CREIGHTON,
R.N., M.S.N., J.D., D. Litt., F.A.A.N.

Distinguished Professor of Nursing, School of Nursing,
University of Wisconsin-Milwaukee, Milwaukee, Wisconsin

W.B. SAUNDERS COMPANY   1986

Philadelphia □ London □ Toronto □ Mexico City
Rio de Janiero □ Sydney □ Tokyo □ Hong Kong

W. B. Saunders Company: West Washington Square
                          Philadelphia, PA 19105

Library of Congress Cataloging in Publication Data

Creighton, Helen.

   Law every nurse should know.

   Includes bibliographical references and index.

   1. Nursing—Law and legislation—United States.   2.
Nursing—Law and legislation—Canada.   I. Title.
[DNLM: 1. Jurisprudence—Canada—nurses' instruc-
tion.   2. Jurisprudence—United States—nurses' in-
struction.   3. Legislation, Nursing—Canada.   4.
Legislation, Nursing—United States.   WY 33 AA1
C9L]

KF2915.N8C7 1986   344.73'0414   85–22183

ISBN 0–7216–1833–2   347.304414

ISBN 0–7216–1832–4 (pbk.)

Editor: Dudley Kay
Developmental Editor: Alan Sorkowitz
Designer: Bill Donnelly
Production Manager: Bill Preston
Manuscript Editor: David Prout
Indexer: Doris Holmes

Law Every Nurse Should Know

Hardcover ISBN 0–7216–1833–2
Softcover ISBN 0–7216–1832–4

Last digit is the print number: 9   8   7   6   5   4   3   2   1

PREFACE

In an era that gives great emphasis to the legal rights of people, the fifth edition of this handbook presents nurses with the basic facts of a wide variety of legal topics in a concise and nontechnical manner. This edition contains 35 percent new material in addition to the Appendix. The purpose is to acquaint nurses with their rights and duties at law so they will conduct themselves at work with more ease and comfort. The right to practice as a registered professional nurse with or without specialization or as a practical/vocational nurse means more to someone who understands the purpose and problems of licensure and the value of certification.

This material has been completely rewritten in the light of recent developments and cases. Nurses who know their contractual rights, duties and remedies are likely to make better, and breach fewer, contracts. Recent as well as older cases involving nurses in negligence and torts show how such problems can and do arise. The ways in which suits originate for such wrongs as assault and battery, false imprisonment, invasion of privacy and defamation of character are illustrated. Such crimes, great and small, that a nurse seems most likely to encounter are presented.

A new chapter dealing with some legal and ethical problems has been added. In vitro fertilization, artificial insemination, surrogate mothers, wrongful birth, wrongful life, Baby Doe cases, terminating life support, organ transplants and the legal aspects of end-stage renal disease and DRGs are covered. To facilitate the work of both undergraduate or graduate students and that of inservice educators and nurses wanting more information on topics, an extensive list of up-to-date references is provided at the end of each chapter. These references are useful and timesaving for those who need additional material and have limited time to review available literature.

Appreciation is expressed to *Nursing Management* and its current editor Leah Curtin for permission to reprint in this book and in its Appendix articles and extracts of articles originally appearing in that magazine.

Any person who writes a book is indebted to others for a great deal of useful assistance and encouragement. In particular, I wish to express my appreciation to my parents, including Mrs. Helen Miller Creighton Reitz who continues to have a sharp, clear mind and lives an active life, for their many sacrifices on my behalf, for the memory of a happy home where life was valued, education encouraged and learning and ethics esteemed. Much credit for encouragement, advice, proofreading and beneficial discussion of current nursing legal problems is due to Catherine Armington, my colleague; and I wish to thank her for all the help and happiness she adds to day-to-day life. For keeping me physically in good working order, I am grateful to Dr. James D. Cox, Professor and Director of

Division of Therapeutic Radiology, and Dr. James M. Cerletty, Associate Professor and Director of Training, Medical College of Wisconsin, Milwaukee. For their prayers and support to the many unnamed Daughters of Charity throughout the world and to the Carmelites of Lafayette, Louisiana. I thank all the thousands of nurses who have attended my seminars, workshops and classes for their questions and encouragement. In addition, I thank Joshua Anderson for serving as my answer to Ponce de Leon's quest.

The faithful guard service of Damn Dog, our Airedale, is acknowledged.

Appreciation is expressed to Mrs. Joan Cincotta for her expert typing of the manuscript and to Mrs. Jean Greve for her expert typing of many articles utilized in *Nursing Management* and the book.

I thank Dr. Norma Lang, Dean of the School of Nursing at the University of Wisconsin–Milwaukee for her encouragement and support in teaching, research and writing. I also wish to thank Dr. Helen Swain, Chairperson of Foundations of Nursing Department, and Mrs. Ellen Murphy, M.S., J.D., CNOR, for sharing material and for encouragement.

Finally, I thank Mr. Dudley Kay, Publisher, Nursing and Allied Health at W. B. Saunders Co., for his kindness and encouragement in the work of updating this book. I also appreciate the interest and work of David Prout, copy editor at W. B. Saunders Co.

HELEN CREIGHTON
2614 North Bartlett
Milwaukee, Wisconsin 53211

CONTENTS

One
LAW AND
SOCIETY

ORIGIN OF LAW: DEFINITION AND SOURCES

The earliest notion of law was not a declaration or decree of a legislative or executive agency. In the early ages, law was the pronouncement of the king or some other ruler, acting according to what was thought to be his "divine right." A body of law developed from an accumulation of judgments arising from particular cases. This practice of building a system of rules and sanctions by the accumulation of case-to-case decisions has remained to this day the unique characteristic of Anglo-American jurisprudence. The body of case law that developed from the adjudications of kings, and later of judges, is known as "the common law." The common law, or judge-made law, is to be contrasted with that emanating from legislative bodies such as Parliament, Congress or city councils; the latter is civil law, also known as "positive law." The law in force today in the United States is a combination of both the common law and legislation, the latter increasing in importance and quantity each year.

The fundamental principles that have guided the growth of American law had their origin in England. As already noted, the king asserted absolute power to dictate the standards of social conduct among his subjects. This power was steadily diminished by demands of influential nobles that the judgment of the monarch be guided by the customs and traditions of his people. Indeed, certain areas of life were placed beyond the reach of the Crown. In 1215 the famous *Magna Charta* was granted by King John of England, and came to be known as the foundation of English constitutional liberty. This landmark in the struggle of human freedom is significant in that it placed effective restraints upon the exercise of governmental power and, at the same time, secured the personal liberty of the subject and his rights to property. Thus, law has a dual function: to confirm certain rights and privileges in the person with means for their enforcement, and to provide a framework of government, together with its powers and restrictions upon the exercise of those powers.

According to Durkheim, law provides a synthetic expression of cultural values. In his opinion, the legal specification of cultural values contributed to social solidarity, for in simple societies criminal law defined and heightened community boundaries, whereas in complex societies the civil law resolved the normative strains created by the division of labor.[1] Weber viewed law as a constructed artifact shaped by the values and interests of particular legal functionaries.[2]

Definition of Law

A workable definition of the term "law" would be: those standards of human conduct established and enforced by the authority of an organized society through its government. Law is not synonymous with custom, although custom plays an important role in creating and enforcing law. Indeed, there are areas of life wherein custom is a much more powerful dictate of human conduct than is the law enforced by the state. However, the point to be emphasized is that there is no law, in the sense in which the term is used here, apart from a government that ordains and enforces the command.

Sources of Law

Statutory law is that law enacted by a legislative body, such as Congress. After enactment, Federal laws are published in the *United States Statutes at Large*. The original copy of the act, with the President's signature, is filed or deposited with the government agency responsible for its administration or enforcement. For example, a pure food law is administered by the Department of Agriculture; a law relating to the national parks is sent to the Department of the Interior. For acts of state legislatures, copies are deposited with the secretary of state of that state. Municipal ordinances are deposited with local authorities. The public generally receives notice of legislation from the daily press and other communication media.

Decisional law is the law announced when courts rule on cases brought before them.

LEVELS OF GOVERNMENT—LAW

The three levels of government in the United States, federal, state and local, are created by law and in turn exercise powers derived from law. Thus, it is said that Americans live under a "government of law, not of men." This means that, before the government may act, it must find some authority for that act in law. The law may take the form of a constitution, a statute, an administrative regulation or a court decision interpreting these forms of law. Hence, the expression "law of the land" means that every citizen shall hold his life, liberty, property and immunities under the protection of general rules that govern society. Furthermore, these rights may not be properly infringed upon unless there has been a proceeding conforming to the law, that is to say, a hearing and inquiry before judgment is rendered at trial.

Federal

The highest form of law in the United States is the Constitution. The Federal Constitution is known as the "organic law"; that is to say, it is law that defines or establishes the very organization of the government. The Constitution provides for the framework of the Federal Government in establishing the three branches, Legislative, Executive and Judicial. The instrument also clothes these branches of government with powers to act, and at the same time places restraints upon the exercise of those powers.

State

In addition to the Federal Government, every state has a constitution. A significant difference in function should be noted: namely, the only powers that the Federal Government enjoys are derived from the positive grants of powers of the Federal Constitution, whereas the state governments enjoy plenary powers subject only to the limitations of the state constitutions, the limitations upon states found in the Federal Constitution and those limitations necessary for the operation of the federal system.

The U.S. Supreme Court ruled that a Federal trial court could not authorize state officials to comply with state law on confinement of mentally retarded patients in a state institution. The Supreme Court ruled that the Eleventh Amendment barred suits against states unless they consented to suit. The Court said that the Eleventh Amendment prohibited the Federal courts from ordering state officials to conform their conduct to state law. The principle of sovereign immunity was a constitutional limitation of the power of Federal courts under the Constitution.[3]

Local and City

Lastly, local governments are creatures of the states that created them, and may exercise only those powers conferred upon them.

TYPES OF LAW

Statutory Law

When Congress exercises the legislative powers conferred by the Federal Constitution, its enactments are known as "statutory law." When a state legislature enacts a law, it is similarly described. Publications containing statutes are referred to as "codes." Thus, the Federal statutes are contained in the United States Code, and those of the various states are contained in similar compilations. The products of law-making power by a city council is known as a "city ordinance."

Administrative Law

Since the turn of the century another branch of public law has become of great importance, that is, administrative law. One may readily understand that when Congress or a state legislature desires to enact a program of regulation of business, or a program to confer benefits upon its citizens, it is difficult for the legislature to foresee the variations necessary for the proper execution of the law. The legislature lacks the time and energy to include all the many details likely to arise when the law is put into operation. The legislature, by way of providing for these eventualities, establishes an administrative agency clothed with power to make rules and regulations that have the force of law. The administrative agencies may also issue orders that have the effect of a court order to take care of violations of its rules and regulations. Actions of the agencies are appealable to the courts. The Interstate Commerce Commission on the Federal level and a bureau of conservation on a state level are examples of administrative agencies.

Public Law

In the preceding paragraph the term "public law" was used. *Public law* is that branch of law concerned with the state in its political capacity, and includes, as noted, constitutional and administrative law. The relationship of the individual or individuals to the state is included in public law, the most striking example of which occurs in enforcement of criminal law.

Criminal Law. Most particularly, *criminal law* deals with acts of offenses against the welfare or safety of the public.

Private Law. By contrast, *private law* refers to that part of the law that is administered between citizen and citizen, or is concerned with the enforcement of rights, duties and other legal relations involving private individuals. Matters of contract law, negligence and agent-principal dealings are areas of private law.

Equity

While the common law system of justice was developing in England, another field of jurisdiction, known as "equity," was growing up beside it. When the application of the civil law became too harsh or when there was no adequate remedy in the common law to satisfy the needs of a petitioner, an appeal was taken to the king. The appeal was made to "conscience," that is to say, to the king's innate sense of justice and right. If the king were convinced that an exception to the common law should be made in the case before him, he would so order. Gradually, separate tribunals were set up, known as "courts of chancery" (because the king appointed a substitute, known as a "chancellor," to hear such matters) or "courts of equity." Equity developed its own set of principles, rules and precedents, and when these clashed with their counterparts in the common law courts, equity was held to prevail. Equity, it was said, acted in accordance with the spirit, not the letter, of the law. It continues to play an important role in the operation of the American judicial system.

STRUCTURE OF AMERICAN GOVERNMENT

The functioning of any system of law is affected by the form of government. The countries of the world today are organized according to either a unitary (also known as "centralized") or a federal form of government. In a unitary state, all governmental powers are vested in the central government, as provided in its constitution, and no subdivisions exist as independent political units. The central government may allocate certain functions to subsidiary units, but such functions are exercised solely by the grace and sufferance of the central power. The United Kingdom, France, Belgium and many other European countries are unitary states. In a federal system the people are not placed under a single governement endowed with full powers exercised from one center. There is a spatial or territoral division of governmental power between the central, or national, government and the constituent units. In the United States, the constituent units are known as "states," in Canada as "provinces" and in Switzerland as "cantons." All these countries and many more are federal in form. The powers of government are divided, some exclusively exercised by the federal or national government, and others exclusively exercised by the state governments.

Powers of Federal and State Governments

The significant fact to note in a federal form of government is that the constituent units are separate and, to a considerable extent, independent political powers. Under the Federal Constitution, the states retain for themselves all powers not specifically conferred upon the Federal Government. Because of the division of governmental power among various jurisdictions within a federal system, laws differ from state to state. Moreover, since there are two sovereigns in a federal system, a conviction under the laws of one (say, the Federal Government) does not preclude a conviction under the laws of the other (state) for the same offense. Finally, some powers may be exercised by both the federal and the state governments, which are called "concurrent powers."

Doctrine of Separation of Powers. The sovereign powers in the United States are divided not only according to territory, that is, federalized, but also internally. This internal division of power is referred to as the "doctrine of separation of powers." Recalling the evils of absolutism in the English experience, the founders of the American government were guided by the truism that "power corrupts and absolute power corrupts absolutely." They believed that one person or one branch of the governement should not enjoy all the power, but that it should be divided so that one branch could serve as a check upon another.

Legislative, Administrative, Judiciary. Consequently, the lawmaking power is conferred upon the Congress, but the Executive can veto legislation, and the Judiciary is empowered to review legislation. Likewise, Congress can withhold funds from, and investigate, the Executive and control the appellate jurisdiction of the federal courts.

Subdivisions of States

As was noted in a preceding paragraph, the third level of government in the United States, municipalities, arises from the power of states to create political subdivisions. These units of local government include counties, cities, towns, townships, boroughs and villages. The designation of a local community may not be indicative of its size. That is to say, there are townships with populations larger than some cities, but since the township has not been chartered by the state as a city it may not use the latter designation. States confer powers upon their subdivisions to make local laws or ordinances, which are operative only within the geographical boundaries of the local communities. Although the Federal Government is powerless to abolish a state by its own act, a state may rescind a charter it had granted to a city and govern the city directly from the state capital. There is no provision in the Federal Constitution about the relationship between the states and their subdivisions.

Courts

Courts are agencies established by the government to decide disputes arising in litigation. The term "court" may be used in another sense as referring to the person or persons hearing the case. More particularly, the court may consist of the judge, the magistrate or the justice. At trials, usually only one judge sits; when cases are taken to courts of appeal, more than one judge hears the appeal.

Types of Courts: Criminal, Civil, Probate. The kind of court in which a case is brought depends on the offense or complaint involved. For example, the proceeding is handled in a criminal court if it involves a traffic violation or the unlawful killing of a person. A claim for damages, by contrast, is a dispute as to the legal rights and duties of individuals in relation to each other, and is known as a "civil action." Actions concerning wills or the estates of decedents are known as "probate proceedings" and, as civil cases, may be heard in courts of general jurisdiction or, in some states, in courts known as "surrogate" or "orphans courts."

Jurisdiction of Courts. There are certain legal principles that guide courts in deciding disputes. First, the court must have jurisdiction over the person or thing involved. This means that the proceeding is commenced in a court in the locality in which the defendant resides or may be served with a summons, or in which the property is situated.

The United States District Courts have original jurisdiction over admiralty cases, bankruptcy cases, postal and banking law cases and crimes involving Federal laws or those committed on the high seas. In addition, they have jurisdiction over cases involving a question of the Constitution, a treaty, a Federal law, or a lawsuit between citizens of different states or between the United States and a state if the amount involved is not in excess of $3000.

The Supreme Court of the United States has original jurisdiction over cases involving ambassadors, public ministers and consuls, and in lawsuits in which the state is a party and the amount involved is over $3000. However, the bulk of its work consists of hearing appeals from the decisions of the circuit court of appeals. A case that involves a constitutional question may be heard directly from the United States District Courts. Cases from state courts that involve the United States Constitution or the constitutionality of any state or Federal law may be brought to the Supreme Court either directly or on appeal.

With our increasingly complex social and economic systems and the explo sion of knowledge in all fields, it is not possible to include within the statutes sufficient detail to cover adequately all situations that may arise in the practical application of the intent of the law. Therefore, the Government has established on a statutory basis a large and ever-increasing number of Federal administrative agencies for the purpose of implementing the intent of legislation. The administrative agency has the power and responsibility to make whatever rules, regulations and standards are necessary to carry out the purpose of the law. However, such powers and responsibilities must be in conformity with existing laws. Several examples of Federal administrative agencies are the Federal Trade Commission, the Social Security Board, the Federal Communications Commission, the National Labor Relations Board and the Interstate Commerce Commission.

The United States is immune from suit unless Congress gives authority otherwise, such as by a private bill device in an individual case of by an act such as The Federal Tort Claims Act. Moreover, the state, which is also a sovereign body, may not be sued without its own consent.

In most states there are county courts that try both civil and criminal cases arising within the county. Usually, there is a limit on the amount of money damages that can be sought in this court.

In villages, towns and rural areas there are Justice of the Peace Courts. These are a part of the state judicial system and may hear civil cases involving small sums of money, try those charged with misdemeanors and conduct a preliminary examination of those accused of felonies.

Generally, state superior courts have only appellate jurisdiction. They are variously called, in different states, "circuit courts," "supreme courts," "district courts" or "courts of common pleas."

Every state has a final court of appeals. Again, its name varies from state to state. It is often called the "Supreme Court," but it may also be known as the "Supreme Court of Errors," the "Court of Appeals" or the "Supreme Judicial Court."

State legislatures, following the pattern of the Federal Government, have created a variety of boards, commissions and administrative agencies to deal with much of the work. Their proceedings are informal, and they are not bound by the rules of evidence. Two examples of such agencies are the Public Service Commission and the Workmen's Compensation Board.

A nursing student filed a suit in a county court for $25,000 in damages for breach of contract against a state regional university. The student claimed to be prevented from obtaining credentials for a nursing degree because of the failure of the university to obtain proper certification for its nursing program. The appellate court in Michigan ruled that all claims for monetary damages against a state instrumentality were under the exclusive jurisdiction of the Court of Claims.[4]

Principle of Stare Decisis. The second principle by which courts are guided is known as *stare decisis*, which is to say, "the previous decision stands." When a previous case involving similar facts has been decided in the jurisdiction, the court will be strongly inclined to follow the principle of law laid down in that prior adjudication. Unless precedents are carefully regarded and adhered to, uncertainty would be both perplexing and prejudicial to the public. However, when the precedent is out of date or inapplicable to the case before the court, the principle of *stare decisis* will not be followed and the court will announce a new rule. The doctrine of *stare decisis* is a salutary one and should not ordinarily be departed from when a decision is of long standing and rights have been acquired under it, unless considerations of public policy so demand.[5]

Recording of Law. Judicial opinions of Federal and state appellate courts are published, but those of trial courts are generally unavailable in this form. By an elaborate system of references and indexes, the many thousands of decisions are kept up-to-date for research and current use.

References

1. Cartwright, B. C., and Schwartz, R. D.: The Invocation of Legal Norms: An Empirical Investigation of Durkheim and Weber. Am. Sociol. Rev., 38:340, 341, June 1973.
2. Ibid., p. 342.
3. Pennhurst State School and Hospital v. Halderman, 104 S.Ct. 900 (U.S. S.Ct. 1984); Citation, 49:56, June 15, 1984.
4. Pacquin v. Northern Michigan University, 262 N.W. 2d 672 (Mich. Ct. of App., 1977). Citation, 37:94, Aug. 1, 1978.
5. Black, H. C.: Black's Law Dictionary, 4th ed. St. Paul, West Publishing Co., 1951, pp. 1577–1578.

General References

Annas, G. J.: How to Find the Law, Nurs. Law Ethics 1(10):5, Dec. 1980.
Mancini, M.: Laws, Regulations and Policies. Am. J. Nurs., 78:681–684, April 1978.

Two
THE PRACTICE
OF NURSING

LICENSURE

Definition

In general, a license is a legal document that permits a person to offer his or her special skills and knowledge to the public in a particular jurisdiction, where such practice would otherwise be unlawful without a license. A license to nurse is granted by the appropriate authority to applicants or candidates who have fulfilled certain established requirements. Such a license permits nurses to practice their profession within the state and gives them the privilege of representing themselves as licensed nurses. A registered nurse has the additional privilege of using the abbreviation "R.N." after his or her name. The rules for licensing have been created by statutes, and in the application of the law there must be no discrimination, improper pressure or arbitrary action. In a case in which applicants failed to show that they had applied within the required time, attended approved schools and gained the requisite experience demanded by the law, applications for licensing as practical and professional nurses without examination were denied.[1]

Purpose

The words "for the protection of the public" explain the reason behind the efforts of nursing, both professional and practical, to require licensure for all nurses by the states wherein they practice.

Exceeding the limits of one's license increases the chance of liability for the nurse and the employer. There was a case in which a practical nurse in a doctor's office administered a polio booster injection to a small child, who suddenly moved; the needle was broken off in the right buttock and, despite surgery, was not located and removed for some months. The parents sued both nurse and doctor for negligence. The trial court exonerated the nurse and doctor but an appellate court reversed the decision, pointing out that under state law only a professional registered nurse may inoculate patients and that the trial judge had failed to so instruct the jury. In addition, the appellate court criticized the lower

8

court for allowing "highly prejudicial" testimony that it was the "custom and practice" in the community for practical nurses to give inoculations, since the practice was contrary to published public policy.[3]

This scope-of-practice problem applies not only to practical nurses but also to some professional nurses who at times take on the duties of pharmacists and others during the night hours, on weekends and so forth. Furthermore, the modern clinical specialist, the occupational health nurse, the school nurse, the public health nurse and other professional nurse practitioners need to review their work periodically in the light of the scope of practice encompassed by their license.

Permissive Licensure

To differentiate mandatory and permissive licensure, the following operational definitions were developed.[4]

> A *mandatory* act requires that anyone who practices nursing according to the definition of the practice that appears in the law must be licensed, the only exceptions being: (1) furnishing nursing assistance in an emergency, (2) practice by student nurses incidental to their course of study, (3) employees of the federal government.*
>
> In a *permissive* act, the titles "registered nurse" and "licensed practical nurse" are protected. The practice of either level of nursing is not prohibited in a permissive act, but an unlicensed person is not entitled to represent himself as an "RN" or an "LPN."† In other words, anyone may, whether licensed or not, practice nursing as long as the unlicensed individual does not call himself an RN or an LPN.

Mandatory Licensure

Licensing laws control the practice of all who nurse "for hire." According to the Boards of Nursing the following jurisdictions have mandatory licensing for R.N.'s and for L.P./V.N.'s: Alabama, Alaska, Arizona, Arkansas, Colorado, Connecticut, Delaware, Florida, Georgia, Guam, Hawaii, Idaho, Illinois, Indiana, Iowa, Kansas, Kentucky, Louisiana, Maine, Maryland, Massachusetts, Michigan, Minnesota, Mississippi, Missouri, Montana, Nebraska, Nevada, New Hampshire, New Jersey, New Mexico, New York, North Carolina, North Dakota, Ohio, Oregon, Pennsylvania, Puerto Rico, Rhode Island, South Carolina, South Dakota, Tennessee, Utah, Vermont, Virgin Islands, Virginia, Washington, West Virginia and Wyoming. The following have a mandatory law for R.N.'s and a permissive law for L.P./V.N.'s: California and Wisconsin. The following states or jurisdictions have a permissive law for both the R.N. and the L.P./V.N.: District of Columbia, Oklahoma and Texas. A mandatory law, though restrictive, does permit relatives or friends to assist others during illness without being penalized by the law. If we believe that only people with certain basic professional education and experience are qualified to carry out professional nursing functions, we must make certain that the laws of our state require all those who perform these functions to meet these standards.

---

*Nurses in the armed forces or those employed by the Federal Government, often subject to transfer, must hold a current state license but not necessarily from the state to which they are assigned.

†L.P.N. is interchangeable with L.V.N. (licensed vocational nurse), which is preferred in some states, e.g., Texas and California.

The National Council Licensure Examination

The detailed test plans for NCLEX-RN and NCLEX-PN determine the examination content that an entry-level practitioner must know in order to be judged minimally competent. Two articles on Developing, Constructing and Scoring the National Council Licensure Examination are found in *Issues* published by the National Council of State Boards of Nursing.[5]

Not only do the various jurisdictions require nurses to obtain a license to practice, but in some states they must also keep their registration up-to-date by re-registering.

Revocation

Nurses who violate specific norms of conduct, such as securing a license by fraud, performance of specific actions prohibited by the Nursing Practice Act, unprofessional or illegal conduct, malpractice and abuse of alcohol or drugs, may have their licenses suspended or revoked by the licensing board in all states. Typically, suspension and revocation proceedings are administrative. To ensure due process, nurses must be notified of the charges in definite terms, so they may prepare a defense. A hearing also must be held at which the nurse is allowed to present evidence.

A private duty nurse, while on duty at a hospital, tampered with tubexes pre-filled with the narcotic Demerol and altered records concerning her administration of Demerol to a patient. After a hearing conducted by the State Board of Nurse Examiners, her license was suspended for a year.[6] In another case, a staff nurse, while assigned to the infant medical and surgical ward, restarted an infiltrated intravenous infusion on an infant in violation of hospital policy and was suspended for three days. Later she forged a physician's name to a patient's medication chart in order to obtain penicillin for a fellow worker and was discharged. Although she obtained employment at another hospital and was promoted to supervisor, her license was suspended for a year.[7] In a third case, a nurse was reprimanded after administering an anesthetic in the absence of a directing physician and in violation of a regulation of the Board of Nurse Examiners.[8]

All violations of the Nursing Practice Act should be reported to the executive secretary of the state board of nurse examiners or similar professional licensing and enforcement groups. The report should include the complete facts of the alleged violation, including the name, time, date and place.

When there has been substantial evidence that a practitioner practiced illegally after her or his license was revoked, the court has upheld the Licensing Board's refusal to restore the license.[9]

In a Connecticut case, a nurse was charged with diverting Demerol to her own use when she charted its administration to a patient. The nurse signed a statement admitting guilt and that she had done the same on a previous occasion. After a hearing before the Board, her license was revoked for failing to adhere to acceptable standards of practice.[10]

In Florida, a registered nurse's license was revoked on a finding of unprofessional conduct in failing to properly chart administration of drugs, in taking a telephone order from a physician for a controlled narcotic with no signed order slip and in sleeping on duty. The nurse waived her rights to an administrative hearing before the Florida Board. A Pennsylvania trial court ruled that the

Pennsylvania State Board of Examiners did not violate her due process right in revoking her license on the basis of revocation in another state.[11]

The Oregon Supreme Court upheld the State Board of Nursing[12] in the revocation of Fern Ward's license, finding that there was substantial evidence that she violated the standard of the profession—in particular, a statute that makes it unlawful for an unlicensed person to misrepresent himself as a licensed professional nurse. The statute also makes it a crime to aid and abet any criminal act. The State Board of Nursing had charged Fern Ward with employing her daughter Karen Ryan as a registered nurse, allowing her to carry out the duties of a registered nurse in both the Oregon City Nursing Home and the Gladstone Convalescent Hospital and recommending her for employment as a registered nurse at the Hillhaven Nursing Home and Hearthstone Convalescent Center. Ward knew or had reason to know that Ryan was not a registered nurse and that such acts were conduct derogatory to the morals and standards of professional nursing.

PROFESSIONAL NURSING PRACTICE

In the United States, each Nursing Practice Act contains a legal definition of nursing practice delineating the area of practice which the law seeks to regulate. It will define "nursing practice," "registered nursing" or "professional nursing," and it is followed by a definition of "practical nursing." La Bar in a 1984 monograph has collected the statutory definitions of nursing practice and analyzed their conformity to certain ANA principles.[13]

Suggested Definition

The suggested definition of professional nursing practice is:

> The practice of nursing means the performance for compensation of professional services requiring substantial specialized knowledge of the biological, physical, behavioral, psychological, and sociological sciences and of nursing theory as the basis for assessment, diagnosis, planning, intervention, and evaluation in the promotion and maintenance of health; the casefinding and management of illness, injury, or infirmity; the restoration of optimum function; or the achievement of a dignified death. Nursing practice includes but is not limited to administration, teaching, counseling, supervision, delegation, and evaluation of practice and execution of the medical regimen, including the administration of medications and treatments prescribed by any person authorized by state law to prescribe. Each registered nurse is directly accountable and responsible to the consumer for the quality of nursing care rendered.

As La Bar states, the definition of nursing practice should be written in terms broad enough to permit flexibility and utilization of nursing personnel, with accountability vested in the professional nurse. Also, the definition should recognize the breadth and depth of educational preparation to justify placing overall responsibility for nursing services in the judgment of the registered nurse. Finally, she states that it is the function of the professional association to upgrade practice, to certify individuals in special areas and to establish the scope and qualifications of each practice area.[14]

Who is the Professional Nurse?

The question of who is considered a professional nurse varies with the date. At the end of the nineteenth century, nurses and other groups looked to professional status and licensure as a means of control over membership in the emerging profession. In 1903, a state registration act was passed in North Carolina and followed in that year by three other registration acts in New Jersey, New York and Virginia.[15] These laws were permissive and regulated only the use of the initials "R.N." They did not define nursing terms of the allowable scope of practice for the profession. Rather, the term "registered nurse" was defined as someone who had completed a regulated and acceptable nursing program and passed a state board examination.

In the second phase in the development of nursing licensure, which began in 1938, the primary goal became mandatory licensure when the first mandatory act was passed in New York. This law established two levels of nurses, registered and practical, and restricted nursing functions to members of these two groups. In 1955, the American Nurses' Association adopted the following definition of nursing practice:

> The practice of professional nursing means the performance for compensation of any act in the observation, care and counsel of the ill, injured, or infirm, or in the maintenance of health or prevention of illness in others, or in the supervision and teaching of other personnel, or the administration of medications and treatments prescribed by a licensed physician or dentist, requiring substantial specialized judgment and skill and based on knowledge and application of the principles of biological, physical, and social sciences. The foregoing shall not be deemed to include acts of diagnosis or prescription of therapeutic or corrective measures.[16]

This definition became the new model for changing nurse practice acts, so that by 1967 some 21 states had incorporated this language either exactly or with slight modification into their state laws. However, the last sentence—the disclaimers in the scope of practice—was out of date at the time it was written, as nurses were already making diagnostic and therapeutic decisions.[17, 18] In 1955, nurses were observing patients, collecting data about their conditions and acting on those decisions to deliver nursing care.

Problems with the restrictive nature of the 1955 definition led the American Nurses' Association in 1970 to amend its definition of nursing to authorize certain acts of diagnosis and prescription. It provided:

> A professional nurse may also perform such additional acts, under emergency or other special conditions, which may include special training, as is recognized by the medical and nursing professions as proper to be performed by a professional nurse under such conditions, even though such acts might otherwise be considered diagnosis and prescription.[19]

The intent of this amendment was to legitimize the nurse's expanded role in providing health care.

Various states have handled the amendment in several different ways. Idaho's law asks the medical and nursing professional organizations jointly to develop areas for expanded nursing responsibility.[20] States such as Maine permit all nurses to act independently of a physician's orders when a physician delegates the authority to act in a specific area.[21] Other states such as New York acknowledge that nurses may practice nursing as a profession independent from medicine. New York states:

The practice of the profession of nursing as a registered professional nurse is defined as diagnosing and treating human responses to actual and potential health problems through such services as case finding, health teaching, health counseling and provision of care supportive to or restorative of life and well being, and executing medical regimens prescribed by a licensed or otherwise legally authorized physician or dentist. A nursing regimen shall be consistent with and shall not vary any existing medical regimen.[22]

Additional changes are anticipated. Several nurses' associations are lobbying in state legislatures for passage of a 1985 proposal that would require all nurses seeking licensure to hold a baccalaureate degree.[23]

During the past two decades the relationship of the various nursing organizations has done much for the improvement of nursing practice. The American Nurses' Association has enunciated standards of practice and developed a certification program. The National League for Nursing has effected improvements through the accreditation of schools of nursing.[24] Other nursing organizations are also active in the improvement of practice.

The ANA defines a standard as an "authoritative statement by which the quality of practice, service or education can be judged."[25] The ANA standards include general standards and assessment factors that can be used to determine whether the standard has been met.[26] For example, one standard for medical-surgical nursing is:

> The collection of data about the health status of the patient is systematic and continuous. These data are communicated to appropriate persons, recorded and stored in a retrievable and accessible system.[27]

Evaluation of fluid and electrolyte balance, metabolic regulation and cardiovascular and respiratory output, and the complete collection of relevant data are assessment factors used in measuring compliance with this standard. For each speciality group developed by ANA, the standards are similar. The following assessment factors may be illustrated by clinical assessment of cardiovascular functions such as chest wall size and configuration, apical/radial pulse, rate, quality, rhythm, Korotkoff sounds, heart sounds and murmurs, pericardial friction rub, thrill, arrhythmias, respiratory rate and quality, chest expansion and configuration, rales, breath sounds, shortness of breath, dyspnea, hemoptysis, eye grounds, blood pressure, bruits, petechiae, edema, urinary output, liver engorgement and enlargement, neck vein distention, fluid and electrolyte balance, visual acuity, syncope, pain, fatigue/activity tolerance, appetite, sleep/rest pattern interruption, laboratory reports such as EKGs, chest x-ray, serum enzymes and arterial blood gases.[28] Thus the standards combined with the assessment factors which follow provide a method of analyzing whether the nursing action complies with what the profession believes to be appropriate standards of care.

The Obstetric, Gynecological and Neonatal Nursing Functions and Standards promulgated by NAACOG[29] are a good example of those developed outside the ANA. In these standards, nursing functions during labor and delivery and after childbirth are set forth in detail. They also list behaviors appropriate for nurses in this area of practice, behavior appropriate for those with special preparation as well as those behaviors considered inappropriate.

Routine functions that are appropriate include:
1. Administering oral, intramuscular or intravenous medications.
2. Starting blood transfusions.
3. Starting and managing oxytocin infusions for induction or augmentation of labor, as ordered by the physician.

4. Performing newborn assessment and identification.
5. Performing newborn resuscitation.
6. Estimating blood loss.
7. Catheterization of patient.

In this same era, a national certification program has developed, and it recognizes the attainment of specialized knowledge and skills beyond those required for safe practice. As Flanagan points out, the ANA certification program was intended to recognize excellence in the clinical practice of nursing.[30] Qualification for certification includes graduation from any basic program, practicing for a given period in the area in which certification is sought and demonstrating excellence through written examinations and written documentation of nursing practice.[31] From the outset, the certification program has been embroiled in controversy. Important opposition to the ANA certification program began with the Academy of Pediatrics, which differed in the degree of independence nurses should be allowed in their practice and in the input physicians were to have in certification measurement tools.[32] This controversy continues today between ANA and NAPNAP.

While there are and have been five ways of entering the profession of nursing to date—the hospital diploma program, the associate degree program, the baccalaureate degree program, the master's degree and the doctoral degree—there has been a marked decrease in the number of hospital diploma graduates within the past 10 to 20 years and a corresponding increase in the number of associate and baccalaureate degree graduates. During that interval, the number of hospital diploma graduates has dropped to approximately 17 percent, the number of associate degree graduates has increased to 49 percent and the number of baccalaureate degree graduates has increased to 33 percent.[33] Recently the nursing profession has begun to differentiate expected levels of performance of nurses. Earlier, it was said that the associate degree graduates were technically skilled; whereas baccalaureate graduates had intellectual and analytical skills. By 1975, Yura stated all nurses have to have the basic technological skills needed to perform routine nursing tasks; in addition, however, the baccalaureate degree nurse has the ability to assess data, choose the correct nursing intervention, carry it out and evaluate it.[34]

Even more recently, the Southern Regional Educational Board's Nursing Curriculum Project stated that nursing care is provided in three settings: primary, secondary and tertiary.[35] Primary care includes the evaluation of the patient's symptoms (both new and old), the referral of patients or clients to other members of the health team and the management of chronic illness.[36] This care may be provided in clinics, in the home and in settings outside the hospital. Secondary care is the care of the patient with a more complex or unusual illness who requires specialized nursing care.[37] The associate degree graduates can carry out standardized plans that are in common use and can work under the supervision of others. On the other hand, the baccalaureate nurses can work in primary, secondary and tertiary care settings and are prepared to work independently.

In *Standards for Nursing Education*,[38] the American Nurses' Association has differentiated the graduates as follows:

Goals for baccalaureate degree nurses include:
    To prepare nurses who demonstrate the ability to use the scientific method and to apply it to nursing care problems.
    To prepare nurses competent to enter professional practice.
    To transmit nursing science.

To demonstrate collaboration among health professionals, nursing team members, and consumers of health services with a view toward improving health and sickness care services and the environments in which students learn.

To exemplify a future orientation by systematic inquiry into and demonstration of means to improve nursing care, education, administration, research and the system of health care. . . .[39]

Goals for associate degree graduates and those receiving diplomas from hospital schools of nursing include:

To prepare nurses competent to enter practice in positions focusing upon direct patient care.

To prepare nurses who understand the parameters of their knowledge and skills and who know when and where to seek consultation.

To transmit nursing science that relates to the role of this graduate.

To demonstrate cooperation among health and nursing team members and clients in order to provide effective health and sickness care services.

To exemplify a future orientation through cooperation in efforts to improve nursing care, education, administration, research and the system of health care. . . .[40]

Boards of nursing, which are composed of both nurses and consumers, help to define professional performance from their own experiences and can powerfully influence the legal aspects of nursing practice.

With these new developments, the status of the nurse as a professional is clearly emerging. It has been a slow process and only recently is the goal being defined.

Professional Versus Institutional Licensure

Within the past few years, the licensure problem has encountered further stress from specialized auxiliary personnel in the health services who perform duties that only licensed professionals were formerly allowed to do. There are inhalation therapists, operating room technicians, EKG technicians, dietetic technicians and so on. When one splits off particular functions for one or another class of auxiliary personnel, this tends to complicate rather than simplify the definition of the scope of practice. There is a conflict between the effective use of personnel and the high quality of personnel needed by modern health care. Hershey points out that, to the extent that other groups such as inhalation therapists and marriage counselors attain by licensure benefits at the expense of the professional nurse, the latter has cause for concern.[41]

In the recent turmoil over institutional licensure versus licensure of the individual professional person, the essential problem remains how to protect the public from unqualified personnel. In People v. Whittaker[42] a neurosurgeon in performing brain surgery used a trained surgical assistant who operated a cranial drill and Gigli saw positioned by the surgeon to bore holes and excise skull flaps during operations. The assistant was found guilty in a jury trial of practicing medicine without a license, and the surgeon was found guilty of aiding and abetting an unlicensed person to practice medicine.

Hershey suggested several years ago that a distinction be made between independent practitioners, such as physicians, who practice in an institution and those who practice as independent practitioners in noninstitutional settings.[43] According to his proposition, so long as persons are practicing in private offices with no required referral to or check by other health professionals, individual licensure is needed to protect the public. On the other hand, Hershey suggests institutional licensure for persons (including professional nurses) who are in an organization, institution or agency which is itself responsible for regulating the provision of services within established state institutional licensing bodies.[44] Such a scheme, he claims, would provide for the effective use of persons and for flexibility, but it is open to serious question as to whether it would provide enough safeguards of quality performance unless there were a huge increase in inspectors of institutions.

The possibility of licensure of health teams working in organized frameworks—in hospitals, extended care facilities, clinics, neighborhood health centers, group practices, laboratories, pharmacies and the multidisciplinary organizations—is suggested by Forgotson and Roemel.[45] Under this scheme, the head of the team would be licensed as an individual who could supervise certain kinds of unlicensed personnel working in the team, provided certain criteria of good patient care were met.[46] Currently, surgical technicians are relieving operating room nurses, orthopedic technicians are helping orthopedists, and various types of aides and technicians are being trained to perform parts of the health care service. Adequate standards of training, qualifications and supervision have not been developed statewide or nationwide for such people, so their work and quality of work vary greatly in different institutions. Therefore, it is proposed that licensing health teams might provide the necessary legal authority for their functioning and the necessary safeguards in patient care. It is suggested, accordingly, that the state agency responsible for setting standards for the operation of health teams should also be responsible for licensure of the facilities. As with Hershey's proposal, this scheme would provide for effective use of persons and for flexibility, but there is serious question as to whether it would provide enough safeguards of quality performance unless there were a very sizeable increase in the number of inspectors of institutions.

Nurses should note that most barriers to their mobility from state to state have been erased through the use of State Board Test Pool Examinations and now NCLEX as a means of evaluating qualifications. Under a scheme of institutional licensure or health team licensure, such as has been proposed, nurses devoid of individual professional licensure would lose their mobility, because a particular institution's or team's evaluation would not be accepted statewide or nationwide.

Professional nurses should know that the American Nurses' Association has reaffirmed its commitment to individual licensure and individual accountability as being essential to safe, high quality care. The American Nurses' Association has gone on record as unalterably opposed to shifting the burden of accountability from individual practitioners to an institution or agency. The National League for Nursing has also taken a strong position in favor of individual licensure. Quality nursing service is the hallmark of the ordinary American hospital, and this has been and is being given by registered professional nurses holding individual licenses. As Regan points out:

> If in any of its dimensions, Institutional Licensure carries with it the potentiality of diluting the quality of nursing service, however attractive the price of such dilution may seem in terms of other conveniences to the institution, the price is too great in the light of the exposure to liability that would result therefrom.[47]

A logical beginning at resolving the conflict over licensure would be to take Roger's suggestion that nursing support two types of licensure: professional as well as technical. This could be coupled with Murray's suggestion that renewal of licensure should be made dependent on recertification.[47a] Although these changes in nursing would have to be accompanied by some sweeping changes in other areas of the health care delivery system, both institutional and personal, this would be a more reasonable and orderly way of proceeding than continuing the haphazard legitimization via licensure of multiple ill-defined new health professionals, or shifting individual licensure and individual accountability to an institution.

Certification

American Nurses' Association

The ANA certification has established a voluntary plan through its division on nursing practice. By means of a specially prepared written examination and a peer review system, nurses are able to qualify for certification provided they meet certain criteria before taking the test.

The *Certification Catalog* describing the criteria for certification lists six steps in the process:

1. *Decide if you are eligible.* To qualify you must have a current license to practice as a registered nurse in the United States or its territories and meet all eligibility requirements specified in the particular area you choose.
2. *Choose the testing location best for you.* There are 67 cities listed in the catalog.
3. *Fill out your application* and any required forms and return them with the $25 application fee.
4. *Prepare for the examination.* The examination fee of $125 is due before the test date. (This fee is $75 for SNA members.)
5. *Take the examination.*
6. *Receive your certificate.* Certification is valid for a five-year period.

Currently, there are 17 specialty areas: clinical specialist in adult psychiatric and mental health, clinical specialist in child and adolescent psychiatric and mental health nursing, psychiatric and mental health nurse, medical-surgical nurse, clinical specialty in medical-surgical nursing, pediatric nurse practitioner, child and adolescent nurse, school nurse practitioner, gerontological nurse, nursing administration, nursing administration advanced, community health nurse, high-risk perinatal nurse, maternal and child health nurse, adult nurse practitioner, family nurse practitioner and gerontological nurse practitioner.[48]

Other Certification. The ANA specialty certification program represents professional organization certification, but there are two other types. An educational institution may, and often does, issue a statement that a student has successfully completed a program of study. Typically, schools of nursing issue a certificate to an individual who, for example, has successfully completed a program in cardiovascular nursing or as a pediatric nurse practitioner. Elsewhere in the United States, one notes mandatory certification in areas such as midwifery, school nursing and, to some extent, public health nursing. It should be noted, too, that several specialty organizations, such as the American Association of Critical Care Nurses, the American Association of Nurse Anesthetists, the American Board for Occupational Health Nurses, the Emergency Room Nurses' Association and the Association of Operating Room Nurses, have certification programs.

Nurses' Rights

In the recent case of *Nelson* v. *Mustian*, an evening supervisor who refused to comply with a dress code that specified only three rings could be worn on duty was terminated.[49]

Our battle for nurses' rights must be centered on significant matters. Fagin in an article on nurses' rights lists the following:

> The right to find dignity in self-expression and self-enhancement through use of our special abilities and educational background.
> The right to recognition for our contribution through the provision of an environment for its practice, and proper, professional economic rewards.
> The right to a work environment which will minimize physical and emotional stress and health risks.
> The right to control what is professional practice within the limits of the law.
> The right to set standards for excellence in nursing.
> The right to social and political action in behalf of nursing and health care.[50]

EXPANDED ROLE OF THE NURSE

In recent years, the profession has shown interest in expanding the role of professional nursing. Two needs that have to be met are: (1) for expanded health services and (2) for preserving the character of nursing. To do this, professional organizations have been developing standards while guarding against accepting functions for which nurses are not prepared. Interdisciplinary committees have contributed to rules for expanded nurse practices. In the Rules and Regulations for about three quarters of the states, Boards of Nursing have dealt with the nurse's expanded role. In other states, the basic definition of the registered nurse has been expanded. Professional nurses in the critical care area are allowed to make complicated judgments and carry out advanced techniques in handling cardiac emergencies. The management of patients with chronic disease in clinics and extended care facilities is handled in many instances by nurse practitioners who have advanced training and who are guided by protocols signed by physicians. In *Family Planning Perspectives*, Donovan provides a summary and discussion of the legislation.[51]

In *Sermchief* v. *Gonzales*, the Missouri State Board of Registration for the Healing Arts threatened to order employees of the East Missouri Action Agency to show cause why their licensed professional nurses should not be found guilty of unauthorized practice of medicine and why their physicians were not guilty of aiding and abetting them. The services routinely provided by the nurses and complained of by the Board included, among others, the taking of history; breast and pelvic examinations; laboratory testing of Papanicolaou (Pap) smears, gonorrhea cultures and blood serology; giving information about and providing oral contraceptives, condoms and intrauterine devices (IUDs); the dispensing of certain designated medications; and counseling services and community education. Both nurses have had post-graduate special training in obstetrics and gynecology. No act is alleged to have done injury or damage to anyone. All acts by the nurses were done pursuant to written standing orders and protocols signed by the appellant physicians, which were directed to specifically named nurses. The Missouri Supreme Court decided in favor of the nurses and physicians. Under the Missouri Nurse Practice Act, a nurse may be permitted to assume responsibilities heretofore considered to be within the field of professional nursing as long as those responsibilities are consistent with her or his "special education, judgment and skill based on knowledge and application of principles derived from the biological, physical, social and nursing sciences."[52] Citations to nurse practice acts in the 40 states that have modernized and expanded their nursing practice laws are found in the references to my article, "More About Nurse Practitioners" (Nursing Management, September 1984).

In a 1981 case, a patient suffered chest pain while riding his bicycle and jogging. Later that night, when he went to the Kaiser Clinic, he was examined by a nurse practitioner who told him he was suffering from muscle spasms and gave him a prescription for Valium. The patient went home, went to sleep and awoke with severe chest pain and returned to the Clinic. He was seen by a physician who ordered a chest x-ray, gave him an injection of Demerol and codeine pills and concluded the patient was having muscle spasms. The next day, the patient returned to the emergency room, was seen by a different physician who ordered an EKG and admitted him to the hospital when the EKG reading showed that he was suffering from an acute myocardial infarction. The patient sued, complaining that his condition should have been diagnosed earlier and that treatment should have been given to prevent the heart attack or at least lessen the residual effects. He was awarded $1,287,733 for lost wages, reduced life expectancy, pain, suffering and medical expenses. The court said that when the patient went to the Kaiser Clinic, he was entitled to the standard of care of a physician. Whether the clinic chose to provide that care through the services of a physician or of a nurse practitioner under the supervision and direction of a physician, the standard of care which the patient was entitled to was the same.[53]

Pre-Employment/Yearly Physicals

Today many pre-employment and yearly physicals are done by nurses who are responsible that they be done correctly. If the examining nurse is an employee of the company, both the nurse and her or his employer (under the doctrine of respondeat superior) are likely to be sued if there is negligence in doing the examination. However, a nurse practitioner, who contracts to do the physicals and is not a company employee, may be considered liable as an independent contractor and sued directly.[54]

In Coffee v. McDonnell-Douglas Corporation,[55] the court observed that employers generally owe no duty to prospective employees to ascertain whether they are physically fit for a job. But, if they assume such a duty, employers are liable if it is performed negligently. In James v. United States,[56] a marine machinist established that he would have benefited from early treatment following discovery and disclosure of a suspected tumor at the pre-employment physical, thus entitling him to $60,000 in damages.

Nurse Midwives

In Nurse Midwifery Associates et al. v. Hibbett, M. D., et al., a physician and several nurse midwives brought an antitrust action against a physician and insurance company, alleging that denial of medical malpractice coverage to the physician who provided medical supervision and services to the nurse midwives violated the Sherman Act.[57] The State Volunteer Mutual Insurance Company agreed to adopt an antidiscrimination policy against physicians who supervise self-employed nurse midwives after the Federal Trade Commission charged that the firm violated antitrust laws.[58]

Prescriptions

In their expanded role, nurses are often unable to function effectively and efficiently, because there is no formal mechanism by which they can write prescriptions. Those states that do authorize such practice use statutes, regulations or protocols to control drugs that a nurse may prescribe. One third of the states have statutory and regulatory recognition of the fact that nurses in expanded roles must be able to write prescriptions: Arizona, Colorado, Connecticut, Florida, Idaho, Mississippi, Missouri, New Hampshire, Rhode Island, South Carolina, Tennessee, Utah, Vermont and Washington.[59]

LICENSED PRACTICAL/VOCATIONAL NURSE

In recent years all states and territories have passed laws controlling practical nursing, and a large number of states have provided for some form of state licensure. There are differences in the laws for the licensure of practical nurses in the various states. Some states have requirements for licensing nursing attendants. Texas licenses trained obstetrical nurses. New Jersey exempts from licensure personnel employed under registered nurse supervision in hospitals, listing specifically ward helpers, attendants, technicians, physiotherapists, and medical secretaries.

The Statement of Functions of the Licensed Practical Nurse[60] gives this role description:

> An LP/VN through education and clinical experience has acquired the necessary knowledge, skill, and judgment to provide nursing care at the direction of a registered nurse, a licensed physician, or a licensed dentist. Through continuing education, the LP/VN prepares to assume progressively more complex nursing responsibilities.
> Functions
> 1. Participates in the planning, implementation, and evaluation of nursing care, and teaches the maintenance of health and prevention of disease.
> 2. Observes and reports to the appropriate person significant symptoms, reactions, and changes in the condition of the patient, and records pertinent information.
> 3. Performs and/or assists in nursing functions such as:
>   a. the administration of medications as prescribed.
>   b. therapeutic and diagnostic procedures.
>   c. procedures requiring the use of medical/surgical aseptic technique.
> 4. Assists with the rehabilitation of the patient and family according to the patient care plan:
>   a. provides support for emotional needs.
>   b. teaches appropriate self-care.
>   c. advocates use of community resources.
> 5. Assists in performing nursing services in specialized units, with appropriate preparation.
> 6. Assumes responsibilities as a charge nurse under direction, with appropriate preparation.

Vocational Responsibilities
The LP/VN
1. Practices nursing according to state law.
2. Performs those nursing functions for which he/she has been prepared.
3. Seeks further growth through educational opportunities.
4. Participates in nursing organizations.

Closing Statement
The LP/VN should be an example of dignity and grace and maintain a spiritual approach to all nursing care.

The definitions of practical nursing found in state licensure laws are similar to the one quoted, which clarifies the type of nursing a practical nurse will do as well as the leadership she will need. It is necessary for practical nurses to understand that they must limit their work to the area of authorized practical nursing. They must realize, too, that no physician or registered professional nurse can give them a right to do more than what legally may be done.

The National Federation of Licensed Practical Nurses (NFLPN) has endorsed two levels of nursing (registered nurse and licensed practical/vocational nurse) and the expansion of L.P./V.N. curriculum programs to at least 18 months. The resolution entitled "Entry into Practice and Licensure" was adopted by the NFLPN House of Delegates at their 1984 convention. It states: "NFLPN believes that it is necessary to upgrade the educational requirements in order to continue to prepare competent, qualified and employable L.P./V.N.'s to assure a higher degree of quality nursing care."[61]

The essential difference between the registered professional nurse and the practical nurse is that, by professional education and training and more refined skills, the registered professional nurse is obliged to evaluate and interpret facts in order to decide necessary action that may be required.

PHYSICIAN'S ASSISTANT

The physician's assistant differs from the nurse in one very important respect: The P.A. has no independent functions. Those articles that describe the primary care role of the physician's assistant list tasks to be accomplished.[62] In contrast to the independence exercised by nurses in their work, Braun and others discuss the independence exercised by physician's assistants and state: "Those tasks that were done frequently and without direct supervision were considered an index of independence."[63] In such a situation, Braun is equating independence with indirect supervision of tasks frequently done, and this is not true independence as compared with that of nurses.

Nurses frequently ask whether they are protected if they carry out the order of a physician's assistant. The Kansas Attorney General has said:

> Any professional or practical nurse performing treatment on a patient as prescribed by a physician's assistant in his written orders is proceeding at his or her own risk insofar as civil liability is concerned in the event.[64]

As a consequence of this interpretation, the Kansas State Board of Nursing has said:

> A professional nurse or a licensed practical nurse must not carry out orders initiated solely by the physician's assistant without direct confirmation of such orders by the licensed physician.[65]

In New York, a 1979 department memo says, in effect, that, when P.A.'s are within their scope of authority properly delegated by a physician, they may supervise nurses executing a medical regimen prescribed by the physician.

In the case of *Washington State Nurses' Association v. Board of Medical Examiners*,[67] the Supreme Court of Washington reversed the judgment of the trial court in favor of the Washington Nurses' Association and ruled that nurses will carry out the medication orders of a physician's assistant. Because every order given by the P.A. is considered as coming from the supervising physician, the regulation has not changed the nurse's position.

In an action brought under the Federal Tort Claims Act to recover damages for alleged medical malpractice in a decedent's wrongful death, the plaintiff decedent became ill en route to a convention and was taken to the Naval Regional Medical Center (NRMC) at Philadelphia. She had an elevated temperature, nausea, vomiting, headache and a feeling of pressure behind the eyes. The decedent was seen by a physician's assistant who prescribed some routine flu medications, because of the prevalence of flu at the time, and who sent her home with orders to return if the symptoms became worse or her temperature became more elevated. Two days later, she returned to the NRMC where she was seen by the physician's assistant and a doctor not licensed in any state. Again, the plaintiff decedent was sent home. Later, during the night, she returned to the NRMC emergency room where she was transferred to another hospital. Following a craniotomy with an evacuation of the hematoma and clipping of the aneurysm, she went into respiratory failure, developed cardiac arrhythmia and died. The U.S. District Court held that the naval hospital acted negligently in failing to have a licensed physician personally examine the patient or review her chart before discharging her after the first emergency room visit and that this was the proximate cause of her death. The surviving spouse was awarded several hundred thousand dollars.[68] Nurses in Pennsylvania are not required to follow medical orders written by physician's assistants.[69]

PARAMEDICS

Paramedics are liable for their own negligence, taking into account their education, experience and the surrounding circumstances. Their employer is also liable, according to the "master-servant" rule (see Chapter 5), for any negligence that they commit in the line of duty.

The administrator of a shooting victim's estate brought a negligence suit against the city and two paramedics employed by its free emergency ambulance program. The paramedics transported the victim to the hospital nearest to the scene of the shooting. When the doctors in the emergency room evaluated the victim and decided to transfer him to a second hospital for care for a thoracic surgeon, the paramedics and their supervisors were not told of the emergency nature of the transfer. Consequently, under their rules, the paramedics refused to transfer the victim to the second hospital. After a delay, the transfer was made by a private ambulance service. The shooting victim died shortly afer arriving at the second hospital. The paramedics were not held negligent in failing to make the inter-hospital transfer.[70]

References

1. Lewison v. Vitti, 356 A.2d 844 (Pa. Commonwealth Ct., 1976). *Citation*, 34:36, Nov. 15, 1976.
2. *Principles of Legislation Relating to Nursing Practice.* New York American Nurses' Association, Rev., Jan. 1958.
3. Barber v. Reiking, 411 P. 2d 861 (Wash., 1966). See *The Physician's Legal Brief* (Schering) 8(7):2, Sept. 1966. Hershey, N.: A Court's View of Mandatory Licensure, *Am. J. Nurs.*, 66:2461, Nov., 1966.
4. Report of AMA Committee on Nursing Mandatory vs. Permissive Licensure for Nurses, *JAMA*, 195:202–23, Feb. 7, 1966. Prepared by Florence M. Alexander, Ph.D., R. N., formerly director of AMA Department of Nursing.
5. Developing, Constructing and Scoring the National Council Licensure Examination, Part I, Issues, 4:1, 3–4, Spring 1983; Part II, 4:1, 6, Summer 1983.
6. Tighe v. Commonwealth of Pennsylvania, State Board of Nurse Examiners, 397 A. 2d 1261 (Commonwealth Ct. of Pa. 1979); *Citation*, 39:95 (Aug. 1, 1979). Creighton, H.: Licensure Problems, *Superv. Nurse*, 11:68–69, Jan. 1980.
7. Ullo v. Commonwealth of Pennsylvania, State Board of Nurse Examiners, 398 A. 2d 764 (Commonwealth Ct. of Pa. 1979); *Citation*, 39:94 (Aug. 1, 1979).
8. McCarl v. Commonwealth of Pennsylvania, State Board of Nurse Examiners, 396 A. 866 (Commonwealth Ct. of Pa. 1979); *Citation*, 39:93–94, (Aug. 1, 1979).
9. Illinois Appellate Court Upholds Dental Board's Refusal to Restore Plaintiff's Dental License, *Am. Dental Assn. J.*, 77:34, July 1968.
10. Leib v. Board of Examiners for Nursing of State of Connecticut, 177 Conn. 78, 411 A. 2d 42 (S. Ct. Conn. 1979). *See also* Arthur v. District of Columbia Nurse's Examining Board, 459 A. 2d 141 (D.C. Ct. of App. 1983).
11. Shoenhair v. Commonwealth of Pennsylvania, Department of State, Bureau of Professional and Occupational Affairs, 459 A. 2d 877 (Pa. Commonwealth Ct. 1983); *Citation*, 48:107, Feb. 15, 1984.
12. Ward v. Oregon State Board of Nursing, 510 P. 2d 554 (Ore. 1973).
13. La Bar, C.: *Statutory Definitions of Nursing Practice and Their Conformity to Certain ANA Principles.* Kansas City, Am. Nurses' Assn., 1984.
14. *Ibid.*, pp. 1–2.
15. Bullough, B.: The Law and the Expanding Role of the Nurse, *Am. J. Pub. Health*, 66:249–253, 1976.
16. Bullough, B.: ANA Board Approves a Definition of Nursing Practice, *Am. J. Nurs.*, 55:1474, 1955.
17. *Op. cit.*, note 15, p. 251.
18. *Cf.* A Revolution in White—New Approaches in Treating Nurses as Professionals, 30 *Vanderbilt L. Rev.*, 839, 842–843, May 1977.
19. D'Amico, D.: Nursing Practice Act Revisions. *AORN J.*, 22:105, July 1970.
20. Idaho Code Ann. Sec. 54–1413 (Bobbs-Merrill Supp., 1976).
21. Maine Rev. Stat. Ann. tit. 32, sec. 2102 (West Supp., 1977). *Cf.*, *op. cit.*, note 32, p. 844.
22. N.Y. Educ. Law, Sec. 6903 (McKinney Supp., 1977).
23. McGriff, E. P., and Simms, Laura L.: Two New York Nurses Debate the NYSNA 1985 Proposal, *Am. J. Nurs.*, 76:930, June 1976. *See also* News, *Am. J. Nurs.*, 77:1093, July 1977.
24. Flanagan, L.: *One Strong Voice.* Kansas City, Am. Nurses Assn., 1974.
25. *Ibid.*, p. 219a.
26. *Standard of Medical-Surgical Nursing Practice.* Kansas City, Am. Nurses' Assn. 1974.
27. *Ibid.*, p. 2, *Cf.*, *op. cit.*, note 18, p. 846.
28. Standards of Cardiovascular Nursing Practice. Kansas City, Am. Heart Assn. Council on Cardiovascular Nursing and Am. Nurses' Assn. Division on Medical-Surgical Nursing Practice, 195, pp. 5–7.
29. Obstetric, Gynecological and Neonatal Nursing Functions and Standards. Chicago, Nurses' Assn. of Am. Coll. Obstet. Gynecol., 1974, p. 12. *Cf.*, *op. cit.*, note 18, p. 847.
30. *Op. cit.*, note 24.
31. *Ibid.*
32. Letter from Dr. Robert Frazier to Fellows of the American Academy of Pediatrics dated Jan. 16, 1974. *Cf.*, letter from Dr. Eileen Jacobi to *Pediatric Nurse Practitioner* and Fellows of the American Academy of Pediatrics dated Jan. 29, 1974. *Cf.*, *op. cit.*, note 18, p. 848.
33. *Facts About Nursing 1982–83.* Kansas City, Am. Nurses Assn., 1983, p. 121.
34. Yura, H.: A Climate to Foster Utilization of the Nursing Process. In *Providing a Climate for Utilization of Nursing Personnel.* New York, Department of Hospital and Related Institutional Nursing Services, Nat. League for Nursing, 1975, pp. 21–22. *Op. cit.*, note 18, p. 850.
35. Southern Regional Educational Board, *Nursing Curriculum Project: Summary and Recommendations.* Atlanta, Southern Regional Educational Board 1976, p. 9.
36. *Ibid.*, pp. 10–11.
37. *Ibid.*, p. 12.
38. *Standards for Nursing Education.* Kansas City, Am. Nurses' Assn., 1975, p. 17.
39. *Ibid.*
40. *Ibid.*, p. 23.
41. Hershey, N.: Who and What Next in Licensure? *Am. J. Nurs.*, 71–105, Jan. 1971.
42. People v. Whittaker, Civil No. 35307, Justice Ct. of Redding Judicial Dist. (Shasta Co., Cal. Dec. 1966).
43. Hershey, N.: Licensing for Health Professionals. *Proceedings ANA Conference for Members and Professional Employees of State Board of Nursing and ANA Advisory Council 1968*, p. 13.
44. Hershey, N.: An Alternative to Mandatory Licensure for Health Professionals. *Hosp. Progr.*, 71:73, March 1969.

45. Forgotson, E., and Roemer, R.: Government Licensure and Voluntary Standards for Health Personnel and Facilities: Their Power and Limitation in Assuring High Quality Care, *Med. Care*, 6:345, 1968.
46. Roemer, R.: Licensing and Regulation of Medical and Medical-Related Practitioners in Health Service Teams, *Med. Care*, 9:42, 47, Jan.-Feb. 1971.
47. Regan, W. A.: Invidual Licensure and Quality Nursing. *Regan Report on Nursing Law*, 14(2):1, June 1973.
47a. Murray, B. L.: A Case for Independent Group Nursing Practice, *Nurs. Outlook*, 20:61, Jan. 1972.
48. The Measure of Distinction among Professionals: Certification, Kansas City, Am. Nurses' Assn., *1985 Certification Catalog*, p. 5–18.
49. Nelson v. Mustian, 502 F. Supp. 698 (D.C. Fla. 1980). Creighton, H.: Violation of Dress Code, *Nurs. Management*, 12:42–44, Oct. 1981.
50. Fagin, C. M.: Nurses' Rights, *Am. J. Nursing*, 75:82, 84, Jan. 1975.
51. Donovan, P.: Medical Societies vs. Nurse Practitioners, *Family Planning Perspectives*, 15:166, 167–168, July–Aug. 1983.
52. Sermchief v. Gonzales, 660 S.W. 2d 683 (S. Ct. Mo. 1983).
53. Fein v. Permanente Medical Group, 175 Cal. Rptr. 177 (Cal. Ct. of App. 1981). Creighton, H.: Nurse Practitioner, *Nurs. Management*, 13:14–15, Jan. 1983.
54. Creighton, H.: Nurse's Responsibility for Pre-Employment/Yearly Physicals, *Nurs. Management*, 13:66–68, May 1982.
55. Coffee v. McDonnell-Douglas Corporation, 105 Cal. Rptr. 358, 503 P. 2d 1366 (S. Ct. Cal. 1972).
56. James v. United States, 483 F. Supp. 581 (U.S. D. C. Cal. 1980).
57. Nurse Midwifery Associates et al. v. Hibbett, M. D., et al. 549 F. Supp. 1185 (U.S. Dist. Ct. Tenn. 1982). Creighton, H.: Insurer Agrees to Cover MDs Supervising Midwives, *Nurs. Management*, 14:18–20, Oct. 1983.
58. Shoulders, C.: Insure MDs Who Oversee Midwives, Firm Reportedly Told, *The Tennessean*, May 20, 1983, p. 1.
59. Cohn, S. D.: Prescriptive Authority for Nurses, *Law, Med. & Health Care*, 12:72–75, April 1984.
60. *Declaration of Functions of the Licensed Practical/Vocational Nurse*, Rev. New York, National Association for Practical Nurse Education and Service, Inc., 1976.
61. LPNs Endorse Two Levels of Nursing, Education, *Am. Nurse*, 16:1, 23, Nov./Dec. 1984.
62. Rothberg, J. S.: Nurse and Physician's Assistant: Issues and Relationships, *Nurs. Outlook*, 21:154–158, March 1973.
63. Braun, J. A., et al.: The Physician's Associate: A Task Analysis, *Phys. Assoc.*, 2:77, July 1972.
64. Legal Implications Relative to Orders from Physician's Assistants, *Kans. Nurse*, 47:1, Aug. 1972.
65. *Ibid*.
66. Communication dated 16 October 1979 from Donald O. Merserve, Associate Attorney, Office of the Counsel, The University of the State of New York, The State Education Department, Albany, New York.
67. Washington State Nurses' Association v. Board of Medical Examiners, 93 Wash. 2d 117, 605 P. 2d 1269 (1980). Creighton, H. Physician's Assistant Medication Orders, *Superv. Nurse*, 12:46–47, Jan. 1981.
68. Polischeck v. United States, 535 F. Supp. 1261 (U.S. D. C. E. D. Pa. 1982). Creighton, H.: Failure to Adequately Supervise PAs, *Nurs. Management*, 13:44–45, Dec. 1982.
69. State Rules Nurses Not Bound by P.A. Orders, *The Am. Nurse*, 14:6, Oct. 1982.
70. Morena v. South Hills Health System, Dr. David Van Thiel, Blair Haynes, Bill McDoodle, and the City of Pittsburgh, 462 A. 2d 680 (S. Ct. Pa. 1983). Creighton, H.: Transporting Accident Patients by Paramedics, *Nurs. Management*, 15:71–73, April 1984.

General References

Cohn, S. D.: Revocation of Nurses' Licenses: How Does it Happen? *Law, Med. & Health Care*, 11:22–24, Feb. 1983.
Cohn, S. D.: Criminal Law and the EMT, *EMT Legal Bull.*, 6:2–6, Fall 1983.
Creighton, H.: Licensure Problems, *Superv. Nurse*, 11:68–69, Jan. 1980.
Creighton, H.: Physician's Assistant Medication Orders, *Superv. Nurse*, 12:46–47, Jan. 1981.
Creighton, H.: Nurse Practitioner, *Nurs. Management*, 13:14–15, Jan. 1982.
Creighton, H.: Failure to Adequately Supervise PAs, *Nurs. Management*, 13:44–45, Dec. 1982.
Creighton, H.: More about Nurse Practitioners, *Nurs. Management*, 15:21–22, Oct. 1984.
La Bar, C.: *Statutory Definitions of Nursing Practice and Their Conformity to Certain ANA Principles*, Kansas City, Am. Nurses' Assn., 1984.
Regan, W. A.: Legal Case Brief for Nurses, N.Y.: Weapon, Marijuana; RN License Suspended, *Regan Rep. Nurs. Law*, 20(12)3, May 1980.
Regan, W. A.: Unprofessional Nursing Conduct: Legal Definition, *Regan Rep. Nurs. Law*, 22(3)2, Aug. 1981.
Regan, W. A.: Nurse Administrators: Unprofessional Conduct, *Regan Rep. Nurs. Law*, 24:4, Sept. 1983.
Salvage, J.: Suitable to Nurse? *Nurs. Mirror*, 152(17)6–7, April 23, 1981.
Trandel-Korenchuk, D. M., et al.: Current Legal Issues Facing Nursing Practice . . . Summary of State Law Treatment of the Expanded Role, *Nurs. Admin. Q.*, 5:77–80, Spring 1981.
Willmott, J.: Why Was Sister Jennings Put on the Carpet? *Nurs. Mirror*, 152(22)9, May 27, 1981.

Three
CONTRACTS FOR NURSING

DEFINITION AND REQUIREMENTS

When a nurse begins to actively practice the profession, she or he will become involved in contracts of one type or another. It is therefore necessary to have at least basic information on contracts and agreements. Moreover, it is of value to know that there is also a remedy at law for one party or the other for the breaking of a legal contract. Nurses should know their rights and, on the other hand, the rights of the other party, so that they may avoid trouble.

Definition

A contract has been defined as a promise, or a set of promises, the performance of which the law recognizes as a duty, and for which the law provides a remedy when the duty is not performed.[1]

Requirements

Every contract, to be enforceable at law, must contain: (1) the real consent of the parties (persons), (2) a valid consideration (something of value), (3) a lawful object (purpose), (4) competent parties (persons with a legal capacity to make a contract) and (5) the form required by law. Under the law of contracts there is a remedy for a breach of contract so that the person who suffers from a broken contract may gain recompense of some sort.

Although every contract is an agreement between two or more parties, not every agreement is a contract. For instance, one may agree to play a musical instrument at a party as a favor for a friend, or a person who has not attended church in years may agree to meet another and to attend a church service with him. If either person to such an agreement, for any reason, failed to do what he had agreed to do, it would not be considered a binding agreement for which he would be liable to penalty under the law. In general, moral agreements, agreements of conscience or agreements involving social obligations are not classified as contracts.

Offer and Acceptance. In any contract there must be an offer and an acceptance. For example, Miss A offers to do or refrain from doing something for Miss B, and Miss B accepts the offer of Miss A. An offer must be definite, it must be communicated by words or actions and it may be withdrawn before it is accepted. If Hospital C telephones Mr. Smith that it has a bed ready for him today, Mr. Smith's coming to Hospital C today is acceptance. Since a person has the right to choose those with whom he will do business, an acceptance of an offer is good only if it comes from the person to whom the offer was made. Another rule provides that acceptance must be unconditional and in accord with the contract's terms as to price, amount, time of delivery and so forth.

The person making the offer can terminate it at any time. It is effective when communication of such termination is received by the person to whom the offer was made. If the person who makes the offer accepts a payment in return for agreeing not to revoke the offer for a certain period of time, the offer is thereby converted into an option. The law treats the option as a binding contract that cannot be terminated during the time period.

Consideration. In addition to the elements of an offer and an acceptance, there must also be "consideration" for the contract. As an example, Mr. Jones, a private patient, enters Hospital C. Care given Mr. Jones by the hospital is "consideration" for his promise to pay proper charges.

As long as the consideration constitutes a bargained-for exchange, its fairness is irrelevant.

In some states, action by a party receiving a gratuitous promise, in reliance on that promise, can be a legally sufficient consideration to make the promise enforceable as a contract. For example, in a New York case, during a construction fund-raising campaign to build a hospital, the defendant doctor was asked to pledge a sum of money. He did so, and paid $500 toward his pledge during the next four years. The hospital then brought suit when he refused to pay the balance of his pledge. The appellate court gave judgment to the hospital for that balance. The court said:

> It is the well established law of this State that charitable subscriptions (pledges) are enforceable on the ground that they constitute an offer of a unilateral contract which, when accepted by the charity by incurring liability and reliance thereon, becomes a binding obligation.[2]

The new hospital was built, so the hospital had fulfilled its obligation under the pledge.

KINDS OF CONTRACTS

There are formal contracts and simple or parol (verbal) contracts as well as express contracts and implied contracts.

Formal Contracts

A *formal* contract is one required by law to be in writing. As an example, each state has its Statute of Frauds, which requires written contracts in specified cases in order to prevent fraudulent practices. Mortgages, deeds and similarly important papers are often printed on a paper on which a seal or the use of the word "seal" shows that it is a contract under seal, another kind of formal contract.

Simple Contracts

Other contracts, whether written or oral, are called "simple" or "parol" contracts.

Express Contracts

An express contract is one in which the conditions and terms of the contract are given orally or in writing by the parties. For example, Hospital C offers Miss Jones, in writing, a position as a staff nurse at a salary of $1000 per month for a five-day week consisting of 40 hours, and Miss Jones accepts the offer in writing. Here, the terms are expressed. It should be pointed out that a contract is not necessarily written.

Implied or Silent Contracts

On the other hand, suppose Miss Jones goes to Dr. Smith's office and Dr. Smith gives Miss Jones professional services, which she accepts. This is an implied contract. Perhaps the greater number of contracts we encounter in daily living are implied. The sale and purchase of many commodities is an example of a simple implied contract. Both a food store and a clothing store offer various items for sale at a price. We expect to and do pay the price asked and then obtain the article. Our contract is completed.

The implied contract may also be referred to as a "silent contract." The consent is silent. For example, Hospital C places all the features of an employment contract before Miss Jones, and after reading it Miss Jones enters on duty. The performance of the act is acceptance. However, one person, by including a statement such as "Unless I hear to the contrary, I will consider my offer accepted by you," cannot make a second person accept the offer through keeping quiet. In other words, silence, unless there is a duty from the circumstances to speak, is not an acceptance of an offer.

Oral contracts are the most common, and many employment contracts fall into this category. The employer and the employee talk things over and come to an agreement as to what services shall be performed for a specified compensation. The terms and payments may be simple or complicated, but they are binding on both parties.

Courts consistently hold that oral contracts for a year or more are void. Parker cities a 1965 decision regarding an oral contract under which a physican was employed by hospital officials for one year at a salary of $28,000.[3] Following a disagreement of the end of six months, the hospital officials discharged the physician after paying him only $12,000. The hospital was held not liable in damages for breaching the oral contract, since a contract for one year was void and unenforceable.

NURSES' CONTRACTS

It has been shown that a contract is an agreement between two or more persons for a consideration. In all contracts, there is mutual consent or a willingness by both parties that the acts will be performed.

When a nurse enters into a professional employment agreement, it is desirable and recommended that it be executed in writing, especially if it is anticipated that it will exist for a period of more than one year. Nevertheless, many nurses err in assuming that since they have no written contract, they have no binding legal commitment. From a legal point of view, there is a binding personal service contract based on mutual understanding and followed by performance of and payment for professional services. The nurse has the duty to perform her assignment in accordance with the standards of nursing practice as defined by the profession and in the nursing practice act of the state. The employer has the duty to provide not only a safe place to work and safe equipment with which to work, but also properly trained and qualified co-workers.[4]

In the case of a private duty nurse's contract, the nurse agrees to serve a patient and the patient agrees to pay the nurse for the service. Possibly the patient has a relative or friend acting for him as his agent, or two persons agree to pay a nurse for the services rendered to the patient. Likewise a nurse may have an agent acting for her. Agreements involving agents will be discussed in subsequent paragraphs.

When a nurse was discharged by a hospital on the basis of a complaint made against her by a patient, the nurse had every legal right to challenge the action of her former hospital-employer and to have her day in court for the purpose of proving her allegations and justifying her complaint.[5] Usually, unless the nursing service has a collective bargaining contract, a nurse can be discharged at will by the hospital-employer, subject only to the protocol set forth in the hospital's personnel policy. However, the average hospital handles the problem of discharging any registered nurse in a sensitive and professional manner.

Definite Commitments

Nurses' contracts should be made as definite as possible concerning the various terms in the offer and acceptance. Otherwise, the law may be called upon to interpret or clarify the uncertainties.

Hours and Salary. If one of the points, such as the amount of daily wage, is indefinite rather than specific, the law determines it according to what is "reasonable." In a given case, reasonableness depends on local custom in such a situation. For instance, if Town A engages a nurse, Miss Jones, as a public health nurse at an annual salary equivalent to that paid by a neighboring community, the fixed terms and usage can be readily ascertained.

For a private duty nurse, the hours and pay are usually inferred. In the absence of an express statement, compensation is at the rate prevailing in the locality.

Length of Contract. Again, unless the patient ends the contract earlier or unless there is a stipulation providing otherwise, the time a contract runs with a private duty nurse generally coincides with the duration of the patient's need or illness. It is the usual assumption that the patient or someone acting for him understands that the nursing service contract of the private duty nurse is on a day-to-day basis and that the nurse will serve as long as the patient desires her services. The prevailing custom is that the patient has the right to terminate the private duty nurse's services at any time, but the nurse does not enjoy the same right.

When a hospital, institution or agency enters into a valid employment contract with a nurse or doctor for a specified time, the party who willfully breaches such contract may be held liable in damages. Thus, in *United States v. Averick* the Veterans Administration sued a doctor for breach of contract and recovered $20,616 in damages.[6] Under the terms of the contract, the physician was to receive medical training in pathology while employed full-time as a physician, with a provision that he was to remain in the employ of the VA for a length of time equal to the residency period after the completion of training. If the physician failed to complete the agreed period of service after his residency, the contract provided for liquidated damages of $492 per month for each month owed but not worked. When the doctor resigned from the VA after four years of training, suit was brought and he was held liable for breach of contract. Similarly, in a case in which an employee was discharged without good cause at the end of six months, whereas he had a written contract of employment for one year at $200 per month, the employer had to pay six months' salary as damages.[7]

Days Off-Duty. At the negotiation of the contract and before entering upon duty, private duty nurses have the right to limit the length of their services on the case, for example, to a week, two weeks or a month, or they may well desire to incorporate specific provisions for "relief" or days off-duty. For example, if a patient, Mr. Brown, makes a contract with a nurse, Miss Jones, for nursing care, Miss Jones cannot as a matter of right, in the absence of a specific provision, take a day off and send another nurse, Miss Smith, as a substitute.

Local Custom. As for the length of time that other contracts for nursing services run, in the absence of a definite statement, local custom is an important factor in the determination. The Dakotas, California and Montana have applicable statutes on this subject. There is also some authority found in court decisions to the effect that, in contracts for services, the period such a contract runs in any event is not less than the salary specified; i.e., so much per week or month may be taken to indicate a hiring for that period. When nurses are employed by hospitals, agencies and institutions, employment by the month is often assumed in the absence of a specific provision or local custom.

As for the wages or salary to be paid for the various nursing services, the inclusion of definite terms in contracts is desirable. In the absence of a provision for a specific amount, the nurse's compensation depends on what is reasonable, which depends on what others in the same area are usually receiving for comparable services. It should be noted that, when such a question arises, the nurse who wants to collect for the services performed has the burden of verifying what is a "reasonable" compensation.

Sometimes, disputes arise as to whether an oral contract for a nurse's services should have been put in writing. In the case of *Cox v. Baltimore*, a nurse made an oral contract to work at $100 a week for the patient for life, and such a contract was held to be valid.[8]

Nurses should be careful in making certain that the "meeting of the minds" with respect to their position, salary and fringe benefits such as vacations, sick leave, education days and so on is reduced to writing when they are first hired for a position. When an employment contract is signed, bilateral obligations arise. As Regan points out, the employer is bound to provide a safe place to work, fellow employees who are capable of doing the jobs assigned to them and equipment and materials that are safe and adequate for the execution of the responsibilities assigned to the employee.[9] Similarly, nurses are expected to have the education and experience that they present as their qualifications, to carry out assigned duties as a reasonable and responsible nurse and to conform to the rules and regulations of the institution or agency. Many misunderstandings that result in negative criticism of persons and institutions will be avoided by a clear written contract.

Teachers' Contracts

In *Lusk v. Estes*,[10] the contract was not renewed for a teacher who expressed concern and dissatisfaction in various forums about community and economic problems affecting students and teachers in the school district and at a particular high school. The court said:

> It can no longer be seriously asserted that teachers have no right to criticize their employers . . . a teacher's employment may not be conditioned upon the surrender of his constitutional rights. A citizen's right to engage in protected expression is substantially unaffected by the fact that he is also a teacher and as a general rule, he cannot be deprived of his teaching position merely because he exercises these rights. . . . Only if the exercise of these rights by the teacher materially and substantially impedes the teacher's proper performance of his daily duties in the classroom or disrupts the regular operation of the school will a restriction of his rights be tolerated.

This decision would be applicable to teachers in nursing education, and the same principles apply to nurses in their positions in hospitals and other institutions.

In *Clark v. Holmes*,[11] an action for damages was brought by a nontenured temporary substitute teacher at a state university for violation of his civil rights by teachers and officials of the university. He was not rehired because he overrode their wishes and judgment as to the proper content of the required health course, and because he engaged in extensive personal counseling of students. The Court of Appeals affirmed a judgment for the defendants, saying:

> We do not conceive academic freedom to be a license for uncontrolled expression at variance with established curricular contents and internally destructive of the proper functioning of the institution.

The demotion of a black woman as high school counselor was upheld as not racially motivated but based on professional incompetence when there was evidence that she kept inaccurate and incomplete records of students' grades, that she allowed students to enter their own grades on permanent records, that she failed to properly follow instructions as to how records should be kept, that she improperly graded achievement tests so that they were unusable and that she encouraged teachers to pass students regardless of whether they actually were qualified.[12]

Explanation of Offer and Acceptance

At times, a nurse's contract or attempt to contract presents a problem because "offer" and "acceptance" are not fully understood. When an offer is made, it is well to realize that it may be withdrawn before it is accepted. For example, if Mr. Brown sends an offer to Miss Jones and then changes his mind before she has accepted the offer, this is his privilege and he incurs no penalty.

Reasonable Period for Acceptance. Moreover, when an offer is made, it is not indefinitely open for acceptance. Either the offer itself states that it must be accepted within a given period or, if no time is set, it is considered open for a "reasonable period." What constitutes a "reasonable period" depends on the circumstances of each case. An offer may be rejected and, in those circumstances, is no longer open for acceptance.

Means Used to Accept Offer. A point of difference as to whether or not an offer has been accepted might arise if a different means were used to accept the offer from that used in making the offer. For instance, if an offer is made in a letter written by some person or agency to a nurse, the law provides that the person making the offer authorize the person receiving the offer to use the same means in sending the acceptance, i.e, by letter through the mail. Under this arrangement, the law considers that acceptance has been made and that the contract is completed when the person receiving the offer replies by the same means, viz., dropping the letter of acceptance (properly addressed and stamped) in the mailbox. On the other hand, if a person mails an offer to a nurse and the nurse replies by wire, the contract is complete only when the person who made the offer receives the wire of acceptance, and not when the nurse sent the telegram. Although to a nurse this may seem like splitting hairs, it is the law of contracts, and since it might be important to the nurse in some cases, she should consider carefully the means by which she replies to an offer.

ILLEGAL CONTRACTS

The question of legality of a contract may arise, for a court will not enforce an illegal contract. The use of fraud (deception, trickery), undue (unlawful) influence or duress (coercion) in securing a contract will make it illegal. An agreement providing for a higher rate of interest than is allowed by law or undertaking to commit a crime is illegal, as is also any attempt to obstruct justice. Of importance to nurses is the fact that in certain states the law requires nurses to be licensed, and if a nurse in such states does not obtain a license, any contract for nursing service that he or she makes may be held illegal.* Furthermore, if a nurse in making a contract claims to be an R.N. or licensed P.N., and in fact is not, the contract is not enforceable even in a state with permissive licensure. In such instances, if the nurse gives nursing service to a patient and the patient does not pay him or her, the nurse may be unable to recover any money for services if the illegality of the contract is set up as a defense.

There are times when two or more persons may undertake a joint responsibility to pay for patient care. For example, two sons may employ and agree to pay for a nurse to care for their father or mother. This is an enforceable agreement, often referred to as a contract for the "benefit of a third person."

AGENT AND PRINCIPAL

Definition

An agent is a person designated by another, called the principal, to do, perform or act in an authorized manner in the name of the principal, but always subject to the control or wishes of the principal.[13] When she or he so acts, the agent binds the principal. It should be noted that one cannot delegate to an agent the performance of an agreement involving personal services.†

A patient in need of nursing service may ask a physician to obtain a nurse. When the physician does so, he or she is acting as the patient's agent. The patient as the principal is bound by the contract. In another instance, the nurse may act as an agent. For example, she or he is requested by a patient to obtain a

---

*See Chapter 2 for an explanation of mandatory versus permissive licensure.

†See Section 17c of Reference 4; also the comment on Sections 400, 401, 406 and 409, which states the consequences that may follow an improper delegation.

nurse and does so. The patient is bound to pay the nurse who has been secured for him or her.

Nurses' Registries

Sometimes an agent, such as a nurses' registry, supplies the nurse requested by the patient. There are different kinds of registries with varying authority and status, and the distinctions should be noted by the nurse.

Official Registry for Nurses. For example, there is the official registry for nurses, which is usually supported to a greater or lesser extent by charges and fees of the nurses it lists. When a patient or someone acting for him or her requests such a registry to obtain a nurse and the registry does so, it is usually regarded as the agent of the patient. Although nurses pay the official registry for having their employment opportunities brought to their attention, customarily they do not give it power to act as their agent.

Hospital Registry. Similarly, hospital registries, whether separate or a part of the hospital service, are not designated by nurses as agents acting for them, but rather become the agent of the patient when asked to supply a nurse.

Nurses' Registry Operated for Profit. When a nurses' registry is operated for profit, customarily there is a contract designating such registry as the agent of either nurse or patient, or both, and specifying the person obligated to pay the registry. The registry for profit has grown in recent years. Typically, it allows nurses to work hours and days of their own choosing. Employee benefits such as social security, vacation, workmen's compensation, unemployment, sick pay, disability and malpractice insurance are expenses that an agency pays.[14]

Gratuitous Agency. In the gratuitous agency, if there is a failure on the part of the agent to secure employment for a nurse, it cannot be considered a breach of contract for which there is a remedy, because there was no contract.

Consideration, as noted, is an essential element of a contract, but consideration is not an essential element in setting up an agency relationship. It should be noted that a contract made by an agent who acts gratuitously is just as binding on the principal as one made by an agent who receives recompense therefor.

Agent's Responsibility

General

If Agent A, while acting for Principal B, injures a third person, Miss Jones, through some negligent act, (1) Agent A himself can be sued for money damages by the third person, Miss Jones, and (2) Principal B, for whom Agent A acted, can also be sued for money damages.

Questions concerning whether or not a person is acting as an agent, and for whom the agent is acting, can be important in situations involving nurses. For example, a patient asked a student nurse to inquire of his doctor whether he might go home, and the student nurse said she would, but negligently failed to do so. In this case, the patient went home after receiving his bill and later found that he had a fractured leg. An action by the patient to recover damages proved unsuccessful, because the court held that the hospital could not be charged with the student nurse's negligence, since she was acting as the patient's agent and not the agent of the hospital.[15]

If a nurse acts as agent, she is responsible for her own negligent acts, regardless of whether she or he acts gratuitously or for pay. Similarly, a nurses' registry is responsible for negligent acts due to a failure to do what can reasonably be expected of such registries. For example, Mr. Brown requested Registry A to send him a nurse, and Registry A sent a nurse who was listed with it. An ordinary reasonable check on the character and credentials usually made by registries would have shown this person to be an alcoholic, but Registry A failed to check. Several days later, Mr. Brown was injured by a wrong medication given by the nurse while she was working under the influence of alcohol. Mr. Brown could bring suit against Registry A as well as against the nurse to recover damages for injury caused by negligence.

Charitable Institutions. One exception to the foregoing example should be noted. If Registry A were a part of a charitable institution, then in states where charitable institutions cannot be sued for negligence, Registry A could not be sued for negligence. Of course, this would not prevent the patient, Mr. Brown, from suing the nurse, but he might have great difficulty in collecting any judgment for damages.

Wife as Agent of Husband. In dealing with agencies, an agency implied by the law must be considered. In some situations, the law implies an agency through which one person may bind a second person to a contract, although the matter has not been considered by the latter. For example, in case of a husband and wife living together, the wife may buy what they need on her husband's credit account. The wife is his agent under these circumstances. If the husband becomes ill or injured and is a patient in a hospital, the wife may continue as his agent, and the law in all likelihood would recognize her authority to engage a nurse needed for his care. The husband, as principal, is bound by the contract to compensate such a nurse. If the wife is the patient, the husband ordinarily is responsible for necessary services (including nursing service) to his wife. In the latter case, it is the husband's legal duty while they are living together to provide for his wife.

The situation is different if the husband and wife are living apart. She may have left him without cause, prompting the husband to give notice that he is no longer responsible for her purchases. In such cases, the husband will not have to pay the wife's bill.

A wife's right to recover damages for loss of consortium is discussed later in the chapter.

Parents as Agents for Minor Children. The court held that the partnership theory in marriage infers that both parents are responsible for the medical, nursing and hospital bills of their minor children.[16]

As the court states in *Kern v. Kern*:

> The duty to provide support for a minor child is based upon the child's incapacity, both natural and legal, and its consequent need of protection and care. At common law, this duty of child support was visited almost exclusively upon the father and was limited to that period when the child remained unemancipated. Today, the obligation of child support is recognized by statute to be upon the mother and father jointly as the natural guardians of their natural and adopted children. (See Sec. 744.301, Fla. Stat. 1977).[17]

As encompassed by the statutory authority and case law, support is defined as the provision of necessary food, clothing, shelter, nursing or medical treatment.[18] Either or both parents have a duty to provide reasonable and necessary medical and nursing attention for their minor children.

Nursing Service, a Necessity. In general, medical, nursing and hospital services are necessities. Parents are legally responsible in most states for providing necessities for their minor children. However, when parents give up control and supervision of a minor who keeps her or his own wages, the minor may be regarded as "emancipated" (freed) even though she or he continues to live at home. In such a case, parents are not liable for services given the child. Also, a nurse cannot charge the parents for services given a married minor child, since marriage emancipates or releases the child from parental responsibility.

INFORMED CONSENT

There is a long history of informed consent dating back to *Slater* v. *Baker* in England (1767), where a surgeon experimented without the patient's consent by stretching the patient's newly healed broken leg with an instrument. There the court said: "It was improper to disunite the callous [i.e., callus] without consent; this is the usage and law of surgeons."[19]

In 1914 in *Schloendorff* v. *Society of New York Hospital*, when a surgeon operated on a woman's tumor without her consent, Justice Cardozo stated: "Every human being of adult years and sound mind has a right to determine what shall be done with his own body; and a surgeon who performs an operation without his patient's consent commits an assault for which he is liable in damages."[20]

In 1915 in *Zoterell* v. *Repp*, where a surgeon performed two major operations that deprived a woman of her ability to bear children, the court went a step further and said: "Consent must be with knowledge and understanding of the operation itself."[21]

In 1939 in surgery resulting in the loss of the right breast in the case of *Valdez* v. *Percy*, the court observed: "Where a person has been subjected to an operation without his consent such operation constitutes technical assault and battery."[22]

In 1957 in *Salgo* v. *Stanford University Board of Trustees*, where the surgeon did not inform the patient of the risk of paralysis in injecting sodium urokon in the course of a translumbar aortography, the court held that a physician must disclose to the patient all the facts necessary to form the basis of an intelligent consent. It added that the physician "may not minimize the known dangers of a procedure or operation in order to induce . . . consent . . . and he must place the welfare of the patient above all else."[23]

In *Dunlap* v. *Marine*, where the patient suffered a cardiac arrest as a result of an injection of a special anesthetic, the court held that there was no deviation from the standard practice in the community in obtaining the patient's consent.[24]

In *Berkey, Dow* v. *Kaiser Foundation*, the patient claimed that an operation to perform an anterior interbody fusion that resulted in injury to major blood vessels was performed without her consent. The court stated: "The plaintiff must establish as part of his burden of proof that the information which was withheld was of such significance that had it been disclosed, consent would not have been given."[25] Thus, a patient must prove that if he had been fully informed, he would not have consented.

In 1972 in *Cobbs* v. *Grant*, where a physician operated on a patient for a duodenal ulcer, the question arose as to whether the action should be one of battery or negligence. The court said that, unless a physician performs an operation for which he has not received the patient's consent, the California courts will proceed under a negligence theory. Based on this approach, it has been found that "the inadvertent failure to disclose a risk of great likelihood could result in a battery, while an intentional failure to disclose a remote risk would constitute, at most, negligence."[26]

The facts of the Cobbs case were that surgery was indicated for the duodenal ulcer, and the family doctor advised the patient in general terms of the risks of undergoing general anesthesia. The surgeon informed Cobbs of the nature of the operation, but not its inherent risks. Nine days after successful surgery, Cobbs had severe abdominal pain and returned to the hospital and had to have his spleen removed. In about 5 percent of such operations, spleen injury happens. Later, Cobbs had severe stomach pains, returned to the hospital and had to have 50 percent of his stomach removed. Still later, he had to return to the hospital for internal bleeding due to premature absorption of a suture. These occurrences are inherent risks of surgery, of which Cobbs was never informed. In order to obtain consent, a physician must divulge "to his patient all information relevant to a meaningful decisional process."[27]

Accordingly, the scope of the physician's duty to disclose also includes any material information that the physician knowns, or should know, that would be regarded as significant by a reasonable person in the patient's position when deciding to accept or reject treatment. In addition, the Cobbs court held that "as an integral part of the physician's overall obligation to the patient there is a duty of reasonable disclosure of available choices with respect to proposed therapy and the dangers inherently and potentially involved in each."[28]

A District of Columbia court held in *Canterbury* v. *Spence* that a physician breached his duty to disclose by failing to warn the patient of a 1 percent risk of paralysis from a laminectomy. In that case, the court held that, to be material, the information must refer to a hazard that the patient had not already discovered.[29]

In *Hunter* v. *Brown*,[30] a woman of Korean ancestry consulted a plastic surgeon, who diagnosed the developing dark spots on her face as chloasma and recommended a dermabrasion. However, he did not inform her of any risks to the procedure, which he performed. When the spots increased, the woman sued the surgeon for lack of informed consent, because evidence indicated that hyperpigmentation is a greater possibility for Oriental patients. The physician countered that it was not good medical practice to tell the woman of the risk. The appellate court reversed the dismissal of the woman's lawsuit and rejected the rule that the necessary scope of disclosure must be established by expert medical testimony. The decision of the court was based on the nature of the physician-patient relationship which inherently demands trust and confidence and imposes a duty on the physician to inform his patient of all risks and material facts. According to the *Hunter* v. *Brown* case, the materiality of the risk or fact is to be determined by applying the standards of a reasonable man, not a reasonable medical practitioner.

In *Wilkinson* v. *Vesey*,[31] the patient claimed that the radiologist failed to secure her informed consent. The Supreme Court of Rhode Island reversed a directed verdict for the radiologist, saying:

> The patient is entitled to receive material information upon which he can base an informed consent. The decision as to what is or is not material is a human judgment, in our opinion, which does not necessarily require the assistance of the medical profession.

In this case, the court said that a reasonable-man standard must be applied as "an objective criterion of whether a risk is material."

The nurse should note that all these cases place the responsibility for informing the patient clearly with the physician, not with a nurse or with an admitting clerk.

The *Truman v. Thomas*[32] case applied the *Cobbs v. Grant* rule to circumstances where a patient refused to submit to a test, a Pap smear, as well as to circumstances where a patient consents to treatment. In previous decisions, a physician had a duty only to warn a patient of risks involved in undergoing treatment or a surgical procedure. Under *Truman v. Thomas*, it is no longer necessary for the physician to administer treatment to a patient in order to be held liable for failing to give full disclosure. As a fiduciary, the physician has an obligation to provide all information material to the patient's decision to accept or reject treatment. *Truman v. Thomas* strengthens the patient's right to decide what will be done to her or his body, including enlightened right of informed refusal.[33]

REAL CONSENT

It has been shown that, to have a contract, there must be two or more persons, an offer, an acceptance and a consideration. In addition, to have a legally enforceable contract, it is often said that there must be real consent, i.e., a "meeting of the minds," revealing the lack of misrepresentation or fraud of real significance. To be able to make valid contracts, persons must have legal capacity.

Disability to Make Binding Contracts

Certain groups of persons are under a disability to make binding contracts, but legal capability is presumed unless one of the following exists: mental incompetence, marital disqualification, infancy, intoxication or drug addiction to a degree precluding legal transactions.

Mental Incompetence. Persons to a contract must be mentally competent, i.e., not suffering from a mental disease or defect. Determining whether a person is mentally competent either for medical or for legal purposes is a thorny and difficult matter, as many nurses realize who have experienced training or duty in psychiatric hospitals. The persons must be capable of understanding the conditions and necessary or natural result of the contract.

The court dismissed the father's petition for commitment of a woman as a mentally ill person when a jury returned a verdict finding that Ms. Levias was mentally ill, but that she was not dangerous to her own life or the lives or property of others.[34]

Legal Insanity. Legal insanity is often determined by the so-called right and wrong test, based on the rule in *M'Naghten's Case*.[35]

> A man is sane when he knows the nature and quality of his acts and knows that they are wrong.

In another decision, the District of Columbia court rejected the existing tests, based on the accused's knowledge of the difference between right and wrong as supplemented by the irresistible impulse test, as the only criterion determining criminal responsibility. The court substituted a rule that an accused is not criminally responsible if his wrongful act is the product of mental disease or mental defect.[36] In a 1976 decision of the District of Columbia Court of Appeals, the court adopted a new standard for an insanity defense, i.e., a person is not responsible for criminal conduct if at the time of such conduct, as a result of mental disease or defect, he or she lacks substantial capacity either to recognize the wrongfulness of conduct or to conform his or her conduct to the requirements of the law.[37] As used in the standard, the terms "mental disease" or "defect" do not include an abnormality manifested only by repeated criminal or otherwise antisocial conduct. As a basis for avoiding a contract, insanity does not mean:

> A total deprivation of reason, but an inability from defect of perception, memory and judgment to do the act in question or to understand its natural consequences.[38]

Also, it must appear that the insanity existed at the time of the particular contract, i.e., that because of the diseased condition of his mind, the person made a contract that he would not have made had he been rational.[39]

As generally used in the popular sense, "insanity" refers to varying degrees of unsoundness of mind, and people realize that sometimes there is a close line between sanity and insanity. Moreover, insanity may be a temporary condition, and a person may have a lucid interval when she or he is considered sane enough to be in a normal state. This makes the matter much more difficult to determine, especially when a person has not been declared insane by a court, since she or he may make a contract during such an interval, and the contract is valid.

Generally, contracts made by an insane person are voidable; i.e., when and if the insane person regains sanity, he or she may affirm or repudiate the contract. However, the other party to the contract cannot use such insanity as an excuse to avoid the contract.

When there is a want of sufficient mental capacity to transact ordinary business and to take care of and manage property, the law will authorize the appointment of a guardian for the patient.[40] If a person is incompetent, but has not been declared so judicially, statutes in the different states provide that an action for the appointment of a guardian may be brought by his next friend, who is either a volunteer or one appointed by the court. After a person has been declared incompetent or insane at law, any contracts she or he makes are void, but the guardian has legal authority to act in her or his place. An insane or incompetent person is liable for personal necessities as well as those of a spouse and minor children. Medical service, including nursing, has been held to be a necessity.[41] In a case decided in 1889, the court held that a husband may not withhold necessary medical assistance for his wife by not giving consent to an operation.[42]

Marital Disqualification. According to the common law (the law prior to passage of a statute), husband and wife were "one"; hence, during the husband's lifetime (unless he were imprisoned for life or deserted her) a married woman had no legal capacity to make a contract, although a single woman had such capacity. At common law, if a married woman wished to make any sort of contract, even if it concerned land and movable articles that she had before marriage or inherited after marriage, she needed the consent of her husband.

The disability of married women has been generally overcome by statutes in each state as society and the economic aspects of life have changed in form and tempo. Under the Married Women's Acts, a married woman can own property in her own name and can, through an express contract, make herself personally liable for necessities supplied to her and her family. However, the nurse should remember that, unless the married woman binds herself personally for nursing services rendered to her, she is not liable for the services.

Loss of Consortium. Consortium is a right that grows out of the marital relation.[43] Historically, the term was used to denote a husband's right (which the law recognized) to have his wife perform all the duties and obligations that she undertook with respect to him at marriage.[44] It included the right to her company, cooperation and aid in every conjugal relation,[45] "conjugal society, affection and assistance of the wife" as one case stated it.[46] Another early American case said that the right of consortium meant comfort in her society in that respect in which a husband's right is peculiar and exclusive.[47] Although early law emphasized loss of services, the concept of consortium has developed to include all the aspects of a marriage relationship, such as love, society, affection, companionship, sex and other attributes.[48] A recent case stated, "Beyond and apart from the legal relationship of the husband to support his wife ... there is in a continuing marital relationship, an inseparable mutuality of ties and obligations, of pleasure, affection, and companionship, which make that relationship a factual entity."[49]

Problems involving the right of consortium are not new. In 1586 the Chomley and Conges case dealt with the possibility of separate causes of action by either spouse.[50] However, at common law, husband and wife were one in marriage, and that one was the husband.[51] Nevertheless, in the ecclesiastical courts, husband and wife were separate persons who could sue and be sued.[52] In the latter courts, a woman could sue for the restitution of conjugal rights, as is interestingly brought out in "The Case of the Lonely Nurse."[53] In the civil courts, the right of the man to sue for loss of consortium was first allowed for intentional torts and then for negligent torts. With the passage of the Married Women's Acts, married women acquired the right to sue and to be sued in their own name. As a result of these statutes, women were able to recover damages for loss of consortium due to injuries done to their husbands by the intentional acts of others that interfered with or damaged the marriage relationship.[54]

Today, the term "consortium" has developed to include the right of the wife to the society and comfort of her husband.[55] It is also a term now used interchangeably, as *Corpus Juris Secundum* states,[56] to denote the affection,[57] aid,[58] assistance,[59] companionship,[60] comfort[61] and society[62] of either spouse; the consort's affection, society and aid;[63] and the person, affection, assistance and aid of the spouse.[64] The loss of any or all of these rights is the loss of consortium.[65]

The Hitaffer decision is the landmark case.[66] In that case, the wife sued her husband's employer for damages for loss of consortium when her husband sustained severe and permanent injuries to his body, as a result of which she was deprived of his aid, assistance, enjoyment and sex relations. The appellate court ruled that the wife had a cause of action. In part the court said:

> It can hardly be said that a wife has less of an interest in the marriage relation than does the husband or in these modern times that a husband renders services of such a different character to the family and household that they must be measured by a standard of such uncertainty that the law cannot estimate any loss thereof. The husband owes the same degree of love, affection, felicity, et cetera to the wife as she to him. He also owes the material service of support, but above and beyond that he renders other services as his mate's helper in her duties, as advisor and counselor, et cetera.[67]

Infancy. At common law, a contract made by a minor was voidable, and a person retained the power to disaffirm a contract until the day before reaching 21 years of age. Following the ratification of the Constitutional amendment that extends the right to vote to 18-year-olds, an increasing number of states are lowering the age of majority for all purposes.

Females attain majority at 18 years of age in Arizona, Arkansas, Connecticut, Delaware, Idaho, Kentucky, Maine, Michigan, Nevada, New Jersey, New Mexico, North Carolina, North Dakota, Oklahoma, South Dakota, Tennessee, Vermont, Virginia, Washington, West Virginia, Wisconsin and Wyoming.[68] Females attain majority in Utah and Oregon at 18 years of age or earlier if married.[69] The age of majority is 19 years in Alaska and Montana, although marriage ends minority in Alaska.[70] Males attain majority at 18 years of age unless emancipated earlier.

Marriage emancipates a minor in Florida, Iowa, Louisiana and Texas.[71] However, an emancipated minor is defined as a high school graduate, a parent or a pregnant female in Alabama and Pennsylvania.[72] Finally, consent at any age for pregnancy or pregnancy-connected care excluding abortion is permitted in Georgia, Kentucky, Missouri and Virginia.[73] It is apparent that the statutes for attaining the age of majority vary from state to state.

Minors

Emancipated-Mature

Whether or not a teenager can lawfully consent to treatment depends on several factors. Historically, except in an emergency, a minor's consent was not a sufficient basis for treatment. In some states a child may petition the court to remove the disability of infancy. In other states, a minor may be emancipated if the parents relinquish their responsibility to control and care for the minor, as well as their rights to his services and earnings. When a minor marries, the parent's control ceases. Today, a mature minor who is not legally emancipated but who understands and appreciates the consequences of treatment is able to give consent in a number of jurisdictions. According to Holder, no cases can be located in which a physician has been found liable to the parent for treating a minor of 14 years or over when the minor gave his consent.[74]

Birth Control. When the United States Supreme Court in *Griswold v. Connecticut*[75] held that a Connecticut statute prohibiting the use of contraceptives interfered not only with the right of privacy of individuals in the marital relationship but also with the physician's right to treat a patient as he or she considered best, most restrictions on giving contraceptives to married people ceased. A later case held that a Massachusetts statute forbidding delivery of contraceptives to unmarried people was invalid since it violated the Fourteenth Amendment's guarantees of equal protection under the law.[76] Elsewhere a Federal district judge stated that a juvenile court has the constitutional power to order a sexually active minor to have an intrauterine contraceptive device regardless of her wishes.[77] A conviction of an Ohio mother for instructing her 16-year-old daughter in the use of contraceptives was reversed on the basis that it violated the mother's freedom of speech.[78]

A Federal appellate court in New York ruled that the HH5 Regulation requiring notice to parents of minors who are prescribed contraceptives was not authorized by statute. The court said it was not intended that the family planning groups directly involve parents or guardians.[79]

In dealing with a minor, the observance of a number of precautions seems advisable.[80] The feasibility of parental consent should be considered. Obtaining and maintaining a complete case history is necessary. An emergency need or judgment of the physician that pregnancy is a health hazard should be recorded.

The minor should sign a consent stating that she knows the problems and consequences of the procedure. Follow-up care when indicated should be insisted upon.

Abortion and Minors. The nurse must check state law concerning minors giving consent for treatment in matters related to pregnancy. In *Ballard v. Anderson*[82] the court held that medical care in connection with pregnancy includes abortion and that a minor can consent to abortion. In the case of *In re Smith*,[83] it was held that the parents of a pregnant minor cannot compel her to have an abortion.

Drug Abuse and Minors. The nurse[84] must check state law concerning minors giving permission for treatment for drug abuse or dependency without parental consent. Increasingly, more states are considering such legislation. However, with the lowering of the age of majority in many states, more people are exempt from facing the problem. In addition, mature minors, married minors and emancipated minors are usually treated without parental consent. If minors seek treatment from a physician for drug dependency, they are likely to receive help whether or not they are able to give consent on their own, because no parental consent is needed in an emergency and the court would order treatment in any narcotic or controlled drug situation if application was made. Statutes requiring physicians to report the treatment of narcotic addicts vary from state to state.[85]

The problem of treatment for venereal disease in minors is comparable to that of drug dependency, because relatively few states have passed laws authorizing the physician to render care in the absence of parental consent. Without such legislation, a physician who treats a minor in the absence of parental consent faces a possible charge of battery.

Minor-Relinquished Child. In the case of *In re Watson* an intelligent and capable unmarried 14-year-old tenth-grade student, who had been counseled by caseworkers and given an opportunity to discuss her situation with empathic persons, signed a petition for voluntary relinquishment of her parental rights. Both she and her mother understood the finality of such a decision, and the court determined that their consents had been intelligently, voluntarily and deliberately given. However, the case was sent back for a determination of whether it was consistent with the Supreme Court decision in regard to due process rights of unwed fathers.[86]

A 14-year-old high school student, when she became pregnant, orally contracted with her parents that, when the child was born, it would be entered on the birth records as the child of her parents, who would bring up the child as their own. When the child was three years old, the girl married a man who knew that the child was that of his wife. They moved to a home of their own and told the child that her "parents" were really her grandparents and that the natural mother was her mother. The court held that, since the mother was only 14 years of age at the time of the original agreement, she could disaffirm the contract upon her attaining majority even if it were considered a valid contract.[87]

Birth Control Pill for Minors. Nurses and physicians frequently encounter in clinics or the doctor's office an unmarried teenage girl who seeks birth control pills to protect her against pregnancy. She is not accompanied by her parent nor does she wish the parent to be contacted for a consent to the requested treatment; hence, two questions arise: (1) Is the teenage girl's own consent legally sufficient for treatment? and (2) Should this request for treatment be brought to the parent's attention?[81]

Whether or not the teenage girl can lawfully consent to treatment generally depends on whether she is an emancipated minor or not. Except in a state that has a statute specifying another age, a person under the age of 18 years is considered a minor or not of age. When a minor marries, the parents' control ceases. When the teenage girl is unwilling to have the physician contact her parents for consent to treat her, he still may lawfully disclose such a request for treatment to them in the typical situation. Whether in fact the physician does disclose to parents the request for a prescription for birth control pills is more a question of discretion than of law.

Voidable or Void Contracts

Contracts made with minors are voidable, but not void. This statement needs explanation, since it may seem contradictory. A voidable contract is one that may be valid in every way except that one of the persons has the option of rejecting it. Such a power is given to the minor who makes a contract. For example, if John Brown, a 17-year-old movie star, contracts with Miss Jones, a nurse, to pay for nursing service for his 16-year-old sister before he becomes 18 years old, he may pay the charges or reject the contract. Obviously, the benefits of nursing service are a consideration that cannot be returned in case he rejects the contract.

A void contract is one prohibited by law or public policy that creates no rights. For example, a contract made by a person legally declared insane is void.

A minor's contract is voidable until he decides to affirm (give positive approval) or avoid it. If the contract concerned personal property (any item of movable or immovable property except real estate or things that are a part of it), the minor could reject it at any time, even before attaining his legal age. The rejection could be verbal (oral) or in writing, or it could be implied from his conduct. Upon rejecting the contract, if the minor has received any of the consideration for the contract, he must return it.[88]

Under statutes today, some contracts made by a minor, such as marriage, enlistment in the armed forces or for necessities to be supplied to him, are obligatory or binding. Among other things, necessities have been held to include medical service.[89] What is a necessity varies somewhat with the person's economic and social status.

The minor is liable only for the reasonable value of necessities supplied to him. For example, when a minor has received necessities, it should be noted that although the "reasonable value" may not exceed the contract price, neither is a "reasonable value" necessarily the contract price. A nurse should be aware of the legal aspects and be careful when making contracts with minors. She should remember that in such a contract, if the minor wants to reject it, the contract is open to investigation and determination by law regarding the necessity of her services and the reasonableness of their value, and that the burden of proving both these facts is on her.[90]

References

1. Cox v. Baltimore & O.S.W.R. Co., 180 Ind. 495, 103 N.E. 337 (1913).
2. Cohoes Memorial Hospital v. Mossey, 266 N.Y.S. 501 (1966).
3. Parker, L. T.: Review of Hospital Lawsuits, Hosp. Topics 43:69, 86, Jan. 1965, and 43:78, Aug. 1965.
4. Regan, W. A.: Contract for Nursing Service, Regan Report on Nursing Law, 4(8):1, Jan., 1965.
5. Fuerst v. Methodist Hospital South, 566 S.W. 2nd 847 (Tenn. S. Ct. 1978). Regan Report on Nursing Law, 19:2, Sept. 1978.
6. United States v. Averick, 249 F. Supp. 237 (1965).
7. Cavalier v. Weinstein, 80 A. 2d 918 (1951).

8. Cox v. Baltimore & O.S.W.R. Co., 180 Ind. 495, 103 N.E. 337 (1913).
9. Regan, W. A.: The R. N. and Her Professional Employment Contract, *Regan Report on Nursing Law*, 12(3)1, Aug. 1971.
10. Lusk v. Estes, etc., 361 F. Supp. 653 (Texas, 1973). *Ed. Ct. Digest*, 18(7):2, July 1974.
11. Clark v. Holmes, 474 F. 2d 928 (Ill. 1972). *Ed. Ct. Digest*, 17(11):6, Nov. 1973.
12. United States v. Board of Education, etc., 469 F. 2d 1315 (Ga., 1972). *Ed. Ct. Digest*, 17(10):2, Oct 1973.
13. *Restatement, Agency*, 1933, Sec. 17c.
14. Our Agency Allows Nurses to Remain Active, *Am. J. Nurs.*, 79:431, March 1979.
15. Bowdich v. French Broad Hospital, 201 N.C. 168, 159 S.E., 350 (1931).
16. Jordan Marsh Co. v. Cohen, 242 Mass. 245, 136 N.E., 350 (1922).
17. Kern v. Kern, 360 So. 2d 482, 484 (Fla. 4th DCA, 1978).
18. State v. Joyce, 361 So. 2d 406 (Fla. 1978).
19. Slater v. Baker, 95 Eng. Rep. 860, 862 (K. B. 1767).
20. Schloendorff v. Society of New York Hospital, 211 N.Y. 125, 129-130, 105 N.E. 92, 93 (N.Y. 1914).
21. Zoterell v. Repp, 187 Mich. 319, 324, 153 N.W. 692, 694 (Mich. 1915).
22. Valdez v. Percy, 35 Cal. App. 2d 485, 491, 96, P. 2d 142 (Cal. 1939).
23. Salgo v. Stanford University Board of Trustee, 154 Cal. App. 2d 560, 578, 317 P. 2d 170, 181 (Cal. 1957).
24. Dunlap v. Marine, 242 Cal. App. 2d 162, 51 Cal. Rptr. 158 (Cal. 1966).
25. Berkey, Dow v. Kaiser Foundation, 12 Cal. App. 3rd 488, 90 Cal. Rptr. 747 (Cal. 1970).
26. Cobbs v. Grant, 8 Cal. 3rd 299, 502 P. 2d 1, 104 Cal. Rptr. 505 (Cal. 1972).
27. Id., p. 242, 502 P. 2d 9, 104 Cal. Rptr. 513.
28. Id., p. 243, 502 P. 2d 10, 104 Cal. Rptr. 514.
29. Canterbury v. Spence, 464 F. 2d 772, 778 (D.C. Cir. 1972).
30. Hunter v. Brown, 484 P. 2d 1162 (Wash., 1971), Affm. 502 P. 2d 1194 (Wash., 1972). Simonaitis, J. E.: Recent Decisions on Informed Consent, JAMA, 221:441–442, July 24, 1972.
31. Wilkinson v. Vesey, 295 A. 2d 676 (R. I., 1972). Simonaitis, J. E.: More About Informed Consent, Part 1, JAMA, 224:1831–1832, June 25, 1973. Informed Consent, *Barnes Hosp. Bull.*, Aug. 1974, pp. 4–5.
32. Truman v. Thomas, 93 Cal. App. 3rd 304, 155 Cal. Rptr. 752 (1979); 27 Cal. 3rd 285, 611 P. 2d 902, 165 Cal. Rptr. 308 (S. Ct. 1980).
33. *Cf.* O'Neil, M.: The Rise of Informed Refusal, 8 *Pepperdine L. Rev.*, 1067–1085 (1981).
34. In re Levias, 517 P. 2d 588 (Wash., 1973).
35. M'Naghten's Case, 10 Cl. & Fin. 200, 8 Eng. Rep. 718 (1843). Barnes: A Century of the M'Naghten Rules, 8 *Camb. L. J.* 300 (1944). The Law and the Mentally Ill, *Ment. Hyg.*, 53:4–40, Jan. 1969. The whole issue discusses various aspects of the topic. Penn, N.

E., et al.: The Dilemma of Involuntary Commitment: Suggestions for a Measurable Alternative, 4–9; Penn, N. E., et al.: Some Considerations for Future Mental Health Legislation, 10–13; Meyer, E. J.: Lawyer in a Mental Hospital, 14–6; Shah, S. A.: Crime and Mental Illness: Some Problems in Defining and Labeling Deviant Behavior.
36. Durham v. United States, 94 App. D. C. 228, 214 F. 2d 862, motion denied 130 Fed. Supp. 445, 45 A. L. R. 2nd 1430 (1954). There has been extensive comment on the case. *See* 53 *Mich. L. Rev.* 963 (1955); 18 *Modern L. R.* 391 (1955); 5 *Catholic U. L. Rev.* 63 (1955), and in the same issue, Cavanagh, A Psychiatrist Looks at the Durham Decision, p. 25.
37. Bethea v. United States, 365 A. 2d 64 (D. C. Ct. of App., 1976).
38. Durrett v. McWhorter, 161 Ga. 179, 129 S.E. 870 (1925).
39. Dewey v. Algire, 37 Neb. 6, 55 N.W. 276 (1893); In re Herr's Estate, 251 Pa. 223, 96 Atl. 464 (1915); In re Halbert's Will, 15 Misc. 308, 37 N. Y. S. 757 (1895).
40. *In re* Wetmore, 6 Wash. 271, 33 Pac. 615 (1893).
41. Snyder v. Nixon, 188 Iowa 779, 176 N.W. 808 (1920).
42. Janneu v. Housekeeper, 70 Md. 162, 16 A. 382 (1889).
43. 41 Corpus Juris Secundum 402: Reppert v. Reppert, 13 A. 2d 705 (Dec., 1940).
44. Ramon v. Ramon, 34 N. Y. S. 2d 100, 110 (N.Y., 1942).
45. Blair v. Seitner Dry Goods Co., 151 N.W. 724 (Mich., 1915); L.R.A., 1915 D 524, Ann. Cas. 1916 D 882.
46. Prettyman v. Williamson, 39 A. 731 (Del., 1898).
47. Bigaouette v. Paulet, 45 Am. Rep. 307 (Mass., 1883).
48. Leaphart, B., and McCann, R. E.: Consortium: An Action for the Wife. 35 *Mont. L. Rev.*, 75, Winter 1973.
49. Deems v. Western Maryland Railway Co., 231 A. 2d 514, 521 (Md., 1967), noted in 13 *Villanova L. Rev.* 418 (1968).
50. Chomley and Conges, 74 Eng. Rep. 748 (Common Pleas, 1586).
51. Blackstone's Commentaries, Sec. 442 (Lewis's ed. 1900).
52. Id., Sec. 444.
53. The Case of the Lonely Nurse: The Wife's Action for Loss of Consortium, 18 *West. R. L. Rev.* 621, 626 (1967).
54. Holbrook: The Change in the Meaning of Consortium, 22 *Mich. L. Rev.* 1 (1923).
55. Henley v. Rockett, 8 So. 2d 852 (Ala., 1942).
56. 41 *Corpus Juris Secundum* 402.
57. CNA Supports Baccalaureate for Entry with Push for Increase in Available Programs, *Am. J. Nurs.*, 79:838, May 1979.
58. Little Rock Gas, etc. Co. v. Coppedge, 172 S.W. 885 (Ark., 1915).
59. Id.
60. Ramsey v. Ramsey, 156 A. 354 (Del., 1931).
61. Id.
62. Id.

63. Seaver v. Adams, 19 A. 776 (N.H., 1890).
64. McGregor v. McGregor, 115 S.W. 802 (Ky., 1909).
65. *Op. cit.*, note 57.
66. Hitaffer v. Argonne, 87 App. D.C. 47, 183 F. 2d 811 (1950), cert. denied 340 U.S. 851.
67. Id., 819.
68. *See* Table on State Laws, *Family Planning Digest,*, 1(6), published by National Center for Family Planning Services, Department of Health, Education and Welfare, Washington, D.C. *See also* Creighton, H.: The New Abortion Ruling, *Supvr. Nurse*, 4:8, 10, July 1973, and Therapeutic Abortion and the Minor, *J. Legal Med.*, 1:36–42, March–April 1973.
69. Ibid.
70. Ibid.
71. Ibid.
72. Ibid.
73. Ibid.
74. Holder, A. R.: Minors and Contraception, JAMA, 216: 2059, June 21, 1971.
75. Griswold v. Connecticut, 381 U. S. 479 (1965).
76. Baird v. Eisenstadt, *CCAI*, July 6, 1970.
77. Young, D. J.: Court Ordered Contraception, *Am. Bar Assn. J.*, 223, March 1969.
78. Ohio v. McLaughlin, 212 N.E. 2d 635 (Ohio, 1965).
79. State of New York v. Heckler, 719 F. 2d 1191 (C.A. 2, N.Y. 1983); *Citation*, 48:134, Apr. 1, 1984.
80. Pipel, H. F., and Wechsler, N. F.: Birth Control, Teenagers and the Law, *Family Planning Perspect.*, 1:29, 1969.
81. Reid, R. L.: Birth Control Pills for Minors, *J. Med. Assn. Georgia*, 57:149–150, March, 1968.
82. Ballard v. Anderson, 484 P. 2d 1345 (Calif. 1971).
83. *In re* Smith, Md. Ct. Spec. App. 41 L W 2202 (1972).
84. Ariz. Rev. Stat. Ann. 544–133.01 (1971 Supp.).
85. Epstein, R. L., and Benson, D. L.: Drug Abuse Treatment and Parental Consent, *Hospitals*, 47:63, Sept. 1, 1973.
86. *In re* Watson, 301 A. 2d 861 (Pa. 1973). *Soc. Welfare Digest*, 19(6):6, June 1974.
87. Rainer v. Rowlett, 502 S.W. 2d 617 (Ark., 1963). *Soc. Welfare Digest*, 19(6):6, June 1974.
88. 1 Williston, *Contracts*, Rev. ed. 1936, Sec. 238.
89. Bishop v. Shurley, 237 Mich. 76, 211 N.W. 75 (1926).
90. Brockway v. Jewell, 52 Ohio St. 187, 39 N.E. 470 (1894).

General References

Bernsweig, E.: Don't Cut Corners on Informed Consent, *RN*, 47:15–16, Dec. 1984.

Creighton, H.: The Right of Informed Refusal, *Nurs. Management*, 13:48–49, Sept. 1982.

Creighton, H.: Nursing School Catalog Is Written Contract, *Nurs. Management*, 15:68–69, Feb. 1984.

Creighton, H.: Both Parents Liable for Payment of Child's Hospitalization, *Superv. Nurse*, 12:12–15, Feb. 1981.

Cushing, M.: Informed Consent and M. D. Responsibility, *Am. J. Nursing*, 84:437–440, April 1984.

Furrow, B. R.: Damage Remedies and Institutional Reform; the Right to Refuse Treatment, *Law, Med. & Health Care*, 10:152–157, Sept. 1982.

Greenlaw, J.: Should Hospitals Be Responsible for Informed Consent? *Law, Med. & Health Care*, 11:173–176, Sept. 1983.

Holder, A. R., et al.: Informed Consent and the Nurse, *Nurs. Law Ethics*, 2:1–2 +, Feb. 1981.

Kapp, M. B.: Legal Guardianship, *Geriat. Nurs.*, 2:366–369, Sept./Oct. 1981.

Manicini, M.: Nursing, Minors and the Law, *Am. J. Nursing*, 78:124–126, Jan. 1978.

Murphy, E.: Informed Consent: Role of the OR Nurse, *Today's OR Nurse*, 5:51–52, March 1983.

Taub, S.: Cancer and the Law of Informed Consent, *Law, Med. & Health Care*, 10:61–66 +, April 1982.

Watson, A. B.: Informed Consent of Special Subjects, *Nurs. Res.*, 31:43–47, Jan./Feb. 1982.

Four
BREACH AND TERMINATION OF CONTRACT

After an agreement has been made between two or more persons capable of contracting who create or intend to create a legal obligation, it is important for the nurse to consider how such a valid contract may be ended.

HOW TO TERMINATE A VALID CONTRACT

Obviously, one way of terminating a contract is for each person to duly *carry out all obligations* in accordance with the contract. Further, the contract may be ended by the release of one person by the other person. Sometimes a contract may be ended by the contracting person's agreeing to *substitute a new obligation* or *new person*. Of particular importance to nurses is the fact that, although you can generally *assign* or *transfer your rights* to receive money under a contract without the consent of the other persons, you cannot assign or transfer duties of a personal nature unless this is acceptable to other persons to the contract. The contract may also provide for termination on the *expiration of a fixed period* or *the occurrence of a particular event*.

UNENFORCEABLE CONTRACTS

A contract may become unenforceable because suits are not brought within the time limit fixed in the *Statute of Limitations*. A malpractice action against a county hospital for a nurse's alleged negligence in giving an injection was barred by the patient's failure to give notice of his claim within 60 days after his alleged injury as required by Iowa law. It did not bar a similar action against the nurse against whom suit was also brought.[1]

Contracts may also be ended because a supervening event makes performance *impossible*. In general, a person is excused from carrying out his obligation or duty in any contract when, through no fault of his own, such performance is *legally* or *physically impossible*. This is the situation in which a nurse is ill or dies, or her patient (on a private duty case) passes away. However, in a case in which a patient paid a physician in advance for treatments to be received, but became too ill to attend the physician's office for the treatments, the physician, having incurred no preparatory expense prior to the patient's disability, was required to return the money paid.[2] If the case had involved a nurse, instead of a physician, under similar circumstances, the court would have probably reached the same decision.

Again, if a nurse is prevented from carrying out her contractual obligations by some supervening event or *"act of God,"* such as a storm or a labor strike, she is excused in a majority of states. Inasmuch as the law is not uniform in all states on this question, the nurse will notice that written contracts often contain a sentence specifically providing for nonliability for performance when performance is impossible. At this point, the nurse is reminded that inconvenience and personal matters other than illness or death do not constitute a legal excuse for failure to carry out a contract. For example, consider the predicament of a nurse, Miss Jones, who lives in a suburb where public transportation facilities are limited and uses her own car for transportation to work. She accepts a position on a monthly basis at Hospital A in the downtown area of a large city. Subsequently, her car is destroyed, and she cannot afford to buy another one for three months. Now it takes Miss Jones 90 minutes instead of 20 minutes to get to work. By riding to work with a neighbor, Miss Jones can save an hour, but she arrives at the hospital 15 minutes late for duty. Nevertheless, Miss Jones decides that this is the only "sensible course of action," and she simply comes to work 15 minutes late. Such tardiness is a breach of contract.

Again, a married nurse, Mrs. Jones, whose two pre-school children are cared for by a maid "living out," accepts a position to work from 7:30 A.M. to 4 P.M. Monday through Friday at Hospital A. One Tuesday morning Mrs. Jones' maid calls and says, "I'm getting married and I'm taking off the rest of the week." Mrs. Jones stays home from her hospital position and cares for her children until her maid returns to work. Any nurse who foresees that circumstances will prevent her or him from carrying out a contract should point them out to the other person to the contract, and reserve the right to stop work or adjust her or his schedule if necessary. If she or he fails to do this and does not perform the services, the hospital may regard the contract as ended. Furthermore, if the hospital sustains a money loss as a result thereof, it may consider the nurse as having broken the contract.

ILLEGAL CONTRACTS

Illegality excuses a nurse from carrying out a contract, as when the subject of the contract is declared illegal.

Contracts in Violation of the Law

For example, suppose a nurse, Miss Jones, makes a contract with Hospital A to serve as head nurse and when on duty to start intravenous infusions on patients and to draw blood for various laboratory tests as ordered when no physician is available. If the state in which Hospital A is located passes a law making it illegal for anyone except a duly licensed physician to do a venipuncture, Miss Jones' performance of her contract is excused.

Consent Obtained by Fraud

In the discussion of the requirement of a legally enforceable contract, it was pointed out that the real consent of the parties is necessary, and that no enforceable obligation is incurred if there is actually no expression of intention.[3] To constitute fraud, there must be a false representation of fact made with the intent that it be acted on by the other party, and such fact must be an inducing cause of the contract. For example, Nursing School C lists an opening for a qualified instructor in nursing fundamentals. A nurse, Miss Jones, makes application for the position and submits, as her own, certain transcripts of university undergraduate and graduate education and published educational articles, all the work of a person with the same name. In view of her apparent education and ability, Nursing School C employs Miss Jones for the position. The fraud in this so-called contract is apparent; a false representation of fact with the intent that it be acted on, and such fact is clearly an inducing element of the contract. In a fraud case involving a physician, the court said that, irrespective of the question of lack of benefit, a practitioner who falsely represents a patient's physical condition in order to induce him or her to contract for services will be denied the right to payment and compelled to refund any money for unnecessary treatment.[4]

Duress

Duress is another matter that will negate real consent of persons to a contract. At common law, duress means actual or threatened violence to or imprisonment of the person or his spouse, parent or child that is brought about by the other contracting party at the time that they make the contract. According to principles established in equity, the branch of law applying ethical or moral standards to disputes, contracts are considered voidable when brought about by forms of coercion and pressure that did not amount to duress at common law. The act complained of must be wrongful to cause duress. For example, in a suit on an agreement in which contracting party A agreed to pay the husband, contracting party B, for medical treatment of B's wife, who was injured by the negligence of the son of party A, in consideration of the husband's promise not to sue the son, the court stated that the husband's threat to exercise a legal right did not constitute "duress,"[5] even if the claims on which the suit was threatened were unfounded and the husband knew it.

A physician's sister failed the Educational Council for Foreign Medical Graduates (ECFMG) examination three times. In 1972 at the request of her husband, the physician took the examination using her sister's name. She passed the examination, and the sister finished her internship and was licensed in 1976. The physician received her medical license in Florida in 1975. Divorce proceedings in 1976 were brought by the physician and her husband. Using his knowledge of the 1972 incident, the husband forced the physician to sign a property settlement and agreement giving him custody of their daughter. In 1978, the physician brought suit to set aside the custody and support agreements on the basis of coercion and duress. The court granted her request. She was reprimanded for taking the ECFMG examination for her sister in 1972.[6]

Undue Influence

When a person is moved by undue influence to make a contract, it may be set aside. For example, an attractive young nurse with a "world of personality" is caring for an 86-year-old patient with a fractured hip when his recovery is interrupted by a stroke. As soon as the patient can talk a little and can use his hand to sign his name, the nurse calls in an attorney and has the patient make a will. In his will, the patient gives half of his property to the nurse. Ten days later, the patient dies. In such a case, the decedent's heirs are likely to question the validity of the will.

Material Misrepresentation

Aside from fraud, a material (significant) misrepresentation does away with real consent and may permit a person to avoid or cancel a contract. For example, if a private duty nurse, Miss Jones, has been engaged to care for a patient represented to her as a surgical case, a colostomy, and the patient is found to be a schizophrenic, Miss Jones may refuse to go on the case. She would not be liable for breach of contract, since there was no real consent, owing to material misrepresentation. For misrepresentation to excuse performance, it must be of such importance that a reasonable person, had he known the situation, would not have made the contract, indicating that the person who desires to negate the contract was in fact misled.

Mistake

Mistake is another matter preventing real consent in the formation of a contract. In general, the question of "mistake" is a difficult one. Obviously, ignorance of a fact is not enough to permit cancellation of the contract. For example, Mr. Smith contracts with Miss Jones for a week's nursing service to be given to his best friend, Mr. Doe. He is bound by the contract even though he did not read it before signing. There may be a mistake about the identity of a contracting person as well as the subject matter.

Informed consent is further discussed in Chapter 3.

DISCRIMINATION

The recent trend has been to outlaw discrimination on the basis of race, creed, color or national origin. In 1896, a state statute requiring segregation of passengers on railroads was held to be valid and nondiscriminatory if equal facilities were at the disposal of each racial group.[7] Fifty years later, the requirement of segregated seating for passengers on interstate buses was held to be unconstitutional. By 1950, racial segregation was enjoined in a state university,[8] and segregated city-owned recreational facilities, even though equal, were prohibited.[9] More recently, school desegregation rulings, public accommodation statutes, employment regulations, open housing laws and so forth have been aimed at eliminating all discrimination insofar as the law can achieve it.

When a unit of government operates a hospital, it must be open to all citizens on the same basis. For many years, a charitable hospital has been open:

> at the call of the afflicted . . . looking at nothing and caring for nothing beyond the fact of their affliction.[10]

Other states for years have required that a hospital, to be tax-exempt, must accept patients without discrimination as to race, creed or color.[11] When the guardian of a severely retarded black child sued a state mental institution to enjoin it from denying him admission on racial grounds, the action against the hospital was dismissed when it proved it did routinely admit black patients but could not accept him because of 100 percent occupancy of all accommodations it had.[12]

In a civil rights action the plaintiffs brought an employment discrimination action involving black nurses against a nonprofit medical center. Extensive, detailed personnel records showed that each plaintiff had been counseled on a number of occasions, and the court found no evidence of an unlawful discrimination with respect to the defendant hospital.[13]

A black registered respiratory therapist who was supervisor of her shift sued a hospital in Texas claiming three instances of racial discrimination in violation of Title VII of the Civil Rights Act of 1964. When she applied for the position of assistant chief therapist, she had never received an unfavorable evaluation. She established a *prima facie* case for promotion, and the reasons advanced against it were pretexts masking racial discrimination. The plaintiff was given $20,123.52 damages and $8,785.95 as attorney's fees and costs.[14]

In a hospital, requiring English as a job qualification does not violate the plaintiff's rights under Title VII of the 1964 Civil Rights Act.[15]

The Federal Court of Appeals decided in *Simpkins v. Moses H. Cone Memorial Hospital* that the separate-but-equal provision of the Hill-Burton Hospital Survey and Construction Act of 1946, under which segregated hospital facilities had been built throughout the South, was unconstitutional. This meant that private, voluntary hospitals that had earlier used any Federal money under the Federal and state plans had to comply with Federal laws made after the hospital buildings was completed.[16] In a later action, a class suit was allowed to compel hospitals who received Hill-Burton funds to provide below cost or without charge a reasonable volume of services to persons unable to pay. Therefore, the court said:

> We hold that the Hill-Burton Act is designed, at least in part, to benefit persons unable to pay for medical services. Such people are not the sole beneficiaries of the Act, but they certainly are the object of much of the Act's concern. We are of the opinion that the Act, by its own terms, makes it plain that persons unable to pay for medical services are one of the chief sets of beneficiaries of this legislation. It is a matter of the clearest logic that the only real beneficiaries of a hospital program are the people who need or may need medical treatment. This includes people of all classes, whether rich or poor.[12]

The Federal Age Discrimination in Employment Act[18] forbids private hospitals who employ 25 or more to "refuse to hire, discharge or otherwise to discriminate against any hospital employee with respect to his compensation, terms, conditions or privileges of employment because of age." Such hospitals also are forbidden to limit, segregate or classify hospital workers in any way that would deprive or tend to deprive any individual of job opportunities or otherwise adversely affect his or her status because of age. "Moreover they are forbidden" to reduce the wage rate of any hospital worker "in order to comply with this act." Also important is the fact that such hospitals are forbidden to "use help-wanted advertisements which indicate any preference, limitation, specification or discrimination based on age." The Act may be difficult to enforce, but it does offer the older nurse, among others, protection against discriminatory practices on account of age.

In October 1978 in Palos Hills, Illinois, two female nurses won an out-of-court settlement case against Christ Hospital and the Evangelical Hospital

Association in a sex bias case on the basis that male employees in the hospital were allowed outside interests to boost their income without hospital interference, but that this privilege had been denied the female employees.[19]

The Supreme Court of the United States ruled that a state statute that excludes males from enrolling in a state-supported school of nursing violates the equal protection clause of the Fourteenth Amendment.[20]

The Michigan Court of Appeals held that a hospital policy that excluded from the delivery room anyone but the expectant mother's husband or member of her "immediate family" violates a state antidiscrimination law.[21]

St. Vincent's Medical Center in Richmond, New York, is appealing the State Division of Human Rights decision that orders it to hire a female employee even though she cannot work on Saturdays. The nurse is an Orthodox Jew forbidden by her religion to perform any work on the Sabbath; the hospital requires its full-time nurses to work weekends on a rotating basis, and would offer her only a part-time or on-call position. The nurse claimed that the hospital discriminated against her for religious reasons.[22]

Epstein and Manson point out that ever since the Department of Health, Education and Welfare published the handicap regulations[23] that implement Section 504 of the Rehabilitation Act of 1973, there has been increasing uncertainty as to what the regulations mean and what should be done to comply.[24] The Department received little guidance on congressional intent in the statute, which states:

> No otherwise qualified handicapped individual in the United States . . . shall, solely by reason of his handicap, be excluded from the participation in, be denied the benefits of, or be subjected to discrimination under any program or activity receiving federal financial assistance.[25]

In Romeo Community Schools[26] the court ruled that, by prohibiting sex discrimination in educational programs receiving Federal financial assistance, Congress intended to protect only the participants in the programs (the students) rather than the school's employees (the teachers). As a consequence, the court struck down the portion of the HEW guidelines under the statute that covered employment practices.

In an action under the Civil Rights Act of 1871 and the Rehabilitation Act of 1973, a case was brought against a college by a licensed practical nurse who, because of hearing disability, was denied admission to the college's nursing program. A decision not to admit the student was made after consultation with the executive director of the state board of nursing, who said that the student's hearing impairment could interfere with the safety of her care for patients in the school's clinical training segments. It was held by the Appeals Court that, under Section 504 of the Rehabilitation Act of 1973, the student should be allowed to enter the R.N. program. However, it was unanimously ruled by the U.S. Supreme Court that colleges and universities do not have to totally disregard physical disabilities when considering prospective students, or make substantial program changes to accommodate the handicapped student. Although the Section 504 regulations require schools to provide such auxiliary aids as taped texts, intrepreters and adapted classroom equipment, the kind of curricular changes that would be necessary to accommodate the student in question were far more than the "modification" that the regulation requires, according to the Supreme Court. Justice Powell also noted that the college would have to significantly lower its educational standards if the student participated, and Section 504 does not intend or require that.[27]

In a case in which a Tennessee university had a policy of limiting the outside income of professors in order to insure that they devote maximal energy to their teaching duties, two professors of medicine at the university were dismissed because they refused to sign income limiting agreements. However, a Federal trial court ruled that they had no civil rights or antitrust claims against the university. The same ruling would hold for nursing faculty.[28]

In another case a medical student has been informed of his school's dissatisfaction with his progress. He had failed at least one major course every year, thus raising questions about his competency, and the Dean of Admissions had written to him six months before he was dropped from school. The highest court of New York ruled that the school had followed proper procedures when it dismissed the student for failure to demonstrate sufficient aptitude for the practice of medicine. The same rule would apply to a nursing student.[29]

In Pennsylvania a state law enabled an eligible institution to receive a grant of up to $400 for each attending student who received a state scholarship, and the law authorized a state agency to determine which institutions were eligible. It was held by the Supreme Court that nursing schools operated by hospitals were not eligible for the grant because they did not meet the independent institution requirement in that they lacked educational charters. Other hospital nursing schools were eligible because they were affiliated with chartered institutions of higher education or had separate charters from their parent hospitals.[30]

When a hospital paid a female occupational therapist asssistant ten cents an hour less than it paid male therapist assistants, a discrepancy that was not justified on the basis of additional duties, and had retaliated against her complaint by offering her a promotion as head of the department with no increase in pay and by placing conditions upon her that were not placed upon the person who eventually held the job, the Commissioner ordered the hospital to cease such discrimination and equalize wage rates, and included an award for back pay plus interest, $2000 in attorney's fees and $2000 for emotional distress.[31] Except for the attorney's fees, the award was upheld by the highest court in Massachusetts.

Comparable Worth

In *Lemmons* v. *City and County of Denver*, starting salaries for parking meter repairmen, tree trimmers and tire servicemen in a male class had beginning salaries from $65 to $319 per month higher than beginning salaries for staff nurses who were in an overwhelmingly female class. In supervisory groups for 35 percent male classifications, less combined education and experience was required than for a head nurse. Despite the overwhelming amount of evidence showing sex discrimination in salaries, the court held that the Equal Pay Act did not include comparing salaries of nurses who were overwhelmingly female with males in unrelated, nonhealth field jobs. In the court's opinion. "comparable worth" meant "equal work" and "equal work meant near identical jobs and functions."[32] A similar outcome was reached in *Spaulding* v. *University of Washington* where nurse educators, almost all of whom were women and paid approximately 35 percent less, were compared with their male counterparts in public health, social work and pharmacy. Such criteria as highest degree held, hours of classroom teaching and hours of clinical supervision per week were used.[33]

Where blacks filled jobs comparable in job evaluation points to whites who filled jobs but received higher pay, the Federal court held there was a violation of Title VII.[34] Where there was an historic policy of the company to segregate men and women warehouse employees and pay women less, the court held there was intentional job discrimination against the women.[35]

In 1982 in *Briggs* v. *City of Madison*,[36] women public health nurses proved they were paid considerably less than public health sanitarians. However, the court found that the jobs were not identical, hence the equal pay for equal work standard of the Equal Pay Act was not met. In its defense, the city admitted that sex was a factor in establishing wages. It claimed that it paid the men higher salaries because there was a shortage of sanitarians, and therefore higher salaries were needed to recruit and retain sanitarians. While the city presented no hard evidence to support its claim, the court held that the city had met the burden of proof of this defense. Thus, the court held that the market rate was a legitimate defense to a *prima facie* case of sex discrimination under Title VII.

In *AFSCME* v. *State of Washington*, the union brought action under Title VII of the Civil Rights Act of 1964 against the state. The state had conducted a job evaluation study comparing predominately male and female jobs in skill, knowledge, mental demands, accountability and working conditions, which found that female jobs having the same number of points as male jobs were paid less. The state court findings were: "State violated Title VII's ban on sex discrimination in compensation, there being past historical discrimination against women in state employment manifested by direct, overt, and institution- alized discrimination that continued after Title VII became applicable to state and there being no legitimate overriding business considerations presented by state." The case is on appeal.

The Supreme Court of the United States has dodged the controversy over the issue of comparable worth. The justices, without comment, rejected in 1984 an appeal by members of the faculty of the University of Washington School of Nursing to the school's wage scale. They brought suit in 1974 under the Equal Pay Act and the 1964 Civil Rights Act, saying men in comparable positions were paid more. The Ninth Circuit Court of Appeals held that the nurses had not shown discriminatory treatment by the fact that the university used prevailing market wages to set salaries for its employees.[38]

Nurse's Aides Versus Orderlies

In one of the early cases,[39] a hospital paid orderlies at a higher rate than nurse's aides, and claimed that the extra duties required of orderlies justified the differential. The hospital asserted that the orderlies put forth extra effort (as in lifting heavy patients), needed more skill (as in catheterizing male patients) and shouldered more responsibility (as in maintaining hospital security). The court held that, if those additional duties did require extra effort, took up a substantial amount of the orderlies' working time and were of an economic value correspond- ing to the additional pay, the orderlies could rightfully be paid more than the nurse's aides. On appeal, the decision in favor of the hospital was reversed and sent back to the district court for a finding of the amount of time and effort that the orderlies spent in performing their extra duties. Thereafter, the district court held that, since the male orderlies spent only 7 percent of their working time on the additional duties and the economic value thereof was not proportional to the pay differential, the employer had discriminated against the aides under the Equal Pay Act.

The vast majority of the cases involving nurse's aides and orderlies have been decided in favor of the female nurse's aides, who as a result have collected back pay and received an equalizing raise in salary. In a second case,[40] the defendant hospital agreed that it had withheld the sum of $9700 due to 161 female nurse's aides as a result of disparity in rate of pay between nurse's aides and orderlies who performed work requiring substantially equal skill, effort and responsibility. In a third case,[41] since the duties of the nurse's aides were substantially equal to those of the orderlies, a hospital was directed to pay the aides stipulated back wages to compensate for wage differentials previously paid the orderlies in violation of the Act. The court held in a fourth case[42] that the equal pay law did not require that the work be identical, but rather that it be substantially equal. The court said that job equality could not be based on job title or classification, but depended rather on actual job requirements and job performance; as a result of the violations involved in the case, the court ordered injunctive relief and payment of $5400 back wages for underpayment of nurse's aides.

There are a few decisions holding to the contrary, including a case[43] in which the court ruled that a wage differential between nurse's aides and orderlies working in the institution concerned was warranted in view of the extensive training of orderlies and the added duties performed by them, such as the insertion of catheters, the lifting of patients, the performance of irrigations, the setting up of oxygen tents and their provision of a psychological influence on patients. The court held that, to the extent that the wage differential resulted from a merit evaluation system that was consistent and had been communicated to the employees, the institution was exempt from the provisions of the Act. The district court mentioned that "the presence of a male orderly represents security to personnel that an aide cannot give," but the Court of Appeals refused "to sanction the concept that only males can perform the work of an orderly."[44] In a situation[45] in which orderlies were responsible for security, worked split shifts and spent approximately 60 percent of their time lifting patients and performing other duties requiring more physical strength than that of a nurse's aide, different hourly wages for aides and orderlies were not held to be solely related to their sex. A similar decision was arrived at in another case.[46]

Maternity Leave

In a Kansas case,[47] the court found the discharge of an unwed, pregnant bookkeeper-clerk to be unlawful sex discrimination. She was reinstated to her former position with back pay, including raises she would have received had she not been unjustly discharged. Following The EEOC guidelines, the court said that there was no relationship between the plaintiff's unwed, pregnant condition and the performance of her duties. and therefore to discharge her because of that condition was unjust.

Following similar reasoning, it has been held that retirement plans may not discriminate as when normal retirement was set for men at 65 years and for women at 60 years.[48] Moreover, the application of Title VII to church administration violates the First Amendment.[49] Under Title VII, a religious organization is allowed to discriminate on the basis of religion only, not on grounds of race, color, sex or national origin.

Transsexuality

A 41-year-old genetic male who had been living and working as a female for 16 years was entitled to surgical expense as "medical assistance" for the purpose of obtaining a sex conversion operation.[50] The court pointed out that medical assistance shall mean payment of part or all of the cost of care, services and supplies that are necessary to prevent, diagnose, correct or cure conditions in the person that cause acute suffering, endanger life, result in illness or infirmity, interfere with the capacity for normal activity or threaten some significant handicap.

A tenured teacher who was 54 years of age, married, father of three children and engaged as a teacher of vocal music (primarily to fourth, fifth and sixth grade children between the ages of 10 and 12) had gender identity problems, underwent sex reassignment surgery and began to live openly as a woman. After surgery she made known her intention of remaining in the school system as a female. When she refused the Board's offer of a one-year contract to teach music as an elective subject in high school, provided she would resign (thus relinquishing her tenure), charges were brought up against her. The Court ruled in favor of the Board, upholding the finding of the State Commissioner of Education that the teacher was incapacitated to teach children in the situation described because of the potential her presence in the classroom presented for psychological harm to the students.[51]

M.T., a transsexual, was born with male physical characteristics and successfully underwent sex reassignment surgery before her marriage to J.T. and while she was living with him. The trial court determined that the plaintiff was a female, the defendant was her husband and there was no fraud, and ordered the husband to pay $50 a week support. On appeal the court ruled that, since the plaintiff had become physically and psychologically unified and capable of sexual activity consistent with her reconciled sexual attributes of gender and anatomy, the plaintiff should be considered a member of the female sex for marital purposes.[52]

Another case involved a 45-year-old transsexual who had undergone hormonal therapy for nine years to assist in developing female characteristics and who was selected as a candidate for sex conversion surgery at a university hospital. The surgery was not performed because the state welfare department concluded that the cost of transsexual surgery was not payable under the medical assistance program. The appellate court found the denial of benefits was arbitrary and unreasonable, and gave instructions that the transsexual be granted medical assistance benefits.[53]

In another case, a transsexual, who was brought up as a male before undergoing sex reassignment surgery, received a female name by court order plus a passport with the newly assumed name and a new photograph. A New York trial court ruled that the city bureau of vital records did not act arbitrarily in refusing to designate the person's sex on an amended birth certificate.[54]

BREACH OF CONTRACT

Definition of Right and Remedy at Law

What do the terms "right" and "remedy at law" mean? Perhaps a nurse is told that she has certain rights under the law. The term "right" is defined to mean that which a person is entitled to have or to do or to receive from another, whose duty is imposed within the limits prescribed by law.[55] As concerns contracts, there exists the right to performance or to sue for a broken contract. Therefore, a nurse needs to know what rights arise in various situations.

A remedy is the means by which a right is enforced or the violation of a right is prevented.* As pointed our earlier, there are several remedies for breach of contract. The party injured by a breach of contract has a right to damages for the loss suffered. Thus, when a breach of contract happens, if the injured party has done a portion but not all of what he was obliged to do by the contract, he can claim the value of what he has done. In certain circumstances, an injured party may get a decree of specific performance of the contract or an injunction to prevent its breach. This remedy is inapplicable to contracts for nursing service.

Consideration has been given to means whereby a contract may be terminated and to situations that legally excuse the performance of a contract for personal services. Attention is directed to what is meant by "breach of contract." If one person to a personal service contract does not perform her or his obligations as required under it, she or he commits a breach of contract unless performance has been excused on one of the grounds noted.

A nurse brought an action alleging termination without cause and a breach of her oral contract of employment. The hospital's response was that the nurse could be dismissed without cause and that she struck a child who was a patient. The findings of the trial court were that the nurse had not struck the child and that any cause for dismissal was to be determined by the employer. The appellate court stated that the trial court should have analyzed hospital policies to determine their effect on the nurse's employment contract. If the nurse could be terminated only for cause, the court erred in concluding that the hospital, instead of the court, should make the final determination.[57]

A respiratory therapist worked for a company that provided respiratory therapy for hospitals that had no respiratory therapy department. The employee was hired as a respiratory therapist by a hospital that had been a customer of the company and had then established its own respiratory therapy department. When the company, in a breach of contract action, sued to enforce the noncompetition clause that the employee had signed, the Supreme Court of Mississippi said that the hospital was not in competition with the company, and therefore the employee did not breach the noncompetition agreement.[58]

Remedies: Damages. Although there are three remedies for breach of contract,[59] the nurse usually is concerned with only one, damages. "Damages" is a term referring to a sum of money awarded to one person because another has disregarded his or her rights as established by law.[60] Damages are given if it is shown that the breach of contract caused money loss to the person who complains.[61] In addition to damages, when there is a material breach of contract, the injured person may choose to reject the contract, provided that the breach "goes to the root of the contract." Specific performance is not ordered in such personal service contracts, nor is it likely that a court would issue an order prohibiting the doing of an act causing a breach of contract for nursing service.

A bus company that failed to deliver a raccoon's head to a laboratory for rabies testing was liable for breach of contract of carriage where the liability was limited to $50, but the case did not give rise to an action for intention to cause emotional distress or for outrageous conduct.[62]

---

*Judge Cothran said: "A remediable right is a legal conclusion from certain stated facts; a remedy is the appropriate legal form of relief by which that remediable right may be enforced."[56]

Where a head nurse in a private psychiatric hospital spoke to someone at the Human Rights Authority, a division of the Guardianship and Advocacy Commission, about rights violations and patient care issues, the Illinois Appellate Court held that findings that the nurse was penalized, sanctioned or restricted as a result of her dealings were not against the weight of evidence. However, reinstatement was not an appropriate remedy where the trial court found that the nurse was insubordinate, disruptive and openly critical of and insulting to employees superior in rank. The court affirmed the finding that the nurse was wrongfully terminated and sent the action back to the trial court on the issue of compensatory damages.[63]

Examples of Breach of Contract

Failure to Fulfill Terms of Contract

Suppose that a nurse was engaged by a hospital, and that among other benefits she was promised a private room and laundry service, neither of which she received. This would be a failure on the part of the hospital to carry out its part of the agreement, and hence it may be said to have breached the contract by not having fully lived up to its obligations.

Again, suppose that a nurse is employed by a Visiting Nurse Association at a salary of $1500 a month, with a month's paid vacation after one year's employment, and an allowance of 23 cents per mile for use of her or his car when used in the line of duty. The nurse works for the Visiting Nurse Association for six months, during which time she or he is required to use a car in answering calls. The association pays her or his salary, but does not reimburse the use of the car. The nurse may enforce her or his right to damages for breach of contract.

Misrepresentation. If a private duty nurse has been engaged to care for a patient and there has been a misrepresentation, knowingly or unknowingly, as to the nature of the case, he or she may refuse to enter duty and will not be liable for breach of contract (as in the earlier example in which the patient was stated to be a surgical case when in fact he also had a severe mental disorder). Nurses may sue for damages if they sustain a money loss because of their inability to obtain another case immediately. On the other hand, if they have rendered some service on the contract before discovering the misrepresentation, they may terminate the contract at once and recover damages for services given. If they continue on the case, the law looks upon this as an agreement to waive the effect of misrepresentation. However, the nurse is somewhat "on the spot." When a nurse has started to give care to a patient before finding out the real situation, she must give the patient time to get another nurse and must be careful not to neglect the patient so as to place him or her in a less favorable condition.

Negligence. In the performance of services, nurses are required to use "due care." They would be responsible if a patient breaks a leg from falling out of bed while delirious because the nurse left her or him unattended for a five-minute cigarette break. Damages would be for lost earnings had she or he returned to work sooner, plus hospital and medical bills. This is nothing more than a modern version of the old statement that:

It is the duty of every artificer to exercise his art right and truly as he ought.[64]

As the court has stated in a modern case:

It is a sound rule of law that one who, by reason of his professional relation, is placed in a position where it becomes his duty to exercise ordinary care to protect others from injury or danger is liable in damages to those who are injured by reason of his failure to exercise such care.[65]

In this connection, it is pointed out that, when nurses are caring for patients and their safety requires someone in attendance, they are bound to use "due care" and to remain until provision is made for their safety. This is true even if they have finished their hours of duty as expressed in the employment contract.

In Dallas, fire department officials fired a nurse who argued with a man over the telephone, scolded him for foul language and delayed sending an ambulance for his dying stepmother who was having trouble breathing.[66]

A licensed practical nurse appealed from a decision of the Civil Service Commission affirming her suspension and termination. The nurse admitted the facts: that she failed to notice that the tube feeding the patient contained acetone or another foreign substance, that she failed to read the label on the bottle, that she filled to notice the odor coming from the bottle, that she failed to follow the doctor's orders concerning the strength of the tube feeding, that in violation of hospital policy she directed a nurse's aide without supervision to hang the tube feeding, and that she allowed her daughter and friend to visit while she was on duty at the hospital. The patient died. Although the nurse was not assured a timely post-termination hearing, she admitted all the factual allegations contained in her letter of dismissal and suffered no injury.[67] Her termination resulted from her own gross negligence. In the suspension or discharge of employees from their jobs, it is important to comply with requirements for a hearing and due process.

TYPES OF ACTIONS BROUGHT AGAINST NURSES

Negligence

Nurses should give some thought to the type of action that may be brought against them by someone seeking compensation for injuries due to a negligent or wrongful act. The persons involved in a lawsuit are the plaintiff,[69] the one who starts an action to obtain a remedy for an injury to his or her rights, and the defendant, who is required to make answer and defend the action or lose by default. The plaintiff's complaint (declaration) has to show a right based on the relationship between plaintiff and defendant, a corresponding duty to the plaintiff imposed upon the defendant by the relationship, a violation of the right and duty and the resulting injury to the plaintiff.[70]

The relation between nurse and patient may arise out of contract, as in the case of a private duty nurse. Therefore, a patient who has suffered injury through the negligence of such a nurse may sue alleging a breach of the contract by which the nurse undertook to care for him or her with due (ordinary) care and skill, as a result of which he or she has sustained a monetary (pecuniary) loss. However, it is well for nurses to realize that, if the patient wishes, when the provisions of the contract are broken, he or she may bring action arising directly out of the breach of duty created by the contract. Or, again, the plaintiff may rely on negligence, simply stating that the defendant has breached the legal duty to use care, resulting in injury to the plaintiff, for which damages are requested.

Tort

The nurse is reminded that choosing the type of action is a practical matter of some consequence. The type of action brought often determines the length of time allowed before it must be commenced by filing a complaint in court. A tort is a legal wrong committed upon the person or property independent of contract. It may be either a direct invasion of some legal right of the person, the infraction of some public duty by which special damage accrues to the person, or the violation of some private obligation by which like damage accrues to the person.[71] For example, if State A has a statute saying that actions for breach of contract may be brought within six years and actions for "tort resulting in personal injury" must be started within two years, the length of time between the injury and the starting of the action is important. If a plaintiff sues in a tort action three years after receiving injuries entitling him to damages, the statute of limitations would be a good defense and would bar compensation. On the other hand, such a plaintiff might have a good action on the breach of contract.[72] It is also important to determine in such a situation whether the court considers the action properly based on a breach of contract rather than a violation of a duty commanded by law. If nurses become involved in a case, they should find out the rule of their jurisdiction, since there is some difference of opinion among the courts. Once an issue is determined on its merits by a court having proper jurisdiction, its judgment is a bar to any further litigation upon the same matter by the same persons. This rule of law is known as res adjudicata.

As previously pointed out, a contract for nursing services is a contract that is personal in nature. The personal services must be given by the nurse making the contract and not by a substitute nurse. For example, Mr. Smith engages a nurse, Miss Jones, to care for him after a heart attack. After working seven days a week for four weeks, Miss Jones feels the need for "time off" and sends Miss Doe, an equally experienced and skillful nurse, to care for Mr. Smith in her place. When the contract contains no provision for a substitute nurse, a breach of contract occurs if a substitute is provided without the consent of the patient. Preventing a person from carrying out a personal service contract, such as one for nursing services, would also constitute a breach of such contract.

UNENFORCEABLE CONTRACTS

Although nurses are primarily concerned with legal contracts, they must be aware that attempts may be made to form unenforceable contracts. Let it be clear that no remedies are provided by law for breach of illegal contracts.

Suppose that a nurse, Miss Jones, promises in exchange for $30 to obtain six ampules of Demerol from a hospital for a man, Mr. Doe, who is a known drug addict. She delivers the Demerol to Mr. Doe, but he refuses to pay her. The law will not compel Mr. Doe to pay her. This contract violates the narcotic laws.

Another example would be that of a contract between Miss Jones, a nurse, and Dr. Doe to assist him in performing an illegal abortion on a patient. The law will not permit Miss Jones in such a case to collect her wages when Dr. Doe refuses to pay for her services. The contract is illegal and void. Contracts to obstruct justice, in fraud of creditors and in excessive restraint of trade are also void, and no remedy may be had for breach of such contracts.

Again, a nurse must be careful not to diagnose diseases or ailments or to prescribe treatments for their relief for compensation; such matters commonly come within the practice of medicine or surgery. A nurse has no license to do these acts, and therefore cannot make a valid contract to do them for compensation.[73] The same interpretation is applied to nurses misrepresenting themselves as having a license in a jurisdiction requiring one. As the court has said in a number of cases, under statutes regulating the right to practice medicine, surgery, dentistry and similar professions, when there has been a failure to comply with the statutory requisites for admission, no recovery can be had for services rendered in a professional capacity.[74] It has been decided the money paid to an unlicensed practitioner may be recovered, at least as long as the agreement to the services remains uncompleted.[75] However, a law prohibiting practice as a nurse, or a person's engaging in the care of the sick as an attendant without a license, does not prevent a recovery for the rendering of services in the nature of nursing as incidental to general employment as a caretaker.[76]

STATUTES OF LIMITATIONS ON DAMAGES

Before the subject of unenforceable contracts is closed, another feature must be discussed. If claims regarding breach of contract are presented after a long delay, the lapse of time may be pleaded as a defense. At (1623) common law, there was no specified time limit to when a person having a cause of action was required to start suit. However, statutes of limitation differing somewhat in their terms have been passed in all states. If there are no express statutory provisions for malpractice actions, actions for damages from injury due to malpractice are governed by the limitations on actions for damages arising out of personal injuries. The time limitation varies in the different states and ranges from one to six years. In the case of a contract, it may depend, among other things, on whether it was a simple contract or a formal one in writing. The time when the statute begins to run is also important: whether from the date of the act causing injury or from the date of the discovery of the cause of injury.

Several decisions show the court's tendency to reckon the statute of limitations from the time of discovery rather than from the date the alleged malpractice was committed. In *Billings v. Sisters of Mercy*,[77] the patient, after undergoing an exploratory operation, sued to recover for damages arising from the discovery of a gauze sponge left in his body in an operation 15 years earlier; the court held that the statute of limitations did not bar the action. In *Rahn v. United States*,[78] a patient with a broken wrist was treated at an Air Force base hospital. When she complained that she was not able to use her hand, the physicians told her that her condition was progressing satisfactorily. Later, when the patient brought a suit against the United States Government for damages owing to loss of the use of her hand, the Georgia two-year statute of limitations was held not to bar the action in view of the concealment of important facts during that period. Until the necessary facts were discovered, the statute did not start to run. In *Phelps v. Donaldson*,[79] a patient expressed dissatisfaction with an orthodontist's work. In that case, the one-year statute of limitations barred his suit when it was brought after that period. In *Gross v. Wise*,[80] a patient sued a physician for malpractice for treatment that extended over three-year period. The court held the reckoning of the statute of limitations as starting from the time of the end of the treatment.

Since in some cities and states it may take four to six years before a personal injury suit comes to trial, the statute of limitations could expire and preclude recovery of medical bills even if the patient eventually wins the suit. This is a serious problem, for the patient's capability of paying for medical care she or he received after being injured often is based on a court's award of damages. A way to protect the hospital's and physician's interests was found by a New York physician who obtained an assignment of an appropriate portion of anticipated damages from his patient as security for payment for treating him after an accident. The physician then notified the defendant's insurer. The physician ultimately secured his money, since his assignment had not ripened into a legal claim until the settlement of the lawsuit.[81]

During the time that a patient is insane, the statute of limitations does not operate. In the case of a patient who suffered postoperative brain damage and who sued a physician after his mental recovery, the court said that the person who is insane at the time of the claimed malpractice has the full statutory period after the disability is removed in which to bring a suit.

Under most statutes of limitation, if a person leaves the jurisdiction or fraudulently hides so that he or she cannot be served a summons, the time limit for an action may be extended. If the person responsible for negligence or breach of contract dies, proceedings should be started against the estate of the deceased or the personal representative authorized to act for the estate within the period allowed by statute.

A 53-year plaintiff, employed as a housekeeper and bartender, was in good health except for severe osteoarthritis in her right hip, for which the defendant surgeon performed a hip prosthesis. During the operation he negligently injured or severed her sciatic nerve, and a result she became crippled and was unable to work. The surgeon falsely told the patient that she was not permanently injured for the purpose of inducing her not to seek medical or legal assistance. This false statement, combined with the fact that the patient did not seek such assistance, was sufficient to state a cause of action for fraud. In this case, the statute of limitations for fraud provided a period of six years after the discovery of the fraud in which to commence the action, whereas the action to recover damages in a medical malpractice case for personal injuries was barred since the plaintiff brought this suit more than three years after the alleged tortious act.[82]

A patient fell and fractured his hip while taking a shower at a city-owned hospital. The Nebraska Supreme Court held that his claim for damages was correctly dismissed because he failed to comply with the law requiring the filing of a negligence suit within one year after claim was accrued.[83]

The statute of limitations is directed at barring the remedy and not the commencement of actions to recover. Therefore, most statutes permit recovery on contract claims after the expiration of the time limit when a person makes a payment or signs a paper acknowledging his debt.

If the relation between nurse and patient arises out of contract, it follows that the nurse's right to salary or wages is governed by the same contract. The performance of duty owed by the nurse, to give nursing services to the patient, must be shown to entitle her or him to receive payment for such services. Failure to pay a nurse for services in accordance with the contrast is a breach of contract for which a nurse may sue.

References

1. Flynn v. Lucas County Memorial Hospital, 203 N.W. 2nd 613 (Iowa, 1973).
2. Bucklin v. Morton, 105 Misc. 46, 172 N.Y.S. 344 (1918).
3. Anson, W. R.: *Principles of the English Law of Contract and of Agency in its Relation to Contract*, 20th ed. New York, Oxford University Press, 1952, p. 144.
4. Barker v. Weeks, 182 Wash. 384, 47 P. 2d 1 (1935).
5. Plunkett v. O'Connor, 162 Misc. 839, 295 N.Y.S. 492 (1937).
6. Farzad v. Department of Professional Regulation, 443 So. 2d 393 (Fla. Dist. Ct. of App. 1983); *Citation*, 49:52, June 15, 1984.
7. Plessy v. Ferguson, 163 U.S. 537, 16 S. Ct. 1138, 41 L. Ed. 256 (1896).
8. Morgan v. Virginia, 328 U.S. 373, 66 S. Ct. 1050, 90 L. Ed. 1317 (1946).

9. McLaurin v. Oklahoma State Regents, 339 U.S. 637, 70 S. Ct. 851, 94 L. Ed. 1159 (1950).

10. Schloendorff v. The Society of the New York Hospital, 211 N.Y. 625, 105 N.E. 92 (1914).

11. San Antonio v. Santa Rosa Infirmary, 259 S.W. 926 (Tex., 1924).

12. Johnson v. Crawfis, 128 F. Supp. 230 (Ark., 1955).

13. Reed, et al. v. Sisters of Charity of the Incarnate Word of Louisiana, Inc., 447 F. Supp. 309 (U.S.D.C.W.D. La. 1978). Creighton, H.: Value of Careful Personnel Records, Nurs. Management, 14:38–40, June 1983.

14. Mitchell v. M. D. Anderson Hospital, 679 F. 2d 88 (U.S. Ct. of App. 5th Cir. 1982). Creighton, H.: Hospital Guilty of Racial Discrimination, Nurs. Management, 14:20–21, March 1983.

15. Garcia v. Rush-Presbyterian–St. Luke's Medical Center, 660 F. 2d 1217 (U.S. Ct. App. 7th Cir. 1981).

16. Simpkins v. Moses H. Cone Memorial Hospital, 323 Fed. 2d 959, 1963. See also Curran, W. J.: The Continuing Legal Saga of Hill-Burton, Am. J. Pub. Health, 60:1845, Sept. 1970.

17. Cook v. Ochsner Foundation Hospital, 319 F. Supp. 603 (U.S. Dist. Ct. E. Div. Law., Div. 1970). See also Regan, W. A.: Law Forum, Hosp. Prog. 52:24, June 1971.

18. Feld, L. G.: Age Discrimination: What Law Says Hospitals Can and Can't Do, Mod. Business Practice, Dec. 1971, p. 63.

19. Nurses Win Sex Bias Case After Four Years, Am. J. Nurs., 79:12, Jan. 1979.

20. Mississippi University for Women v. Hogan, 102 S. Ct. 331 (S. Ct. 1982).

21. Whitman v. Mercy Memorial Hospital, 339 N.W. 2d 730 (Ct. App. Mich. 1983).

22. Nurse Who Can't Work on Her Sabbath Fights for Right to Work Full Time, Am. J. Nurs., 77:12–14, Jan. 1977.

23. Nondiscrimination on the Basis of Handicap in Programs and Activities Receiving or Benefiting from Federal Financial Assistance, Fed. Reg., 42:22676–22694, May 4, 1977.

24. Epstein, R. L., and Manson, L. A.: First Questions on the HEW Handicap Regulations, Hospitals, 51:57, Oct. 1, 1977.

25. United States Code Sec. 794.

26. Romeo Community Schools v. HEW, 14 EDP Par. 7704 (E.D. Mich., 1977). Epstein, R. L., and Manson, L. A.: First Questions on the HEW Handicap Regulations, Hospitals, 51:57, 60, Oct. 1, 1977.

27. Southeastern Community College v. Davis, 99 S. Ct. 2361 (U.S. Sup. Cut., 1979). High Court Upholds School's Rejection of Deaf Applicant, Am. J. Nurs., 79:1344, Aug. 1979.

28. Gross v. University of Tennessee, 448 F. Supp. 245 (D.C. Tenn., 1978); Citation, 38:22, Nov. 1, 1978.

29. Sofair v. State University of New York Upstate Medical Center College of Medicine, 377 N.E. 2d·730, 406 N.Y.S. 2d 276 (N.Y. Ct. of App., 1978); Citation, 38:22, Nov. 1, 1978.

30. Commonwealth of Pennsylvania, Higher Education Assistance Agency v. Abington Memorial Hospital, 387 A. 2d 440 (Pa. Sup. Ct., 1978; rehearing denied, 1978); Citation, 38:21–22, Nov. 1, 1978.

31. Bournewood Hospital, Inc. v. Massachusetts Commission Against Discrimination, 358 N.E. 2d 235 (Mass. Sup. Jud. Ct., 1976).

32. Lemmons v. City and County of Denver, 620 F. 2d 228 (U.S. 10th Cir. Ct., 1980); Cert. denied 449 U.S. 880 (U.S. Sup. Ct. 1980).

33. Spaulding v. University of Washington, Docket No. C74–91 M. (W.D. Wash. 1981).

34. Vuyanich v. Republic National Bank, 505 F. Supp. 224 (N.D. Tex. 1980). Aff'd. on rehearing 521 F. Supp. 656 (N.D. Tex. 1981).

35. Taylor v. Charlie Brothers Co., 489 F. Supp. 498 (W.D. Pa. 1981).

36. Briggs v. City of Madison, 536 F. Supp. 435 (W.D. Wis. 1982).

37. AFSCME v. State of Washington, 32 FEP Cases 1577 (U.S. Dist. Ct. W. Dist. Wash. 1983).

38. High Court Avoids Comparable Worth, Milwaukee Journal, Nov. 26, 1984. p. 1, 12.

39. Hodgson v. Brookhaven General Hospital, 436 F. 2d 719 (15th Cir. Texas, 1970).

40. Hodgson v. Lancaster Osteopathic Hospital, 3 CCH Empl. Prac. Dec. 8309 (E.D. Pa., 1971).

41. Hodgson v. Beverly Enterprises, 4 CCH Empl. Prac. Dec. 7849 (E.D. Cal., 1972).

42. Hodgson v. Cheviot Hills Convalarium, 4 CCH Empl. Prac. Dec. 7679 (C.D., 1972).

43. Hodgson v. Golden Isles Nursing Home d/b/a Golden Isles Convalescent Center, 3 CCH Empl. Prac. Dec. 8108 (S.D. Fla., 1971).

44. 5 CCH Empl. Prac. Dec. 8027 at 6776.

45. Schultz v. Royal Glades Inc., 3 CCH Empl. Prac. Dec. 8313 (S.D. Fla., 1971).

46. Hodgson v. William and Mary Nursing Hotel, 3 CCH Empl. Prac. Dec. 8194 (N.D. Fla., 1971).

47. Doe v. Osteopathic Hospital of Wichita, 33 F. Supp. 1354 (D. Kansas, 1971).

48. EEOC Decision No. 72–0702 CCH EEOC Dec. 6320 (Dec. 27, 1971).

49. McClure v. Salvation Army, 323 F. Supp. 110 (N.D., Ga., 1971); Aff'd 460 F. 2d 553 (5th Cir., 1972).

50. Denise R. v. Lavine, 364 Y.Y.S. 2d 557 (N.Y. Sup. Ct. App. Div. 2d Dept., 1975); Sex Problems Court Digest, 6:1, July 1975.

51. In re Grossman, 316 A. 2d 39 (New Jersey, 1974); Sex Problems Court Digest, 5:1, June 1975.

52. M.T. v. J.T., 355 A. 2d 204 (N.J. Super. Ct. App. Div., 1976).

53. Doe v. State of Minnesota, Department of Public Welfare, 275 N.W. 2d 816 (Minn. St. Ct. 1977); Citation, 36:46, Dec. 1, 1977.

54. Anonymous v. Mellon, 398 N.Y.S. 2d 99 (N.Y. Sup. Ct., 1977); Citation, 36:45, Dec. 1, 1977.

55. Atchison & N. R. Co. v. Baty, 6 Neb. 37, 29 Am. Rep. 356 (1877). See also Coke: 2 Institutes of the Laws of England; or a Commentary upon Littleton, 1812, *345(a).

56. Ebner v. Haverty Furniture Co., 138 S.C. 74, 136 S.E. 19 (1926).

57. Falls v. Lawnwood Medical Center, 427 So.

2d 361 (Fla. Dist. Ct. of App. 1983); *Citation,* 48:23, Nov. 1, 1983.

58. Riddel v. Respiratory Care Services, 355 S. 2d 1376 (Miss. Sup. Ct., 1978); *Citation,* 37:84, July 15, 1978.

59. Williston: *Contracts,* rev. ed. 1936, pp. 683–688.

60. Prosser: Torts. Hornbook, 1955, Sec. 2; Morris: Punitive Damage in Tort Cases. 44: *Harv. L. Rev.* 1173 (1931); Simpson: *Handbook of the Law of Contracts.* Hornbook, 1955, Secs. 148–157; Rubin: May a Person Be Convicted of a Felony and Yet Escape Civil Liability Therefore? 10 *Marq. L. Rev.* 113 (1926).

61. McQuaid v. Michou, 85 N.H. 299, 157 Atl. 881 (1932); Burns v. American Nat. Ins. Co., 280 S.E. 762 (Tex. Civ. App., 1936).

62. Gibson v. Greyhound Bus Lines, Inc., 409 F. Supp. 321 (D.C. Fla., 1976); *Citation,* 48:78, Jan. 15, 1984.

63. Witt v. Forest Hospital, Inc., 450 N.E. 2d 811 (Ill. App. Ct. 1983); *Citation,* 48:78, Jan. 15, 1984.

64. Fitzherbert: *Natura Brevium,* 94 D. 208 D (1534).

65. Davis v. Rodman, 147 Ark, 385, 227 S.W. 612 (1921).

66. Nurse in Dallas Discharged, *The Houston Post,* Mar. 17, 1984.

67. Burnett v. Department of Health and Human Resources, 425 So. 2d 245 (La. Ct. of App. 1982). Creighton, H.: Is Termination Proper? *Nurs. Management,* 15:50–51, Jan. 1984.

68. Singely v. Bigelow, 108 Cal. App. 436, 291 Pac. 899 (1930).

69. Pomeroy: *Code Remedies,* 5th ed. 1929, Secs. 62–81.

70. *Id.,* Sec. 2.

71. Prosser: *Torts.* Hornbook, 1955 Sec. 1; Stone: Touchstones of Tort Liability, 2 *Stan. L. Rev.* 259 (1950). Radin: A Speculative Inquiry into the Nature of Torts. 21 *Texas L. Rev.* 697 (1943).

72. Boane v. Austin, 156 Tenn. 353, 2 S.W. 2d 100 (1928).

73. People ex rel. Burke v. Steinberg, 73 N.Y.S. 2d 475 (N.Y.C. Mag. Ct., 1947).

74. Whitehead v. Coker, 16 Ala. App. 165, 76 So. 484 (1917); Rubin v. Douglas, 59 A. 2nd 690 (D.C. Munic. Ct. 1948); Hoxsey v. Baker, 216 Iowa 85, 246 N.W. 653 (1933); Katsafaros v. Agathakos, 52 Ohio App. 290, 3 N.E. 2d 810 (1935).

75. Deaton v. Lawson, 40 Wash. 486, 82 P. 879, 2 L.R.A. (N.S.) 392 (1935).

76. Marker v. Cleveland, 212 Mo. App. 467, 252 S.W. 95 (1923); *see* Physicians and Surgeons, 48 C.J. 1159, Sec. 168, n. 59, Failure to register or record license; *see also* "Witnesses," 70 C.J.S. 1027, Sec. 1225, Asking or examining witnesses as to inconsistent or contradictory statements.

77. Billings v. Sisters of Mercy of Idaho, 86 Ida. 485, 389 P. 2d 224 (1964).

78. Rahn v. United States, 42 A. 2d 200, 80 A. 2d 368, 222 F. Supp. 775 (1963).

79. Phelps v. Donaldson, 243 La. 1118, 150 So. 2d 35 (S. Ct. of La., 1963).

80. Gross v. Wise, 18 A D 1097, 227, N.Y.S. 2d 523, 239 N.Y.S. 2d 954 (1963).

81. Bernstein v. Allstate Insurance Co., 228 N.Y.S. 2d 646 (Civ. Ct. N.Y.C., 1968).

82. Volk v. McCormick, 165 N.W. 2nd 185 (Wis. 1969). *See also* Regan, W. A.: Law Forum, *Hosp. Prog.* 52:16, Feb. 1971).

83. Campbell v. City of Lincoln, 240 N.W. 2d 339 (Nebr. Sup. Cit., 1976).

General References

Alessi, D. J.: *Proving Sex-Based Wage Discrimination Under Federal Law.* Kansas City, Am. Nurses' Assn., 1983.

Bernstein, A. H.: Informed Consent, *Hosp. Medical Staff,* 13:2–6, Nov. 1984; 13:4–8, Dec. 1984.

Creighton, H.: Is Termination Proper? *Nurs. Management,* 15:50–1, Jan. 1984.

Creighton, H.: Comparable Worth Cases, Part I, *Nurs. Management,* 15:21–22, Oct. 1984.

Creighton, H.: Comparable Worth Cases, Part II, *Nurs. Management,* 15:20–22, Nov. 1984.

Creighton, H.: Hospital Guilty of Racial Discrimination, *Nurs. Management,* 14:20–21, March 1983.

Creighton, H.: Value of Careful Personnel Records, *Nurs. Management,* 14:38–40, June 1983.

Cushing, M.: Informed Consent and M.D. Responsibility, *Am. J. Nursing,* 84:437–440, April 1984.

Felui, A. G.: The Risks of Blowing the Whistle, *Am. J. Nursing,* 83:1387–1388, Oct. 1983.

Finch, J.: Law and the Nurse 6. Damages, Who Carries the Can? *Nurs. Mirror,* 153(2)33–34, July 1, 1981.

Finch, J.: From Day One to Retirement . . . Law and the Nurse, *Nurs. Mirror,* 155:19, Dec. 1, 1983.

Finch, J.: Reasonable Standards . . . in Determining Negligence and Awarding Damages, *Nurs. Mirror,* 156:38–39, Feb. 23, 1983.

Lewis v. St. Charles Parish Hosp. Service District, 337 So. 2d 1137 (La. Sup. Ct. 1976); *Citation,* 34:108, Feb. 15, 1977.

Regan, W. A.: Hospital Employees, Religious Rights, *Regan Rep. Nurs. Law* 20(9)2, Feb. 1980.

Five
THE NURSE'S LEGAL STATUS & HOSPITAL LIABILITY

TYPES OF RELATIONSHIPS FOR SERVICES PERFORMED

The relationship between parties whereby a nurse, for example, performs services for another person may fix the limitations of liability in a legal action to recover damages caused by wrongful or negligent acts. The existence of a certain relationship may also determine whether a certain person is entitled to rights and benefits given to "employees" by various Federal and state laws. It follows that the meanings of the terms "employer" and "employee" are important. In some employment situations nurses may be employees, whereas in others they may be independent contractors, and it is important to know the difference. In general, when one person performs services for another, the parties in various relationships may be classified under the headings "employer and employee" and "employer and independent contractor."

Employer and Employee

Again, the nurse is reminded that each person is personally liable for negligent acts.[1] In addition, an employee may make the employer liable as well. In the latter case, a person injured by an employee's negligent act may be able to bring an action against both employer and employee, and thereby increase the chance of collecting. The person injured by an employee's negligent act may not collect twice for the same injury, but he may bring actions against separate defendants. Since it is not always possible to make a clear-cut test of a relationship, the nurse needs to know the factors involved. Generally speaking, the employer has the "right to control" and to direct another in the performance of the work,

62

including the details and means by which the work is to be done. It is not necessary that the employer actually direct or control the way in which the services are performed; it is enough that the employer is legally entitled to do so.[2]

In a doubtful case, the relationship has to be determined in the light of the facts. In a negligence case brought against a surgeon operating on a patient, the *surgeon was held not liable* when injury resulted to the patient because a scrub nurse at the hospital had used a different machine from the one the surgeon ordered. The court expressed the opinion that the scrub nurse, in setting up the operating room, was not an employee of the surgeon, since the hospital could direct how such work should be done.[3] A different relationship exists when a nurse is supplied by the hospital to assist the surgeon in an operation.[4] Then, it is the duty of the surgeon, in using the nurse furnished by the hospital, to see that every act necessary for the operation and under his supervision is properly done. In such a case, the nurse is working under the surgeon's orders, he controls her acts, and thereby the surgeon becomes the employer.

A person becomes an employee, generally speaking, when he performs services for another who has the "right to control" what is done and how it is to be done. An employee is one who works for wages or salary in the service of an employer. The power to discharge is that of the employer,[5] although in some instances this is modified by law. As the Social Security Act points out, other factors characteristic of an employer are the furnishing of tools and a place to work to the person who performs the services. It is important to realize that the controlling factor is the relationship that actually exists, and not the terms by which the persons are described.

Nursing Students as Employees. One of the uncertain areas of the law is the vicarious responsibility of hospitals and health agencies for nursing students who are acquiring clinical experience while caring for patients. In the absence of payment a student would probably not be classified as an employee. Some years ago in hospital diploma programs, when nursing students received a stipend, they were considered to be employees except for social security purposes. (See Nursing Students, Chapter 6.)

Workmen's Compensation Laws. These laws, with some exceptions, provide a fixed schedule of economic and medical benefits to employees or their dependents in case of industrial accidents or disease.[6] Workmen's Compensation Laws do away with the requirement of proof that the employer was negligent or that the employee was free from contributory negligence. To determine whether they qualify for this protection, nurses must first know if they are employees and if their employers are covered by these laws.

In *Denver v. Pollard*,[7] a public health nurse employed by the City and County of Denver worked in proximity to patients infected with beta streptococcus. When she became infected, suffered from rheumatic fever and as a result was forced to leave her work, she brought suit before the Industrial Commission to obtain weekly compensation. It was granted.

Likewise, the defenses of assumption of risk and negligence of a fellow employee are eliminated. Also, Workmen's Compensation Acts prevent court actions for injuries and provide instead a simple administrative procedure for securing compensation awards. Many Workmen's Compensation Laws exclude casual employees; hence, private duty nurses employed on different cases for short periods generally are not eligible.

In *Twin City Fire Insurance Co. v. Graham*,[8] an operating room nurse who suffered an injury while on a break was entitled to workmen's compensation, according to a Georgia appellate court.

In *Russell v. Camden Community Hospital et al.*,[9] a nurse's aide who contracted tuberculosis while working at a community hospital did not have to prove that she was exposed to the disease for 60 days in order to recover compensation under the occupational disease statute, the highest court in Maine ruled. The commissioner found that the claimant had attended a patient at the Camden Community Hospital, named Elis J. Talamine, who was suffering from a caseating tuberculous ulcer. From the hospital records, it appears that the claimant applied an ointment to the infected area on several occasions during the 20 days Mr. Talamine was in the hospital. Dr. Martin stated that the opportunity for contracting tuberculosis increased with the intimacy of contact with a tuberculosis sufferer. The commissioner concluded that because of the claimant's direct contact with the tuberculosis organism, "it is more probable than not" that her infection with tuberculosis resulted from attending to Mr. Talamine.

In *Lewis v. St. Charles Parish Hospital Service District et al.*,[10] a black woman who had been employed as a hospital maid was found to be totally disabled within the meaning of the Workmen's Compensation Law by the Louisiana Supreme Court. The woman, as a result of regular exposure to a detergent germicide that contained a phenolic chemical, suffered 75 percent loss of pigment on the back and palm of her right hand and 50 percent on her left hand. As the court pointed out, her severely discolored, diseased-appearing hands narrowed her employment opportunities.

To recover damages for psychological injuries under any workers' compensation statute, the claimant must show that he sustained trauma in the course of his employment and that this injury proximately caused the resulting psychological disability.[11] Awards have been made for neurosis[12] and suicide.[13]

Where a worker who was only 15 percent physically disabled claimed permanent disability because of his fears that cancer would result from continuing to work, the Montana Supreme Court held that occupational disease includes "all diseases arising out of or contracted from and in the course of employment." The court held that the question for the occupational disease medical panel was whether the claimant, in fact, was totally disabled because of his psychological impairment.[14]

In the case of a nurse at a VA medical center who filed a compensation claim in 1981 for pulmonary tuberculosis contracted after exposure to a patient and co-worker who had the disease, the Office of Workers' Compensation found that he "was not within the time limits which begin to run when the employee becomes aware ... of a possible relationship between his disease and his employment."[15]

When a nurse died in an automobile collision while on his way to a hospital shift assigned by his employer, a temporary agency, the Texas appeals court found that travel time was part of their oral employment contract and an exception to the "going and coming" rule. It awarded the widow and daughter compensation.[16]

Where a nurse's assistant who was required to undergo antituberculosis therapy as a necessary condition of the employment contract sustained injuries including blurred vision and a partial paralysis on her left side, she could recover workers' compensation benefits.[17] When a company required one of its employees, a musician, to undergo various inoculations and he contracted encephalitis, the resulting incapacity was held to be compensable.[18]

Employer and Independent Contractor

The law defines an independent contractor as a person contracting with another to do something, but not controlled by the other, nor subject to the other's "right to control" with respect to his or her physical conduct in the performance of the undertaking (work or service).[19] Applying this definition to the nurse, it becomes apparent that if a nurse is subject to control by another merely for the result of the work, and not for the means by which the result is reached, she or he may be an independent contractor.

Private Duty Nurses. Most of the nurses who are in this class are professional nurses acting as private duty nurses. As independent contractors, nurses are answerable for any wrong they may commit, and the hospital in which they are working is not liable. For example, in an action by a patient to recover for burns occurring after an operation, it was shown that these burns were caused by electric pads placed upon the patient by a special duty nurse, and the hospital was held not to be liable. Here, the injury occurred as a part of the professional treatment by someone not subject to control or direction by the administrative officers of the hospital.[20]

When the patient engages a special duty nurse, the latter is an independent contractor and is legally responsible for fulfilling the job duties.[21] This question arose in a New York case over injury to the patient, and the nurse was held liable as an independent contractor,[22] although the hospital paid the nurse and collected from the patient. It seems to be a general rule that a hospital is not responsible by contract or in tort for acts of surgeons, physicians or special nurses who take care of patients in the hospital.[23]

The private duty nurse or other nurse who is serving as an independent contractor in a hospital has certain rights and may expect certain conditions from the hospital. In order to render proper services, she or he can expect the hospital to supply suitable and necessary equipment. Moreover, the nurse can rightfully expect the hospital to keep its premises and equipment in a reasonably safe condition. She or he can also expect that the hospital will require employees to use reasonable care in their work.[24] If the nurse suffers injury because of the hospital's failure to provide suitable conditions, recovery on the claim may be prevented if the hospital is a charitable institution.

Agents. An agent may be an employee or an independent contractor, depending on the type of relationship entered into with his principal. Thus, an agent would be an independent contractor if he or she were engaged in an independent trade, business or occupation and agreed to perform work or services with no control by the principal over the way in which the details were carried out. However, at any one time, a person cannot be both an employee and an independent contractor.

Liability of Supervising Nurses. As the profession of nursing continues to grow, the professional registered nurse is having to assume more responsibility for supervising the work of graduate nurses, student nurses, practical nurses and others who help the patient. In this connection, a supervising nurse may be liable for the negligence of others to whom she or he has assigned certain duties.* For example, when a nurse supervisor failed to call a physician for three days after a general duty nurse reported that a patient recovering from an operation

---

*In *Blyth* v. *Birmingham Waterworks Co.*[25] Judge Alderson stated: "Negligence is the omission to do something which a reasonable man, guided upon those considerations which ordinarily regulate the conduct of human affairs, would do or do something which a prudent and reasonable man would not do."

showed signs of pathology, the supervising nurse was held liable.[26] The law requires that each person act with due care toward other persons, i.e., the care that would be used by an average, careful nurse supervisor. To illustrate further, judgment for damages was entered against a supervising nurse in charge of unused sponges in surgery when it appeared that the death of a patient was due to an infection arising from a sponge left in the abdomen. The evidence showed that the person to whom the count was assigned was not competent without immediate supervision, which was lacking.[27]

If a registered nurse assigns student or vocational nurses to duties that are beyond their ability to carry out, and negligence occurs, the registered nurse is responsible. This rule is based on the fact that nurses should not assign duties that they know (or should know) the person selected is incompetent to perform because of inexperience or insufficient education. In other words, nurses should not assign duties that a person could perform only under adequate supervision, and then fail to provide it, in accordance with the standard of care used by an average, careful supervisor in similar circumstances.

Although lack of adequate nursing supervision is frequently cited by courts as a direct contributing cause of accidents with resulting injuries to patients, there is little by way of setting forth legal measurements for adequate nursing supervision in the cases or the law. Guidelines vary with changing circumstances from one hospital or health provider institution to another. As Regan says, in the final analysis it is the experience and judgment of the director of nursing services that form the basis for defining what nursing supervision must consist of in a particular hospital.[28] Accordingly, the decision of the director of nursing services should be controlling in the distribution of nurses and patients throughout the hospital when, in his or her judgment, adequate supervision requires personnel changes.

The National Labor Relations Board essentially has thrown out the argument that the mere presence of supervising nurses in a state nurses' association means that the group cannot fairly represent staff nurses in collective bargaining, in the case of *California Nurses Association* v. *Sierra Vista Hospital*, San Luis Obisbo.[29] This decision revokes an earlier one, the Anne Arundel case in Maryland, which said that certification of nurses' associations as collective bargaining units hinged on the SNA delegating authority to autonomous chapters.

HOSPITAL LIABILITY

The "Master-Servant" Rule

Respondeat superior (literally, "let the master answer") is a legal principle that makes an employer liable for the wrongful acts of any employee. Also called the master-servant rule, it can apply to the relationship between a principal and an agent as well. For example, whenever a person is injured by an employee as a result of negligence in the course of the employee's work, the employer is responsible to the injured person. In this situation, the injured person may sue both the employee and the employer and thus has a better chance of being compensated for his injury. However, a double recovery is not allowed.

It is pointed out that the relationship of employer and employee is not negated by the fact that the employee is doing work of a technical or highly skilled nature that the employer could not do himself.

> The aviation company which employs an aviator to fly an aeroplane on a difficult course is liable for his negligence. . . . Similarly, a steamship company is liable for the negligence of the certified shipmasters who are navigating its ships. In such cases, the employers are liable, even though they cannot tell their servants how to perform the tasks they have employed them to do, and would, in fact, make themselves criminally liable if they attempted to do so.[30]

The significance of this theory is apparent in connection with claims against hospitals. For example, in a Georgia hospital, a newborn baby who needed a blood change-over operation was strapped in an incubator by nurses for surgery. Owing to error, the baby's foot rested against a bare light bulb used to heat the incubator, and as a result of the burns she lost the major portion of her foot. The defendant hospital was held liable for the negligence of its nurse employees.[31]

A physician, too, has been held liable in a $25,000 judgment when an office nurse's report slowed therapy and the patient died.[32] The toddler had been seen by the physician that morning, at which time his condition was diagnosed and he was treated with antibiotics. Some two hours later, the mother returned with the boy and told the nurse she thought he had convulsions and was dying. The physician was at lunch, and the nurse called him to report what the mother said, but added that she (the nurse) thought his condition was about the same as earlier in the morning. Leaving the receptionist in charge, the nurse also went to lunch. Some minutes later the little boy, lying on the examining table, vomited and his respirations became scarcely visible. Although the receptionist called the physician, he arrived after the boy had died. At trial, there was a preponderance of evidence that the probable cause of death was the negligence of the nurse.

According to the doctrine of *respondeat superior*, a shortage of nurses can be risky for the hospital. The legal standard of care requires that there always be sufficient personnel to meet the apparent physical needs of patients (see JCAH Standards of Nursing Service III). This applies to all employees, including nurses from other countries and student nurses being used as registered professional nurses, as well as when there are more nurse's aides and practical nurses than R.N.'s, which often happens on evening and night shifts.[33] Employers are not responsible when they employ independent contractors to act for them unless there are special circumstances, as when the employer fails to use proper care in selecting a competent contractor. Employees are also liable for acts of independent contractors when work is "extra hazardous," e.g., the use of scaffolding to paint a building.

"Captain of the Ship" Doctrine

In view of the Texas Supreme Court decision of January 15, 1977, the "captain of the ship" doctrine is a false issue.[34] The basic issue of this case[35] was whether merely being present in the operating room makes a physician legally liable for the negligence of other persons. The court announced that operating room surgeons and hospitals are subject to the same principles of agency law that apply to others, i.e., they are liable only for those whose conduct they have the right to control. In a second case,[36] the court reiterated its previous decision and noted:

The essential inquiry should be whether or not the surgeon had the right to control the assisting nurses in details of the specific acts raising the issue of liability.[37]

Under various legal doctrines, there is a history of the operating surgeon having vicarious liability imposed on him for the negligent acts of those assisting him during an operation.[38-40] Surgeons are liable both for personal negligence[41] and, like any other person, for the acts of their agents.[42] Surgeons are responsible for their employees[43] and for those who act on their direct orders in the operating room.[44] Also, the "borrowed servant" doctrine makes the surgeon responsible for whomever he or she has an immediate right to control during surgery.

Several courts apply the "captain of the ship" doctrine in the strict sense where a master has control or an immediate right of control over the performance of the negligent acts of the alleged servant. However, reality is at odds with the captain of the ship doctrine in its broader form, which assumes a master-servant relationship merely from the presence of the surgeon and that, after entering the operating room, she or he has complete right of control over the other personnel there. An assumption that the surgeon is controlling the nurses, or has the right to do so, merely because they are in the operating room is far beyond the original scope of the "borrowed servant" doctrine, according to a Colorado case.[45]

In a Texas case,[46] the court held that there was evidence to support the jury finding that the nurses who counted sponges were not the borrowed servants of the surgeon.

Surgery is now a team effort, carried out by professionals, each trained in his or her own special area. Surgeons no longer "borrow" hospital employees; instead, the hospital is supplying certain services directly to the patient through its own specially educated employees. A more detailed account of this doctrine has appeared in an article in *Supervisor Nurse*.[47]

Understaffing—Float Nurse

Understaffing is not exclusively the concern of administrators, but staff nurses are troubled by the effect it will have on their liability and the quality of patient care.

In *St. Joseph's Hospital v. Pennsylvania Labor Relations Board*,[48] three R.N.'s were on duty at 7:00 A.M. in the hospital's ICU, which had two patients and a third soon to arrive. Upon her arrival, one R.N. left and reported to the third floor. At 7:10 A.M., the director of nursing telephoned the unit and requested a second R.N. to be sent to the third floor. At 7:25 A.M., one R.N. had the director paged and she arrived at 7:30 A.M. After discussing the staffing in ICU, i.e., the prudence of leaving one R.N. with three high-risk patients, the director assured the nurses that she bore the responsibility when an R.N. is pulled from a unit. At 7:45 A.M., one of the two R.N.'s left for the third floor. At the end of the day, both nurses were discharged for insubordination by the director. Both brought complaints to the Pennsylvania Labor Relations Board, which ruled that the hospital should offer to reinstate them along with back pay. This ruling was affirmed by the Court of Common Pleas of Luzerne County, but on appeal, the Commonwealth Court of Pennsylvania reversed the decision and recognized the duty of nurses to execute orders given to them by their administrative superiors. It said that orders must be carried out promptly and that failure to carry out such orders in this situation (which lasted over a half-hour) can appropriately be termed insubordination.

Where the only available delivery room nurses were occupied with a complicated emergency delivery, the jury found that they were not negligent in failing to make a vaginal examination of a pregnant patient when she came to the hospital.[49]

A delirious patient admitted to a hospital with a high fever was seen standing on a balcony and calling for a ladder. A physician ordered that someone should stay with him. The charge nurse telephoned the patient's wife to get a family member to stay with the patient, since no nurses were available, but refused the wife's request to remain with him for five or ten minutes until his mother arrived. The nurse refused due to understaffing. During this time, the patient fell from the balcony and was injured. There was a jury verdict for the plaintiff. On appeal, the court reviewed the staffing on the unit, which consisted of a ten-bed ward and nine private rooms with a charge nurse, a new R.N. assigned for orientation, an L.P.N. and an aide. When the accident occurred, the staff was engaged in routine duties that could have waited, such as the L.P.N. leaving for supper.[50]

According to JCAH Nursing Service Standard III, a sufficient number of qualified registered nurses shall be on duty at all times to give patients the nursing care that requires the judgment and specialized skills of a registered nurse. Also, there shall be sufficient nursing personnel to assure prompt recognition of an untoward change in a patient's condition and to facilitate appropriate intervention.[51]

A critical care nurse in California was asked to go to the emergency room. She agreed to float on the condition that she receive an orientation to the area. Because no orientation was provided, she did not go; however, she resigned before she was fired and successfully sued the hospital for $1,000. So, it appears that a nurse who is floated to another unit is entitled to an orientation.

Where an obstetrical specialty nurse was floated to the emergency room as a fill-in for an absent emergency room nurse, and the doctor ordered 50 milligrams of lidocaine to be administered to a patient having an acute myocardial infarction, and the nurse erroneously injected 800 milligrams of lidocaine, the patient suffered a grand mal seizure and had a cardiac-respiratory arrest and died. The estate's suit against the hospital and nurse was settled for $255,000.[52] The liability of this nurse and her employer should serve as a warning.

While it is often true that, if nurses want a job, they had better float to a floor where they are asked to go, they should tactfully—but clearly—state their qualifications, area of proficiency and lack of experience (if such is the case) in the area of proposed assignment. This will help nursing management to make appropriate assignments. In addition, a nurse who is transferred (even temporarily) should ask for an orientation to the new area.

Types of Hospitals

It is often difficult to decide whether a person is an employee or an independent contractor, and this question often arises in connection with the wrongful acts of nurses in hospitals. Generally speaking, the most important criterion in deciding this question is the "right to control" or to supervise the details of performing the services.

Recovery for negligence is further complicated in the United States since hospitals are divided into three classes: public (government) hospitals; private, nonprofit charitable hospitals; and private hospitals run for profit (proprietary hospitals). The liability of a hospital as an employer varies with its classification. Since nurses frequently practice in a hospital, it is important for them to know the difference between a voluntary, nonprofit charitable institution and a private, profit-making hospital. The former type is far more numerous than the latter.

Immunity of Charitable Hospitals

A hospital operated as a "charitable" institution does not, of course, treat and care for patients free of charge. Such charitable hospitals may incidentally have nonpaying patients, but for the most part they charge standard fees for services rendered. Important factors in deciding the classification include the purpose of the hospital, the type of organization and its character as set forth in the charter or articles of incorporation. In a charitable hospital, any funds over and above expenses usually go to the maintenance fund for expansion of facilities or for research in health problems in order to further the purposes of the institution.

The immunity of charitable institutions for employee negligence has been based on different theories: that public policy supports an immunity; that the assets of the institution, being impressed with a trust for a charitable purpose, may not be used otherwise; and that patients who voluntarily enter assume the risk and waive claims for injuries.[53] For example, in a state where a charitable institution has immunity, a patient was unable to collect damages from a hospital for a burn caused by a nurse's negligence in placing a hot water bottle.[54] But a charitable hospital was held liable to a paying patient when a student nurse who had been in training only seven months administered morphine, instead of a given dose of codeine, to a six-year-old boy who had been apparently recovering from an operation, but who died as a result of the morphine.[55] In another type of case, a charitable hospital protected by liability insurance has been held liable for negligence in care and medical treatment.[56] There is a conflict in the decisions of the various states as to whether or not the beneficiaries of the charity may recover for injuries due to negligence when it is not shown that there was negligence in selecting the employee.[57]

The nurse should note, however, that the trend of recent decisions is toward discarding the immunity rule and toward holding charitable institutions liable for the negligent acts of employees. It is appropriate for patients to receive damages since any hospital can buy malpractice insurance. This view was adopted when a charitable hospital was held liable under the master-servant rule after a private duty nurse suffered permanent injuries from a swinging door owing to a student nurse's negligence.* Another charitable hospital was held liable for a patient's injuries after being thrown from a stretcher when a nurse's aide lost control over it.[59] California, Minnesota and Arizona have also decided

---

*In this case, Judge Rutledge states: "The law's emphasis ordinarily is on liability, not immunity, for wrongdoing. . . . Charity is generally no defense. When it has been organized as a trust or corporation, emphasis has shifted from liability to immunity. The conditions of law and of fact which created the shift have changed. The rule of immunity is out of step with the general trend of legislative and judicial policy in distributing losses incurred by individuals through the operation of an enterprise among all who benefit by it rather than in leaving them wholly to be borne by those who sustain them. The rule of immunity itself has given way gradually but steadily through widening, though not too well or consistently reasoned, modifications. It is disintegrating. . . .

"To offset the expense will be the gains of eliminating another area of what has been called 'protected negligence' and the anomaly that the institutional doer of good asks exemption from responsibility for its wrong, though all others must pay. The incorporated charity should respond as do private individuals, business corporations and others, when it does good in a wrong way."[58]

cases in which charitable hospitals, as employers, have been liable for the negligence of nurses.

The trend to limit the charitable immunity of voluntary, nonprofit hospitals continues. The West Virginia Court has followed a similar action taken recently by the Supreme Court of Pennsylvania, which held that a paying patient may sue a charitable institution for negligence. A partially paralyzed patient with impaired vision, who was being prepared by an orderly for a tub bath, fell against a steam radiator. While the orderly went for assistance, the patient remained on the hot radiator and sustained third-degree burns. The patient claimed that he was injured from the hospital's negligence in employing and retaining incompetent help. The hospital claimed immunity from damage suits, but the court rejected this claim.[60]

Liability of Government or Public Hospitals

Before concluding this discussion of legal status, another situation that should be mentioned is the nurse's employment in government establishments. An increasing number of nurses enter this growing field. The question arises, "What liability falls on the government or public hospital in the various situations involving wrongs of their employees, such as nurses?" The usual answer is, "None at all." In our country, neither the United States nor the individual states can be sued without their consent. The general rule also supports the view that the maintenance of a hospital by a local unit of government is a governmental function. By contrast, employees of state or local government hospitals have to answer any charge of negligence and to pay damages to the patient if the suit is decided against them. In the case of the Federal Government, the Federal Torts Claims Act (FTCA) of 1945, with the exception of certain classes of claims specifically enumerated, confers a general waiver of Government immunity from suits for wrongs arising from the negligence of Federal Government employees.[61]

When a member of the military service dies in a U.S. hospital owing to the negligence of the hospital physicians and others, the dependents cannot recover damages for wrongful death in a suit against the United States.[62] In one case, a soldier underwent surgery while in the Army. Later, when he had another operation at a Veterans Administration hospital, a towel 30 inches long and 18 inches wide, marked "Medical Department U.S. Army," was removed from his stomach.[63] Again, the court held that the United States was not liable in damages under the FTCA for such negligence.

It was held that an Army surgeon was not liable for negligence in rendering services to an enlisted solider who claimed that the surgeon left sutures in the kidney area that caused him to have a second operation and to have the kidney removed.[64] Although the government does not permit recovery under the FTCA, the military services do not leave those permanently injured in the line of duty uncompensated.

In a case in which the regulations did not permit admitting a patient suffering from alcoholism to a veterans hospital, the court held that the doctor's duty did not go beyond a careful and safe delivery of the patient into competent hands.[65]

The United States has been held liable in a record judgment to an ex-sailor for negligent treatment at a Naval hospital during World War II.[66] As a part of his treatment at the hospital, a radioactive substance was inserted into his nose so that x-ray films could be taken. Following the treatment, the substance was not removed. The patient went to a VA hospital after receiving a medical discharge from the Navy, and his records were transferred. Over a period of time he made a number of visits to the hospital, but was not told of any danger from the substance in his nose. Eventually, when the patient had a tooth extracted, a biopsy of the material surrounding it revealed that cancer had developed as a result of the radioactive substance irritating a pre-existing malformation in the nose. Radical surgery for the condition was carried out, causing disfigurement. The award of $725,000 was settled for $200,000 less, and thus an appeal was barred.

Another large malpractice award was received by an Army veteran who was paralyzed after he had lung surgery at a VA hospital.[67] During his military service he had contracted tuberculosis, for which surgery was advised. Near the conclusion of surgery, a resident, to control some bleeding, placed Oxycel gauze in the region of the intervertebral foramen, which caused spinal canal obstruction and paralysis.

The United States also has been held liable in damages to minor children orphaned by the slaying of their mother when an Air Force psychiatrist was negligent and did not inform his successor of violent threats made by the airman against his wife.[68] Without this information, the new psychiatrist had the airman released from the hospital after a few days; the airman's duty assignment gave him access to weapons, one of which he used to kill his wife.

The United States also has been held liable in damages to a veteran for the partial paralysis of his leg, which occurred as a result of excessive pressure exerted by a defective tourniquet during surgery at a VA hospital.[69] During the procedure, the orderly continued for some minutes to pump air into a pneumatic tourniquet applied to the patient's thigh before he told the surgeon that the pressure gauge on the cuff was not working. Use of obviously defective equipment renders the employee and employer liable for the negligence.

Negligent use of proper equipment also renders the person liable. A retired Marine Corps sergeant received a $60,000 award against the United States for loss of visual acuity, classified as industrial blindness in the injured eye, due to a Navy physician's negligence in placing a heated tonometer on the patient's eyeball.[70]

However, a patient who is injured during the course of his hospitalization is not necessarily entitled to damages. During a grand mal epileptic seizure, a patient in a VA hospital fell from his bed and fractured his hip. Since he had been ambulatory on the day of the fall, the side-rails on his bed had been removed. Considering all the circumstances, the court held that he was not entitled to legal relief.[71]

When a patient in a Government hospital is injured while performing work for the hospital, he can sue and recover under the FTCA rather than accept the compensation provided by the Federal Employee's Compensation Act.[72] A patient at a U.S. Public Health Service hospital who was injured while working at a pants-pressing machine claimed the Government was negligent in not keeping it properly repaired.

A Government hospital was not liable when a black plaintiff suffered total depigmentation allegedly due to sleeping tablets known as Doriden. The tablets were given to him at the outpatient department of the VA regional office when he complained of difficulty in sleeping in addition to an ulcer.

> The Court has come to the conclusion that the plaintiff has failed to prove, by preponderance of the evidence, malpractice on the part of the government physicians. Although the expert testimony of the plaintiff's medical witness is

sufficient to support a finding of proximate cause, there is no proof that the V.A. doctors, whom the plaintiff has alleged to have consulted, departed from recognized medical standards in their dealing with the plaintiff.

The Court's sympathies are with this plaintiff. From the evidence, it appears that the depigmentation has had a severe effect on his personality and life, and that he has had a difficult time adjusting thereto. It is, however, this Court's duty to apply the law of evidence, and the Court finds that the plaintiff has failed to sustain his burden of proof.[73]

Employees in Government hospitals must consider carefully their responsibility for the care of dependents of military personnel. The standard of care required everywhere is reasonable care in accordance with the patient's apparent physical needs. Nurses in Government hospitals should not relax in their professional practice and assume that no one can sue them or their employer. Pursuant to enabling legislation, the U.S. Government and many political subdivisions permit lawsuits. In one case, parents who brought suit on behalf of their infant daughter for injuries resulting in permanent blindness, allegedly due to the negligent use of forceps by an Air Force physician at a base hospital during delivery, were awarded $100,000 damages.[74] Likewise, in the case of a premature girl born at a U.S. Naval hospital who was seriously deformed after contracting osteomyelitis, the court held that the Government was negligent in permitting an inexperienced nurse, who had worked in a hospital where there were sick children, to work in a premature babies' nursery without giving her a physical examination, including a throat culture, and that such negligence had resulted in transmitting hospital staphylococcus to the baby.[75] However, in another case, a nurse administered intramuscular injections in each buttock of an infant at an Army hospital, and the child later sustained a weakening right leg and footdrop that required extensive treatment; the lawsuit brought by the parents, who claimed that the injection by the nurse was done negligently and injured the sciatic nerve, failed.[76]

Where a child suffered from rubella syndrome after Army medical personnel failed to advise the mother of her positive rubella test administered when she was only one month pregnant, the court ruled that parents' recovery for the wrongful life of the child should include all expenses associated with rearing the child.[77]

The United States was held liable to a patient's wife for losses caused by her husband's suicide when VA hospital staff failed to take appropriate precautions. For six years, the patient had suffered recurrent depression that required psychiatric care. The admitting psychiatrist diagnosed a depressive reaction, but the patient was assigned to a seventh-floor room without any restrictions or special supervision. That evening, he complained of being more depressed and, the next day, leaped to his death from an unsecured window.[78]

When a four-month-old child was given DPT immunization injection, oral polio serum and a typhoid injection in adult doses by an airman at an Air Force base, resulting in continual grand mal seizures for a period of time and permanent mental retardation, an award of more than $700,000 was not excessive, a Federal appellate court in Rhode Island ruled. The girl was 12 years old at the time of the trial and had the mentality of a four-and-one-half-year-old child. The suit was filed within two years after the parents discovered the cause of the convulsions, and the Air Force dispensary records were unavailable until some ten years after the inoculations.[79]

A mental patient fled from a VA hospital after being admitted for threatening to blow up a VFW hall and being placed on an open ward because it was felt that he was not dangerous to himself or others. After returning and leaving the hospital a second time, he shot and killed a man on the street. A Federal trial court in Missouri found that the hospital was not negligent in either diagnosis or supervision, and that the victim was contributorily negligent.[80] While the victim was driving his car, the patient, carrying a rifle, had stopped in front of the car, pointed the rifle toward the windshield and continued walking. Instead of telling the police about the patient, the driver returned to where the patient was walking, shouted a remark and asked why he was pointing a gun at people. The patient then shot him.

Another case involved two specialists, practicing urologists who served as consultants to a VA hospital on a contractual basis, one for 11 years and one for 19 years. They reported that the urologist who became chief of the urology section of the hospital lacked professional competence and ability to work in harmony with hospital personnel, communicate with patients or supervise other physicians and that he was incompetent as a specialist in urology owing to his slowness and so forth. An Illinois appellate court ruled that they were absolutely immune from liability for defamatory statements made in the line of duty.[81]

A voluntary patient in a VA hospital left two days after admission, traveled to the town where his family lived and was run over and killed by a train. In a suit to recover for the patient's death, the VA staff was held to be not negligent in failing to notify his relatives as soon as he left the hospital without authorization, since the hospital could not legally force a voluntary patient to remain there.[82]

A patient's widow brought suit under the Federal Tort Claims Act, claiming that VA hospital personnel had inadequately trained her and her husband and had given them a nonfunctional dialysis unit. As a result, her husband, who had polycystic kidney disease, died of renal failure. The Federal trial court entered a judgment in favor of the Government. After a full trial, the court concluded that there had been no inadequacy in training and that, during the ten months in which the patient underwent biweekly hemodialysis at the hospital, both he and his wife were instructed in the operation, maintenance and supervision of the treatment.[83]

A patient who received a swine influenza immunization at the office of a private physician and within six hours was left with some paralysis in her body, loss of vision and inability to speak, sued four swine influenza vaccine manufacturers for $6,675,210. The U.S. Government intervened to substitute itself in place of the four defendants and moved to dismiss the suit on the grounds of the patient's failure to file an administrative claim. In ordering the suit dismissed, the court said that the Swine Flu Act has three basic effects: (1) It creates a cause of action against the United States for injuries from swine influenza inoculation, (2) it abolishes suits against the manufacturers and (3) it makes the Federal Tort Claims Act applicable to suits based on swine influenza inoculations. The Act was constitutional and applied to the patient's claim. The FTCA required an administrative claim to be filed before suit could be filed; since this was not done, the suit had to be dismissed.[84]

To alleviate a hearing problem, a patient had a stapedectomy in a VA hospital. Since he experienced vertigo and continued loss of hearing, the prosthesis was removed in a second operation, and it was found that the hearing loss was due to granuloma. He brought a suit under the FTCA, contending that failure of the government physician to warn him of the risks of granuloma constituted negligence. The issue then arose as to whether a government physician's failure to warn of the risks attendant to surgery constituted misrepresentation under the FTCA. If it was misrepresentation, the patient would be barred from bringing suit against the United States because of a specific exclusion in the language of the FTCA, which said that the Act would not apply to any claim arising out of assault, battery, false imprisonment, false arrest, malicious prosecution, abuse of process, libel, slander, misrepresentation, deceit or interference with the contract rights. The U.S. Court of Appeals ruled in favor of the patient, holding that failure to warn of risks attendant to surgery did not constitute a misrepresentation under the FTCA.[85]

In another VA hospital case, the court held that a physician was not negligent in view of the fact that aseptic necrosis was a very uncommon complication of steroid therapy, whereas permanent loss of vision, loss of consciousness and sudden death could have occurred had there been no treatment.[86]

In 1977, a man sued the United States, charging that he was disabled by diabetes mellitus, which he allegedly had when he was inducted into the Army in 1952. His claim was that the Army induction physicians failed to administer tests for diabetes, that the negligence of the Army doctors resulted in his failing to get the proper medical treatment for his condition and that his condition was aggravated by service in the line of duty. The position taken by the Court was that the plaintiff's failure to file a claim for a specific amount of money to the appropriate Federal agency within two years after the claim accrued resulted in the tort claim against the United States being barred forever.[87]

A Federal appellate court ruled that a $1 million award for a patient's pain and suffering was not excessive where he was rendered a quadriplegic after a procedure at a VA hospital. Because of an arthritic spinal condition, a World War II veteran took an early retirement. In 1978, he fell and sustained a nondisplaced fracture of the cervical spine. A halo brace and vest were put on his head and neck under the direction and supervision of a VA hospital. During the procedure, he felt an electric shock through his body, and this later developed into a complete paralysis despite a surgical laminectomy. A malpractice suit under the FTCA was brought by the patient. He recovered $464,730 in damages and $1 million in general compensatory damages for pain and suffering.[88]

Another VA hospital was held negligent in failing to raise the bedrails on an 83-year-old heart patient's bed. He required brain surgery for a fractured skull and subdural and cerebral contusions. Permanent injuries included speech aphasia and a general partial paralysis of his right side. In a suit under the FTCA, he was awarded $80,000. The nurses who attended the patient testified he was alert, oriented and cooperative and that raising the bedrails was not necessary. The court said that, considering the patient's age and physical condition and the medications given to him, failure to use bedrails was just plain negligence.[89]

The Gonzalez bill was passed by both the House of Representatives and the Senate in September 1976, and on October 8, 1976 President Ford signed the bill into law.[90] The first paragraph of this bill states:

> The remedy against the United States provided by sections 1346(b) and 2672 of title 28 for damages for personal injury, including death, caused by the negligent or wrongful act or omission of any physician, dentist, nurse, pharmacist, or paramedical or other supporting personnel (including medical and dental technicians, nursing assistants, and therapists) of the Armed Forces, the Department of Defense, or the Central Intelligence Agency in the performance of medical, dental, or related health care functions (including clinical studies and investigations) while acting within the scope of his duties or employment therein or therefor shall hereafter be exclusive of any other civil action or proceeding by reason of the same subject matter against such physician, dentist,

nurse, pharmacist, or paramedical or other supporting personnel (or the estate of such person) whose act or omission give rise to such action or proceeding.[91]

Immunity for National Guard medical personnel while they are acting within the scope of their duties during training exercises,[92] and for NASA medical personnel while they are acting within the scope of their employment,[93] is also provided by the amended bill.

Nurses and all other Government employees should give careful consideration to the effect of false statements of ex-veterans. It has been held that a nurse who was an ex-veteran would be denied the benefits of the Veteran's Preference Act if she ever denied being a veteran.[94]

Immunity of States and Subdivisions. A state government cannot be sued without its consent. The admission of a state's liability for the negligence or wrongful act of its employees or agents is comparatively recent. Three states, Illinois, Michigan and New York, now have a court of claims to handle such suits. Among the remaining states, a few have a constitutional provision barring recovery against the state; a number by statute permit certain suits against the state under specified conditions; but most of the other states have not legislated on the subject.

In the U.S. form of government, county, township, borough, municipal and village governments are subdivisions of the state created by law. Generally, in the absence of a specific law, such units are not liable for damages arising from the negligent performance of a governmental function. According to the weight of authority, a jurisdiction is performing a governmental function in maintaining a hospital. Accordingly, recovery against a city hospital for an unauthorized autopsy, because of a nurse's error, was denied.[95] In some states, whether or not the patient pays for his services determines whether a hospital is being operated in a governmental or proprietary capacity. For example, when a county hospital accepted patients who were able to pay for hospitalization, it was held liable for damages caused by negligence.[96]

A county that operates a hospital for paying and nonpaying patients has been held liable to a private patient paying the usual charges who sustained severe burns when an employee negligently and carelessly placed a bedpan of boiling water under her.[97] In other states, the rule is not changed because the patient in a county or city hospital pays for his services. Thus, a Texas court held that the city government was not liable for injury to a patient through negligence of a student nurse employed by the hospital. In its opinion, the court said:

> The city's maintenance of the hospital for purposes of conserving public health, receiving indigent patients, and applying money receipts to expenses, is the exercise of a governmental power so that the city is not liable for hospital employee's negligence resulting in injury to patients.[98]

A California court did not hold the county hospital responsible for injuries sustained when a delirious patient was left unattended for a short time.[99] However, the nurse was held liable for her act of negligence.

Whether a private hospital and its employees are liable for injuries resulting from negligence depends on whether the employee exercised ordinary care at the time that the injury occurred.[100] It has been held that a private hospital is under a duty to furnish competent nurses.[101] The question of whether a nurse is an employee or not, and as to what constitutes ordinary reasonable care under the circumstances, has been discussed previously.

Psychiatric Hospitals

Abuse of Patients. A practical nurse at Eastern State Hospital, who was attempting to get a recently admitted voluntary patient to take her place in a line of patients going to their evening meal, pushed her; she fell, fractured a femur and subsequently had urinary troubles. The patient sued the nurse and recovered a judgment of $10,000. Although the Washington appellate court sent the case back for a new trial on account of various errors, it does indicate the willingness of juries to hold nurses liable for rough and abusive treatment of patients.[102]

    Negligent Treatment. The next of kin sued for negligent mistreatment of a schizophrenic patient's diabetes and excessive doses of an experimental drug that caused organic brain damage. The patient's physician stated that the diabetes had been controlled at all times and that proper tests were made. The court found no evidence to support either allegation, and a verdict for the state upholding the lack of negligence was affirmed.[103]

    A patient with a medical history of epileptic seizures and suicide attempts in Hudson River State Hospital was found lying prone across the head of the bed, with part of her body on top of a radiator. She was experiencing a seizure when found by a nurse. Because the nurse was unable to lift the patient, she attempted to move the bed, and the patient fell to the floor. With the help of other nurses the patient eventually was placed back in bed, but had suffered serious burns on her back and the back of her arms. There was evidence that, on the day the accident occurred, the patient was found with her bed turned around in the room so that the side usually against the side wall was against the outside wall, and that both side-rails, which had been raised, were down. The court held that, since the patient had moved herself to a position in front of a window and near the radiator and lowered the side-rails, recovery could not be based on the doctrine of res ipsa loquitur.[104] The court decided that the nurses acted in a reasonable manner in their attempts to handle the emergency that confronted them.

    A patient sued a county hospital and a registered nurse to recover damages for the nurse's alleged negligence in giving an injection that caused serious injury. Although a malpractice action against the county hospital was barred by the patient's failure to give notice of his claim within 60 days, such notice requirement did not bar the action against the nurse.[105]

    A psychiatric nursing attendant at the Anoka State Hospital was found asleep in a lounge chair in a dimly lit television room by his supervisor accompanied by another orderly. The State Civil Service Board sustained the hospital's action in dismissing the attendant, saying that the cause or reason for dismissal must be related to the manner in which he performed his duties, and the evidence showed substantial reason for dismissal.[106]

    A registered nurse in a state institution for the mentally retarded ordered paraldehyde to be given to an unruly patient, but unknown to the nurse the medication was four times as strong as it was supposed to be. The patient became ill and was taken to another hospital, where she died five days later of pneumonia. A conviction of involuntary manslaughter was reversed in view of evidence that, if the overdose was the real cause of death, it would have occurred in four to six hours. The registered nurse ordered medications to be given to patients as required, under general directions of a physician who was located at another hospital.[107]

    There was a judgment for the hospital when a patient, left alone unattended and unrestrained and acting under the compulsion of her mental and emotional illness, inflicted serious damage on both of her eyes and rendered herself blind. Suit was brought against the hospital for damages for the alleged negligence of nurses and attendants in not preventing this unfortunate occurrence. The court said:

> It would appear that the only certain way to keep a conscious mental patient from injuring himself or someone else would be to bind his hands and feet. That method of restraint, however, would not be tolerated except for brief periods of time in extreme cases. The objective is treatment, not merely incarceration. Treatment requires the restoration of confidence in the patient. This, in turn, requires that restrictions must be kept at a minimum. Risk must be taken or a case left as hopeless.[108]

Patient's Refusal of Treatment or Medication. A Colorado appellate court said that a patient who was mentally incapable of deciding whether to refuse medical treatment still had a right to refuse an involuntary antipsychotic medication. There was no emergency and the order was in effect as long as the patient was certified without any provision for review. The patient was a paranoid schizophrenic and was involuntarily committed.[109]

The Arizona appellate court held that a 31-year-old patient who had spent most of the previous decade in various penal and psychiatric institutions and who was involuntarily committed but not judged incompetent could refuse psychotropic medication. The court said there were only two circumstances in which such a patient could be subjected to psychotropic medications against his will: (1) an emergency or (2) as part of a written treatment plan and according to regulations published by the department of health services and written hospital procedures. Neither condition applied to this patient.[110]

Committed mental patients, according to the highest court of Massachusetts, have a right to refuse antipsychotic medication.[111] In its opinion, an involuntarily committed patient is competent to make treatment decisions. According to that court, incompetence must be determined by a judge, and only after a patient is judged incompetent can he be forcibly administered antipsychotic drugs. In a nonemergency situation, there is no state interest great enough to permit involuntary administration of drugs. In an emergency, and to prevent the immediate, substantial, and irreversible deterioration of a serious mental illness, forcible treatment is permissible.

A Federal appellate court in New Jersey ruled that involuntarily committed mental patients have a constitutional right to refuse administration of antipsychotic drugs. The court said that the proper standard for determining whether drugs can be administered against the patient's will was one based on accepted professional judgment. In the state administration bulletin, the procedures were outlined, and this satisfied the due process requirements for applying the professional judgment standard. According to the bulletin, the physician was required to explain the reasons for the medication, to specify risks and benefits, to have procedures for patient consultation with family members, and to provide for a review by other professional staff and meetings with the treatment team. The action was brought by a patient in a state mental institution during his twelfth hospitalization after an involuntary mental commitment.[112]

A New York court has held that a mentally ill patient, if capable of making a decision, may refuse electroshock therapy, even though that decision may prove unfortunate.[113]

Standard of Care. If the ordinary standard of due care is not observed, then in the absence of an immunity statute, recovery is allowed. Thus, the administratrix of an estate was allowed to recover damages when her husband was killed in an automobile wreck caused by a mental patient, known to be dangerous, who assaulted and overpowered an attendant, escaped from the hospital, stole a car and was being chased by the Highway Patrol. The court found that the hospital was negligent in failing to provide the number of attendants necessary to prevent such an escape.[114]

A patient was admitted to the adult psychiatric unit of a hospital pursuant to a court order obtained by his wife. Seven days later, he was released upon the recommendation of his psychiatrist. A week later, he attempted suicide by dousing himself with gasoline and setting himself on fire. In a malpractice action, he was awarded $564,225. The psychiatrist made no effort to obtain the patient's medical history, including a medical discharge from the Army and the records of the VA hospital, which state he attempted suicide on three occasions. After admission, a nurse reported that he became quite restless as though he were hallucinating, but no inquiry was made by the nurse or doctor about these auditory hallucinations.[115]

Where a patient had been approved for discharge, he remained in the hospital for 41 days thereafter. During this time he became assaultive, required physical restraint and suffered seizures. These incidents indicated a deterioration in the patient's condition, and recovery was allowed.[116]

A Federal trial court in New York held that a hospital psychiatric clinic does not have to provide special care for a patient in a coma after a second suicide attempt.[117]

The Washington Supreme Court held that psychiatrists have a duty to take reasonable precautions to protect anyone who might foreseeably be endangered by a patient's drug-related mental problems. Patients were considered potentially dangerous especially if they stopped taking prescribed antipsychotic medication and used "angel dust" again.[118]

In a suit against two psychologists for failure to diagnose and to warn of a patient's dangerousness, a woman, who was shot after throwing herself over her three-year-old son to save his life and prevent serious injuries to him, was able to bring a suit for professional negligence, which in California is governed by the three-year statute of limitations.[119]

Negligent Discharge. When a mental patient who is released with the expectation that he can adjust to normal life assaults another person, the usual rules of negligence law generally apply to the hospital and its employees who released him.[120] Statutes in some states, however, confer immunity on both the physician and the state.

In a wrongful death action against a psychiatrist at a state mental hospital, the jury awarded the patient's aunt $500,000 in damages when she had alleged that a negligent discharge was the cause of her sister's death and that the psychiatrist had failed to warn the mother of the danger her son posed. The psychiatrist was aware that the patient had threatened his mother for money and that he had no money when he entered the hospital.[121]

A father and two sons received a jury award of $92,300 in a wrongful death action against five physicians who discharged the father's son from a hospital. After telling his grandparents that he planned to "knock them off and take the Toyota," the patient was committed to a state mental hospital. Some four months later, the clinical director suggested the patient be discharged to save the money it would cost to transfer him to another hospital. Not long afterward, the patient shot and killed his mother and brother. Standards of care were not followed.[122]

The Montana Supreme Court ruled that a section of the state statute prohibiting recovery from the state for noneconomic damages and limiting the amount of economic damages was unconstitutional. A woman sought damages for injuries suffered when she was attacked by a patient who had escaped from a state mental hospital five years earlier. The man was allegedly a violent and dangerous criminal. She suffered severe emotional injuries that would significantly affect her ability to live a happy and fulfilling life.[123]

Right to Treatment. If the person accused of crime pleads mental incompetency, as a defendant did in a trial for willful evasion of income taxes, he is stopped from objecting to further psychiatric examination under court order.[124] A court-appointed psychiatrist testifies as an expert for the court and not as a witness for either party.[125] Whether an accused has a right to have his attorney present at a compulsory psychiatric examination is not settled. Pursuant to the Sixth Amendment, an increasing number of courts hold that the accused is entitled to have a lawyer present when he is interviewed by a court-appointed psychiatrist.[126] At any hearing involving his sanity, the accused is entitled to have his lawyer present.[127]

When a person accused of a crime is ruled unfit to stand trial and is confined to a mental institution against his will, he has a right to treatment. In *Rouse v. Cameron* the court said:

> [T]he purpose of involuntary hospitalization is treatment, not punishment. Absent treatment, the hospital is transformed into a penitentiary where one could be held indefinitely for no convicted offense.[128]

In this case the accused, who was arrested for a misdemeanor carrying a maximal sentence of a year, had been in the hospital for four years at the time of decision. In a class action brought by guardians of a number of inmates in Alabama state mental institutions, the court ruled that the plans in the hospitals failed to conform to any known minimal standard established for treatment, and that each inmate had a constitutional right to treatment that would give him a realistic opportunity to improve. The court gave the state six months to produce a treatment plan that would meet its requirements, in the absence of which it would appoint experts to devise one.[129]

Nurses should note that a similar class suit brought on behalf of the mentally retarded held that minimal standards to ensure provision of essential care and training for mental retardates are mandatory, and that no default can be justified by lack of operating funds.[130] In addition, the Pennsylvania Association for Retarded Children won a class action suit to force the public school system to provide a free public education for all retarded children.[131]

In New York, boys committed to a training school have a constitutional right to rehabilitative treatment. From the evidence produced in the case of the Goshen Annex for Boys, the court concluded that the use of isolation, of hand and feet restraints and of Thorazine or other tranquilizing drugs to control excited behavior in children was unconstitutional.[132]

Confinement. In state mental hospitals, several patients had been ordered discharged pending placement. The patients had been institutionalized for an average of 30 years each and were not capable of carrying on an independent and self-sufficient life. For confinement, a showing that the patient was likely to pose a threat to himself or others was required. The court held that the state could continue their confinement on a conditional basis to protect their essential well-being.[133]

Damages for Involuntary Commitment. In a suit under the Civil Rights Act for deprivation of their liberty without due process of law, a couple who were involuntarily committed to separate detoxification centers were entitled to $250,000 in compensatory and $12,000 in punitive damages, a Federal trial court ruled. While preparing to leave for a Christmas party, the couple, who were not intoxicated and who had received no notice of any proceedings against them, were arrested and confined to a detoxification center. The orders were issued by a judge without a hearing. The basis of the commitment was statements made by the couple's 15-year-old daughter to two social workers. Later, the daughter testified she wanted to be placed in a foster home so she could "get away with a lot more," such as staying out at night. The social workers had not verified the girl's statements about her parents. Later, the county dismissed its case against them.[134]

Confidentiality of Staff Conferences. A Federal appellate court in Maryland ruled that transcripts of staff conferences at a psychiatric hospital were inadmissible as evidence under a state law protecting the confidentiality of medical review committee proceedings. The sister of a chronic schizophrenic and administratrix of the patient's estate brought an action against the hospital and physicians for malpractice and invasion of privacy for administering psychotherapy and other forms of psychiatric therapy to the patient.[135]

Psychiatric Nurses. Psychiatric nurses are considered one of the four major types of psychotherapists, and the question is whether they have a duty to warn possible victims when the therapist believes that a client may cause harm to others. Kjervik's position is that the psychiatric nurse is legally and morally bound to take steps to prevent a homicidal client from carrying out a serious threat.[136]

Malpractice Insurance

It is well for nurses employed in Government as well as non-Government hospitals to realize that the consistent practice of their profession in the proper manner is the strongest safeguard against damage suits. In addition, they may carry malpractice insurance for personal protection. The cost of such insurance, particularly when obtained through the American Nurses' Association, is modest. In an era when the number of lawsuits against hospitals, physicians and nurses is increasingly markedly, this type of protection seems desirable. Such insurance provides three benefits to the policy holder: (1) In the event of an award of damages against the nurse, the insurance pays any sum within the specified limits of the policy, (2) it pays the cost of the lawyer furnished to defend a nurse who is sued in a civil court for an alleged injury resulting from his or her professional work and (3) it will pay for a nurse's bond, if required, during an appeal. Not all lawsuits involving nurses result in an award against the nurse; but, as Grace Barbee, former lawyer for the California Nurses' Association, so aptly remarked, "It can be expensive to prove your innocence."

Many nurses work under the impression that they are protected by the hospital's insurance policy. Before relying exclusively on such insurance coverage, the prudent nurse should examine a copy of the policy to be certain of the extent of the coverage and of whether such insurance simply protects her or his interests to the extent necessary in the course of protecting the hospital's interests.

A good feature for nurses to look into is the matter of insurance. Nurses' malpractice or professional liability insurance pays the damages (to the extent of the face value of the policy) awarded by the court, and it also provides expert legal counsel to defend a claim and pays the cost of such defense. Such policies may be secured in amounts ranging from $300,000/$1,000,000 and upward for a relatively small premium. A $300,000/$1,000,000 policy means that the insurance company will pay up to $300,000 in damages to any one person who is injured as a result of the nurse's real or alleged malpractice, and it will pay up to $1,000,000 in damages in any one year on all claims involving the insured nurse. It is the view of many authorities that all registered nurses should carry malpractice insurance to cover the cost of expert legal counsel and to pay possible claims for damages. At times, it has been necessary for a nurse to prove that she was not negligent, and this litigation can be costly.

When the representatives of the insurance carrier declined to accept a pre-trial offer to settle out of court for $45,000 in a malpractice suit, which came to trial and resulted in a $120,000 judgment, a physician succeeded in making his insurance carrier pay $50,000 more than his original $70,000 policy allowed.[137]

When a radiologist's radioactive protective cart was negligently pulled and struck a nurse, his professional liability insurance did not cover the incident.[138]

An employee cannot always rely on his employer's insurance. Sometimes a nurse may feel more secure than the facts warrant when she thinks that her employer's malpractice insurance will cover the personal liability of the employed nurse. This is seldom the case, according to the findings of one article.[139] Nurses desiring protection should take out their own malpractice insurance. The American Nurses' Association sponsors a group plan that is available to any member on an individual basis. Some of the states have group plans, such as the California State Nurses' Association.

The recent changing patterns of nursing activities contribute to increased exposure to lawsuits. A number of years ago, the court held that it was a matter of common knowledge that the welfare of the patient was as much the responsibility of the nurse as of the physician.[140] Today, nurses have increased legal responsibilities when they carry out a great variety of new procedures, give new drugs and are responsible for the supervision or teaching of assorted personnel and patients. These are increased legal responsibilities. Then, too, this is an age of specialists; for example, nurses give care in coronary care units and in intensive care units where patients may receive organ transplants, undergo renal dialysis, receive hyperbaric care or obtain treatment for severe neurologic or other problems. The nurse who is thus engaged as a specialist is expected to possess the qualifications of a person ordinarily practicing in that specialty. Although in some states the nurses' hospital and medical associations have worked together constructively to delineate what the professional nurse may do by way of nursing care in critical patient care situations, other states have taken no action to clarify the gray area between nursing and medical practice.

At least one attorney who works in the field considers professional liability insurance a "must" for every licensed nurse and states that the amount depends on three factors: (1) the type of nursing a particular nurse does, (2) the geographical area and (3) the inclination of patients in the area to sue nurses.[141]

CIVIL RIGHTS ACT

The Civil Rights Act of 1964 forbids discrimination against any person on the grounds of race, color or national origin in relation to any program that receives Federal assistance.

Civil Rights

A 1971 Supreme Court decision ruled that a company cannot require employees to hold a high school diploma or pass an intelligence test as a condition to a job promotion unless such standards are "significantly related to successful job performance."[142] The Court did say that tests and other conditions for advancement may be used provided they relate directly to an employee's ability to perform the job. In the North Carolina case, the company had agreed to permit interdivision promotion, but required that candidates have a high school diploma and submit to two professionally prepared aptitude tests. The Court found that persons in this company, who were promoted to positions similar to the one in question before the diploma/intelligence test requirement, were now performing satisfactorily and that, if an employment practice that operated to exclude blacks could not be shown to be related to job performance, the practice was prohibited.

The predetermined racial admissions policy in a state university law school was upheld when the State Supreme Court ruled that the so-called preferential minority admissions policy was not a form of invidious racial discrimination, since the goal of the policy was not to separate the races but to bring them together. The school policy in considering race for determining admissions had the requisite connection between the racial classification used and the compelling state interest to have a racially balanced student body at the school.[143]

The U.S. Supreme Court in a 5 to 4 ruling held that a medical school's special minority admissions program violated Title VI of the 1964 Civil Rights Act, and affirmed a lower court order directing the school to admit an applicant who sued for "reverse discrimination."[144] Justice Powell, for the majority, said:

> The guarantee of equal protection cannot mean one thing when applied to one individual and something else when applied to a person of another color. If both are not accorded the same protection, then it is not equal.
> Preferring members of any one group for no reason other than race or ethnic origin is discrimination for its own sake. This the Constitution forbids.

In another case, a transsexual who was legally a male but was living as a female prior to his sex change surgery sued for discrimination after he was fired from his job as a waitress. A Federal trial court in Maryland found that the Civil Rights Act of 1964 did not protect transsexuals from employment discrimination.[145]

The discharge of a nursing assistant from a Veterans Administration hospital in a Civil Rights action was based on patient abuse and was not motivated in any way by racial discrimination or prejudice. Testimony as to the abuse of patients by the nursing assistant on several occasions was offered by eyewitnesses as well as by VA investigators.[146]

Labor Relations and Collective Bargaining

Prior to 1974, nonprofit hospitals were exempt by the Taft-Hartley Act from the jurisdiction of the National Labor Relations Board. After that date, hospitals are subject to the NLRB and employees have the right to bargain collectively. Any discrimination against employees due to union activities comes within the jurisdiction of the NLRB. In *NLRB v. Baptist Hospital, Inc.*,[147] the hospital prohibited solicitation by employees at all times in any area of the hospital that was used by or accessible to the public—including entrances, corridors, cafeteria, public restrooms and sitting rooms on patient floors. After the matter was presented before it, the court allowed solicitation in the first-floor lobby, gift shop and cafeteria. (Collective bargaining by nurses is discussed in an article in the Appendix.)

A nurse is entitled to a hearing before discharge. In a 1976 case,[148] the appellate court found that governing commission rules required that even a probationary employee be afforded a hearing, and that a sufficient record must be preserved for a court to determine whether just cause for discharge had been shown. The court further stated that if the commission conducted the required hearing within a time established by the trial court, it would purge itself of the contempt charge. This charge grew out of the governing commission's seven month failure to hold a hearing ordered earlier by the trial court to be held within 15 days.

See also cases under Workmen's Compensation, pp. 63ff.

Supervisor Membership in ANA.* The ANA does qualify as a labor organization under NLRA. In *Mercy Hospitals of Sacramento, Inc.*,[149] it is brought out that Sec. 2(5) of the NLRA defines a labor organization as:

> any organization of any kind . . . in which employees participate and which exists for the purpose, in whole or in part, of dealing with employers concerning grievances, labor disputes, wages, rates of pay, hours of employment, or conditions of work.

A professional association must admit that it is a labor organization in order to come within the jurisdiction of the NLRB for the purpose of obtaining a representation election. While the state nurses' associations and ANA, as a public relations matter, rather grudgingly concede they are labor organizations, they seek to persuade members and potential members that they are not *unions*, an unpopular self-concept among most professional nurses.

A supervisor is defined by Sec. 152(11) of the NLRA as:

> Any individual having the authority, in the interest of the employer, to hire, transfer, suspend, lay off, recall, promote, discharge, assign, reward, or discipline employees, or responsibly to direct them, or to adjust their grievances, or effectively to recommend such action, if in connection with the foregoing exercise of such authority is not of a merely routine or clerical nature, but requires use of independent judgment.[150]

As a consequence of the professional nursing associations, as labor organizations, representing the nurses in collective bargaining, some hospitals have requested and have required nursing supervisory personnel and the director of nurses to give up membership in their state nurses' association and in the ANA as a condition of continued employment.

As the U.S. Supreme Court said in *Florida Power & Light Co. v. IBEW*,[151] the employer is at liberty to demand absolute loyalty from his supervisory personnel by insisting, on pain of discharge, that they neither participate in nor retain membership in a labor union. (See *Beasley et al. v. Food Fair of North Carolina, Inc.*[152]) Alternatively, an employer who wishes to do so can permit his supervisors to join and retain their membership in labor unions, resolving conflicts that may arise through the traditional procedures of collective bargaining.[153] In the light of these U.S. Supreme Court decisions, it is not unlawful for a supervisor or a director of nursing services to belong to a labor organization, but whether such membership is permitted is a matter of hospital or agency policy.

In *Coamo Knitting Mills, Inc.*,[154] the NLRB held that encouraging an employee to join a labor organization does not in itself violate Sec. 8(a)(2) of the NLRA.

---

*This section first appeared as an article in *Supervisor Nurse*, 7:48–53, July 1976.

Hence, even if a professional organization qualifies as a labor union, continuing to encourage nurses to belong to their professional association would not seem to involve a legal problem.

Neutrality on Religious Matters

In *Williams* v. *Eaton*,[155] several black athletes were dismissed from a football team following a dispute over their intention to wear black armbands during a football game with Brigham Young University. The court upheld the school's dismissal of the athletes from the team, because the state and Federal constitutions mandate complete neutrality on religious matters and would have been violated by the armband display, which expressed opposition to the religious beliefs of the Church of Jesus Christ of Latter-day Saints on racial matters. The court said that the trustees' decision "protected against invasion of the rights of others by avoiding a hostile expression to them by some members of the university team. It was in furtherance of the policy of the religious neutrality by the State."

References

1. *Restatement, Torts* 1934, Sec. 281.
2. Curry v. Bruns, 136 Neb. 74, 285 N.W. 88 (1939).
3. Clary v. Christiansen, 83 N.E. 2d 644 (Ohio Ct. of App., 1948).
4. Armstrong v. Wallace, 8 Cal. App. 2d 429, 37 P. 2d 467, motion denied in part, affirmed in part, 47 P. 2d 740 (1935).
5. Jefferson Electric Co. v. National Labor Relations Board, 102 F. 2d 949 (C.C.A., 1939).
6. 4 Schneider's Workmen's Compensation (1940 & supp. to date); Virginia Workmen's Compensation Law Secs. 30–32; Wisconsin Workmen's Compensation Act Sec. 102.44 and Table I; Texas Employer's Liability and Workmen's Compensation Insurance Laws, tit. 130, Rev. Civ. Stat. Tex., art. 8306 Secs. 8–12 and Daily and Weekly Compensation Table and Table I; Pennsylvania Workmen's Compensation Act (Act of June 2, 1915–P.L. 736 as re-enacted and amended by Act of June 4, 1937-P.L. 1552), art. 3, Secs. 306, 307; Pennsylvania Occupational Disease Act, art. 3 Secs. 301–309.
7. Denver v. Pollard, 417 P. 2d 231 (Colo., 1966).
8. Twin City Fire Insurance Co. v. Graham, 130 Ga. App. 318, 228 S.E. 2d 355 (Ga. Ct. App., 1976); *Citation*, 34:96, Feb. 1, 1977.
9. Russell v. Camden Community Hospital et al., 359 A. 2d 607 (Me. Sup. Jud. Ct., 1976); *Citation*, 34:96, Feb. 1, 1977.
10. Lewis v. St. Charles Parish Hospital Services District et al., 337 So. 2d 1137 (La. Sup. Ct. 1976).
11. Miller, C. D.: Recovery for Psychic Injuries under Workers' Compensation, *Law, Med. & Health Care*, 9:25–27, 41, Dec. 1981.
12. Burlington Mills Corp. v. Hagood, 13 S.E. 2d 291 (S. Ct. Va. 1941).
13. Kahle v. Plochman, Inc., 428 A. 2d 913 (S. Ct. N.J. 1981).
14. McMahon v. Anaconda Company, 678 P. 2d 661 (S. Ct. Mont. 1984).
15. L. J. Reesor and Veterans Administration, 33 Empl. Comp. App. Bod. 1780, Aug. 19, 1982. Sosin, J. S.: What to Do If You Are Hurt on the Job, *RN*, 47:13–15, Oct. 1984.
16. United States Fire Insurance Co. v. Brown, 654 S.W. 2d 566 (Tex. Civ. App. 1983).
17. Maher v. Workmen's Compensation Board, San Clemente General Hospital, 33 Cal. 3d 729, 661 P. 2d 1058 (S. Ct. Cal. 1983). Creighton, H.: Recovery for On-The-Job Injuries or Illness, *Nurs. Management*, 15:70–71, March 1984.
18. Roberts v. U.S.O. Camp Shows, Inc., 91 Cal. App. 2d 884, 205 P. 2d 1116 (Cal. App. 1949).
19. Restatement, Agency. 1933 Sec. 2(3); see also Secs. 220, 250, 251.
20. Ware v. Culp, 24 Cal. App. 2d, 22, 74 P. 2d 283 (1938).
21. Williams v. Pomona Valley Hospital Assn., 21 Cal. App. 359, 131 Pac. 888 (1913).
22. Kamps v. Crown Heights Hospital, Inc., 251 App. Div. 849, 296 N.Y.S. 776, affirmed 277 N.Y. 86 (1937).
23. 60 A.L.R. 303; Annotation on Moody v. Industrial Accident Commission, 204 Cal. 668, 269 Pac. 542 (1928).
24. Hughes v. President and Directors of Georgetown College, 33 Fed. Supp. 867, affirmed 130 F (2d) 810 (D.C. Cir., 1942).
25. Blyth v. Birmingham Waterworks Co., 11 Exchequer 781, 156 Eng. Rep. 1047 (Exchequer, 1856). See *also* Osbourne v. Montgomery, 203 Wis. 223, 234 N.W. 372 (1931), and Charbonneau v. MacRury, 84 N.H. 501, 153 Atl. 457 (1931).
26. Valentin v. La Société Française de Bienfaisance Mutuelle de Los Angeles, 76 Cal. App. 2d 1, 172 P. 2d 359 (1946).
27. Piper v. Epstein, 326 Ill. App. 400, 62 N.E. 2nd 139 (1945).
28. Regan, W. A.: Supervision in Nursing: Legal

Significance, *Regan Report on Nursing Law*, 12(5):1, Oct. 1971.

29. Sierra Vista Ruling Supports SNA's NLRB Revokes Earlier Decision, *Am. J. Nurs.*, 79:1027, 1052–1055, June 1979.
30. Goodhart: Hospitals and Trained Nurses, 54:*Law Q. R.*, 560 (1938). Gold v. Essex, C. C. (1942) 2 K.B. 293.
31. Porter v. Patterson and Emory University, 107 Ga. App. 64, 129 S.E. 2d 70 (1962).
32. Crowe v. Provost, 52 TN. Appeals 397, 374 S.W. 2d 645 (1963).
33. Regan, W. A.: Nurse Shortage Remedies Can Be Risky, *Regan Report on Nursing Law*, 5(8):1, Jan. 1965.
34. Hall, W. T.: What's Happened to the "Captain of the Ship" Doctrine? *Texas Nursing*, Texas Nurses' Association, Austin, Feb. 1977, p. 13.
35. Sparger v. Worley, *Tex. Sup. Ct. J.*, 20:143–149, Jan. 15, 1977.
36. Ramone v. Mani. *Tex. Sup. Ct. J.*, 20:149–150, Jan. 15, 1977.
37. *Supra*, note 35, p. 144.
38. Payne, W. H., and Mayes, K. M.: Vicarious Liability and the Operating Room Surgeon, *S.T.L.J.*, 17:367–398, 1976.
39. Henrickson, C. W., and Laughlin, N. C.: The Sponge Count, the Surgeon's Vicarious Liability and Other Fictions, *Federation Ins. Coun. Q.*, 25:34–44, Fall 1974.
40. Svete, I. E.: Physician's Liability for Torts of Hospital Employees, *Clev.-Mar. L. Rev.*, 18:308–318, May 1969.
41. Burke v. Washington Hosp. Center, 475 F. 2d 364 (D.C. Cir., 1973); Conrad v. Lakewood Gen. Hosp., 410 P. 2d 785 (Wash., 1966); Nicholsen v. Sisters of Charity, 463 P. 2d 861 (Ore., 1970).
42. Restatement (Second) of Agency, Sec. 1 (1958).
43. Porter v. Puryear, 262 S.W. 2d 933 (Tex., 1953) aff'g. 258 S.W. 2d 182 (Tex. Civ. App.) Amarillo, 1953.
44. Moore v. Lee, 211 S.W. 214 (Tex., 1919) rev'g. 162 S.W. 437 Tex. Civ. App. (Dallas, 1914).
45. Beadles v. Metayha, 135 Colo. 366, 311 P. 2d 711 (Colo., 1957).
46. Ramone v. Mani, 535 S.W. 2d 654 (Tex. Civ. App., 1975).
47. Creighton, H.: Captain of the Ship Doctrine, *Supervisor Nurse*, 8:63, 66–67, Aug. 1977.
48. St. Joseph's Hospital v. Pennsylvania Labor Relations Board, No. 442, Jan. Term, 1975. See the Record and Brief filed for the Pennsylvania Labor Relations Board.
49. Nelson v. Peterson, 542 P. 2d 1075 (Utah 1975).
50. Horton v. Niagara Falls Mun. Med. Ctr., 380 N.Y.S. 2d 116 (Ct. App. N.Y. 1976).
51. *Accreditation Manual for Hospitals*. Chicago, JCAH, 1983.
52. Dessauer v. Memorial General Hospital and Glorious Bourque, 628 P. 2d 337 (Ct. App. N. Mex. 1981). Creighton, H.: Liability of Nurse Floated to Another Unit, *Nurs. Management*, 13:54–55, March 1982.
53. Cook v. John N. Norton Memorial Infirmary, 180 Ky. 331, 202 S.W. 874 (1918).
54. Roosen v. Peter Bent Brigham Hospital, 235 Mass. 66, 126 N.E. 392 (1920).
55. Sessions v. Thomas Dee Memorial Hospital Assn., 94 Utah 460, 51 P. 2d 229 (1938).
56. O'Connor v. Boulder Colorado Sanitarium Assn., 105 Colo. 259, 96 P. 2d 835 (1939).
57. Scott, A. W.: *Law of Trusts*, vol. III. Boston, Little, Brown & Co., 1939, Sec. 402, p. 2148 ff.
58. *Supra*, note 24.
59. Ray v. Tucson Medical Center, 72 Ariz. 22, 230 P. 2d 220 (1951). *See also* Spencer: Ray v. Tucson Medical Center, a Re-appraisal of the Tort Liability of Charities, 24 *Rocky Mt. Law Review* 71 (1951). Haynes v. Presbyterian Hospital Assn., 241 Iowa 1269, 45 N.W. 2d 5 (1950): Malloy v. Fong, 232 P. 2d 241 (1951) reversing 37 Cal. 2d 356, 220 P. 2d 48.
60. Adkins v. St. Francis Hospital of Charleston, W. Va., 143 S.E. 2d 154 (W. Va., 1965).
61. 60 Stat. 812; 28 U.S.C. Secs. 1291, 1346, 1402, 1504, 2110, 2401, 2402, 2411, 2412, 2671, 2680.
62. Van Sickel v. United States, 56 Ca. R. 81, 285 F. 2d 87 (U.S. Ct. of App., 9th Cir., Calif., 1960). *See also* Feres v. United States, 340 U.S. 135 (1950) concerning a serviceman in the United States who "while on active duty and not on furlough, sustained injury due to negligence of others in the armed forces."
63. Jefferson v. United States, 77 F. Supp. 706, aff'm 178 F. 2d 518, 71 S. Ct. 153 (1950).
64. Bailey v. E. Van Buskirk, 375 F. 2d 72, 345 Fed. Rep. 2d 298 (U.S. Ct. of App., 9th Cir., 1965).
65. Murray v. United States, 16 CCH Neg. Cases 522 (U.S. Ct. of App., 4th Cir., 1964).
66. Schwartz v. United States, 16 CCH Neg. Cases 2d 1227 (USDC-Pa., 1964).
67. Christopher v. United States, 237 F. Supp. 787, 16 A. 23, 19 A. 2d 1893, 32 A. 2d 1262 (U.S. Dist. Ct. E.D. Penna., 1964).
68. Underwood v. United States, 1A, 2 222, 356 F. 2d 92 (U.S. Ct. of App., 5th Cir., Ala., 1966).
69. Brown v. United States, 5 CCH Neg. Cases 2d 1086 (USDC-N.Y., 1956).
70. Owen v. United States, 251 F. Supp. 38 (1966).
71. Greenberger v. United States, 17 CCH Neg. 2d 1254 (USDC-N.Y., 1965).
72. United States v. Martinez, 334 Fed. (2d) 728 (U.S. Ct. of App., 10th Cir., Colo., 1964).
73. Finley v. United States, 314 F. Supp. 905 (Dist. Ct. N. Dist., Ohio, 1970).
74. Larabee v. United States, 13 CCH Neg. 2d 1001.
75. Kapuschinsky v. United States, 248 F. Supp. 732 (1966).
76. Evans v. United States, 212 F. Supp. 648 (D.C., Mass., 1962) 15 CCH Neg. 2d 989 (U.S. Ct. of App., 1st Cir., 1963).
77. Robak v. United States, 658 F. 2d 471 (U.S. Ct. App., 7th Cir., 1981).

78. Dinnerstein v. United States, 486 F. 2d (C.A. 2, 1973); *Citation*, 28:170–171, March 15, 1974.

79. Caron v. United States, 548 F. 2d 366 (C.A. 1, R.I., 1976); *Citation*, 35:41, June 1, 1977.

80. Voss v. United States, 423 F. Supp. 751 (D.C., Mo., 1976); *Citation*, 35:43, June 1, 1977.

81. Savarirayan v. English, 359 N.E. 2d 236 (Ill. Ct. of App., 1977); *Citation*, 35:25, May 15, 1977.

82. Castillo v. United States, 406 F. Supp. 585 (D.C. N.M., 1975).

83. Kyslinger v. United States, 406 F. Supp. 800 (D.C., Pa., 1975); *Citation*, 33:77, July 15, 1976.

84. Sparks v. Wyeth Laboratories, Inc., 431 F. Supp. 411 (D.C., Okla., 1977).

85. Ramirez v. United States, 567 F. 2d 854 (U.S. Ct. of App., 9th Cir., 1977).

86. Niblack v. United States, 483 F. Supp. 383 (U.S. Dist. Ct. D., Colorado, 1977); *Pub. Health Ct. Dig.*, 24:5, Oct. 1978.

87. Knight v. United States, 442 F. Supp. 1069 (U.S. Dist. Ct. S.C., Nov. 22, 1977); *Regan Rep. Med. Law.*, 11:2, April 1978.

88. Siverson v. U.S., 710 F. 2d 557 (C.A. 9, 1983); *Citation*, 48:29, Nov. 15, 1983.

89. Wooten v. U.S., 574 F. Supp. 200 (D.C. Tenn. 1982), Aff'm. 722 F. 2d 743 (C.A. 6, Tenn. 1983); *Citation*, 49:42, June 1, 1984.

90. 2 CCH Cong. Index 4993 (Oct. 27, 1976).

91. Act. of Oct. 8, 1976, Pub. L. No. 94–464 §1, 90 Stat., 1985.

92. *Id.* §2.

93. *Id.* §3.

94. Vigdor v. United States Civil Service Commission, 254 Fed. 2d 333 (1958).

95. Schwab v. Connelly, 116 Colo. 195, 179 P. 2d 667 (1947).

96. Henderson v. Twin Falls County, 56 Idaho 124, 50 P. 2d 597 (1935).

97. Hernandez v. The County of Yuma, 91 Az. 35, 369 P. 2d 271 (1962).

98. City of McAllen v. Gartmen *et ux.*, 81 S.W. 2d 147, affirmed 107 S.W. 879 (Ct. Civ. App., Tex., 1937).

99. Griffin v. County of Colusa et al., 44 Cal. App. 2d 915, 113 P. 2d 270 (1941).

100. Dahlberg v. Jones, 232 Wis. 6, 285 N.W. 841 (1939); Wetzel v. Omaha Maternity, etc., 96 Neb. 636, 148 N.W. 582 (1914).

101. Goldfoot v. Dofgren, 135 Ore. 533, 296 Pac. 843 (1931).

102. O'Donoghue v. Riggs, 440 P. 2d 823 (Wash., 1968).

103. Saron v. State of New York, 263 N.Y.S. 2d 591 (N.Y., 1965).

104. Wendover v. State of New York, 313 N.Y.S. 2d 287 (N.Y., 1970); Regan, W. A.: Law Forum, *Hosp. Progr.*, 51:43, Dec. 1970.

105. Flynn v. Lucas County Memorial Hospital, 203 N.W. 2d 613 (Iowa, 1973).

106. Hagen v. Civil Service Board, 1964 N.W. 2d 269 (Minn., 1969).

107. State v. Comstock, 70 S.E. 2d 648 (W. Va., 1952). See Holder, A. R.: Criminal Prosecution for Patient's Death, *J.A.M.A.*, 222:1341, 1342, Dec. 4, 1972.

108. Gerba v. Neurological Hospital, 1967 CCH Neg. 1660. See also *Regan Report on Nursing Law*, 8(5):3, Oct. 1967.

109. People of the State of Colorado in the interest of Medina, 662 P. 2d 184 (Colo. Ct. of App. 1982); rehearing denied 1982; certiorari granted, Colo. Sup. Ct. 1983; *Citation*, 48:45, Dec. 1, 1983.

110. Anderson v. State of Arizona, 663 P. 2d 570 (Ariz. Ct. of App. 1982); rehearing denied 1983; review denied 1983; *Citation*, 48:45, Dec. 1, 1983.

111. Rogers v. Commissioner of the Department of Mental Health, 458 N.E. 2d 308 (Mass. Sup. Jud. Ct. 1983): *Citation*, 49:53–54, June 15, 1984.

112. Rennie v. Klein, 720 F. 2d 266 (C.A. 3, N.J. 1983): *Citation*, 48:136, April 1, 1984.

113. N.Y. City Health & Hosp. Corp. v. Stein, 335 N.Y.S. 2d 461 (N.Y., 1972).

114. Dunn v. State, 312 N.Y.S. 2d 61 (N.Y. 1970).

115. Bell v. New York City Health and Hospitals Corporation, 456 N.Y.S. 2d 787 (N.Y. Sup. Ct. App. Div. 1982). Creighton, H.: Negligence in Releasing Psychiatric Patient, *Nurs. Management*, 14:53–54, Nov. 1983.

116. Homere v. State of New York, 48 A.D. 422, 370 N.Y.S. 2d 246 (N.Y. 1975).

117. Katepoo v. New York Hospital, 562 F. Supp. 875 (D.C., N.Y. 1983): *Citation*, 48:42, Dec. 1, 1983.

118. Petersen v. State, 671 P. 2d 230 (Wash. S. Ct. 1983).

119. Hedlund v. Superior Court of Orange County, 669 P. 2d 41, 194 Cal. Rptr. 804, (Cal. S.C. 1983); *Citation*, 48:37–38, Dec. 1, 1983.

120. Holder, A. R.: Improper Release from Mental Hospital, *J.A.M.A.*, 220:897, May 8, 1972.

121. Davis v. Lhim, 335 N.W. 2d 481 (Mich. Ct. of App. 1983); rehearing denied 1983; *Citation*, 48:37–38, Dec. 1, 1983.

122. Durflinger v. Artiles, 563 F. Supp. 322 (D.C. Kans. 1981): *Citation*, 48:39, Dec. 1, 1983.

123. White v. State of Montana, 661 P. 2d 1272 (Mont. S.C. 1983): rehearing denied 1983; *Citation*, 48:40, Dec. 1, 1983.

124. United States v. Baird, 414 F. 2d 700 (ECA 2, 1969). *See* Holder A. R.: Compulsory Psychiatric Examination, *J.A.M.A.*, 220: 1277, May 29, 1972.

125. Massey v. State, 177 S.E. 2d 79 (Ga., 1970).

126. People v. Abdul Karim Al-Kanani, 260 N.E. 2d 496 (N.Y., 1970).

127. Commonwealth *ex rel* McGurrin v. Shovlin, 257 A. 2d 902 (Pa., 1969).

128. Rouse v. Cameron, 373 F. 2d 451 (D.C., C.A., 1966). *See also* Holder, A. R.: The Right to Treatment, *J.A.M.A.*, 220:1165, May 22, 1972.

129. Wyatt v. Stickney, 325 F. Supp. 781 (D.C., A6, 1971).

130. Wyatt v. Stickney, 344 F. Supp. 387 (Ala., 1972).

131. Pennsylvania Assoc. for Retarded Children v. Commonwealth of Pennsylvania, David H. Kurzman et al., Civil Action No. 71–42,

Order Injunction and Consent Agreement, Oct. 7, 1971. See Curran, W. J.: Rights for Retarded: A Landmark Decree, Am. J. Pub. Health, 62:264, Feb. 1, 1972.

132. Pena v. N.Y. State Div. for Youth, 419 F. Supp. 203 (U.S.D.C., S.D., N.Y., 1976).

133. In the Matter of S.L., 462 A. 2d 1252 (N.J. Sup. Ct. 1983); Citation, 48:46, Dec. 1, 1983.

134. Dick v. Watonwan County, 562 F. Supp. 1083 (D.C. Minn. 1983); Citation, 48:43, Dec. 1, 1983.

135. Kappas v. Chestnut Lodge, Inc., 709 F. 2d 878 (C.A. 4, Md. 1983); Citation, 48:44, Dec. 1, 1983.

136. Kjervik, D. K.: The Psychiatric Nurse's Duty to Warn Potential Victims of Homicidal Psychotherapy Outpatients, Law, Med., & Health Care, 9:11–16, Dec. 1981.

137. Price v. Neyland, 320 F. 2d 674 (1963).

138. Hartford Casualty Insurance Co. v. Shehata, 427 F. Supp. 336 (Ill. 1977).

139. Barbee, G. C. When Is the Nurse Held Liable? Am. J. Nurs., 54:1343–1346, 1954.

140. Miller v. Mohr, 198 Wash. 619, 89 P. 2d 807 (1939).

141. Insurance: A "Must" for Every Licensed Nurse, Regan Report on Nursing Law, 10(3):1, Aug. 1969.

142. Griggs v. Duke Power Co. (N.C., 1971). See also Supreme Court Major Civil Rights Decision Affects All Employees, Hosp. Management, April 1971.

143. DeFundis v. Odegaard, 507 P. 2d 1169 (Wash., 1973): Ed. Ct. Digest, 17(12):1, Dec. 1973.

144. Regents of the University of California v. Bakke, Docket No. 76–811 (U.S. Sup. Ct., 1978); Citation, 37:85–86, Aug. 1, 1978.

145. Powell v. Read's Inc., 436 F. Supp. 369 (D.C., Md., 1977).

146. Rozier v. Roudebush, 444 F. Supp. 861 (D.C., Ga., 1978); Citation, 37:108, Aug. 15, 1978.

147. NLRB v. Baptist Hospital, Inc., 61 L. Ed. 2d 251 (S. Ct. 1979).

148. People of the State of Illinois et rel. Miselis v. Health and Hospitals Governing Commission, 358 N.E. 2d 1221 (Ill. Ct. of App., 1976).

149. Mercy Hospitals of Sacramento, Inc., 217 NLRB No. 131 (1975).

150. 61 Stat. 138, 29 U.S.C. Sec. 152(11).

151. Florida Power & Light Co. v. International Brotherhood of Electrical Workers, Local 614 et al., 417 U.S. 790 (1974).

152. Beasley et al. v. Food Fair of North Carolina, Inc. et al., 416 U.S. 653 (1974).

153. Bernstein, A. H.: Responsibilities of Professional Societies, Hospitals, 50:135, Feb. 1, 1976.

154. Coamo Knitting Mills, Inc., 150 NLRB 579 (1964).

155. Williams v. Eaton, 468 F. 2d 1079 (Wyo., 1972).

General References

Age Discrimination & Nurses, Pamphlet No. 4, Texas Nursing, 58(1)28–29, Jan. 1984.

Analysis of Workers' Compensation Laws, Chamber of Commerce of the United States (1615 H Street N.W.), Washington D. C.

Bernzweig, E. P.: When In Doubt—Speak Out, Am. J. Nursing, 80(6)1175–1176, June 1980.

Cole, R.: Patient's Rights to Refuse Antipsychotic Drugs, Law, Med. & Health Care, 9:19–22+, Sept. 1981.

Creighton H.: Comparable Worth Cases, Part I, Nurs. Management, 15:21–22, Oct. 1984.

Creighton, H.: Comparable Worth Cases, Part II, Nurs. Management, 15:20–22, Nov. 1984.

Creighton, H.: Forced Medication of Mental Patients, Nurs. Management, 12:72–73, Sept. 1981.

Creighton, H.: Rights of Mental Patients, Superv. Nurse, 12:16–27, May 1981.

Creighton, H.: Collective Bargaining, Superv. Nurse, 11:61–62, Sept. 1980.

Creighton, H.: P.H.N. as Interested Person, Superv. Nurse, 11:13–14, Nov. 1980.

Creighton, H.: Malpractice Insurance, Nurs. Management, 12:15–16, Dec. 1981.

Creighton, H.: Liability of Nurse Floated to Another Unit, Nurs. Management, 13:54–55, March 1982.

Creighton, H.: Negligence in Releasing Psychiatric Patient, Nurs. Management, 14:53–54, Nov. 1983.

Creighton, H.: Recovery for On-the-Job Injuries or Illness, Nurs. Management, 15:70–71, March 1984.

Cushing, M.: Malpractice: Are You Covered? Am. J. Nursing, 84:985–986, Aug. 1984.

Greenlaw, J.: Understaffing: Living with Reality, Law, Med. & Health Care, 9:23–24+, Sept. 1981.

Horsley, J. E.: Legally Speaking: Think Twice before You Give that Advice, RN, 43(9)94–98, Sept. 1980.

Nurses & Job Discrimination Using the EEOC, Pamphlet No. 3, Texas Nursing 58(1)28–29, Jan. 1984.

Philpott, M.: Legal Liability and the Nursing Process. Toronto, W. B. Saunders Company Canada Ltd., 1985.

Regan, W. A.: Psychiatric Assessment—RNs v. Psychologists, Regan Rep. Nurs. Law, 21(4)2, Sept. 1980.

Regan, W. A.: Nurses' Rights in Collective Bargaining, Solicitation, Regan Rep. Nurs. Law, 22:2, Jan. 1982.

Regan, W. A.: Restraining Patients in Psychiatric Units, Regan Rep. Nurs. Law, 23:2, July 1982.

Sosin, J. S.: What to Do If You're Hurt on the Job, RN, 47:13–15, Oct. 1984.

Taub, S.: Psychiatric Malpractice in the 1980s: A Look at Some Areas of Concern, Law, Med. & Health Care, 11:97–103, June 1983.

Six
NURSES' RIGHTS AND LIABILITIES IN RELATION TO THEIR POSITION AND STATUS

NURSES' RIGHTS AND LIABILITIES

In any occupation, the person who works and the persons for whom the work is done must "keep the law." The practice of nursing is no exception. Suits at law fall into two classes of actions: those involving a breach of contract; and those involving torts, or injuries or wrongs to the person or property of another. Those actions in which a nurse is one of the parties are frequently suits either involving disagreements over contracts for personal services or for damages for injuries as a result of negligence to the person or property of another. Situations resulting in claims for damages can be handled by a lawsuit or settlement. Laws of different states vary considerably as to the liability that can be imposed for the injuries and wrongs done by another, for example, as an employee or agent.

General

It is important to keep in mind that liability for negligence does not depend on a legal relationship or a contract between the persons. A nurse who in some manner causes injury to a patient can be sued for damages by the patient, regardless of who may employ the nurse or whether the services are given for pay or given gratuitously. As pointed out before, a nurse may also be sued in some cases for breach of contract to give proper nursing care. Whether the nurse is an independent contractor, agent or employee is important in ascertaining the liability of other persons in addition to the nurse in damage suits arising from negligence. The employer's degree of control, the type of business, the basis and method of payment, the place and the equipment are some factors considered in differentiating employees from independent contractors.

The nurse is reminded that negligence must be determined from all the circumstances.[1] The question arises whether the nurse acted as a person with average skill in her calling, placed in similar circumstances, would have acted, or whether he or she used less care, judgment or skill. Moreover, the nurse is cautioned that it is not necessarily enough to do what is ordinarily done, because no one can claim that he or she is not liable for failure to use due care on the grounds that others are just as careless.

Care in Emergency Situations

The nurse should know that, whatever moral or humanitarian obligations there may be, there is no obligation or duty in the absence of a statutory provision to give care to a person in an emergency.[2] For example, in some states there is a law expressly requiring that a person involved in an automobile accident in which persons are injured must not leave without giving aid. However, when an obligation is undertaken voluntarily, it becomes one's duty to give every necessary service that the situation calls for. For example, the court has stated that no one is obliged by law to assist a stranger, even though he can do so by a word and without the slightest danger to himself, but once he has undertaken to give assistance, the law imposes on him a duty of care toward the person assisted.[3]

Another circumstance that may affect liability or negligence is whether the act was done in an emergency situation. Under emergency circumstances, a nurse, like any other person, may perform a medical act to preserve life and limb. Either law or custom exempts such actions from coming within the medical practice acts. However, whether there is in fact an "emergency" is a question that has to be decided in light of all the circumstances. Nurses are reminded that, in view of their education, training and experience, a higher degree of care will be expected than from an ordinary person who acts in an emergency. In other words, they will be expected to act like an ordinary nurse under similar circumstances.

Good Samaritan legislation is designed to encourage volunteer first aid in emergency situations. However, such statutes offer little help in determining whether or not a true emergency exists. Since numbers of apparent emergencies are borderline situations, the decision that a real emergency exists is important for two reasons: It typically relieves the first aider of the consequences of her or his acts (except for willful misconduct), and certain statutory restrictions on performing medical acts are suspended for the emergency. The determination that a particular set of facts constitutes an emergency is legally correct only when it can be shown that reasonable and prudent persons would have reached the same decision under the same or similar circumstances. Moreover, at the time of a trial, which is generally several years later, the emergency character of many situations may seem less than at the time of occurrence. Thus, the need for a first aider to evaluate correctly emergency situations as judged at a later time by reasonable and prudent persons, is not relieved by Good Samaritan laws and, in fact, may be a deterrent to intervention.[4]

However, in Vermont you must be a Good Samaritan. The nurse, doctor or anyone else who comes along is now required by Vermont law to render aid in an emergency on pain of criminal penalty. In 1983, Minnesota added a provision to its Good Samaritan statute that creates a duty to help persons exposed to "grave physical harm." It provides a fine up to $100 for people who fail to aid others in an emergency and relieves Good Samaritans of liability when they render emergency aid.[6]

The professional nurse in the emergency room must make rapid decisions, screen patients, have knowledge of how to assist in all types of emergency care and be able to deal appropriately with people under stress.[7] Both professional nurses and their personnel must be prepared to render effective nursing care in emergencies. Consequently, they must have knowledge about various types of emergencies, and they must keep abreast of new developments in this field. When the emergency patient arrives, emergency drugs, equipment and supplies must be on hand and in working order for immediate use.

Nurses should know that neither they nor their employer incurs tort liability unless there has been a deviation from certain standards. To specify precisely what is expected in the way of nursing care is not easy. If a hospital participates in Medicare or Health Insurance for the Aged, one must know the following "Conditions for Participation":

    1. Standard A. Factor 3. The emergency service is supervised by a qualified member of the medical staff and the nursing functions are the responsibility of a registered professional nurse.
    2. Standard C. Factor 1. The medical staff is responsible for insuring adequate medical coverage for emergency services.
    3. Standard C. Factor 2. Qualified physicians are regularly available at all times for the emergency service, either day or on call.
    4. Standard C. Factor 3. A physician sees all patients who arrive for treatment in the emergency service.
    5. Standard C. Factor 4. Qualified nurses are available on duty at all times, and in sufficient number to deal with the number and extent of emergency services.

These provisions cover the matter of staffing in the emergency room, which at various times has been a matter of concern. Furthermore, as Dr. Letourneau has pointed out, any deviation from these standards may lead to a presumption of negligence.[9]

Many times the emergency room nurse must make decisions as to whether an emergency exists. In one case, an action was brought for wrongful death of an infant who died shortly after treatment had been refused at a private hospital that maintained an emergency ward.[10] The infant, who had a temperature and diarrhea and had not slept for two nights, was brought in by his parents, who told the nurse that the child was under the care of two doctors and showed her the medicine prescribed. The nurse explained to the parents that the hospital could not give treatment because the child was under the care of a physician and that the medicine of the hospital might conflict with that of the doctor. She did not examine the child, but tried unsuccessfully to get in touch with his doctors. She suggested that the parents bring the child to the pediatric clinic the next morning. During the night, the baby died of bronchial pneumonia. An order for summary judgment for the hospital was denied, and the court said the question was whether the nurse's determination not to have the infant examined by an intern was within reasonable limits of judgment of a graduate nurse, even though mistaken, or whether she was derelict in her duty as a graduate nurse in not recognizing an emergency from the symptoms related to her.

In a New York case, a widow sought recovery of damages for wrongful death from a hospital and a physician for failure to render necessary emergency treatment to a patient who came to the emergency room after awakening with severe pains in his chest and arms.[11] He mentioned that they were members of the Hospital Insurance Plan (HIP). The nurse stated that the hospital had no connections with HIP and did not take care of HIP patients. The nurse did call a HIP doctor, and let the patient describe his complaints to him. The doctor told him to go home and return when HIP was open. After that, the nurse refused to summon another doctor to examine the man. Thereafter, the man and his wife returned home, where he died before help could be secured. The New York Supreme Court reversed the trial court's verdict for the hospital, and said that there was a question whether the physician who talked to the decedent, and the hospital's nurse who allegedly refused to have the decedent examined, were negligent.

In another case, in which a patient with a myocardial infarct was brought to the emergency room and examined by the nurses, they decided there was no emergency and a physician was not called.[12] Later, he was examined by a physician, who had him admitted to the hospital as an emergency patient; he died two days later. The nurses erred in making a decision that was not theirs to make. However, the hospital was not held liable, since physicians testified that the delay in admitting the patient made no difference in his death.

Every professional nurse in the emergency room should know the *Standards for the Emergency Department*, published by the American College of Surgeons, which states:

> The function of an emergency department is to give adequate appraisal and initial treatment or advice to every person who considers himself acutely ill or injured and presents himself at the emergency department door.[13]

Since many emergency rooms are clogged with patients with assorted minor ailments, and it appears that many come in the evenings because they find emergency room hours more convenient than clinic hours, it seems necessary to point out to the professional nurse the necessity of establishing some system of priorities, such as that of triage. Otherwise, if a "first come, first served" basis is used, a person with a severe myocardial infarction or a depressed skull fracture may have to wait for long periods in the emergency room while physicians examine numbers of patients with common colds, minor cuts, sprains and so forth. Such an arrangement scarcely meets the standard required by the law of what an ordinary, reasonable and prudent person would do. In an emergency patients should be allowed to leave only after they have been seen, examined and offered reasonable first aid.

Refusal to Treat. Whether a nurse who denied hospital admission to a woman in active labor accurately reported the doctor's telephone orders, and whether failure to accurately report constitutes negligence, were questions of fact for the jury when the woman sued for damages. The patient was having 30-second contractions every two or three minutes, and there was a small amount of bright red show when she came to the emergency room at 2 A.M. The nurse stated that, when she reported this by telephone to the physician assigned to the emergency room duty he said, "Tell the patient to get in touch with her own doctor." However, the doctor stated, "I told the nurse to have the girl call her doctor at Garland and see what he wanted her to do." The baby was born while the woman was on her way to the doctor at Garland.[14]

A verdict was affirmed against a hospital where a man who sustained a back injury in an automobile accident came to the hospital at 4:30 A.M. complaining of the injury and stating that his back might be broken. The nurse told him to wiggle his toes, and then telephoned the doctor on call for emergency room duty, saying that she could find nothing wrong with him and that he and his friends had been drinking. The patient was given medicine for pain and was refused admission. After he found blood in his urine the following day, he was taken to another hospital, where it was found he had a broken back. The doctor at the first hospital said that he told the nurse to admit the man and have x-rays and other diagnostic tests made on him. He denied that the nurse told him the man was complaining of a back injury and could not walk.[15] The difficulty an emergency room nurse may encounter as a result of telephone orders is evident from these cases.

In a similar case a pregnant woman visiting in a small Ohio town for a funeral went to the emergency room of the local hospital and said that she did not think she could get home to Illinois before her baby was born. The small hospital had only four physicians on its staff. The first physician on call told the emergency room nurse that he did not accept "walk-in OB's," and the second physician refused to see the woman. The woman did get home, where her baby was born during the night without medical help. She called an ambulance, which came immediately, but she was dead on arrival at Owensboro Hospital. The court said that because hospital rules required a physician's order before a patient could be admitted, and because the nurse could not force either doctor to accept the woman as a patient, the nurse had done all she could to help and that, therefore, both the hospital and the nurse were entitled to have the complaint dismissed as a matter of law.[16]

More than 70 years ago, in the case of *Schloendorff* v. *Society of New York Hospital,*[17] Justice Cardoza said:

> Every human being of adult years and sound mind has a right to determine what shall be done with his own body; and a surgeon who performs an operation without his patient's consent commits an assault, for which he is liable in damages.

On the right of the patient to refuse treatment, the general rule is clear. Regardless of the opinion of his or her physician concerning the advisability of treatment, a patient may refuse to permit any medical or surgical procedure to be performed. The difficulties arise in exceptional cases.

In emergency situations, physicians have considerable discretion and latitude. Where a patient is unconscious and immediate treatment is indicated, the law presumes that if the patient were conscious he or she would consent. If a child requires emergency treatment and parents are unavailable, the law presumes the parents would give consent.

In *Wallace* v. *Labrenz*[18] it has been held that the courts can order compulsory medical treatment of children for any serious illness or injury. However, a parent may refuse to provide nonessential treatment and this is liberally construed.

Nurses and physicians should remember that elderly persons continue to be competent adults until or unless they are judged incompetent. In *Maxwell* v. *Maxwell,*[19] a father won a false imprisonment suit against a middle-aged son who had the father confined to a VA hospital for mental incompetence. It is worth noting also that even where, as in *Winters* v. *Miller*,[20] a person may be judged incompetent to handle money matters, she or he may be considered competent to give or withhold consent to medical treatment.

The individual's right to refuse treatment is quite broad.[21] It is based on the legal right of a person to decide what treatment is appropriate for his or her body.

Where a physician refused to treat a semicomatose brittle diabetic woman brought into a hospital's emergency room and there was a 45-minute delay before another doctor treated the patient and she died, her husband sued for damages. The Appellate Court of Arizona observed that the physician may have contracted away his right to refuse to treat a patient when he agreed to be the doctor "on call" in charge of the emergency room of the Mohave General Hospital, particularly in view of the fact that he was paid $100 a day to perform those services.[22]

An 11-year-old boy was struck on the head in a fight during a softball game. The injured boy fled on his bicycle despite the supervisor's efforts. The boy's parents were divorced, and on the day in question he accompanied his father to San Francisco where they were to spend the weekend. Because the boy was in pain, they wound up in the hospital emergency department. Within two hours of his injury, the boy was examined by two nurses, an intern and a pediatric resident. It was decided that the boy should be admitted for observation since, although x-ray films did not show a skull fracture, other signs of intracranial bleeding were evident. Because the boy was not under the care of a private practitioner who had hospital privileges, an admitting office employee advised the intern that admission was not possible. The director of the hospital's pediatric outpatient clinic was asked by the resident to assist in admitting the boy. Although the director did not examine the boy, he talked with the father and decided that he would be a competent observer of the boy's symptoms. Instructions to the father were that he should watch for dilation of the pupils, and that the boy could be roused from sleep for this purpose. A sheet of symptoms that would indicate the boy's need to return to the hospital, customarily given to parents in similar circumstances, was not given to the father. Some hours later, the son returned to the hospital, had neurosurgery and was comatose for days. The boy eventually recovered most of his mental faculties, but his body was paralyzed and he was mute. The amount of damages assessed was over $4 million, which was not considered excessive by the appellate court.[23] Failure to properly instruct the patient and family can be costly.

Emergency Services Management. According to JCAH Standards for Emergency Services, a well-defined plan for emergency care, based on community need and on hospital capability, shall exist within every hospital. Large hospitals that provide a wide variety of services can, and usually do, provide effective emergency care for any type of patient. On the other hand, hospitals that offer only a partial range of services may operate only a limited emergency service and must arrange for the transfer or referral of certain patients to other hospitals. Other institutions such as very small hospitals and specialty hospitals may refer all emergency patients. However, the referring hospital must institute essential lifesaving measures and provide emergency procedures that will minimize aggravation of problems during transportation.

In *Methodist Hospital* v. *Ball*,[24] the hospital was held liable for damages when a 16-year-old accident victim waited for 45 minutes without examination or treatment. The intern had believed bystanders that the youth was drunk and sent him to another hospital, where the patient died of a ruptured liver. Where a patient has been accepted for treatment, then due care in diagnosis and treatment is necessary. In *Joyner v. Ochsner Medical Foundation*,[25] where an accident victim was given emergency treatment for lacerations, bruises, damage to teeth and possible head injuries, his wife could not pay the $100 deposit for his admission to the hospital. Ochsner Medical Foundation contacted the Veterans Administration Hospital, which agreed to accept him as a patient, and he was transferred there. The court held that Ochsner Foundation Hospital was not liable for not admitting him for inpatient treatment.

Staffing shall be related to the scope and nature of the needs anticipated and the services offered. The results of poor staffing in the emergency room is illustrated by *Maidma v. Glendora Community Hospital*[26] where an eight-week-old infant was brought to the hospital with complaints of vomiting and difficulty in breathing. An obstetrics resident on call in the emergency room gave him an injection of penicillin and sent him home. The baby was brought back to the hospital the next day with a temperature of 106° and was seen by a radiology resident, who ordered cold packs for the temperature and an oral electrolyte solution for the dehydration. Two hours later, the pediatrician arrived and sent him to intensive care. As a cutdown was done, the baby sustained cardiac arrest. Although revived, he was severely mentally retarded and had quadriparesis. A substantial settlement was made.

In *Glavin v. Rhode Island Hospital*,[27] a patient injured his hand in an industrial accident and was admitted to the hospital. The intern on call was assigned to the patient. The intern, being unable to stop the flow of blood, put a tourniquet on the patient's arm but did not summon assistance. It was held in this case that the patient's injury was such that, according to the hospital's rule, a surgeon should have been summoned and the intern's failure to do so was the causative negligence for which the hospital was liable.

In emergencies when the patient requires immediate care to preserve life and health, the physician is reasonably privileged to treat the patient. In *Luka v. Lowrie* where surgery was performed on the mangled foot of a 15-year-old accident victim, the court said:

> In emergencies, a surgeon may lawfully perform and it is his duty to perform such operations as good surgery demands without the consent of the patient.[28]

In certain situations, capacity to consent has been found lacking. In most instances where intoxicated persons cannot authorize treatment, an emergency exists. This is true also of many mentally incompetent persons.

In *Thomas v. Corsa*,[29] a judgment of $99,609.24 was affirmed against a doctor and a hospital where there was a failure to report vital signs and take appropriate action in treating an automobile accident victim. The patient was brought to the emergency room at 11:10 P.M. with an abrasion of the frontal scalp and inability to move the right leg. The emergency room nurse telephoned the on-call physician, informed him of the patient's vital signs and said the patient had been hit by a car. He was admitted to the hospital and given medication for relief of pain; however, the nurse's testimony conflicted with that of the doctor as to the telephone orders. The court said that if the physician had performed his duty to personally attend the patient, and if the nurse had reported his vital signs at 12:05 A.M., the patient's life might have been saved. Again, the nurse should note the problems that arise with telephone orders.

In *New Biloxi Hospital v. Frazier*,[30] a patient with a gunshot wound was kept in an emergency room, and two nurses looked at him but did nothing to stop his bleeding. A pool of blood 30 inches in diameter formed, and a physician ordered him transferred to the Veterans Administration Hospital when he was in shock. The patient died, and the court allowed a recovery, holding that a hospital giving emergency treatment is obliged to do what is immediately necessary to preserve life, limb and health of the patient.

In *Garcia* v. *Memorial Hospital*,[31] a Texas appellate court ruled that the parents of a child who died when a municipal hospital did not have a pediatric endotracheal tube to assist in the child's breathing could maintain a wrongful death suit against the hospital.

The JCAH says that emergency policies shall be approved by the medical staff and by the hospital management. Moreover, the written policies shall be reviewed periodically, revised as necessary and dated to indicate the time of the last review. Written procedures are to be developed that are based upon these policies.

The JCAH states that the medical record shall contain: adequate patient identification; information concerning the patient's arrival, means of arrival, and by whom transported; pertinent history of injury or illness including first aid or emergency care prior to his or her arrival at the hospital; significant clinical, laboratory or x-ray findings; diagnosis, and treatment given; condition of the patient on discharge or transfer; and the final disposition. It states that the record is to be signed by the physician in attendance who is responsible for its clinical accuracy. Finally, the JCAH states that emergency room medical records shall be used to evaluate regularly the quality of emergency medical care.

The JCAH standards for emergency services are an efficient outline for quality emergency room service and good professional relationships in the emergency room. The JCAH is a recognized standard-setting organization for hospitals in the United States.[32]

Care of Psychiatric Patients

A psychiatric patient suffering from a schizo-affective disorders and depression was undergoing Glissando therapy, which includes medications, electroshock therapy and restraint for four or five hours. She fell and broke her hip after the ninth treatment, but could not recover damages where it was shown that the ties on a restraining sheet were tied in accordance with the recognized method of keeping a patient in bed after electroshock therapy, and the only established standard of care was used.[33]

A patient with a history of suicidal tendencies was admitted to a unit that provided no special nursing or custodial care. Several days later he lost his scheduled time for hydrotherapy when he left his room, and the nurse found him playing checkers in the recreation room. Shortly thereafter a nurse, looking out a fourth-floor window, saw him hang by his hands from a window and then drop to the roof of a building. Although he died from the effects of the fall, the court ruled in favor of the hospital and its employees in a damage suit, since in the absence of anything to put the nurse and attendants on notice that the patient was likely to climb over the parapet of a roof, they could not be expected to anticipate and prevent such an action.[34]

The degree of care a nurse or attendant must use in caring for mental patients varies with their condition. Thus, in a case in which the condition of a patient who was hospitalized for the treatment of mental disorders was improving, the court did not hold the hospital liable when one day he ran away from an attendant, jumped in a water tank and drowned.[35] However, in another case, the condition of a hospitalized mental patient was steadily deteriorating. He had delusions and wanted to leave the hospital. One afternoon, when out for a walk with an attendant, he suddenly ran into the street and was seriously injured by a truck. The court ruled that he had established a *prima facie* case of negligence on the part of the hospital.[36]

The Kansas court reversed a judgment in favor of a hospital and granted a new trial to a psychiatric patient who sustained injuries when he fell out of a window. He had been transferred from the psychiatric service and had undergone prostatic surgery. His family stayed with him for two nights. When they left, the daughter told the charge nurse that the patient was confused and needed watching, and that his side-rails should be up. She was told that he would be watched. Not long afterward he was found lying on a roof beneath the bathroom window. He had a medical order for bathroom privileges, and the nurse on duty was not a psychiatric nurse, knew little about depressive patients, had just returned from vacation and had not received any special instructions regarding the patient from the nurse she relieved.[37]

In an action by a psychiatrist to enjoin the state from enforcing a Connecticut law requiring physicians to report the names of, and other information about, "drug-dependent" persons to the State Health Commissioner, it was held that the law was constitutional. Whatever protection there is against disclosure of a patient's communications exists solely through laws of individual states; there is no Federal constitutional right to such privileges.[38]

A plantiff was awarded $15,000 damages when no medical or eyewitness testimony was offered to justify extreme forms of control such as being locked in her cell in solitary confinement, beaten and subjected to other abuses during her nine years in a New York state hospital. The court said that, although detention in a state hospital may be necessary, unnecessary punishment and cruelty, if proved, constitute malpractice. In this case the court found that the patient was subjected to such cruel and unusual punishments as to constitute assaults upon her.[39]

A New York court ruled that compensatory damages in excess of $25,000 were excessive and the patient was not entitled to punitive damages in a malpractice action against her psychiatrist for having sexual intercourse with her as part of her therapy.[40] The court said that she could recover only for the aggravation of her long-standing mental disorders.

In a class action suit challenging medication and seclusion policies in a state institution for the mentally ill in Massachusetts, the appellate court held that a physician's findings of possible harm to the patients from antipsychotic medication is outweighed by the need to prevent violence, and that the unavailability of less restrictive means is a necessary prerequisite under the Due Process Clause, for forcible administration of such drugs. Also, a judicial determination of the patient's incapacity to make treatment decisions is a necessary prerequisite, under the Due Process Clause, for forcible nonemergency administration of antipsychotic drugs to state mental patients.[41] In an Ohio case, the court held that the state mental hospital's administration of mood-altering drugs to patients without their informed consent violates "liberty" interests guaranteed by the Due Process Clause, unless patients present danger to themselves or others.[42] A state may not constitutionally confine, without cause, individuals who are not dangerous and who can safely survive in freedom by themselves or with the help of willing and responsible family members or friends, even if their behavior is somewhat abnormal.[43]

PROFESSIONAL REGISTERED NURSES' LEGAL STATUS

By way of clarifying a nurse's legal status, professional registered nurses may be grouped into two classes based on the type of work performed. According to the American Nurses' Association[44] the first group consists of those who actually practice nursing: the general duty nurse, private duty nurse, public health staff nurse, school nurse, industrial nurse and office nurse. It is true that they may have additional duties as well, but in the aggregate this group consists of persons who not only are nurses, but also give nursing care to individual patients. A second group consists of persons who are primarily concerned with other aspects of nursing that further the patient's care and welfare and who handle such related matters as supervision, administration, consultation and education. This group does not usually give individual care to patients but prepares and assists other nurses to do so by handling necessary administrative and supervisory matters.

Although there are nurse practice acts in every state that outline precisely what nurses may do, these do not define or set forth their duties except in general terms. However, it is evident that a nurse must not do any act that might be interpreted as the practice of medicine;[45] and the nurse's acts, aside from emergency situations, must be performed under the direction or supervision of a licensed physician.[46] From the decided cases, it appears that licensed nurses may do all those professional acts that they ordinarily and customarily are taught in schools of nursing approved by the jurisdiction, if the acts are done to a patient in accordance with the direction and supervision of his or her physician.

Doctor's Orders

Nurses must obey the orders of the physician in charge of a patient, unless an order would lead a reasonable person to anticipate injury if it were carried out.[47] However, this does not mean that a nurse can go ahead and, willy-nilly, carry out the doctor's orders unquestioningly. For example, in a case in which a nurse was giving a hypodermoclysis and noticed that the patient was not properly absorbing the fluid, she was held liable for negligence since she neither discontinued the treatment nor called a doctor.[48] On going to a hospital, physicians have the right to assume that the nurses in the hospital who are neither directly employed by them nor working directly under them are competent.[49]

There is a conflict of authority and opinion on the question of whether or not a nurse is protected when she acts upon the orders of an unlicensed physician, such as an intern. On the whole, interns are not licensed to practice medicine, although, as in New York, they may be expressly allowed to do so within a hospital.[50] Whether an intern or resident is the agent of the patient's physician depends on whether or not the physician has the right to direct not only the work to be done, but also the details of doing it. If the intern is an agent of a licensed physician acting within the scope of his employment when giving orders to the nurse, the nurse is protected. In any event, it would seem advisable for a nurse to know the legal status of an intern in the particular jurisdiction in which she works.

Telephone Orders

Telephone orders constitute a real problem for nurses in a number of situations. The best interests of the patient, physician, nurse and hospital or other agency are served by having all physician orders in writing. When physicians telephone an order, they should sign it on their next visit. The nurse accepting the telephoned order should read it back to the physician to make certain she or he has correctly written it down. Granted, anyone can make an error. Studies show that fewer errors are made by those who have more education and who are more knowledgeable about drugs. The person who takes the telephone order should sign the name of the physician per his or her own name. However, if the nurse has any question about the suitability of an order in view of the patient's apparent condition, he or she should ask a resident physician to examine the order and to check that it is not inconsistent with the patient's needs. When a problem appears, the order should be verified with the prescribing physician.

In *Childs* v. *Greenville Hospital Authority*, whether a nurse who denied hospital admission to a woman in active labor inaccurately reported the doctor's telephone orders, and whether failure to accurately report constitutes negligence, were questions of fact for the jury when the woman sued for damages.[51] In *Cortez* v. *Chi*, a family in a wrongful death action successfully sued a physician who repeatedly gave telephone orders at 3:00 A.M., 6:00 A.M. and 7:45 A.M. but who did not come to see a child with a temperature of 106.4° F.[52] In *Thomas* v. *Corso*, the administratrix of an accident victim's estate made a substantial recovery where there was conflicting testimony between the doctor and nurse about telephone orders and failure to report vital signs and to take appropriate action. As Regan has stated, the "telephone–medicine man" jeopardizes his license, the licenses of cooperating nurses and the health and safety of his patients.[53]

True, in an emergency the telephone order may be the only way to secure needed medical advice. In situations such as an ill seaman on a ship without a physician, telephone orders are necessary and the court will uphold those who act upon them.[54] Nevertheless, nurses and doctors should limit telephone orders to true emergencies in which there is no alternative, since using the telephone as a substitute for the physician's actually seeing and evaluating the patient can lead to serious error and may border on malpractice.[55]

It has been suggested that the problem could be alleviated by recording the physician's telephone conversation. This raises another legal difficulty. Evidence obtained by using voice-recording equipment is generally inadmissible in court unless: (1) the person whose conversation is being recorded is informed of that fact at the time of the telephone call and told that the evidence thereby obtained may be used in a court of law or (2) the recording is made through a connector provided by the telephone public utility company that automatically produces a distinctive recorder tone that is repeated at intervals of approximately 15 seconds. The Wisconsin statute applicable to recorded telephone conversation is an example of this law.[56]

The California Appellate Court has held that an identification based on a "voice print" was improperly admitted in evidence. The "voice print" technique is not generally accepted at present by the scientific community.[57]

Transcribing Orders

In many hospitals today, ward secretaries or clerks transcribe orders. It is important that they be thoroughly instructed in transcribing the order as it is written by the physician. Moreover, ward secretaries or clerks should know that at law everyone is liable for her or his own errors and that they can be sued for negligence. The requirement that a transcribed order must be countersigned by a professional registered nurse is common. If the nurse countersigns an order incorrectly transcribed by the ward secretary or clerk, she or he is liable for her error. However, if the nurse also errs, this does not relieve the ward secretary or clerk of responsibility for the original error. If two persons both make an error, both can be sued; in addition, if they are employees of a hospital or other agency, then, pursuant to the doctrine of *respondeat superior*, it, too, can be sued.

PERSONAL LIABILITY

Nurses should remember that they are liable for their own negligent acts. Consequently, if they carelessly injure their patient's property, such as his personal belongings, they may incur liability. When a patient wearing two rings underwent surgery in a private hospital, and one ring disappeared while she was unconscious, the hospital was held liable, although the surgeons and nurses present said they did not know what became of the missing ring. The patient said that on admission she was asked to surrender only her money for safekeeping; however, there was a duty to protect her other property while she was helpless.[58] the court stated that the liability of the hospital for its employees, nurses and physicians was like that of a railroad or steamship company to passengers for the acts of its employees. Also, a hospital was held liable when a patient sued for damages for the loss of his bridgework through the negligence of a nurse.[59]

When a patient dies, the nurse should know that the property of the deceased may be given only to the legal representative of the estate who can produce a certified copy of his or her appointment as executor or administrator. As a practical proposition, considering the risks involved, articles of little or no value may be turned over to the decedent's family or next of kin and a signed receipt obtained. However, in the case of valuables, the nurse should realize the risk in any failure to observe the law.

In the eyes of the law, the licensed nurse's work is based on skills acquired through education and training. A typical statute is that of Maine, which expresses the nurse's status as follows:

> The registration and certification of professional trained nurses is to designate by public registry and certification those nurses for whose qualifications the state is willing to vouch, and to prevent others who are not entitled to it from falsely claiming such sponsorship.[60]

Nurses are personally liable in a civil action if a patient is injured because of incompetence or carelessness in the performance of their skills and duties. If their negligent acts show a wanton and reckless conduct or disregard for human life, such a degree of negligence is considered "gross negligence," which the law views as criminal. Reference to specific skills and duties will aid in spelling out the degree of care and prudence demanded by the law.

Charts[61]

Concise and adequate charting is one of the largest problems in nursing. Since memories are fleeting and distractions cause most nurses to interrupt their train of thought, promptly charting significant items is very important. It is one way not to forget communications between the physician or other members of the health team. In order to minimize the margin of error in implementing the physician's orders, it is important that everything be in writing for the guidance of all nursing staff.

A patient with suicidal tendencies and a long history of mental illness was admitted to the hospital for treatment of physical injuries after a suicide attempt. The doctor noted on the patient's progress chart that he should have round-the-clock attendants, but did not order any special precautions or notify the attending nurses (including private duty ones) of the patient's suicidal tendencies. There was also no notation to that effect on the doctor's orders on the chart. A private duty nurse left the patient alone momentarily and he leaped to his death. The widow filed a wrongful death action. Such omissions in communications between physicians and nurses lead to tragic results.[62] From a summary judgment for the doctor, the case was returned for trial.

In a Maryland case, a woman whose two small children had a rash on their chest accompanied by a high fever took them to a hospital emergency room. She told the nurse on duty that she had removed two ticks from Kenneth, but the nurse did not tell the emergency room physician about the ticks. The doctor decided the children had measles and prescribed aspirin and that the boys be kept in a darkened room. Two days later, the rash had spread to the arms and legs and the fever had not subsided. The children were brought back to the emergency room where another doctor was unsure of the measles diagnosis and instructed the family to see their pediatrician. When the latter examined the boys the next day, he advised the parents to keep the boys in a darkened room and to notify him of any change. Four days later, the children's condition was much worse, but the family was unable to reach the pediatrician. On the following day, Ernest was found dead and Kenneth was taken to a hospital in another town. Two ticks were removed from him, and he was treated for Rocky Mountain spotted fever and recovered. An autopsy revealed Ernest died of Rocky Mountain spotted fever. The Court of Special Appeals entered judgment in favor of the parents against the first hospital. The nurse's failure to notify the physician about the removal of ticks from one of the boys constituted a violation of her duties as a nurse.[63]

In an Oregon case, a patient sued a hospital and a doctors' clinic for medical malpractice causing permanent brain damage and received an award of $750,000. Expert witnesses testified that the patient most probably suffered a period of respiratory depression at the conclusion of anesthetic in the recovery room. In the recovery room, the nurses had charted his pulse and blood pressure every 15 minutes but not the rate and depth of his respirations, despite the fact that the chart provided a place specifically for this purpose. This omission was the pivotal point of the case, according to the court.[64]

As mentioned in an earlier section, a widow in a malpractice action against a physician and hospital secured a verdict for $99,609.24 as a result of the lack of charting.[65]

Charting is evidence of anything that a person can see, hear, feel or smell. The importance of charting is emphasized by the general ANA *Standards of Nursing Practice*, Standard I, which states:

> The collection of data about the health status of the client/patient is systematic and continuous. The data are accessible, communicated, and recorded.[66]

This includes assessment, the plan of nursing care and how it is implemented. Patient teaching should be specific. Evaluation of the patient's condition on admission, periodically during his or her stay and at the time of discharge should also appear on the record. Nurses' notes are probably the best evidence we may have of the real situation in our search for truth.

In *Cooper v. National Motor Bearing Co.*,[67] an employee brought a lawsuit for damages against a company and an industrial nurse for a malpractice action arising out of her treatment of a puncture wound, which he sustained in the forehead. At the time of the accident, he went to the dispensary, and she swabbed and bandaged the wound but did not probe it for possible foreign matter. Eventually, the wound healed, but a small red area remained, and it began to spread and become puffy. After 10 months of treatment, the employee requested that the nurse send him to the doctor. A laboratory examination showed a malignant growth which was removed by surgery. The nurse and her employer were both held liable in damages.

In *Garafola v. Maimonides Hospital of Brooklyn et al.*,[68] three days after having a cesarean section, a patient complained of soreness in her jaw and in opening her mouth. Although she was given several medications by a nurse and resident, they did not tell her physician about her complaint. When the physician finally discovered the patient's symptoms on a visit, he administered tetanus antitoxin and remained with her until her death that night. The appellate court affirmed a judgment that the hospital was liable for the failure of its employees to give timely notification ot the doctor of the patient's condition.

Adams v. State of Washington[69] involved a state mental hospital where a patient cut her hand by ramming it through a plate glass window. She threw herself from the treatment table when she was having the wound sutured and a light cast applied. Close surveillance was maintained on the day shift, but at the change of shift no report of these events was made by the day nurses to the evening nurses, who consequently relaxed the supervision of the patient. About 4:30 P.M. the patient was seen walking on the grounds toward a busy boulevard. When a car came along, the patient hurled herself in front of it and was seriously injured. A $275,000 suit against the state hospital was awarded to the patient.

It is clear that the nurse who has collected important information about the patient's health status must communicate it to the physician and other members of the health team as set forth in standard I of the ANA *Standards of Nursing Practice*.

In regard to charts, nurses have important responsibilities. On each sheet of the chart, the name of the patient and the date should be properly filled in for identification. Since erasures in records may create suspicion as to the reason for the change, it is preferable to make none, but rather to draw one line through the incorrect matter, add the date and signature of the person doing so and then add the correct material. As one writer has pointed out in discussing hospital records, the charts of every hospital should be kept in order to show that consent to surgery was given by the patient before the administration of narcotics or sedatives.[70] Otherwise, as in a California case, if a patient has not signed a consent form prior to receiving sedatives and narcotics, the reality of consent may be effectively questioned. Since nurses customarily get the patient's signature on the consent form for surgery, they should be aware of this point. The doctor's problem with informed consent has been discussed in Chapter 3.

The California Hospital Association publishes a Consent Manual, which is brought up to date every two years. A consent is valid in the hospital for a reasonable period of time.

In negligence actions against doctors, nurses and hospitals, the nurse should realize the value of complete charting. For example, when it is customary for a physician to visit hospital patients each morning, consider the effect in a malpractice action of a nurse's chart that did not record these visits for four or five days at a time. Again, for their own protection, nurses should chart routine procedures. For example, if a nurse is being questioned as to why the chart does not show that she checked the color of the patient in the parts affected by a cast, it is discouraging to her defense if she says, "Oh, I know I did it; I always do; that's why I don't chart it."

A careful and detailed notation of the facts surrounding an accident helped a Mississippi registered nurse successfully defend herself in a lawsuit brought against her by a patient. The ambulatory patient had requested her nightly medication, and as the nurse was giving it, the patient somehow fell and fractured her femur. The patient claimed that the nurse caused the accident by whirling her around, striking her and knocking her down. The patient had cerebral arteriosclerosis, which affected the accuracy of her testimony.[71]

Accurate, truthful nurses' notes, which record what the nurse has observed and heard first-hand, are of great value. In some instances, the patient's lack of obedience to doctor's orders may indicate contributory negligence. In other cases, repeated complaints warn of problems that may be avoided by early intervention. Considerable care must be exercised when using a streamlined system of predetermined signs and symbols, which may not accurately reflect pertinent observations of the patient's condition, the nurse's evaluation thereof or the overall plan of nursing care.

In a 1965 case, the appellate court ruled that the trial court committed serious error in not admitting to evidence the nurse's notes.[72] The plaintiff obtained an award for $4500 in a malpractice suit but the nurse's notes on the plaintiff's chart for the days in question indicated that he slept well, was up and around as he chose and made no complaints, so it was prejudicial to exclude them. Although nurses' notes on a chart are bulky and the storage of medical records requires valuable space, they should be preserved at least for the statutory period in which a suit could be brought against the hospital, personnel and doctors. The need for microfilming at least selected records warrants careful consideration.

The case of *Engle* v. *Clark et al.* deserves mention for the excellence of the nurses' charting and nursing care.[73] The patient had undergone surgery to correct an epigastric hernia and, after a downward postoperative course, died. A malpractice suit was brought and, in finding for the doctor, the court said:

> The patient did not have a special nurse but received excellent attention from hospital personnel. At 3 P.M. he was nauseated and was given Dramamine. At 4 P.M. Mrs. McReynolds, the supervising nurse on duty from 3–11 P.M. was concerned over his progress. He was cold, clammy, pale, restless, and sweating profusely. McReynolds telephoned Dr. Scott at his office. He instructed her to go ahead and give the patient a medication (Dramamine) and said he probably would come to the hospital later in the afternoon. Glucose was administered at this time, and blood pressure stood at 120/80. The patient was nauseated at 5 P.M. and 6 P.M. his color was still more pallid; he was cold, in an anxious state, and there was a 10-point downward change in blood pressure.

The entire record, only a portion of which is quoted, reflects good nurses' charting, which greatly aided the court in its search for true facts.

On the other hand, in another lawsuit against the state for damages following the death of a mentally ill girl, the chart showed that the patient's temperature was 101.8° F on March 13 and 104° F on March 16, without any effort at treatment or any nurses' notes for March 14 and 15. It was held to be evidence of the hospital's lack of ordinary and reasonable care of the patient.[74]

Several California decisions have upheld the right of any patient to obtain hospital medical records on request.[75] Nurses as well as physicians and hospitals will have to adapt to this change.

Gabrial has pointed out that the following medicolegal cases may need reference to the nurses' notes or observations: (1) personal injury cases, such as traffic victims; (2) insurance cases when patients try to collect; (3) workmen's compensation cases; (4) will probates in which nurses' notes may show the condition of the patient with respect to consciousness or testamentary capacity; and (5) criminal cases.[76] In order to avoid lawsuits and charges of negligence, the nurses' charting on such patients must be complete and pertinent.

Medical Records. At least in California, new court decisions will require more accurate and circumspect record-keeping, since any patient has the right to obtain hospital medical records on request.[77]

In *Johnson v. Woman's Hospital*[78] a mother of several girls gave birth to a boy in the sixth month of term, and he died shortly thereafter. A nurse advised the family that disposal of the body could be handled either by the hospital or by a family burial. The nurse said that the hospital would take care of everything properly, so the Johnsons agreed to let the hospital do it. The nurse took the infant's body, placed it in a jar of formaldehyde and forwarded it to the pathology laboratory for disposition as a surgical specimen. Later, the body in the jar of formaldehyde was returned to the floor with a notation that, because of its size and age, it could not be disposed of as a surgical specimen. The pathologist's report was attached to Mrs. Johnson's medical chart, and she was given the chart to hand to the doctor when she returned for her six-weeks' checkup. Mrs. Johnson looked over and read her chart and inquired about the pathologist's report. The doctor advised Mrs. Johnson to see the nurse about the matter and sent his nurse to accompany her. The nurse on the floor exclaimed that she had been looking for Mrs. Johnson, that she had her infant's body and that it had been preserved. She took Mrs. Johnson back to a refrigerator, removed the jar of formaldehyde containing the shriveled body of her baby and handed it to her. After this, Mrs. Johnson had nightmares, insomnia, depression and required psychiatric treatment. In a suit for breach of contract to bury and for outrageous conduct, Mr. and Mrs. Johnson received substantial damages.

With respect to patients' access to their own medical records, there is a paucity of literature. A search of the literature since 1965 reveals only Fleischer's "Ownership of Hospital Records and Roentgenograms." In *Wallace v. University Hospitals of Cleveland.*[79] the court held that since hospital records are essential to proper administration, they are the property of the hospital; however, the patient has a property right to the information contained in the report. As a practical matter, this property right constitutes the right to inspect and copy. In the Wallace case, the plaintiff had sought a mandatory injunction compelling the defendant hospital to allow her to examine her medical records with a view toward filing a suit against a third party, and the injunction was granted. In a leading Oklahoma case of *Pyramid Life Insurance Co. v. Masonic Hospital Association,*[80] a similar holding was arrived at. Therefore, once a patient is discharged (except a mental patient), it appears that he or she has a right to the information in his or her medical record and that, as a practical matter, this constitutes a right to inspect and copy. However, in all but nine states, patients can obtain their medical records only by instituting legal action. Medical records should be written with the patient's right to the information in mind.

In *Gotkin* v. *Miller*[81] where a psychiatric patient was writing a book about her experiences and wanted to compare her own recollections of various incidents with material contained in hospital records, the U.S. District Court decided that medical records are the property of the institution that compiled them and not the patient's because of the confidential information they contain.

Medical/Nursing Staff Committee Reports. Judging by *Spears* v. *Mason, M.D., et al.,*[82] a case involving infection following surgery, the court will open medical/nursing staff committee reports to the public on a basis of producing only those portions that pertain to the particular case or the patient's period of hospitalization. Hospitals and other health care institutions should exercise considerable discretion in producing medical/nursing staff committee reports even when the public demands them for use in lawsuits. Even judicial orders should be challenged through proper channels to press home the point of limited access to confidential matters.

Incident Report

An incident report or unusual occurrence form[83] was designed to serve four functions: (1) improving the management and treatment of the patient; (2) inservice education of residents, nurses and others; (3) administrative supervision; and (4) medicolegal coverage. By careful wording chosen to avoid the implication of blame and retribution, by routing it through key members of the teaching and administrative staff and by classifying the incident for statistical tabulation, the form provided for these requirements.

The first responsibility of the nurse is to cooperate in the incident-reporting process, i.e., to be exact and truthful. In incident reports, opinions and judgment should be avoided. Incident reports should contain facts and are a means of informing administration and risk management of any untoward happening. Generally, these are screened by an administrative officer or risk manager who reports some to the insurance carrier and withholds others as not having sufficient legal implications to warrant reporting of the incident to the carrier. Incident reports must be carefully monitored, since the usual liability insurance policy gives the carrier the option of not defending the case if the hospital knew or should have known of the incident and failed to notify the insurer promptly. Nurses must not fail to report an incident or, worse yet, deliberately attempt to cover up an incident. This is a breach of a contractual obligation with the employer, who has a right to assume that all employees will comply with the health care facility's policy of promptly reporting all untoward incidents through internal channels. The person with first-hand information should make the report. The filing of an incident report should not be mentioned on the chart.

In some states, incident reports can be used as evidence in litigation. In *Sierra Vista Hospital* v. *Superior Court,*[84] the hospital administrator had specific instructions from the hospital's insurance company to complete the confidential report and to send it to the insurance company. The order applied to all incidents that could lead to litigation, and the general practice was to prepare one copy and to send it to the insurer, which the director of nursing and administrator did. The report was labeled "Confidential Report of Incident (Not a Part of the Medical Record)." The court held that the report was confidential, i.e., that the original reporter's intent controls confidentiality and that explicit notice is needed from the insurer to the insured that such reports are to be used for legal purposes.

The Supreme Court of Colorado in *Bernardi v. Community Hospital Association*[85] considered whether a report about a patient's footdrop, which occurred in the hospital, was privileged. In that case, three copies of the incident report were made—one was placed on the patient's chart, one was sent to the hospital administrator and the other to the director of nurses. Such reports were available for routine inspection by the hospital's attorney regarding threatened or actual lawsuits. There was no plan that showed a definite intent to seek legal advice. The former general counsel could not vouch for the primary purpose of the incident report. In this situation, the incident report was not held privileged.

Subjecting a patient to the wrong surgery or treatment and losing or damaging a patient's personal property, such as dentures or jewelry, are some of the more common types of incidents. Since dissatisfied patients are the source of malpractice claims, the nurse, ombudsman or patient advocate should provide information about complaints to administration and risk management so that any potential problem receives prompt attention. The Medical Malpractice Commission in the early 1970s reported that some 60 to 80 percent of all malpractice claims could be alleviated by good public relations.

In a hospital where a patient had a back operation, the head nurse administered an injection ordered by the surgeon. The needle broke off in the patient's buttocks, but the nurse did not report the incident to anyone in the hospital and did not tell the patient. If prompt action has been taken, the needle could easily have been removed without causing additional problems. The imbedded needle caused a severe infection and was very difficult to remove. In addition, the patient had thrombophlebitis as a result. When the patient sued the nurse and the hospital for damages, the court found that the nurse's failure to report the incident was so far below the standard of care required of a head nurse that a cause of action was stated on whether the hospital was negligent in putting her in a supervisory position.[86] This particular hospital in North Carolina was protected by the doctrine of charitable immunity unless it was negligent in the selection and retention of employees.

A Florida appellate court ruled that, where reports referred to incidents in which patients fell from their beds and wheelchairs while in the hospital and the hospital presented no evidence to show that the reports were privileged records prepared in anticipation of litigation, a patient suing the hospital for malpractice was entitled to inspection of the incident reports.[87]

DEFENSE IN COURT ACTIONS FOR NEGLIGENCE

It is instructive to consider the defenses a nurse may have to actions for damages due to injuries caused by negligence.

Idiosyncrasy

Generally, a claim of idiosyncrasy (peculiarity of constitution) of the patient can be a defense to negligence. The meaning of this claim is that the patient had some peculiarity that made him unusually susceptible to a treatment or drug that in normal persons would be reasonably safe, and that the peculiarity was of such a kind that the nurse, using average care and skill, could not have discovered it. For example, when a patient who obtained x-ray treatment sued for damages for burns, the court said that a patient assumes the risk of burn from proper x-ray treatment, but the physician incurs liability for causing negligent burns.[88] The same result would be true if the defendant were a nurse. However, by express provision of law, the defense that one has assumed the risk is done away with in cases coming within the Workmen's Compensation Laws.

Remoteness of Cause of Injury

Again, the nurse might claim remoteness of cause of injury as a defense. For a negligence to be actionable, the breach of duty must be the "proximate cause of injury"; i.e., one that in the usual course of events would not happen in lieu of the cause. For example, suppose a patient who was incapable of using sound judgment was placed in a sanitarium; assume further that one day the patient wandered away and onto a railroad track where a train struck and killed him, whereupon the patient's executor brought an action for damages against the head nurse. In such a case, the negligent acts of the head nurse were not the proximate cause of death, but only a condition that made a fatal injury possible.[89]

Contributory Negligence

Contributory negligence has been defined as "conduct on the part of the plaintiff contributing as a legal cause to the harm he has suffered which falls below the standard to which he is required to conform for his protection."[90]

A frequent defense interposed is that of contributory negligence. Contributory negligence is used to describe any unreasonable conduct on the part of the patient that is the cause of injury, whether the nurse is also negligent or not. For example, suppose a patient sued a nurse for damages due to burns caused by negligently applying an electric heating pad. Assume further that the evidence showed that the patient's physician had ordered hot moist packs and the use of an electric heating pad to keep the packs hot. The evidence, moreover, showed that the patient had control over the switch to the electric heating pad and that he used it without difficulty for four days, but later went to sleep with the switch on and suffered some burns. Since the patient's negligence contributed to his injury, the case against the nurse would be dismissed.[91]

In a case in which a nurse's aide emerged from a utility room without looking into the corridor and sustained injuries when she collided with a delivery man carrying a vase of flowers, she was denied recovery in a lawsuit because she was guilty of contributory negligence.[92] The court said:

> As a nurse's aide, aware of the use of the corridor for disabled patients in wheelchairs, nurses, doctors, delivery men and the like, she had a duty to determine before emerging from the door whether there was anyone in the corridor with whom she would collide.

When the patients of a deceased two-and-one-half-year-old child brought a malpractice action against the doctor for damages for wrongful death of the child in his office, and the physician alleged the contributory negligence of the parents in caring for the child, the jury exonerated the physician.[93] The child was brought to the doctor with a boil on her left shoulder. He administered penicillin and ordered hot packs applied every three to four hours and a check on the child's temperature with a baby fever thermometer. The hot packs were not applied as ordered, since the child spent time with each of the parents (who were separated);

the temperature was taken with an ordinary oral thermometer; and the child was allowed to play outside. An autopsy showed anaphylaxis due to Xylocaine used before opening the boil and to toxemia caused by bacteria from the abscess.

Judgment was entered for the defendant doctor in a suit brought by a patient for damages for ruptured ear drums in which he was contributorily negligent in insisting that the nurse wash the wax from his ears.[94]

A hospital patient suffering from a severe gouty arthritic condition had been admonished several times not to get out of bed without ringing for assistance, and had been provided with standard equipment in keeping with his requirements. However, he disregarded instructions, got out of bed unassisted, went to the bathroom across the hall from his room and, as he was returning to his room, fell and fractured his hip; he later died of pulmonary embolism following hip surgery. No damages could be recovered owing to his own contributory negligence, and the hospital was cleared of negligence.[95] It is noted in this case that the hospital is responsible for providing adequate equipment and personnel. Also, the nursing service has a parallel responsibility to record the information that a patient has been told of medical orders restricting his activities and that needed nursing assistance would be provided. These matters were evident in the present case. The nurses' notes on his chart indicated that (1) the patient was alert and aware of his surroundings and (2) he had been repeatedly warned to stay in bed and to call for assistance as needed. When it can be shown that an accident would not have occurred except for the carelessness of an alert, conscious patient, the importance of evidence of some negligence on the part of the hospital is sharply lessened.

A Louisiana appellate court affirmed a trial court's decision that a patient was not contributorily negligent for failure to read a prescription label. The patient had undergone oral surgery, and her dentist prescribed Percodan for pain. At the pharmacy when her name was called, she picked up the bag that was labeled with her name and her dentist's name and went home. She had been taking the medicine for three days before her niece observed that the label on the prescription container bore another person's name. The bottle contained Meticorten, not Percodan. The trial court awarded the patient $4500 in a suit against the pharmacy. The court said that she was not contributorily negligent, considering her postoperative condition and the fact that she did see her name on the prescription bag. After taking the Meticorten, she suffered from weakness, nausea and hypertension for several weeks; she also suffered pain as she was not taking the prescribed analgesic.[96]

A patient who alleged negligence on the part of a hospital when he set fire to his bed and suffered personal injuries simply because he was "helplessly intoxicated" at the time was not free from contributory negligence. He had managed to procure matches in spite of being restrained by a strap. The appellate court found that the matter of intoxication did not, as a matter of law, provide an absolute excuse for failure to act as a reasonably careful person would act.[97]

However, the nurse is reminded that, by express provision of law, the defense of contributory negligence is done away with in cases coming within the Workmen's Compensation Laws.

Statute of Limitations

The statute of limitations as a defense to an action to recover damages for negligence has already been discussed in Chapter 4.

Release Agreement

There is an old maxim to the effect that one who consents to an act that is *prima facie* wrongful cannot afterward complain of it. However, it is pointed out that contracts that "contract out" liability for negligence are looked upon with disfavor by the law. In some jurisdictions, one cannot avoid liability for negligence by contract.[98] In any jurisdiction, such a contract would be strictly interpreted against the person claiming it as a defense. However, the nurse is reminded that a contract for indemnity from such liability is valid.

Sometimes a release may be a good defense against an action for damages for injuries caused by negligence. For example, a patient who released an automobile driver from liability for an accident was unable to bring an action against the physician for negligence in caring for the injury, because these damages could have also been recovered from the driver.[99] Or again, suppose that a nurse agrees to give up her or his right to compensation, in return for which a patient agrees to release the nurse from possible legal action. The nurse could use such an agreement as a defense in any action the patient might bring later.

Registered nurses are reminded that they are professional people and that their status has been elevated in recent years. As a consequence, nurses' earnings have increased, and this may give a new direction to damage suits. Perhaps in bygone years the patient did not think it worthwhile to seek damages from nurses on account of their mistakes. Today this viewpoint has changed. Nurses who make careless mistakes cannot depend on being "let off," but will have to face their responsibility.

EMPLOYER-EMPLOYEE (MASTER-SERVANT) RELATIONSHIPS

General Duty Nurse in Hospital

General duty nurses usually perform their duties as employees of the hospital or institution that engages their services.[100] The contract does not indicate a nurse-patient relationship; but the nurse's wages are paid by the employer, who furnishes a place of employment and necessary working equipment, and the nurse's services are carried out in relation to the general business of the employer. It is generally considered that the hospital-employer not only controls the work to be done, but also has authority to supervise and regulate the means by which it is done.

General Duty Nurse to Physician or Patient

When a hospital assigns a general duty nurse to a physician or a patient, the nurse is in a different status. She or he is no longer a general duty nurse in the hospital, but an employee of the physician or a special duty nurse of the patient. For example, a court has held that, when a hospital nurse was under the operating surgeon's special supervision and control during an operation, although she was not in his regular employment, the relationship of master and servant existed.[101] In another case, a patient who sustained a fractured rib as a result of a nurse's applying pressure to her body during delivery was denied recovery in a lawsuit against the hospital.[102] The Vermont Supreme Court held that the doctor, who was not selected or employed by the hospital, had complete control and supervision of the nurses in the delivery room, and that the hospital therefore was not responsible for the negligent performance of the nurse in carrying out his order. However, in the absence of a specific contract, a physician is not responsible for the negligent acts of a nurse in treating a patient after the operation unless he undertakes to continue his control of the nurse.[103]

Nonetheless, in New York, nurses, performing routine duties, such as giving a bedpan, are employees or servants of the hospital. But when nurses are carrying out their professional acts concerned with patients' medical or nursing needs, i.e., following physicians' orders, they may be independent contractors.[104] Sometimes the question of the relationship between the parties becomes a question of fact for the jury to decide. The standards for various general duty nurses have been developed by the American Nurses' Association.[105]

Liability of Employer

When the general duty nurses are considered employees, the question whether, in addition to themselves, their employers are liable in damages for their acts may be governed by whether the employer is a governmental, charitable or profit-making institution. For example, when a nurse was lowering a hospital bed by mechanical means and did not warn the patient of the hazards, which resulted in injury to his fingers, so that they later had to be amputated, the hospital was held liable for the nurse's carelessness.[106]

In an era of nursing shortages, employers should bear in mind that from the legal standpoint there must be sufficient nurse coverage to meet the apparent needs of the patients. To meet hospital needs, nurses have been recruited from overseas as well as from within the United States. Greater use of practical nurses, nurses prepared in associate degree programs and nursing students (who work for pay outside school hours) has followed. Inactive nurses have been encouraged to return to work, and in some instances refresher courses have been provided to facilitate their return to active duty. It is important for directors of nursing, hospital administrators, nursing home administrators and others to realize that the doctrine of *respondeat superior* applies to all employees.

PRIVATE DUTY NURSE

In the ordinary case, the law looks upon the private duty nurse (or special duty nurse) as an independent contractor, who is not under the control of the patient as to the details of the nursing services. The American Nurses' Association provides the following definition:

> A private duty nurse is a registered professional nurse who independently contracts to give expert bedside nursing care to one patient. This permits the nurse to utilize professional knowledge and skills to the fullest extent and to assume responsibility for the total nursing care of the patient.[107]

Among the more important functions in supervising patients, private duty nurses are expected to plan patient care; to observe, evaluate and report symptoms and reactions; to carry out independent nursing procedures; and also to perform treatments under the direction or supervision of a licensed physician.

It is important for them to keep adequate and accurate records for the benefit of the patient and all medical and nursing personnel connected with his or her care.

Private duty nurses have the right to sue patients who fail to pay their wages or who wrongfully discharge them in violation of the terms of the employment contract. They are also liable to patients for any breach of contract or any wrongs or acts of negligence.

Although private duty nurses are independent contractors, the supervising nurse in a hospital may give advice from time to time about their patients. Private duty nurses and their patients must comply with the hospital's rules and regulations if they wish to use its facilities, but the hospital has no right to dismiss private duty nurses or to take a patient away from them or to reassign them to the care of others.[108] The acts of a private duty nurse do not make the hospital liable, since she or he is not an employee, nor subject to its control.[109] When a person wrongfully interferes with a private duty nurse's right to work in a hospital or institution, he is liable in an action for damages based thereon.[110] A private duty nurse is entitled to damages for injuries caused by the negligence of a hospital or its employees, servants or agents.[111]

As long as private duty nurses were selected and paid by the patient, family or doctor, there was no question about their status as independent contractors. Now that private duty nurses are usually obtained from a nurses' registry, and the hospital may insist that its approval be obtained for anyone who is allowed to care for patients in it or that a nurse be under the supervision of the hospital's nursing supervisor, private duty nurses may be regarded as hospital employees. In *Emory University v. Shadburn*, in which the hospital selected the private duty nurse, received payment for her services and later settled with her, the hospital was held liable for her negligence.[112] If the trend toward hospitals' responsibility for all nursing care becomes the general rule, the status of private duty nurses is likely to change. To date, they have generally been denied the benefits of workmen's compensation when injured on duty in the hospital.[113]

A 65-year-old licensed practical nurse coming to work who was injured in a fall on the icy sidewalk outside a nursing home was denied a recovery of damages. Although the defendant nursing home had the duty to exercise ordinary care to keep the premises in a reasonably safe condition and to give warning of any hidden defects, so as not to expose the nurse to unnecessary danger, both the nurse and the nursing home had knowledge of the icy conditions.[114]

A practical nurse injured her back in a hospital while helping an elderly patient from a whirlpool bath. This injury prevented her from performing heavy tasks and she was awarded workmen's compensation benefits for total disability.[115] The order was affirmed on appeal.

When an experienced practical private nurse was hurt while attending to a patient in a wheelchair in a Maryland nursing home, she was held not to be an employee and not entitled to recover workmen's compensation.[116] The court pointed out:

> The most important and really decisive common law test is whether there is a right to control and direct the worker in the performance and manner of doing his work.

It also listed some other criteria, such as selection and engagement of the worker, power of dismissal and payment of wages. In conclusion, the court said that the private duty nurse was not an employee of the home.

Private duty nurses, whether employed by physicians or self-employed, should be required to apply for appointment to the nursing staff of the hospital in much the same way that physicians make staff applications. The application of the private duty nurse should then be referred to a nurses' credentials committee for evaluation and confirmation of the privilege to work in the hospital. This would cover the private scrub nurses of surgeons as well as other private duty nurses. Regan states that the nurse should be identified, screened, appointed and privileged before being permitted to provide OR nursing services.[117]

COMMUNITY HEALTH NURSE

Consumers are the clients or patients in a community health nursing practice, and they may be individuals, family members, students or industrial workers from a variety of settings. The responsibility and accountability of the nursing care such consumers receive belong to the professional nurse and nonprofessional assistants. Nursing practice includes assessment, planning, implementation and evaluation; and the focus of standards is on practice rather than the practitioner.[118]

Community health staff and school nurses are employees of a department of health, board of education or voluntary agency. In order to carry out or complete the contract for rendering nursing services, the principal who is legally responsible for the same must, as a practical necessity, get an agent or agents to carry out the details. As previously discussed, the relationship between principal and agent makes the principal liable for the acts of agents when they are acting within the scope of their employment. The community people represented by the board of health or education may be regarded as the principal, and the health officer, nurses and other employees may be considered the agents thereof. In cases in which the courts have held that the authority for appointing the health officer was the same as that for appointing nurses and other employees, the health officer was held to be an employee under the direction, supervision and control of the board of health.[119]

The community health, public health or school nurse may conduct the physical examination of children in the public schools. Since government agencies may not be legally liable for damages of employees in the absence of a statutory provision for the same, and since a government cannot be sued without the express consent of the government, the employee may be the only one from whom a recovery in damages for negligent or wrongful acts may be obtained.

Again, the health staff nurse is reminded of the necessity and value of keeping adequate and accurate records. For example, in one case, a visiting nurse's records were used as evidence in an action.[120]

The case of *Denver v. Pollard*[121] has significance for all occupational and community health nurses. In that case, a community health nurse employed by the City and County of Denver came into close physical contact with individuals infected with beta streptococcus. When she became infected, suffered from acute rheumatic fever and was forced to leave her work in January 1963, she brought a suit before the Industrial Commission. Her employers were ordered to pay her weekly compensation for the period of her disability.

In another case in which a community health nurse was assaulted and sustained a dislocated shoulder, facial cuts and bruises inflicted by a person residing in the home of a patient being visited, he was tried and convicted of assault with intent to commit rape.[122]

Some years ago, a local welfare department nurse's license was revoked for acts derogatory to the morals and standing of the profession of nursing.[123] This particular nurse visited patients without the knowledge and consent of their doctors and without the patients' request. She also told some of them that their diagnoses were incorrect and gave her own. In addition, there was evidence that she had used unwarranted and unprofessional language in criticizing patients and doctors.

Regan reports that a U.S. public health nurse was held liable when serious nerve injury resulted from her carelessly administered infusion while she was assisting in a mass inoculation program following a devastating flood in a midwestern community.[124]

School nurses who work alone much of the time and do not have a physician nearby for ready consultation must still use prudence and report observations they make while discharging their duty to the physician. Regan[125] reports that, when a school nurse informed a girl's parents and the school principal of what appeared to be a venereal disease, and a later medical examination reported a negative finding, the nurse was sued for defamation of character.

Several recent decisions may affect the work of the community health nurse. The U.S. Court of Appeals decided that a manufacturer of Sabin polio vaccine could be held liable for damages to an adult who contracted paralytic poliomyelitis apparently as a result of receiving Sabin Type III vaccine in a mass immunization program.[126] It held that the drug company had a duty to warn people, either itself or through purchasers, of the dangers involved in taking the vaccine. How this decision will affect mass immunization programs is not yet certain. The regional medical programs will probably benefit from another decision, in which the court required an anesthesiologist practicing in a smaller city to meet the general standard of care applicable to all specialists in his field regardless of where they were located.[127] Furthermore, the court stated that it would apply this rule to general practitioners.

The crux of the community health or visiting nurses' problems lies in good judgment and adequate written nursing policies that define the limits of services. The Visiting Nurse Service of New York allows only two visits to a patient without medical supervision.[128]

When students are working under the supervision of nurses in the agency, then under the master-servant doctrine (respondeat superior) the agency can be held liable if they negligently injure a patient. When a college or university sends its own instructor with nursing students who care for patients in the agency, and she or he is in control of the students, it is likely that the instructor and college or university would be liable if a student nurse were to negligently injure a patient. On the other hand, if the agency is, to some appreciable extent, jointly in control of the nursing students, it could also be held liable.

Recording telephone orders on a form, dating them and sending them to the physician for written confirmation is a method that helps considerably to secure written orders. The necessity for securing written consents for treatment of minors or for photographs of patients is the same in a public health agency as in a hospital. The Visiting Nurse Service of New York extended its liability insurance to cover volunteers who take patients out-of-doors, and also invited their legal counsel representatives from the State Board of Examiners of Nurses to meet with representatives of the administrative staff and director of the home aide program to make certain that that program was on a sound legal basis.

Community health nurses and others who use agency or hospital automobiles will find the case of *Sadler v. Draper*[129] instructive. An action was brought for damages for personal injuries sustained from being struck by an automobile owned by Sadler in charge of his employee and driven by a third party. The plaintiff charged that the dealer, via his employee acting in the scope of his employment, negligently entrusted the automobile to another driver knowing that the driver was unfit, reckless and a habitual drunkard, and that the dealer's negligence through his employee was the cause of the injuries sued for. The award of $85,000 for multiple fractures of pelvic bones, hip joints, a punctured bladder and multiple compound fractures of both legs was upheld. Various agency policies limiting the use of automobiles to certain drivers, and in some instances rather strictly limiting the passengers who may be transported in such agency cars, are related to the agency's liability and liability insurance coverage, and should be adhered to.

Is a community health nurse who uses medical reports an "interested person" at law in a case determining the rights of a patient?

In *Hoppe v. State of Iowa*,[130] a county health nurse and district adoption and foster care specialist, who both used medical reports concerning a mother with a history of waywardness, mental problems and child abuse, were called upon to testify. The case involved the termination of Rita Hoppe's relationship with her ten-year-old son. According to the court, compiling and using the reports in connection with their official duties was enough to qualify the nurses as "interested persons," and they could properly testify in connection with their official duties. The Supreme Court of Iowa upheld the judgment of the lower court.

In an earlier case, *Minnesota Public Interest Research Group v. Minnesota Department of Labor and Industry et al.*,[131] the Minnesota Supreme Court held that the research group was an "interested person" and had standing to sue. An "interested person" is entitled to request a public hearing on proposed standards affecting the Minnesota Occupational Safety and Health Act of 1973. The Act's purpose, promoting standards consistent with the latest scientific research, would be frustrated by construing it so narrowly that only employers and employees directly affected by proposed standards could request hearings.

As families suffer increasingly from divorce, child abuse and alcohol and drug abuse, these problems and others frequently appear in the reports and records of community health and hospital nurses, who could be subpoenaed to produce their records and to testify in court. For purposes of pre-trial discovery, the records will have to be produced and the nurses will have to testify, as in the Hoppe case. The records ordinarily cannot be withheld under the claim of confidentiality.[132] Community health nurses as well as other nurses will have to write records with a view to the possibility that the record may be subject to adversarial legal review.

EDUCATORS AND ADMINISTRATIVE NURSES

Educators or instructors of nursing are employees of the institution engaging their services. In recent years, there have been a multiplicity of lawsuits by dissatisfied nursing students against their instructors and the educational institutions. (See cases under "Nursing Students" in Chapter Five.) Instructors must keep their education up-to-date. They are responsible for accurate, current material. Therefore, they should keep a dated outline of material presented in classes and conferences together with the references used. In the clinical area, an anecdotal record evaluating students' performance, discussions and individual conferences should be maintained as a basis for the clinical grade. Realistically, instructors must be aware that more students are bringing lawsuits challenging their grades. At the beginning of a course, the instructor should provide students with an overview of the content, objectives and means of evaluation as well as a timetable of tests and the due date for projects or papers, attendance requirements and so on. By clarifying expectations, dissatisfaction that can later lead to lawsuits can be eliminated. In addition, it is pointed out that clinical nursing instructors have an obligation to maintain clinical competency. This can be done, for example, by working as a staff nurse during summer vacations or by working four hours per week as a clinical nurse throughout the academic year. Experience and current clinical competency as well as education are factors that lawyers probe in court cases. An article on Patient Teaching is in the Appendix.

In bachelor's degree programs, qualified instructors are generally required to have a master's degree, and the trend for new faculty is to require that the master's degree be in nursing. The emphasis on doctoral preparation for faculty members should be noted. This same increase in qualifications is also being demanded by more associate degree and hospital diploma programs. In *Swett v. Vermont State College*, a faculty member, who had a bachelor's degree in nursing and a master's degree in education, was hired in 1979. Although she proved an excellent teacher and had superb evaluations, her contract was not renewed. She was informally advised that her lack of a master's degree in nursing was the basis of the nonrenewal. The Court upheld the college's decision.[133]

As employees, teachers and educational administrators have the same rights as other employees on contract and under the Social Security and compensation laws. Although such persons may have more education, training and experience in their profession than the average nurse, the employer's right to control their actual performance of the details of their work is the chief basis for believing that such nurses are employees. Instructors should give thought to carrying professional liability insurance.

The Ingham County, Michigan, Circuit Court upheld a ruling by the Michigan Employment Security Commission Appeal Board granting a nurse instructor the right to receive unemployment benefits while seeking employment in her specific area of practice.[134]

OCCUPATIONAL HEALTH NURSES

See the article in Appendix, "Occupational Health Nurse's Liability."

OFFICE NURSES

Office nurses engaged by a physician, surgeon or dentist are usually regarded as employees. The fact that the physician supplies the place of work and necessary equipment and materials, pays their salary and directs their nursing services is usually considered as an employer-employee relationship. In this situation, the employer as well as the nurse employee may be liable for injury or wrong committed by the nurse. For example, a patient at the suggestion of a doctor submitted to diathermic treatment by the physician's employee. After adjusting the electrodes on the patient's body, the employee left the room, and after the lapse of some time returned and turned off the electricity, having forgotten about the patient, so that the patient was burned. The physician was liable to the patient in damages for injuries caused by the negligence of the employee.[135] However, in another case, the nurse was under the direction and control of a surgeon during an operation, and he ordered a 1 percent procaine solution; a solution of formaldehyde was negligently prepared in its place and given to him for use. The court held that the surgeon was entitled to rely on the care and skill of trained nurses and similar persons and was not liable for such negligence.[136] The same result, it would seem, would hold in the case of an office nurse whom the employer selected with due care and in the absence of any indication alerting him or her about the employee's incompetence. When a woman who had brought her child to a physician's office was requested by the nurse to assist in holding another child on an x-ray table, and in so doing was injured by burns and a fall, she recovered damages from the physician for the nurse's negligence.[137] In a case in which a doctor's office assistant, who was a high school graduate and who had worked previously as a hospital aide for two years, treated a patient involved in an industrial accident on 12 out of 17 visits by soaking, bathing and rebandaging a badly injured hand, and the patient sustained permanent damage, the court held that the care of the physician and his assistant was not comparable with that ordinarily given in the community.[138]

In an action against a physician and his office nurse, an award of $25,000 for the death of a 22-month-old boy was held not excessive when he died apparently from aspirating vomitus when left unattended on his back by the nurse.[139] Earlier in the morning the child had been treated by the physician, and was brought back to the office by his mother, who thought he was much worse. She told the nurse that she believed the child had had a convulsion. When the office nurse called the doctor, she told him the child seemed to be in about the same condition as earlier in the day, so the doctor had his lunch before returning to the office. Then the office nurse went to lunch, leaving the receptionist in charge. Some minutes later, the child vomited while lying on his back on the treatment table, and died within a few minutes. A policeman uncle who happened to come in was unsuccessful in reviving him with artificial respiration. Had the nurse been present when the child vomited, there were a number of things she could have done, such as turn him on his side, extract the vomitus and, in an emergency, give a stimulant. The functions and duties of an office nurse include carrying out doctor's orders, nursing procedures, charting and recording, and health guidance and supervision and direction of ancillary workers.

A decision against a nurse and her doctor employer was affirmed in a case in which the nurse, using a Stryker saw on medical orders to remove a plaster of Paris cast from the arm of a patient, cut the arm. During the procedure, the patient complained strenuously that her arm was being cut, but the nurse told her it was only the heat of the blade and admitted at trial that, despite the patient's complaints, she continued to use the same amount of pressure in handling the saw. The court held that, when the patient complained of injury, the nurse failed to follow the recommended procedure that other nurses would have used.[140]

A plaintiff who had a history of chronic earaches went to his doctor's office to have the wax washed from his ears. The doctor was not there, and the plaintiff insisted that the nurse perform the procedure. After arguing with the plaintiff for a while, she undertook the procedure, and both his eardrums were ruptured. The plaintiff was held to be contributorily negligent and could not recover damages.[141]

Some office nurses are now nurse clinicians or practitioner assistants or associates, and their role is expanded compared with that of other office nurses. These nurses may interview and admit patients, take medical or interval histories, organize and record data, make observations, do physical examinations and record the findings, make nursing diagnoses and suggest treatment.[142] In addition, they have much of the responsibility for teaching patients and helping them to identify problems. They may change dressings, remove sutures and casts, order x-rays and laboratory work and do laboratory screening procedures.

It should be noted that the specialist is required to exercise a higher degree of skill when working within her or his speciality than would be demanded of a general practitioner. If nurses held themselves out to be specialists in a certain area, they will normally be held to the standard of a specialist. This higher standard would prevail even though they are not certified in one of the areas established by the American Nurses' Association. Even though they were not certified, the fact of self-representation would be sufficient to hold them to the higher standard.

To recognize excellence in the practice of nursing, the American Nurses' Association is putting into operation its certification program. (See the discussion on certification in Chapter Two.) Licensed registered nurses who can demonstrate knowledge and excellence in current practice are eligible for certification irrespective of the basic program they have completed. Every five years, certified practitioners must submit evidence that they have maintained high standards of practice as a requirement for re-certification.

If the locality rule is applied, a person making a claim against a nurse has to secure testimony from another nurse who is familiar with the standards in that particular community. Many times, nurses from the same community are reluctant to testify against a colleague, so that a claim may fail for lack of proof. If the standard used is that of a specialist, the court is less likely to use the locality rule. With board certification and regional and national meetings for various specialty groups, and the availability of national journals in the specialty areas, it is feasible to hold a specialist to a nationwide or regional standard of care rather than that of the local community. In turn, this makes it easier for a plantiff to secure expert testimony.

In an action to recover damages from two pediatricians for failure to make a timely diagnosis of PKU on a patient in the late 1950s, the Michigan Supreme Court ruled against the pediatricians, saying:

> The reliance of the public upon the skills of a specialist and the wealth and sources of his knowledge are not limited to the geographic area in which he practices. Rather his knowledge is his specialty. He specializes so that he may keep abreast.

In that Detroit case, the physician expert witnesses were drawn from the Chicago and Los Angeles areas.[143]

On appeal, a court affirmed an award of $150,000 to a patient and $60,000 to his wife for loss of consortium against a hotel and the estate of a "nurse" who died before trial, and reversed it as to the physician, remanding the case for a new trial on his liability. When the patient fell in his hotel room, he hit his head, complained of a headache, became nauseated and vomited, and there was a bruise on the back of his head. In response to a call to the hotel management for a physician, the "nurse" came, took his temperature, pulse and blood pressure, and told him to stay in bed for 12 hours after she had learned that he had a heart condition and was on anticoagulant therapy. During the night, the patient vomited four or five times, and he became comatose later the next day. Upon hospitalization, a subdural hematoma was removed, but the patient suffered residual brain damage. The nonlicensed nurse was permitted and authorized by the physician to perform duties that under state law could be done only by licensed physicians. The "nurse" was left in charge of the medical department at night with the knowledge and consent of the hotel's management. When guests requested medical assistance at night, the "nurse" saw them and a $15 charge was added to the guest's bill. The physician provided the "nurse" with a list of specialists to whom she could refer guests, but he did not review her evaluations.[144]

NURSE PRACTITIONER

See "Expanded Role of the Nurse" in Chapter Two.

CRITICAL CARE NURSE

First, what is the primary responsibility of the R.N. in the critical care unit? Basically, the legal responsibility of critical care nurses is the same as that of any other nurse, i.e., they are responsible for their own conduct, including any negligence or tort. It has been said that "the essence of critical care nursing lies not in special environments or amid special equipment but rather in the decision making process of the nurse and her willingness to act upon her decision."[145] Nurses in the critical care unit must have sufficient knowledge to assure a reasonably correct judgment in decision-making. This means that the critical care nurse must understand human physiology, major pathophysiology and signs and symptoms of assorted impending crucial complications; be able to make an assessment of the total body systems; and be familiar with supporting pharmacological therapy, including contraindications and side-effects.

Critical care nurses must also understand the complicated electronic devices used to determine various physiological parameters (of which the electrocardiographic monitor is only one example). In addition, they must know how and when to institute emergency measures in the absence of the physician. When a pre-set alarm system, e.g., on an electrocardiographic monitor or a respirator, warns of a potentially life-threatening situation, nurses must be available to respond quickly. In other words, there are legal implications involved in the use of such equipment, i.e., that the user will be present and will take appropriate action when needed. This sophisticated equipment requires a trained and experienced R.N. to care for patients adequately; the L.P.N. and aide are useful auxiliary nursing personnel, but are not prepared to replace the R.N. even on a temporary basis. Further, one must keep in mind that such machines are not infallible; malfunctions may occur and therefore the R.N.'s frequent assessment of the patient takes precedence.

If the R.N. in the critical care unit is "pulled" to respond to an emergency elsewhere in the hospital, her or his own patients may suffer from the reduced available staff, which cannot effectively meet all essential needs as they arise. Critical care nurses cannot serve two masters simultaneously: the needs of the patients on their own unit and the emergency requirements of an "arrested" patient elsewhere in the hospital. No set of guidelines or job description should place them in this dilemma. Although the individual critical care nurse who carries out the assignment as made is not likely to be held legally liable for nonfeasance in the critical care unit while being temporarily reassigned to an emergency situation elsewhere, the employer and the individual responsible for the reassignment might be liable, depending on all the circumstances. However, a written policy based on deliberately removing a critical care R.N. for temporary work elsewhere does not seem to be in the best interest of patient care.

The hazards of accidental electrocution inherent in the use of any electrical appliance for patient care are increased if, for any reason, nursing care is not quickly available on a critical care unit. Barnett cites the case of a 53-year-old patient who was admitted to an ICU with a diagnosis of a myocardial infarction.[146] The patient was in an electrically operated bed and had leads from an electrocardiographic monitor attached to his chest. He used a urinal and, while attempting to return it to his bedside table, spilled the urine over his lap and the hand control of the bed. Thereupon he experienced an electrical shock that produced ventricular fibrillation, and cardiac resuscitation was needed to revive him. This situation illustrates the dangers involved in the use of electrical equipment. They should not be increased by patients attempting to help themselves owing to a shortage of nursing staff.

Second, if a supervisor relieves a critical care nurse so the latter may go to the cardiac arrest scene, what is the responsibility of each nurse? The law requires that each nurse act with due care toward other persons in the situation. If the critical care nurse is relieved to go to the scene of the arrest, he or she is being temporarily reassigned to that scene and must go and perform his or her duties as an ordinary, reasonable critical care nurse. The primary responsibility of the nurse supervisor is to determine which of the patient's needs can safely be entrusted to others, and whether the person to whom the duties are delegated is competent only if personally supervised. If a supervisor elects to cover the unit during the absence of the critical care nurse, the supervisor must be competent to carry out the latter's duties. If a situation arises in the critical care unit that the supervisor is unable to handle adequately and the other nurse is absent, the supervisor is responsible for his or her own actions, and the employer is also responsible on the theory of *respondeat superior.*

The classification of CPR as an emergency measure has affected nurses, and the American Nurses' Association has encouraged state groups to develop joint CPR policies. Joint policy statements by the state nurses' association, state medical society and state hospital association have been issued in many states.

With authorization, nurses who work in critical care areas assume responsibility for certain procedures that previously have been considered medical practice, and they have to be aware of the legal implications of such work. Besides securing adequate training, hospital or agency approval and the legal protection supplied by the employer, the critical care nurse should also secure personal liability insurance for the most complete protection in the event that a malpractice action is brought.

Because of the specialized nature of the critical care unit and its legal implications, unprepared or inadequately prepared nurses of whatever rank should not be assigned to it, even during a crisis. Therefore, it does not seem wise to designate a critical care R.N. as one of the members who must respond to a cardiac arrest elsewhere in the hospital. Whipple states that, because successful resuscitation from cardiac arrest requires extremely early intervention by at least two trained individuals, two staff members must be available at all times in a critical care unit regardless of size, and that at least one of them should be an R.N.[147] He further indicates that, in larger units, the nurse-to-patient ratio should be 1:2.5, although in special situations the ratio could be 1:1.5 or 1:1. He also points out the less-appreciated fact that the critical care unit nursing staff should be relieved at mealtime and coffee breaks by specially trained personnel. Therefore, the nursing supervisors and others who may provide critical care unit coverage must be specifically trained, experienced and exposed to the inservice teaching activities of such a unit.[148]

Third, if the critical care R.N. does not respond to a cardiac arrest elsewhere in the hospital, what problems arise if personnel who are not "monitor-oriented" try to participate intelligently in the arrest?

If adequately trained R.N.'s do not respond to emergencies outside their location, nursing care and legal problems may conceivably arise if an emergency patient suffers from the lack of essential nursing care. However, this does not imply that the critical care R.N. is the one who should answer the call for help. Whipple and others believe proximity to a medical ward to be an important consideration in critical care unit locations, and that improved staffing can result if the nursing service of the critical care unit, the progressive coronary care area and the adjacent medical ward are all linked together administratively.[149] In this situation, good nursing care can be developed and maintained if a few teaching and supervisory nurses remain permanently assigned to the critical care unit and the other nurses rotate between an adjacent progressive coronary care–general medical ward and the critical care unit. This rotation gives more varied nursing experience and yet maintains critical care unit skills. With this pattern of staffing, a competent and experienced R.N. from the progressive critical care unit or the general medical unit could respond to the cardiac arrest elsewhere in the hospital rather than an R.N. from the critical care unit. Even the smaller hospitals must recognize the need for an adequate number of R.N.'s and supplemental personnel who are "monitor-oriented" as well as trained and experienced in CPR.

Recovery Room Problems*

In one celebrated case,[150–152] two nurses on duty in the postanesthesia recovery room (PAR) thought they had things under control. Two patients were in the PAR and the five operating rooms were booked for that morning. At about 10:25 A.M., Nurse M, with the full knowledge and approval of her supervisor, left for a coffee break. Not long thereafter, a third patient was brought in and Nurse S started to attend to him, but she had to leave him because Patient L was returned to the PAR. Next was the arrival of a fifth patient accompanied by his anesthetist, Dr. T, and a nurse. Dr. T gave an order for an injection of Demerol to be given immediately to the restless Patient R. Nurse S, without completing her check of

---

*In the preparation of this material, byline credit is given Catherine L. Armington.

Patient L, left to give the injection to patient R. Just as she was completing the injection, Nurse S answered a telephone call, which was from an ill nurse who wanted someone to pick up her paycheck. Upon returning to Patient L, Nurse S noted that the patient was not breathing and called Dr. C, who was in the PAR making a telephone call. About this time, Nurse M returned from her coffee break. Extensive, permanent brain damage was sustained by Patient L as a result of insufficient oxygen while she was still under the influence of anesthesia in the recovery room.

Usually, there were two registered nurses on duty in the PAR, and these nurses were expected to take their coffee breaks before any patients arrived. Otherwise, they could obtain relief by calling for a substitute while they went on their coffee break. Relief for nurses in the PAR was a responsibility of the nursing supervisor.

The functions of the PAR and its staffing were discussed by the trial judge as follows:

> The function of this room is to provide highly specialized care, frequent and careful observation of patients who are under the influence of anesthesia. They remain in this room until they have regained consciousness and their bodies return to their normal functions. Respiratory arrest is not an uncommon occurrence in the PAR room and therefore the personnel in this room must be watchful and alert at all times in order to protect the patients in this labile and vulnerable stage. The nurses in this room are there for the purpose of promptly recognizing any respiratory problem, cardiovascular problem, or hemorrhaging. They are expected to take corrective action and/or to summon help promptly.
>
> [I]t is my opinion that this is the most important room in the hospital and the one in which the patient requires the greatest attention because it is fraught with the greatest potential dangers to the patient. This known hazard carries with it, in my opinion, a high degree of duty owed by the hospital to the patient. As the dangers of risk are ever-present, there should be no relaxing of vigilance if one is to comply with the standard of care required in this room....
>
> The prevailing standard of care in the PAR room as far as numbers of staff personnel is a ratio of one registered nurse for each three patients in the recovery room, but with always a minimum of two registered nurses present regardless of the number of patients in the room. Some hospitals utilize nurses' aides in these rooms as assistants to the registered nurses. In either case the prevailing medical opinion points out the necessity of always having a minimum of two staff bodies in the PAR regardless of the number of patients therein with the ratio of one for three.

The court held Nurse S negligent in failing to provide the required observation of Patient L and in leaving her unobserved for a period of longer than the three to four minutes, as claimed. Nurse S, as the nurse in charge, was also negligent in agreeing to the absence of Nurse M for a coffee break without arranging for relief. Nurse M was held negligent in leaving the PAR at the time she did. The hospital was held liable in damages for the negligence of these nurse employees. (See also *Stears v. Park Avenue Hospital*, where an L.P.N.'s error in the recovery room led to a large award.)

In "Post-Surgical Nursing and the Law," Regan cites two additional cases resulting in patient injuries in the recovery room.[153] In one, a recovery room nurse noticed that a six-year-old child who had undergone eye surgery was trying to reach the bandages on both eyes, so she applied restraining boards to both arms. During this time, the child's mother, who was at the bedside, stated that the child complained of the restraints hurting her arms and that they were checked infrequently. When the restraints were removed 18 hours later, there was damage to the child's left arm requiring treatment by an orthopedic surgeon.

In a lawsuit that followed, the court said that the jury could have considered the hospital nurses to be negligent in failing to prevent the child from struggling against the boards. A greater standard of care should be utilized in the treatment of the very young or very old.

In the case of seven-year-old Lisa Bernardi, who had surgery for an abscessed appendix, the physician ordered an injection of tetracycline every 12 hours. During the evening following surgery, a recovery room nurse negligently injected a dose of the tetracycline into or near the sciatic nerve, causing the patient to have a complete footdrop and to lose permanently the normal use of her right foot. The court held the hospital responsible for the acts of the nurse.

In *Peacock* v. *Piper*,[154] a three-month-old plaintiff was admitted to Madigan Army Hospital for breathing difficulties, and a tracheotomy showed a swelling in her throat. A month later, she had surgery for removal of the obstruction, which was a benign tumor of the larynx. After surgery, three physicians left verbal and written orders for the recovery room care of the baby. About two hours after she was returned to the recovery room, the baby had some kind of attack and her heart stopped beating. Mouth-to-mouth resuscitation was given by an Army nurse, and her heart started beating after a nearby physician ran to the recovery room, opened her chest and gave heart massage. Whether the episode had any connection with the subsequent palsy condition of the baby was a matter of conflict between the medical witnesses at the trial. A jury's verdict for the defendants was returned by the trial court.

In *Hunt* v. *Gerber*, the death of the appellant's decedent in the recovery room was held not to be the fault of the hospital or the surgeon. The court said:

> The appellant was charged with the duty of coming forward with proof of the standard of care as well as the breach of that standard and demonstrating that such breach was the proximate cause, or facts from which it could be reasonably inferred that such breach was the proximate cause of the decedent's death. In the face of these deficiencies, we think the trial judge was correct in rendering the summary judgment. The fact that the decedent died, regrettable as it is, does not necessarily establish negligence on the part of the hospital or the doctor.[155]

As Regan says, there should be standing orders for specific situations in the recovery room.[156] When there is a life and death emergency in the PAR, as elsewhere, anyone can do anything reasonable to save the life of someone in jeopardy.

PRACTICAL/VOCATIONAL NURSES

General Liability

Next, we may consider further the status of a practical or vocational nurse. As discussed in Chapter 2, the practical nurse is one prepared to share in the care of the sick, in rehabilitation and in prevention of illness, always under the care of a licensed physician or a registered professional nurse. Practical nurses, like other nurses, are responsible for their own wrongful and negligent acts. For example, if a practical nurse applied a hot water bottle to a patient and the patient was burned, the practical nurse would be liable; her or his power of observation and attention to detail, even without elaborate training, would prevent such results. Practical nurses may not exceed their authority in the practice of nursing, and they are liable for unauthorized practice of medicine.[157] The provisions of the licensure act and the extent of their education and training in an approved school are factors governing their practice of nursing.

Although practical nurses may be employed to give nursing care in private homes, institutions and health agencies to a variety of chronically ill, aged or convalescent patients, they are reminded that they work only under direct orders of a licensed physician or under the supervision of a registered professional nurse. For their own protection, as well as that of their patients, practical nurses should be careful to observe such limitations. Like professional nurses, they must realize that no one can give them the right to do more than they are authorized by law to do.

In particular, they should realize that the scarcity of available registered nurses does not permit them or technicians or aides to carry out functions that are recognized as within the exclusive area of registered professional nursing.[158] The tendency of some hospitals, nursing homes and other institutions to ask practical nurses and others to carry out duties beyond the scope of their educational preparation, experience and licensure is to be deplored. In the event of a lawsuit, practical nurses will find themselves in difficulties if they have assumed the responsibilities of a registered professional nurse, since someone who assumes such a role is held to its standard of performance.[159] In some institutions, this problem is particularly acute on the evening and night tours of duty.

Following a prostatectomy, a patient's doctor telephoned the hospital and gave an order for Levophed to the practical nurse, who was the only one on duty at the time. He neglected to warn her about the drug or to state that only a resident physician should administer the drug. When the patient sustained permanent arm damage as a result of an improper transfusion or failure to keep the needle in place, a sizable award against the hospital was upheld. The doctor was ruled not liable, on the grounds that he was entitled to rely on the competency of the hospital staff in carrying out his order.[160] Practical nurses, like other employees, render their employers as well as themselves liable for their negligent acts in the course of their employment.

Practical nurses may sue or be sued for breach of a contract for personal services. The same rules for the negotiation and performance of contracts apply to them as to others. For example, if a patient fails to pay their wages or dismisses them in breach of contract, practical nurses have a cause of action. In an emergency, a practical nurse, like any other person, may give medical care. But again, whether there is an emergency in fact depends on all the circumstances.

Expanding L.P./V.N. Roles

Today the licensed practical/vocational nurse is a very important member of the health care team who renders good, safe nursing care to many patients in hospitals, nursing homes, doctors' and dentists' offices, public health agencies and other community health services. To the public, the L.P./V.N. is a highly visible nurse who gives direct nursing care to patients.

State law and national health commissions have recognized the rights of L.P./V.N.'s to perform certain functions if three basic conditions are met: (1) they must have appropriate and recognizable education or training for the task; (2) if the task is a medical one, they need a doctor's order; (3) the task must be one that appropriately trained nurses in the institution perform. These conditions must be included in a written policy of the institution, established by a committee composed of representatives from the medical staff, the department of nursing and the administration, and the policy must be made available to the total medical and nursing staffs.

In accepting responsibilities, it is important that L.P./V.N.'s be familiar with the legislative and judicial decisions that govern their legal right to perform these tasks. Basically, such legal decisions deal with seven broad areas of practical nurse responsibility.

In planning nursing care, one must take into account the patient's condition and plan safe and reasonable nursing care to meet her or his known needs. Planning, supervising and helping to implement the over-all nursing care of patients is the L.P./V.N.'s responsibility in many hospitals (especially on the afternoon or night shifts), in nursing homes, in patients' homes and in public health and community agency work. Many times the L.P./V.N. must evaluate the patient's needs for medical care, execute medical orders or ordinary nursing procedures, support the patient's adaptation to the illness or injury and coordinate the patient's care in relation to routine hospital, nursing home or other agency activities.

This nursing care must be safe and must meet patient needs, as has been emphasized in many legal decisions, such as *Granite Home v. Schwartz*.[161] In this case, damages were recovered from a nursing home where an 89-year-old patient died from chemical pneumonia after he drank kerosene from a brown jug left lying around the premises.

Assessment of Patient's Needs. L.P./V.N.'s must observe patient symptoms and reactions. In other words, they must assess patients' needs. In a case in which a patient died from loss of blood when he was brought to an emergency room following a stab wound, the nurse called a doctor but took no measures to stop the bleeding. The patient was transferred to another hospital without receiving emergency care, and his heirs subsequently recovered damages for his death.[162]

Recording and Reporting Observations. L.P./V.N.'s are responsible for promptly and accurately recording and reporting their observations, assessment and nursing activities. Many statutory definitions of nursing specifically include this area within the language of the statute. Judicial decisions also deal with the right of physicians to rely on the facts contained in nursing records relating to temperature, respiration, pulse and other physical conditions.[163]

As the case of *Joseph v. W. H. Groves Latter-day Saints Hospital et al.* showed, factors regarding the general condition of patients such as complaints, sleep and activity may be essential information to prove their case.[164]

Responsibility for Procedures and Techniques. The practical nurse is responsible for an ever-widening area of practice involving nursing procedures and techniques. A judgment for $700 was affirmed against a hospital and a nurse for injuries sustained when the nurse put hydrochloric acid in the patient's nose instead of nose drops.[165]

L.P./V.N.'s, like all nurses, are personally responsible for all the nursing procedures they perform, and in addition the employer or principal is liable for the torts committed by the employee or agent in the course of that employment or agency. (A tort is a wrong committed by a person involving injury to another for which the law provides a remedy by allowing those injured to sue for damages for injuries incurred.)

Supervision of Aides. It appears that an ever-growing area of practical nursing involves the supervision of nursing aides, orderlies and others involved in contributing to the care of the patient. If an L.P./V.N. is in charge of a floor or a nursing team, and in reality she is in many situations, then in those situations she is supervising others. The basic responsibility of the individual nurse, whether R.N. or L.P./V.N., who is required to supervise others is to decide which of the patient's needs can be assigned to others, and whether the person to whom the work is assigned is competent only if personally supervised. Supervising nurses can be held liable for the negligence of another nurse to whom they assign duties that the latter is incompetent to perform because of lack of education or experience. In one case, a patient who had almost recovered from a sciatic nerve injury was being taken to the physical therapy department on a stretcher by a nurse's aide. The aide lost control of the stretcher on a ramp, it rolled around and overturned, and the patient fell on the floor and was injured. The patient recovered damages for his injuries.[166]

Patient Education. An ever-expanding area of nursing activity involves teaching patients and their families how to care for themselves, maintain their health, prevent disease or injury and rehabilitate themselves. L.P./V.N.'s are caring for patients with diabetes, those who have a colostomy, new mothers, those who have had a stroke or a broken hip and those who must use crutches, a cane or a walker. In many instances the L.P./V.N. is the only nurse rendering patient care, and therefore he or she must teach patients how to care for themselves.

In one case, a nurse was held not liable for damages where she had taught a mother how to use a heating pad correctly on a child's neck in order to localize pus, since the injury was caused by the negligent manner in which the mother carried out these instructions.[167]

Executing M.D.'s Orders. The L.P./V.N. carries out the physician's orders and those of the registered nurse in charge. The minimal legal requirements to carry out a physician's order are: (1) that the L.P./V.N. act under the direction or supervision of a licensed physician, (2) that the order be legal and (3) that the L.P./V.N. understand the cause and effect of the order before carrying it out.

AIDES, ORDERLIES AND ATTENDANTS

Aides, orderlies and attendants, as is true of everyone else, are responsible at law for their own actions, including negligence. In addition, when a person is injured by an aide, orderly or attendant as a result of negligence in the course of the employee's work, the employer is also responsible to the injured person. In a case in which a doctor wrote an order "May dangle PRN" for a 67-year-old woman who was paralyzed from the waist down and who was responding satisfactorily to treatment for decubitus ulcers and persistent fever, a nurse's aide helped her to a dangle position on the side of her bed and then left her sitting alone, contrary to the doctor's orders. The patient recovered $208,000 damages when she fell and was injured.[168] She had asked for some writing paper, and the nurse's aide left her alone in order to fill this request. The patient sustained an impacted fracture of the leg, which had to be amputated. The injury was not discovered for several days, since the paralyzed patient had no-sensation of pain and x-rays were not taken at the time of the accident. Aides, orderlies and attendants must be sufficiently informed of patients' conditions so as not to leave them alone when they need assistance.

When a patient who had undergone eye surgery was being moved from one hospital building to another, the stretcher slipped while being lifted by an ambulance attendant and a hospital attendant whose help he had recruited, and the patient's eye was injured as a result. He could not recover damages for negligence based on the grounds that the city ordinance required the ambulance to have two attendants. The court held that the ordinance was concerned only with the cleanliness of drivers and their ability to give first aid, and hence both the hospital and ambulance company were found not liable for damages.[170]

Many of the problems of supervising aides, orderlies and attendants can be eased appreciably through adequate training and proper assignments. Nurses who supervise the work of these personnel are responsible for their assignment of duties to them and for supervising their performance. This means that the duties assigned must be within the scope of the education and experience of the assignees, and it means a decision is necessary as to whether they are safe and competent to perform these duties *only* if under immediate supervision—in which case, immediate supervision must be given.

A paying patient, who was blind and partially paralyzed, was taken in a wheelchair by an orderly to a bathroom and, while being prepared for a bath, fell against a steam radiator and sustained third degree burns, allegedly because the orderly went for help instead of moving the patient immediately. The patient was allowed to sue the voluntary hospital for negligence.[171] He charged that the charitable hospital was negligent in employing and retaining the services of the orderly, who was incompetent for the work and who had been released from the penitentiary only a few weeks previously, after serving a sentence of several years for commission of a felony.

The need for proper training of aides and orderlies is apparent from the next two cases. A stroke patient who suffered a broken leg while being turned by a nurse's aide in a hospital bed recovered substantial damages.[172] A judgment for the hospital was reversed and a new trial ordered where a patient sued for injuries incurred while being catheterized by an orderly, and three urologists testifed that the injury was due to the failure of the orderly to use the catheter properly.[173]

In a case in which warm compresses properly applied aggravated a pre-existing cellulitis and infection that had symptoms similar to a second-degree burn, the nurse's aide and her employer were cleared in a lawsuit claiming damages for negligence resulting in burns.[174]

The dismissal of an attendant from a children's psychiatric hospital was sustained following a hearing under the Civil Service Law. The attendant struck a 13-year-old agitated boy in the abdomen after disarming him when the boy was threatening other patients with a chair leg. The boy was not very strong, and a nurse who heard the commotion was able to remove him from his ward and calm him down without the use of excessive force. The attendant was also guilty of tardiness and numerous unexcused and unexplained absences as well as the physical abuse of patients.[175]

The Minnesota Supreme Court upheld the dismissal of a psychiatric technician from his position in the maximum security ward at Anoka State Hospital when his superior, accompanied by another orderly, found him asleep and snoring in a lounge chair in the dimly lit television room. At a hearing before the state Civil Service Board, the plaintiff employee insisted he was awake at all times.[176]

When a paramedical employee pulling a food cart collided with and injured a healthy 70-year-old plaintiff while the latter was legally on the hospital premises, use of the *res ipsa loquitur* doctrine placed an unfair burden on the defendants. A judgment for such plaintiff was reversed and the case sent back for a new trial. Nevertheless, it should be pointed out that paramedical and other hospital employees must exercise ordinary prudent, reasonable care not to injure patients, visitors and others in the hospital.[177]

An incontinent cardiovascular patient sustained fatal burns when he was left on a commode unattended and restrained while the nurses' aide attended other patients. In a suit to recover damages for conscious pain and wrongful death, a judgment in favor of his estate was reversed and a new trial ordered, but the court said that "the trial judge properly charged the jury that it was the duty of the defendants to use reasonable care in looking after the safety of their patients." Under the circumstances, if the time interval was adequately defined, the jury might well consider the knowledge of the nurse's aide and find that it was imprudent for him to leave the patient unattended and restrained on a commode while he was busy preparing and serving lunch for other patients.[178]

In a nursing home, a patient was senile and almost totally helpless physically. The employees (nurses and aides) of the nursing home knew of her condition and usually put side-rails on her bed at night. However, one night the aides accidently omitted putting the side-rails in place, and the patient fell and was injured. The nursing home was held liable for the negligence of the aides.[179]

A patient who was in the hospital for rehabilitation owing to weakness in her arm and leg was being pushed to lunch in a wheelchair; as the aide pushed the chair up to the table, she turned it so the patient's arm, resting on the arm of the chair, was pinched against the table. Although no incident report was filed, the appellate court ruled that the patient's testimony was sufficient to raise a *prima facie* case of simple negligence committed by the hospital aide in the course and scope of her employment. From a directed verdict for the hospital, on appeal, the case was sent back to the lower court for trial.[180]

An Ohio case[181] illustrates the problem of overutilization of the aide while a hospital unit is understaffed. A schizophrenic patient, who had told her husband she was contemplating suicide and made two attempts in the hospital to jump out of a window, was kept in a security room with the door locked at night. She was assigned for morning care to the nurse's aide. The aide carried out the morning care, asked a nurse whether the door could be left open and received an affirmative reply but was not told of the patient's history. A short time later the patient jumped to her death from a ninth-floor solarium window. In reversing a directed verdict for the hospital and remanding the case for a new trial, the court said that the patient was assigned to the sole care of a nurse's aide who had two days' experience after two weeks' training and who was not advised of the patient's history, so that reasonable minds could differ as to whether the hospital exercised reasonable care under the circumstances. It happened on a weekend day when there was absenteeism and the nurse in charge was having a sprained ankle treated in the emergency room.

A patient was awarded $4000 after being injured when an orderly dropped his leg, which was covered by a full-length cast.[182] The patient's physician was not notified until 24 hours later.

NURSING STUDENTS

It is important for nursing students, as is true of other persons, to remember that they are personally liable for their own wrongs and negligent acts. The fact that they are students and may be of "minor" age does not exempt them from liability or responsibility for their actions. If student nurses enjoy employee status, they may make others liable, too, for their negligent acts. In cases that come to trial, the facts relating to the student nurse's admission, experience record and efficiency ratings may be presented in detail for consideration as to whether she or he acted like an ordinary, reasonable, prudent nursing student under the circumstances.[183]

When nursing students in the course of their clinical experience in hospitals or other agencies perform duties that are within the scope of professional nursing, these acts must be carried out with the same degree of competence as if done by a registered professional nurse. In other words, patients must not be subjected to a lower standard of nursing care because they have nursing students caring for them. When nursing students are negligent in the performance of their duties, patients may bring a lawsuit for damages.

It is pertinent to point out that instructors are responsible for their assignments and for reasonable and prudent supervision of nursing students. Accordingly, if they were to assign nursing students to perform duties for which the students had not been trained, or were to neglect or omit to supervise their performance to ensure professional competence, the instructors could be held liable. The inherent responsibility of nurses who supervise others—whether they be nursing students, registered professional nurses, practical nurses, aides, orderlies or attendants—is to determine which of the patient's needs can be safely entrusted to a particular person, and whether or not the delegated person is competent only if personally supervised. An integral part of a clinical instructor's duty is to supervise the fitness and competency of nursing students who give nursing care to patients, and any negligence in failing to supervise in accordance with the standard of a reasonable and prudent clinical instructor is the basis of liability.[184]

When a first-year student in a hospital in which first-year students were permitted to give injections under supervision gave one to a patient hospitalized with Buerger's disease, and injured his right sciatic nerve, the patient recovered a substantial judgment because the defendant hospital had not provided adequate supervision.[185]

Nursing students should bear in mind that they are responsible for their own actions and liable for their own negligence.[186] As has been pointed out in the preceding discussion, nursing students are required to adhere to the same standard of care as the ordinary, reasonable and prudent professional nurse. Consequently, if nursing students know they are inadequately prepared for a particular assignment or duty or need additional supervision, they should inform the person responsible for their assignment and for supervision of the matter.

In past years, nursing students in a diploma program in a hospital school of nursing were considered employees of the hospital when they were doing nursing in the institution, under its direction and for its benefit.[187] However, the nursing student may not be an employee. Today nursing students in associate degree and collegiate programs typically receive no stipend from the college and provide their own room, board and laundry and usually pay some tuition fees. When nursing students are in the hospital practice area, the faculty of the college teaches them, and the hospital simply provides clinical experience, without giving any compensation to the students or making any service demands. In such instances, the nursing student would not seem to be an employee of the hospital, but might be held to be an employee of the college. A patient who suffered injuries as a result of manipulation by a student of osteopathy recovered damages from the college, and the court said that a student in a clinical situation must be given reasonable guidance and supervision.[188]

As previously pointed out, the nursing student was expressly exempted by law from the Social Security program.

Qualifications for Clinical Practice

A concerned head nurse, a first-line supervisor of a busy 60-bed medical unit, asks: "Since I am ultimately responsible for the nursing care of patients on my unit, what are my rights with respect to accepting only nursing students with satisfactory preparation for clinical experience? Recently we had on our unit two serious medication errors involving digitalis and morphine which were made by nursing students, one of whom had a grade of D in Pharmacology and the other a C− in the same subject. In my opinion, neither student should have been assigned to medications." A second question comes from a chairman of a department of nursing and allied health who wants to know the responsibilities and rights of a chairman when a student in the program has such a poor state of health as to endanger the patients.

The nursing students in each example were either from a collegiate or from an associate degree program using the facilities of the hospital as a practice area in which the college's own faculty teach the students. These programs are supported by tax funds, grants and tuition. Students live on campus or at home and not in the hospital, and the clinical experience is planned to meet the students' needs without recompense of any kind from the hospital. Under such circumstances, there is no employer-employee relationship between the hospital or school and the student.

However, there is a contract between each school and the hospital governing the rights of both parties. Under the terms of this contract, the hospital agrees to accept a number of nursing students accompanied by their instructors for clinical experience in either all units or specific units of the hospital for a given time. Pursuant to the terms of the same contract, the school undertakes to send only students whose health and scholastic progress meet the test of an ordinary, reasonable and prudent nursing student in the clinical experience situation. Each party to the contract is liable for any breach thereof.

As the representative of the hospital administration, head nurses are entitled to assurance that the nursing students assigned to their units have satisfactory educational preparation. Whether this information is supplied by the school on each student, or whether the level of preparation and health is assumed by the hospital administrator as required in the contract, seems immaterial so long as the head nurse has the assurance that the nursing students actually caring for the patients on the unit have been screened by the school.

In an opinion a court has stated, "It is not sufficient to say that a nurse is competent simply because she is capable of discharging the manual duties incumbent upon her as a nurse. If she is lacking in educational preparation, if she is guilty of indiscretion that impairs her physical or mental status, if she is lacking in that moral character which imbues the patient with confidence, then it cannot be said that she is a competent person to be placed in charge of a helpless patient."[189]

Every patient has the right to the sevices of a reasonably competent nurse, and to expect from a nursing student the same standard of care that he or she would receive from a registered professional nurse. If nursing students without apparent satisfactory educational preparation come to a hospital or other agency unit for clinical experience, the head nurse should immediately report the matter to the authority in the hospital and the educational unit with a request that, in the interest of safe and adequate nursing care of patients, such students should not be allowed to proceed with clinical practice. A record of the request should be filed by the head nurse.

If nursing students make a medication error or are otherwise involved in an untoward incident in the hospital, they should complete, sign and file an incident report with Nursing Service. As a part of that report, many hospitals will request the name of the clinical instructor and head nurse on duty on the unit at the time of the incident. It is important for nursing students to appreciate that legally they are responsible for their own errors while giving care as a part of their educational experience.

Since nursing students are also responsible to the school, they must complete whatever form the school and its insurer have devised for notification of possible liability. It is the duty of the clinical instructor to make sure that the nursing student in due course completes, signs and files such a form. Regrettably, some clinical instructors are remiss in making certain that the school's insurer has timely notification. Such clinical instructors and their nursing students must realize that every professional liability insurance policy contains a cooperation clause that calls for the fair and frank disclosure of information reasonably demanded by the carrier, as well as the opportunity to make prompt and complete investigation of any alleged claims and assistance in securing witnesses.

Following the same reasoning, the chairperson of a department of nursing who is ultimately responsible for the assignment of nursing students to a clinical area also has the responsibility of ensuring that the nursing students are in good health and free from health hazards that may endanger patients. It follows that it is the right of the chairperson not to assign any student whose poor health would endanger a patient to a clinical area.

In 1966, the parents of a baby girl born prematurely at a U.S. Naval Hospital recovered damages for her injuries and deformity as a result of osteomyelitis in the hips caused by a staphylococcus infection. In that situation, one nurse in the nursery had a positive nose culture for staphylococcus, and it was shown that she did not receive a physical examination when reporting on duty at this hospital, although she had had one shortly before leaving her previous post of duty.[190]

The policy of most schools of nursing in giving special attention to the health of nursing students engaged in the care of infants is consistent with the result obtained in the above case.

Admission

In *Davis v. Southeastern Community College*, an L.P.N., afflicted with a severe hearing disability and considered as a handicapped person under the Rehabilitation Act of 1973, brought an action against a community college, claiming that the school had denied her equal protection of the law and due process in denying her admission to a program for the education of registered nurses. Davis could be responsible for speech only when the speaker got her attention and allowed her to look directly at him. In settings such as the operating room, intensive care or postnatal care unit, doctors and nurses wear surgical masks that make lip reading impossible. In many situations, a registered nurse is required to follow a physician's instructions instantly, e.g., in procuring various instruments and drugs, and the physician would be able to get the nurse's attention only by vocal means. The court held that Davis's handicap actually prevents her from safely performing in both her training program and her proposed profession. She could continue to serve as a licensed practical nurse, since the necessary constant supervision required in that role provides some assurance of safe practice. The school was upheld in denying her admission.[191]

A student in the School of Graduate Studies at Case Western Reserve sued in tort and contract, seeking to have the university reinstate her as a graduate student and to admit her as a Ph.D. candidate in nursing and for damages. She claimed the assistant dean had failed to properly supervise the procedure for evaluating her examination and that the two faculty members were personally prejudiced against her. A requirement for admission to candidacy for the degree is successful completion of a three-part written examination. The student passed one part on the first attempt, a second part on a second attempt, declined to take the third part a third time and was terminated. In cases involving academic decisions, colleges and universities are not subject to the supervision or review of the courts to ensure the uniform application of their academic standards.[192] In another case the appellate court reversed a decision of the district court compelling a university to grant a degree to a foreign student who twice failed to pass a required comprehensive examination.[193]

Grades/Progression in Program

A student, who earned a D in a required nursing course and failed another course the following term, was not permitted to graduate because of the college's written policy requiring at least a C grade in every required nursing course. The student sued the school. The court said that the grades and the basis on which they were given to the plaintiff are not the subject of judicial scrutiny and that the consequences are not the result of arbitrariness or capriciousness.[194]

In *Lyons v. Salve Regina College*, a nursing student brought an action against the college alleging that the college's refusal to allow the student to continue her studies toward a degree in nursing constituted a breach of contract. The student received a grade of F in a required course and could no longer continue her studies toward a nursing degree. She graduated from the college with a degree in psychology and sought monetary damages and an order requiring the college to change her course grade from an F to an "incomplete" and to reinstate her in order to complete her nursing degree. After several appeals within the institution, the Appeals Court held that the college did not breach its agreement with the student when the dean rejected the recommendation of the majority of the Grade Appeals Committee and refused to change the student's grade.[195]

In the *Horowitz* case, a medical student, who ranked first on Part I of the National Board Examinations for Medical Students and second on Part II and ranked second in quarterly exams at the medical school, was dismissed after numerous conferences for unacceptable clinical performance. The decision rested on the academic judgment of school officials that she did not have the necessary clinical ability to perform adequately as a medical doctor and was making insufficient progress toward that goal. This was a U.S. Supreme Court decision. The nursing instructor can fail a student on unsatisfactory clinical performance. It is a subjective judgment based on accepted professional standards. There should be a number of well-documented faculty-student conferences where the student is apprised of the reasons for her or his unsatisfactory evaluation and the ultimate outcome. A review of the case at several levels ensures fairness.[196]

An action was brought for a preliminary injunction on a civil rights complaint against a community college for delaying a student's graduation from nursing school. Approximately two months into the second semester of the program, the student fractured and dislocated his ankle and had to wear a cast and to use crutches, and later a cane, to move about, which made it impossible for him to continue in the program. The school officials confirmed the decision of the instructor and dean of students that the student would not be permitted to participate in the clinical course and would be required to repeat it. The injunctive relief was denied.[197] As these cases illustrate, nursing students are not reluctant to resort to the courts to assist in enrollment, to compel a teacher to raise a grade or to block withdrawal from a program.

Where a medical student allegedly cheated on an examination and then lied about it, he was entitled to a hearing before being expelled, a Federal appellate court for Nebraska ruled.[198]

School Catalog

In *University of Texas Health Science Center at Houston* v. *Babb*, the Texas Appellate Court held that a school's catalog constitutes a written contract between the educational institution and the student who enters under its terms. In this case, the student nurse entering the nursing school under the 1978–79 catalog had a right to rely on its terms. Although later amended, this catalog permitted a student to complete the degree requirements within a six-year period. In addition, the 1978–79 catalog did not permit the school to dismiss a student based on the number of bad grades that the student made; it only required a student to maintain a 2.0 G.P.A. In the case of this student nurse, the court held that the commitment made by the University of Texas to her in the 1978–79 catalog controlled their relationship as long as she remained a student in the School of Nursing program.[199]

Cheating

By obtaining answers to two questions from the professor supervising the examination, a nursing student allegedly cheated and was found guilty of academic dishonesty by the student court. A faculty panel found her not guilty. She was found guilty and given a failing grade by the vice chancellor. Because the course was a prerequisite for nursing school, she was not registered for the next semester. The Federal appellate court for North Carolina upheld the appellate and trial courts granting her an injunction and reinstating her as a student in good standing pending resolution of her claim that the university violated her due process rights.[200]

Rights of Expelled or Suspended Students

In *Brookins* v. *Bonnell*[201] a nursing student who allegedly failed to submit a physical examination report, failed to report previous attendance at a hospital school of nursing or to provide a transcript of records and failed to attend class regularly was expelled from a community college. The court held that a student dismissed from a public college because of disciplinary misconduct is entitled to a due process hearing, but one dismissed solely because of academic failure is not entitled to such hearing. The nursing student, who was expelled for disciplinary reasons, was entitled to a hearing, but he was denied a preliminary injunction for immediate reinstatement because of the unlikelihood of success in the ultimate action.

In *White v. Knowlton*[202] the court dismissed the complaint of six West Point cadets seeking injunction against separation from service for violation of the cadet honor code in having cheated on a physics examination. Hearings had been held and each cadet was found guilty of cheating.

An injunction was granted to a student in *Paine v. Board of Regents, etc.,*[203] when school rules required an automatic suspension for two years of any university student "placed on probation for or finally convicted of the illegal use, possession and/or sale of a drug or narcotic." Such rules were held to be unconstitutional because they did not provide for a hearing that would afford the student an opportunity to establish that he or she posed no substantial threat of influencing other students to use, possess or sell drugs or narcotics. It was also held that there was a denial of equal protection by the rule, because students convicted of other offenses were given a hearing at which evidence could be offered in extenuation and mitigation and at which a flexible range of penalties could be given.

In a case in which students had been suspended from school without being given hearings in violation of their constitutional rights, the U.S. Court of Appeals held that they should have been awarded damages even though no pecuniary loss was shown, and that they were also entitled to special damages for loss of school days.[204]

The District of Columbia appellate court held that a university followed proper procedures in suspending a medical student for one year for cheating.[205] During his sophomore year the student was accused of cheating, and a Judiciary Board composed of four faculty members and four students, hearing the charges when two of the four students were absent, found him guilty of cheating and recommended his indefinite suspension. The decision was affirmed by the Board of Appeals, also composed of four faculty members and four students, when one of the student members was absent. When both boards overruled the student's objection to their composition, he filed a suit against the university seeking $100,000 damages and an injunction against his suspension. A preliminary injunction was denied by the trial court. Meanwhile, the student was readmitted to medical school to repeat his entire sophomore year on probation. After he failed four subjects, his enrollment was terminated. When the trial court heard the case, it decided that he had been given appropriate hearings and that his academic failure was not related to the cheating incident. The decision was affirmed by the appellate court, which said that the composition of the two boards was not so deficient as to invalidate their decisions.

When a private, nonmatriculated college student, who went to school part-time, claimed that she had been arbitrarily suspended in violation of due process, the court rejected the complaint. The college faculty doubted the student's fitness, both academically and emotionally, and their misgivings were not without a real basis. In part, the court stated that it has long been established that due process constitutional guarantees are not applicable when a student is dismissed or suspended for academic deficiencies, and that judicial officials are not as well qualified as academicians in determining scholastic aptitude. The court pointed out that there are many cases holding that a student is entitled to full due process, notice and hearing if suspended or expelled for disciplinary reasons from tax-supported colleges or universities; however, student disciplinary procedures in private institutions will be circumscribed by constitutional safeguards only if the state is involved in the activities of the college in a meaningful way.[206]

When a former dental student sued a private university for breach of contract in dismissing him before graduation, a Federal trial court in Georgia said that respect for the discretion of those best qualified to make such judgments dictated that the university, and not the Federal courts, should determine the qualifications of students to continue their postgraduate education.[207]

Student Rights

The right of New Hampshire University students to organize a homosexual organization and to function on a university campus, as well as their rights of access to university facilities and media in order to sponsor and participate in social functions, was upheld by the court.[208]

A similar action was brought by an association of university students interested in homosexual rights, which was seeking registration as a student organization and the attendant privileges.[209] The university's refusal to register the association under the same terms and conditions as its other organizations was ruled by the Court of Appeals to be a violation of the Federal Constitution.

A New York appellate court ruled that a law school student, who was a patient, did not have a right to continue his twice-weekly pick-up privileges at a methadone clinic. The 32-year-old patient had been addicted to heroin since the age of 15 and had not controlled his addiction until voluntarily submitting to methadone treatment. He returned to high school, graduated with honors, graduated *cum laude* from Fordham University and was a third-year law student at the time of trial. All patients were ordered on a daily schedule by the director of the clinic. The student brought suit claiming that daily visits interfered with his studies. The court held that the director's professional judgment concerning the frequency of personal visits was not arbitrary or capricious.[210]

When a student filed a $5 million suit against his high school district for failing to teach him basic reading and writing skills, the New York appellate court ruled that he had no cause of action against the high school for educational malpractice. According to the ruling, courts were an inappropriate forum to test the efficacy of educational programs and pedagogical methods.[211] This would seem to apply also to schools of nursing.

TECHNICIANS

Where a student during on-the-job training as a laboratory technician suffered serious injuries when an acid container burst, her only remedies lay under the Workmen's Compensation Act, because she was ruled an employee of the hospital.[212]

A 38-year-old truck driver sustained a fracture and dislocation of C6–C7 in a motorbike accident and was taken to a hospital emergency room. While the physician was consulting an orthopedist, two x-ray technicians with the assistance of an emergency room nurse attempted to apply traction in order to obtain x-ray films. The patient screamed, arched his back and went limp during the procedure; he suffered quadriparesis and received a settlement of $1.5 million.[213] He contended that the x-ray technicians were negligent in failing to comply with the procedure manual and in manipulating him and taking x-rays without the physician's knowledge.

A California appellate court ruled that x-ray technicians certified by the American Radiography Technologists must take a state examination in order to be licensed to use x-rays on human beings.[214]

References

1. Fowler v. State, 78 N.Y.S. 2nd 860 (Ct. Cl., 1948).
2. 2 *Restatement, Torts*, Sec. 314.
3. Malloy v. Fong, 37 Cal. 2d 356, 220 P. 2d 48, 233 P. 2d 241 (1951).
4. *Cf.* Question for Good Samaritan: Is This Emergency Really Real? *Ohio Nurses Rev.*, 41:13–14, Jan. 1966.
5. Emergencies and the Law, *Emergency Medicine*, 3:216, Jan 1971.
6. Health Briefs, *Law, Med., & Health Care*, 11:227, Oct. 1983.
7. Creighton, H.: Legal Responsibilities of the R.N. in the Emergency Room, *Mississippi RN*, 30:35–40, Oct. 1968. Lambertsen, E. C.: *Education for Nursing Leadership*. Philadelphia, J. B. Lippincott Co., 1958, pp. 165–166.
8. Social Security Administration. *Document HIM-1*, p. 35, 1966.
9. Letourneau, C. U.: Legal Aspects of the Hospital Emergency Room, *Hosp. Man.*, 103:55–60, March 1967; 103:39–41, April 1967.
10. Wilmington General Hospital v. Manlove, 54 Del. 15, 174 A. 2d 135 (1961).
11. O'Neill v. Montefiore Hospital et al., 11 A.D. 2d 231 202 N.Y.S. 2d 436 (1960).
12. Ruvio v. North Broward Hospital District, 186 So. 2d 45 (1966).
13. American College of Surgeons: *Standards for the Emergency Department*. Approved by the Board of Regents, Feb. 23–24, 1963.
14. Childs v. Greenville Hospital Authority, 469 S.W. 2d 399 (Texas, 1972).
15. Citizens Hospital Association v. Schoulin, 262 So. 2d 303 (Ala., 1972).
16. Hill v. Ohio County, 468 S.W. 2d 306 (Ky., 1971).
17. Schloendorff v. Society of New York Hospital, 211 N.Y. 125, 105 N.E. 92 (1914).
18. People *ex rel.* Wallace v. Labrenz, 411 Ill. 618, 104 N.E. 2d 769, cert. denied 344 U.S. 824 (1952).
19. Maxwell v. Maxwell, 177 N.W. 541 (Iowa, 1920).
20. Winters v. Miller, 206 F. Supp. 1158 (E.D. N.Y., 1969) rev'd on other grounds 446 F. 2d Cir., 1971); cert. denied 404 U.S. 985 (1971).
21. Law, S. A.: The Patient's Right to Refuse Treatment, *Hosp. Med. Staff*, 5:1–7, Oct. 1976.
22. Hiser v. Randolph, 617 P. 2d 774 (Ct. App. Ariz. Div. 1, Dept. C., 1980). Creighton, H.: Refusal to Treat Patient, *Superv. Nurse*, 12:67, 70, April 1981.
23. Niles v. City of San Rafael, 42 Cal. App. 3rd 230 (1974). Bernstein, A. H.: A Pair of Malpractice Cases, Law in Brief, *Hospitals*, 77:91, July 1, 1977.
24. Methodist Hospital v. Ball, 362 S.W. 2d 475 (Tenn., 1961). Armington, C. L.: Legal Implications in Emergency Services, *Nurs. Clin. North Am.*, 9:445, 448, Sept. 1974.
25. Joyner v. Ochsner Medical Foundation, 230 So. 2d 913 (La., 1970); Armington, C. L.: Legal Implications in Emergency Services. *Nurs. Clin. North Am.*, 9:445, 449, Sept. 1974.
26. Maidma v. Glendora Community Hospital, Cal. Super. Ct., Los Angeles Co., Docket No. EAC 12392, June, 1973; *Citation*, 27:161–162, Sept. 15, 1973. Creighton, H.: *Law Every Nurse Should Know*, 3rd ed. Philadelphia, W. B. Saunders Co., 1975, p. 136.
27. Glavin v. Rhode Island Hospital, 12 R. I. 411 (1979); Wasmuth, C. E.: *Law for the Physician*. Philadelphia, Lea & Febiger, 1966, p. 119.
28. Luka v. Lowrie, 171 Mich. 632; 108 N.W. 94; 7 L.R.A. (NS) 290 (1912).
29. Thomas v. Corso, 288 A. 2d 379 (Med., 1972); *Op. cit. supra*, note 26; Creighton, H.: *Law Every Nurse Should Know*, 3rd ed. Philadelphia, W. B. Saunders Co., 1975, p. 84.
30. New Biloxi Hospital v. Frazier, 146 So. 2d 882 (Miss., 1962). Creighton, H.: *Law Every Nurse Should Know*, 3rd ed. Philadelphia, W. B. Saunders Co., 1975, p. 83.
31. Garcia v. Memorial Hospital, 557 S.W. 2d 859 (Tex. Ct. of Civil Appeal, 1977); *Citation*, 36:111, Mar. 1, 1978.
32. *Cf.* Regan, W. A.: Emergency Unit Management: Legal Aspects, *Regan Rep. on Nurs. Law*, 17:1, April 1977.
33. Constant v. Howe, 436 S.W. 2d 115 (Tex., 1968).
34. Shocky v. Washington Sanitarium, 11 CCH Neg. 2d 1302. See also *Regan Rep. on Nurs. Law*, 11(11)3, April 1971.
35. James v. Turner, 201 S.W. 2d 691 (Tenn., 1942).
36. Noel v. Menninger Foundation and Albert E. McCalg, d.b.a. McCalg Plumbing Co., 299 P. 2d 38 (Kans., 1956).

37. Avey v. St. Francis Hospital, 1968 CCH Neg. 3675; *Regan Rep. on Nurs. Law,* 9(3)3, Aug. 1968.
38. Felber v. Foote, 321 F. Supp. 85 (U.S. Dist. Ct. Conn., 1970).
39. Morgan v. State, 319 N.Y.S. 2d 151 (N.Y., 1970).
40. Roy v. Hartogs, 381 N.Y.S. 2d 587 (N.Y. Sup. Ct., 1976).
41. Rogers v. Orkin, 478 F. Supp. 1342 (U.S. D.C. Mass.) 1979; Creighton, H.: Rights of Mental Patients, *Superv. Nurse,* 12:16–17, May 1981.
42. Davis v. Hubbard, 49 Law Week 2215 (U.S. D.C. N. Ohio Sept. 16, 1980).
43. O'Connor v. Donaldson, 422 U.S. 563 (U.S. C.A. 5th Cir. 1975).
44. American Nurses' Association: Statement of Functions, *Am. J. Nurs.,* 54:868–871, 994–996, 1130, 1954.
45. People ex rel. Burke v. Steinberg, 73 N.Y.S. 2d 475 (Mag. Ct. N.Y.C., 1947).
46. Thomson v. Virginia Mason Hospital, 152 Wash. 297, 277 Pac. 691 (1929).
47. Byrd v. Marion General Hospital, 202 N.C. 337, 162 N.E. 738 (1932).
48. Parrish v. Clark, 107 Fla. 598, 145 So. 848 (1933); see also Wood v. Miller, 158 Ore. 444, 76 P. 2d 963 (1938).
49. Morrison v. Henke, 165 Wis. 166, 160 N.W. 173 (1916)
50. Education Law, N.Y. Consolidated Laws Service (Issue 2, 1955) Tit. 8, Art. 131, Sec. 6512, 21, 22, 1(j).
51. Childs v. Greenville Hospital Authority, 479 S.W. 2d 399 (Texas, 1972).
52. Cortez v. Chi, 167 Cal. Rptr. 905 (Ct. of App. 4th Dist. Div. 2, 1980). Creighton, H: Telephone Orders, *Superv. Nurse,* 12:48, 52 March 1981.
53. Thomas v. Corso, 288 A. 2d 379 (Md. 1972); *Regan Rep. on Nurs. Law,* 12:3, May 1972.
54. Forestel v. United States, 261 F. Supp. 269 (1966).
55. *Cf.* Regan, W. A.: Telephone Orders and Legal Risks, *Regan Rep. On Nurs. Law,* 8(1):1, June 1967; Nursing Judgment vs. Medical Judgment, *Regan Rep. on Nurs. Law,* 9(4):1, Sept. 1968; Nurses, Diagnosis and the Law, *Regan Rep. on Nurs. Law,* 8(5):1, Oct. 1967.
56. Wisconsin Statutes, 1967, Sec. 885. 365 Recorded telephone conversations: (1) Evidence obtained as the result of the use of voice recording equipment for recording of telephone conversations, by way of interception of a communication or in any other manner, shall be totally inadmissible in the courts of this state. (2) Subsection (1) shall not apply where: (a) Such recording is made in a manner other than by interception and the person whose conversation is being recorded is informed at that time that the conversation is being recorded and that any evidence thereby obtained may be used in a court of law; or such recording is made through a recorder connector provided by the telephone public utility in accordance with its tariffs and which automatically produces a distinctive recorder tone that is repeated at intervals of approximately 15 seconds.
57. People of the State of California v. King, 72 Cal. Rptr. 478 (Cal., 1968).
58. Vannah v. Hart Private Hospital, 228 Mass. 132, 117 N. E. 328 (1917). *See also* Gray, A. W.: Protecting Patients' Property, *Mod. Hosp.,* 78:58, Feb. 1952.
59. Yohalem v. Yasuma, 165 Misc. 435, 300 N.Y.S. 929 (N.Y. City Ct., 1937).
60. 2 Rev. Stat. Maine c. 69, Sec. 7 (1954); Snelson v. Culton, 141 Me. 242, 42 A. 2d 505 (1945).
61. Creighton, H.: Nurse's Charting, Part I, *Superv. Nurse,* 11:42–43, May 1980; Creighton, H.: Nurse's Charting, Part II, *Superv. Nurse,* 11:61–62, June 1980.
62. North Miami General Hospital and Travelers Indemnity Co. v. Michael Gilbert and National Guaranty Insurance Co., 360 S. 2d 426 (Dist. Ct. App. Fla. 3rd Dist. 1978); See also Charting M.D./R.N. Communication Errors, *Regan Rep. on Nurs. Law,* 20:1, Oct. 1979.
63. Ramsey et al. v. Physician's Memorial Hospital, Inc., et al., 373 A. 2d 76 (1977).
64. Thomas H. Wagner v. Kaiser Foundation Hospitals et al., 285 Or. 81, 589 P. 2d 1106 (S. Ct. Ore. 1979). *See also* Drug Errors and Reversal Therapy: Legalities, *Regan Rep. on Nurs. Law,* 19:1, March 1979.
65. Thomas v. Corso, 265 Md. 84, 288 A. 2d 379 (1972).
66. *Standards of Nursing Practice.* Kansas City, American Nurses' Association, 1973.
67. Cooper v. National Motor Bearing Co., 136 Cal. App. 2d 229, 288 P. 2d 581, 51 A.L.R. 2d 963 (1953).
68. Garafola v. Maimonides Hospital of Brooklyn et al., 253 N.Y.S. 2d 856, aff'd 279 N.Y.S. 2d 523, 226 N.E. 311 (1967).
69. Adams v. State of Washington, 1967 CCH Neg. 1821. *Regan Rep. on Hosp. Law,* 8:3, Oct. 1967.
70. Burrell, H.: Legal Hazards of Inadequate Hospital Records, *Mod. Hosp.,* 66, 70–72, March 1946.
71. Clinical Problem . . . Unjustified Patients' Complaints, *Regan Rep. on Nurs. Law,* 11(9):4, Feb. 1971.
72. Spoar v. Fudjack, 24 A.D. 731, 263 N.Y.S. 2d 340 (1965).
73. Engle v. Clarke et al., 346 S.W. 13 (Ct. App. Ky., 1961).
74. Soto v. State, 55 Misc. 2d 1035, 286 N.Y.S. 993 (1968).
75. *Supra,* note 23.
76. Gabriel, A.: Medico-Legal Cases on Nurses' Charting, *St. Thomas Nur. J.,* 5:273–274, Dec. 1966.
77. Greyhound Corp. v. Superior Court of State of California in and for the County of Merced, 15 Cal. Rptr. 90:364 P. 2d 266 (1961).
78. Johnson v. Woman's Hospital, 527 S.W. 2d 133 (Tenn. 1975). Creighton, H.: Medical

Records, Patient Access, *Superv. Nurse,* 7:64–66, Sept. 1976.

79. Wallace v. University Hospitals of Cleveland, 164 N.E. 2d 917 (Ohio, 1959).

80. Pyramid Life Insurance Co. v. Masonic Hospital Association, 191 F. Supp. 51 (W.C. Okla., 1961). Creighton, H.: Patient's Access to His Own Medical Records, *Superv. Nurse,* 4:12, 6, May 1973.

81. Gotkin v. Miller, 379 F. Supp. 859 (U.S. D.C.—E.D. of N.Y., 1974). *See also* Regan, W. A.: Law Forum. *Hosp. Prog.* 56:40–42, March 1975.

82. Spears v. Mason, M.D., et al., 303 So. 2d 260 (La. 1974); Creighton, H.: Medical/Nursing Staff Committee Reports, *Superv. Nurse,* 6:12–13, Oct. 1975.

83. Fullerton, D. T., May, P. R. A., and White, R.: The Unusual Incident Report—A Teaching and Therapeutic Device, *J. Psychiatr. Nurs.,* 3:258–268, May-June 1965.

84. Sierra Vista Hospital v. Superior Court, 248 Cal. App. 2d 359, 56 Cal. Rptr. 387 (Cal. 1967).

85. Bernardi v. Community Hospital Assn., 166 Colo. 280, 443 P. 2d 708 (Colo. 1968). Creighton, H.: Incident Reports Subject to Discovery? *Nurs. Management,* 14:55–56, Feb. 1983.

86. Helms v. Williams, 166 S.E. 2d 852 (N.C., 1969). *See* Holder, A. R.: Negligent Selection of Hospital Staff, JAMA, 223:833–834, Feb. 12, 1973.

87. Hospital Corporation of America v. Dixon, 330 So. 2d 737 (Fla. Dist. Ct. App., 1976).

88. Ballance v. Dunnington, 241 Mich. 383, 216 N.W. 329 (1928).

89. Hebel v. Hinsdale Sanitarium and Hosp., 2 Ill. App. 2d 527, 119 N.E. 2d 506 (1954). The fact situation of this case is similar to, but not identical with, the illustration.

90. 2 *Restatement, Torts,* Sec. 463.

91. *Cf.* Dittert v. Fischer, 148 Ore. 366, 36 P. 2d 592 (1934).

92. Mayer v. Reyes & Co., 13 CCH Neg. Cases 2d 1475 (La. Ct. App., 4th Cir.) 1962.

93. Puffinberger et al. v. Day, Calif. Dist. Ct. App., No. 6845 (1963).

94. Brockman v. Harpole et al., 44 P. 2d 25 (Ore., 1968).

95. Jenkins v. Bogalusa Community Med. Center et al., 340 So. 2d 1065 (La., Dec. 20, 1976). Regan, W. A.: Law Forum, *Hosp. Prog.,* 58:29–32, Aug. 1977.

96. Davis v. Katz & Bestoff, Inc., 333 So. 2d 698 (La. Ct. App., 1976); *Citation,* 34:1–2, Oct. 15, 1976.

97. Brown v. Decatur Memorial Hospital, 367 N.E. 2d 575 (Ill. App. Ct., 1977); *Citation,* 36:43, Dec. 1, 1977.

98. 17 C.J.S. 644. *Contracts Sec. 262*: Agreements Exempting from Liability for Negligence.

99. Thompson v. Fox, 326 Pa. 209, 192 Atl. 107 (1937).

100. Wright v. Conway, 34 Wyo. 1, 242 Pac. 1107 (1926); Brox v. Omaha Maternity General Hospital, 96 Neb. 648, 148 N.W. 575 (1914).

101. McCowen v. Sisters of Most Precious Blood of Enid, 208 Okla. 130, 253 P. 2d 839 (1953).

102. Minogue v. Rutland Hospital, Inc., 119 Vt. 336, 125 A. 2d 796 (1956).

103. Meadows v. Patterson, 21 Tenn. App. 283, 108 S.W. 2d 417 (1937), 19 Tenn. L.R. 368 (1946).

104. Schloendorff v. Society of New York Hospital, 211 N.Y. 125, 105 N.E. 92 (1914).

105. *Standards.* Kansas City, American Nurses' Association, 1974.

106. Welsh v. Mercy Hospital et al., 65 Cal. App. 2d 473, 151 P. 2d 17 (1944).

107. *Op. cit.,* note 44 at page 869.

108. Brown v. St. Vincent's Hospital, 222 App. Div. 402, 226 N.Y.S., 317 (1928).

109. Canney v. Sisters of Charity of House of Providence, 15 Wash. 2d 325, 130 P. 2d 899 (1942).

110. Owen v. Williams, 322 Mass. 356, 77 N.E. 2d 318 (1948).

111. Bowers, R. D.: Legal Status of Private Duty Nurses, *Am. J. Nurs.,* 48:624–626, 1948. *See also* Hughes v. President and Directors of Georgetown College, 33 F. Supp. 867, aff'm., 130 F. 2d 810 (D.C. Circ., 1942).

112. Emory University v. Shadburn, 47 Ga. 643, 171 S.E. 192, aff'd 180 S.E. 137 (Ga., 1933). Bugalari, J. E.: Courts Put Private Duty Nurses' Blunders on Your Doorstep., *Mod. Hosp.,* 108:87–89, Jan. 1969.

113. Mautino v. Sutter Hospital Ass'n., 296 Pac. 76 (Cal., 1931).

114. Wrenn v. Hillcrest Convalescent Home, 270 N.C. 477, 154 S.E. 2d 483 (1967).

115. 203 A. 2d 511 (Pa., 1966). See also *Nursing Homes.,* 15:41, June 1966.

116. Edith Anderson Nursing Homes, Inc. v. Bettie Walker, 232 Md. 442, 194 A. 2d 85 (1963).

117. Regan, W. A.: OR Nursing Law. *AORN J.,* 26:978, 981, Nov. 1977.

118. Standards: *Community Health Nursing Practice.* Kansas City, American Nurses' Association,, 1973, p. 3.

119. Scofield v. Strain, Mayor et al., State *ex rel.,* Reilly v. Hamrock, Mayor et al., 142 Ohio St. 290, 51 N.E. 2d 1012 (1943).

120. McCarthy v. Maxon, 134 Conn. 170, 55 A. 2d 912 (1947).

121. 417 P. 231 (Colo., 1966).

122. State v. Hyde, 158 N.W. 2d 134 (Iowa, 1968).

123. Stefanik v. Nursing Educational Committee, 37 A. 2d 661 (R.I., 1944).

124. Regan, W. A.: Clinical Problem—Public Health Nursing, *Regan Rep. on Nurs. Law,* 5(11):4, April 1965.

125. *Ibid.*

126. Davis v. Wyeth Laboratories, Inc. and American Home Products Corp., 399 F. 2d 121 (Ct. App., 9th Cir., 1968).

127. Brune v. Belinkoff, 235 N.E. 2d 793 (Mass., 1968).

128. Fillmore, A.: The Visiting Nurse Service

and the Law, *Nurs. Outlook*, 12:28–32, June 1964, p. 30.

129. Sadler v. Draper, 46 Tenn. App. 1, 326 S.W. 2d 148 (1959).

130. Hoppe v. State of Iowa, 289 N.W. 2d 613 (S. Ct. Iowa, 1980).

131. Minnesota Public Interest Research Group v. Minnesota Department of Labor and Industry et al., 249 N.W. 2d 437 (S. Ct. Minn. 1976).

132. Regan, W. A.: Public Health Nursing: Child Custody Proceedings, *Regan Rep. Nurs. Law*, 21:4, July 1980.

133. Swett v. Vermont State College, 448 A. 2d 150 (Vt. S. Ct. 1982). See also *In re* Esther Swett, 4 Vt. Lab. Rel. Bd. Op. 98 (1981). Creighton, H.: Education of Instructors, *Nurs. Management*, 14:48–49, May 1983.

134. Precedent-Setting Ruling Favors Michigan Nurse, *Am. J. Nurs.*, 78:558, 583, April 1978.

135. Wemmett v. Mount, 134 Ore. 305, 292 Pac. 93 (1930).

136. Hallinan v. Prindle, 220 Cal. 46, 11 P. 2d 426 (modified); 17 Cal. Ap. 2d 656, 29 P. 2d 202 (rev'd); 69 P. 2d 1075 (aff'm in part, rev'd in part, 1936).

137. Kelly v. Yount, 338 Pa. 190, 12 A. 2d 579 (1940).

138. Delany v. Rosenthal, 347 Mass. 143 81 A. 2d 547, 196 N.E. 2d 878 (1964).

139. Crowe v. Provost, 52 Tn Apeals 397, 374 S.W. 2d 645 (1963).

140. Thompson v. Brent, 245 So. 2d 751 (La., 1971).

141. Brockman v. Harpole et al., 444 P. 2d 25 (Ore., 1968).

142. Biggs, B.: Nurse-Clinician-Practitioner-Assistant-Associate, *Am. J. Nurs.*, 71:1936, Oct. 1971.

143. Naccarato v. Grob, 180 N.W. 2d 788 (Mich., 1970).

144. Stahlin v. Hilton Hotels Corp. 484 F. 2d 580 (C.C.A. 7, 1973); *Citation*, 28:117–118, Feb. 1, 1974.

145. Hudak, C. M., et al.: *Critical Care Nursing*. Philadelphia, J. B. Lippincott Co., 1973, p. 1.

146. Barnett, F. J.: Micturition Death, *MXR*, 1(5)7, Dec., 1971. *N. Engl. J. Med.*, 281:31, 1969.

147. Whipple, G. H., et al.: *Acute Coronary Care*. Boston, Little, Brown and Co., 1972, p. 97.

148. *Ibid.*

149. *Op. cit.*, note 147, p. 178.

150. Laidlaw v. Lion Gate Hospital, 70 W.W.R. 727 (1969).

151. Hershey, N.: Prudence and the Coffee Break, *Am. J. Nurs.*, 70:2389, Nov. 1970.

152. Negligence in the Recovery Room, *Can. Nurse*, 66:26, July 1970.

153. Regan, W. A.: Post-Surgical Nursing and the Law, *Regan Rep. on Nurs. Law*, 13:1, Oct. 1972.

154. Peacock v. Piper, 504 P. 2d 1124 (Wash. 1973). Regan, W. A.: Law Forum, *Hosp. Prog.*, 54:12–13, June 1973.

155. Hunt v. Gerber, 16 CCH Neg. Cases 2d 1250, Fla., 1963. Hayt, E.: Hospitals and the Law, *Hosp. Man.*, 98:20, Nov. 1964.

156. Regan, W. A.: Clinical Problems, *Regan Rep. Nurs. Law*, 10:4, May 1970.

157. *Supra*, note 45.

158. See Regan, W. A.: Surgical Nursing—Current Trends, *Regan Rep. on Nurs. Law*, 6(11):1, April 1966.

159. Barber v. Reiking, 411 P. 2d 861 (Wash., 1966). The court said: "In accordance with the public policy of this state, one who undertakes to perform the services of a trained or graduate nurse must have the knowledge and skill possessed by a registered nurse."

160. Baidach v. Linden General Hospital. *Regan Rep. on Nurs. Law*, 2(1):3, June 1961.

161. Granite Home v. Schwartz, 364 S.W. 2d 309 (Ark., 1973).

162. Frazier v. New Biloxi Hospital, 182 So. 372 (Miss., 1967).

163. Emory University v. Shadburn, 180 S.E. 137 (Ga., 1933).

164. Joseph v. W. H. Groves Latter-day Saints Hospital et al., 318 P. 2d 330 (Utah, 1957).

165. Neel v. San Antonio Community Hospital, 1 Cal. Rptr. 313 (1959).

166. Ray v. Tucson Medical Center, 230 P. 2d 220 (Ariz., 1951).

167. Bernard v. Gravois, 20 So. 2d 181 (Ct. App. La., 1944).

168. Hialeah Hospital, Inc. v. Johnson, 268 So. 2d 424 (Fla., 1972).

169. *Supra*, Note 166.

170. Boie-Hansen v. Sisters of Charity, 314 P. 2d 189 (Calif., 1957).

171. Adkins v. St. Francis Hospital of Charleston, W. Va., 143 S.E. 2d 154 (W. Va., 1965).

172. St. John's Hospital and School of Nursing of Tulsa v. Chapman, 1967 CCH Neg. 1586 (Okla., 1967).

173. Hyland v. St. Mark's Hospital, 1967 CCH Neg. 1442 (Utah, 1967).

174. Clovis v. Hartford Accident, 223 S. 178 (La., 1969).

175. Hayes v. Mashikan, 333 N.Y.S. 2d 862 (N.Y., 1972).

176. Hagen v. Civil Service Board, 164 N.W. 2d 629 (Minn., 1969).

177. Duncan v. Queen of Angels Hospital, 90 Cal. Rptr. 157 (Cal., 1970).

178. Elliott v. Tempkin et al., 1969 CCH Neg. 4641.

179. Powell v. Parkview Estate Nursing Home, Inc., 240 So. 2d 53 (La., 1970).

180. Cleaver v. Dade County, 272 So. 2d 559 (Fla., 1973); *Citation*, 27:57, June 1, 1973.

181. Johnson v. Grant Hospital, 286 N.E. 2d 308 (Ohio, 1972).

182. Hansen v. Downey Community Hospital (Cal. Super. Ct. Los Angeles Co., Docket No. SWC 2811, July 31, 1973); *Citation*, 28:121–122, Feb. 1, 1974.

183. Miller et ux. v. Mohr et al., 198 Wash. 619, 89 P. 2d 807, 105 P. 2d 32 (1939).

184. Lesnik, M. J., and Anderson, B. E.: *Nursing*

Practice and the Law, 2nd ed. Philadelphia, J. B. Lippincott Co., 1955, pp. 270–271.

185. Regan, W. A.: Your Legal Liability When Supervising, *RN*, 32:44, 68, Jan. 1969.

186. *Cf.* Hershey, N.: Student, Instructor, and Liability, *Am. J. Nurs.*, 65:122–123, March 1965.

187. Hewett v. Woman's Hospital Aid Assn., 73 N.H. 556, 64 A 190 (1906); Bernstein v. Beth Israel Hospital, 236 N.Y. 268, 140 N.E. 694 (1923).

188. Christensen v. Des Moines Still College of Osteopathy, 82 N.W. 2d 741 (Iowa, 1957).

189. Norfolk Protestant Hospital v. Plunket, 173 S.E. 363 (Va., 1934).

190. Kapuschinsky v. United States, 248 F. Supp. 732 (U.S. D.C., S.C., 1966).

191. Davis v. Southeastern Community College, 424 F. Supp. 1341 (U.S. D.C., E.D. N.C. 1976); Creighton, H: Nursing Students as Litigators, *Nurs. Management*, 13:63–64, Oct. 1982.

192. Doris G. Nuttelman v. Case Western Reserve University et al., 560 F. Supp. 1 (U.S. D.C. Ohio, 1981). Creighton, H.: Right of Nursing Student to Pursue Higher Degree, *Nurs. Management*, 14:16–17, Dec. 1983.

193. Mahavongsanan v. Hall et al., 529 F. 2d 448 (5th Cir. 1976).

194. Hubbard v. John Tyler Community College, 455 F. Supp. 753 (U.S. D.C., E.D. Va. 1978).

195. Lyons v. Salve Regina College, 565 F. 2d 200 (U.S. Ct. App. 1st Cir. 1978).

196. Board of Curators v. Horowitz, 98 S. Ct. 948, 435 U.S. 78, 55 L. Ed. 124 (U.S. S. Ct. 1978); Creighton, H.: Students' Unsatisfactory Clinical Performance, *Nurs. Management*, 13:47–49, Feb. 1982.

197. Grimard v. Carlston et al., 567 F. 2d 1171 (U.S. Ct. App. 1st Cir. 1978).

198. Corso v. Creighton University, 731 F. 2d 529 (C.A. 8, Neb. 1984).

199. University of Texas Health Science Center at Houston v. Babb, 646 S.W. 2d 502 (Tex. Ct. of App. 1982); rehearing denied 1983.

200. Jones v. Board of Governors of the University of North Carolina, 704 F. 2d 713 (C.A. 4, N.C. 1983); *Citation*, 48:24, Nov. 1, 1983.

201. Brookins v. Bonnell, 362 F. Supp. 379 (Pa. 1973).

202. White v. Knowlton, 361 F. Supp. 445 (N.Y. 1973).

203. Paine v. Board of Regents, etc., 355 F. Supp. 199 (Tex. 1972).

204. Piphus v. Carey, 545 F. 2d (U.S. Ct. of App. 7th Cir. Ill. 1976).

205. Pride v. Howard University, 384 A. 2d 31 (D.C. Ct. of App. 1978).

206. Tedeschi v. Wagner College, 402 N.Y.S. 2d 967 (S. Ct. Richmond Ct. N.Y. 1978).

207. Jansen v. Emory University, 440 F. Supp. 1060 (D.C. Ga. 1977).

208. Gay Students Organization v. Bonner, 367 F. Supp. 1088 (N.H. 1974).

209. Gay Alliance of Students v. Matthews, 544 F. 2d 162 (U.S. Ct. of App. 4th Cir. 1976).

210. Harris v. Warde, 235 N.Y.S. 2d 283 (N.Y. Sup. Ct. 1977).

211. Donohue v. Copiaque Union Free School District, 407 N.Y.S. 2d 874 (N.Y. Sup. Ct. App. Div. 1978).

212. Wright v. Wilson Memorial Hospital, Inc., 226 S. E. 2d (N.C. Ct. App., 1976); *Citation*, 34:35, Nov. 15, 1976.

213. Robbins v. Mad River Community Hospital (Cal. Super. Ct. Humboldt Co. Docket No. 54275, 1976); *Citation*, 34:30, Nov. 15, 1976.

214. Antoine v. Dept. of Public Health, 108 Cal. Rptr. 689 (Cal. Ct. App. 1973); Citation, 29:32, May 1, 1974.

General References

Annas, G. J.: The Law of Emergency Care, *Nurses Law Ethics*, 3:5 + , June/July 1981.

Annas, G. J.: The Registered Nurse and Aid in Emergency, *Aust. Nurses J.*, 9(9)75–76, April 1980.

Bennett, H. M.: The Legal Liabilities of Critical Care: The Good Samaritan Act, *Crit. Care Nurse*, 3:24, May/June 1983.

Bernstein, A. H.: Medical and Nursing Students v. Their Schools, *Hospitals*, 56:98–102, April 1, 1982.

Bowyer, E. A.: The Liability of the Occupational Health Nurse, *Law, Med. & Health Care*, 11:224–226, Oct. 1983.

Cohn, S. D.: Legal Issues in School Nursing Practice, *Law, Med. & Health Care*, 12:219–221, Oct. 1984.

Creighton, H.: Nurse's Charting—Part I, *Superv. Nurse*, 11:42–43, May 1980.

Creighton, H.: Nurse's Charting—Part II, *Superv. Nurse*, 11:61–62, June 1980.

Creighton, H.: Telephone Orders, *Superv. Nurse*, 12:48, 52 March 1981.

Creighton, H.: Students' Unsatisfactory Clinical Performance, *Nurs. Management*, 13:47–49, Feb. 1982.

Creighton, H.: Nursing Students as Litigators, *Nurs. Management*, 13:63–64, Oct. 1982.

Creighton, H.: Incident Reports Subject to Discovery? *Nurs. Management*, 14:55–57, Feb. 1983.

Creighton, H.: Education of Instructors, *Nurs. Management*, 14:48–49, May 1983.

Creighton, H.: Right of Nursing Student to Pursue Higher Degree, *Nurs. Management*, 14:16–17, Dec. 1983.

Creighton, H.: Patient Teaching, *Nurs. Management*, 16:15–20, Jan. 1985.

Creighton, H.: Occupational Health Nurse's Liability, *Nurs. Management*, 16:49, 52–53, Feb. 1985.

Cushing, M.: An Occupational Nurse's Liability, *Am. J. Nursing*, 81:2207, Dec. 1981.

Cushing, M.: Gaps in Documentation, *Am. J. Nursing*, 82:1899–1900, Dec. 1982.

Finch, J.: Law and the Nurse 7: The Law and the Learner, *Nurs. Mirror*, 153(3)34–35, July 15, 1981.

Greenlaw, J.: Documentation of Patient Care: An

Often Underestimated Responsibility, *Law, Med. & Health Care,* 10:172–174, Sept. 1982.

Groat, L. et al.: Your Responsibility in Documenting Care, *AORN J.,* 37:1174+, May 1983.

Horsley, J. E.: Charting Nasty Truths with an Absence of Malice, *R.N.,* 46:16, July 1983.

Langslow, A.: Medical Records—A Few Problems in Confidentiality, *Aust. Nurses J.,* 11:39–41, June 1982.

Murphy, E.: Documenting OR Nursing Care, *Today's OR Nurse,* 5:47–48, May 1983.

Philpott, M.: *Legal Liability and the Nursing Process.* Toronto, W. B. Saunders Co., 1985.

Podratz, R. O.: A Student Nurse Sues, *Am. J. Nursing,* 80:1604–1605, Sept. 1980.

Poteet, G. W., and Pollack, C. S.: When a Student Fails Clinical, *Am. J. Nursing,* 81:1889–1890, Oct. 1981.

Regan, W. A.: Surgeons Who Edit Nurse's Notes Are Out of Line, *AORN J.,* 31:78–79, Jan. 1980.

Regan, W. A.: Record Keeping Requirements for Orthopedic Implants, *AORN J.,* 21:230+, Feb. 1980.

Regan, W. A.: Will Documenting Problems Jeopardize Physicians, Hospital? *AORN J.,* 31:881+, April 1980.

Regan, W. A.: Charting: Importance of Nurse's Notes, *Regan Rep. Nurs. Law,* 20(12)1, May 1980.

Shaeffer, M. S.: Legally Speaking: To Avoid a Lawsuit Keep the Record Straight, *R.N.,* (11)81–84, Nov. 1981.

Seven
NEGLIGENCE
AND
MALPRACTICE

This chapter describes a variety of cases involving negligence or malpractice in the field of nursing so that nurses may know the basis of some claims against them.

DEFINITION OF NEGLIGENCE AND MALPRACTICE

Negligence has been defined as the omission to do something that a reasonable person, guided by those considerations that ordinarily regulate human affairs, would do, or as doing something that a reasonable and prudent person would not do.[1]

Malpractice has been defined as any professional misconduct, unreasonable lack of skill or fidelity in professional or judiciary duties, evil practice or illegal or immoral conduct.[2] Moreover, nurses should understand the meaning of malpractice as it applies to physicians, i.e., bad, wrong or injudicious treatment resulting in injury, unnecessary suffering or death to the patient, and proceeding from ignorance, carelessness, want of proper professional skill, disregard of established rules or principles, neglect or a malicious or criminal intent.[3] Since nurses are closely associated with physicians, and since malpractice suits are indeed numerous, if nurses understand the nature of the problem and the acts of commission or omission that give rise to the suits, they may the better cooperate with physicians and others in minimizing the difficulty. In a previous chapter, the matter of the completeness and accuracy of records demonstrated how helpful the nurse could and should be in this regard.

A tenured teacher was discharged after a hearing by the board in which he was found guilty of "immorality" in having made advances to female students.[4] The court held that the statute permitted discharge for "immorality" and "other good and just cause" and that it was not unduly vague or overbroad, since a teacher could be expected to know what actions would fall within its meaning.

141

Although the specification of charges used the term "unprofessional conduct" and did not mention "immorality," the court ruled that the teacher had been adequately apprised of the charges, which included an exact description of the alleged improper conduct.

Poor public relations is the leading cause of lawsuits, according to the Medical Malpractice Commission. The nurse's attention is called to the fact that malpractice suits generally come from patients who have poor results from treatment. Friendly patients who feel that nurses and doctors have done their best are not likely to sue. Hence, the need for tactful handling of patients who are dissatisfied with their care and progress should be evident to a nurse. Moreover, since nurses may spend more time than physicians in rendering care to patients, their handling of patients and families may be of great importance. The way they relate to these people may make the difference between a suit and refusal to sue a physician for malpractice.

Generally, suits based on negligence or malpractice are brought in civil courts to recover damages for the injuries claimed. However, when the negligence or malpractice amounts to wanton and reckless conduct or shows a disregard of human life, the law regards it as criminal and the action is handled in criminal courts. Discussion and illustration of the latter classification are reserved for the next chapter.

Malpractice claims give rise to such questions as whether or not the nurse is solely responsible for the alleged act, omission or other wrongs, and how the physician and hospital are implicated, if at all. A point for the nurse to remember is that, in states in which the governmental or voluntary charitable institution is exempt from liability, injured patients have only the nurse, doctor or other individual from whom they may seek to recover damages for an alleged, negligently caused injury.

LIABILITY FOR NEGLIGENCE/STANDARD OF CARE

Everyone has a duty to behave as a reasonably prudent person would act in similar circumstances. This means that individuals must handle themselves and their property so as to avoid injury to the person or property of others. In a civil action for damages based on negligence, the person sued must have done or failed to do some act that he or she was under a duty to do, and there must be an injury to the person bringing suit that can be traced directly to the breach of this duty. For example, in New York, a parent sued a physician and a hospital for damages for mental pain and suffering caused by alleged negligence, carelessness and breach of contract. In this case, the acts complained of were that the father was told that his child, born in the hospital, was a girl, but later was told that the child was a boy. The court dismissed the action on the grounds that, in the absence of physical injury, the complaint was not sufficient to state a cause of action in tort. Also, it failed to state a cause of action for breach of contract.[5] Even though this action was dismissed, the fact that a legal action was brought will tend to make busy nurses, who frequently handle inquiries concerning patients over the telephone or in person, attentive both to their replies and to the person to whom they are addressed.

In one case, a mother being discharged from the hospital following childbirth was given an infant purported to be her own. Some time later, the parents discovered that the nurse had given them the wrong baby. They brought the error to the hospital's attention and were given another child who, the hospital stated, was their baby. The parents were denied a recovery of damages.[6] Although the court agreed that the action complained of was negligence, still, in the absence of proof of any physical suffering, an award was not permitted for mental suffering alone.

When an 89-year-old patient in a nursing home died from pneumonia caused by the ingestion of kerosene, a verdict against the nursing home for damages for his death was upheld.[7]

The parents of a boy recovered in excess of a quarter of a million dollars in damages against a hospital for the negligence of the nurses that resulted in injuries to their child at birth.[8] Specifically, they charged that nurses in the hospital's delivery room in 1957 had delayed the baby's birth by pressing a towel against his head until an obstetrician arrived. As a result, they claimed, oxygen to the baby's brain was cut off; he is retarded and will require special care for life.

Hospital nurses were cleared in the death of a patient from pulmonary edema shortly after a blood transfusion was completed, in a case in which the attending physician set the amount of blood to be administered at 1000 ml, started the procedure and set the stopcock at the desired rate of flow. The nurses kept the patient under observation for five to 15 minutes.[9]

The New York and California courts have allowed recovery of damages for mental anguish. In 1959, a patient collected $15,000 for cancerphobia resulting from a physician's warning that a radiation burn might lead eventually to cancer. A California mother who was seven months' pregnant when she saw an ice truck run over her small son was severely shocked, and received damages when the court said:

> No immutable rule calls for physical impact to justify recovery for emotional distress.[10]

However, in another suit against a doctor and hospital for psychic injury because of alleged erroneous diagnosis and treatment, the case was dismissed.[11] The diagnosis was that an arrested pulmonary tuberculosis condition had become active, and that the germs were in the stomach and might have reached the intestine. The patient claimed he had undergone unnecessary chemotherapy. He was well at the time of trial, and the court felt that the doctor's error (if he was in error) was understandable, if not an error of judgment.

Negligence and related problems in the operating room are discussed monthly by Murphy in the *AORN Journal*.

A nurse anesthetist who was assisting at a cesarean section slipped on blood and tissue and fell, breaking three previous spinal fusions. She sued, claiming that the hospital and circulating nurse were negligent in not cleaning the floor. However, the hospital was not held liable since the circulating nurse could not stop her other duties during a critical part of the operation to wipe the floor, and the nurse anesthetist, who was not sterile at the time, could have wiped the floor.[12]

The Supreme Court of Michigan ruled that the statute of limitations for malpractice does not bar an action for negligence of registered nurses. Following a heart attack, a patient was given injections of an anticoagulant drug that caused swelling, discoloration and disability of his arms. The court found that the three-year statute of limitations applicable to negligence by a nurse was also applicable to the employer, whose liability was based on the doctrine of *respondeat superior*.[13]

COMMON ACTS OF NEGLIGENCE

Foreign Objects Left in Patients

One of the most common acts of negligence in surgical cases in the past has been the overlooked sponge. Either nurses failed to make a check on the number of sponges or there was an error in their sponge count, and the surgeon closed the incision with a sponge or sponges left inside the patient. As a result, infections and delayed recoveries or even death ensued, and then there would be actions for damages for negligence.

In a California case in which a sponge was left in a patient and the surgeon neither counted the sponges himself nor required a nurse to do so, the charitable hospital was held not liable for the acts of the nurses, since they were under the control of the surgeon. However, the surgeon was liable for the negligent act.[14]

On the other hand, in another case, an action was brought against a nursing student and others for damages relating to a patient's death. In this case, a student nurse simply passed out sponges to a surgeon during the operation, but did not count them afterward. A supervising nurse was responsible for the sponge count at the conclusion of the operation, and reported that the count was correct, when in fact a sponge had been left in the patient. The nursing student was held not liable, but the supervising nurse was held liable.[15]

Out of an award of $36,000, a scrub nurse and a circulating nurse had to pay $4000 apiece in a case in which a laparotomy sponge was left in a patient during abdominal surgery although they had reported the sponge count correct.[16] Since the surgeon had ordered the metal rings removed from the sponges, which was a safeguard provided by the employer, he became the nurses' special employer during the surgery and was liable with them.

In a sponge count error during a cholecystectomy performed on an air freight handler, in a total verdict of $12,500 for the patient, 65 percent was assessed against the defendant surgeon and 35 percent against the nurses employed by the hospital.[17]

A patient underwent a successful operation to remove three-fourths of his stomach. However, it was discovered that a needle had been left in his stomach, and a second operation was necessary to remove it. The appellate court ruled that the patient was entitled to recover damages from the surgeon, his assistant, the hospital's surgical resident and the hospital, but the operating room supervisor was not held liable. The court said,

> Every defendant in whose custody the plaintiff (Bowers) was placed for any period of time was bound to exercise ordinary care to see that no unnecessary harm came to him and each would be liable for failure in this regard.

The operating room supervisor was not liable because she had assigned two competent nurses to the operation, was not present at the operation nor at any other place with the plaintiff and had no control over him.[18]

Burns

Along with missing sponges, at the head of the list of negligent acts frequently charged to nurses, are burns of one kind or another from hot water bottles, heating pads, inhalators, contact with steam pipes, radiators, scalding hot water, douches, sitz baths, sweat cabinets and solutions that are either too hot or of improper concentration for the purpose. Nurses, notwithstanding the stage of their training, may be liable for certain acts. It does not require a technical education to know that very hot objects burn persons. Consequently, if a nursing student with only a little professional education and training or a practical nurse were to fill a hot water bottle with excessively hot water and place it against an unconscious person causing a burn, she or he would in all likelihood be deemed liable for such an act. In other words, it is questionable whether an ordinary nurse of similar training using due care in such circumstances would thus burn a patient with a hot water bottle; if not, the nurse who did burn a patient is liable for her or his failure to use that degree of care.

When a patient sustained a third-degree burn because a surgeon placed a hot metal gag in her mouth during a tonsillectomy, a verdict in favor of the surgeon and instrument nurse, but against the hospital, was returned by the jury. According to testimony, it was the duty of the circulating nurse to have available a basin of water for cooling instruments after their sterilization, and its negligent omission was the cause of the accident.[19]

A patient, who was paralyzed, could not remove his pipe from his mouth safely and had a speech impediment, was left alone while smoking his pipe, which fell from his mouth, set fire to the bed and resulted in serious burns. He received a judgment against the hospital.[20] Nurses have a duty to protect the patient from any known danger.

The court ruled that the government was liable to the administratrix of the estate of an 83-year-old patient who was senile, generally non compos mentis and suffering from a possible cerebral vascular accident when he was burned while in the bathtub at an Army hospital.[21] The injuries were caused by the negligence of hospital employees in allowing scalding water to stand in the hot water pipe leading directly into the bathtub, and in the course of a struggle with the attendant assisting him from the tub, the patient had accidentally turned on the hot water.

A paying patient in a hospital conducted for profit by a municipality in Oklahoma recovered damages for injuries due to burns caused by a hot enema negligently administered by a registered nurse.[22]

In a case in Virginia, $13,000 damages were awarded to a woman patient for burns of tissue caused by negligence in injecting dye into a vein before taking x-rays, and in applying a hot water bottle that resulted in a partial disability of the patient's arm and in physical and neurotic ailments that might never improve. The intern and nurse were held to be employees of the hospital and not independent contractors. Both were considered to be working directly under the hospital's supervision and control, and acting on behalf of the hospital. The court distinguished no substantial difference in their relation to the patient.[23]

The hospital was not exempt from liability in an Oklahoma case in which a nurse burned a patient by placing an unguarded lamp globe on her body without direction, but while in the presence of a physician. In this case, the physician was working directly over the patient immediately after an operation, attempting to save her from heart failure. The emergency required all his attention, and it was necessary to leave the other details of postoperative care to the nurse.[24]

On the other hand, when a patient was instructed in the operation of an electric heating pad and successfully operated it for three days, neither the nurse nor the hospital were held liable for burns caused by the pad when the patient went to sleep while the current was turned on. Here, the nurse could plead contributory negligence as a defense to the patient's claim.[25]

When a nurse placed a steam vaporizer on the side of the bed where the bathroom was located and a patient tripped over it and was injured, the court held that negligence could be inferred from the nurse's failure to put the vaporizer on the opposite side of the bed.[26] The nurse is required to use reasonable judgment in carrying out a doctor's order.

A cautery machine had malfunctioned, so a nurse checked it. Thereafter it was used during a hemorrhoidectomy, and the patient was burned on the chest where the electrode was placed. In the patient's suit against the surgeon for damages, the court said he was not negligent and pointed out that the hospital owned the machine and that the operating room nurses, not the surgeons, were trained to set it up. The court held that, when technical equipment and personnel to man it are furnished by the hospital, the doctrine of *respondeat superior*, by which a surgeon is held to be the "captain of the ship," does not apply. Although the hospital in this case would have been liable, it was not a party defendant.[27]

A patient undergoing surgery on a rectal fissure had benzalkonium chloride applied to the area. It dripped onto the drapes, which caught fire when cautery was used, with the result that the patient was badly burned. A verdict was returned against the hospital, which was liable for the nurse's negligence in failing to remove drapes when she should have known they were soaked.[28] Similarly, in a case involving burns on the patient's breast when too much disinfectant had been applied to her skin and ignited on contact with cautery, the court found the surgeon not liable for the nurse's negligence since he was not obliged to supervise something as elementary as the application of disinfectant.[29]

Falls

Possibly next in frequency are suits for damages against nurses and hospitals by patients who have fallen out of bed and as a result suffered injuries. Sometimes the patient may be one who is allowed to get up, but who falls while getting out of a high hospital bed. Accidents of this kind often occur with elderly persons, those who have had sedatives, postoperative patients who have not fully recovered from anesthesia, blind persons, semiconscious persons or sufferers from dizziness.

Side-rails and other restraints, when ordered, prevent or reduce the hazard of such falls. It would almost seem unnecessary to say that, when unconscious or partially conscious patients are returned to their beds after an operation, in the absence of a qualified attendant giving constant attention, the side-rails should be put up immediately. Such a precautionary measure is at times neglected, and this in turn leads to falls, injuries and lawsuits for resulting damages. In some hospitals, it is routine to place side-rails on the beds of all postoperative or irrational patients, and at night on the beds of all patients who are over 65 or under six years of age. In New York, it is considered an administrative act, and the hospital is liable if a nurse fails to carry out the instructions of a physician to use side-rails as a precaution for the patient's protection against falling from bed.[30] Certainly, delirious patients need side-rails and constant care to prevent accidents.

In recent cases, courts are finding that hospitals have a duty to take reasonable precautions in order to safeguard patients who are likely to injure themselves. Full-length side-rails on both sides of the bed probably are needed for the elderly, the debilitated, the very obese, post-surgical patients, the confused, the heavily sedated or those for whom side-rails would be added protection. Any omission of side-rails, when the patient's condition would seem to warrant it, must be on the written order of the attending physician.[31]

A patient was hospitalized for surgery and a skin graft to her hand and was given a postoperative injection for pain. Because a nurse raised the railing only on the left side of the bed, the patient sustained multiple injuries when she fell in the bathroom. The patient was awarded $14,623 when the court ruled that the hospital employees had breached their duty to the patient and that such breach was the proximate cause of her injuries.[32]

A nurse attending a mother during labor negligently failed to summon an intern in sufficient time for delivery, and the resident seemingly misunderstood the urgency of the call. As the result of a fall, the baby suffered a birth injury, and the parents recovered substantial damages on behalf of the infant girl.[33]

Several days after surgery, a 93-year-old patient fell from a hospital bed and fractured her hip. She was awarded damages for the hospital's failure to protect her from falling out of bed.[34]

A substantial verdict was rendered in behalf of a patient known to have neurologic problems who fell and sustained serious injuries when she was unattended and became dizzy in the hallway en route from the bathroom during the night.[35]

A verdict for damages was reversed in a case in which a patient failed to show that a fall from the examining table in the emergency room of the hospital was due to negligence of the hospital.[36] The patient had been brought to the emergency room following a heart attack. She could not prove that she had been unconscious when left unattended. There was some evidence that she was conscious and had been secured to the table by a belt, and that the side-rails of the table had been raised.

An award of $115,000 to a widow for the wrongful death of her husband was not excessive in a case in which the hospital's technicians had left the patient alone on an x-ray table when he was in a sleepy, tired and dazed condition and under the influence of drugs.[37] The court held that the technicians should have foreseen that the patient, who was complaining of nausea, would attempt to go to the bathroom and would be likely to injure himself in so doing because of the effect of the drugs.

A judgment for injuries sustained in a fall from bed was affirmed for a 73-year-old man who suffered a heart attack and was taken to the defendant hospital. His daughter testified that he was "dazed" and "didn't know where he was."[38] The court held that the jury could find that the patient's conduct was a result of drugs or a mental condition caused by the heart attack, and not a result of his conscious volition.

How long a patient may be safely left alone by the nurses depends on the facts of each case. A woman was given three grains of Tuinal, Phenergan and 50 mg of Demerol and scopolamine before delivery and 2 ml of 2× Deladumone afterward, and was left alone in a private room for an hour and five minutes, during which time she fell out of bed and was injured. The court took the view that the patient was not alert owing to heavy sedation and was not properly attended.[39]

An award of damages for pain and suffering was affirmed against a nursing home when a frail 77-year-old bedridden patient fell from her bed and was injured. The accident occurred about 10:30 P.M., and the patient was found a few minutes later by the nurse on duty who, with the assistance of an aide, placed the patient back in bed and raised the side-rails. In making out her report the nurse noted that the patient suffered abrasions and cuts on her face, but apparently suffered no serious injuries, and added, "does not complain of pain—hard to determine." The trial judge concluded from the testimony of other witnesses on the staff that the side-rails of the patient's bed were down at the time of the accident, and a night table, which usually stood close to her bed to prevent her from falling, was not in its customary position. After the fall, pain medications were administered at 12:10 A.M., 12:30 A.M., and 4:00 A.M., at which time the nurse noted that the patient's left foot and ankle appeared swollen. When the registered nurse came on duty at 7 A.M. the next morning, she determined that the patient's leg was broken above the ankle and called the doctor. The patient's daughter brought the action to recover damages from the nursing home after her mother died several weeks later from other causes.[40]

A judgment in favor of a patient's visitor was affirmed by the Arkansas Supreme Court when she opened a door out over stairs and fell. The hospital exit had no landing on the same level, and people had to step down immediately to the first step. The court ruled that the hospital's failure to install a platform that was as wide as the door and that extended out to a distance equal to the width of the door, so as to conform to the state health department regulations, was evidence of negligence.[41] Nurses who worked on this floor and knew the hazard such a doorway presented, and also the safety engineer, should have warned hospital administration of the danger and sought to eliminate it.

An unescorted 53-year-old patient suffering from severe hypertension and cerebral arterial spasms went to the bathroom on the fourth morning of her hospital stay, and became ill and faint. She fell to the floor and, after an undetermined length of time, made her way back to her bed. While unconscious on the bathroom floor, she sustained a severe burn on her arm and back caused by an uncovered steam radiator that produced a temperature of 208°F to 281°F. The Minnesota Supreme Court held that questions of whether a foreseeable risk existed which created a duty that the hospital breached, and whether the hot radiator was so located and the facilities so designed as to present a danger to ill and infirm patients, were questions for a jury to decide.[42]

A patient suffering from pneumonitis was admitted to the hospital acutely ill, feverish, lacking in coordination and with blurred vision. He was placed in a private room that had a small balcony with a railing 2 or 3 feet high. Not long before the subsequent accident, he was seen on the balcony calling for a ladder from construction workers, who notified hospital personnel. The nurse returned the disoriented patient to his room, placed a Posey belt and cloth wristlets on him and notified his physician, who told the nurse to keep an eye on him. The nurse then called the patient's wife at her place of work to come and sit with him, as none of the hospital staff was free to do so. The wife told the nurse she would call her mother and ask her to go to the hospital immediately, and asked the nurse to have someone watch him until her mother arrived. However, the patient fell from the balcony just before his mother-in-law arrived. The New York appellate court affirmed a judgment for the plaintiff, finding the hospital negligent in failing to supervise the patient until the arrival of his mother-in-law.[43]

A 76-year-old patient who was debilitated from loss of blood, disoriented and sedated fell out of her hospital bed. In a suit to recover damages on the grounds that she had not been properly restrained or provided with adequate nursing supervision, the jury decided against the patient. It was necessary to present evidence as to the proper application of a restraint and proper nurse supervision.[44]

In a suit against a nursing home, $25,000 was awarded to an 82-year-old patient who suffered injuries and $7500 was awarded to her conservator on claims of breach of contract, negligence and fraud. The patient, who was senile and mentally incompetent but could walk with assistance at the time she entered the home, stopped walking during her stay and developed leg contractures and sores on one hip. When she was transferred to a new nursing home, a nurse requested an x-ray examination, which showed the patient to have a broken hip. It was alleged that the first nursing home negligently permitted the patient to fall and break her hip, and court made the awards as described.[45]

Under the Federal Torts Claims Act, a patient who suffered injuries after a practical nurse in a VA hospital sent him to a laboratory unassisted was awarded $12,000.[46] The patient had entered the hospital because of a knee problem. Prior to the accident, a sign was placed on his bed forbidding unassisted ambulation. However, he said that, despite his protest, the nurse ordered him to go to the laboratory unassisted. The patient eventually required amputation of his little finger as a result of his fall.

Failure to Observe and Take Appropriate Action

Nurses who disregard a mother's pleas and who fail to observe and evaluate a child's condition and secure timely medical assistance may make the hospital liable for actionable negligence.[47] There was testimony that a 13-year-old rheumatic fever patient was coughing almost constantly, that her nails turned blue and that her heart pounded until the mattress shook over a six-hour period, while the distraught mother's pleas for help brought little except personal reprimands. Eventually, when the supervisor of nurses found the mother crying in a hallway and hurried to the child's room, the physician in charge of the patient was summoned. Despite intensive care and the efforts of the doctor and special duty nurses, the child died the following day.

A college football player sustained a broken leg. It was placed in a cast at a community hospital. The foot became cold two days later, there was a foul smell in the room for two weeks and eventually the leg had to be amputated at a medical center to which the patient was transferred. He recovered damages.[48] Not long after the cast was applied, the patient complained of pain, and his toes were swollen and became dark. The cast was cut several times, and in so doing the leg was cut. After two weeks, the patient was transferred to a medical center. The community hospital was held liable under *respondeat superior* because the nurses either did not observe, or at least failed to report, patient problems that were overlooked or not thought to be significant by the doctor. The physician himself settled out of court; he had no specialty training and had not secured consultation.

A mother, following delivery of her daughter, died of a hemorrhage from a laceration of the cervix. The nurse had not taken her pulse, blood pressure, temperature or respiration or called her doctor, even though she was aware that the bleeding was more than normal postpartum flow, and realized in time that the patient's condition was critical. The higher court reversed a verdict in favor of the nurse, hospital and physician.[49] The court said:

> We are satisfied that the evidence was sufficient to support a finding that the nurses, Lee and Kiese, were negligent. . . . Conceding that Dr. Ashley was negligent, still if nurse Lee had called the doctor at 10:30 P.M., when she was aware the condition of the patient was critical, who can say the same result would have occurred.

A baby vomited and choked on one of its first feedings, causing oxygen deprivation that led to residual brain damage. The court held that whether the nursery personnel left the baby without attention for an unreasonable and unsafe period of time was a question for the jury to decide, and reversed a summary judgment for the hospital.[50] The medicolegal aspects of the missing registered nurse have been discussed by various writers.[51]

In a wrongful death action, the parents of a stillborn child contended that the mother was not properly monitored, observed or treated when she came in experiencing severe back pains near her EDC (Expected Date of Confinement). Consequently, during the next 24 hours, her uterus ruptured and the baby was delivered stillborn. The Missouri Supreme Court ruled that the word "person" in the wrongful death act included a viable fetus.[52]

A young married woman received an award of damages for injuries and permanent scarring in a case in which a nurse did not discontinue an injection of saline solution under the patient's breasts for hypodermoclysis after it became evident that it was adversely affecting the unconscious patient.[53] Nurses who carry out any medical order must exercise reasonable judgment. When there are changes in the patient's condition that would indicate some change in therapy, they are expected to communicate with the physician for modification or confirmation of written orders. If she or he is not available, they must seek instructions from another physician.

Wrong Medicines: 5R's

Another group of common negligent acts includes wrong medicines, wrong dosage, wrong concentration of the proper medicine, misreading labels, neglecting to check labels, administering medicine to the wrong person and similar errors. The 5R's of medication are that: (1) the right medicine (2) be given to the right person (3) in the right dose (4) by the right route (5) at the right time.

The parents of an infant daughter in a wrongful death action recovered damages from a nurse and doctor for her accidental death due to an overdose of digitalis. With respect to the nurse, the court said:

> As laudable as her intentions are conceded to have been on the occasion in question, her unfamiliarity with the drug was a contributing factor in the child's death. In this regard we are of the opinion that she was negligent in attempting to administer a drug with which she was not familiar. . . . Not only was Mrs. Evans unfamiliar with the medicine in question but she also violated what has been shown to be a rule generally practiced by the members of the nursing profession in the community and which rule, we might add, strikes us as being most reasonable and prudent, namely, the practice of calling the prescribing physician when in doubt about an order for medication.[54]

A patient became violently ill as a result of a licensed practical nurse's mistakenly administering internally a potassium permanganate pill meant for external use. The patient could not recover damages from a charitable hospital where the nurse had completed a prescribed course for vocational nurses, had received a license from the state to practice nursing and had been practicing continuously for over three years.[55]

A judgment for $700 was affirmed against a hospital and nurse for injuries sustained when the nurse put hydrochloric acid in a patient's nose instead of nose drops.[56]

A passenger on a bus, injured when the driver lost consciousness and the bus struck a telephone pole, recovered a substantial sum from the bus company and driver. The latter's lapse of consciousness was attributed to the side-effects of the drug Pyribenzamine, which his doctor had prescribed.[57] The patient had been given no warning of the side-effects and had taken his first pill on the morning of the accident. The value of instructing patients who are to take their own medications—the teaching function of nursing as well as that of physicians—seems apparent.

When the parents of an infant sued a physician and an assistant physician for crippling damage to the infant's leg as the result of a nursing student's erroneously injecting a drug into the muscles of the infant's buttocks, the physicians settled out of court for $10,000.[58] The nursing student ignored a warning on the ampule that the drug was for intravenous use only.

The Court of Appeals ruled that the allegation of a child's mother that the amount of Demerol given the child following surgery was greater than the amount the nurse charted was sufficient to raise an issue of fact.[59] The child had died following an injection of Demerol administered after a tonsillectomy and circumcision.

When a paying patient sued a county in Idaho for damages for an injury caused by the wrong solution administered by a nurse employed by a hospital, the patient was allowed to recover damages from the county. In this instance, the nurse negligently supplied boric acid solution for injection in the patient's thigh instead of the saline solution requested.[60] In the majority of states, a person may not sue the government or a political subdivision of the state government without its consent, in the absence of an express statutory provision.

In Oklahoma, a patient brought suit for damages for injuries caused by a nurse who did not follow the physician's directions in administering a hypodermic injection into the patient's hips instead of her arms. Abscesses resulted. However, when it was not shown that similar injuries would not have followed an injection in the patient's arm, the court held that, as a matter of law, the negligence of the nurse was not the proximate cause of the injuries.[61] However, the case serves to illustrate the point that the nurse should carry out the doctor's orders. Had this nurse done so, she would have avoided the accusation of negligence and also the time, trouble and expense involved in the court action.

In a case in which a nurse negligently administered a solution of 10 percent sodium hydroxide instead of an 85 percent saline solution as part of a gastric analysis, causing serious injuries and some permanent disability, the patient was awarded $162,500 damages.[62]

In another case, a verdict for $750,000 against a drug manufacturer and judgment in favor of all other defendants was upheld. The patient had fallen from a ladder, fracturing his pelvis and some ribs. After several days, he began to exhibit symptoms of fat embolism, which the doctor treated with dextran, a blood plasma expander. Another doctor order a blood sugar test, which a hospital laboratory technician performed, using the Hycel P.M.S. blood glucose test, which gave a reading of 200 mg. The doctor had not checked to determine if the patient was receiving a substance that would interfere with the blood sugar test. The technician testified that a reading of 65 to 110 mg is normal. The patient was treated with large doses of insulin, and brain damage resulted from the excessive insulin. The interference caused by the dextran gave the inaccurate reading, but the manufacturer failed to give any warning to the hospital personnel of the false elevation problem caused by the drug's interference with the blood test.[63]

Injection. A 65-year-old, self-employed pest exterminator suffered a neuroma as a result of an injection that was given too low in the buttock by a nurse in a hospital. It struck the sciatic nerve and caused a permanent limp, which prevented the patient from carrying on his business, and he was awarded $17,706.[64]

A physician in treating a patient for coronary disease prescribed that heparin be administered subcutaneously every six hours. A nurse, Ms. Stern, R.N., employed by the Hahnemann Hospital, injected the heparin directly into the femoral nerve at a site on the front portion of the thigh 10 inches above the kneecap, and the patient sustained permanent injuries resulting from the injection. The physician was not held liable, but personal liability was imputed to the nurse, and agency liability to her hospital employer.[65]

A motorist spent most of a day in a tavern and became intoxicated; in trying to find his way home that night with his grandson as passenger in the car, he drove into a ditch. The grandson was taken to a hospital for treatment of his injuries, and a nurse negligently injected a drug into his buttocks, thereby injuring a nerve and causing permanent footdrop. The motorist having paid $11,200 and the hospital $25,000, the motorist was entitled to indemnity from the hospital.[66]

A prescribed drug was erroneously administered intravenously in a carrier of succinylcholine instead of normal saline solution while a patient was recuperating from an operation. The patient went into respiratory arrest not long after the nurse gave the injection, and he died five days later. Both parties agreed that the erroneous injection of the muscle relaxant was the cause of death. When the patient's widow sued the insurer, recovery was precluded by a policy exception involving medical and surgical treatment. According to the court, death was caused by an "accident" that occurred in the course of administering medical treatment.[67]

Twenty thousand dollars was awarded to a patient who sustained a permanent footdrop and atrophy of the calf of his leg as the result of a nurse's negligently placing an injection in the wrong area of his buttock.[68]

A hospital patient received an injection of fluid for a diagnostic test from a nurse, and thereafter infection arose in her arm, followed by thrombophlebitis. She recovered damages on the doctrine of res ipsa loquitur, since the procedure was under the hospital's control and there was some evidence of failure to maintain sterility.[69]

Drug Dispensing and Administration. With the complexity of modern medical care and the shortage of highly trained personnel, there is an increased tendency for physicians to shift some of their obligations toward their patients onto the professional nurse, who in turn passes along some of the tasks to the practical vocational nurse. The legal implications of these changes are important, since it is basic in the law that increased authority necessarily carries increased responsibility, and this increased responsibility and liability cannot be averted.

At the same time, hospital pharmacists must realize that their legal liability extends beyond the proper filling of prescriptions. The move to incorporate them as a member of the health team is well under way, and their utilization as consultants and resource persons is increasing every day.

In hospital, clinic and nursing home practice, the professional nurse must be careful to differentiate between drug administration and drug dispensing, in order not to violate the Pharmacy Practice Act. It is legal, Swafford points out,[70] for a nurse to take from the pharmacy to the nurses' station one dose of a drug for a particular patient, or a pharmacy-prepackaged and properly labeled nurses' station medication container, since this is drug administration. On the other hand, it is not legal for a nurse to fill or refill a nurses' station container or any other container with the drug specified, because such an act is dispensing and may be performed legally only by a licensed pharmacist in accordance with the state's Pharmacy Practice Act.

Having determined the difference between *dispensing* and *administering* medications, consideration should be given to the degree of care and skill required in carrying out these acts.

The parents of an infant daughter, in an action for wrongful death, recovered damages from a nurse and doctor for their infant's accidental death caused by an overdose of digitalis.[71] The patient was a three-month-old baby with a congenital heart condition. At the time of the baby's admission, it was agreed that her mother would continue to administer her daily dose of Lanoxin, and the nurses would not administer this drug unless the physician wrote a special order. On the fateful day, the physician wrote: "Give 3.0 cc (ml) Lanoxin today for one dose only." The assistant director of nursing, while on her rounds checking the various units, found the nurse in the pediatric unit busy with an emergency and her desk stacked with patient's charts. The assistant director thereupon decided to help out, and on checking the charts found that the 3 ml of Lanoxin had not been given. She was familiar only with the injectable form of Lanoxin, and not with the pediatric elixir of Lanoxin intended for oral use. It did occur to her that 3 ml of Lanoxin was a large dose for a small three-month-old infant, and she discussed the matter briefly with a registered nurse and a nursing student working there. After getting two ampules of the injectable Lanoxin, she questioned a consultant on the baby's case and was told that, if 3 ml was what the attending physician ordered, that was what he meant to give. Thereafter, the nurse administered 3 ml of the injectable form of Lanoxin, which was about five times the strength of 3 ml of the elixir, and an hour later the baby died. The law requires that a nurse check a drug order with the prescribing physician when faced with a question, doubt or apparent error in the order.

As Willig has stated, the following acts are specially prohibited by the new amendments to the Federal laws, and apply to the nurse's handling of all prescription drugs:

1. Compounding or dispensing the designated drugs except by authorized parties, for legal distribution and administration.
2. Distributing the drugs to any persons who are not licensed or authorized by federal or state law to receive them, such as persons outside the physician-patient relationship. Penalties for selling or giving the drugs to minors without a prescription are especially severe.
3. Possession of stimulant or depressant drugs as authorized by law, that is, as a patient, or incidental to the legal dispensing or administration of the drugs.
4. Making, selling, keeping or concealing any counterfeit drug equipment, and the doing of any act which causes the sale of a counterfeit drug. This includes buying amphetamine derivatives, such as desoxyepedrine, and labeling and dispensing them as trade-marked (brand-named) product to patients inside or outside the hospital.[72]

In an excellent article on "The Nurse's Viewpoint of Pharmacy in a Hospital,"[73] Ritter suggests practical ways of relieving a nurse from pharmacy work on evenings and weekends. She also states that, with a shortage of professional nurses available to give nursing care, patients are being denied many hours of such care for which they or the government taxes are paying dearly, while the nurses are tied up doing pharmacy work. Ritter further points out that such nurses are illegally dispensing drugs.

Dispensing drugs as part of a professional nurse's responsibility has been discussed by lawyers.[74]

Failure to Monitor Oxytocin Injection. When a patient was admitted to a hospital for the birth of her fourth child, hospital records showed that oxytocin was administered to induce labor. The patient's chart contained no indication of a check between 2:30 A.M. and 5:15 A.M. Following delivery, the patient began heavy intrauterine bleeding, and after a attempted repair of the tear in her uterus had failed to stop the bleeding, a total hysterectomy was done. During the latter procedure, the patient receiving 6½ pints of blood and contracted hepatitis. As a result of the medication administered for the hepatitis, she sustained a partial hearing loss in both ears. The appellate court affirmed a verdict of $40,000 against the physicians and the hospital for failure to monitor the administration of the oxytocin.[75]

Mistaken Identity. Mistaken identity can plague nurses and hospitals in a variety of situations. A patient recovering from a nephrectomy and almost ready for discharge was given a blood transfusion, which an intern and nurse told her was supplied by her daughter, Lillian, despite her protest that she did not have a daughter. When she suffered chills and rising temperature due to incompatible blood, the transfusion was stopped. She then became mentally ill and underwent psychiatric care in a state hospital. A judgment for $6500 damages was affirmed.[76] The transfusion had been ordered for another woman on the same floor of the hospital.

A mix-up of hospital charts on the way to an operating room led to wrong surgery being performed on two patients, and resulting lawsuits. One with a normal gallbladder was operated upon for her gallbladder instead of a breast biopsy, and one with a malfunctioning gallbladder had an incision for breast biopsy. The patient who had the wrong cholecystectomy sued and recovered compensatory damages from the surgeon who opened her abdomen and from the hospital; an award of punitive damages was not allowed.[77]

Administration of Blood

The question frequently arises as to whether a registered professional nurse who has had adequate instruction and experience may start and administer blood transfusions under the direction of a physician. It is pertinent to remind nurses of what Emanuel Hayt has said repeatedly:

> There is probably no biologic product in medical therapy that carries with it more possible sources of dangerous error than blood.[78]

When hospital policy or the law does not preclude nurses from carrying out some procedure, and when they have had adequate instruction and experience, the general rule is probably that they can perform the procedure under the direction and supervision of a licensed physician.

At the same time, it is pointed out that what registered professional nurses may do legally and what it is desirable for them to do may be quite different matters. With respect to cutdowns, except in a dire emergency when no physician is available, the nurse should not make an incision to reach a vein.[79]

The patient's name and hospital number should be attached to each unit of blood, and the information should be carefully verified with the patient's identification armband. During the transfusion, the patient should be observed carefully; if there are any untoward symptoms, reactions or complaints from the patient, the transfusion should be stopped, the physician notified and further direction requested. It is an obligation of the nurse to make certain that every requisition for blood has the patient's complete name and hospital number.[80]

A patient who was recovering from surgery was informed by a hospital nurse and intern that she was to have a blood transfusion. The intern started the transfusion and the patient suffered a reaction to it, followed by other ills. The transfusion had not been ordered for her by the attending physician, and the hospital was held liable.[81] The court went on to say that the patient was entitled to be protected from trespass and assault if it could be reasonably anticipated, and that the wrongs were due to the very person whom the hospital employed to care for patients.

In an action against a blood bank by a hospital patient for breach of implied warranty—the patient contracted hepatitis after she received blood transfusions—the judgment was in favor of the defendant.[82] Furnishing blood to a patient for a transfusion charged for by the hospital does not constitute a sale, and the patient cannot recover for breach of implied warranty of its fitness for use.

An erroneous blood transfusion sensitized a girl's blood, and the condition was detected eight years later during testing for pregnancy. Despite exchange transfusions administered after delivery, her child was born with permanent brain damage. The court ruled that the precise harm that occurred to the baby was reasonably foreseeable by doctors and hospitals. The claim therefore was for prenatal injuries to the surviving infant, which is a recognized cause of action in Illinois.[83]

In an action by a patient who contracted serum hepatitis subsequent to a blood transfusion, there was a judgment for the defendants, namely, the hospital where the transfusion took place and the blood bank. The court held that no showing was made that accepted medical standards were not followed in screening and testing the blood and in administering the transfusion.[84]

Failure to Communicate

Three days after a cesarean section a patient complained of soreness in her jaw and in opening her mouth. Although a nurse and a resident gave her several medications, they did not notify the physician of her complaint. When the physician finally discovered his patient's symptoms on a visit, he administered tetanus antitoxin and remained with her until her death that night. The appellate court dismissed the charge against the physician, and affirmed a judgment that the hospital was liable for the failure of its employees to give timely notification to the doctor of the patient's condition.[85]

A patient in a Washington state mental hospital cut her hand when she rammed it through a glass window. When she was taken to a treatment room to have it sutured and a light cast applied, she threw herself from the treatment table. The doctors discussed putting her in a closed ward but decided that, since this would be evidence to the patient of regression, they would keep her on the open ward under close observation. On the day shift, close surveillance was maintained, but at the change of shift no report of these events was made to the evening group, who consequently relaxed the supervision of the patient. About 4:30 P.M. the patient was seen walking on the grounds toward a busy boulevard.

When a car came along, the patient hurled herself in front of it and was seriously injured. A $275,000 suit against the state hospital for damages for such injuries was maintained by the patient.[86]

The case of *Karrigan v. Nazareth Convent and Academy* concerned hospital nurses who repeatedly observed adverse reactions in a patient from whom a surgeon had removed a T tube after a cholecystectomy. The Kansas Supreme Court stated that a jury might well have found that a 10½ hour delay in reaching the surgeon was plainly unreasonable and constituted negligence on the part of the nursing service.[87]

A mother who noticed that two of her children, both boys, had a chest and head rash accompanied by high fever took them to the emergency room of a hospital, where she told the nurse on duty that she had removed two ticks from the head and stomach of one son. The nurse did not tell the emergency room physician of the tick history that the mother had related to her. The physician, deciding that the children had measles, prescribed aspirin and instructed that the boys be kept in a dark room. When the rash spread to the arms and legs and the fever had not subsided, the parents brought the boys back to the emergency room. They were seen by a second physician, who was unsure of his tentative diagnosis of measles and referred them to their pediatrician. When the latter examined the boys, he advised that they be kept in a dark room and that he should be notified of any change. One of the boys was found dead the following day, and two ticks were removed from the body of the second boy. Subsequently, the second boy was treated for, and cured of, Rocky Mountain spotted fever. The first child died of Rocky Mountain spotted fever, according to an autopsy. In a lawsuit brought by the parents, the Circuit Court of Clavert County entered judgments N.O.V. in favor of the hospital and physician. The Court of Special Appeals affirmed the judgment in favor of the physician, but vacated that for the hospital, entering judgment for the parents. The court said:

> Evidence supported finding that the failure of the nurse to notify physician of patient history involving removal of ticks from one of the boys constituted a violation of her duties as a nurse, and failure to relate the information to the physician was a contributing proximate cause of death of one child and serious illness of the other.[88]

A patient suffering from a comminuted compound fracture of the right wrist, a posterior dislocation of the right elbow and a compression fracture of the second lumbar vertebra had a cast applied to the arm, extending from above the elbow to below the knuckles. For the first two days, all apparently went well; however, he alleged that treatment by nurses and hospital personnel during the next 24 hours, when he was taken to another hospital, deviated from hospital policy and constituted negligence. Several nurses testified to the swollen and black condition of the patient's arm, from which a foul-smelling substance was draining, and to the fact that the patient had a high temperature and was sometimes delirious. The treating physician was called by one nurse, who reported some of the symptoms and told him that the patient could not retain orally administered antibiotics. She did not report the delirium, and did not call the departmental chairman when the physician failed to act on the information. According to hospital policy as set out in the department of nursing's manual, registered nurses who had reason to question care provided to any patient were required to direct the question to the attending physician. Thereafter, if they felt the question was not satisfactorily answered, they were to report this to the departmental chairmen. According to a specialist in infectious diseases who had the patient transferred to the second hospital where hyperbaric oxygen treatments were available, an important 24 hours was lost by the nurse's alleged failure to report the patient's condition. The arm had to be amputated at the shoulder joint. In a lawsuit against the physician and the hospital, the patient was awarded $333,000 and his wife $1320. The appellate court reversed the trial court's judgment in favor of the hospital, and reinstated the jury's verdict.[89]

Delay in Obtaining Help

A Louisiana appellate court ruled that two physicians, an anesthesiologist and a hospital were not liable as there was no unreasonable delay in obtaining help for a patient with a breathing problem after a thyroidectomy. Late in the day after surgery, the woman developed stridor. Her anesthesiologist was called by a nurse, but he was administering blood to an 80-year-old patient with a history of a heart difficulty and could not come immediately. The nurses initiated an emergency procedure known as "Dr. Quickstep" to obtain help for the patient. A nurse brought a crash cart and the emergency room physician tried twice unsuccessfully to intubate her. Finally, the anesthesiologist came and inserted the endotracheal tube. The patient suffered permanent brain damage from lack of oxygen and died almost a year later.[90]

Defects in Equipment

Defects in equipment may cause injury. If the defects are obvious, the nurse is thereby warned against using the equipment, but the nurse cannot be held responsible for awareness of hidden defects in equipment. A hospital that furnishes defective equipment is liable to the patient who is injured by the same.[91] If nurses use obviously defective equipment, they will be liable to a patient for injuries caused by the same. Nurses' training and experience familiarize them with supplies and equipment that are of an acceptable standard.

The danger of infection from the use of an unsterile needle is a matter of common knowledge. A nurse's use of such a needle in all probability would be considered negligent. In cases involving physicians, the courts have so held.[92]

An older hospital visitor, who was injured when the chair in which she sat collapsed, recovered damages from the hospital because no one made regular inspections in order to discover and repair defective conditions.[93]

A judgment for a patient was affirmed when a nurse made a long cut on the patient's arm with a Stryker saw while removing a plaster of Paris cast. The nurse at trial admitted that, despite the presence of blood and the patient's complaints of pain, she continued to use the same amount of pressure in handling the saw. The court held that the nurse did not carry out the recommended procedure that other nurses would have followed when the patient complained of injury.[94] In using any equipment, a nurse must exercise reasonable judgment.

In a case in which hospital nurses failed to notify a physician of the symptoms of his patient, the court set aside a jury's $104,000 verdict in favor of the hospital and against a physician. The nine-year-old boy, who sustained a fractured left femur, was taken to the hospital, where the physician ordered both legs placed in Bryant's traction. The boy continued to complain of pain. His right foot became swollen, and on the tenth day another physician noticed that both legs had become gangrenous. As a result, the right leg had to be amputated, and muscle and tissue were removed from the left leg. While the trial was being conducted, the hospital's insurance carrier settled for $104,000 and the physician's insurance carrier for $75,000.

A patient in a hospital in Guam was electrocuted when he touched a metal water pipe while simultaneously touching a window frame. An electric current from an air conditioner, resulting from a defective capacitor, was found to be passing through the frame. In a suit by the widow and son against the manufacturer, the appellate court affirmed a decision for the manufacturer after he introduced credible evidence that environmental factors in Guam, such as exceptional salinity, dustiness and humidity in the air, could have caused the defect in the capacitor six weeks after installation. Such a verdict would not necessarily relieve the hospital of liability.[96]

A 37-year-old man was suffering from a gunshot wound in his neck, and the bullet had severely damaged his spinal cord. During the first few days of treatment, a general surgeon and a neurosurgeon formed an opinion that the patient would be a permanent paraplegic, but the neurosurgeon noted on the hospital record that the patient had sensation in his feet. Four days later, when the patient was transferred to a special bed, a nurse failed to check the position of an "essential bolt," so that when the bed was rotated the patient fell. Thereafter, he lost all sensation in his feet and had increased pain. A Florida appellate court affirmed the judgment of the trial court as to the liability of the hospital, but found the $325,000 damages award to be excessive.[97]

A hospital orderly was awarded $5743.90 when he was injured by an exploding glass jar attached to an oxygen tank as he was about to insert an oxygen tube into a patient. He brought a products liability suit against the supplier of the oxygen services, claiming that it provided defective equipment and failed to perform its maintenance contract properly.[98]

A $12.5 million malpractice award was upheld by a Florida appellate court, and the patient's attorney's fees were lowered to $1.5 million. The 30-year-old patient had been placed on a respirator after an automobile accident. Before the hospital staff discovered that the respirator had malfunctioned, the patient sustained irreversible brain damage that left her half-blind, bedridden and in pain. She could recognize people and responded to sounds and touch.[99]

A patient suffered numbness in her lower leg and foot following a gynecological operation. According to hospital records, the condition was caused by pressure on the peroneal nerve during surgery. After reaching a settlement with the hospital, the patient also sued the doctor on the theory that he was responsible for negligent placement of the safety strap on her prior to surgery. Both the doctor and the operating room nurse testified that it was the circulating nurse who placed the safety strap on patients. A summary judgement for the physician was affirmed.[100]

Allowing Relatives to Help

Although parents, spouses, relatives and friends who assist in caring for a patient may be psychologically and emotionally comforting, the nurse must remember that they may complicate the liability problem. When an accident occurs, certain questions inevitably arise, such as whether the act done by the relative was one that should have been done by a nurse. In the matter of negligence, it is possible for a relative as well as a nurse to be negligent. If patients are injured as a result of the relative's negligence, can they recover damages from the hospital? Relatives concerned with the patient's comfort may do things contrary to the doctor's orders—matters of diet, turning and coughing patients and self-help as a part of rehabilitation are examples of areas in which relatives, at times, may undo a part of the plan of therapy. In any event, rules for relatives should be reviewed by the hospital or agency legal counsel.[101]

In *Williams* v. *Sisters of the Incarnate Word*,[102] a 13-year-old girl was admitted to the hospital to undergo tests relative to symptoms of dizziness and fainting. Her parents obtained cots and spent the night in their daughter's hospital room. The next morning a nurse's aide asked if the child needed any assistance in taking her daily bath or shower. All witnesses at the trial agreed that the mother informed the nurse's aid that she (the mother) would help her daughter if any assistance was required.

Thereafter, both of them entered the bathroom, and the patient proceeded to shower while her mother stood by to assist. After showering, the girl dressed in the bathroom and walked toward the hospital bed. She became weak and dizzy and fell, striking her mouth on the edge of the table and damaging several teeth. The nurse's aide was not present in the hospital room at the time of the incident. After the patient's mother offered help with the shower, the nurse's aide reasonably assumed that the patient was in good hands and continued her routine morning rounds. The trial judge found the hospital was not guilty of any negligence that caused injury to the plaintiff's daughter, and this verdict was affirmed on appeal.

In *Hunt* v. *Bogalusa Community Medical Center*, the Supreme Court of Louisiana stated the duty of a hospital toward its patient:

> A hospital is bound to exercise the requisite amount of care toward a patient that the particular patient's condition may require. It is the hospital's duty to protect the patient from dangers that may result from the patient's physical and mental incapacities as well as from external circumstances peculiarly within the hospital's control. A determination of whether a hospital has breached the duty of care it owes a particular patient depends upon the circumstances and facts of that case.[103]

In *Goodeaux* v. *Martin Hospital, Inc.* the oft-quoted limitation on the hospital's duty has been recently reiterated:

> On the other hand, a private hospital is not an answer of a patient's safety, and the rules as to the care required are limited by the rule that no one is required to guard against or take measures to avert that which a reasonable person under the circumstances would not anticipate as likely to happen.[104]

(See *Avey* v. *St. Francis Hospital*,[105] a case dealing with a psychiatric patient. See *Duling* v. *Bluefield Sanitarium, Inc.*,[106] a case of a pediatric patient.)

In *Norton* v. *Argonaut Insurance Co. et al.*,[107] in a suit against a hospital, a registered nurse and a physician for the wrongful death of a three-month-old girl, an award of approximately $26,000 was amended to approximately $11,000 and affirmed. The fatal error was made by the nurse who did not check an unclear order with the prescribing doctor. The mother usually gave the medication.

In summary, the matter of family help with a hospitalized patient, where doctors request that the patient's family be allowed to perform certain tasks, is controversial. Legally, this has not been criticized in the cases. Where members of the nursing team offer to assist patients in such activities as bathing, feeding and walking, it is acceptable for apparently capable family members to help. As in the Williams case, the hospital is not liable if the patient sustains injury due to the family member's error. This assumption of risk by a family member volunteering to carry out a personal function unassisted by willing members of the nursing team should be noted. But nurses would be negligent in assuming that the presence of a family member in a patient's room obviates their own responsibility to help the patient in daily activities such as bathing.

Loss of or Damage to Patients' Property

Nurses may be accused of negligence in the care of a patient's property. Possibly, the item most frequently involved is the patient's dentures. In the course of their training, nurses have been taught some simple but effective method of handling dentures to prevent damage and loss, such as placing them in a transparent container or one conspicuously labeled for the purpose. It is a wise nurse who adheres to such a practice in his or her work. However, if a denture is wrapped in a piece of tissue or paper towel, it is easy to understand how such a crumpled handful of apparent trash may subsequently be thrown out. Alternatively, the denture may be damaged if it is placed where a heavy tray or other heavy object may be placed on it. In some modern dentures, the plastic used will crack if subjected to extremes of heat and cold.

Nurses' liability for the negligent loss of or damage to a patient's property is based on their duty as a person, trained or untrained, to act as a reasonable and ordinary prudent person. Since nurses customarily must from time to time handle patients' personal belongings, they must use reasonable care in placing them in drawers and lockers. Not only are nurses personally liable for their acts of negligence in regard to a patient's property, but if they are an employee or agent they may render their employer liable as well.

Bailment. At this point, it should be mentioned that, when a patient deposits personal property such as money, rings or watches with another, a bailment is created. The person who deposits the property is a "bailor," and the person with whom the property is deposited is a "bailee." A bailment is a contract in which property is deposited for keeping and is to be delivered at a certain time to the bailor on her or his order, and payment made for such service. In a typical hospital situation, however, the depositing of a patient's property with the hospital or a nurse represents a gratuitous type of bailment, whereby the nurse or hospital agrees to care for such property. In this case, if the patient's property is injured or lost, there is an action for damages for negligence. As previously discussed, once a person undertakes to do an act or to give a service, she or he must use due care.

Elopement

If a patient elopes from an institution, nurses and their employers will be held liable only to a degree that is commensurate with the patient's known condition.

Today, the primary purpose of hospitalization for mental illness is considered to be the rehabilitation of sick persons so that they may return to the community as useful and healthy citizens. The problem still remains as to just how this hospitalization should be carried out. The current concept of treating the mentally ill is to allow them as much freedom as possible in order to restore their self-confidence and to resocialize them. When the patient's history and chart show past suicidal tendencies, he or she should be kept under the closest supervision.[108] The report of another case[109] contains a court's discussion of various factors involved in suicide, and Scheidman[110] notes that about 80 percent of persons with suicidal tendencies give some advance warning.

In a Washington case,[111] the plaintiff patient and her husband recovered $275,000 for injuries she incurred in an accident following an elopement from a state mental health hospital. Owing to a communication failure, the degree of supervision required of ordinarily prudent nurses in light of the patient's morning conduct was not in force in the afternoon; hence, the elopement, which culminated in injuries that resulted in the hospital's liability.

A government hospital is under the same duty as a nongovernmental hospital to exercise due care in safeguarding veterans with suicidal tendencies.

The relatives of an 81-year-old man brought a suit against a rest home to recover damages for his wrongful death when he was found dead in a wet grassy area near a river bank at the northern boundary of the property.[112] The patient had been a resident for about six months and enjoyed walking around the nursing home and its grounds. Exits from the nursing home were unlocked in accordance with the fire laws that required the provision of escape routes in case of fire. The attending physician had not limited the patient's activities. The court had to consider whether or not the home was negligent in permitting him to get out of the building and wander to his death. It was held that, although a nursing home has a duty to provide a reasonable standard of care, this does not include having a nurse or attendant following each patient around at all times. The verdict was in favor of the nursing home.

What about the "walk-away" patient, the person who has a tendency to wander off unsupervised? As with many other difficult problems, this becomes a matter of judgment for nurses. They cannot permit a patient to wander off aimlessly, yet they could face a lawsuit for false imprisonment if they restrained a competent resident against his or her will. The nurse should recall the language of the standard of care: "such reasonable care as his known condition may require, the degree of care being in proportion to his recognized physical or mental ailments."[113] Therefore, the more serious the patient's disability, the more care is required not only to prevent his or her elopement and possible injury but to cover all other risks as well.

In reviewing over 1000 incident reports pertaining to a sizable psychiatric unit of a very large general hospital, it was found that approximately 12 percent involved elopement. Interestingly enough, not one of the elopement incidents resulted in any harm or injury to the patient. It might be pointed out that the overwhelming majority of the patients in this institution were younger people with a reasonably good prognosis. This one study seemed to indicate that the elopement problem was not uncommon, but that the rate of injury resulting therefrom was low, at least among younger patients with a good prognosis.

Judicial opinion appears to be in agreement with most physicians that, although strict confinement undoubtedly affords greater safeguards, nevertheless, the closer the supervision, the fewer will be the number of patients who are cured.[114] With respect to the elopement problem, nurses and their employers should take comfort in the fact that, if they use such reasonable care as the patient's known condition may require, they are not likely to be held liable if she or he escapes and as a result is injured.

In one case of elopement, a patient had been confined for several days in the county hospital with a diagnosis of psychosis. After escaping, he felt sick, and told a police officer what he had done. The officer took him to the city hospital emergency room and left him with a nurse while he telephoned to verify whether the patient had escaped from the county hospital. The patient, finding himself alone in the emergency room after examination, left and jumped in front of a subway train, with the result that his leg was crushed and had to be amputated. He was awarded $300,000 in damages for personal injuries against the county hospital, City of New York and City Health and Hospital Corporation. A nurse testified that, under such circumstances, hospital procedure would have required that the officer be asked to guard the patient until he was seen by a physician and proper arrangements could be made to transfer him to a hospital with a psychiatric facility, as necessary.[115]

See Chapter 6 for additional cases concerning psychiatric patients.

Incompetent Physician

The Washington Supreme Court concluded that a physician's suspension was justified for the following reasons: serious alteration of a patient's chart, non-cooperation with nursing and record-keeping staff and a questionable tubal ligation under local anesthetic without a full surgical crew in violation of the hospital rules.[116] When nurses are confronted by a physician who violates hospital rules and regulations, they should make out an incident report with the date and facts and file it with nursing service for appropriate follow-through action by administration. If the situation involves immediate surgery, as in this case of the tubal ligation, immediate contact through the supervisor with the director of nursing service is necessary.

See also the case of *Farrell* v. *Kramer* where a nurse reported to the medical society a physician whom she considered to be giving inadequate postoperative care to a patient.

Where a comatose patient with shallow breathing was brought to the emergency room of a hospital as a result of an unintentional drug overdose, an endotracheal tube was inserted to improve the breathing, and she was transferred to intensive care. Five days later, when the doctor ordered a nurse to remove the tube, problems were encountered and a tracheostomy had to be done. As a result, scar tissue formed, the patient's voice was reduced to a whisper and she breathed partly through her nose and partly through a hole created by the tracheostomy. A verdict for $150,000 against the hospital was affirmed on appeal. There was negligence on the part of the nurses and inhalation therapist in not reporting to their supervisor when they were aware that the endotracheal tube was being left in a patient longer than the customary three or four days.[117]

A plaintiff patient was admitted to the hospital with a broken wrist and dislocated elbow. A cast was put on the wrist, and the arm began to swell and turned black. The patient became delirious. Although the nurses observed the patient's worsening condition and reported some of the symptoms to the physician, they did not report the delirium. When the doctor did nothing further, the nurses did not call the hospital authorities. The West Virginia Supreme Court upheld a verdict against the hospital.[118] In *Toth* v. *Community Hospital at Glen Cove* where premature infants were blinded by too high a concentration of oxygen being administered for too long a time, the court said that it became the duty of the nurses to inform the attending physician and, if he failed to act, to advise the hospital authorities so that appropriate action might be taken.[119]

For other cases concerning whether the nurse should report negligence in medical treatment, see *Farrell* v. *Kramer* and *Darling* v. *Charleston Memorial Hospital* reported elsewhere in this book.

Nosocomial Infections

According to Fifer, a 5 percent incidence of nosocomial infections in short-term general hospitals translates to 1.5 million infections annually, which result or contribute to 14,000 deaths and cost $1 billion annually.[120] While nosocomial infections are numerous, it is usually difficult or impossible to establish the element of proximate causation. Hence it is difficult for patients to get damages for hospital-acquired infections. To establish negligence, four elements of the tort must be proved: (1) There must be a duty toward the plaintiff, (2) the defendant must have failed to perform the duty that was owed, (3) it must be proved that the defendant's failure was the proximate or direct cause of the plaintiff's injuries and (4) actual damages must have occurred as a result of the injury.[121]

In *Bartlett* v. *Argonaut Insurance Co.*, the patient and her husband sued the hospital for damages resulting from her contracting an infection with *Staphylococcus aureus coagulase* positive after an operation. The Arkansas Supreme Court affirmed a judgment in favor of the hospital's insurance carrier, since the staph germ that caused the infection could have entered the body in many ways and from many sources.[122] In another hospital malpractice suit, the doctrine of *res ipsa loquitur* did not apply because the mere occurrence of an infection in a patient's arm was not enough to imply negligence, and any verdict would have been based on mere speculation about the cause of the infection.[123]

In a medical malpractice case brought by a patient and her husband against a hospital and doctor for damages from an infection and for loss of consortium, the hospital had stored both sterile and nonsterile needles in the same cabinet, and the physician had allegedly used a nonsterile needle in performing a liver biopsy. The court held that expert testimony was not essential to the jury's determination that hospital storage was inconsistent with their obligation to use due care.[124] Other cases such as *Helman* v. *Sacred Heart Hospital* and *Kapuschinsky* v. *United States* are discussed elsewhere in this book.

In *Robey* v. *Jewish Hospital of Brooklyn*,[125] damages for the infection of a newborn were sought in an action for negligence. The hospital had admitted the infant's mother immediately prior to the birth, although there was an infection affecting infants in the hospital, about which the expectant mother was not notified. The court ruled that the record failed to show any actionable negligence on the part of the hospital.

In *Scott* v. *Salem County Memorial Hospital*,[126] a patient, who was struck by a car which broke her leg, was admitted to the hospital where the defendant orthopedist set the leg and applied a cast. The patient was not seen by a physician for several days. Gas gangrene had set in the leg by the time the patient was seen, and the leg had to be amputated. The patient brought a lawsuit against the hospital and both physicians. According to expert witnesses, the patient's condition was caused by failure to bivalve the cast at the first sign of a problem, and after 12 to 16 hours the problem was irreversible. The expert witnesses testified that the orthopedic physicians were negligent in failing to see her by that time. No evidence was produced showing either nerve or vascular damage in the original injury. A cause of action was stated, said the court.

In *Defalco* v. *Long Island College Hospital*,[127] 75-year-old Vincent Defalco was admitted to the hospital for the surgical removal of a senile cataract in his right eye. A witness testified that, while visiting the patient in the hospital, she had observed a nurse pick up an eye patch that had fallen to the floor and apply it directly to the patient's right eye. The patient argued that the jury might infer that the fallen eye patch picked up *Enterobacter* and *Staphylococcus albus* germs from the floor and caused the infection that resulted in the loss of his eye. The trial court awarded the patient $375,000. This judgment was reversed by the Supreme Court, which held that the occurrence of a postoperative hyphema was no basis for an automatic inference of negligence.

Cardiac Arrest

Insurance carriers for two hospitals and anesthesiologists agreed to payment of lifetime annuities to children suffering brain damage as a result of cardiac arrest. In one case, a licensed practical nurse in a recovery room who was occupied with another patient left a nine-year-old girl who had a tonsillectomy unattended for 10 to 25 minutes. Finally, when the practical nurse noticed that the patient was pulseless and apparently in cardiac arrest, she ran to an adjoining suite for the anesthesiologist instead of immediately giving resuscitation. Although the anesthesiologist came immediately and worked on the girl and she lived, she suffered general paralysis and had little mental ability. In settlement, the hospital's insurance carrier purchased an annuity providing $1350 monthly, to be increased 7¾ percent annually, and guaranteeing an extra $100,000 if one of the parents survives the daughter. The parents were also paid $150,000, which included payment from the anesthesiologist's insurance carrier. In addition, the patient's attorney received $300,000 as his fee.[128]

In another case, an eight-week-old infant was brought to the hospital with complaints of vomiting and difficulty in breathing. His temperature was normal, his pulse 180 and his respirations 42. The physician on duty in the emergency room, an obstetrics resident from another department, prescribed an injection of penicillin and sent him home, noting that the baby had a possible respiratory infection and otitis media. On the following day when the baby was brought back, the emergency room was staffed by a radiology resident supplied by an independent organization. At that time, the baby's temperature was 106°F and he was dehydrated, so cold packs were ordered for the temperature and the on-call pediatric resident was notified. The latter claimed that, since he was not told of the urgent problem, he ordered an oral electrolyte solution. However, the baby was unable to suck the fluid from the bottle. When the pediatrician arrived some two hours later, he rushed the baby to intensive care. As a cutdown was done, the baby sustained a cardiac arrest. Although he was revived, he was severely mentally retarded and had quadriparesis. Settlement included payment of $400 per month increasing to $1350 per month after three years, $25,000 to the child's mother and $240,000 in attorney's fees.[129]

The death of a 39-year-old legal investigator from a cardiac arrest while being prepared for a hemorrhoidectomy, again in an intensive care unit, resulted in a $1,200,000 settlement against an anesthesiologist and a hospital. Negligence in the medication administration before anesthesia, and delay in detecting the arrest and in corrective procedures undertaken, was alleged.[130]

Pronouncing the Patient Dead

The literature contains many articles discussing the time at which death occurs. Whether a nurse may pronounce a patient dead is a vexed question, particularly in nursing homes and extended care facilities.

Traditionally, death has been said to have occurred, both medically and legally, whenever both the lungs and the heart have irrevocably ceased to function.[131] This occurrence has usually been called "clinical death." However, two modern procedures have made further study of the time of death necessary: the ability to maintain by artificial means the circulation of oxygenated blood through tissues of the body that have been irreversibly injured, and the use of cadavers' organs for transplants. Consequently, there is some need for a new definition of death,[132] and for this to become a part of the law for the guidance of those who must make death or time-of-death determinations.

The law provides that death is to be pronounced before artificial means of supportive respiratory and circulatory function are terminated, and before any vital organ is removed for purposes of transplantation.

Irreversible coma has been defined as a new criterion of death by a faculty committee of the Harvard Medical School. The committee gives these characteristics of a permanently nonfunctioning brain: (1) unreceptivity and unresponsivity, (2) no movements of breathing, (3) no reflexes and (4) a flat electroencephalogram.[133] In addition, it would be necessary to report that the patient was not on hypothermia or anesthetic drugs that could depress the central nervous system.

Upon a review of some of the definitions and concepts of death, it should be stated that the determination of an overall concept of death remains a medical judgment, as does the actual diagnosis of death under whatever the concept of death may be. The statement on death by the 22nd World Medical Assembly in Sydney, Australia, in August 1968, states that the determination of time of death is, and should remain, the legal responsibility of the physician.[134]

What the nurse should do is chart the time, and the signs and symptoms, and the action taken, for example:

3:08 A.M. Respirations ceased, no carotid or apical pulse.

3:10 A.M. Pupils dilated. Dr. John Doe notified.

This question arises because nurses are increasingly being asked to carry out tasks at hours, times and places that the physician finds inconvenient. Whether nurses will continue to spend much of their time and effort in a dependency relationship with the medical profession is a moot issue at the present time.

RES IPSA LOQUITUR RULE

The law has a rule known as res ipsa loquitur, or "the thing speaks for itself," which may be applied to certain negligence cases. Three conditions are necessary before this rule may be applied: (1) that in the ordinary course of affairs the accident would not have occurred if reasonable care had been used, (2) that the thing that caused the accident was under the exclusive control of the defendant and (3) that the plaintiff did not contribute to the occurrence of the accident.[135] When the plaintiff proves that these conditions exist, it is regarded in some states as circumstantial evidence of negligence, which judge or jury may accept or reject. In other states, it is held to create a presumption of negligence.

Thus, judgment was entered for parents who sued a hospital and physicians to recover damages for malpractice resulting in the loss of a two-day-old boy's glans penis as a result of circumcision.[136] Judgment was also affirmed for a plaintiff who developed fever and chills and a urinary infection after a cystoscopic examination.[137] However, in an action to recover damages for a burn allegedly caused by the application of hot water bottles during a surgical procedure, the verdict was in favor of the doctor and hospital, as there was evidence that the injury might have resulted from other causes not attributable to any negligence on the part of the defendants.[138]

MALPRACTICE

Cause for Damages

As Eccard has stated, there are three questions that must be answered to determine whether a nurse is liable for malpractice: What kind of an act is complained of? What are the qualifications of the nurse who did the act? Where was the care carried out?[139] In answering the first question, lawyers and courts should look to the ANA standards of nursing practice. The general standards of nursing practice apply to all nurses, whereas the specialty standards apply only to nurses who work in the particular area under consideration. For instance, the collection of data on vital signs is something expected of all nurses according to the generic standards of nursing care.

In *Wagner* v. *Kaiser Foundation Hospitals*[140] a patient was awarded $750,000 by an Oregon court for permanent brain damage in connection with his eye surgery. In the recovery room, the rate and depth of his breathing were not charted despite the fact that the form provided a place for this. The court said: "If the Recovery Room nurses had properly monitored the rate and the depth of the patient's breathing, they would, in the normal course of events, have discovered what was happening and would have had time to give him oxygen so as to prevent brain damage."

The second question concerning the qualifications of the nurse who performed the act points out that, while deviation from the standard of care would establish liability for all nurses, a nurse with more education can be expected to use more expertise. Lawyers, courts and all of us must discard the notion that a nurse is a nurse is a nurse. When we recognize differences in the education of nurses, then the nurse with a baccalaureate or higher degree, who has the ability to assume independent roles in the expansion of nursing practice, will be exposed to greater liability than the nurse from the associate degree or hospital diploma program. While malpractice was not the issue in *Lyons* v. *Salve Regina College*,[141] it does show the accountability of a dean and faculty, who typically must have a master's degree in nursing. There, a student sued a college claiming its refusal to allow her to continue nursing studies constituted a breach of contract. The student's progress had been evaluated by faculty with a baccalaureate degree in nursing and who almost certainly had a master's degree, too. The judgment of the nursing faculty and the dean, who had at least a baccalaureate and higher degrees, was upheld by the court. As more lawyers and the courts become aware of the differences in nurses' education, this issue will become important in malpractice litigation. It is only a matter of time before educational differences will be used the same way as the distinction between general practitioners and specialists in medical malpractice cases.

The third question concerns where the act was carried out. If the nursing care was carried out in a specialty area or by a nurse practitioner, the care may have been given by a clinical nurse specialist. Typically, the clinical nurse specialist has a master's degree and, with this advanced preparation, has the ability to act in a more independent manner than a nurse with a baccalaureate degree, an associate degree or a hospital diploma. In many clinics for the chronically ill, such as a diabetic or a hypertensive clinic, clinical specialists assess and evaluate the patients. If nurses make errors in assessment or evaluation, their liability is measured not only by their education but by the independent judgments they are permitted to exercise. In occupational health and in public health, nurses also exercise a great deal of independent judgment, as medical guidelines are usually broad and general. In the hospital setting, a nurse's education and ability should be utilized effectively. Those patients who have well-defined and predictable illnesses or conditions should be cared for by the associate degree and hospital diploma nurses. Those patients in critical care whose conditions are unpredictable should be cared for by graduates with a baccalaureate or higher degree, because their additional education enables them to respond to such situations. Again, this is something that consumers, lawyers and courts have not focused sufficient attention upon in malpractice litigation.

In the future, certification will be another factor in judging the approximate standard of care for nurses. Corresponding to their additional education and experience, they have additional expertise and more responsibilities. A number of groups in addition to the ANA are concerned with certification, and the criteria used by the particular group must be used to measure the accountability of the nurse who is certified by the group.

As nurses assume more independent roles, they will become more accountable for their actions. This has considerable implication for cost containment. As long as nurses are hospital employees, then according to the doctrine of *respondeat superior*, the hospital will be liable for acts of nursing malpractice. When hospital attorneys and other lawyers recognize that nursing standards are a means of determining potential liability and that nurses with independent functions are responsible for them, nurses will be given more independence in their work.[142] This economic factor will ultimately result in a change of who speaks for nursing, since when nurses speak for themselves, they are liable for the same.

Some authorities believe that the differences between negligence and malpractice are not too well distinguished, and that it is preferable to consider malpractice synonymous with professional negligence. In a California case, the court defined malpractice in relation to a nurse:

> Malpractice is the neglect of a physician or nurse to apply that degree of skill and learning in treating and nursing a patient which is customarily applied in treating and caring for the sick or wounded similarly suffering in the same community.[143]

On the other hand, it would seem that malpractice also denotes a stepping beyond one's authority with serious consequences.

The Surgeon's Own Nurse

How much responsibility do operating room supervisors have when surgeons bring in their own nurses, instruct them in what to do during surgery and allow them to close a patient's skin after an incision while the surgeon has coffee?

Traditionally, surgeons have been granted authority to exercise control over all activities and personnel in the operating room during surgery.[144] This means that persons associated with the surgical operation have been under their direct supervision. In a Georgia case,[145] the court stated that a surgical operation begins when the incision is made and ends when the wound has been properly closed. During that interval of time, by the rule of respondeat superior, surgeons are held liable for the acts of their "employees." An employer is one who has the right to direct and control a person who performs services, both as to the result to be achieved and as to the means used to achieve it. An employee is a person subject to such direction in his or her work.

The courts are inclined to hold that, in the operating room, the employer-employee relationship exists between surgeons and their assistants.[146] According to a Florida case, when a patient is treated by a nurse furnished by the hospital but who is under the direct supervision of the surgeon, the nurse acts as the agent of the surgeon.[147] The hospital is not liable for nurses' actions while they serve under the surgeons' directions, nor is the hospital liable for the surgeons' negligence.

The Vermont Supreme Court held that a doctor, who was not selected or employed by the hospital concerned, had complete control and supervision of the nurses in the delivery room, and that the hospital therefore was not responsible for the negligent performance of a nurse in carrying out his order. In this case, a patient who had suffered a fractured rib as the result of a nurse's applying pressure to her body during delivery was denied recovery in a lawsuit against the hospital.[148]

When surgeons bring in their own nurses, there is no doubt that they are the employer of the nurse. Accordingly, surgeons, on the theory of respondeat superior, are vicariously liable for the negligent acts of their nurse-employees, so long as the nurse-employees are working for them and not independently.

If the surgeon's nurse, when in the operating room, does not adhere to the policies and procedures approved by the medical board for the care and safety of patients, the supervisor or charge nurse in the operating room should make a report of any problem through appropriate channels to the hospital administrator.

The task of closing the surgical wound goes beyond the usual role of the nurse assisting the surgeon in the operating room. Whether such activity is encompassed within the expanded role of the nurse is another matter. If so, does such a nurse have the necessary training and education for the task, and do the written policies of the hospital permit nurses with comparable training to perform such work on a physician's order? Although one may point out that custom and practice in a community may coincide with the nurse's work in closing the skin, a cautious approach to such activities is advised. Licensure of physician assistants, which is provided by a number of states, is another answer to the problem.

Failure to Exercise Due Care

In a malpractice suit against a hospital, a registered nurse and a physician, it was alleged that the surgeon was operating to remove a cyst from the wall of an abdomen. He ordered the preparation of a 1 percent procaine solution. A solution of formaldehyde was negligently prepared in its place and handed to him by the nurse. The court held that the surgeon was allowed to rely on the skill and care of trained nurses and similar persons. The nurse was held liable by the court on the grounds that she did not read the label on the formaldehyde bottle, and because she knew that the physician was going to use the solution he had ordered to produce local anesthesia on the patient.[149] In short, nurses as professionally educated persons must exercise all the due care and reasonableness associated with the education of members of their profession. In the case cited, in which the nurse was aware of the purpose for which the solution was to be used, and by education knew (or should have known) the properties of formaldehyde and procaine, she was not justified in unquestioningly heeding the surgeon's order even if she understood him to say formaldehyde instead of Novocain. On the other hand, if she handed the surgeon a syringe full of a drug without reading and checking the label, she was not using the due care of an ordinary, reasonable and prudent professional registered nurse under similar circumstances.

In the case that follows, a physician was sued for alleged negligence of his nurse, but held not liable. The nurse took out of a medicine cabinet a bottle labeled "silver nitrate," the percentage of which was illegible. Knowing that a solution of only 1 percent (customarily used in a newborn's eyes) was usually kept there, she filled a dropper and instilled it while the doctor held open the infant's eyes. It was in fact a 30 percent solution, and impaired the infant's vision.[150] Again, nurses are reminded in their education that they are customarily taught to read the label three times on a medicine container, and to use no medicine from a container the label of which is illegible. The wisdom of adhering to such education and standards of care is obvious.

In an action for damages against an Indiana private hospital, the plaintiff sued because of malpractice in diagnosis and treatment of injury of the patient's left hip. The owner or proprietor of the hospital, which is operated for private gain and not for charity, was liable for the injury sustained by the patient as a result of the negligence of nurses or other employees.[151]

The plaintiff in another case sued a hospital and doctors for the death of a 12-day-old child as a result of what was claimed to be malpractice in permitting a baby to become infected with impetigo, and negligence in treating the infection and in discharging the plaintiff's wife and baby while the infant was still suffering with impetigo. A judgment of $6000 was awarded. Since nurses care for newborn infants, and since such nursing service is frequently given to babies in a nursery situation at hospitals, the responsibility, duty, failure and liability of a nurse are apparent.[152]

Emotional Damages

Some recent cases have allowed compensation for emotional damage. Certain standards have been formulated by the California courts, which will recognize a parent's cause of action when: (1) the emotional shock suffered by the parent results also in physical harm, (2) the parent was near the scene of the negligent act and (3) the parent's emotional trauma resulted directly from observing the incident. In California, a foster mother who had contemplated adoption of a three-year-old child held the child while dye was injected for diagnostic purposes. Because the dye contained 50 percent instead of 5 percent glucose, it caused the child to convulse and suffer blindness, quadriplegia, severe retardation and death ten months later. As a result of observing the incident and its aftermath, the mother became depressed, lost considerable weight and was bedridden. Thus, her claim satisfied the standards and was allowed to proceed to trial.[153]

However, in Pennsylvania, unless the viewer of the negligence was in the "zone of danger" at the time, i.e., was in fear of being physically injured by the negligent party, he cannot recover for his emotional damage and related physical ailments. Thus, if the California case had occurred in Pennsylvania, the mother would not have received compensation because the improper injection into her child did not place the mother in fear of physical injury to herself.[154]

A Local Versus a National Standard

Ever since the *Small* v. *Howard*[155] case of 1880, in which the court ruled that a village practitioner would be required to have only knowledge and skills comparable to those of other practitioners of ordinary ability and skill in "similar localities, with opportunities for no larger experience," the community test of malpractice has been generally applied as the legal standard for physicians, nurses and others. When the court held the physician guilty of malpractice in making a mistake in diagnosis and medical mismanagement in the care of a child born of parents with Rh factor blood incompatibility, it said:

> To fasten liability in a malpractice case, the patient must prove by a preponderance of evidence the recognized standard of medical care in the community, and that the physician being sued departed from that standard in treating the patient.[156]

However, this precedent was overruled by the *Brune* v. *Belinkoff* decision, in which the court required the anesthesiologist practicing in a smaller city to follow a general standard of care applicable to all specialists in his field. Furthermore, the court stated that it would apply the same rule to general practitioners.[157] This decision should help the regional medical programs to attain the goal of bringing the latest and best in modern health care to practitioners in all areas of the country.

ARBITRATION

As an alternative to malpractice litigation for settling disputes, arbitration is not an innovation of the past few years. A few states had arbitration statutes in the 19th century, but most of the legislation was enacted following World War I. In the early 1920s, the first Uniform Arbitration Act came into existence, and the American Arbitration Association was established in 1926.

The Medical Malpractice Commission found that only a small fraction of malpractice claims were submitted to arbitration. Based on some studies on arbitration done for the Commission and a discussion of the countrywide experience with arbitration, the Commission stated that contractual arbitration as an innovative method of settling malpractice disputes "is an important development that justifies continued experimentation and study prior to universal adoption."[158] Statutes that permit medical malpractice claims to be settled through arbitration exist in 33 states today.

Since there has been a continuing rise in the number of malpractice claims and in the size of the awards, and since this has resulted in sharply increased malpractice insurance premiums for hospitals and physicians, arbitration as an alternative has received more attention. In a San Francisco case, an 11-year-old boy who was injured in a schoolyard fight and became a quadriplegic as a result of emergency room negligence was awarded in excess of $4 million in a malpractice action against a hospital, a pediatrician and the school district.[159] In a Los Angeles case, a nine-year-old girl who had undergone a tonsillectomy was left unattended in the recovery room for 10 to 15 minutes while the only nurse present, a licensed practical nurse, was busy caring for another patient. The girl apparently suffered a cardiac arrest some minutes before it was discovered, and as a result had permanent brain damage. The parents received $150,000 and the patient's attorney $300,000, and the patient was guaranteed a monthly income for life with initial payments of $1350 monthly, to be increased 7¾ percent annually. There was also a guarantee of $100,000 if one of the parents were to survive the child.[160]

Persons who are in favor of arbitration state that it results in a speedier settlement of claims; saves the time of the litigants, witnesses and attorneys; employs the services of better-prepared and experienced decision-makers, such as lawyers and physicians; utilizes informal proceedings without the technical rules of evidence; and results in a final decision from which there is very limited appeal.[161] The nonpublic nature of arbitration also spares the reputation of professionals who are charged with fault.

Those who oppose arbitration as a substitute for malpractice litigation state that arbitation may encourage small claims and nuisance claims; may lead to more compromise judgments; may actually increase the size of awards; since the decision-makers may put a higher value on pain, suffering and the loss of income; and, because of its nonpublic nature, tends to protect those at fault by sparing them the pressure of publicity that many times forces an improvement in health care. Also many people in addition to trial lawyers feel that there is no better way of resolving complicated cases than by the "harrowing and winnowing" of adversary proceedings in a court.

For the arbitration of future disputes, the American Arbitration Association recommends the following standard arbitration clause for insertion in contracts:

> Any controversy or claim arising out of or relating to this contract, or breach thereof, shall be settled by arbitration in accordance with the Rules of the American Arbitration Association, and judgment upon the award rendered by the Arbitrator(s) may be entered in any Court having jurisdiction thereof.[162]

When parties agree to arbitration under these Rules or when they provide for arbitration by the American Arbitration Association, the duties of the AAA under these Rules may be carried out through the Tribunal Administrator or such other officers as the AAA directs. The AAA establishes and maintains a National Panel of Arbitrators and appoints arbitrators from the panel, unless the parties have appointed an arbitrator or have provided some other method of appointment of an arbitrator. It is necessary to select a mutually agreeable arbitrator for each case. Arbitration under the AAA rules may be started by the initiating party giving notice to the other party of her or his intention to arbitrate, which notice shall contain a statement setting forth the nature of the dispute, the amount involved and the remedy sought; or by filing at any Regional Office of the AAA two copies of said notice, together with two copies of the arbitration provisions of the contract, along with the appropriate administrative fee as provided in the Fee Schedule.[163]

The time and place for each hearing are fixed by the arbitrator, who mails each party a notice thereof at least five days in advance unless the parties by mutual agreement waive such notice or modify the terms. At the hearing, any party may be represented by counsel. If a party intends to be so represented, he or she is to notify the other party and the AAA at least three days prior to the date set for the hearing at which the counsel is to appear, unless the arbitration is initiated by counsel or an attorney replies for the other party. If a stenographic record or an interpreter is requested, the AAA makes the necessary arrangement for such services, and the requesting party pays the cost. Although persons with a direct interest in the arbitration are entitled to attend hearings, it is within the discretion of the arbitrator to determine the propriety of the attendance of any other persons. Although an arbitrator may take an adjournment at the request of a party or on his or her own initiative, he or she shall take one when all the parties agree to the same. At his or her discretion, the arbitrator may require witnesses to testify under oath. If there is more than one arbitrator, all decisions of the arbitrators must be at least by a majority.

At the hearing, the complaining party presents her or his claim, proofs and witnesses, who are subject to questions or other examination. The defending party then presents her or his defense, proofs and witnesses, who likewise are subject to questions or other examination. Exhibits offered by either party may be received in evidence. The relevancy and materiality of all evidence offered is judged by the arbitrator, and conformity to legal rules of evidence is not necessary. Parties may offer such evidence as they desire, and shall produce such additional evidence as the arbitrator may consider necessary to an understanding and determination of the dispute. When the law authorizes an arbitrator to subpoena witnesses or documents, she or he may do so on her or his own initiative or at the request of any party. When an arbitrator considers it necessary to make an inspection or investigation in connection with the arbitration, she or he directs the AAA to advise the parties of her or his intentions, and any party who so desires may be present at such inspection or investigation.

When all parties have no further proofs to offer or witnesses to be heard, the arbitrator declares the hearings closed. If briefs are to be filed, the hearings are declared closed as of the final date set by the arbitrator for the receipt of the briefs. The arbitrator shall make the award promptly and, unless otherwise agreed by the parties or specified by the law, no later than 30 days from the close of the hearings. The Commercial Arbitration Rules are rather more detailed than the synopsis given, but the reader can appreciate that arbitration, as opposed to litigation in court, is comparatively simple, quick, inexpensive and much less public an affair. It is quite likely that a nurse asked to be a witness at an arbitration hearing will find it a less traumatic experience than being a witness in malpractice litigation in a court.

The Ross-Loss group has dealt with 35 claims alleging malpractice since 1964. The claimant won $70,000 in one case, and the medical group won two and paid nothing. The remaining 32 claims were all settled in advance of arbitration. Although arbitration is claimed to be speedy, one of the three cases took 42 months from the occurrence of the incident to final determination. When a dispute reaches the stage of the arbitration panel, it moves rapidly, but it is getting to that final stage that takes so long.

Nurses should follow the development of arbitration as a possible alternative to the present malpractice litigation in the courts.

PROFESSIONAL LIABILITY INSURANCE

Coverage by Employer

While nurses are on duty in the hospital and to the extent that they function within the assigned job, the hospital liability insurance is adequate coverage. If a patient is injured as a result of a nurse's negligence on the assigned job, the hospital's liability insurance would defend her or him and the hospital. However, there are many situations in which nurses may practice nursing off the job.

Many nurses have been told that if they do carry their own professional liability insurance, their hospital's malpractice insurance carrier may not be liable if they are sued by a patient for negligence. This may be true, as the case of *Jones v. Medox, Inc.* illustrates.[164]

Even if a hospital does protect its employees with a professional liability policy, nurses should realize that in a number of instances they will be carrying out duties under the direction or supervision of a physician or surgeon, and will be considered temporarily as his or her special employee. Now, although the physician or surgeon likely carries malpractice insurance that covers him or her and any person for whom he or she is legally liable, it would not cover the individual liability of such an employee (employees are always personally liable for their own negligence). It is infrequent that the physician's liability policy protects the nurse; hence, his or her own individual liability policy is desirable.

Occupational health nurses will find that industry may not have professional liability insurance, and that if it does, their personal liability may not be included. Since occupational health nurses work more on their own, and the physician is not so readily available in case of need, they should consider seriously the need for their own professional liability coverage.

Nurses' Own Professional Liability Insurance

When nurses plan to secure professional liability insurance, they should shop for a policy that will best protect them. Quite often, nursing organizations offer nurses a group liability insurance policy. Heinz cites the following statement from the policy of a major company as one that offers the nurse good protection:

> To pay all loss by reason of the liability imposed by law upon the insured for damages on account of professional services rendered or which should have been rendered by the insured or any assistant to the insured during the term of this policy including the dispensing of drugs or medicine or any counterclaims in suit brought by the insured to collect fees providing such damages are claimed under any of the foregoing.[165]

Professional liability insurance (malpractice insurance) can be obtained through the state nurses' association, the American Nurses' Association, the National League for Nursing and through most of the nursing specialty organizations, such as the Association of Operating Room Nurses, the Critical Care Nurses and the American Association of Nurse Anesthetists. The price of the professional liability insurance through such groups is quite reasonable. While there is some element of duplication if the employing hospital or other agency provides malpractice coverage, it is far better to have duplicate coverage than for some part of one's liability to be uncovered. The personal professional liability policy provides not only a source of funds to pay judgments or out-of-court settlements, but also good quality legal talent to defend the nurse and to post bond while appealing a case.

SUBSTANTIAL AWARDS

In 1969, a physician examined a baby, found that he had a severe croup or cough and recommended that he be sent to the hospital. The suit alleged that, when the infant arrived at the hospital, the nurse without authorization placed him in a steam room where his heart stopped beating for several minutes, as a result of which he suffered permanent brain damage and lost the use of his limbs. According to the experts who testified at the trial, the boy actually suffered epiglottitis, a dangerous form of croup that can cause a child to strangle if not treated properly. The proper treatment would have been to insert a tube down the throat to allow breathing, the experts said. The boy, now five years old, is mentally retarded and without the use of his limbs, and attends a school for the handicapped. The parents filed suit in 1970 against the hospital, the nurse and the pediatrician. In the circuit court the parents were awarded $1 million in damages; no damages were assessed against the physician.[166]

A 79-year-old patient who suffered amputation of his right hand, allegedly as a result of negligent nursing care, was awarded $40,000 against the hospital to which he had been admitted with pneumonia. On the second day, the patient complained of coldness and numbness in his right hand, and an R.N. and a L.P./V.N. were unable to obtain a blood pressure reading in the right arm. The following day, the patient complained to a nurse that there was pain in his right arm, which felt cold and numb, and said that a blood pressure cuff had been left on his arm for an extended period. Thereafter, on this third day, an R.N. telephoned the physician to report the patient's complaints, and the physician prescribed codeine and Tylenol. At the trial, the physician claimed that the nurse mentioned only the pain, not the coldness and numbness. On the fourth day, the nurse noticed that the patient's hand was cyanotic and mottled, but did not call the physician because the chart indicated he had been notified of the patient's condition. Later the same day when the physician visited and saw the cyanosis and mottling, he called a vascular surgeon, who ordered 4000 units of heparin to be administered. Nevertheless, the hand finally had to be amputated.

At the trial, an internist testified that the failure to obtain a blood pressure reading indicated occlusion of the right brachial artery, and said that the standards of nursing practice required notification of the physician at that time. In his opinion the hand, or part of it, could have been saved had the heparin been administered on the evening of the second day, or even as late as the third day. An R.N. testified that the failure to enter observations in the nursing notes and to notify the physician that the patient's complaints were medically significant constituted less than the proper standard of nursing care. For the hospital, two vascular surgeons testified that the occlusion did not occur until the fourth day, and in their opinion the earlier administration of heparin would not have changed the outcome. The verdict was against the hospital only, and not any other party.[167]

The state supreme court affirmed a jury verdict of $22,500 in favor of a patient and against a hospital in a case in which the patient, following a hemorrhoidectomy, suffered a fat necrosis and additional hospitalization as a result of subcutaneous Dramamine administration in the area of the left hip. The correct way to administer the drug hypodermically is to inject it into the muscle. The hospital tried to defend itself on the basis that the prescribing physician did not specify that the Dramamine was to be given intramuscularly. The doctor's order was placed over the telephone. The patient was a woman of appreciable girth, and in the opinion of the court, competent and experienced nurses should have known that the proper way to carry out the order was to give the drug intramuscularly.[168]

A 73-year-old arthritic patient recovered damages for injuries sustained in a fall while being transferred from a chair to a bed.[169]

Survivors of a 78-year-old man, who was recovering from surgery and died from injuries when he fell over a railing guarding a staircase, recovered damages from a hospital.[170]

When a patient suffering a stab wound was given an intramuscular injection of an antibiotic, the nurse struck his sciatic nerve. His right leg was damaged and footdrop resulted. The patient recovered substantial damages from the hospital and nurse.[171]

Taking into account court costs and attorney's fees, the total costs in each of these cases are appreciably higher than the awards. Once again, the value of a nurse's carrying professional liability insurance should be apparent.

NURSE'S FREEDOM OF SPEECH

A Pennsylvania case[172] deals with a nurse exercising her freedom of speech. A psychiatric nurse worked at a state hospital for five years, ending in August 1972. During that time, she became increasingly concerned about violations of the standards of safe and acceptable patient care. Observed violations by the nurse included "the staff's failure to protect patients from homosexual abuse by other patients and from sexual exploitation by outside workmen; improper nonpsychiatric medical care; allowing patients to keep medication in their rooms; locking up fire extinguishers; leaving blank prescription forms, signed in advance by physicians, in unlocked drawers for nurses to fill out on weekends; and chronic absenteeism on the part of the hospital's medical staff." When the nurse's repeated complaints to her superiors were to no avail, she resigned.

Two weeks later, the nurse was hired as a supervisor of nurses at the inpatient unit of a community mental health center at a salary of $10,500 per year. The center's salaries are paid out of public funds. During the interval between jobs, the nurse had given an interview to a reporter for a city newspaper in which she discussed the conditions she observed, and criticized the care given to patients at the state hospital. Nine days after beginning her employment at the center, an article about the state hospital based on the nurse's interview appeared in the city newspaper. On the following morning two nurses at the center showed the article to the director of nurses, and told him that they and other members of the staff were upset about its publication. The director discussed the matter with his higher authorities, whose reaction was that the nurse should be discharged immediately. Upon returning to his office, the director summoned the nurse to tell her of the decision. In response to her inquiry as to whether the decision could be reconsidered, the director said it was final and there was no possibility of reconsideration. Thereafter, the nurse left the center.

Following her dismissal, the nurse was unable to secure another job as a supervisor of psychiatric nurses or as a psychiatric nurse. Then, for 2½ months, she worked as a geriatic nurse in a nursing home at a reduced salary. Her actual wage loss from the center was $213.75 per week, and at the time of the appeal this amounted to $3687.50.

The community mental health center had no formal grievance procedures at the time of the nurse's discharge. The joint executive committee held a meeting the following day at which they discussed various topics and drew up formal grievance procedures, which were published and distributed to employees. An executive was directed to contact the discharged nurse and explain the newly adopted procedures, but he failed to do so. In mid-October, the chairman of the personnel committee upon instructions wrote to the nurse briefly about the avenues of appeal available to her, and gave her 15 days in which to file an appeal. The nurse did not answer the letter because it was written on colored personal stationary with the chairman's name at the top and his home address, without indication of his position. She thought it was one of a number of letters she had received from a variety of concerned private citizens.

The nurse instituted a lawsuit against the community mental health center, and was joined by the Commonwealth of Pennsylvania in a *parens patriae* action, with the American Civil Liberties Union and the Pennsylvania Nurses Association as *amici curiae*. The lawsuit alleged deprivation of constitutional rights in connection with the termination of the nurse's employment at the center, and asked for damages and injunctive relief, including the nurse's reinstatement.

The defendants gave two reasons for the nurse's discharge: (1) inadequate performance of her job duties and (2) "staff anxiety" caused by the publication of the newspaper article. However, the court found that the allegations of inadequate performance were afterthoughts to justify the dismissal, rather than reasons for it. Moreover, evidence failed to show that the center staff members were upset at the appearance of the article, or that the plaintiff's statements to press and staff reaction to her comments would have interfered with her performance of her daily duties at the center. As the court said; "if the defendants and their staff were upset, it was because they were uneasy about having in their midst an outspoken, forthright person who had aired her grievances against her former employer in what they regarded as an unprofessional manner. Their anxiety was caused, in other words, by their proximity to a person who was engaging in precisely the sort of free and vigorous expression that the First Amendment was designed to protect."

The court said that a public employer may not, as a condition of employment, require an employee to surrender all First Amendment rights she or he would otherwise possess. It added that this does not mean that a public employee may never be restricted in her or his freedom to comment on public issues if these comments adversely affect an important interest of her or his employer.

In this case, the court cited with approval material from *Pickering* v. *Board of Education*,[173] the First and Fourteenth Amendments of the U.S. Constitution, *Board of Regents* v. *Roth*[174] and *Joint Anti Fascist Refugee Committee* v. *McGrath*.[175]

In analyzing the case, the court found that the community mental health center summarily fired the nurse not, as they claimed, to preserve a proper therapeutic environment, but because they wanted to rid themselves of an outspoken employee and to allay the personal uneasiness of some of their staff members. Against this, the court said, must be weighed the interests of the plaintiff in avoiding the loss of her job and the consequent injuries of such loss. Second, the nurse had a very real interest in avoiding the damage to her professional reputation that a summary dismissal could and did cause. Third, the nurse had an extremely important interest in having a prior hearing. Again, the court pointed out that, if an employee is to be dismissed for reasons touching on the free exercise of her First Amendment rights, the requirements of procedural due process are stringent indeed.

The court ordered the defendants to reinstate the nurse as supervisor of nurses in the inpatient unit of the community mental health center, or in a position at the parent center of equal rank and pay. It also ordered the defendants to pay the nurse $3687.50 in back wages and $213.75 a week until reinstatement. Further, the court enjoined the defendants from interfering in any way with the nurse's exercise of her First Amendment rights.

Several lessons are to be learned from the case. Nurses and their employers should note that courts will examine the real, as well as the alleged, reasons for dismissal of an employee. A public employer may not, as a condition of employment, require employees to surrender all First Amendment rights they would otherwise possess. Although this does not mean that public employees may not be restricted in their freedom to comment on public issues if their comments adversely affect an important interest of their employer, the problem is to arrive at a balance. In order to determine whether a hearing is required before an employee is discharged from a publicly supported institution, the court must weigh the institution's interest in summary dismissal against the grievous loss that the employee may suffer and the employee's interest in avoiding that loss. The pre-discharge hearing test is a strict one, and is constitutionally dispensable only if the employer's interest is important and significantly outweighs the employee's interest.

The case does not uphold nurses who irresponsibly or capriciously criticize hospitals, but it does recognize that nurses, as is true of all employees, enjoy freedom of speech guaranteed by the First Amendment, and that employers may not compel nurses as their employees to surrender such rights as a condition of employment. When there is a decision to discharge a nurse, there must be a formal grievance procedure and an opportunity for a fair, impartial hearing, if the employee wishes to avail himself or herself of such a procedural due process.[176]

SOME PRECAUTIONS TO OBSERVE

Nurses must learn the basic facts of their profession; they must learn to observe, evaluate and judge a patient's condition. In addition, they must learn to perform their duties with at least the care of the ordinary, reasonable and prudent nurse in those particular circumstances. They must realize that they are personally responsible for their own wrongful or negligent acts, and that as an employee or agent they may render their employer liable.

If in doubt about a written order from a physician, nurses should make sure that they understand it before attempting to carry it out. The situation is somewhat like the story of the bad egg: If there is any doubt about it, there is no doubt about it. They should secure an interpretation or verification of the order if it is not clear. There are tactful ways of securing explanations.

If, in pursuit of their nursing assignments, nurses notice an adverse effect of a medicine the doctor has ordered administered to a patient, they should not continue to carry out orders blindly, but should report adverse effects immediately and request further orders. Part of the nurse's duty is to observe symptoms and reactions and report them.

Nurses, the same as any other person in the course of everyday human activities, may render medical care in an emergency, and in so doing they would not be liable for violating medical practice acts.

Nurses are not authorized to give medical opinions either before a case is brought up in court or in testimony at a trial. Like any other witness on the stand, nurses may state what they have seen, heard or done.[178]

We have previously mentioned the fact that insurance is available for the protection of the nurse. Some authorities believe that all registered nurses should carry malpractice insurance to cover the cost of expert legal protection and to pay possible claims for damages.

References

1. Prosser: *Torts* (Hornbook, 1964), Sec. 35, 36. Cf. *Restatement, Torts*, Sec. 281 Palsgraf v. Long Island R. Co., 248 N.Y. 339, 162 N.E. 99, 59 A.L.R. 1263 (1928).
2. Napier v. Greenzweig, 256 Fed. 196 (2d Cir., 1919); Forthofer v. Arnold, 60 Ohio App. 436, 21 N.E. 2d 869 (1938).
3. Rodgers v. Kline, 56 Miss. 808, 31 Am. Rep. 389 (1879).
4. Kilpatrick v. Wright, 437 F. Supp. 397 (U.S. Dist. Ct. M. D. Ala., 1977); *Education Ct. Dig.*, 22:1, Aug. 1978.
5. Kaufman v. Israel Zion Hospital, 183 Misc. 714, 51 N.Y.S. 2d 412 (1944).
6. Espinosa v. Beverly Hospital et al., 249 P. 2d 843 (Calif., 1953).
7. Granite Home v. Schwartz, 364 S.W. 2d 309 (Ark., 1963).
8. Deutsch v. Doctors Hospital, *The AMA News*, Oct. 4, 1965, p. 2.
9. Powell v. Fidelity & Casualty Co. of New York, 185 So. 2d 324 (1966).
10. Amaya v. Home Ice, Fuel & Supply Co., 23 Cal. Rptr. 131 (1962).
11. Kraus v. Spielberg and Jewish Hospital of Brooklyn, 37 Misc. 2d 519, 236 N.Y.S. 2d 143 (1962).
12. Makolondra v. St. Therese Hospital (Ill. Cir. Ct., Cook Co., Docket No. 71C–668, Apr. 27, 1973); *Citation*, 27:150, Sept. 1, 1973.
13. Kambas v. St. Joseph's Mercy Hospital of Detroit, 205 N.W. 2d 431 (Mich. Sup. Ct., 1973); *Citation*, 27:87–88, July 1, 1973.
14. Armstrong v. Wallace, 8 Cal. App. 2d 429, 37 P. 2d 467, 47 P. 2d 740 (1935).
15. Piper v. Epstein, 326 Ill. App. 400, 62 N.E. 2d 139 (1945).
16. Martin v. Perth Amboy Hospital et al., 1969 CCH Neg. 4385 (N.J.).
17. Hestbeck v. Hennepin County, 212 N.W. 2d 361 (Minn., 1973).
18. Bowers v. Olch, 260 P. 2d 997 (Calif., 1953).
19. Quinby v. Morrow et al., 340 F. 2d 584 (U.S. Ct. App., 2d Cir., Vt., 1965).
20. Hospital Authority of St. Mary's v. Eason, 148 S.E. 2d 499 (Ga., 1966).
21. Kopa v. United States, 236 F. Supp. 189 (D.C. Hawaii, 1964).
22. City of Shawnee v. Roush, 101 Okla. 60, 223 Pac. 354 (1924); *Hospitals*, X:82–83, Feb. 1936.
23. Stuart Circle Hospital Corporation v. Curry, 173 Va. 136, 3 S.E. 2d 153 (1939).
24. Flower Hospital v. Hart, 178 Okla. 447, 62 P. 2d 1248 (1936); *Hospitals*, XI:106, April 1937.
25. Dittert v. Fischer, 148 Ore. 366, 36 P. 2d 592 (1934); *Hospitals*, XIII:99, Feb. 1939.
26. Clark v. Piedmont Hospital, 117 Ga. App. 875, 162 S.E. 2d 418 (Ga. Ct. App., 1968).
27. May v. Broun, 492 P. 2d 776 (Ore., 1972).
28. Bing v. Thunig, 143 N.E. 2d 3 (N.Y., 1957).
29. Nichter v. Edmiston, 407 P. 2d 721 (Nev., 1965). See Holder, A. R.: Electrosurgical Instruments, *JAMA*, 223:111, Jan. 1, 1973.
30. Gordon, Adm. v. Harbor Hospital, Inc., 275 App. Div. 1047, 92 N.Y.S. 2d 1010 (1949).
31. Creighton, H.: Are Side Rails Necessary? *Nurs. Management*, 13:45–48, June 1982.
32. Avilez v. South Jefferson General Hospital, 403 So. 2d 1260 (La. Ct. of App., 1981).
33. Garfield Memorial Hospital v. Marshall, 204 F. 2d 721 (U.S. Ct. App., D.C., 1953).
34. Washington Hospital Center v. Martin, 454 A. 2d 306 (D.C. Ct. of App., 1982); *Citation*, 47:84, July 15, 1983.
35. Cardamon v. Iowa Lutheran Hospital, 128 N.W. 2d 226 (Iowa, 1964). Regan, W. A.: Hospital Negligence Cases in the Court, *Hosp. Prog.*, 42:62–63, 128, June 1961.
36. South Broward Hospital District v. Schmitt, 172 So. 2d 12, cert. dism. 174 So. 2d 726 (Fla., 1965).
37. Hospital Authority of Hall County v. Adams, 110 Ga. App. 848, 140 S.E. 139 (1964).
38. Rhodes v. Moore et al., 239 Ore. 454, 398 P. 2d 189 (1965).
39. Vick v. Methodist Evangelical Hosp., 1966 CCH Neg. 273 (Ky., 1966).
40. Powell v. Parkview Estate Nursing Home, Inc., 240 So. 2d 53 (La., 1970). See also *Silver Threads*, Feb. 1971, p. 10.
41. Fidelity Insurance Co. v. Lynch, 455 S.W. 2d 79 (Ark., 1970).
42. Elm v. St. Joseph's Hospital, 180 N.W. 2d 262 (Minn., 1970). Regan, W. A.: Law Forum, *Hosp. Prog.*, 52:26, 31, March 1971.
43. Horton v. Niagara Falls Memorial Medical Center, 380 N.Y.S. 2d 116 (N.Y. Sup. Ct. App. Div., 1976); *Citation*, 33:66, July 1, 1976.
44. Howard v. Research Hospital and Medical Center, Inc., 563 S.W. 2d 111 (Mo. Ct. App., 1978); *Citation*, 37:102–103, Aug. 15, 1978.
45. Koblitz v. Laguna Beach Nursing Home (Cal. Super. Ct., Orange Co., Docket No. 238715, 1976); *Citation*, 35:29, May 15, 1977.
46. Thompson v. United States, 368 F. Supp. 466 (D.C. La., 1973); *Citation*, 29:25–26, May 1, 1974.
47. Duling v. Bluefield Sanitarium, Inc., 149 W. Va. 467, 142 N.E. 2d 754 (1965).
48. Darling v. Charleston Memorial Hospital, 211 N.E. 253 (W. Va., 1965). *Regan Rep. on Nurs. Law*, 5(9):3, Feb., 1965; Hershey, N.: Hospital's Expanding Responsibility, *Am. J. Nurs.*, 66:1546–1547, July 1966.

49. Goff v. Buchanan Hospital, 333 P. 2d 29 (Cal. App., 1959). Parker, L. T.: Liable for Negligence of Nurse, *Hosp. Topics*, 37:60–61, Dec. 1959.
50. Sprick v. North Shore Hospital, 121 So. 2d 682 (Fla., 1960). *See also* Holder, A. R.: Birth Injuries, *JAMA*, 219:129, Jan. 3, 1972.
51. McWilliams, R. M.: Medico-Legal Aspects of the Missing R.N., *AORN Journal* 18:767–770, Oct. 1973; Hershey, N.: Prudence and the Coffee Break, *Am. J. Nurs.*, 70:2389–2390, Nov. 1970; Rosovsky, L. E.: The Law and the Coffee Break, *Can. Hosp.*, 49:48–49, Dec. 1972.
52. O'Grady v. Brown, 654 S.W. 2d 904 (Mo. S. Ct., 1983); *Citation*, 48:117, Mar. 1, 1984.
53. Parrish v. Clark, 107 Fla. 598, 145 So. 848 (1933).
54. Norton v. Argonaut Insurance Co., 144 So. 2d 249 (Ct. App., La., 1962).
55. Penaloza v. Baptist Memorial Hospital, 304 S.W. 2d 203 (Tex., 1957).
56. Neel v. San Antonio Community Hospital, 1 Cal. Rptr. 313 (1959).
57. Kaiser v. Suburban Transportation System, 398 P. 2d 14, Amended 401 P. 2d 350 (Wash., 1965).
58. O'Neil v. Glens Falls Indemnity Co., 35 Am. Law Rep. 452, 310 F. 2d 165 (U.S. Ct. App., 8th Circ., 1962).
59. Ward v. Henderson et al., 110 Ga. App. 780; 140 S.E. 2d 92, 142 S.E. 2d 244, 143 S.E. 2d 44 (Ga., 1965).
60. Henderson v. Twin Falls County, 56 Idaho 124, 50 P. 2d 597, Aff'm. 80 P. 2d 801 (1938).
61. Masonic Hospital Assoc. of Payne County v. Taggart, 171 Okla. 563, 43 P. 2d 142 (1935).
62. Gault v. Poor Sisters and St. Joseph Hospital, 1967 CCH Neg. Cases 1223.
63. Kincl v. Hycel, Inc., 372 N.E. 385 (App. Ct. Ill. First Dist., 1977); *Pub. Health Ct. Dig.*, 24:4, Oct. 1978.
64. Lewis v. Northridge Hospital (Cal. Super. Ct. Los Angeles Co., Docket No. NWC 24536, Dec. 11, 1973); *Citation*, 29:29, 1974.
65. Muller v. Likoff, 310 A, 2d 303 (Pa., 1973); Regan, W. A.: Law Forum: Nurse Implicated in Femoral Nerve Injury, *Hosp. Prog.*, 55:28, 35–36, May 1974.
66. Hunt v. Ernzen, 252 N.W. 2d 445 (Iowa Sup. Ct., 1977).
67. Reid v. Aetna Life Insurance Co., 440 E. Supp. 1182 (D.C. Ill., 1977); *Citation*, 37:9, April 15, 1978.
68. Wilmington General Hospital v. Nichols, 210 A. 2d 861 (Del., 1965). *See also* Regan, W. A.: Nursing Policy and Hypodermic Injections, *Regan Rep. on Nurs. Law*, 6(2):1, July 1965.
69. Southern Florida Sa. v. Hodge, 215 So. 2d 753 (Fla., 1968).
70. Swafford, W. B.: Legal Aspects of Drug Distribution and Administration, *Hosp. Management*, 102:64, Nov. 1966.
71. Norton v. Argonaut Ins. Co., 144 So. 2d 249 (Ct. App., La., 1962).

72. Willig, S. H.: *The Nurse's Guide to the Law*. New York, McGraw-Hill Book Co., 1970, p. 200.
73. Ritter, J.: The Nurse's Viewpoint of Pharmacy in a Hospital, *Weather Vane*, 38:9, 11, June 1969.
74. Kinkela, G. G., and Kinkela, R. V.: Dispensing Drugs: A Professional Nurse's Responsibility, *J. Nurs. Adm.*, 3:7, Jan./Feb. 1973.
75. Stack v. Wapner, 368 A. 2d 292 (Pa. Super. Ct., 1976); *Citation*, 35:38, June 1, 1977.
76. Necolayeff v. Genesee Hospital, 61 N.Y.S. 2d 832 (N.Y., 1946).
77. Ebaugh v. Rabkin, 99 Cal. Rptr. 706, 1972. *See* Bergen, R. P.: Mistaken Identify, *JAMA*, 221:747, Aug. 14, 1972.
78. Hayt, E. et al.: *Law of Hospital and Nurse*. New York, Hospital Textbook Co., 1958, p. 198.
79. Op. Atty. Gen. 368 (N.Y., 1942).
80. Champer, J.: Historical and Legal Aspects of Blood Transfusions, *Hosp. Management*, 85:50, Feb. 1958.
81. *Supra*, note 76.
82. Whitehurst v. American National Red Cross, 1 Az. App. Rep. 326, 402 P. 2d 584 (1965).
83. Renslow v. Mennonite Hospital, 351 N.E. 2d 870 (Ill. App., 1976).
84. Martin v. Southern Baptist Hospital, 352 So. 2d 351 (Ct. App., 4th Circ., La., 1977); *Pub. Health Ct. Dig.*, 24:1, Nov. 1978.
85. Garafola v. Maimonides Hospital of Brooklyn et al., 253 N.Y.S. 2d 856, Aff'd 279 N.Y.S. 2d 523, 226 N.E. 311 (1967).
86. Adams v. State of Washington, 1967 CCH Neg. 1821; *Regan Rep. on Hospital Law*, 8:3, Oct. 1967.
87. Karrigan v. Nazareth Convent and Academy, Inc., 510 P. 2d 190 (Kans., 1973). Regan, W. A.: Law Forum: Nursing Service Ruled Negligent for Delay in Notifying Physician, *Hosp. Prog.*, 54:12, 14–16, Oct. 1973.
88. Ramsey et al. v. Physicians Memorial Hospital, Inc., et al., 373 A. 2d 76 (Md., 1977). Creighton, H.: Nurse's Failure to Communicate, *Superv. Nurse*, 8:10–11, Dec. 1977.
89. Utter v. United Hospital Center, 236 S.E. 2d 213 (W. Va. Sup. Ct. App., 1977); *Citation*, 36:1–2, Oct. 15, 1977.
90. Battles v. Aderhold, 430 So. 2d 307 (La. Ct. of App., 1983); *Citation*, 48:66, Jan. 1, 1984.
91. Woodhouse v. Knickerbocker Hospital, 39 N.Y.S. 2d 671, Aff'm 43 N.Y.S. 2d 518 (1943).
92. Clemens v. Smith, 170 Ore. 400, 134 P. 2d 424 (1943).
93. Dwyer v. Jackson, 20 Wis. 2d 318, 121 N.W. 2d 881 (1902).
94. Thompson v. Brent, 245 So. 2d 751 (La., 1971).
95. Garfield Park Community Hospital v. Vitacco, Ill. Cir. Ct. Cook Co., Docket No. 69 L-8335, Mar. 1, 1973; *Citation*, 28:131, Feb. 15, 1974.
96. Quichocho v. Kelvinator Corporation, 546 F. 2d 812 (C.A. 9, Guam, 1976).
97. University Community Hospital v. Martin,

328 So. 2d 858 (Fla. Dist. Ct. App., 1976); *Citation*, 33:67–68, July 1, 1976.

98. James v. Keefe and Keefe, Inc., 379 N.Y.S. 2d 576 (N.Y. Sup. Ct. App., 1975).

99. Florida Medical Center, Inc. v. Von Stetina, 436 So. 2d 1022 (Fla. Dist. Ct. of App., 1983), rehearing denied; *Citation*, 48:61, Jan. 1, 1984.

100. Boza v. Schiebel, 308 S.E. 2d 510 (N.C. Ct. of App., 1983); *Citation*, 49:43, June 1, 1984.

101. Regan, W. A.: Family Care No Substitute for RN Service, *Regan Rep. Nurs. Law*, 5(6):1, Nov. 1964.

102. Williams v. Sisters of the Incarnate Word, 341 So. 2d 1299 (Ct. of App. 3rd Cir. La., 1977). *See also* Regan, W. A.: Law Forum, *Hosp. Prog.*, 58:29, Dec. 1977.

103. Hunt v. Bogalusa Community Medical Center, 303 So. 2d 745 (S. Ct. La., 1974).

104. Goodeaux v. Martin Hospital, Inc., 333 So. 2d 717 (La. App. 2d Cir., 1976).

105. Avey v. St. Francis Hospital, 1968 C.C.H. Negl. 3675.

106. Duling v. Bluefield Sanitarium, Inc., 142 S. 2d 754 (S. Ct. of App. W. Va., 1965).

107. Norton v. Argonaut Insurance Co. et al., 144 So. 2d 249 (Ct. App. 1st Cir. La., 1962).

108. Baker v. United States, 226 F. Supp. 120 (S.D. Iowa, 1964), Aff'd 343 F. Supp. 222 (8th Circ., 1965).

109. Frederic v. United States, 246 F. Supp. 368 (D. La., 1965).

110. Scheidman, E.: Preventing Suicide. *Am. J. Nurs.*, 65:111, May 1965.

111. Adams v. State of Washington, 1967 CCH Neg. (1921).

112. Nichols v. Green Acres Rest Home, 245 So. 2d 544 (La., 1971). See also *Regan Rep. on Nurs. Law*, 11(12):3, May 1971.

113. Blaes, S. M.: Nursing Home and the Law of Negligence, *Nursing Homes*, 17:8–12, 1968.

114. Gregory v. Robinson, 338 S.W. 2d 88 (Mo., 1960). *See* comments of Judge Eager. *See also* Bernzweig, E. P.: *Legal Aspects of PHS Medical Care*. Washington, D.C., Public Health Service Pub. No. 1468, 1968, pp. 58–59.

115. Torres v. City of New York, 396 N.Y.S. 2d 34 (N.Y. Sup. Ct. App. Div., 1977); *Citation*, 36:6, Oct. 15, 1977.

116. Ritter v. Board of Commissioners of Adams County Public Hospital District, 96 Wash. 2d 503, 637 P. 2d 940 (Wash. Sup. Ct., 1981). Creighton, H.: When Physician Violates Hospital Policies, *Nurs. Management*, 13:61–63, Aug. 1982.

117. Poor Sisters of St. Francis Seraph v. Catron, 435 N.E. 2d 305 (Ct. App. Ind. 2nd Dist., 1982); Creighton, H.: Should Nurses Report Negligence in Medical Treatment? *Nurs. Management*, 14:47–49, Jan. 1983.

118. Utter v. United Hospital Centre, Inc., 236 S.E. 2d 213 (S. Ct. W. Va., 1977).

119. Toth v. Community Hospital at Glen Cove, 22 N.Y., 2d 255, 239 N.E. 2d 368 (Ct. App. N.Y., 1968).

120. Fifer, W.: Infection Control as a Quality Control in an Integrated Hospital Quality Assurance Program, *Amer. J. of Infection Control*, 9:120, Nov. 1981.

121. Creighton, H.: Liability for Infection Control, *Nurs. Management*, 13:42–44, Nov. 1982.

122. Bartlett v. Argonaut Insurance Co., 523 S.W. 2d 385 (S. Ct. Ark., 1975).

123. Wilson v. Stilwill, 92 Mich. App. 227, 284 N.W. 2d 773 (Ct. App. Mich., 1979).

124. Suburban Hospital Assn., Inc. v. Hadary, 22 Md. App. 186, 322 A. 2d 258 (Ct. of Special App. Med., 1974).

125. Robey v. Jewish Hospital of Brooklyn, 280 N.Y. 533, 21 N.E. 694, 254 App. Div. 874 (1939).

126. Scott v. Salem County Memorial Hospital, 280 A. 2d 843 (N.J., 1971).

127. Defalco v. Long Island College Hospital, 383 N.Y.S. 2d 859 (N.Y. 1976); *Regan Rep. on Nurs. Law*, 18:3, Oct. 1977.

128. Stears v. Park Avenue Hospital, Cal. Super. Ct. Docket No. EAC 9578, May 1973; *Citation*, 27:161, Sept. 15, 1973.

129. Maidma v. Glendora Community Hospital, Cal. Super. Ct., Los Angeles Co. Docket No. EAC 12392, June 1973; *Citation*, 27: 161–162, Sept. 15, 1973.

130. Burke v. Kessler (Fla. Cir. Ct. Dade Co., Case No. 72–12726, 1973); *Citation*, 27:100, July 15, 1973.

131. Sadler, A. M., and Sadler, B. L.: Transplantation and the Law: The Need for Organized Sensitivity, 57 *Georgetown Law Journal*, 5:27 (1968). *See also* Waltz, J. R., and Inbau, F. E.: *Medical Jurisprudence*. New York, Macmillan Publishing Co., 1971, p. 228.

132. Williamson, W. P.: Life or Death, Whose Decision? *JAMA*, 197:793, 1966.

133. Report of the Ad Hoc Committee of the Harvard Medical School to Examine the Definition of Brain Death: A Definition of Irreversible Coma, *JAMA*, 205:337–340, Aug. 5, 1968.

134. Quoted in Wecht, C.: Attorney Describes Current Efforts to Establish Uniform Guidelines (in death and transplantation), *Hospitals*, 43:54–57, Nov. 1, 1969.

135. Prosser, W. L.: *Handbook of Law of Torts*. Sec. 43. St. Paul, Minn., West Publishing Co., 1941.

136. Valentine v. Kaiser Foundation Hospital, 15 Cal. Rep. 26 (1961).

137. Moore v. Belt, 34 Cal. 2d 525, 203 P. 2d 22, 212 P. 2d 509 (1949).

138. Wallstedt v. Swedish Hospital, 220 Minn. 274, 19 N.W. 2d 426 (1945).

139. Eccard, W. T.: Revolution in White, 30 *Vanderbilt L. Rev.*, 839, 851, May 1977.

140. Wagner v. Kaiser Foundation Hospitals et al., 589 P. 2d 1106 (S. Ct. Ore., 1979). Drug Errors and Reversal Therapy: Legalities, *Regan Rep. Nursing Law*, 19:1, March 1979.

141. Lyons v. Salve Regina College, 565 F. 2d (U.S. Ct. App. 1st Cir. R.I., 1977); *Education Ct. Dig.*, 22:4, Aug. 1978.

142. *Supra*, note 139, *cf.* pp. 878–879.

143. Valentin v. La Société Française de Bien-faisance Mutuelle de Los Angeles, 76 Cal. App. 2d 1, 172 P. 2d 359 (1956).
144. Wasmuth, C. E.: *Law for the Physician.* Philadelphia, Lea & Febiger, 1966, p. 121.
145. Akridge v. Nobel, 41 S.E. 78 (Ga., 1902).
146. Bradford, A. L., and Carlson, P. A.: Captain of the Ship. *Insurance Counsel Journal* 156 (1960); The Borrowed Servant Doctrine As It Applies to Operating Surgeons, 19 *Southwestern Law Journal* 179 (1965).
147. Wilson v. Lee Memorial Hospital, 65 So. 2d 40 (Fla., 1953).
148. Minogue v. Rutland Hospital, Inc., 125 A. 2d 796 (Vt., 1956).
149. Hallinan v. Prindle, 220 Cal. 46, 11 P. 2d 426 (modified); 17 Cal. App. 2d 656 (rev'd), 62 P. 2d 1075 aff'm in part (rev'd in part, 1936). See Gordon, Turner and Price: Medical Jurisprudence (1953), p. 148, for an interesting comment and comparison with English cases.
150. Covington v. Wyatt, 196 N.C. 357, 145 S.E. 673 (1928).
151. Iterman v. Baker, 214 Ind. 308, 11 N.E. 2d 64 (1937).
152. Criss v. Angelus Hospital Association of Los Angeles et al., 13 Cal. App. 2d 412, 56 P. 2d 1274 (1936).
153. Mobaldi v. Board of Regents of the University of California, 127 Cal. Rpt. 720 (Cal. App., 1976).
154. Scarf v. Koltoff, 45 Law Week 2203 (Pa. Super. Ct., 1976); Bernstein, A. H.: Hospitals Face Increasing Exposure to Liability, *Hospitals*, 51:106, 108, Sept. 1, 1977.
155. Small v. Howard, 128 Mass. 131 (1880).
156. Price v. Neyland, 320 F. 2d 674 (U.S. Ct. App. D.C., 1963).
157. Brune v. Belinkoff, 235 N.E. 2d 793 (Mass., 1968).
158. *Report of the Secretary's Commission on Medical Malpractice.* Washington, D.C., Department of Health, Education and Welfare, Government Printing Office, 1973, Pub. No. (05 73–88), p. 96.
159. Niles v. City of San Rafael School District, Cal. Super Ct., San Francisco Co., Docket No. 624337, Feb. 5, 1973; *Citation*, 28:49, Dec. 1, 1973.
160. Stears v. Park Avenue Hospital, Cal. Super. Ct., Los Angeles Co., Docket No. EAC 9578, May 1973; *Citation*, 27:161, Sept. 15, 1973.
161. United Steel Workers v. Warrior and Gulf Navigation Co. (U.S. Sup. Ct., June 20, 1957).
162. Commercial Arbitration Rules of the American Arbitration Association as amended and in effect Nov. 1, 1973. New York, American Arbitration Association, 1973, p. 2.
163. Id., p. 3.
164. Jones v. Medox, Inc., 430 A. 2d 488 (D.C. Ct. App., 1981).
165. Heinz, C. H.: Professional Liability Insurance for Nurses, Nurs. Clin. North Am., 2(1):177, March 1967.
166. $1 Million Malpractice Award, *Chicago Tribune*, July 19, 1974.
167. Walton v. Providence Hospital, Cal. Super. Ct., Alameda Co., Docket No. 433105, March 14, 1974; *Citation*, 29:106, July 15, 1974.
168. Barnes v. St. Francis Hospital and School of Nursing, Inc., 507 P. 2d 288 (Kansas, 1973); Regan, W. A.: Law Forum, *Hosp. Prog.*, 54:10, 12–16, Aug. 1973.
169. Martin v. Intercommunity Hospital, Cal. Super. Ct., Solano Co., Docket No. 53711, Jan. 26, 1973; *Citation*, 28:56, Dec. 1, 1973.
170. Leibel v. St. Mary's Hospital of Milwaukee, 203 N.W. 715 (Wis. S. Ct., 1973); *Citation*, 27:58–59, June 1, 1973.
171. Massey v. Heine, 497 S.W. 2d 564 (Ky. Ct. App., 1973).
172. Commonwealth of Pennsylvania ex rel. Linda Rafferty et al. v. Philadelphia Psychiatric Center et al., 356 F. Supp. 500 (U.S.D.C.-E.D., Pa., 1973).
173. Pickering v. Board of Education, 391 U.S. 563, 568, 88 S. Ct. 1731, 1734, 20 L.Ed. 2d 811 (1968).
174. Board of Regents v. Roth, 408 U.S. 564, 577, 92 S. Ct. 2701, 2709, 33 L.Ed. 2d 548 (1972).
175. Joint Anti Fascist Refugee Committee v. McGrath, 341 U.S. 123, 168, 71 S. Ct. 624, 95 L.Ed. 817 (1951).
176. Cf. Regan, W. A.: Law Forum. *Hosp. Prog.*, 54:32, Nov. 1973.
177. City of Miami v. Oates, 152 Fla., 21, 10 So. 2d 721 (1942).

General References

Allen, P.: Legal Controversies in Nursing: Doing What Is Right, *AORN J.*, 31(5)158+, April 1980.
Bell, N. K.: Whose Anatomy Is at Stake? *Am. J. Nursing*, 81:1170–1172, June 1981.
Bennett, H. M.: Negligence, Part I, *Crit. Care Nurse*, 3:8, July/Aug. 1983.
Creighton, H.: Nurses and the Malpractice Law, Part I, *Superv. Nurse*, 11:36–37, July 1980.
Creighton, H.: Nurses and the Malpractice Law, Part II, *Superv. Nurse*, 11:44–46, Aug. 1980.
Creighton, H.: Refusal to Treat Patients, *Superv. Nurse*, 12:67+, April 1981.
Creighton, H.: Are Side Rails Necessary? *Nurs. Management*, 13:45–48, June 1982.
Creighton, H.: When Physician Violates Hospital Policies, *Nurs. Management*, 13:61–63, Aug. 1982.
Creighton, H.: Liability for Infection Control, *Nurs. Management*, 13:42–44, Nov. 1982.
Creighton, H.: Insurer Agrees to Cover M.D.'s Supervising Midwives, *Nurs. Management*, 14:19–20, Oct. 1983.
Creighton, H.: Transporting Accident Patients by Paramedics, *Nurs. Management*, 15:71–73, April 1984.
Cushing, M.: A Judgment on Standards, *Am. J. Nursing*, 81:797–798, April 1981.
Finch, J.: Law and the Doctor: Judgment or Damnation, *Midwife Health Visit. Community Nurse*, 19:58–59, Feb. 1983.

Finch, J.: The Arthur Judgment, *Nurs. Mirror*, 153(21)1203, Nov. 18, 1981.

Fince, J.: Law and the Nurse 5. From All Points of View, *Nurs. Mirror*, 153(1)29–30, July 1, 1981.

Furrow, B. R.: Diminished Lives and Malpractice, *Law, Med. & Health Care*, 10:100–174, June 1982.

Gouge, R. L.: Legally Speaking: The MD-Patient Relationship Still Sacred, *R.N.*, 43(4)71–74, April 1980.

Greenlaw, J.: When Leaving the Siderails Down Can Bring You Up on Charges, *R.N.*, 45:47–48, Dec. 1982.

Hart, M.: To Count or Not to Count, *AORN J.*, 31(5)775–778, April 1980.

Kucera, W. R.: Famous Last Words: "But the Doctor Said," *AANA J.*, 48(5)448–450, Oct. 1980.

Kucera, W. R.: Imputed Negligence: The Captain of the Ship is Sinking, *AANA J.*, 48(2)162–164, April 1980.

Kucera, W. R.: Judging the Nurse: A Standard of Care, Yes, But Which One? *AANA J.*, 48(4)392–394, Aug. 1980.

Kucera, W. R.: *Res ipsa loquitur*, "The Thing Speaks for Itself". . . Especially Regarding the Unconscious Patient, *AANA J.*, 49:287–289, June 1981.

Langlow, A.: The Nurse 8, The Law: Drugs and the Need for Systems, Part II, *Aust. Nurses' J.*, 10(11)22–24, June 1981.

McLain, N. B.: Risk Management in the Operating Room, *AORN J.*, 31(5)873+, April 1980.

Philpott, M.: *Legal Liability and the Nursing Process*. Toronto, W. B. Saunders Co., 1985.

Regan, W. A.: Is Hepatitis Carrier Liable for Infection of Surgical Patient? *AORN J.*, 32(6)952–954, Dec. 1980.

Regan, W. A.: What Is Liability of OR Staff in Cardiac Arrest? *AORN J.*, 21(4)639–640, March 1980.

Eight

TORTS AS A SOURCE OF OTHER CIVIL ACTIONS

TORT

At the outset, it may be well to differentiate torts from crimes. A tort is a legal wrong, committed against a person or property independent of contract, which renders the person who commits it liable for damages in a civil action. There are many types of torts, but we are interested in the ones most frequently encountered by nurses. A tort or legal wrong may consist of a direct invasion of some legal right of a person, the violation of some public duty by which special damages come to a person or the violation of some private duty by which damages come to a person.[1]

According to the law of torts, a person, A, is liable for invading (encroaching upon) the interest of another person, B: (1) if the interest invaded is protected against the unintentional invasion, (2) if the conduct of person A is negligent in regard to such an interest, (3) if such conduct is a legal cause of the invasion and (4) if person B has not disabled himself by his conduct so that he is prevented from bringing an action.

By contrast, a crime is defined as any wrong that is punishable by the state. For an act to be a deliberate crime, at least two elements are necessary: evil intent (mens rea) and a criminal act. However, there are crimes in which the matter of intent is not spelled out; that is, when there is some grossly negligent act or when the person is ignorant of the law.

CIVIL ACTION

At this juncture, it is advisable to give a brief account of how a civil action proceeds, without attempting a detailed description. In a civil lawsuit, the plaintiff is sometimes a "petitioner" and the defendant the "respondent." For the court to acquire jurisdiction (a legal right to hear the case), a summons is served on the defendant. A summons is a written notification, signed by the proper officer, served on a person requesting him or her to appear in court on a specified day to answer to the plaintiff upon pain of judgment against the defendant for default (failure) in not showing up.[3] Pleadings in the case are the papers stating the claims of the plaintiff and the defenses of the defendant.

Before the defendant may be brought to a civil trial, a complaint setting forth the cause of action in legal form must be served upon him. Sometimes the details of the claim are given in a bill of particulars. Then, in return, the defendant sets forth an answer in which he or she may deny any or all of the plaintiff's charges and offer certain specific defenses, such as the statute of limitations. Alternatively, the defendant may admit all the plaintiff's charges and file a demurrer, which means that, assuming the truth of the charges stated, the charges do not state a cause of action, and hence the plaintiff should not be allowed to proceed further. The defendant may also set up a counterclaim for damages from the plaintiff. After the pleadings have been made, either the plaintiff or the defendant may serve notice of trial on the other.

Witnesses are served a subpoena, a summons to attend court under a penalty for failure, such as punishment for contempt. At this point, nurses are reminded that one of the obligations or duties of a citizen is to aid the administration of justice and to appear in order to testify to their knowledge of facts. When witnesses must bring certain records, they are served a subpoena known as a *subpoena duces tecum*. The constitutional right of trial by jury may be waived if both the plaintiff and the defendant agree to do so; in that event the case is tried only before a judge. The right to a trial by jury does not exist in every type of case, but in this brief overview, exceptions and details are omitted. If the trial is by jury, the jurors are selected and sworn (i.e., they take an oath). The trial judge handles questions of law and some questions of fact. Other matters, such as the amount of damages, the trustworthiness of witnesses and the important question of choosing between conflicting accounts of the events, are left for the jury to decide.

At a civil trial, the plaintiff's lawyer outlines her or his case and calls witnesses. The witnesses are first examined by the plaintiff's lawyer, and then may be cross-examined by the defendant's lawyer. After this, they may be re-examined by the plaintiff's lawyer. When the plaintiff has finished presenting her or his case, the defendant's lawyer may ask that the suit be dismissed on the ground that the plaintiff has failed to state a case for the defendant to answer. If this is refused, the defendant's case is presented in the same way as was the plaintiff's case. Then follows argument by the lawyers, a "summing up" to the jury. The court instructs the jury as to the law and possible verdicts, after which the jury leaves the courtroom. The jury, in the jury room, weighs the facts and arguments. The jurors return when they are ready either to give a verdict or to state that they cannot reach an agreement. At times, verdicts of juries are set aside as contrary to the law or evidence. One or both of the parties may appeal the decision of a lower court to a higher court.

ASSAULT AND BATTERY

A recital of civil actions other than negligence or malpractice may now be set forth. Assault and battery are two words we often hear together, but they have separate meanings. Assault is the unjustifiable attempt to touch another person or the threat to do so in such circumstances as to cause the other reasonably to believe that it will be carried out.[4] Battery means the unlawful beating of another or the carrying out of threatened physical harm. It includes every willful, angry and violent or negligent touching of another's person or clothes or anything attached to his person or held by him.[5]

A woman confined to a New York State Hospital for nine years recovered $15,000 damages where no medical eyewitness testimony was offered to justify her being locked in her cell in solitary confinement and being beaten and subjected to other abuses. The court ruled that, although detention in a state hospital may be necessary, unnecessary punishment and cruelty, if proved, constitute malpractice. It found that the patient was subjected to such cruel and unusual punishments as to constitute assaults upon her.[6]

Lack of Consent or Privilege

The lack of consent or privilege is an important part of the meaning of assault. Consent is a defense to an action when a person is charged with intentionally interfering with either a person or his property.[7] However, if a person in his actions goes beyond the limits to which a person consented, he may be liable. Also, if the person who does consent is known to be an infant, mentally incompetent or intoxicated—matters that make a person incapable of giving consent—the consent is not a valid defense. At times, too, physicians and nurses have learned "the hard way" that the fact that treatment is desirable does not allow one to go ahead without the consent of the patient or someone entitled to give consent for her or him. However, as explained elsewhere, in an emergency nurses may do what they can to save life and limb, even in cases in which they have no consent or can obtain none. Consent may be given by conduct as well as by express words. For example, in a case in which a person held up his arm to be vaccinated, the court said he would not be heard to deny that he had consented.[8] Consent to an act that is *prima facie* (on the surface of it) actionable will afterward deprive a person of the right to complain of it. Although consent may be given by words or implied by conduct, it must be free, and the person must understand what she or he is doing.

Duty to Secure. Nurses are concerned about consent forms, and rightly so. In recent years more and more lawsuits have alleged lack of consent. To begin with, the nurse should know that the attending surgeon has the duty of informing the patient concerning the nature of the proposed surgical procedure.[9] This must be done by a physician and it cannot be delegated to a nurse. Ward secretaries, aides or nurses can fill out the consent form, and any of these people may witness the patient's signing the consent. Preferably, nurses or physicians should present the form to patients for their signature, since they can more readily appraise the conditions at the time. If patients' sensoria are clouded by medications, such as narcotics, or if they do not know the essential information pertaining to the surgery, they cannot give a valid consent for it. Moreover, the consent must be voluntary, for it is an established principle of law that adults of sound mind have the right to decide what shall or shall not be done to their bodies. In the case of a married woman, her consent is all that is required by law. However, when the surgery affects the sex functions or may result in the death of an unborn child, then as a matter of good public relations the spouse's consent is desirable. Although oral consent, if proved, is valid, written consent is highly desirable and quite generally required by hospitals. Written consent is presumed to be valid, but oral consent may be difficult to prove.

In an emergency, consent may be implied if immediate surgery is necessary to save the patient's life and an express consent cannot be obtained. Consent never authorizes unnecessary surgery.

Emancipated and Mature Minors. If the patient is a minor, or at least not a mature or emancipated minor, consent for surgery must be obtained from the parent or guardian. In the case of children whose parents are separated or divorced, consent must be obtained from the parent who has custody. For years, in most states, physicians were liable to charges of assault and battery if they treated a minor without the parents' consent, except in an emergency. In accident cases, such as one in which amputation was necessary to save a 15-year-old boy whose foot was mangled,[10] or one in which a seven-year-old sustained a comminuted fracture of the elbow,[11] consent is implied in the law. Also, in a case in which a school principal failed to locate the mother and took a seven-year-old child with a fractured forearm to a doctor's office for treatment, the court held that the physician was justified in proceeding without the parents' consent.[12]

However, when a visiting nurse took a nine-year-old boy to a city doctor, who sent him to a hospital with the request that his tonsils and adenoids be removed, and no one secured the permission of the parents for surgery, the court allowed nominal damages in a suit against the surgeon.[13] Although the boy was accompanied by a 15-year-old brother, such a sibling cannot give a valid consent in lieu of the parents, and this was not an emergency situation.

In the case of a mature minor, his consent may be sufficient, as it was when a 19-year-old boy had a tumor removed from his ear.[14] More recently, in the case of an 18-year-old who had plastic surgery performed on her nose without the consent of her parents, the court held that an unemancipated minor may consent to a "simple operation."[15] However, the parents' responsibility for a child's health and welfare is supported by law, and most physicians and many agencies are reluctant to interfere.

The whole issue of parents' constitutional rights versus a child's right of protection was reviewed in a recent Wisconsin case in which the mother of a six-year-old black boy with sickle cell anemia refused to give her consent for a splenectomy and other blood procedures recommended by attending physicians, and the State Child Welfare Division filed a petition alleging neglect in failing to provide care for her child's health. The mother objected as a Jehovah's Witness on religious grounds and also:

> because of risks of adverse effects and because medical opinion could not assure her with any certainty that such transfusions would save the life of her child or substantially benefit his health and welfare.[16]

Although the religious objections were overruled, the court found that the mother's:

> reservations and objections to the proposed treatments were made in good faith, entirely apart from her objections for religious reasons.[17]

They dismissed the petition against her.

However, a Maryland law[18] makes provision for physicians to examine and treat minors for venereal disease without consent of their parents or guardians. Both Massachusetts and Connecticut have somewhat similar statutes.[19] Since many physicians report that minors seek medical prescriptions for "the pill" to prevent conception or for treatment of an illegitimate pregnancy, these statutes are significant, and both nurses and physicians will be obliged to keep their knowledge current in this area.

Religious Objections. In one case, the Supreme Court of Illinois held that the appointment of a conservator and authorization of transfusions of whole blood to a ward without giving notice to her or to her husband interfered with their basic constitutional rights. The couple had notified the physician and hospital of their belief that the acceptance of blood transfusions constituted a violation of the law of God, no minor children were involved and there appeared otherwise no clear and present danger to society.[20]

In a Texas case,[21] the U.S. District Court for the Southern District of Texas upheld a state judge's action in ordering temporary removal of an infant from his parents' custody to that of the Child Welfare Unit and empowering the Unit to provide necessary emergency medical treatment. The parents, who were Jehovah's Witnesses, refused to consent to a blood transfusion needed because of the Rh negative factor in their child's blood. The court said that, although parents may be free to become martyrs themselves, they are not free to make martyrs of their children before the latter have reached the age of full and legal discretion.

When operating room supervisors are or ought to be aware of the performance of an unusual surgical procedure, they are responsible for notifying the nursing supervisor if the consent for surgery lacks reference to such a procedure.[22] When a minor died following a very unusual surgical procedure for scoliosis, and the surgeon had not informed the parents about it, although the hospital knew he had used it for several years, both the surgeon and the hospital were liable in damages.[23] Nurses who find themselves unexpectedly assisting a surgeon who is doing something unusual, or something that is even in violation of hospital rules, must continue to assist the surgeon, for to do otherwise might jeopardize the patient's life. However, after surgery, they should report the matter to their superior in the chain of command.

It is sometimes difficult for a nurse to realize that persons do not have to accept treatment and to be healed, and that treatment must not be forced upon them. In discussing consents, Grace Barbee, lawyer for the California Nurses' Association, cites a Long Island case in which the physician thought a patient who had been seriously ill should be motivated to get out of bed and walk. All efforts to motivate him failed, so the physician threw back the bed covers, and he and the nurse slid the patient to the floor, carefully walked him around and then put him back in bed. Some days later, the patient was discharged. However, the patient sued the physician and hospital for damages for assault and battery, and the court allowed the suit on the grounds that the patient had an absolute right to refuse to be touched.[24]

The Supreme Court affirmed an appeals court ruling that compelling a mental patient to take medication over religious objections is a violation of First Amendment rights.[25] The case was brought by Miriam Winters, after her discharge from the state hospital, against New York's Bellevue Hospital and the Central Islip State Hospital. The plaintiff contended that her rights were violated when she was given medication at the hospitals despite her objections, and that this ran counter to her beliefs as a Christian Scientist. She asked damages and an injunction against such treatment in the future. The doctors had diagnosed the patient as a chronic paranoid schizophrenic. The state argued that constitutional guarantees of freedom of religion could not "be used as a cloak for a person with a contagious or infectious disease" and said the same principle applied to mental illness.

Research Consents

If nurses are not to share the headlines with other clinical investigators,[26] they must secure the patient's consent in research. Any research should provide the subject patient with sufficient information to make a knowledgeable decision as to whether he or she wishes to participate in the study. The abuses in drug evaluation studies prompted the Food and Drug Administration to issue specific guidelines on how patient consent is to be obtained:

> The patient must have the legal capacity and freedom of choice to give consent, and . . . he must be given necessary information about the investigational drug. This information must include the purpose of the drug, the duration and method of use, hazards expected (including the fact that the patient may be used as a control), alternative therapy available, if any, and possible effects upon his health.[27]

The guidelines say that the "not feasible" exemption will be:

> limited to cases where the patient cannot communicate or is otherwise unable to give his informed consent, his representative is not available, and it is necessary to use the drug without delay.

A patient brought a million-dollar suit against the Memorial Hospital for Cancer and Allied Diseases, the Memorial Sloan-Kettering Cancer Center, the Sloan-Kettering Institute for Cancer Research and the James Ewing Hospital, a city institution, charging that he was injected with live cancer cells. He had been suffering from cancer for some years. The experiments were part of a ten-year study by the Sloan-Kettering Center designed to test the speed and manner in which debilitated noncancerous patients reject cancer implants.[28]

The Federal Code identifies six elements of informed consent:

> A fair explanation of the procedures, to be followed, their purposes, and the identification of any procedures that are experimental.
> A description of any attendant discomfort and risks reasonably to be expected.
> A description of any benefits reasonably to be expected.
> A disclosure of appropriate alternative procedures that might be advantageous for the subject.
> An offer to answer any inquiries about the procedure.
> An instruction that the person is free to withdraw consent and discontinue participation in the project or activity at any time without prejudice to the subject.[29]

Examples of Assault and Battery

Freedom from contact with another person is one of our personal rights, and this applies to the nurse-patient relationship. When persons come to the hospital, they presumably consent to be treated, and at times this involves contact with another person. However, they may have some ideas of their own, may wish to refuse certain contacts and may say so. For example, they may refuse a back rub or an intramuscular injection of a drug. In such a case, if the nurse, for instance, knowing that a paralyzed patient has refused to consent to such an injection, nevertheless comes toward him with 2 ml of penicillin in a syringe with a No. 22 needle in her hand as though she were going to give him an injection, she has threatened or assaulted him even though she has said nothing. If she follows through, still without his consent, and gives him the injection, the nurse has committed a battery.

Nurses may be liable on a charge of battery if they do anything improper in handling or treating an unconscious patient. One does not need to be in actual person-to-person contact to commit a battery. If a person strikes another with a stick or rolled paper, or forcibly removes clothing without the other's consent, it may be an act of battery.

In a Pennsylvania case, an agent of an artificial limb company falsely represented himself as a physician to a woman who had lost one leg and wore an artificial one, and she was persuaded therefore to undress so that he could determine how it fitted. Under these circumstances, the fraud negated her consent, and the man was held guilty of indecent assault.[30] Most actions involving assault and battery are brought as civil actions to recover damages, but this example illustrates how they may be criminal proceedings, with the state prosecuting a person for his act.

In a New York case, the parents of an 11-year-old boy sued physicians to recover damages for the boy's death, on the grounds that the physicians had performed an unnecessary operation without the consent of the patient, of his parents or of a person in whose custody the boy was. The doctor offered evidence that the boy had blood poisoning, that he acted in an emergency and that the use of chloroform as an anesthetic was reasonable, although it proved fatal to the boy because of status lymphaticus. The judgment was for the physicians.[31]

The defendant in a Louisiana case was infuriated one morning by the way the plaintiff drove his car, and followed him to a parking lot in the city. A fight followed, during which the plaintiff had his clothes torn and his face bruised. An award of $350 for unprovoked assault and battery was held not excessive in view of the plaintiff's injuries, embarrassment and humiliation, in addition to damage to his clothing. The court observed:

> No provocative acts, conduct, former insults, threats, or words, if unaccompanied by an overt act of hostility, will justify an assault, no matter how offensive or exasperating, nor how much they can be calculated to excite or irritate.[32]

An Iowa case concerned an action for damages for assault and battery wherein the plaintiff offered evidence that the defendant maliciously assaulted him, causing severe pain, injury and humiliation and necessitating medical treatment, and disabled him from attending his business for five days. A verdict of $500 actual damages and $500 exemplary damages was upheld.[33]

In a Tennessee case, a corporation and doctors employed by the corporation in a dispensary for treating employees were held not liable for damages. The plaintiff charged that her examination by the physicians, since they lacked a state license to practice medicine, was really assault and battery, even though she had voluntarily submitted to the examination on the supposition that the physicians were licensed. The plaintiff did not claim any negligent acts on the part of the physicians in their diagnosis or treatment, nor did she claim that the corporation was negligent in selecting the doctors. The court said that failure to comply with a licensing statute might subject a person to criminal prosecution. Nevertheless, to sustain a civil action on these facts, the plaintiff must show that the result complained of was due to negligent or unskilled treatment.[34]

As one writer has pointed out in discussing torts, it is justifiable to violate a police regulation in order to save a life.[35] As a parent may use reasonable force in the correction and punishment of a child, so may military officers use similar disciplinary authority. In some jurisdictions, a school teacher also may use disciplinary measures involving reasonable force or restraint to maintain morale and order. Likewise, a person may, if necessary, use reasonable force in resisting an unlawful arrest.

In discussing intent in tort actions, a well-known authority has said that a person intends a result when she or he acts in order to achieve it or when the result is certain to follow her or his acts.[36]

Persons acting unlawfully, or not conducting themselves properly, may be ejected forcibly from a building if necessary. This could happen to nurses who were incompetent or who conducted themselves unprofessionably, e.g., reporting for work inebriated or not leaving quietly if requested to by the hospital.

In an action by a patient against a sanitarium for injuries (including a fractured jaw when he was struck by an employee upon the chin), an adverse judgment was affirmed because it appeared that the attendant committed assault and battery in his own necessary self-defense.[37]

A patient who sustained a fractured jaw when assaulted and beaten by an attendant who objected to his tapping his foot on the floor at the Brooklyn State Hospital, to which he was confined, recovered $3000 damages for pain and suffering.[38] The court stated that the state must exercise reasonable care to protect its patients from injuries, with such attention to their safety and the safety of others as their mental and physical condition, if known, may require. New York is one of the few states that permits patients in the state hospitals to bring suit against the state.

Where a patient sued a hospital and a physician for malpractice and assault, the court ruled that the alleged intentional sexual assault by the doctor employed in the hospital could not be interpreted as an act in furtherance of the business of the hospital, so that there was no basis for a cause of action against the hospital.[39]

Nurses have been concerned about whether they could draw a blood sample when requested by the police in the absence of the patient's consent. In *Schmerber* v. *State of California*, the Supreme Court of the United States ruled that the tests made on a blood sample drawn by a physician in a hospital from a person arrested by the police were admissible evidence in a court action.[40] Nurses should check on the law in the state in which they are working, as such laws vary. Whereas Kansas rules that a blood sample is not to be drawn if a person objects, although such refusal is a basis for suspending his driver's license,[41] New York exempts physicians, registered professional nurses and their employers from liability if they draw a blood sample without the person's consent at the request of the police.[42]

When a 27-year-old unmarried patient consulted a physician for severe ower abdominal pain during her periods, he proposed exploratory surgery to remove adhesions and the endometrioma. During surgery, the physician found that her reproductive organs were so distorted by adhesions that he felt she was already sterile. After consulting with the assisting surgeon, he performed a total hysterectomy. There was no life-threatening situation. The Louisiana Supreme Court ruled that the physician was liable for battery for performing the hysterectomy without the patient's consent.[43]

A former nurse's aide at a Glendale nursing home in Wisconsin pleaded no contest to a charge of misdemeanor battery of a nursing home resident. She was accused of sticking a 76-year-old female resident in the buttocks over 50 times with a pin and holding a pillow over the woman's face.[44]

ABUSE

Child Abuse

Not all parents are reasonable and prudent, let alone loving; a few frankly abuse their children in fits of anger or for various other reasons. Therefore, all states in recent years have enacted laws to encourage or compel people to report any suspected case of child abuse to the police or child welfare agency, and these laws provide immunity from civil and criminal suit for those who do. Nurses as well as physicians are required in many states to report suspected child abuse victims. In particular, emergency room nurses and physicians must be alert to the problem. Along with the reporting required by law, the nurse who is knowledgeable in the services of community agencies may often refer these people to those equipped to help them deal with their problems. The nurse will find the Child Abuse Prevention and Treatment Act helpful to an understanding of Federal law on the subject.[45]

Statutes give juvenile courts jurisdiction over "neglected" children in every state, and mistreatment is a form of neglect. In some states, the emphasis is on the behavior of parents, e.g., whether they are cruel to a child. In other states, the emphasis is on the child's environment and whether it is unsuitable, owing to the neglect of one or both parents. What the statute of a particular state emphasizes is important, since it tells what must be proved to spell out a neglect case. In any neglect or child abuse case, two questions have to be answered: (1) What actually happened? and (2) Do the facts presented amount to neglect or abuse?

Evidence is a problem, and situations about which objective proof cannot be produced cannot be remedied through the court. However, at least in one state, circumstantial evidence may shift the burden of a satisfactory explanation to the parents. For instance, In the Matter of S., the court said:

> [T]he proceeding . . . was initiated undoubtedly by a consensus of view, medical and social agency, that the child Freddie, only a month old, presented a case of a battered child syndrome. Proof of abuse by a parent or parents is difficult because such actions ordinarily occur in the privacy of the home without outside witnesses. Objective study of the problem of the battered child . . . has pointed up a number of propositions, among them, that usually it is only one child in the family who is the victim; that the parents tend to protect each other and resist outside inquiry and interference; and that the adult who has injured a child tends to repeat such action and suffers no remorse from his conduct.
>
> Therefore in this type of proceedings affecting a battered child syndrome, I am borrowing from the evidentiary law of negligency the principle of "res ipsa loquitur" and accepting the proposition that the condition of the child speaks for itself, thus permitting an inference of neglect to be drawn from proof of the child's age and condition, and that the latter is such as in the ordinary course of things does not happen if the parent who has the responsibility and control of the infant is protective and nonabusive. And without satisfactory explanation, I would be constrained to make a finding of fact of neglect on the part of the parent or parents and thus afford the court the opportunity to inquire into any mental, physical or emotional inadequacies of the parents and/or to

enlist any guidance and counseling the parents might need. This is the court's responsibility to the Child.[46]

In such situations, the juvenile court may order protective supervision of the child so that his or her situation may be improved through casework techniques and the use of other community resources. In some states, the welfare department is required to investigate and offer social services to families where child abuse is alleged.[47]

As Cheney has pointed out,[48] the problem of safeguarding legal rights in providing protective services is a thorny one. In those states that have no statutes for providing protective services in child neglect cases, under juvenile court laws, the parent is protected from state power by the requirements of due process of law. However, in protective services, the social worker who is part of an administrative agency is authorized to supervise the home as the court may order, and the standards of care expected of the family are set by the agency at its discretion. The presence of a stranger (the agency worker) in the home may deprive parents of liberty without due process of law. In addition, the due process requirement raises the family's right to counsel at a hearing. Because juvenile court hearings do not have to provide a defendant with the same safeguards as are necessarily provided in a criminal action, providing the family with counsel in the form of a lawyer is not mandatory. As a consequence, many feel the legal maxim that "every man is entitled to his day in court" is not carried into effect, and that administrative agencies with supposedly benevolent intentions negate legal rights in a number of instances.

The fact that the actions of the protective services are not without question or criticism by various members of society is illustrated by some of the following cases. A complaint of neglect was brought because a child's parents advocated Communism,[49] because their interracial marriage affected the family-community relationship[50] and because they neglected the child's religious instruction.[51] While one family was petitioning for a reversal of a decision denying them the return of their children because their house was too small, they lost half of them through adoption.[52] Also, one agency petitioned to remove a child from his home because his mother visited taverns.[53] Therefore, as Cheney points out, the best way to assure both that due process of law is followed and that the values on which decisions are made are clearly stated is to provide parents with counsel.[54] Legal procedures are not impediments to timely correction of this social ill of child abuse, but rather help to make certain that the decisions of protective services are based on relevant criteria.

School nurses should protect themselves from possible lawsuits by making certain that their reports are made only to designated individuals within the school system. Since school nurses are often among the first people to know of child abuse, their reports on this matter are important.[55]

Foster parents were convicted of manslaughter in the death of a four-year-old child who died from a hematoma caused by a subdural hemorrhage and aggravated by a second skull injury. The child's body showed marks of over 150 bruises of varying ages. The parents stated that the child was extremely clumsy and sustained the injuries in two falls down the stairs.[56]

A father was convicted of manslaughter in the first degree when a six-month-old baby boy died of a skull fracture and a spiral fracture of the leg when left with his father while his mother went to a laundromat. According to the mother, the father had a temper and the baby's crying annoyed him.[57] The parents were not married, and the father said the baby rolled off a bed.

The father of a child was convicted of killing her with karate chops to the liver and kidneys, and three physicians testified that she was the victim of the battered child syndrome. The father, who was skilled in karate, admitted that he practiced karate on her and encouraged her siblings to follow his example.[58]

The problems that a physician encounters with child abuse are documented by Holder in an article in the *Journal of the American Medical Association*.[59] The nursing responsibility in child abuse is discussed by Friedman and others in an article in *Nursing Forum*.[60]

In the case of *Landeros v. Flood*,[61] a mother brought her 11-month-old child to the San Jose Hospital for examination, diagnosis and treatment. At that time, the plaintiff baby was suffering from a comminuted spiral fracture of the right tibia and fibula, which apparently had been caused by a twisting force. Her mother had no explanation of this injury. The baby also had bruises over her entire back and superficial abrasions on other parts of her body. In addition, she had a nondepressed linear fracture of the skull, which was in the process of healing, and was tearful and apprehensive when approached. It was further alleged that proper diagnosis of the baby's condition would have included taking x-rays of her entire skeletal structure, and that this would have revealed the skull fracture. The defendants negligently failed to take such x-rays and thereby negligently failed to diagnose her battered child syndrome. It was further alleged that proper medical treatment would have included reporting the injuries to local law enforcement authorities or the juvenile probation department. This would have resulted in an investigation by the concerned agencies, followed by a placement of the baby in protective custody until her safety was assured. The defendants negligently failed to make such a report.

The complaint further stated that, as a result of the preceding negligence, the plaintiff was released from San Jose Hospital without proper diagnosis and treatment of her battered child syndrome and was returned to the custody of the mother and her common-law husband, who resumed physically abusing her.

Two months later, the baby was brought in for medical care to a different doctor at another hospital. She had sustained traumatic blows to her right eye and back, puncture wounds over her lower left leg and across her back, severe bites on her face, and second- and third-degree burns on her left hand. This time, the battered child syndrome was immediately diagnosed and reported to local police and juvenile probation authorties. Following hospitalization and surgery, she was placed with foster parents, who subsequently undertook to adopt her. The foster parents on behalf of the child brought a damage action against the first hospital and the physician who had treated her.

The baby's natural mother and common law husband fled the state but were apprehended, returned for trial and convicted of the crime of child abuse.

In *People v. Jackson*,[62] the Court of Appeals held as admissible the testimony of a physician identifying the typical elements of the battered child syndrome:

> (1) The child is usually under three years of age; (2) there is evidence of bone injury at different times; (3) there are subdural hematomas with or without skull fractures; (4) there is a seriously injured child who does not have a history given that fits the injuries; (5) there is evidence of soft tissue injury; (6) there is evidence of neglect.

From the *Landeros v. Flood* case as well as other cases, it seems clear that doctors, nurses and other professionals who deal with injured children and their troubled families leave the responsibility of reporting evidence of possible child abuse to the proper authorities.

While undergoing treatment for her injuries, a four-year-old child-abuse victim told a physician and nurse that she was injured when "my mommy beat me." The Wyoming Supreme Court ruled that the child's statements were admissible under the treatment and diagnosis exception to the hearsay rule. The mother's conviction for child abuse was affirmed.[63]

Patient Abuse

The abuse of patients—striking out against patients who annoy, irritate and frustrate members of the nursing team—is unfortunately not as uncommon as nurses would like to believe it is. Among other authors, Ken Kesey in *One Flew Over the Cuckoo's Nest*[64] and Mary Jane Ward in *The Snake Pit*[65] portray the abuse of patients in psychiatric hospitals, where the situation has repeatedly occurred for many years. The celebrated case of *Commonwealth of Pennsylvania ex rel. Linda Rafferty et al. v. Philadelphia Psychiatric Center et al.*[66] involving a nurse's freedom of speech grew out of a psychiatric nurse's observation of violations at Haverford State Hospital over a five-year period. Infractions included the staff's failure to protect patients from homosexual abuse by other patients and from sexual exploitation by outside workmen as well as other types of negligence and neglect by nursing and medical staff. The report on Haverford State Hospital found that the nursing and medical staff were, if not directly abusive, at least accessories to those who did abuse patients.

An article by Susan Jacoby, "Waiting for the End: On Nursing Homes," in *The New York Times Magazine*,[67] described, among other regrettable conditions in extended care facilities and nursing homes, the abusive treatment received by some very elderly patients.

Nurses should realize that abusive treatment can and does occur in any portion of a hospital: medical, surgical, obstetrical, pediatric, psychiatric, emergency room, recovery room or other clinical areas in which patient's anxiety might cause them to behave in a provoking manner. Both verbal and physical abuse are always a distinct possibility.

In her discussion of verbal abuse, Nations cites threatening words that cause patients or their family members to feel fearful or intimidated; words of coercion that tend to leave a patient without freedom to act or to decide; words of extortion that attempt to illegally deprive patients of their money or property; words of vulgarity that may be construed as offensive or threatening; and derogatory words that cause patients to feel ridiculed.[68]

A patient, who was 108 years old, suffered aggravation of the senility process, bruises on her arms, chest and right eye and diminished alertness as a result of mistreatment by a nurse's aide in a convalescent hospital.[69] The California jury awarded $27,000 damages, including $2000 in general damages and $25,000 in punitive damages. The trial revealed that the hospital negligently hired a young nurse's aide with one year of experience who had been fired from another convalescent hospital for alleged mistreatment of patients.

In an article by August Gribbin on "Neglected Heroes,"[70] one finds the story of a 24-year-old soldier who was manning a machine gun on a moving jeep that hit a land mine in South Vietnam. He is now almost entirely paralyzed, and aides must clothe him, feed him and swing him in and out of bed on a special lift. The veteran says that one aide, who had idly ignored his repeated calls for help at the Hines (Ill.) VA Hospital, finally put him in the lift and whispered, "You ever say a word or complain, and I'll let your ass fall from this thing one day."

Another determined Vietnam-combat artilleryman damaged his spinal cord in a stateside accident and is now a paraplegic. He left the VA Hospital in Memphis, because he was allegedly given no rehabilitation training and was punished for too much candor. "They punished me by keeping me in bed except for an hour a day."[71] This situation involved both negligence and punishment by staff.

In the case of a New York patient,[72] a quadriplegic confined to a wheelchair brought an action against the state claiming that a therapeutic aide had struck him in the face. While no one witnessed the incident, the patient suffered a cut tongue, a small abrasion over his left eye and a bruise on his forehead. According to the aide, the patient had been injured in a fall from his wheelchair. The court of claims, after a hearing, said that the evidence supported the patient's claim of being assaulted by the aide and awarded him $526.64 for his injuries and the hospital bill for treatment. The court of claims also concluded that he was entitled to $5000 in punitive damages for the hospital's reckless conduct. On the day of the incident, testimony showed that the aide had reported to work under the influence of alcohol and in an emotionally unstable condition. In addition, the hospital had been aware of the aide's alcohol problem when it hired him, and it continued to employ him after other incidents involving alcoholism.

In Alabama,[73] a patient brought suit against a county for sexual assault allegedly committed on him by a county hospital employee in the course of his duties. The state supreme court set aside the precedent of immunity for government subdivisions (in this case the county) and ruled, in effect, that the plaintiff patient could sue the county for alleged wrongdoing.

In New York,[74] the dismissal of an attendant from a children's psychiatric hospital was sustained following a hearing under the Civil Service Law. The attendant struck an agitated 13-year-old boy in the abdomen after disarming him when the boy was threatening other patients with a chair leg. The boy was not very strong, and a nurse who heard the commotion was able to remove him from the ward and calm him down without the use of excessive force.

Physical abuse of patients is not always easy to detect. Patients may be intimidated into not reporting it, or the injuries may be reported as the result of a patient's fall, for example. If reported by the patient, the account may be attributed to senility, paranoia or other delusions or the unreliability of youth. Even with professional nursing staff who have higher education and experience, abuse can be a problem, although it is usually a greater problem with nonprofessional nursing staff.

Abusive Patients

A patient suffering from acute and chronic alcoholism was admitted to a hospital at the request of the county sheriff's department. He was examined by a physician who prescribed Valium and restraints, if needed. Later in the evening, the patient awakened and threatened to leave, abused the nurses and attempted to physically assault those who came near him. At the hospital's request, the sheriff's department took the patient, who had not been regularly discharged, from the hospital to the jail and put him to bed. The following morning, the patient was found shaking uncontrollably and having trouble breathing, so he was returned to the hospital where he died soon after arrival. In an action brought by the patient's children against the hospital, the appellate court affirmed a verdict in favor of the hospital.[76]

In an action by a patient against a sanitarium for injuries including a fractured jaw when he was struck by an employee on the chin, an adverse judgment was affirmed because the attendant apparently committed assault and battery in his own necessary self-defense.[77]

On the other hand, nurses may have to defend themselves against patients who might assault or strike them. Everyone is allowed to defend himself from unlawful attack even, for example, in a psychiatric setting. However, only those steps necessary for self-protection or the aid of another are permitted. Self-defense is said to extend to the use of reasonable force that appears to be necessary for protection against the threatened interference.[78] A few cases illustrating action involving assault follow.

A person is allowed to defend another person by use of force reasonably necessary to prevent a threatened attack when the defense would be allowed by ordinary social custom.[79] Also, anyone who has real or personal property is allowed to defend it by the use of force that appears reasonably necessary to prevent threatened interference with his or her possession.[80]

When a private duty registered nurse was injured by an alcoholic patient who hit her on the head with a table lamp, she sued him for assault.[81] The state supreme court reversed a verdict for the patient and ordered a new trial, stating that the nurse assumed the risk of injury if she could have prevented it by the exercise of due care, or if it was not an unreasonable risk for her to accept in the course of her duty. A private duty nurse is an independent contractor. Consent is a defense to assault and battery cases as well as to others, unless the consent is against the policy of the law. The defense of assumption of risk comes from the common law rule of *volenti nonfit injuria,* i.e., to one who consents no wrong is done.

Alcohol/Drug Abuse

Federal statutes protect certain patient records, particularly those related to alcohol and drug abuse. Only on a court order or with a specific release from the patient should information on these records be released.

An estimated 75,000 nurses with alcohol or drug problems are found in the United States today. An increasingly common experience of working nurses is the use of mood-altering drugs. Jessup reports that 67 percent of the license probations and 83 percent of the license revocations of registered nurses in a recent six-month period in California were drug-related.[82] From September 1980 to August 1981, the Council of State Boards of Nursing reported that 649 nurses lost their licenses in this country as a result of chemical dependency.[83] Dismissing nurses rather than referring them for treatment will only remove them from one hospital and place them in another until their dependency is discovered again. Nurses have three responsibilities in regard to the chemically dependent nurse: (1) that patients are not placed in jeopardy by the unrecognized and untreated illness of a nurse; (2) that standards of integrity and practice within the profession are maintained and (3) that colleagues who are ill receive the care and effective action they need.[84] A variety of treatment choices include specialized inpatient facilities, community detoxification centers, outpatient services at mental health clinics, private therapists, Alcoholics Anonymous, Narcotics Anonymous and diversion programs mandated by the courts.[85] In Milwaukee, the DePaul Rehabilitation Hospital has an Impaired Nurse Program. In dealing with such nurses, the supervisor's major concern must be with job performance.[86]

A registered nurse who diverted the painkilling drug Demerol to her own use (which must have resulted in protracted pain to those patients for whom the drug was prescribed) had her license suspended for one year.[87] In another case, a registered nurse in Alabama substituted a quantity of unknown pills for Tylenol #3 tablets. After a hearing, the board of nursing concluded that she was guilty of unprofessional conduct of a nature likely to deceive, defraud or injure the public in matters relating to health, and her nursing license was revoked.[88]

Those nurses who work with alcoholics will be interested in the *Powell* v. *State of Texas* decision. Although the court recognized alcoholism as one of the most serious social and public health problems today, it described professional knowledge of the subject as "comparatively primitive." Consequently, the court refused to rule that the criminal punishment of a chronic alcoholic for public drunkenness was unconstitutional. Said the court:

> One virtue of the criminal process is, at least, that the duration of penal incarceration typically has some outside statutory limit. . . . therapeutic civil commitment lacks this feature; one is typically committed until one is "cured." Thus, to do otherwise than affirm [the conviction of Powell], might subject indigent alcoholics to the risk that they may be locked up for an indefinite period of time under the same conditions as before, with no more hope than before of receiving effective treatment and no prospect of periodic "freedom."[89]

To convict an ambulance driver of driving while under the influence of liquor, some courts require chemical evidence and others merely use common sense.[90]

FALSE IMPRISONMENT

False imprisonment means the unjustifiable detention of a person without a legal warrant, within boundaries fixed by the defendant, by an act or violation of duty intended to result in such confinement.[91] For example, to confine a patient by unjustifiably locking him in a room is a false imprisonment. If it is accompanied by unjustifiable forcible restraint or threat of restraint, it is an assault. In regard to nurses and other medical personnel, the charge of false imprisonment may arise in the case of mental patients. A right existed at common law to confine insane persons in order to prevent injury to themselves or others or to prevent property damage. However, this right existed only for the length of time required to get legal authority for the person's restraint. By statutes in the various states today, procedures have been devised for committing persons who are mentally deranged and for caring for their property.

Another way in which a charge of false imprisonment may arise against a nurse may be for detaining a patient for payment of a bill. Nurses, for example, may detain patients for a few minutes to check on whether they have paid their bills, and this is looked on as reasonable and permissible. Nurses may not, however, lawfully detain patients longer, whether or not they have paid the bill. The detention of patients for failure to pay their bill would be false imprisonment. There are other remedies at law available to a person for collecting wages, payment for services and hospital charges.

For example, a sane person was kept for 11 hours in a hospital against her will for failure to pay a bill. There was evidence that one of the nurses told her she would be tied to the bed if she did not keep quiet, and that the door was locked. The plaintiff recovered money damages.[92]

In another case, a dentist claimed that a patient in his office owed him $33 for denture work. The patient asserted that the fees amounted to $22; the dentist locked the door to compel her to pay what he claimed or return the denture. The patient sued him for damages for false imprisonment, and the dentist was adjudged liable.[93]

A suit against a hospital for false imprisonment of a child was dismissed in a case in which the mother, who had come to take her child home from the hospital, was delayed 30 minutes while she arranged for payment of her child's bill.[94] Since there was no threat that the child could not leave the hospital unless the bill was paid or secured, the charge of false imprisonment was not supported.

A patient discharged from Mattewan State Hospital was awarded $300,000 in damages for false imprisonment.[95] The facts of the case show that he had been committed to this hospital for the criminally insane with a diagnosis of a paranoid condition with chronic alcoholism in May 1947, when he was incompetent to stand criminal trial for assault with a knife. At the trial, various psychiatric witnesses testified that, with proper treatment, he should have been discharged within two years at the most and sent back for trial. Acordingly, he was given damages for the balance of his 12 years and four months of confinement. The case stands for the right to treatment. If this case is followed, patients can sue for a writ of *habeas corpus* and compel their release from a psychiatric hospital on the grounds of no or inadequate treatment.

Saralee Maniaci, a former student, sued Marquette University for false imprisonment and libel and a physician for malpractice, and asked for $300,000 in damages from each for being placed in a hospital mental ward when she tried to quit college without saying where she was going. As a 16-year-old boarding student living far from her parents, she was blocked by university officials who first wanted to contact her parents. The doctor said she told him that she was going to work in a nightclub and support herself. She was released the next morning when her father called and demanded that she be freed.[96]

A patient brought a lawsuit for damages for false imprisonment, assault and battery, negligence and breach of contract against a hospital and two physicians. Involuntary admission was alleged, and there was a question concerning whether she had properly demanded her release and whether it was refused for reasonable and sufficient cause; hence a summary judgment in favor of the hospital was reserved.[97]

A 67-year-old patient who had Parkinson's disease, arthritis, heart trouble, a hiatal hernia, voice impediment and a history of alcoholism was admitted to a nursing home. Thereafter he was locked up and kept for 51 days, during which time he demanded his release and attempted to escape. Eventually he escaped, hitched a ride to the home of a friend and brought suit against the nursing home for false imprisonment. He was awarded $12,000.[98]

A housewife living with her husband and children, and considering a divorce, was taken on a court order at the instigation of her husband from her home to a private psychiatric hospital. She was allowed no communication in or out for several weeks and was given, over her objection, a tranquilizer ordered by the psychiatrist. The hospital was found liable for false imprisonment, and the unconsented application of medication by the nurses who held the patient down constituted assault and battery.[99]

When two aides attempted to help a patient to a sitting position in a hospital, he kicked one in the stomach; the aide then threw tea at him and he threw soup at her. Not long afterward, the patient attempted to leave the hospital in his trousers and shirt and with only one shoe, and was forcefully restrained by a physician. Upon consultation with a staff psychiatrist, the patient was transferred to a mental institution. In a suit brought by the patient against the doctor for assault and false imprisonment, the court ruled in favor of the doctor.[100]

LOSS OF CONSORTIUM

A wife may sue in at least 26 states and the District of Columbia for loss of consortium as a result of negligent injury to her husband. A decision denying a wife's damages for loss of consortium after her husband was injured in an automobile accident was reversed.[101] See *Hospital Authority of Hall County v. Adams* and *Stahlin v. Hilton Hotels Corp.*

THE RIGHT TO PRIVACY AND ITS PROBLEMS

The so-called right of privacy is the right to be left alone or a right to be free from unwanted publicity. Some form of privacy right is recognized by statute in four states (New York, Oklahoma, Utah and Virginia) and by judicial decision in 30 other states.[102] In 1890, Warren and Brandeis in an influential article entitled "The Right of Privacy,"[103] which appeared in the *Harvard Law Review*, surveyed those cases in which damages had been awarded for defamation, breach of confidence or some implied contract or invasion of a property right. They decided that many of the cases were grounded upon a separate and broader principle of privacy that deserved to be recognized. In *Pasevich v. New England Life Insurance Co.*,[104] the court held that invasion of privacy was a separate and compensable tort.

A review of privacy cases reveals that there are four aspects of the right of privacy. One is the unauthorized appropriation of the plaintiff's personality for commercial purposes, as in *Roberson v. Rochester Folding Box Co.*[105] There, the defendant used the picture of an attractive girl without her permission to advertise its flour. In *Griffin v. Medical Society of State of New York*,[106] the plaintiff alleged that the plastic surgeons had taken photographs at the commencement of treatment and that the society's journal had published four of the pictures, without her permission, in the article "The Saddle Nose." The judge allowed the suit. In *Ettore v. Philco Television Broadcasting Corp.*,[107] a large number of cases are cited and described.

A second privacy tort includes gross intrusions into a person's seclusion, such as peering into a window[108] or phone tapping.[109] A third privacy tort includes placing someone in a position that is false and embarrassing, such as signing another's name to a letter, telegram or petition that misrepresents his or her views on a subject.[110] A fourth aspect, particularly important to nursing and medicine, is compromising the ordinary decencies applying to private, although not necessarily defamatory, information. In *Barber v. Time Inc.*,[111] the news magazine in an article in the medicine section identified a woman, had a picture of her in a hospital gown and gave the details of her symptoms caused by a pancreatic condition: uncontrollable gluttony, i.e., "eats for ten." The patient sued on the right of privacy theory and collected $1500 damages.

In the course of medical treatment, a patient has the right to privacy. In *Feeney v. Young*,[112] a patient may have agreed before undergoing a cesarean section to allow the surgeon to take a motion picture for use at a medical society meeting. However, the patient had a cause of action when the physician and the motion picture producer made a film called *Birth* and exhibited it publicly in two New York theaters.

In *Bazemore v. Savannah Hospital*,[113] the parents of a deceased child sued the hospital and others for an injunction and damages in connection with the unauthorized newspaper publication of a picture of their son who had been born with his heart on the outside of his body. The parent's complaint, alleging mental anguish and invasion of privacy caused by the hospital's unauthorized actions, stated a good cause of action, according to the Georgia Supreme Court.

A Federal judge in *Banks v. King Features Syndicate, Inc.*[114] severely criticized two osteopathic surgeons who turned over x-rays showing a 6-inch hemostat that had been in the patient's abdomen for four years. It was the basis of a lawsuit for violating the patient's right to privacy.

In *Doe v. Roe*,[115] a psychoanalyst wrote a book that was actually a case history of a patient and her family. The book was advertised in daily newspapers and sold in ordinary bookstores. While the psychiatrist had made some attempt to conceal the patient's identity, the patient had the right to an injunction to prevent further sale of the book in order to protect her rights to privacy and to confidentiality in the physician-patient relationship.

Nurse researchers should become familiar with the experience of other social scientists. The American Political Science Foundation in 1973 initiated a research project to investigate problems surrounding the establishment and maintenance of confidential relationships between scholarly researchers and research subjects.[116] The Russell Sage Foundation funded the project, which included all the national social science associations as co-sponsors.[117] They collected approximately 250 untoward incidents involving the confidentiality of social science resources and data. Among these was the Popkin Case, where a political scientist's research sources were subpoenaed and he was subsequently imprisoned for contempt of court for refusal to breach confidences.[118] Several incidents have included a threat of subpoena directed toward a political sociologist investigating attitudes toward court-ordered school busing,[119] the subpoenaing of two policy analysts for research sources,[120] the subpoenaing of a political economist for testimony and the subpoenaing of research notes related to a study of a public utility's decision-making.[121] Other incidents have involved refusals to provide access to governmental data[122] and problems encountered in concealing subject identities published in research findings.[123]

The study of social scientists' problems concluded that some legal immunity was needed for researchers in order to protect their records and their research subjects from judicial and governmental intervention. The immunity is needed not only because of incidents such as those cited but, as Fields points out, because of problems of subpoenas, threats of subpoenas, informal pressures to reveal data, increased Federal regulation of projects and the growing public reluctance to participate in research.[124]

In addition, the study quoted a United States District Judge, Charles B. Renfew, in *Richards of Rockford, Inc. v. Pacific Gas and Electric Co.*,[125] who denied a motion to compel Professor Mark Roberts of Harvard University to testify and to produce documents concerning confidential interviews:

> Society has a profound interest in the research of its scholars' work which has the unique potential to facilitate change through knowledge.... Compelled disclosure of confidential information would, without question, severely stifle

research into questions of public policy, the very subjects in which the public interest is greatest.[126]

Approximately 73 percent of the researchers responding to the survey felt that legal protection was desirable to help persuade people to participate in research projects. In the survey of researchers, 7.3 percent of them had experienced some problems of confidentiality in their research.

A woman's complaint against a man for contracting genital herpes stated a cause of action. The woman sued for damages for negligence, alleging that the man injured her by having sexual intercourse with her at a time when he knew or should have known that he was a carrier of a venereal disease. She also alleged battery and fraud in that he misrepresented himself as being free of venereal disease. The man contended that the right of privacy protected him and that it was not the court's business to supervise promises between consenting adults as to the circumstances of their private sexual conduct. The court held that the right of privacy is not absolute and, in some cases, is subordinate to the state's fundamental right to enact laws promoting public health, safety and welfare, even if such laws invade an offender's right of privacy. It was pointed out by the court that genital herpes is a serious and incurable disease, stating that the constitutional right of privacy did not protect the man.[127]

DEFAMATION

Defamation is another type of wrongful action. Nurses should be careful in their personal statements, especially regarding patients, doctors, hospital supervisors and fellow workers. Unquestionably, one way that nurses sometimes get into trouble is by making unguarded derogatory remarks. Granted, legal actions arising therefrom are the exception; nevertheless, the volume of criticism of such conduct is appreciable. As a student, each nurse has been taught that it is wrong to discuss patients except insofar as their care necessitates such discussion in a professional setting.

The invasion of a person's interest in his or her reputation and good name by communication to others of anything that tends to diminish the value or esteem in which he or she is held, or to arouse adverse feelings against him or her, is defamation.[128] Defamation consists of publication of matter that tends to lower the reputation of a person or to cause ordinary reasonable persons to shun him or her. Nurses may defame patients, or vice versa. Not every mention of a person's affairs is defamatory, but only such things as engender derogatory opinions of him or her in others. For example, to say that a patient had a common cold or fractured arm could hardly be considered defamatory. On the other hand, to say that a patient had a venereal disease would be defamatory. Likewise, to say that a patient had a mental disease or some unpleasant physical deformity might be considered defamatory. In many jurisdictions, to publish that an unmarried woman is pregnant is defamatory, since it carries a charge of immoral behavior.[129] It is also defamatory to cast any reflection on a person's fitness or ability for his work.

As Prosser points out, a certain amount of vulgar name-calling is tolerated, on the theory it will necessarily be understood to amount to nothing more.[130] In *Notarmuzzi v. Shevack*, a landlord and tenants exchanged abusive epithets in a heated backyard squabble. The tenants said: "I'll get out as soon as I get my $300 bonus back from you, you black marketeer." The landlord said: "You are a bleached-blond bastard, a goddamn son of a bitch, and a bum and a tramp; get the hell out of the house."[131]

In *Barry* v. *Baugh*,[132] a nurse brought a defamation action charging Dr. Baugh had slandered her during a consultation concerning the commitment of her alcoholic husband to a mental institution. In the course of a telephone conversation with a county official, the physician referred to Mrs. Barry (the nurse) as "crazy". As a result of this statement, the nurse sued for $5000 for mental pain, shock, fright, humiliation and embarrassment resulting from the defendant's false, wanton, intentional, voluntary, malicious and willful misconduct. The nurse claimed that, if the physician's statement were made known to the public, her job and reputation would be affected adversely. The judgment for the physician was affirmed, the court holding that the physician's statement concerning the nurse did not constitute slander because the physician was not referring to the nurse in a professional capacity.

All nurses should appreciate that governance of the tongue is necessary if they are to avoid legal proceedings due to thoughtless, careless or provocative words.

Slander and Libel

Under the title of defamation, the law in many states draws a distinction between slander and libel. Slander is the oral defamation of a person by speaking unprivileged or false words by which his or her reputation is damaged.[133] Libel is printed defamation by written words, cartoon, effigies and such representations as cause a person to be avoided, ridiculed or held in contempt, or tend to injure him or her at work.[134]

Neither of these two types of defamation of character applies to remarks between two persons that are directed at each other. There must be a third person to hear or read the comment before it can be considered "published." For instance, a nurse might make a contemptuous remark about a patient, physician or another nurse, and this would not constitute slander unless it were made in the presence of a third person.

Similarly, a statement is not libel even if it is written to another, provided it is not seen by a third person. Some jurisdictions consider a letter "published" even if the writer only dictated it to a secretary. A nurse should realize, too, that some kinds of defamation are actionable without proof of damage. For instance, statements that affect persons in their profession or business or imply that they are connected with a serious crime would be slander.[135] Some slanderous words—for instance, those imputing lack of chastity to a woman—are made criminal by special laws in some jurisdictions.

A nurse recovered $5000 damages in a slander action against a staff doctor at the Cary Memorial Hospital in Caribou, Maine. A feud raged between the doctor and the nurse after the nurse was dismissed by the hospital for unprofessional conduct when she became openly critical of the doctor's postoperative treatment of a patient. The charges that she brought against the doctor were dismissed by the Grievance Committee of the Aroostook County Medical Association. Some time later, she was re-employed by the hospital on the stated condition that she would not discuss hospital business outside the hospital. When the physician learned that the nurse had been re-employed, he called the administrator and said:

> I wanted to ask you if you would stoop so low as to hire that creep, that malignant son of a bitch, back to work for you in the hospital.

He added:

> She was unfit for the care of patients . . . he could prove that . . . and that he intended to make an issue of it.

The nurse learned of these remarks and brought suit against the doctor. If actual malice is shown, the plaintiff may recover compensatory damages and punitive damages. A jury verdict of $17,500 was reduced to $5000 since provocation, although no excuse for slander, is a mitigating factor in assessing punitive damages.[136]

When a physician became chief of the urology section of a VA hospital, and numerous complaints were made about his capabilities, an Illinois appellate court ruled that two federally employed urologic specialists serving in a contractual capacity were absolutely immune from liability for defamatory statements made against the physician in the line of duty, with or without malice. The consultants alleged that the physician was too slow in surgery; was unable to perform major surgery; was incapable of performing surgery without the assistance of other physicians; and lacked professional competence and ability to work in harmony with hospital personnel, communicate with patients and supervise other physicians. The physician had charged the consultants with libelous and slanderous statements.[137]

According to the minutes of a staff meeting, one physician said of another, "One does not get a free ride with a M.D. degree, not here. . . . If one wants a security blanket, go get a government job." A few weeks later, the physician spoken of was dismissed from the staff, where his privileges had been suspended at local hospitals for failure to keep his charts up to date. Also, a grievance alleging that he charged excessive fees had been filed with the county medical society. A New Mexico appellate court ruled that the first physician did not slander the second one.[138]

Excuses

The greater the publicity given to a defamatory statement, the greater is the damage to the plaintiff's reputation. A defamatory statement may be excused or justified by showing that the person who made it was not moved to do so by a spirit of injury but for a nonmalicious, justifiable purpose, e.g., proof of consent, truth, privilege or fair comment.

There are circumstances in which a legal or moral duty exists for a person to pass on information of a defamatory nature to another. A nurse may feel obliged to give a confidential report to a person entitled to it. For example, a director of nursing service in a hospital who has personal knowledge of the character and qualifications of a nurse, Miss Jones, may give his or her fair opinion of Miss Jones to a potential employer.

It is not difficult to decide when there is a legal duty to speak. The nurse must do so when required to give evidence in court and when it is reasonably necessary for the patient's own sake, as in the case of a patient with a deranged mind. However, to decide when a person has a moral or social duty to speak is considerably more difficult. Perhaps the only guide in such situations is to ask whether an ordinary, reasonable person under the circumstances would feel obliged to speak.

Again, persons may make a statement to protect their reasonable interests, as in self-defense. An assistant director of nursing service may complain to the director of nursing service about the work of a certain practical nurse on duty in the hospital, but she or he would not be justified in complaining about irrelevant matters.

Truth. In U.S. law, in the absence of a privileged communication, truth is a good defense in a civil suit for libel or slander. Nurses should remember, however, that if they resort to truth as a defense, they must prove the whole defamatory statement to be true and not merely a part of it. Also, if a person relies on the defense of truth and fails to prove it, that action would seem to increase the amount of damages that the plaintiff might sue for, since it shows persistence in the defamation and probably gives it wider publicity.

It would seem pertinent at this point to remind nurses of the wisdom of thinking before they speak. Many former student nurses will recall two of my favorite quotations, one attributed to the late president Calvin Coolidge:

I notice that what I have not said, never gets me into any trouble.

The second is attributed to Halleck and Franz, authors some years ago of a grade-school text on American history:

The sphinx of Egypt looks wise enough to solve any question and has maintained its reputation through the centuries by saying nothing.

To be sure, there is at times a duty to speak, and then one should.

Many times it has been remarked that more needless actions are brought for defamation than for any other cause. Before initiating suit, one should consider whether it is honestly worth the trouble, time and expense involved. However, if a defamation is particularly damaging one may be impelled to bring an action in order to clear one's good name, even if recovery would be extremely unlikely.

Under the common law, truth is not a defense to a criminal libel action. In criminal actions, if the publication of the statement is for a justifiable and not a malicious purpose, truth is an available defense.

Privilege. In discussing "privilege," an authority on torts has said that a person may be privileged to publish defamation for protection or furtherance of public or private interests recognized by law.[139] He observed that in one group of actions, such as legal and legislative proceedings, publications made with the consent of the plaintiff, communications between husband and wife and circumstances in which executive officers are charged with important responsibilities, there is an immunity from responsibility without regard to the defendant's motive or reasonableness. In another set of situations, however, there is a limited or conditional privilege, and the defendant's immunity depends on good motives and reasonable behavior. Here, by way of illustration, the author cites communications between those having a common interest for the advancement of that interest, publication made to proper persons in the public interest, publications to protect or advance an important interest of the person or a third person in circumstances in which an ordinary reasonable person would consider herself or himself under a moral or legal obligation to do so, and in accounts of proceedings of public interest.[140]

Before the conclusion of this section on wrongs against persons, privileged communications should be discussed further. There are certain classes of confidential or privileged communications between persons who stand in a confidential or fiduciary (founded on or holding in trust) relationship to each other, and for the sake of public policy and the good of society, the law will not permit them to be divulged or allow them to be inquired into in a court of justice.[141] Examples of such communications are those between husband and wife, attorney and client and a clergyman and someone who seeks counsel.

The common law does not recognize the physician-patient relationship as confidential or privileged. Privilege between a physician and a patient is based on the idea that the physician cannot give adequate care to a patient without the patient's completely disclosing the facts relating to the ailment. In about two thirds of the states, there are statutes providing for privileged communications between a physician and a patient. Generally, these statutes confer a qualified type of privilege.

States conferring a physician-patient privilege include New York, Ohio, Indiana, Illinois, Michigan, Wisconsin, Minnesota, North Dakota, South Dakota, Iowa, Missouri, Kansas, Nebraska, Oklahoma, Arkansas, Mississippi, Colorado, Wyoming, Utah, Montana, Idaho, Washington, Oregon, California, Arizona, Alaska and Hawaii. The District of Columbia also allows the physician-patient privilege.

New Jersey has passed a law to protect the confidentiality of communications between a physician and patient.[142] Massachusetts also has enacted a statute to protect the confidential communications between patients and psychotherapists.[143]

In one case, an accident victim was in the hospital, and her physician requested Dr. Murtagh, a neurosurgeon, to examine her. When he did so, Dr. Murtagh decided that, although the patient had sustained a moderately severe whiplash injury to the neck and spine, there was a marked hysterical element present that was more severe since the patient was emotionally unstable. Dr. Erickson, employed by the defense attorneys to interview doctors of injured patients, obtained a report from Dr. Murtagh without the patient's permission to give such information. In his report, for which he was paid $50 by the doctor for the defense attorneys, Dr. Murtagh stated:

> It is my opinion that there was a very mild musculo-ligamentous strain at the time of the accident but no neurogenic involvement, nothing to suggest permanent neurologic sequelae, and that the prognosis for recovery of this mild strain should be very good. Her somatic symptoms, however, have been perpetuated by an underlying pre-existing anxiety neurosis and hysteria, centered about an hysterical personality.

Affirming a motion for a new trial because of the verdict inadequacy, the court scored the physicians on privileged communications, saying:

> We are of the opinion that members of a profession, especially the medical profession, stand in a confidential or fiduciary capacity as to their patients. They owe their patients more than just medical care for which payment is exacted; there is a duty of total care; that includes and comprehends a duty to aid the patient in litigation, to render reports when necessary and to attend court when needed.

It also said:

> The doctor, of course, owes a duty to conscience to speak the truth; he need, however, speak only at the proper time. Dr. Erickson's role in inducing Dr. Murtagh's breach of his confidential relationship to his patient is to be and is condemned.[144]

In Louisiana, no physician-patient privilege exists, according to the appellate court. A husband who was legally separated from his wife sued for custody of the two minor children, alleging that the mother was in a psychiatric hospital and unable to care for them. The mother claimed privilege of the information between a physician and a patient. The court ruled that the issue could not be satisfactorily determined without a full disclosure of the findings of the medical expert who had examined and treated the defendant.[145]

A New York family court, in a child protection proceeding, ruled that the interests of allegedly neglected children outweighed the policies of confidentiality of the records of a patient with a history of alcohol and drug abuse and of the physician-patient relationship. The patient apparently was the children's mother, and the court ordered that her records be produced for use and also gave permission for examination of the results of all her urine tests.[146]

In Georgia, the privilege applies only to communications between a patient and a psychiatrist, and in both Virginia and North Carolina disclosure can be ordered when it is needed in administering justice. Privilege is limited to vital statistics in Kentucky; in Pennsylvania, to information that tends to blacken the character of the patient; and in New Mexico to workmen's compensation claims and loathsome diseases. In West Virginia, privilege is allowed only in the justice court.

A mental patient was committed to the hospital after pleading not guilty by reason of insanity to charges of arson and attempted arson. It was held that the physician-patient and psychologist-patient privileges were not absolute, and would yield to discovery of essential information by the attorney general to determine whether the patient was still too dangerous to be at large.[147]

As a rule, communications to a nurse are not privileged except by statutes in New York, Arkansas, New Mexico and Wisconsin which have changed the common law rule and have expressly included a professional registered nurse in their scope. As a court in Arkansas pointed out in a suit by a physician against the father of a patient to collect for services to the patient, a statute declaring physicians and nurses to be privileged from compulsion as witnesses concerning certain kinds of testimony has no application to the testimony of a nurse as to a conference between the defendant father of the patient and a plaintiff physician regarding his agreement to pay the physician for the patient's operation.[148]

Although a nurse is not specifically mentioned in a privileged communications statute, courts have held that professional nurses assisting physicians are their agents and, therefore, when so acting, stand in the same confidential relation to the patient as the physician.

According to a Nebraska decision, a professional nurse assisting a physician to whom a confidential communication is made by a patient is the agent of the physician. Accordingly, doctors or their agents shall not be allowed, in giving testimony, to disclose any confidential communication entrusted to them in a professional capacity and that was necessary and proper to enable them to carry on their work according to the usual course of practice. In an action against a railroad company by the administrator of a patient who was a brakeman and had been injured and paralyzed, a judgment in a trial in which such persons had given testimony was reversed.[149]

However, when the information is acquired by a professional nurse unconnected with the patient's treatment and diagnosis, the rule does not hold that the nurse is an agent of the physician and, as such, is prohibited from disclosing confidential communications. In an action to set aside and cancel a deed of property valued at $100,000 to a husband, it was alleged that the woman patient was mentally incompetent at the time of executing the deed and that the deed was procured through fraud and undue influence. It was further alleged that the deed was never delivered, and that if it was delivered it was not to take effect until after the death of the patient. The nurse's testimony tended to show that the patient knew what she was doing, intended to act as she did when she executed the deed and that it was delivered to the husband. A judgment for the defendant husband was affirmed.[150] In this case, the communications of a patient to a nurse were not necessary to enable the physician to prescribe or treat the patient and were not within the privileged communication law.

In regard to practical nurses, it would seem that, since they are neither "professional" nor "registered," no communication between the patient and them is privileged. Consequently, they may be called in an action to testify about what they know. In a case in which the plaintiff physician recovered a judgment for services to the defendant's wife, the court said that a nurse who is not registered or professional can properly give testimony of conversations between physician and patient about the patient's condition and its cause.[151]

In some states, there is no law allowing privileged communications between a physician and patient, and hence no law cloaking as privileged any communications between patient and nurse. In an action for damages for death of the plaintiff intestate while riding in an automobile that was struck by a train at a crossing, the court noted that, under the common law still in force, confidential communications between physician and patient arising from professional relations were not privileged. The section of the civil code making privileged all communications to an attorney by a client, or to a clergyman when made in confidence, was inapplicable between a physician and a patient.[152] Also, in a homicide action concerning a husband who had fatally shot his wife, resulting in a first-degree murder charge, part of the evidence revealed that the wife was pregnant and did not want a child, whereas the husband did want a child. Communications between physician and patient (wife) as to the pregnancy, during which the wife told the doctor that she wanted him to terminate the pregnancy and that he had consented, were admissible. Communications between patient and physician were not privileged in Alabama.[153]

Where a psychiatrist was hired by the state to examine a defendant to determine his state of mind at the time he shot another person, the doctor's testimony was admissible in evidence and a conviction of first-degree manslaughter was upheld. In Oregon, the physician-patient privilege, under the terms of the statute, does not apply in a criminal case.[154]

From 1969 until 1973, an employee worked as a ward clerk at "X" Hospital. When she returned to work following an automobile accident, she was told to report for her annual physical examination, and as part of it she furnished blood and urine samples. The urinalysis revealed morphine sulfate, and a check showed that no drugs that were prescribed following the automobile accident contained morphine sulfate. Thereafter, her employment was terminated for having violated a work rule forbidding personal use or abuse of drugs. The employee filed a defamation of character lawsuit against the hospital. After her dismissal, she testified that she applied to five hospitals and an employment agency for work. At "Y" Hospital, she listed "X" Hospital as her last employment and revealed that she had been dismissed for violating a work rule. At the trial, the employee indicated that the personnel director at "Y" Hospital was told that she had been terminated for violating a work rule and was not rehirable. The trial court concluded as a matter of law that the employee did use morphine, and that the employee herself published the reasons for her termination to "Y" Hospital. The Court of Appeals, affirming a judgment for the defendant, said that, in general, a qualified privilege is recognized where the public interest in activities that presuppose frank communication on certain matters between persons standing in particular relationships to each other outweighs the damage to individuals when good-faith, but defamatory, statements are made relative to the problems of those employees involved. The court said:

> Qualified privilege extends to all communications made in good faith upon any subject matter in which the party communicating has an interest, or in reference to which he has a duty to a person having a corresponding interest or duty. And this privilege embraces cases where the duty is not a legal one, but where it is of a moral or social character.[155]

Where insanity is asserted as a defense and defendants offer evidence to show their insanity in support of the plea, a complete waiver of the patient-physician privilege is effected. A defendant was convicted of the murder of his wife by striking her about the head with a metal fireplace poker and stabbing her with a large meat fork. After indictment, he was found mentally unfit to stand trial and was committed to the state hospital for the criminally insane. He was later certified as capable to conduct his defense, and the prosecution produced a psychiatrist who had treated him at the state hospital and who testified that he was, in fact, a malingerer and sane at the time of the slaying (the issue of the defendant's waiver of the physician-patient privilege). The court affirmed the conviction and held that the physician-patient privilege was waived, since the patient had pleaded insanity and introduced evidence to that effect.[156]

Research grant documents on studies conducted by the Psychopharmacology Research Branch of the National Institute of Mental Health on the drug treatment of school- and preschool-age children with learning difficulties or behavioral disorders, particularly hyperkinesis, are subject to disclosure.[157]

Statements Actionable *Per Se*

As previously mentioned, the words of a statement in some cases are "actionable per se"; that is, the words are actionable in themselves, and damages are presumed and need not be proved. Several actions of this type include accusation of unfitness for a trade or profession, immorality, commission of a serious crime or having venereal disease. If a physician untruthfully accused a nurse to a third person of unskillfulness because a patient was injured by failure to turn him properly, his words probably would be sufficient to constitute slander. The court considered it slander when a defendant doctor said of a nurse:

> Many have perished for want of her skill.[158]

In another case, a doctor sued for slander when the defendant in connection with a confinement case said:

> I heard Doc A was drunk that night and wasn't able to go.

The court held that such a statement was prejudicial to the plaintiff in his profession and actionable as slander.[159]

In an action for libel against a hospital and its secretary in his individual capacity, a physician based his complaint on letters dictated by the defendant secretary to his stenographer. One such letter on the hospital letterhead and signed by the defendant read:

> Dear Sir:
>   I am calling your attention to the unpaid hospital bill of Julia Sagert, amounting to $301.24.

As this girl received treatment following a criminal operation for which you were responsible, we hereby request and demand you make immediate payment of this bill. If you fail to do so, we will institute criminal proceedings and use our best efforts to see you are committed to the state penitentiary.

This is a final notice and your immediate attention is requested.[160]

The plaintiff, alleging that he was seriously injured and had lost gains and profit in his practice, asked for $10,000 damages. The court said that if the expression in the letter "for which you were responsible" referred to the statement "the unpaid hospital bill," found in the first paragraph, and not to the expression "criminal operation," found in the second paragraph immediately preceding the matter in controversy, it could be shown in defense or mitigation of damages. Also, the court said that if the secretary of the board of trustees of the hospital while in the discharge of duties published a libel, the hospital, in addition to the secretary, was liable for such act and that the hospital was not immune from liability because it was a nonprofit charitable organization.

COPYRIGHT AND PHOTOCOPYING

The extensive use of photocopying of copyrighted materials has created a serious infringement problem with the rights of publishers and authors. Nurses, particularly those in nursing education and inservice education, have occasionally duplicated and distributed multiple copies of pertinent articles without the permission of, and in violation of the rights of, the publisher and author.

In 1976, Congress passed the first revision of the copyright law since 1909. This contains provisions that could end much of the free photocopying of copyrighted articles done by nurses, students, teachers, researchers and libraries.

How much photocopying of material is permitted under the new copyright law?

The guidelines state that for use in their professional work, teachers or research scholars will be allowed to *make a single copy*, without charge, of:

○ A chapter from a book;
○ An article from a periodical or newspaper;
○ A short essay, story or short poem;
○ A chart, graph, diagram, drawing, cartoon, or picture from a book, periodical, or newspaper.[161]

A teacher may make multiple copies for classroom use only, and not to exceed one per student in a class, of the following:

○ A complete poem, if it is less than 250 words and printed on not more than two pages;
○ An excerpt from a longer poem, if it is less than 250 words;
○ A complete article, story, or essay, if it is less than 2,500 words;
○ An excerpt from a prose work, if it is less than 1,000 words or 10 percent of the work, whichever is less;
○ One chart, graph, diagram, drawing, cartoon, or picture per book or per periodical.[162]

For brief works of which multiple copies can be made *only* for classroom use, the guidelines define "brief" as 2500 words of a complete article or story in prose and 1000 words or 10 percent of a longer work.[163] However, no photocopying of "consumable" works, such as workbooks or standardized texts, is allowed.

To be permissible, photocopying has to be spontaneous, i.e., "the decision to use the work and the moment of its use, for maximum teaching effectiveness, are so close in time that it would be unreasonable to expect a timely reply to a request for permission."[164]

Things that a teacher may *not* do are:

○ Make multiple copies of a work for classroom use if it has already been copied for another class in the same institution;
○ Make multiple copies of a short poem, article, story, or essay from the same author more than once a class term, or make multiple copies from the same collective work or periodical issue more than three times a term;
○ Make multiple copies of works more than nine times in the same class term;
○ Make a copy of works to take the place of an anthology;
○ Make a copy of "consumable" materials, such as workbooks.[165]

The new law does bar "the systematic reproduction or distribution" of materials.[166] It is pointed out that a periodical can be copied free for interlibrary loan use up to six times a year. When a periodical is more than five years old, it does not have to be counted.

It might be noted that works sponsored and paid for by a government agency, unless classified, cannot be copyrighted at present, and they can be freely duplicated.

Nurses should study these provisions of the new copyright laws and strictly adhere to them. When articles are reproduced, it is imperative that the name of the author, the article and the periodical as well as its volume, page and date be shown on the reproduced copy. Failure to observe this rule in duplicating materials has led to a great mass of duplicated material used by nurses that does not identify the source from which it was taken. Sometimes, even the author's name is not shown. As a result, some very worthwhile periodicals that publish quality articles receive very little recognition. In addition, undated duplicated material is frequently used by nurses when the information is obsolete. Authors are amazed at seminars and workshops to find many nurses who do not realize that new editions of textbooks are expected to contain at least 35 percent new material, and hence earlier editions of the book often differ appreciably from a current one.

In utilizing copyrighted material, nurses should form the habit of giving credit to authors for their ideas. Considerable work, research and effort go into the production of written material, and it is discouraging and disheartening to see it being used without credit to the originator.

RESTRAINTS

The problem of the use of restraints at times confronts nurses who care for disoriented, irrational and restless patients. Whatever restraint is used should be adequate for the purpose, but the same type may not always be needed. In some situations, besides restraints, continuing observation by some member of the nursing team may be necessary for the safety of the patient. Therefore, the nurse must know when and how to use restraints correctly; depending on the circumstances, there may or may not be a medical order. Even when patients are restrained, many accidents happen, hence one must realize that the use of restraints imposes an obligation on the nurse to observe the patient more frequently and carefully.[167]

A recovery room nurse placed restraining boards on the arms of a six-year-old girl who had had eye surgery, and she struggled against them. When the restraints were removed on the following day, there was limited motion in one arm, which a doctor concluded could have resulted from either the child's struggle or the tightness of the restraint. The appellate court, in reversing a dismissal of the complaint, commented that a greater standard of care should be exercised in the treatment of the very young or very old, especially if they are under sedation or semiconscious.[168]

An unattended and unrestrained patient suffering from mental and emotional illness so seriously damaged both of her eyes as to make herself blind. A judgment for the hospital was given in a $150,000 damage suit, the court saying that the objective of hospitalization is treatment and that restrictions must be kept at a minimum if the patient's confidence is to be restored.[169]

Even though a nursing restraint proved faulty for keeping an electroshock patient in bed after treatment, the patient could not recover for injuries when ties on a restraining sheet were fastened in accordance with the recognized method of keeping a patient in bed after electroshock treatment, and when the only standard of care established was used in treating and restraining the patient. The patient, who was suffering from depression and schizo-affective disorder, was receiving Glissando therapy, a part of which is electroshock therapy and restraint of the patient for four to five hours. The patient broke her hip when she fell out of bed.[170]

Following cataract surgery, an 81-year-old patient became confused, disoriented, hallucinatory and violent and in a struggle with an attendant suffered a fractured hip. The patient was awarded $22,763 damages against the hospital, which was found negligent in failing to provide necessary restraints such as a Posey belt.[171]

A three-judge Federal Court in Connecticut ruled that a mental hospital may hold a patient against his will for 45 days without a decision on his mental competency. The New Britain Legal Aid Society in behalf of nine patients had challenged the state's emergency commitment law under which a single physician may declare a person "dangerous to himself or others," commit him to a hospital and have him detained without further investigation for 45 days. While the case was being heard, the General Assembly reduced the period by 15 days for future commitments.[172]

STERILIZATION

Sterilization is a procedure that renders the individual unable to produce offspring. As a voluntary procedure, it has received increased attention in recent years, partly because certain private and governmental agencies advocate birth control to limit the size of families. There are no case decisions declaring voluntary sterilization illegal or against public policy.

In voluntary nontherapeutic sterilization, physicians have been warned by the AMA to obtain the consent of the patient's spouse because of the legal argument that husband and wife have a mutual interest in each other's ability to procreate. Also, Howard Hassard, counsel for the California Medical Association, has advised physicians against performing a sterilization until the law is more definitive:

except when it is therapeutically indicated or in accordance with a statute.[173]

In a Pennsylvania case, a man had a vasectomy performed because he and his wife wanted no more children. Afterward, the wife became pregnant and they had another child, whereupon he sued the physician for breach of contract for money damages to rear and educate the child. The court held that to allow such damages would be against public policy.[174]

In *Christensen v. Thornby*,[175] a vasectomy was performed on a husband since further pregnancies would endanger his wife's health; it was held to be not against public policy, and the court's opinion seems to indicate that consent alone is sufficient.

Eugenic sterilization to prevent procreation of the unfit, such as the feeble-minded, the mentally ill, habitual criminals and sexual deviates, is provided in more than half of the states.

In therapeutic sterilization, the whole or an important part of the reproductive system is removed in order to preserve the life or health of the patient. If the surgery is performed after consultation with another physician or specialist and with the consent of the person (and, if the patient is married, the consent of the spouse), few lawsuits arise. However, the medical profession does not always agree on the grounds for therapeutic sterilization. Surgery to reduce the spread of cancer in the breast or prostate gland is almost universally accepted, but there is great difference of opinion as to whether, say, inactive tuberculosis or mild diabetes is a proper ground for therapeutic sterilization.

Aside from the law, there are moral and religious objections to contraceptive sterilization, and if such operations are permissible in a hospital or doctor's office and the physician is willing to peform them, the religious convictions of patients should not be disregarded.

In *Wyatt v. Aderholt et al.*,[176] the court set forth at length the required standards for sterilization of mentally retarded residents of the Alabama state retardation facilities.

Whether a sterilization procedure may be done on a minor is a changing concept at law. Where the parents of a severely mentally retarded 13-year-old girl who lived at home requested court approval for her sterilization, the judge refused the order since in the absence of specific legislative authority a judge does not receive judicial immunity therefor.[177]

In Ohio, no state statutes defined the term "feeble-minded" or authorized sterilization of mentally retarded persons. Nevertheless, a probate court judge ordered a sterilization performed on a 17-year-old girl who had the mentality of a nine-year-old and an I.Q. ranging from 57 to 59, and who had been brought before the juvenile court three times in a year. Later, she filed a $3 million lawsuit against the judge, gynecologist and others, claiming that the sterilization deprived her of her constitutional rights. The case, which was settled in a Federal Court for an undisclosed sum, seems to imply that, in the absence of statutory authority, the state cannot order sterilization for eugenic purposes.[178]

The New York Surrogate Court denied authorization to a mother for sterilization of a severely retarded 16-year-old girl. The girl functioned below the level of a five-year-old but was attractive and well-developed, and attempts had been made to seduce her. The mother said the daughter would be entirely unable to care for a baby. The court ruled that, in the absence of any statute authorizing the procedure, determination of such a fundamental right could not be left to the courts on a case-by-case basis, and that the courts lacked jurisdiction to make this irreversible decision.[179]

The Unplanned Child

The legal consequences of a child born after an unsuccessful sterilization merit discussion. A Los Angeles Superior Court jury awarded a woman $42,000 to raise her unplanned son until he is 21. The judgment was given against a pharmacy that gave the woman sleeping pills instead of birth control pills, as a result of which she gave birth to a son. The mother said that the child "is not unwanted, but he is unplanned."[180]

In another case, a husband had a vasectomy to protect his wife from the dangers of further childbearing. Subsequently the couple had another child, and the wife survived without any problems or complications. The court held that the couple suffered no damages in having another child. The language in the opinion supports the conclusion that consent alone is sufficient to allow a sterilization operation in Minnesota.[181]

When birth control pills are prescribed, the doctor should make it clear that there is no guarantee that the person taking them will not conceive a child.

In a Pennsylvania case, a husband, because he believed it necessary for economic reasons to limit the size of his family, had a vasectomy. Later, a normal child was born to his wife. In the lawsuit for damages that followed, the court held that it would be against public policy to permit a recovery of damages in such a situation, and said:

> We are of the opinion that a contract to sterilize a man is not void as against public policy and public morals. . . . It is only when a given policy is so obviously for or against the public health, safety, morals or welfare that there is virtually unanimity of opinion in regard to it, that a court may constitute itself the voice of the community in declaring such policy void. . . . It is the faith of some that sterilization is morally wrong whether to keep wife from having children or for any other reason. Many people have no moral compunctions against sterilization. Others are against sterilization, except when a man's life is in danger, when a person is low mentally, when a person is a habitual criminal. There is no virtual unanimity of opinion regarding sterilization. . . :
>
> However, on the issue of damages, the Court is of the opinion that to allow damages for the normal birth of a normal child is foreign to the universal public sentiment of the people. . . . Many people would be willing to support his child were they given the right of custody and adoption, but according to plaintiff's statement, plaintiff does not want such. He wants to have the child and wants the doctor to support it. In our opinion to allow such damages would be against public policy.[182]

An Illinois case, which reached a different result, made a distinction. This lawsuit was brought for breach of contract rather than negligence, since the wife claimed that the surgeon had stated that the operation would make her husband sterile. The couple had had two retarded children and sought the services of a physician to avert the procreation of more handicapped children. Following the husband's vasectomy, the couple had a third retarded and deformed child. In this case, the court ruled that the complaint stated a good cause of action. The case involved a sterilization undergone not for convenience, but because of the wish not to create more disabled children.[183]

Wasmuth cites a case involving a surgeon who, while performing an abdominal operation, intended to ligate the fallopian tubes but through an oversight failed to do so. The plaintiff patient was awarded the verdict and a judgment for all pain and suffering, mental and physical, together with loss of services and any other loss or damages apparently resulting from the negligence of the surgeon. In this case, the surgeon failed to perform the operation that he had intended and had agreed to perform, and thus was held liable.[184]

Bernstein has discussed sterilization as an enforceable right.[185]

The Roman Catholic View

The Roman Catholic Church has stated:

> Direct sterilization, namely the practice that aims to make procreation impossible, is a grave violation of moral law and therefore illicit.

Sterilization is licit when a pathological condition makes the removal of an organ necessary for the preservation of the patient's life and health. If the purpose of the operation is to prevent the inconvenience or dangers of childbearing, it is illicit.[186] A hysterectomy is permitted only if the pathology of the patient warrants it. Removal of the ovaries, or oophorectomy, for the prevention of metastasis or in the treatment of cancer of the breast is permissible upon consultation and prudent medical advice; the purpose is to prevent spread of the disease, not contraception.[187] Similarly, when a no less drastic and equally effective procedure is reasonably available, orchidectomy may be done when it offers some hope of benefit, as long as the purpose is not contraception.[188] Vasectomy should not be performed unless there is sufficient medical reason.

The Roman Catholic Church opposes eugenic sterilization of the mentally defective and physically diseased as a mutilation of a person guilty of no crime and one whom the state should not punish because of his or her misfortune.[189] The licitness of punitive sterilization performed on criminals as a penalty for their crimes is disputed by moralists. Again, Healy points out that it seems to be illicit to sterilize criminals for sex crimes, because it leaves the sex organs otherwise intact, and hence encourages rather than deters the sex offender in his crime.[190] Today, in the media some Roman Catholics are challenging this point of view.

WRONGFUL DEATH

A number of civil actions are brought to recover damages for wrongful death if a statute permits such action. For example, parents brought a suit to recover for the wrongful death of an 8½-year-old child who was mentally and physically unable to care for himself. The child's condition was known to an attendant, who nevertheless was negligent in her attention; as a result, the child was scalded when he fell into a bathtub of hot water while he was an inmate at a state institution. He died from burns after four days. The parents recovered damages for the child's personal suffering and for funeral expenses.[191]

When a baby died during the delivery process, a Florida appellate court ruled that the child was not born alive and that the father had no cause of action for wrongful death. The baby's head emerged during the delivery, but its shoulders were too wide to allow further passage. The attempts of two other physicians who were summoned to assist were unsuccessful. About 20 minutes later, the fetal heartbeat tones disappeared; the physicians concluded that the child could not be born alive and turned their attention to saving the mother. Upon receiving permission from the father, the child's head was severed and the rest of the body removed by cesarean section. The child's head and torso weighed 14 lb, 8 oz. The cause of death was listed as cardiovascular failure due to, or as a consequence of, strangulation. The father had sought to recover damages for the child's wrongful death in a malpractice suit against the hospital and his wife's treating physician. He charged that they negligently failed to recognize in advance that a cesarean section would be needed. The court held that generally the umbilical cord must be severed after expulsion of the child from the mother's body, and the child must have independent circulation of blood, in order to constitute a live birth.[192]

A California appellate court held that an arbitration agreement signed by a hospital patient did not bar a wrongful death suit by the deceased patient's husband and son. According to the court, a patient's agreement to arbitrate her possible cause of action was not effective to bar the constitutional and procedural rights of the decedent's heirs in their own independent action.[193]

There are a number of other civil actions brought to recover damages following gross negligence, abortion, apparently aggravated assault and so forth. Actions of this nature will be discussed later in connection with crime (Chapter 9). In Chapter 7, under Negligence, a number of cases resulting in wrongful death are cited.

AUTOPSY PROCEEDINGS

When a patient dies, it is often necessary from a legal point of view, or desirable from an informational or learning standpoint, to do an autopsy. The nurse should know something about this subject. There is no right of property in a corpse.[194] An autopsy is the dissection of a dead body for the purpose of inquiring into the cause of death. In general, persons have a right to dispose of their own body, and the laws and decisions tend to uphold their desires. A patient's surviving spouse, children, next of kin or friends, are generally entitled to receive the corpse intact for the purpose of burial. Unless there is a statutory exception or consent, any willful mutilation of a patient's body, such as an autopsy, gives rise to an action for damages.

Generally speaking, persons will not be penalized if they secure consent in good faith for an autopsy from a relative or other person who appears to be responsible for the burial. The nurse is reminded that, more than once, there has been a legal dispute over just who is entitled to a dead body. Persons so entitled include the surviving spouse, an adult child, parent or guardian, the nearest relative or friends. However, such persons are not necessarily consulted in this order. For example, a person who has taken no interest in a patient during his lifetime can hardly expect to be consulted when the patient dies. More often than not, the first person sought is a relative with whom the patient lived. Generally, at the time of admission to a hospital, a patient is required to list his next of kin. It is reasonable that hospital personnel, including nurses, should accept such a person and not be expected to look elsewhere.

With respect to a dead body, an operation generally accepted by custom is legal. The work of embalmers and the customary post-mortem examinations made for medical and scientific purposes are legal, provided due consideration is given to provisions in the will of the deceased or the desires of the next of kin.

In cases of deaths from violence or suspicious circumstances, at common law a coroner was required to hold an inquest and seek evidence to prevent a wrongdoer's escaping justice.[195] To determine whether a death is caused by natural or other means, the coroner may perform an autopsy. Today, in many states, the reporting of cases to a coroner or medical examiner is governed by statutory law. Some of the deaths that commonly must be reported include those due to suicide, homicide, abortion or accident; those occurring after a patient has been under a doctor's care or in a hospital for a short time; those that are unexpected; and those that are likely to be followed by criminal action. The coroner or medical examiner has the right to determine whether an autopsy will be performed and can proceed without the consent of the patient's spouse, next of kin or friends.

An insurance company may request to examine the body of an insured person and, if not forbidden by law, may do an autopsy to determine whether death was a result of any cause excluded from coverage under its contract with the insured. However, unless an insurance company secures a valid consent, it has no standing at law to demand an autopsy.

By way of illustration, a case concerning the Denver General Hospital may remind the nurse of what may happen. Two men in adjoining beds died at about the same time. A nurse, following the usual custom, prepared death tags, but through mistake or negligence attached a tag prepared for the other man to the body of the plaintiff's husband. The other man's family gave consent for an autopsy, and as a result of the nurse's error in tags the body of the plaintiff's husband was sent to the morgue and an autopsy performed. The plaintiff sued the hospital, hospital manager, coroner and pathologist for damages for the unauthorized autopsy. The pathologist was held not liable under the circumstances, since he proceeded with due care and without wrong intent on the basis of the information as usually supplied. The hospital as a governmental institution was immune. The hospital manager and coroner were not associated with this particular autopsy.[196] The nurse whose negligent actions were the proximate cause of the dispute was not sued in this action. However, the case illustrates how a nurse may incur liability to suit, and it confirms the need to exercise reasonable care in all nursing work.

TRANSPLANTATION OF ORGANS

Cardiac transplantation, often presented as a tense and emotional drama by the media, has stimulated the public to think about the legal and ethical problems involved.

The Organ Procurement and Transplantation Act, a new Federal law aimed at making more organs available for transplants, went into effect in January 1985. In addition to making it illegal to buy or sell organs, the bill allocates $25 million over three years to:

1. Help fund local organ procurement agencies around the country.
2. Launch a national computerized network to find and place organs that cannot be used regionally.
3. Create a scientific registry to monitor all U.S.A. transplant results.
4. Set up a 25-member task force to identify ways to increase organ supply.[197]

This legislation is in response to extensive media publicity concerning transplants and a report that there are 7000 kidney patients on the transplant list, between 50 and 75 patients at any one time awaiting a heart transplant, about 200 waiting for liver transplants, many more awaiting corneas and dozens of other patients waiting for pancreas or for combined heart and lung transplants.[198]

The Commissioners on Uniform State Laws made important advances in the Uniform Anatomical Gift Act, 1968, which eliminates the chief legal constraints without compromising other important rights and sensitivities.[199] This Act solves a number of problems: Section 2(a) provides that any person of sound mind and 18 years of age or more may give her or his body or any part of it for purposes listed in the Act, Sections 3, 4(c) and (d), the gift to become effective after death. Under English common law, the next of kin had the right to possession of the body for burial, so that a person had no say in the disposal of her or his body.[200] Furthermore, since the next of kin are the ones who have control over the dead body, Section 2(b) gives them authority to donate the body or a part thereof and, to resolve possible disagreements, provides an order of priority among them. Section 2(e) gives control to the wish of the donor if there is a difference between the donor's plans and those of relatives, and Section 2(d) permits whatever examination is needed to ascertain whether the proposed gift is medically acceptable for use. Section 7(b) states:

> The time of death shall be determined by a physician who attends the donor at his death, or, if none, the physician who certifies the death. This physician shall not participate in the proceedings for removing or transplanting a part.

Section 7(c) protects all persons, including physicians, from liability in civil and criminal actions. However, the Act does not purport to decide other problems, such as the time of death and criteria for selecting recipients, which are the work of allied disciplines.[201] The adoption of this Act has been supported by the American Medical Association, the American Heart Association, the Eye Banks Association of America, The National Kidney Foundation and many other organizations. (See Chapter 11 for more information on organ donations.)

Background

The initial guidelines for clinical research that protect patients and physicians were developed during the Nuremburg Trials that followed World War II, when the public was shocked by the experimentation carried out by Nazi physicians. Growing out of that situation was the Declaration of Helsinki, which contains recommendations for the guidance of doctors in clinical research, and which was adopted by the World Medical Association in 1964. The basic principles set forth in that declaration are:

> 1. Clinical research must conform to the moral and scientific principles that justify medical research and should be based on laboratory and animal experiments or other scientifically established facts.
> 2. Clinical research should be conducted only by scientifically qualified persons and under the supervision of a qualified medical man.
> 3. Clinical research cannot legitimately be carried out unless the importance of the objective is in proportion to the inherent risk to the subject.
> 4. Every clinical research project should be preceded by careful assessment of inherent risks in comparison to foreseeable benefits to the subjects or to others.
> 5. Special caution should be exercised by the doctor in performing clinical research in which the personality of the subject is liable to be altered by drugs or experimental procedure.[202]

An editorial in the *New England Journal of Medicine* states:

> The principles involved are, in substance, that the subject of an experiment involving any risk must stand to benefit by it; that his informed consent must be obtained to the fullest degree possible; finally and more important than any

specific rules that have yet been devised, the investigator must be "intelligent, informed, conscientious, compassionate, responsible."[203]

Time of Death

The time of death is the subject of much discussion and many articles. *Black's Law Dictionary* defines death as:

> The cessation of life; the ceasing to exist; defined by physicians as the total stoppage of the circulation of blood, and a cessation of the animal and vital functions consequent thereupon, such as respiration, pulsation, etc.[204]

This definition was used in at least two cases.[205] In 1968, the definition of irreversible coma, formulated by a committee at the Harvard Medical School, gave these characteristics; (1) unreceptivity and unresponsivity, (2) no movements of breathing, (3) no reflexes and (4) flat electroencephalogram.[206] The statement on death by the Twenty-second World Medical Assembly in Sydney, Australia, in 1968 states that the determination of the time of death is and should remain the legal responsibility of the physician.[207] It points out that two modern procedures have made further study of the question of the time of death necessary, viz., the ability to maintain by artificial means the circulation of oxygenated blood through tissues of the body that have been irreversibly injured and the use of cadavers' organs for transplants. Furthermore, it states that if transplantation of an organ is involved, the decision that the donor is dead should be made by two or more physicians who are not connected with the transplantation procedure.

Living Donor

Transplants of kidneys, corneas, skin and bone have been done many times, and some with a fairly high degree of success, without causing the mind-searching engendered by heart transplants. Unlike kidney transplants, for example, the number of heart and liver transplants has been limited because death is inevitable for the donor. However, when the kidney transplant involves the removal of one kidney from a living donor, the additional risk of serious complications or death to a living donor must sufficiently justify injuring a healthy person to improve the well-being of another.[208] The degree of success of renal transplants, coupled with the minute decrease in the donor's life expectancy, is suggested as justifying the renal transplant procedure.[209] However, the thorny problem of "Who among us is to decide who will be donor and who a recipient?" remains.

In *Sirianni* v. *Anna*,[210] the plaintiff voluntarily donated a kidney to her son, who needed it to save his life. She alleged that malpractice occurred in the removal of her son's kidney. Although the son survived and his claim for damages was settled, the mother still sued the surgeon, claiming that her own health had been impaired by the unnecessary loss of her donated kidney. The court did not permit the mother to recover damages.

In the matter of transplants, it is interesting to note that the Internal Revenue Service Ruling 68–452 provides that a donor's travel, medical and hospital expenses are deductible medical expenses of the recipient if the latter pays for them.

Ethics

A brief word concerning the ethical aspects of transplants seems necessary. The American Medical Association has published *Ethical Guidelines for Organ Transplantation*.[211] One prominent Presbyterian minister has said:

> There are no moral or ethical implications involved in an actual organ transplant.[212]

The view of S. S. Kety is:

> The moral obligation of performing all human experiments, with due regard to the sensibility, welfare, and safety of the subject, must not be violated. As phrased by Claude Bernard in 1856, "Christian morals forbid only one thing, doing ill to one's neighbor." So among experiments that may be tried on man, those that can do only harm are forbidden, those that are harmless are permissible, and those that may do good are obligatory.[213]

Concerning organ transplantation among the living, Lowery points out that there are two schools of thought. One group holds that transplantation of organs among the living is immoral, and their reasoning is:

> Man is the only administrator of his life and bodily functions; his power to dispose of these things is limited. He can allow serious self-mutilation when it is for the good of his own person, because that is reasonable administration. But he cannot allow serious self-mutilation for the benefit of another person.[214]

The second school of thought holds that organ transplantation among the living

> is morally justifiable provided it confers a proportionate benefit on the recipient, without exposing the donor to a greater risk of depriving him completely of an important function.[215]

This brief citation of the ethical views of various thinkers is intended merely to show the reader that there is a considerable variety and diversity of opinion upon this topic.

References

1. Prosser: *Torts*, 3rd ed., 1964, Sec. 1, 2 Baudry-Lacantinerie: *Précis de droit civil*, 7th ed. par. 1346–1347. Lee: *Torts and Delicts*, 27 *Yale L.J.* 721 (1928). *Salmond on the Law of Torts*, 9th ed., 1936, Secs. 3–5.
2. *Restatement*, Torts, Sec. 281.
3. Clark: *Law of Code Pleading*, 2nd ed. 1947 Sec. 13, 64.
4. *Supra*, note 1, Sec. 10. Carpenter: Intentional Invasions of Interest in Personality, 13 *Ore. L. Rev.* 227, 275 (1934).
5. Pollock: *Torts*, 14th ed., 1939, p. 170; Miller: Criminal Law. Hornbook, 1936, 191; Assault and Battery, Civil Liability 1(b), 6 C.J.S. 796.
6. Morgan v. State, 319 N.Y.S. 2d 151 (N.Y., 1970).
7. *Supra*, note 1, Sec. 18.
8. O'Brien v. Cunard S.S. Co., 154 Mass. 272, 28 N.E. 266 (1891); 13 L.R.A. 329.
9. Hughes, J. J., Jr.: The Hospital, the Physician and Informed Consent, *Hospitals*, 42:66–70, June 16, 1968. This article contains a review and citation of a number of cases.
10. Luka v. Lowrie, 171 Mich. 122, 136 N.W. 1106 (1912).
11. Jackovach v. Yocom, 212 Iowa 914, 237 N.W. 444 (1931).
12. Wells v. McGhee, 39 So. 2d 196, (La., 1949).
13. Zoski v. Gaines, 271 Mich. 1, 260 N.W. 99 (1935).
14. Bakkar v. Welsh, 144 Mich. 632, 108 N.W., 94 (1906).
15. Lacey v. Laird, 166 Ohio 12, 139 N.E. 2d 25 (1956).
16. Russell, D. H.: Law, Medicine and Minors, *N. Engl. J. Med.*, 278:779–80, April 4, 1968. Brown, H. G.: Parental Right to Refuse Medical Treatment for Child, *Crime and Delinquency*, 12(4):377–385, Oct. 1966.
17. *Ibid*.
18. Laws of Maryland, Ch. 468, Sec. 1 (1968).
19. Massachusetts General Laws, Ch. 1, Sec. 117 (1954); Connecticut, Public Act No. 206 (1968). *See* Russell, D. H.: Law, Medicine, and Minors, Part 1, *N. Engl. J. Med.*, 278:35–36, Jan. 4, 1968.
20. Brooks Estate v. Brooks, 32 Ill. 2d 361, 205 N.E. 2d 435 (1965).
21. Lacy v. Judge Robert Lowry, Harris County Hospital District et al., U.S.D.T. No.

74–H–124, March 16, 1977; Law News, *Hosp. Prog.*, 58:19, Aug. 1977.

22. Regan, W. A.: O.R. Nursing and Unorthodox Surgery, *Regan Rep. on Nurs. Law*, 7(5):1, Oct. 1966.

23. Fiorentino v. Wenger, 26 A.D. 2d 693, 262 N.Y.S. 2d 557 (1966).

24. Barbee, G. C.: Consents: The Nurse's Role in Obtaining and Using Them, *Hosp. Forum*, 9:23–24, Sept. 1966.

25. Court Backs Civil Rights for Patients, *Milwaukee Journal*, Dec. 9, 1971, p. 16.

26. Lear, J.: Experiments on People—The Growing Debate, *Saturday Review*, July 2, 1966, pp. 41–43.

27. Clarke, A. R.: Patient Consent in Research, *Nurs. Forum*, VI(1):11, 118, 1967. *See also* Downs, F. S.: Ethical Inquiry in Nursing Research, *Nurs. Forum*, VI(1):12–13, 1967.

28. Cancer-Implant Test Brings Threat of Million-Dollar Suit for Damages, *The Physician's Legal Brief*. Bloomfield, N.J., Shering Corp., 1964.

29. U.S. Department of Health, Education and Welfare. OPRR Reports: *Code of Federal Regulations 45 CFR 46*. Washington, D.C., U.S. Government Printing Office, Rev. Jan. 11, 1978, p. 3. Stites, L.: Protecting Research Subjects, *Am. J. Nurs.*, 79:1139–1140, June 1979.

30. Commonwealth v. Gregory, 132 Pa. Super. 507 (1911).

31. Wood v. Wyeth, 106 App. Div. 21, 81 N.Y.S. 1148, 94 N.Y.S. 361 (1905).

32. Beaucoudray v. Hirsch, 49 So. 2d 770 (Ct. App., La., 1951). See also this subject in 6 C.J.S. 807.

33. Main v. Ellsworth, 237 Iowa 970, 23 N.W. 2d 429 (1946).

34. Martin v. Carbide & Carbon Chemicals Corp. et al., 184 Tenn. 166, 197 S.W. 2d 798 (1946).

35. Beale: Justification for Injury, 41 *Harv. L. Rev.* 553 (1928).

36. *Supra*, note 1, Sec. 8. Hall: Interrelations of Criminal Law and Torts, 43 *Col. L. Rev.* 753, 967 (1943).

37. Nelson v. Rural Educational Assn. et al., 23 Tenn. App. 409, 134 S.W. 2d 181 (1939).

38. Sarlat v. State of New York, 52 Misc. 2d 240, 275 N.Y.S. 2d 293 (1966).

39. Hoover v. University of Chicago Hospitals, 366 N.E. 2d 925 (Ill. App. Ct., 1st Div., 1977); *Sex Problems Court Digest*, 9:6, Aug. 1978.

40. 384 U.S. 757 (1966). *See also* discussion by Hershey, N.: When Police Ask for Blood Sample, *Am. J. Nurs.*, 68:540–541, March 1968, which points out that the decision does not necessarily prevent an action for battery.

41. Kan. Stat. Ann. Sec. 8–1001 (Suppl., 1967).

42. N.Y. Law Ch. 615 (1966).

43. K. J. Pizzalotto, M.D., Ltd. v. Wilson, 437 So. 2d 859 (La. St. Ct. 1983); rehearing denied, 1983; *Citation*, 48:110, March 1, 1984.

44. Ex-nurse's Aide Enters No Contest Plea, *Milwaukee Sentinel*, Sept. 14, 1983.

45. Child Abuse Prevention and Treatment Act, Public Law 93–247, 93rd Congress, S. 1191, U.S., Congress Senate, Jan. 31, 1974.

46. In the Matter of S., 259 N.Y.S. 2d 164 (Fam. Ct., 1965).

47. Paulsen, M. G.: Legal Protections Against Child Abuse, *Children*, 13:43–48, March/April, 1966.

48. Cheney, K. B.: Safeguarding Legal Rights in Providing Protective Services, *Children*, 13:87–92, May/June, 1966.

49. In re Dubin, 112, N.Y.S. 2d 267 (1952).

50. Murphy v. Murphy, 143 Conn. 600, 124 A. 2d 891 (1956).

51. Hunter v. Powers, 135 N.Y.S. 2d 371 (1954).

52. Savery v. Eddy, 242 Iowa 822, 45 N.W. 2d (1951).

53. State v. Greer, 311 S.W. 2d 49 (Mo., 1958).

54. *Op. cit.*, note 48.

55. School Nurses' Responsibilities Viewed, *CNA Bulletin*, 63:7, June 1967.

56. State of Washington v. Parmenter, 444 P. 2d 680 (Wash., 1968).

57. State of Minnesota v. Loss, 204 N.W. 404 (Minn., 1973); *Citation*, 27:159–160, Sept. 1, 1973.

58. People of the State of New York v. Eisenman, 351 N.E. 2d 429, 385 N.Y.S. 2d 762 (N.Y. Ct. App., 1976); *Citation*, 34:10, Oct. 15, 1976.

59. Holder, A. R.: Child Abuse and the Physician, *JAMA*, 222:517–518, Oct. 1972.

60. Friedman, A. L. et al.: Nursing Responsibility in Child Abuse. *Nurs. Forum*, 15:(1)95–112, 1976.

61. Landeros v. Flood, 17 Cal. 3d 399, 551 P. 2d 389 (Cal. 1976).

62. People v. Jackson, 18 Cal. App. 3d 504, 506, 95 Cal. Rptr. 919 (Cal. 1971).

63. Goldade v. State of Wyoming, 674 P. 2d 721 (Wyo. S. Ct. 1983); rehearing denied, 1984; *Citation*, 49:48, June 1, 1984.

64. Kesey, K.: *One Flew Over the Cuckoo's Nest*. New York, Viking Press, 1962.

65. Ward, M. J.: *The Snake Pit*. New York, New American Library, 1973.

66. Commonwealth of Pennsylvania *ex rel* Linda Rafferty et al. v. Philadelphia Psychiatric Center et al., 356 F. Supp. 500 (U.S.D.—C.E.D. Pa., 1973).

67. Jacoby, S.: Waiting for the End: On Nursing Homes, *The New York Times Magazine*, March 31, 1974, p. 13.

68. Nations, W.: What Constitutes Abuse of Patients? *Hospitals*, 47:51, 52, Dec. 1, 1973.

69. Galaz v. Seacrest Convalescent Hospital (Cal. Super. Co., Los Angeles Co., Docket No. SOC 35022, Dec. 10, 1974); *Citation*, 31:64, July 1, 1975.

70. Gribbin, A.: Neglected Heroes, *National Observer*, 11:1, May 20, 1972.

71. *Ibid.*, p. 10.

72. Hayes v. State of New York, 363 N.Y.S. 2d 986 (N.Y. Ct. of Claims, Jan. 29, 1975); *Citation*, 31:67, July 1, 1975.

73. Lorence v. Hospital Bd. of Morgan County, 320 2d 631 (S. Ct. Ala., Oct. 2, 1975); *Sex Problems Court Digest*, 7:4, Feb. 1976.

74. Hayes v. Mashikan, 333 N.Y.S. 2d 862 (N.Y., 1972).

75. Morgan v. State, 319 N.Y.S. 2d 151 (N.Y., 1970).

76. Maddox v. Houston County Hospital, 158 Ga. 283, 279 S.E. 2d 732 (Ct. of App. Ga., 1981). Creighton, H.: Unruly Patients, *Nurs. Management*, 13:15–16, July 1982.

77. Nelson v. Rural Education Assn., et al., 23 Tenn. App. 409, 134 S.W. 2d 181 (Ct. of App. Tenn., 1939).

78. *Supra*, note 1, Sec. 19. *See also* Perkins: Self-defense Re-examined, 1 *USCLA Rev.* 133 (1954).

79. *Supra*, note 1, Sec. 20.

80. *Supra*, note 1, Sec. 21.

81. Burrows v. Hawaiian Trust Co., 49 Hawaii Rep. 351, 417 P. 2d 816 (1966).

82. Jessup, M.: Chemical Dependency: Looking after the Nurse, *California Nurse*, 78(7)8, 1983.

83. Green, P.: Chemical Dependency in the Nursing Profession, *Kansas Nurse*, 58(1)17–18, 1983.

84. *Ibid.*, p. 18.

85. De Garmo, P., et al.: Substance Abuse: An Occupational Hazard among Nurses, *Oregon Nurse*, 48(5)8+, 1983.

86. Jefferson, L., and Ensor, B. E.: Help for the Helper: Confronting a Chemically Dependent Colleague, *Am. J. Nursing*, 82:574–577, April 1982.

87. Conlon v. Commonwealth State Board of Nurse Examiners, 449 A. 2d 108 (Pa. 1982); *Regan Rep. Nurs. Law*, 23(6)2, July 1982.

88. Smith v. State of Alabama, 435 So. 2d 108 (Ala. 1983); *Regan Rep. Nurs. Law*, 24(6)4, Nov. 1983.

89. 88 S. Ct. 2145 (Tex., 1968).

90. Zebell v. Krall, 348 Mich. 282, 83 N.W. 2d 288 (1957).

91. *Supra*, note 1, Sec. 12. Harper: Malicious Prosecution, False Imprisonment, and Defamation, 15 *Tex. L. Rev.* 156 (1937).

92. Gadsden General Hospital v. Hamilton, 212 Ala. 531, 103 S. 553 (1925). *See also* Analysis of Legal and Medical Considerations in Commitment of the Mentally Ill, 56 *Yale L. J.*, 1178 (1947).

93. Salisbury v. Poulson, 51 Utah 552, 172 Pac. 315 (1918).

94. Bailie v. Miami Valley Hospital, 221 N.E. 2d 217 (Ct. Common Pleas, Ohio, 1966).

95. Whitree v. State of New York, 290 N.Y.S. 2d 486 (1968).

96. Ex-MU Student Says She Was Imprisoned, *Milwaukee Journal*, Part 2, August 5, 1969, p. 9.

97. Rice v. Mercy Hospital Corp., 275 S. 2d 566 (Fla., 1953); *Citation*, 27:103, July 15, 1973.

98. Big Town Nursing Home v. Newman, 461 S.W. 2d 195 (Tex., 1970).

99. Stowers v. Ardmore Acres Hospital, 172 N.W. 2d 497 (Mich., 1969); Regan, W. A.: Law Forum, *Hosp. Prog.*, 51:32, July 1970.

100. Felton v. Coyle, 238 N.E. 2d 191 (Ill., 1968); *Regan Rep. on Nurs. Law*, 9:1, Aug. 1968.

101. City of Glendale v. Bradshaw, 503 P. 2d 803 (Ariz., 1972); *Citation*, 27:101, July 15, 1973.

102. *Supra*, note 1, Sec. 831–832.

103. Warren, S. D., and Brandeis, L. D.: The Right of Privacy, 4 *Harv. L. Rev.* 193 (1890).

104. Pasevich v. New England Life Ins. Co., 50 S.E. 68 (S. Ct. Ga., 1904).

105. Roberson v. Rochester Folding Box Co., 64 N.E. 442 (Ct. App. N.Y., 1902).

106. Griffin v. Medical Society of the State of New York, 11 N.Y.S. 2d 109 (S. Ct. N.Y., 1939).

107. Ettore v. Philco Television Broadcasting Corp., 229 F. 2d 481 (3rd Cit., 1956).

108. Note: Crimination of Peeping Toms and Other Men of Vision, 5 *Ark. L. Rev.* 338 (1951).

109. La Crone v. Ohio Bell Tel. Co., 182 N.E. 2d 15 (Ohio App., 1961).

110. Wigmore, J. H.: The Right Against False Attribution of Belief or Utterance, 4 *Kentucky L. Rev.* No. 8, 3 (1916).

111. Barber v. Time, Inc., 1594, W. 2d 291 (S. Ct. Mo., 1942).

112. Feeney v. Young, 181 N.Y.S. 481 (N.Y., 1920).

113. Bazemore v. Savannah Hospital, 155 S.E. 194 (S. Ct. Ga., 1930).

114. Banks v. King Features Syndicate, Inc., 30 F. Supp. 352 (S.D. N.Y., 1939).

115. Doe v. Roe, 345 N.Y.S. 2d 560 (N.Y. 1973).

116. Carroll, J. D., and Knerr, C. R.: The APSA Confidentiality Social Science Research Project: A Final Report, *Political Science*, 9:416–419, Fall 1976.

117. A detailed summary of findings and a sample survey instrument may be obtained from J. D. Carroll, Principal Investigator, Research Data Project, and Chairman, Department of Public Administration, the Maxwell School, Syracuse University, or from C. D. Knerr, Research Associate and Assistant Professor, Department of Political Science, University of Texas at Arlington.

118. Carroll, J. D.: Confidentiality of Social Science Research Sources and Data: The Popkin Case, *Political Science*, 6:268–270, Summer 1973.

119. *Supra*, note 117, Research Data Project Case 023.

120. Tyler, R. M., and Kaufman, D.: The Public Scholar and the First Amendment, 49 *George Washington L. Rev.* 995–1023, July 1972.

121. *Supra*, note 117, Research Data Project Case 043.

122. *Supra*, note 117, Research Data Project Cases 158, 162, and 163.

123. *Supra*, note 117, Research Data Project Cases 049, 058, 093, 100, and 105.

124. Fields, C. M.: Growing Problem for Re-

searchers, *Chronicle of Higher Education*, 14(10)1, 15, May 2, 1977.

125. Richards of Rockford, Inc. v. Pacific Gas and Electric Co., (N. Dist. Calif. No. 3-74-0578 CBR, May 20, 1976).

126. *Id.*

127. Kathleen K. v. Roberts B., 198 Cal. Rptr. 273 (Cal. Ct. of App. 1984); *Citation*, 49:56-57, June 15, 1984.

128. *Supra*, note 1, Sec. 92. *Restatement, Torts*. Sec. 559 Holdsworth: Defamation in the Sixteenth and Seventeenth Centuries, 40 *L.Q. Rev.* 302, 397 (1924); 41 *L.Q. Rev.* (1925). Carr and "The English Law of Defamation," 18 *L.Q. Rev.* 255, 388 (1902). Donnelly: History of Defamation, 1949 *Wis. L. Rev.* 99. Yankwich: Certainty in the Law of Defamation, 1 *U.S.C.L.A. Rev.* 163 (1954).

129. Alpin v. Morton, 21 Ohio St. 536 (1871).

130. Prosser, W. L.: *Handbook of the Law of Torts*, 4th ed. St. Paul, West Publishing Co., 1971, p. 742.

131. Notarmuzzi v. Shevack, 108 N.Y.S. 2d 172 (1951), p. 174.

132. Barry v. Baugh, 111 Ga. App. 813, 143 S.E. 2d 489 (1965).

133. *Supra*, note 1, Secs. 93-96. *Restatement, Torts*, Sec. 568. Donnelly: Defamation by Radio: A Reconsideration, 34 *Iowa L. Rev.* 12 (1948); 1 *Duke B. J.* 218 (1951).

134. *Supra*, note 1, Secs. 93-96.

135. Russell, I.: *Crimes*, 8th ed., 1923, p. 983.

136. Farrell v. Kramer, 159 Maine 387, 35 A. 2d 218, 193 A. 2d 560 (1963).

137. Savarirayan v. English, 359 N.E. 2d 236 (Ill. App. Ct., 1977); *Citation*, 35:25, May 15, 1977.

138. Proper v. Mowry, 568 P. 2d 236 (N. Mex. Ct. App., 1977); *Citation*,36:38, Dec. 1, 1977.

139. *Supra*, note 1, Sec. 95. Evans: Legal Immunity for Defamation, 24 *Minn. L. Rev.* 607 (1940).

140. *Supra*, note 1, Sec. 95.

141. 1, 3 Scott: Trusts (1939, 1954 Supp.) Secs. 2.5, 495. 1 *Restatement, Trusts*, Sec. 2(b); also Sec. 170 (1) (2). 1 Restatement Agency. 1933 Sec. 13—Agent as a fiduciary.

142. New Jersey Session Laws, C. 185 (N.J., July 19, 1968).

143. Massachusetts Session Laws, C. 418 (Mass., June 18, 1968).

144. Alexander v. Knight, 177 A. 2d 142 (Pa., 1962).

145. Boulward v. Boulward, 153 So. 2d 182 (La., 1964).

146. In the Matter of the Doe Children, 402 N.Y.S. 2d 958 (N.Y. Family Ct., 1978).

147. State of New Hampshire v. Kupchun, 373 A. 2d 1325 (N.H. Sup. Ct., 1977).

148. Cleveland v. Maddox, 152 Ark. 538, 239 S.W. 370 (1922).

149. Culver v. Union P.R. Co., 112 Neb. 441, 199 N.W. 794 (1924).

150. Meyer v. Russell, 55 N.D. 546, 214, N.W. 857 (1927).

151. Hobbs v. Hullman, 183 App. Div. 743, 171 N.Y.S. 390 (1918). Judgment reversed for other error.

152. Louisville & N.R. Co. v. Crockett's Adm'x., 232 Ky. 662, 24 S.W. 2d 580 (1930).

153. Dyer v. State, 241 Ala. 679, 4 So. 2d 311 (1941).

154. State v. Wright, 572 P. 2d 669 (Ore. Ct. App., 1977); *Mental Health Ct. Dig.*, 21:5, June 1978.

155. Merritt v. Detroit Memorial Hospital, 265 N.W. 2d 124 (Mich. Ct. App., 1978); *Regan Rep. on Hosp. Law*, 18:4, June 1978.

156. People v. Abdul Karium Al-Kanai, 351 N.Y.S. 2d 969 (N.Y., 1963).

157. Washington Research Project, In. v. Dept. of H.E.W., 366 F. Supp. 929 (D.C., 1973).

158. Flower's Case, Cro. Car. 211, 79 Eng. Rep. 785 (1632).

159. Amick v. Montross, 206 Iowa 51, 220 N.W. 51 (1928).

160. Rickbeil v. Grafton Deaconess Hospital et al., 74 N.D. 525, 23 N.W. 2d 247 (1946).

161. Winkler, K. J.: A Sweeping Revision of the Copyright Laws, *Chronicle of Higher Education*, 14:1, 12, Oct. 11, 1976.

162. What Teachers and Libraries Can and Can't Do Under the New Law, *Chronicle of Higher Education*, 14:1, 12, Oct. 11, 1976.

163. *Op. cit.*, note 161, p. 1.

164. *Ibid.*

165. *Op. cit.*, note 162, p. 1.

166. *Op. cit.*, note 161, p. 12.

167. Regan, W. A.: Nursing Liability for Restraint Accidents, *Regan Rep. on Nurs. Law*, 8(6):1, Nov. 1967.

168. Moore v. Halifax Hospital, 202 So. 2d 568 (Fla., 1967).

169. Gerba v. Neurological Hospital, 1967 CCH Neg. 1660 (Mo.).

170. Constant v. Howe, 436 S.W. 2d 115 (Tex., 1968).

171. Methodist Hosp. v. Knight, 1969 CCH Neg. 4571 (Tenn.).

172. Court Rules on Holding Mental Patients without Hearing, *Am. J. Nurs.*, 73:1258, July 1973.

173. Legal Risks Involved in Sterilization Cited by California Lawyer, *Physician's Legal Brief*, 9(4):3, April 1967.

174. Shaheen v. Knight, 6 N.Y.C. 19, 11 Pa. D&C 2d 41 (1957).

175. Christensen v. Thornby, 192 Minn. 123, 255 N.W. 620 (1934).

176. Wyatt v. Aderholt et al., 368 F. Supp. 1383 (Ala., 1974).

177. In the Matter of S.C.E., 178 A. 2d 144 (Del. 1977).

178. Wade v. Bethesda Hospital, *Columbus Evening Dispatch*, Ohio, March 29, 1972; *Citation*, 27(5):65, July 15, 1973.

179. Application of A.D., 394 N.Y.S. 2d 139 (N.Y. Surrogate's Ct., 1977).

180. Wins Case, *Milwaukee Journal*, Nov. 26, 1971, p. 16, col. 2.

181. Christensen v. Thornby, 225 N.W. 620 (Minn., 1934).

182. Shaeheen v. Knight, 6 Lyc. 19, 11 Pa. Dist. & Co. R 2d 4 (1957).

183. Doerr v. Villate, 222 N.E. 767 (Ill., 1966).

184. Wasmuth, C. E., and Wasmuth, C. E., Jr.: *Law and the Surgical Team*. Baltimore, Williams and Wilkins Co., 1969, pp. 122-123.

185. Bernstein, A. H.: Law in Brief: Sterilization: An Enforceable Right? *Hospitals*, 48:96–99, 112, May 1, 1974.
186. Healy, E. F. S.J.: *Medical Ethics.* Chicago, Loyola University Press, 1956.
187. *Ibid.*
188. *Ibid.*
189. *Ibid.*
190. *Ibid.*
191. Johnsen v. State, 176 Misc. 347, 27 N.Y.S. 2d 945 (1941).
192. Duncan v. Flynn, 342 So. 2d 123 (Fla. Dist. Ct. App., 1977).
193. Rhodes v. California Hospital Medical Center, 143 Cal. Rptr. 59 (Cal. Ct. App., 1978).
194. *Supra,* note 1, Secs. 11, 37. *Restatement, Torts,* Sec. 868. Fryer: *Readings on Personal Property.* 3rd ed. 1, Recent Case Notes, 9 *Ind. L.J.* 177 (1933–1934).
195. Polk County v. Phillips, 92 Tex. 630, 51 S.W. 328 (1899).
196. Schwalb v. Connely, 116 Colo. 195, 179 P. 2d 667 (1947). *See also* Hasselbach v. Mt. Sinai Hosp., 173 App. Div. 89, 159 N.Y.S. 376 (1916).
197. New Law May Increase Human Organ Donations, *USA Today,* Nov. 14, 1984, p. 6D.
198. *Ibid.*
199. Sadler, A. M., Jr., Sadler, B. L., and Stason, E. B.: Uniform Anatomical Gift Act: Model for Reform, *JAMA,* 206:2501–2506, 1968. Curran, W. J.: Law-Medicine Notes: Uniform Anatomical Gift Act, *N. Engl. J. Med.,* 280:36, 1969.
200. Stason, E. B.: Role of Law in Medical Progress, *Law & Contemp. Prob.,* 32:573–596, 1967.
201. Stickel, D. L.: Ethical and Moral Aspects of Transplantation, *Monogr. in Surg. Sc.,* 3:267–301, 1966. Report of the Ad Hoc Committee of the Harvard Medical School to Examine the Definition of Brain Death: A Definition of Brain Death, *JAMA,* 205:337–340, Aug. 5, 1968.
202. Wolstenholme, G. E. W., and O'Connor, M. (eds.): *Ciba Foundation Symposium: Ethics in Medical Progress, with Special Reference to Transplantation.* Boston, Little, Brown & Co., 1966.
203. Experimentation in Man, *N. Engl. J. Med.,* 274:1382–1383, June 16, 166.
204. *Black's Law Dictionary,* 4th ed. St. Paul, West Publishing Co., 1951.
205. Thomas v. Anderson, 96 Cal. App. 2d 371 (1950). Smith v. Smith, 229 Ark. 579, 317 S.W. 2d 275 (1958).
206. Report of the Ad Hoc Committee of the Harvard Medical School to Examine the Definition of Brain Death: a Definition of Irreversible Coma, *JAMA,* 205:337–340, Aug. 5, 1968.
207. Quoted in Wecht, C.: Attorney Describes Current Efforts to Establish Uniform Guidelines (in Death and Transplantation), *Hospitals,* 43:54–57, Nov. 1, 1969.
208. Conn, J., Jr.: Difficulty in Establishing Goals for Clinical Efforts, *Hospitals,* 43:49–50, Nov. 1, 1969.
209. *Ibid.*
210. 285 N.Y.S. 2d 709 (Sup. Ct. Niag. City., 1967).
211. Ethical Guidelines for Organ Transplantation, *JAMA,* 205:341–342, Aug. 5, 1968.
212. McCleave, P., D.D.: Clergyman Says "Moral Problems" Stem from Emotions, Not Ethics, *Hospitals,* 43:53–54, Nov. 1, 1969.
213. Page, I. H.: The Ethics of Heart Transplants, *JAMA,* 207:109–113, Jan. 6, 1969.
214. Lowery, D. L.: Questions about Organ Transplants, *Liguorian,* 56(3)12–15, March 1968.
215. *Ibid.*

General References

Creighton, H.: The Expert Witness, *Superv. Nurse,* 11:71–72, April 1980.
Creighton, H.: Unruly Patients, *Nurs. Management,* 13:15–16, July 1982.
Cushing, M.: Whose Best Interests: Parents vs. Child Rights, *Am. J. Nursing,* 82:313–314, Feb. 1982.
Dean, K. A.: The Nurse as Witness: Deposition, *Focus Crit. Care,* 10:20–22, June 1983.
Greenlaw, J.: Ethical Dilemmas: Reporting Incompetent Colleagues II: Will I be Sued for Defamation? *Nurs. Law Ethics* 1(5)5–6, May 1980.
Kreitzer, M.: Symposium on Child Abuse and Neglect: Legal Aspects of Child Abuse: Guidelines for the Nurse, *Nurs. Clin. North Am.,* 16:149–160, March 1981.
Langslow, A.: Where Do I Stand? The Nurse and the Law, *Aust. Nurses' J.,* 10(8)26–28, March 1981.
Langslow, A.: The Nurse and the Law: Judgment and Counter Judgment, *Aust. Nurses' J.,* 11(8)28–30, March 1982.
McCracken, J.: Child Abuse Has No Class, *Crit. Care Update,* 7:19–21, Dec. 1980.
Morris, W. A.: Legally Speaking: 1001 Ways to Land in Court, Part Two, *R.N.,* 44(8)67–72, Aug. 1981.
Northrop, C., et al.: The Nurse as Expert Witness, *Nurs. Law Ethics,* 2:1+, March 1981.
Philpott, M.: *Legal Liability and the Nursing Process.* Toronto, W. B. Saunders Company Canada Ltd., 1985.
Regan, W. A.: Drug Abuse by RNs, Unprofessional Conduct? *Regan Rep. Nurs. Law,* 21(1)2, June 1980.
Shindul, J. A., et al.: Legal Restraints on Restraint, *Am. J. Nursing,* 81:393–394, Feb. 1981.
Southby, J. R.: Legal Considerations for Nurse Researchers . . . Adherence to Ethical Codes, *AORN, J.,* 33:1278–1280+, June 1981.
Wiemerslage, D.: Torts: Doctrine of Precedent, *Crit. Care Update,* 9:27–37, Oct. 1983.

Nine
CRIMES: MISDEMEANORS AND FELONIES

Nurses, like other citizens, may subject themselves to criminal prosecution either by doing something that the law defines as a criminal act, or by omitting to do an act that the law requires and the omission of which the law declares to be a crime. Moreover, a person does not have to do something immoral or wicked for the law to regard the act as criminal. For example, if a state, using its police power, makes it mandatory for all nurses who practice nursing for hire to obtain a license, and provides that willful violation of such law shall constitute a misdemeanor, then nurses who render nursing service for pay without securing a license are guilty of a crime, even though they may not intend to do wrong. Again, some acts of negligence are so gross or wanton in character as to be classified as crimes.

DEFINITION OF CRIMINAL ACTIONS

Criminal actions deal with acts or offenses against the public welfare. These are considered offenses against the state, and vary from minor, petty offenses and misdemeanors to felonies. A misdemeanor is a general name for every sort of criminal offense that does not in law amount to the grade of felony. A felony in many states is defined as any public offense for the conviction of which a person is liable to be sentenced to death or to imprisonment in a penitentiary or state prison.[1] A felony implies that the crime has more serious consequences or is of a more atrocious nature than a misdemeanor.

A felony at common law was an offense that brought about a total forfeiture of either a person's land or goods of both, and to which capital or other punishment might be added according to the degree of guilt. In American law, the word "felony" has no clear, definite meaning at common law, but it includes offenses of considerable gravity. A crime is not a felony unless it is so declared by statute or it was so at common law.[2] In the U.S. Criminal Code,[3] all offenses that are punishable by death, by imprisonment for one year or more or by a fine in excess of $1000 are felonies; all other offenses are misdemeanors. For example, if a nurse were convicted of performing an illegal abortion, that act would be a felony. On the other hand, if a nurse were convicted of unlawfully taking a $3 bottle of wine from a patient's locker, that would be a misdemeanor.

Every adult person of sound mind recognizes the acts of murder, rape, manslaughter, robbery and larceny as crimes. Likewise, assault may be a criminal offense as well as the basis of a tort action for damages, as may most crimes.

Certain wrongs are identified as crimes because they are regarded as harmful to public health, welfare, safety or security. In the last analysis, public policy or the will of the people as expressed by law determines what shall be classified as criminal wrong. In the United States, by virtue of the police power, Congress has the power to decide which wrongs are crimes in Federal matters, and each state legislature has the power to declare which wrongs will be classified as crimes within its jurisdiction. Because public policy as expressed by law determines the category of crimes, acts that are criminal in one country may not be so in another. As a society or a state grows, the pressure to express its standards of social conduct in law increases.

A person sometimes hears or sees the term "moral turpitude," which refers to an act of baseness, vileness or depravity in social and private duties.[4] Crimes involving moral turpitude are acts that are bad in themselves, such as rape, robbery and murder.

REQUIREMENTS FOR CONVICTION

Criminal offenses are composed of two elements: a criminal act and a criminal intent. In order to convict a person of a crime, both must be proved beyond a reasonable doubt. A criminal offense is either some act that the law forbids or the omission of some act that the law requires.

Criminal intent is the state of mind a person has at the time that the criminal act is committed; this means knowning that an act is not lawful and deciding to do it anyway. To be criminal, an act must be defined as a crime by law. When there is an actual doing of a criminal act, the courts, except in specific intent crimes, presume a criminal intent unless the person who is acused of the crime attempts to show that at the time such criminal action was committed it was an involuntary act, or that he was not capable of understanding or deciding the essential character of the act and its unlawful nature. To prove the same, he may offer evidence showing insanity, necessity or compulsion, accident, mistake of fact or infancy. Although an act may be recognized as criminal, nevertheless, if a person is able to prove to the satisfaction of the court the lack of criminal intent due to one or more of the conditions cited, the court will decide he or she did not commit a criminal offense and will declare the person not guilty. In other words, although the law may presume intent upon the doing of a particular act, it cannot presume intent on the part of persons who are incapable of it.[5]

ARGUMENTS AGAINST CRIMINAL INTENT

Insanity

As a defense to a crime in criminal law, insanity has been defined as such a deranged condition of the mental and moral faculties as to make a person incapable of knowing whether her or his acts are right or wrong.[6] Statutes have been passed in a number of states providing for medical examination of accused persons when there is a question concerning their sanity. Experts are often requested to examine accused persons and to testify during the trial about their sanity at the time of examination and also to speculate about their mental state when the crime was committed. In some states, in addition to the "right and wrong test," there is an "irresistible impulse test."[7] An irresistible impulse is symptomatic of mental disease that causes a person to commit an act despite her or his ability to differentiate between right and wrong. As pointed out in the discussion of contracts, where it was mentioned that an insane person could not make a valid contract, the whole problem of whether or not a person is insane is often difficult to determine. However difficult insanity may be to ascertain, an insane person cannot be legally charged with criminal intent.[8]

In a Mississippi case, on appeal, the court ruled that it was an error to deny a motion to have a defendant charged with a capital murder where a pre-trial examining psychiatrist found him able to distinguish between right and wrong with respect to the particular crime. The court also refused to abandon the M'Naghten Rule—the right and wrong test for insanity—and to accept the American Law Institute's Test. The latter would relieve a defendant of responsibility for criminal conduct:

> if at the time of such conduct as a result of mental disease or defect he lacks substantial capacity either to appreciate the criminality (wrongfulness) of his conduct or to conform his conduct to the requirements of law.

The court stated that such a rule, in effect, would provide for the acquittal of those who commit criminal acts and assert that they did so because of so-called uncontrollable urges or irresistible impulses. The court added that although the M'Naghten Rule may not be a perfect means to test criminal responsibility, it is the safest of the rules proposed.[9]

The District of Columbia Court of Appeals, in affirming a defendant's conviction of first-degree murder of his wife, *did* adopt the American Law Institute's Test (quoted above) for an insanity defense. As used in the standard, the terms "mental disease" or "defect" do not include an abnormality manifested only by repeated criminal or otherwise antisocial conduct.[10]

Where a 17-year-old juvenile was tried as an adult and convicted of felony murder, burglary and felony theft after beating a woman to death, an instruction to the jury to use the M'Naghten Rule rather than the proposed American Law Institute Model Penal Code Test in considering a defense of insanity was not error, according to the Kansas Supreme Court.[11] Not long before the murder, the youth had consumed an eight-pack of 7 oz beer and had taken "three hits" of amphetamines. The psychiatrists essentially agreed that the accused knew the difference between right and wrong at the time of the crime, but that when he began to hit the woman he was unable to control his behavior during the passion of the moment.

Necessity or Compulsion

Necessity is a defense to a charge of criminal intent and action. There are occasions when nurses must defend themselves from attack and infliction of bodily harm by a violent patient. If they are able to prove that in defending themselves they used only the force necessary to repel the attack, they are not guilty of criminal intent, despite the injuries inflicted upon their assailant.

Accident

If an act is an accident, this might relieve one of criminal intent. For example, assume that a nurse was out playing golf, and he hit a ball which, after striking a tree, bounced off, striking a child and seriously injuring the eye. The nurse did nothing a reasonable person would not do in the circumstances, and yet an accident resulted; the injury was due neither to criminal intent nor to gross negligence.

Mistake of Fact

Suppose a hospital pharmacy put up boric acid solution and dextrose solution in similar bottles, similarly labeled, except that the boric acid bottle label said "For external use only." Assume further that newborn babies were customarily fed 5 percent dextrose solution. Assume, too, that a druggist's helper mistakenly filled a dextrose bottle with boric acid and that a nurse fed the solution to several babies, who died.[12] The nurse would not be responsible for their deaths. Her action, due to a mistake of fact, lacked criminal intent.

Infancy

The law recognizes that criminal intent may be absent because of a person's infancy. Although children may be convicted of crimes, those under 7 years of age generally are conclusively presumed to be unable to differentiate criminal right and wrong in the legal sense. Hence, if a five-year-old who was at times jealous of his baby sister fed her ten pink aspirin tablets as "candy," and the sister was harmed thereby, it would be presumed that the little boy had entertained no criminal intention. Also, minors between 7 and 14 years of age in many states are chargeable only with juvenile delinquency, not crime.

DISTINCTION BETWEEN CRIMINAL LIABILITY AND TORT

Criminal liability is to be distinguished from tort liability. In a criminal action, the state seeks the punishment of the wrongdoer. In a tort action, which is a civil action, the person who has been wronged seeks to be compensated for the injury or wrong he or she has suffered on account of the acts of the wrongdoer. The same set of circumstances, such as negligence causing the death of a person, may give rise to both a criminal action and a civil action, but these actions are tried in different courts with different procedures. In criminal cases, there is a heavy burden on the prosecution to prove its case beyond a reasonable doubt, whereas in civil actions the plaintiffs have only to show a preponderance (excess of weight or influence) of evidence in their favor. Therefore, it may happen that a person may escape punishment for a crime and yet be liable in a civil suit arising out of the same event.

In a California case, under a statute which provided that, when the death of a person is caused by a wrongful act of another, her or his heirs may maintain an action against the person causing the death, an administrator brought a civil suit against a private hospital, physician and head nurse for damages for a wrongful death. The deceased patient had been a cook who earned high wages and sent most of them to his mother in Italy. After some years, he decided to make a trip to Italy, and apparently became so excited and nervous about the trip that it was necessary to take him to a private hospital. The evidence tended to show that the patient was not violent, but that he was merely excitable and had sudden outbursts—a condition that frequently yields to rest and treatment. Evidence also established that the sanitarium was equipped with restraining straps, which were not used, and that the patient's death resulted either from excessive use of ether or from the application of a tourniquet that consisted of a towel placed about his neck. There was considerable evidence concerning a violent struggle, that four or five persons were subduing him and that most of the contents of a 1-lb can of ether were used. The struggle lasted some time. A $15,000 award to a mother with a life expectancy of 13 years was held not excessive.[13] Although this is a civil action and no mention is made of a criminal action against the doctor and nurse, it illustrates the possibilities of nurses (as well as others) rendering themselves liable.

All criminal actions are brought in the name of the state, such as State versus Staples. By contrast, a civil action is, for example, Jennie Jones, plaintiff, versus Sue Smith, defendant. It is a principle of U.S. law that, in any legal action, "every person is entitled to his day in court." It is hoped that this brief outline of the conduct of civil actions will give the nurse some appreciation of how this right is secured for each person, both citizen and alien.

CRIMINAL COURT PROCEDURE

Briefly, the procedure at a criminal trial is as follows. The accused person is brought before the court, and the indictment or charges are read aloud. The office of the grand jury is to examine the basis on which a charge is made by the state.[21] After this, the accused person is asked whether he pleads guilty or not guilty. If he pleads guilty, and if the court is satisfied that he knows full well the meaning of what he says, it may sentence him. However, the court, if it is considering a capital punishment offense, must ignore a plea of guilty and enter one of not guilty. In any very serious case, the court may ignore the accused person's plea of guilty and enter a plea of not guilty. Under U.S. criminal laws, a person is always presumed innocent until proved guilty beyond a reasonable doubt. In very serious cases, the court enters a plea of not guilty in an accused person's behalf, even when he pleads guilty, in order to put on the prosecutor the burden of proving him guilty beyond a reasonable doubt. When the accused person is thus arraigned (called before the court to answer to an indictment), preparations for the trial are made.

If it is a jury trial, the jurors are then selected and sworn in to give a true verdict. The prosecutor opens the trial with a statement in which she or he outlines the important features of the case; then, the witnesses are called. A witness is examined and then cross-examined by the defense attorney. The witness may be re-examined by the prosecutor, followed by a re–cross-examination. After the state's case has been presented, the attorney for the accused may request the court to dismiss the case and discharge the accused on the ground that no case has been made against him or her. If the court agrees, it directs the jury to return a verdict of not guilty; otherwise, the trial proceeds, and witnesses are called for the defense. They are examined by the defense attorney; then, they may be cross-examined by the prosecutor, and again they may be re-examined by the defense. When the entire defense has been heard, the prosecutor and the defense attorney each address the jury in summation. The court then instructs the jury and asks them to consider their verdict. The jurors retire to a designated room to do so. If the accused person is found not guilty, he or she is discharged. If a guilty verdict is returned, the presiding judge pronounces sentence. After a person has been tried on a criminal charge and either discharged or convicted, he or she may not be tried on that same charge again by the same sovereign. If a person is tried in a lower court, he or she may, as a rule, appeal to a higher court if some error in the proceedings can be shown.

PRINCIPALS OR ACCESSORIES

Principals in Felonies

Attention is directed at this point to the persons concerned in the commission of felonies. They are either principals or accessories.[14] In misdemeanors and in treason, the distinction between principals and accessories is not recognized. A person who actually performs the act, either acting alone or through an innocent agent, is a principal in the first degree.[15] A person who is either actually or constructively present, and who is aiding and abetting (i.e., encouraging or supporting) another in the commission of an act, is a principal in the second degree.[16] There must be a common interest of unlawful purpose between the principals at the time the act is done. To illustrate, a person who mixed Paris green and water in a cup and placed it within reach of another person who, in turn, drank it and died, aided and abetted the killing and was guilty of murder.[17] A female friend who simply accompanies a woman who undergoes an illegal abortion is not an associate in guilt.[18] But a person, say, who lent her home to a woman so that she could have an illegal abortion performed, would be a party to the crime.*

Accessories to the Crime

A person who was absent when an act was done—but who obtained, advised, ordered or encouraged the principal to commit it—is an "accessory before the fact."[19] A person who for the purpose of defeating justice receives, comforts, assists or relieves another person and, at the time he or she does so, knows that the other person has committed a felony, is an "accessory after the fact."[20] It is pertinent to note that a person who removes evidence after a crime is an accessory after the fact. To illustrate, a women tells her lover she is pregnant and asks his help, and he gives her a piece of paper on which is written the name and address of a person who performs illegal abortions. If, in addition, he gives her the exact amount of money to pay such a person, then the lover, although not present at the illegal abortion, may be considered an accessory before the fact. As another example, a jeweler who helps another to dispose of a large quantity of gems, which he knows to be stolen goods, is an accessory after the fact. In most jurisdictions, a parent or spouse is immune from prosecution

---

*In the District of Columbia, a woman who has an illegal abortion performed on herself is not an accomplice.

as an accessory after the fact. To be punishable as an accessory to a criminal act, assistance or participation must be shown.

CRIMES

Murder

Murder is the unlawful killing of a human being with intent to kill. In every case, murder is a very serious crime, the penalty for which may be death, life imprisonment or a lesser punishment. There can be no consent to killing a person. In passing, it seems instructive to remind nurses that in the United States euthanasia (an act or practice of painlessly putting to death persons suffering from an incurable or a distressing disease) is murder according to U.S. law.[22] Also, it is murder when a death occurs as a result of an illegal abortion.

Homicide and Murder. Sometimes nurses use the words "homicide" and "murder" interchangeably, but they have different meanings. Homicide is the killing of one human being by another, and it may be justifiable, excusable or felonious.[23] The homicide is regarded as justifiable in executing a death sentence, in suppressing a riot, in preventing a felony and, in some cases, in defending oneself, one's home or others.[24] An example of an excusable homicide would be a killing done in necessary, reasonable self-defense or by an unavoidable accident.[25]

On the other hand, murder, properly speaking, is the unlawful killing of one human being by another with "malice aforethought."[26] Malice aforethought indicates purpose and design in a person's action, in contrast to accident. To exhibit malice aforethought, a person does not necessarily have to intend to kill another or to do it deliberately, but in general it is enough if, at the time that the crime was done, the person intended serious bodily harm or knew that serious bodily harm or death would probably result from her or his acts. The commission of a felony that results in death also constitutes murder.

A chiropractor was convicted of murder in the death of an eight-year-old patient. The court reversed the judgment owing to prejudicial erroneous instructions to the jury. There was evidence that removal of a cancerous eye was necessary to save the child's life, but the chiropractor, with reckless and wanton cupidity, falsely represented himself to the parents as being able to cure cancer. He induced the parents to forego the operation and submit the child to his treatment. Thus, the child's life was shortened; the elements of first-degree murder were present. However, the evidence could also have been weighed and accepted as showing second-degree murder or manslaughter. The felony murder rule was prejudicially erroneous since it bound the jury by conclusive presumption if they found the felony of theft by false pretense.[27]

When 35 patients at the VA hospital in Ann Arbor suffered 51 cardiopulmonary arrests during July and August 1975, there was an intensive epidemiological and criminal investigation. A grand jury returned an indictment charging two government nurses with five counts of murder and ten counts of unlawfully mingling a poison in the food and medicine of certain patients. In the first trial, the nurses were convicted of murdering the patients by injecting Pavulon, a muscle-relaxing drug, into the victims' intravenous apparatus. The prosecutor made improper statements to newspaper reporters during the trial, and implied to the jury that the nurses had some duty to bring forth evidence of their innocence. A Federal Court in Michigan ruled that the nurses were entitled to a new trial.[28] Thereafter, there was a motion and order of dismissal of indictment and cancelling bond on February 1 and 6, 1978.[29]

A former nurse's aide was convicted of murder in the first degree for injecting an elderly patient with a fatal dose of lidocaine, a heart-regulating drug, and was sentenced to life imprisonment. He failed to establish that his due process rights were violated by failure to grant a change of venue.[30]

A California nurse was convicted of murdering 12 elderly patients with massive doses of lidocaine.[31] A Superior Court judge gave him 12 death sentences. An appeal to the state supreme court is automatic.[32]

A Texas vocational nurse was convicted of fatally injecting a 15-month-old girl with a drug.[33] The nurse was sentenced to the maximum prison term of 99 years by a jury.[34]

First- or Second-Degree Murder. From reading and conversation, nurses have heard such terms as first-degree murder, second-degree murder and manslaughter. Usually the distinction is not clear to them. In some states, the crime of murder is divided into first-degree murder, which generally means malice aforethought plus premeditation and deliberation, and second-degree murder, which is killing without premeditation or deliberation.[35] In other states, there is no distinction between first- and second-degree murder.

Murder in the second degree occurs where there is no deliberately formed design to take life or to perpetrate one of the enumerated felonies as is required for the first degree. Rather, there is a purpose to kill (or at least to inflict the particular injury without caring whether it causes death or not) formed instantaneously in the mind, and where the killing was without justification or excuse, and without any such provocation as would reduce the crime to the grade of manslaughter.[36]

Manslaughter. By way of distinction, manslaughter means an unlawful killing of a human being without malice aforethought.[37] For example, the killing may take place during a sudden quarrel, or may occur unintentionally while the person is doing some unlawful or lawful act. If the manslaughter is the result of an intentional killing without malice, it is called "voluntary"; but when the manslaughter is the result of an act without malice, and is an unintentional killing, it is called "involuntary." By way of illustration, death resulting from a person's negligently leaving poison where it may endanger life was held to be involuntary manslaughter,[38] similarly, a death due to reckless driving is usually held to be involuntary manslaughter.[39]

The Pennsylvania appellate court ruled that a wife had a duty to obtain medical aid for her husband when it became apparent that he was in serious need of medical attention. The husband, who was a diabetic, was attempting to withdraw from insulin treatment because of religious beliefs. He found the insulin had been removed from the refrigerator when he decided to take it. Despite apparent symptoms of lack of insulin, no medical assistance was sought and he died. The court found the wife guilty of involuntary manslaughter.[40]

A case most frequently mentioned occurred in 1929. A surgeon ordered a head nurse to prepare, as an anesthetic, a 10 percent cocaine solution with Adrenaline for a tonsillectomy patient; the nurse repeated the order. After the injection, the patient convulsed and died. The doctor meant procaine in the order instead of cocaine. Here was a situation in which the nurse should have questioned the order. By reason of her training, education and experience, she should have recognized that the order was incorrect. Not only was the nurse negligent, but her conduct amounted to gross negligence. She was convicted of manslaughter.[41] The lesson of this case should be thoroughly understood by all nurses.

Concerning this case, students frequently inquire why the nurse was convicted instead of the doctor. The answer is that the negligent act of the nurse caused the patient's death. The surgeon was also negligent, but his negligence in itself did not cause the death. In all likelihood, the case would not have arisen had the head nurse been alert and said, for example, "Pardon me, Doctor, did you say 10 percent procaine?" It bears repetition that persons are always personally answerable for their own torts and negligent acts. The negligent act in this case reached the level of crime. Failure to consider cause and effects that careful nurses ought to know and to recognize gives rise to liability.

Conviction of voluntary manslaughter was affirmed where a three-year-old girl died beause of traumatic injury to the brain inflicted in a beating by her stepmother. The physician testified as to her physical injuries, and the child's father and a neighbor testified that the woman had given the child a beating in the preceding weeks.[42]

A registered nurse was convicted of involuntary manslaughter, but the appellate court reversed the decision. As the nurse in charge of a state institution for the mentally retarded, she ordered medications given to patients as required under the general directions of a doctor located at another hospital. One day she ordered paraldehyde given to an unruly patient, and unknown to her the medication was four times the correct strength. As a result the patient became ill, was taken to another hospital and died five days later of pneumonia. Since medical testimony indicated that if the overdose of medicine was the cause of death, the patient would have died in four to six hours, then, without more evidence as to the precise cause of death, the court would not sustain the conviction.[43]

Nurses take courses in pharmacology, pharmacodynamics, anatomy, physiology and other subjects, and therefore are required to have a knowledge of cause and effect in executing orders. On occasion, though seldom, physicians have made errors in ordering medicines. The well-trained, alert, thinking nurse will tactfully check any obvious discrepancy. With a knowledge of the average therapeutic dose, the maximal dose, the effects of the drug and the age, sex and condition of the patient, the nurse's action, if there is an apparent discrepancy in an order, must be judged by what the average, reasonable and prudent nurse would do in such circumstances.

Gross Negligence

As noted before, ordinary negligence is not a crime. However, when the negligence is extremely careless or reckless, with disregard for human life, it becomes something more serious, viz., gross negligence. As has been stated, at least two elements are necessary for deliberate crime: evil intent and criminal action. There are crimes in which the matter of intent is not spelled out, such as some grossly negligent acts in which the person is ignorant of the law.

As has been pointed out, criminal or gross negligence is a commission or omission of an act, lawfully or unlawfully, in which such a degree of negligence exists as may cause a serious wrong to another. To illustrate, a paying patient in a charitable hospital, through the negligence of a nurse, was given a medicine that in fact has been intended for another patient in an adjoining room. The medicine proximately caused serious injury to the plaintiff, including the death of her baby. In a civil action for damages against the hospital, a judgment for the defendant was affirmed, since it was immune from liability as a charitable institution.[44] Nevertheless, the negligence of the nurse in question is readily apparent.

In another case in which a mother died after childbirth, a judgment for damages against a private hospital was affirmed, since there was sufficient evidence to sustain a finding that a nurse was negligent in failing to observe post-partum eclampsia and in not notifying the attending physician.[45]

In another case, a physician ordered a nurse to give a sitz bath to a patient. The nurse prepared the bath negligently, and as a result the patient was severely scalded.[46] Although the case does not state whether the nurse was a student nurse, practical nurse or graduate nurse, the finding of negligence on the part of the nurse would have been the same. Ordinary persons are presumed to know the dangers of excessively hot water in giving baths, and failure to act in accordance with such common knowledge, when others are injured as a result, constitutes criminal negligence. In this case, since the action was brought against two doctors in the hospital rather than the negligent nurse, the verdict was for the defendant.

The Louisiana appellate court ruled that a licensed practical nurse was guilty of gross negligence during the tube feeding of a patient and was properly terminated from her position. She failed to notice that the patient received acetone or another foreign substance in her tube feeding. She also failed to carry out the physician's order to give Isocal at full strength. In addition, she allowed her daughter and a friend to visit her while she was on duty. This was a violation of hospital policy and sound nursing practice. The patient died. The nurse admitted all the facts, and her suspension and termination were affirmed by the court.[47]

Fraud

An osteopathic physician and his assistant were convicted of 22 counts of submitting false and fraudulent claims to the Bureau of Public Assistance of Los Angeles County for treatment of public welfare patients, and of conspiracy to submit such claims. The conviction was reversed when the court held that admission of the physician's private medical records, taken under a search warrant, to prove that he had presented false claims for treatment of public welfare patients and had conspired to present false claims, violated the physician's constitutional privilege against self-incrimination and his privilege against unreasonable search and seizure.[48]

Assault and Battery

In criminal law, an assault is an attempt or offer, with force or violence, to inflict a physical injury upon another. It must consist of an overt (apparent) act; words are not enough.[49] There is a split of authority in the cases, but it would seem that a general criminal intent is enough. Battery is an assault in which any force, however slight, is actually applied to another. A general criminal intent is sufficient for the crime.[50]

In a New York case, the administratrix recovered damages in a civil suit for the death of her husband from:

> intra-abdominal hemorrhage, shock, and fractured ribs caused by external violence.

The patient had been suffering from paranoid schizophrenia, and died as a result of negligence of the attendants of the Hudson River State Hospital at Poughkeepsie. The court said that the attendant violated rules and regulations of his department, and:

> visited entirely unnecessary force toward, if not actually venting personal animosity toward a patient, while ample means were available to him of suppressing the patient however strenuous his resistance might have been.

In this case, it was brought out that the attendant had a record of conviction for:

> crime of willfully inflicting harsh, cruel and unkind treatment and neglect of duty toward an incompetent person.[51]

Robbery

Robbery is a felony at common law, and is a crime against the person and property. The taking of personal property of another person from him or in his presence, by either violence or intimidation and against his will, constitutes robbery.[52] Larceny at common law is obtaining personal property of another by trespass in taking and carrying away of it, together with a felonious intent to deprive the person of ownership.[53]

In a Massachusetts case, a civil action was brought against a private hospital for loss of a ring while the plaintiff was undergoing an operation. There was evidence that the plaintiff had engaged accommodations at the hospital for her operation and had also contracted for nursing before, after and during the operation. Furthermore, there was evidence that one of the operating room nurses stole a ring from the plaintiff's hand while the plaintiff was under the influence of ether. It was held that there was a violation by the hospital of its duty toward the plaintiff under its contract with her, and that the plaintiff could sue only for breach of the defendant's contractual duty.[54] The wrongdoing of the nurse was obvious, although the case was one for civil damages.

Burglary. Burglary is breaking into and entering the house of another with intent to commit a felony therein, whether the felony is actually committed or not.[55] A hospital dietician informed a security officer that her superior had money from the previous year's United Fund campaign, and at the suggestion of, and in the company of, a hospital security officer she entered into the desk of her immediate superior and searched it. The New Hampshire Supreme Court ruled that the search was not unauthorized. Because of the search, however, the dietician was demoted to a lower position. On appeal, the demotion was reversed, and the court ordered that the dietician be reinstated to her former position and given back pay and benefits.[56]

Larceny. In a Medicaid fraud case, a physician's conviction on 28 counts of grand larceny was affirmed, but a New York appellate court ordered that he should be resentenced. The physician had submitted invoices seeking reimbursement for services not rendered.[57]

Mayhem

Mayhem was a crime at common law that was the same as "maim," and it involved a violent injury to another, rendering him less able to fight, to annoy his enemy or to defend himself.[58] In most jurisdictions of the United States, it is a felony. For example, when a stepfather scalded a boy's feet, and the skin came off the toes so that, except for medical treatment, they would have grown together, it was held to be mayhem.[59]

Rape

The act of having unlawful carnal knowledge of a woman by force and against her will is rape.[60] It has been held that, when there is the slightest penetration, the crime is committed. The force may be either actual or constructive, as when it is induced by fear or intimidation. A man was convicted of the rape of a patient in a state mental health facility even though he did not know that the victim was a patient there.[61]

In *McKinney v. State*,[62] the conviction of a man for the statutory rape of his 14-year-old adopted daughter was affirmed. The girl testified that she had been having intercourse with him since she was 10 or 11 years old. The other three adopted daughters also testified he had sexual intercourse with them on numerous occasions over a period of years while they were living at home; such evidence was admitted only as evidence of intent. The court said the issue of consent could not arise since the offense is complete with or without the consent of the girl. A similar case involved the conviction of a stepfather for statutory rape of a nine-year-old stepdaughter. The girl's vagina was dilated to adult size, the mother testified that her daughter had complained to her for ten months of similar conduct and her 14-year-old brother had witnessed an act of sexual intercourse performed on his sister some months earlier.[63]

Sexually Dangerous Person. Where a defendant pleaded to indictments charging "assault to rape," an unnatural act, assault and battery with a dangerous weapon and furnishing liquor to a minor, the Massachusetts Appeals Court upheld an appeal from an order for commitment as a sexually dangerous person. It held that such a commitment must be based on evidence of repetitive acts of sexual misconduct that are also violent, or on evidence of behavior that is compulsive and violent.[64]

Sexual Sociopath. The Nebraska Supreme Court confirmed a conviction for rape and robbery, stating that the evidence warranted a finding that the defendant was a sexual sociopath who would not be benefited by treatment, and who should be committed in accordance with the sexual sociopath statute for an indefinite period in the state penal and correctional complex.[65] When the defendant is found to be no longer a sexual sociopath, any sentence the court may impose for the original conviction may not exceed the maximum sentence for the sexual crime of which he is found guilty.

Where a plaintiff, convicted of two rapes within five months, contended he should have been placed on probation to receive outpatient treatment, the Wisconsin Supreme Court upheld his commitment to the Central State Hospital for specialized treatment under the Sex Crime Act.[66] The court indicated that the Department of Health and Social Services recommends such treatment under the Sex Crime Act only when the behavior for which the person is convicted is the result of sexual psychopathology, or when the person is dangerous to society and is treatable.

Where a defendant had pleaded guilty to charges of indecent exposure and of fondling the sexual organs of a minor boy under the age of 16, the court confirmed the defendant as an untreatable sexual sociopath and confirmed his commitment to the State Penal and Correctional Complex, where sexual sociopaths are held separate from other prisoners.[67] The court said that the laws covering the habitual offender and the sexual sociopath are alike in that both are for the protection of society. In the case of the former, the law offers protection from a dangerous criminal offender; in the case of the latter, from a person who is found dangerous to society by reason of his sexual proclivities. For one, the purpose of incarceration is punishment; for the other, the purpose is treatment.

Defective Delinquent. The State of Maryland has held that a person who comes within the definition of defective delinquent must remain incarcerated until his demonstrated persistent, aggravated antisocial or criminal behavior caused by an "intellectual deficiency or emotional imbalance or both," and constituting an actual danger to society, is not by reason of passage of time or treatment, or both, likely to recur, therefore making his release reasonably safe for society.[68] In this case, the defendant had pronounced sexual urges that were directed toward children. The defendant had entered a plea of guilty of perverted practice, and was determined to be a defective delinquent and committed to an institution.

Bastardy–Fornication

A bastard is an illegitimate child born of an unlawful intercourse and before the lawful marriage of its parents.[69] This is the opposite of legitimacy, a condition of being born in wedlock. The bastardy process is a method provided by statute of proceeding against the putative father to secure a proper maintenance for the child. Fornication is unlawful sexual intercourse between two unmarried persons.[70] Adultery is the voluntary sexual intercourse with a person other than the offender's husband or wife.[71] Sodomy has been defined as carnal copulation by human beings with each other against nature, or with a beast.[72]

In *Commonwealth* v. *Rankin*,[73] a conviction for bastardy was reversed, and a conviction for fornication affirmed, where the evidence tended to prove that the child's mother had intercourse with more than one man during the time within which the child could have been conceived. In a bastardy prosecution, the state must prove an act of intercourse between the plaintiff and the defendant, and the conception of the child as a result of that act. In all criminal cases, the state has the burden of proving the elements of the offense beyond a reasonable doubt. Both bastardy and fornication are crimes in Pennsylvania.

In *Commonwealth* v. *Pizzimente* a conviction was affirmed for getting the complainant pregnant.[74] Although the complainant was a married woman, her testimony alone was sufficient to overcome legitimacy.

When an abortion clinic was being sued for damages resulting from an unsuccessful abortion and subsequent birth of a child, it filed a third-party complaint against the child's unwed father alleging that his negligent failure to employ a method of contraception was the legal cause of any injuries suffered by the child's mother. A Florida appellate court upheld the trial court, ruling that the only cause of action against the father was that of bastardy.[75]

Legitimacy. Where a child is born eight months after marriage, there is a presumption of legitimacy.[76] If a man, A, marries a woman, B, who is pregnant with a child fathered by another, C, and such child is born during the marriage of A and B, it does not legitimatize the subsequently born child.[77]

Controlled Substances

Every practicing nurse encounters situations that require knowledge of, or familiarity with, controlled substances regulations. Federal and state laws dealing with controlled substances are complex, but it is incumbent on nurses to know their responsibilities and limitations under the regulations.

The Comprehensive Drug Abuse Prevention and Control Act of 1970, generally called the Controlled Substances Act, replaced almost all pre-existing Federal laws dealing with narcotics, stimulants, depressants and hallucinogens. Drugs covered under the Controlled Substances Act include not only narcotics but also central nervous system stimulants, depressants, hallucinogenic drugs and some tranquilizers.[78] The drugs covered by this Act are classified in five schedules. Schedule I drugs have no accepted medical use in the United States and are not routinely encountered in nursing or health care practice. Schedule II drugs include those formerly known as Class A narcotics and the amphetamines and methamphetamines. In addition, the drugs amobarbital, methylphenidate, pentobarbital, phenmetrazine and secobarbital are in this schedule. Schedule III drugs include those formerly known as Class B narcotics, depressant non-narcotic drugs such as glutethimide and methyprylon, and short-acting barbiturates not listed in Schedule II. Schedule IV drugs include longer-acting barbiturates such as phenobarbital and barbital, tranquilizers such as meprobamate, and depressant drugs such as chloral hydrate, paraldehyde and ethchlorvynol. Schedule V drugs include those formerly known as "exempt narcotics" such as codeine-containing cough syrups.

The Controlled Substances Act was enacted to improve the administration and regulation of manufacturing, distribution and dispensing of these controlled substances by providing a closed system of distribution for legitimate handlers of the drugs. The purpose of the closed system is to reduce the widespread diversion of these drugs from legitimate channels to the illicit market. Persons authorized to prescribe or dispense controlled substances are required to register with the Drug Enforcement Administration (DEA). Such registration must be renewed annually or returned upon discontinuance of practice by a registrant. A nurse is not authorized to become registered as one who dispenses controlled substances. Every physician, dentist, veterinarian or other practitioner authorized to dispense and prescribe controlled substances must be registered with the DEA. "Administer" is defined as instillation of a drug into the body of a patient by a practitioner or his or her authorized agent. Although nurses administer medications including controlled substances, they are not authorized by state law to do so except pursuant to the order of a physician. Controlled substances are administered by nurses as agents of the physician.

When controlled substances are stored on nursing units, they should be kept in locked cabinets so that only authorized persons have access to them. Since the Federal Government passed the Controlled Substances Act, various states have enacted mini–Controlled Substances Acts to replace former narcotic and depressant-stimulant laws.

A violation of the Harrison Narcotic Law in Arizona has been held to be an offense involving moral turpitude within the statutory definition of unlicensed professional conduct. For the violation, the person's license to practice medicine was revoked.[79] It would seem that similar conduct on the part of a nurse would bring an equivalent penalty.

There are certain practical rules that the nurse who administers narcotics should know. Any P.R.N. order for a narcotic drug must be rewritten every 72 hours. A standing order, meaning a drug dose administered for the physician by a nurse without first obtaining a signed order for each hospital patient, is not permitted for narcotic drugs. In an emergency, a verbal order for narcotic drugs is permitted if the nurse makes note of the nature of the emergency on the chart and the physician validates the order within 24 hours.

When a dose of a narcotic is refused by the patient, then in the presence of a witness, it should be placed in the sewage system. If a dose of a narcotic drug is contaminated or wasted, the nurse should make an entry in the record explaining how the dose was disposed of, and the entry should be signed by a witness.

Narcotics Violation. Where a licensed practical nurse removed meperidine and morphine from the narcotics cabinet, refilling the drug containers with either Compazine or water to conceal the theft, and retained them for her own use, the state commissioner of health assessed her $150 for violation of the Public Health Law. The same nurse was also charged with administration of a narcotic drug to a patient more than 72 hours after a physician's order; she conceded the violation and was not penalized.[80]

A Georgia appellate court upheld the conviction of a physician to a prison sentence of 15 years where he had prescribed narcotics in exchange for sexual favors and merchandise secured through forged checks.[81]

Public Nuisance. A court granted an injunction permanently enjoining defendants from operating a methadone clinic at a particular location in such a manner as to constitute a public nuisance.[82] The record showed there was illegal drug traffic on the premises, which in some cases involved clinic employees, as a result of which there was a police raid and a number of arrests made. There was also evidence that some 46 ambulance calls were made to the clinic over a six-month period, and that at least half of them related to an overdose of drugs. By way of contrast, a number of other clinics were operating in the neighborhood without major difficulties or complaints.

ADMINISTRATION OF ANESTHESIA BY NURSES

The right of a properly trained nurse to administer anesthesia is no longer a legal question. The practice of medicine involves three things: judging the nature of a disease or injury by its signs and symptoms, deciding upon the proper remedy and prescribing it. The nurse who administers a prescribed anesthetic to a patient in the presence of, and in accordance with, a surgeon's directions is held not to practice medicine.[83] The attorneys general of New York,[84] Iowa,[85] South Dakota[86] and other states have stated that administration of anesthesia by a registered nurse under the direction of a licensed physician is the practice of nursing and not medicine. Questions relative to nurse anesthetists administering endotracheal and spinal anesthesia should take into account the adequacy of their training, since there is no legal provision that distinguishes these from other types of anesthesia.[87]

Nurse anesthetists, like other nurses, are responsible for their own acts.

Their acts are also the responsibility of their employers under the master-servant relationship.[88] If the nurse is a hospital employee, his or her acts while administering anesthesia are charged to the surgeon on the "borrowed servant" doctrine.[89] When the act complained of arises from the use of a piece of monitoring equipment, there may be a question as to who is responsible: the manufacturer, the supplier, the hospital, the owner or the user. Resolving the question depends on the exact facts of the situation as well as the law of agency.[90]

References

1. Perkins, R. M.: *Criminal Law*. Mineola, N.Y., Foundation Press, 1969, p. 12.
2. *Id.*, p. 626.
3. United States Code (1952 ed.) tit. 18, Sec. 1; 4 *Federal Practice and Procedure*, Rules ed. Sec. 1912.
4. *Supra*, note 1, p. 626. *In re* Henry, 15 Idaho 755, 99 Pac. 1054 (1909).
5. Intent in statutory cases, i.e.: "willfully," United States v. Sioux City Stock Yards Co. 162 Fed. 556 (C.C.A., 1908); "knowingly," State v. Smith, 119 Tenn. 521, 105 S.W. 68 (1907).
6. M'Naghten's Case, 10 Cl. & Fin. 200, 8 Eng. Rep. 718 (1843). Barnes: A Century of the M'Naghten Rules, 8 *Camb. L. J.* 300 (1944). *Supra*, pp. 858, 860.
7. Keedy: Irrestible Impulse as a Defense in the Criminal Law, 100 *U. Pa. L. Rev.* 956 (1952).
8. State v. Brown, 36 Utah 46, 93 Pac. 521, 102 Pac. 641 (1909).
9. Hill v. State, 339 S. 2d 1382 (Miss. S. Ct., 1976).
10. Bethea v. United States, 365 A. 2d 64 (D.C. Ct. App., 1976).
11. State of Kansas v. Smith, 574 P. 2d 548 (Kan. Sup. Ct., 1977); *Citation*, 37:94, Aug. 1, 1978.
12. Sutton's Adm. v. Wood, 120 Ky. 23, 85 S.W. 201 (1905).
13. Bellandi v. Park Sanitarium Ass'n., 214 Cal. 472, 6 P. 2d 508 (1931).
14. *Supra*, note 1, pp. 623, 643, 667.
15. *Id.*, p. 656.
16. *Id.*, p. 657.
17. People v. Roberts, 211 Mich. 187, 178 N.W. 690 (1920).
18. People v. McGonegal, 136 N.Y. 62, 32 N.E. 616 (1892).
19. *Supra*, note 1, p. 663.
20. *Id.*, p. 667.
21. Underhill: *Criminal Evidence*, 4th ed. 1935, Sec. 75 (70).
22. *Supra*, note 1, p. 86.
23. *Supra*, note 1, pp. 28–106.
24. *Id.*, pp. 379, 1001.
25. *Id.*, p. 1001.
26. *Id.*, p. 48.
27. People v. Phillips, 42 Cal. Rptr. 868 (1965).
28. U.S. v. Narisco, 446 F. Supp. 252 (D.C. Mich., 1977); *Citation*, 37:88, Aug. 1, 1978.
29. U.S. v. Narisco, Crim. Nos. 76–80884 D1 (Clerk of Court, Detroit, Mich.). *See also* Ann Arbor VA Nurses Freed from Charges. News, *Am. J. Nurs.*, 78:348, March 1978.
30. Hargrave v. Landon, 584 F. Supp. 302 (D.C. Va., 1984); *Citation*, 50:48, Dec. 1, 1984.
31. *USA Today*, p. 3A, March 30, 1984.
32. *Houston Post*, p. 17A, June 16, 1984.
33. *Milwaukee Sentinel*, p. 2, part 1, Feb. 16, 1984.
34. *Milwaukee Sentinel*, p. 2, part 1, Feb. 17, 1984.
35. *Supra*, note 1, p. 89.
36. *Black's Law Dictionary*, 4th ed. St. Paul, Minn., West Publishing Co., 1951, p. 1171.
37. *Supra*, note 1, pp. 51, 96.
38. Rex v. Grout, 6 Car. & P. 629, 172 Eng. Rep. 1394 (1834).
39. Lee v. State, 1 Cold 62, 41 Tenn. 42 (1860).
40. Commonwealth of Pennsylvania v. Konz, 402 A. 2d 692 (Pa. Super. Ct., 1979); *Citation*, 40:60, Dec. 15, 1979.
41. Somera Case, G. R. 31693 (Philippine Is., 1929). Grennan, E. M.: The Somera Case, *Int. Nurs. Rev.*, 5:325–334 (1930).*
42. State of Oregon v. Blocher, 499 P. 2d 1346 (Ore. Ct. App., July 27, 1972).
43. State v. Comstock, 70 S.E. 2d 648 (W.Va., 1952); Holder, A. R.: Criminal Prosecutions for Patient's Death, *JAMA*, 222:1342, Dec. 4, 1972.
44. Enell et al. v. Baptist Hospital, 45 S.W. 2d 395 (Tex. Ct. App., 1931); *Hospitals*, XIII: 107, Aug. 1939.
45. Hansch v. Hackett, 190 Wash. 97, 66 P. 2d 1129 (1937). *See also* Valentin v. La Société Française de Bienfaisance Mutuelle, 76 Cal. App. 2d 1, 172 P. 2d 359 (1946).
46. Perinowsky v. Freeman, 4 F & F 977, 176 Eng. Rep. 873 (1866).
47. Burnett v. Department of Health and Human Resources, 425 So. 2d 245 (La. Ct. of App. 1982); *Citation*, 47:81, July 15, 1983.
48. People v. Thayer, 44 Cal. Rept. 718 (1965).
49. *Supra*, note 1, p. 132.
50. *Id.*, pp. 115–116.
51. St. Pierre v. State, 33 N.Y.S. 2d 151 (Ct. Cl., 1942).
52. *Supra*, note 1, pp. 190, 281.
53. *Id.*, p. 234.

---

*Unfortunately, the case was not reported either in the *Official Gazette* or in the *Philippine Reports*. Miss Daisy C. Bridges, Executive Secretary of the International Council of Nurses in 1956, and Miss Julia V. Sotejo, Dean of the College of Nursing, University of the Philippines, kindly cooperated with me in endeavoring to locate all possible source material on this case.

54. Vannah v. Hart Private Hospital, 228 Mass. 132, 117 N.E. 328, L.R.A. 191 A. 1157 (1917).
55. Black's Law Dictionary, 4th ed. St. Paul, Minn., West Publishing Co., 1951, p. 247.
56. Morse v. Personnel Commission, 374 A. 2d 1176 (N.H. Sup. Ct., 1977); Citation, 36:48, Dec. 1, 1977.
57. People of the State of New York v. Chaitin, 462 N.Y.S. 2d 61 (N.Y. S. Ct. App. Div., 1983); Citation, 48:70, Jan. 1, 1984.
58. Supra, note 1, pp. 185, 187.
59. State v. McDonie, 89 W. Va. 185, 109 S.E. 710 (1921).
60. Supra, note 1, p. 152. See also Rape or Suspected Rape Cases, J. La. State Med. Soc., 119:319–320, Aug. 1967.
61. Guinyard v. State of South Carolina, 195 S.E. 2d 392 (S.C. Sup. Ct., 1973).
62. McKinney v. State, 505 S.W. 2d 536 (Tex., 1974); Sex Prob. Ct. Digest, 5(6):4, June 1974.
63. Miller v. State, 202 S.E. 2d 682 (Ga., 1973); Sex Prob. Ct. Digest, 5(6):6, June 1974.
64. Commonwealth v. Jarvis, 307 N.E. 2d 844 (Mass., 1974).
65. State v. Irwin, 214 N.W. 2d 595 (Neb., 1974).
66. Cousins v. State, 214 N.W. 2d 315 (Wis., 1954).
67. State v. Little, 261 N.W. 2d 847 (Nebr. S. Ct. 1978); Mental Health Ct. Dig., 22:6, Sept. 1978.
68. State v. Lewis, 314 A. 2d 716 (Md., 1974).
69. Black's Law Dictionary, 4th ed. St. Paul, Minn., West Publishing Co., 1951, p. 192.
70. Id., p. 781.
71. Id., p. 71.
72. Id., p. 1563.
73. Commonwealth v. Rankin, 311 A. 2d 660 (Pa., 1973); Soc. Welfare Dig., 19:6, May 1974.
74. Commonwealth v. Pizzimente, 306 N.E. 2d 279 (Mass., 1974); Soc. Welfare Dig., 19:4, May 1974.
75. Ladies Center of Clearwater, Inc. v. Reno, 341 So. 2d 543 (Fla. Dist. Ct. App., 1977).
76. Ripplinger v. Ripplinger, 511 P. 2d 82 (Wash., 1973).
77. Taylor v. Taylor, 279 So. 2d 364 (Fla., 1973).
78. Controlled Substances and the Registered Professional Nurse, The Interpreter, 56:1, Aug. 1974; Health Law Center: Problems in Hospital Law, 2nd ed. Rockville, Md., Aspen Systems Corp., 1974, pp. 180 ff.
79. Garlington v. Smith, 63 Ariz. 460, 163 P. 2d 685 (1945).
80. Forbes v. Ingraham, 338 N.Y.S. 2d 955 (N.Y., 1972); Citation, 27:107, July 15, 1973.
81. Geiger v. State of Georgia, 199 S.E. 2d 861 (Ga. Ct. App., 1973); Citation, 28:174, March 15, 1974.
82. People v. HST Meth., Inc., 352 N.Y.S. 2d 487 (N.Y., 1974).
83. Frank v. Smith, 194 S.W. 375 (Ky., 1917). See also Chalmers-Francis v. Nelson, 57 P. 2d 1312 (Cal., 1936). Hayt, E.: The Law and the Practice of Anesthesia, J. Am. A. Nurse Anesthetists, 32:373–379, Dec. 1964.
84. Op. Atty. Gen. of N.Y., Nov. 15, 1933.
85. Rep. of Atty. Gen. of Iowa on Registered Nurses: Administration of Anesthetics, June 27, 1946.
86. Op. Atty. Gen. of South Dakota, June 3, 1964.
87. Op. Atty. Gen. of N.Y., Sept. 3, 1957.
88. Prosser, W. L.: Handbook of the Law of Torts, 3rd ed. St. Paul, Minn., West Publishing Co., 1964, p. 470. Mecham, F. R.: Outlines of the Law of Agency, 4th ed. Chicago, Callaghan and Co., 1952, p. 327. Wasmuth, C. E.: Anesthesia and the Law. Springfield, Ill., Charles C Thomas, 1961, p. 33.
89. Wasmuth, op. cit., p. 41.
90. Dornette, W. H. L.: Monitoring the Anesthetized Patient: Practical Aspects and Legal Connotations. J. Am. A. Nurse Anesthetists, 36:420–425, Dec. 1968.

General References

Bryant, S. K.: Beware of Undocumented Claims of Credentials, AARTIMES, 7(5)19, 21, May 1983.

Criminal Law and the EMT, EMT Legal Bull., 6(4)2–6, Fall 1982.

Donovan, P.: Judging Teenagers: How Minors Fare When They Seek Court-authorized Abortions, Fam. Plann. Perspect., 15(6)259–267, Nov./Dec. 1983.

Gargaro, W. J., Jr.: Criminal Prosecution for Discontinuance of Life Support, Part 4, Cancer Nurs., 7(1)57–58, Feb. 1984.

Hospital Safety Programs: Employees are Entitled . . . Some Female in Your Hospital Will Be Assaulted, Roughed Up or Possibly Raped, Regan Rep. Nurs. Law, 23(5)2, Oct. 1982.

Kalisch, B. J., et al.:When Nurses are Accused of Murder: The Melodramatic Effects of Media Coverage, Nursinglife, 2:44–47, Sept./Oct. 1982.

Lippe, D.: Security Investigating New Tactics as Violent Crime Plagues Hospitals, Mod. Healthcare, 12:72 +, April 1982.

RNs and Criminal Assault: Legal Rights, Regan Rep. Nurs. Law, 23:2, Sept. 1982.

Stone, A. A.: The Insanity Defense on Trial, Hosp. Community Psychiatry, 33:615–616, Aug. 1982.

Theft in Hospitals: Investigations and Accusations, Regan Rep. Nurs. Law, 21:2, April 1981.

Ten
WITNESSES, DYING DECLARATIONS, WILLS AND GIFTS

Nurses are often unmindful of the fact that their profession makes them liable at times to be called upon to testify in regard to some matter in a legal proceeding. In general, the nurse should realize that a witness is required to testify to facts; the jury and the court must form an opinion of their own and are not interested in the witnesses' opinions on the matters in dispute. If the problem is one that requires special study or experience to form a sound opinion, the opinion of an expert witness who has such special experience or study is pertinent and admissible. As we have previously pointed out, witnesses are not required to appear and testify and are not liable to penalty for failure to do so, unless a subpoena is served on them, summoning them to court on a certain day to give evidence. If, for reasons beyond their control, witnesses are unable to respond to the subpoena, they should take steps to notify the court as quickly as possible. For attendance at court, witnesses are paid a fee.

DUTIES OF A WITNESS

Witnesses, before giving evidence, are required to swear or solemnly affirm that they will tell the truth, the whole truth and nothing but the truth. If, after taking an oath, witnesses make a statement that is false or which they do not know or believe to be true, they are guilty of perjury, which is a crime. Provided that witnesses act reasonably, they are protected from a civil action for damages when they make a defamatory statement in evidence. In general, witnesses cannot be required to answer any question if their answer would subject them 241 to criminal prosecution; they are privileged not to answer the question. This is known as the privilege against self-incrimination. Although it is the duty of the judge to tell witnesses that they do not have to answer such a question, witnesses are reminded to be alert, to protest any such question and to ask whether they must answer it. Since a person is allowed to attack the credibility of his or her opponent's witness, a nurse can appreciate how the problem arises as to whether a particular question is privileged on the ground of incriminating the witness, or is a legitimate question to attack the credit that might be given to the witness's evidence.

Witnesses are under a duty to do all that they can to assist the course of justice. Nurses are reminded that, unless a person is impartial, assisting justice is well-nigh impossible. They know only too well the human tendency to see and hear only what a person wants to see and hear.

Witnesses should speak loudly enough to be readily heard. They should give a simple, direct answer to the question asked and no more. Loquacious, chatty answers not only consume the valuable time of the court, but also often form a basis for a protracted, difficult cross-examination. Nurses should use words and terms that the average person will understand. For example, the witness might tell a juror that on May 25 the skin around the plaintiff's right eye was tumefied and contused or that on May 25 the plaintiff had a black eye. Suffice it to say that the ordinary reasonable person knows what you mean by a black eye.

LAW OF EVIDENCE

After this brief discussion of witnesses, a few words about evidence are in order. Several volumes would be needed for any detailed discussion of the law of evidence, but a few points may help the nurse's understanding of this important phase of law.

Tangible Evidence

Evidence is any type of proof legally presented at the trial of an issue by the act of the parties, and through the medium of witnesses, documents, concrete objects, records and so forth, for the purpose of persuading the jury or court as to their contention.[1] In a legal case, evidence is admissible when it is of such a kind that the court is obliged to receive it. The court, for example, will take judicial notice of facts and matters of common and general knowledge, such as that aspirin and citrate of magnesia are drugs.[2]

Another kind of evidence is the testimony of witnesses. For example, testimony that the adjustment of splints and bandages upon a plaintiff's injured arm was so tight that there was no allowance of space for swelling was admissible evidence.[3] However, in this connection it is pointed out that statements of a self-serving nature are not admissible as evidence, nor may a witness introduce evidence that is irrelevant or immaterial to the issues (matters in dispute) of the case. The judge or jury (if it is a trial by jury) decides on the weight to be given to testimony of witnesses and the witnesses' credibility. Statements against self-interest are admissible. Witnesses may refresh their memory by looking over records or charts made by them at a time when the facts were fresh in their minds. If a nurse is a witness, he or she cannot read statements from nursing books to a jury. Witnesses may exhibit other material objects to the senses. For example, in a Maryland case, a plaintiff was allowed to show her injured knees to the jury.[5]

"Hearsay" Evidence

Perhaps the nurse has heard of "hearsay evidence." This is the name for testimony given by a witness that is simply a repetition of what she or he has heard others say, and it is not admissible. For instance, when a plaintiff gave testimony as to what a nurse who had helped at an operation on the plaintiff later told her about the way the operation was done, the testimony was not admissible.[6] In other words, the plaintiff was not testifying from her personal knowledge, but simply repeating what she had heard another say; hence, it was hearsay evidence and not admissible.

Truth Serum and Lie Detector Tests

Nurses frequently inquire about the admissibility of "truth serum" tests and lie detector tests as evidence of a person's guilt in connection with a crime. In fact, the courts usually reject such tests.[7] However, evidence of a urinalysis test for alcohol is admissible in many jurisdictions.

DYING DECLARATIONS

Perhaps a few words about dying declarations may be instructive to a nurse. A statement concerning the cause of his injury or illness made by a person who believes he or she is dying and has no hope of recovery is a dying declaration. Generally, dying declarations may be admitted in cases of murder or felonious homicide. For example, the court allowed a defendant to show the dying declaration of the dead person when the defendant was being prosecuted for the killing of that person.[8] A dying declaration may be verbal, but the person receiving it should put it in writing either while it is being made or soon afterward. The person's actual words should be written down, and, if possible, the dying declaration should be read back to the person to see whether it is correct. If possible, the person making the dying declaration should sign the statement, and persons present should witness the signature.

WILLS

The topic of dying declarations leads to that of statements of testamentary (pertaining to a will) character. On the following pages, the question of who may make a will and the elements of testamentary capacity are discussed. Wills that are made orally are called "nuncupative wills." As a well-known authority on wills has stated, the statutes of most states with certain restrictions recognize an oral will for disposing of personal property as valid.[9] Common restrictions are that the will be made during the person's last illness, that it be done in the place in which he died, that he shall have asked one or more of the required witnesses to witness the will, that the matter of the will be put in writing within a given number of days, that the will be offered for probate (official proof) within a specified time and that the amount of property passing by an oral will be generally limited.[10] A nuncupative will, dictated by a person in his last illness before the required number of witnesses and later recorded, is valid.[11]

LAW REGARDING WILLS

A brief review of the law regarding wills may be of interest to the nurse. Nurses are not trained in the techniques or the law of executing a will, and therefore should not offer to perform this service for others. If a patient asks them for such help, the best thing is to advise the patient to consult an attorney. Nurses have no more right to engage in the practice of law than they have to engage in the practice of medicine. However, since nurses frequently care for patients who are near death, when there is no time to consult an attorney, a nurse may assist the patient with a will. It is to help a nurse in such "emergency" situations that a limited amount of material on the topic is offered.

A will is a declaration of a person's mind as to what is to be done after his death with his property. A will may be revoked during his lifetime. It is operative for no purpose until his death, and it applies to the situation as it exists at his death.[12]

Disposal of Property

In connection with wills, the nurse is likely to encounter a number of special terms such as "real property" and "personal property." Real property is land and generally whatever is erected on, growing on or fastened to it.[13] Often, in a general way, real property is therefore regarded as "immovables." Personal property is everything that is owned that does not come under the denomination of real estate. Again, personal property is sometimes spoken of as "movables." Under personal property, a nurse may hear of "corporeal" personal property, which includes movable and tangible things such as furniture, animals and merchandise; and "incorporeal" personal property, which consists of such items as stocks, patents and copyrights.[14] A person is said to "bequeath" personal property by will, whereas a person is said to "devise" real property.

Factors Necessary for a Valid Will

A person must have testamentary capacity to make a valid will, and this is determined by a person's mental ability to make a will.

Sound Mind. To execute a valid will, one must be of "sound mind"; however, a person does not have to have an above-average or even average mentality.[15] For the purpose of making a will, a person has a sound mind only when he can understand and carry in his mind in a general way the following: the type and amount of his property; the persons who are the natural objects of his generosity, and their claims on him; and the disposition he is making of his property.[15] In addition, he must be able to appreciate such factors in relation to each other and to make an orderly desire as to the disposition of his property.[16] If a person lacks the above qualifications, he is not mentally competent to make a will.[17] However, a person may have a guardian and may lack ability to transact some other business, and yet have testamentary capacity. The nurse's attention is also invited to the fact that illiteracy, moral depravity, extreme old age, severe illness and great weakness do not necessarily disqualify a person from making a will.[18] A person with epilepsy has been held capable of making a valid will,[19] as have a person with a brain tumor[20] and a person with apoplexy.[21] In other words, though the mental power may be reduced below the ordinary standard, if there is enough intelligence to understand the act of making a will in the different aspects already mentioned, there is capacity to make a will.[22]

A son and daughter challenged the capacity of a testatrix to make a will. The 83-year-old woman had become feeble, and her memory and sight had deteriorated two years before her death. She had delusions about being mistreated by her daughter and about people trying to get her money, and left the bulk of her estate to a church that she had not previously mentioned. The court held that she was not mentally competent to execute a will.[23]

Testamentary Capacity. Where the natural sons of a decedent introduced psychiatric testimony that their mother did not know the true relationship between herself as mother and her sons as sons, it did not negate her testamentary capacity since the following questions could be answered in the affirmative: (1) Did the testator at the time he executed the will understand the nature of the act he was performing; (2) at that time, did the testator understand the character of his property; and (3) at that time, did the testator recollect his relationship to the natural objects of his bounty and to those who would naturally have some claim to his remembrance?[24] As the court stated, the test of testamentary capacity is not whether the testator appreciated the moral obligations and duties toward such heirs in some standard fixed by society, courts or psychiatrists.

In a contest to a will, the court ruled that, although the deceased had suffered from schizophrenia, he was mentally competent at the time he executed his will. In addition, the testator was not unduly influenced when he executed his will leaving all his property to his mother, who did not know he had made his will until she received it in the mail. A will made by an insane person may be valid if made during a lucid interval. It must be established by clear and convincing proof.[25]

Freedom from Fraud and Undue Influence. It is also necessary, in order for the will to be valid, that a person be free from the effect of fraud and undue influence when he made the will. Obviously, when a patient is in a weakened condition, it might be possible for a person to induce the patient to make him or her a beneficiary in the will. Heirs at law or beneficiaries under earlier wills of the deceased, or in general anyone who will be directly benefited by setting aside a will, may contest it.[26] Frequently, relatives of the deceased and others who think that they should have benefited by the will, or those who have been named and think that they have been treated unfairly, take the matter to court.

Legal Age Requirement. In many states, minors, unless they are married, are not considered competent to make a will.

Intestacy

Persons who die without a will are said to die intestate. Their personal property and the real property of a person who makes a nuncupative will are distributed according to the law of intestacy.

Execution of a Will

Statutes govern the formalities[27] for the execution of a will. Ordinarily, a will must be in writing. Nuncupative wills, for obvious reasons, tend to be frowned upon by courts. A will must be signed; however, a mark is sufficient (it would have to be properly identified by one who could write). A person does not have to write his full name. In most states, two competent witnesses are required to sign the will, whereas a few states require three witnesses. If more than the required number of witnesses sign a will, it is not made invalid by their doing so. The person making the will should sign it before the witnesses subscribe; a few states require that the person making the will should sign it in the presence of the witnesses to it. In some states, statutes expressly require that a person making a will request the witnesses to act as witnesses. In the absence of an express statutory provision, it usually is not required that the person making the will publish (tell the witnesses) that the document is her or his will. The witnesses must sign the document with the intention of giving validity to such a document as the act of the person making the will.

The nurse should know that it is practically a universal requirement in the statutes that the witnesses should all be present at the same time, and should sign the will in the presence of the person making the will. For example, if a blind person is making a will, he and his witnesses should all be present at the same time. He should sign his will, and the witness should sign it "in his presence," which is sufficient, although the blind person cannot actually "see" the witnesses do it. Witnesses to a will should not be beneficiaries under the will, because in most jurisdictions it does affect their right to take under the will if there are not a sufficient number of witnesses who do not stand to benefit by the will.

For the nurses' protection, they should make a notation on the patient's chart of his or her apparent mental and physical condition at the time of making the will, and also the fact of making the will. Such records may be important if the will is later contested.

Before the property of the deceased reaches those named in the will, it must pass through the hands of the executor. The executor is in a position of trust. Besides distributing the assets of the deceased, the executor is responsible for paying, out of the estate assets, any taxes and debts of the deceased. Executors may be appointed and bonded, or they may be appointed to serve without bond. A bond is an insurance agreement pledging surety for financial loss caused to another by the act or default of a third person. The fee charged varies according to the value of the estate.

If a beneficiary dies before the will is executed, the bequest lapses. It ceases to take effect, and the property named in the bequest passes to whoever has been left the residue of your estate. Some lawyers advise clients "to give everything away twice," i.e., "I leave my house at 35 Bell Street, Washington, D.C., to my son, John Doe if he be alive. If he is dead, I leave such residence to the Richard Roe University."

Anyone who cares what happens to their property after their death—and who wishes to minimize the effort, delay and expense of the administration and distribution of their property—needs to have a will.[28]

St. Mary's Hospital of Milwaukee has developed a useful guide for making a will, and with their permission it is reprinted.

GUIDE FOR MAKING A WILL

Date _____

Full Name _____
First   Middle   Last

Present Address _____
Street   City   State   Zip

Permanent Address (if residence address is only temporary)

_____

Married _____ Single _____ Date of Birth _____

Children (Grandchildren, if applicable)

Name	Relation	Age	Address
_____	_____	____	_____
_____	_____	____	_____
_____	_____	____	_____
_____	_____	____	_____
_____	_____	____	_____
_____	_____	____	_____
_____	_____	____	_____
_____	_____	____	_____

Do you have a will now in force? _____ (Please attach copy)

Present Inventory of Estate

Real Estate Owned

Address	Value	Title in your name only?
_____	_____	_____
_____	_____	_____

Personal Property (Household furniture, automobile, equipment, jewelry, etc.)

_____

_____

_____

_____

Cash

$ _____ Bank _____ Address _____

$ _____ Bank _____ Address _____

Savings Accounts

Bank _____ Address _____

Loan Company _____ Address _____

List any government bonds, stocks, real estate mortgages owned.

_____

_____

_____

Amount of Insurance

Company	Beneficiary	Amount
_____	_____	$_____
_____	_____	$_____
_____	_____	$_____
_____	_____	$_____
_____	_____	$_____

Type of policy *(20 pay life, whole life, endowment, group, etc.)*

_____

_____

_____

Social Security No. _____

If retired on company pension plan, explain benefits

_____

_____

Estimated Debts and Mortgages against your Estate

Debt or Mortgage to:	Amount
_____	$_____
_____	$_____
_____	$_____

How do you want your estate to be distributed?

Specific Legacies, etc.

Person	Property or Articles Bequeathed
_____	_____
_____	_____
_____	_____

Residue

Person	Proportionate Share or Percent
_____	_____
_____	_____
_____	_____

How do you want churches or charitable organizations to share in your estate?

Name of Organization and Address	Amt. or Percent
_____	$_____
_____	$_____
_____	$_____
_____	$_____
_____	$_____

Name of Executor Preferred _____

Address _____

Bonded _____ No Bond _____

Other Information:

The drafting of your will is, of course, a task for your attorney. This guide will serve as a worksheet in your discussion with him or her.

Example of a Will. The following example will illustrate the formalities for the execution of a will:[29]

Last will and testament of _____ . I, _____ , of (or "residing in") the city (or as the case may be) of _____ , county of _____ , state of _____ , being of sound mind and disposing mind and memory, and not acting under duress, menace, fraud or undue influence of any person whomsoever, do make, publish and declare this my last will and testament, and I do hereby expressly revoke all other and former wills and codicils to wills made by me.

First. I direct my executors hereinafter named to pay all my just debts and obligations, including the expenses of my last sickness, as soon after my decease as is practicable.

Second. I bequeath the following property to the persons hereinafter named.

   1. To _____ , my _____ automobile.

   2. To _____ , my household furniture consisting of

_____ .

   3. To _____ , _____ .

Third. I bequeath the following sums of money to the persons and associations hereinafter named:

   1. To _____ , _____ dollars.

   2. To _____ , _____ dollars.

Fourth. I devise the following real property to the persons hereinafter named:

   1. To my wife, _____ (name), _____ (describe property).

   2. To my son, _____ (name), _____ (describe property).

   3. To my daughter, _____ (name), _____ (describe property).

Fifth. (If any property devised or bequeathed in trust) I devise and bequeath to _____ (or " _____ and _____ " or the like) _____ (describe property) in trust, however, for the following purposes, viz., _____ .

Sixth. (If there is a trust) the trustees shall be bound to observe the following instructions in handling the property devised and bequeathed to them in trust thereby:

   1. _____ .

   2. _____ .

   3. _____ .

Seventh. (If a trust is included) Upon final termination of this trust, I give, bequeath and devise as follows: _____ .

Eighth. All the rest and residue of my estate, of every kind and description, whether real, personal, or mixed, wherever located, I give, bequeath and devise to _____ (or add: "in trust for the following purposes." etc.).

Ninth. I hereby nominate and appoint _____ (or " _____ and _____ " or the like) to be the executor of this my last will and testament, and direct that he (or "each") be required to furnish a bond as such in the sum of _____ dollars (or direct that he [or "they"] shall not be required to give any bond [or "bonds"] as such executor [or "executors."]).

Tenth. My executor (or "executors") is (or "are") hereby empowered and authorized to _____ .

In witness whereof, I, (followed by the name of the testator), have hereunto set my hand this _____ day of _____ , 19___ , at the city (or as the case may be) of _____ , county _____ , state of _____ . Signed, sealed, published, and declared by testator, _____ , as and for his last will and testament, in the presence of us, who, at his request, in his presence, and in the presence of each other, have hereunto subscribed our names as witnesses this _____ day of _____ , 19___ .

Insurance policies upon a person's life constitute a valid nontestamentary arrangement, although the insured person retains the right to change the beneficiary.[30]

Holographic Will. A will that is entirely written, dated and signed by the same person making the will is called a holographic will. By statute, in 19 states holographic wills are valid without formal attestation, i.e., without subscribing witnesses.[31]

Incompetent's Estate

Where a mother died leaving her estate by will to her three adult sons in equal shares, and one son was a patient at a state hospital from August 1953 to November 1971, the question certified to the court was: Is the debt incurred by such son as a patient of the New Hampshire Hospital to be paid from his derivative share of the mother's estate, or is the debt the direct responsibility of the son's estate? The court ruled that it was a direct responsibility of the incompetent son's estate, which could then reimburse itself from the son's share of the mother's estate. At common law, the general rule is that there is no liability on the part of a parent for the support of a mentally incompetent adult offspring confined to a public institution. In this case the court decided that, lacking a clear intent of the legislature to alter the common law rule that the patient and his own estate are primarily liable for his care and treatment, the court would not imply the change.[32]

Living Wills

Living wills are a directive from competent, seriously ill persons to medical personnel and family or those responsible for their care regarding the treatment they wish to receive when they become incompetent to make decisions for themselves. Statutory provisions of living wills vary widely from state to state. Usually laws require that the living will be in writing and witnessed by two persons who are 18 years or older. Anyone 18 years of age or older and of sound mind may execute a living will. States with right-to-die laws are: Alabama, Alaska, Arkansas, California, Delaware, Florida, Idaho, Illinois, Kansas, Mississippi, Nevada, New Mexico, North Carolina, Oregon, Texas, Vermont, Virginia, Washington and Wisconsin as well as the District of Columbia. In some states, the directive is only advisory. In other states it is binding, but there is no penalty for noncompliance. In still other states, it is binding and considered as unprofessional conduct for the physician not to comply. All statutes provide immunity from civil and criminal liability to personnel and facilities that participate in good faith in withholding or withdrawing treatment from a patient in compliance with a living will. A nurse who receives a copy of a living will should notify the attending physician and place the document in the medical record. Cohn states it is legally as well as ethically necessary that a nurse raise questions about the applicablity or inapplicability of the living will.[33]

Living wills are discussed in more detail in Chapter 11. Georgia, Tennessee and West Virginia also have right-to-die laws.

GIFTS

The nurse should realize that a will is not the only way of disposing of a person's property. Another method is by gift. The four legal requirements for a gift are:

(1) The gift must consist of personal property; (2) there must be an intention to make the gift; (3) there must be an indication of transfer of control over such property; and (4) there must be acceptance by the recipient.

The kinds of gifts with which a nurse might be especially concerned are those made by dying patients. Gifts made by a person because of approaching death or a belief in approaching death are called gifts *causa mortis*, which are revocable and subject to the claims of the donor's creditors without proof of intent to defraud them.[34] Such gifts are limited to personal property. On a number of occasions, a nurse may be asked to witness the making of such gifts and to testify to the same. As with the execution of a will, the law will not acknowledge the validity of a gift made by someone who does not know what she or he is doing. If patients make a gift, they must intend and realize the consequence of their act. Moreover, they must do it freely, without undue influence or fraud. If a nurse doubts that a patient has the ability to understand what she or he is doing, the nurse should say so openly and positively. Again, nurses should make notes of the patient's condition and reactions for the record.

References

1. Wigmore: 1 Evidence, 3rd ed. 1940, Sec. 1. McCormick: *Handbook of the Law of Evidence*. Hornbook, 1954.
2. People v. Garcia, 1 Cal. App. 2d 761, 32 P. 2d 445 (1934).
3. Klodek v. May Creek Logging Co., 71 Wash. 573, 129 Pac. 99 (1913).
4. Farmer v. Williams, 92 Vt. 132, 102 Atl. 932 (1918).
5. Zeller v. Mayson, 168 Md. 663, 179 Atl. 179 (1935).
6. Cook v. Coleman, 90 W. Va. 748, 111 S.E. 750 (1922).
7. *See* A.L.R. 2d 1310 for annotations and compilations of cases on this topic.
8. People v. Costa, 67 Cal. App. 175, 227 Pac. 201 (1924).
9. Atkinson: *Wills*. Hornbook, 1937, Sec. 135.
10. *Id.*, Sec. 135, notes 98 and 99; Sec. 4, note 73. Bordwell: Statute Law of Wills, 14 *Iowa L. Rev.*, 1, 172, 283, 428 (1928–29).
11. Starks v. Lincoln, 316 Mo. 483, 291 S.E. 132 (1927). For nuncupative wills in Louisiana, *see* 5 *West's Louisiana Stat. Ann.*, c. 6, Sec. 2, art. 1574 (1952 ed. and 1955 suppl.). Lemann: Testamentary Transfer Simulations, 29 *Tul. L. Rev.*, 55 (1955).
12. *Supra*, note 9, Sec. 1. *See also* Restatement, Property, 2nd ed., 1954, Sec. 8; and Burby: *Real Property*, 2nd ed., 1954.
13. 1 Restatement, *Property*, 2nd ed., 1954, Sec. 8. *See also* Secs. 14–18; Moynihan: Law of Real Property, c. 1. 2 Secs. 1–3 (1940).
14. 2 Kent Comm. 12th ed. 1884, Sec. 340.
15. *Supra*, note 9, Sec. 51.
16. *In re* Whitworth's Estate, 110 Cal. App. 256, 194 Pac. 84 (1931).
17. *In re* Halbert's Will, 15 Misc. 308, 37 N.Y.S. 757 (1895).
18. *Supra*, note 9, Sec. 53.
19. *In re* Derusseau's Will, 175 Wis. 140, 184 N.W. 705 (1921).
20. *In re* Fricke, 64 Hun 639, 19 N.Y.S. 315 (1892).
21. Cheney v. Price, 90 Hun 238, 37 N.Y.S. 117 (1895).
22. Wood-Renton: Testamentary Capacity in Mental Disease, 4 *Law Q. R.*, 442 (1888). Green: Public Policy Underlying the Law of Mental Incompetence, 38 *Mich. L. Rev.*, 1189, 1217 (1940).
23. Matter of Will of Worrell, 241 S.E. 2d 343 (Ct. App., N.C., 1978); *Mental Health Ct. Dig.*, 22:3, Sept. 1978.
24. *In re* Estate of Weil, 518 P. 2d 995 (Ariz., 1974).
25. Matter of the Estate of Gentry, 573 P. 2d 322 (Ct. App., Ore., 1978); *Mental Health Ct. Dig.*, 21:4, June 1978.
26. *Supra*, note 9, Sec. 99. Powell and Locker: Decedents Estates, 30 *Col. L. R.*, 919 (1930).
27. *Supra*, note 9, Sec. 62–72.
28. Creighton, H.: You and Your Will, *Nurs. Management*, 14:51–52, Sept. 1983.
29. 9 Nichols: Legal Forms Annotated (1936 ed.) 465; (1950 suppl.) 441.
30. *Supra*, note 9, Sec. 39.
31. *Id.*, Sec. 75. See comprehensive note on holographic wills, 28 *Yale L. J.*, 71 (1918); Parker: History of the Holographic Testament in the Civil Law, 3 *Jurist*, 1 (1943); 7 *Mont. L. Rev.*, 76 (1940).
32. *In re* Houghton Estate, 314 A. 2d 674 (N.H., 1974).
33. Cohn, S. D.: The Living Will from the Nurse's Perspective, *Law, Med. & Health Care*, 11:121–124, 136, June 1983.
34. *Supra*, note 9, Sec. 45. Mechem: Delivery in Gifts of Chattels, 21 *Ill. L. Rev.*, 341, 356 (1926).

General References

Brent, E. A.: Think! Before you Witness that Will, *R.N.*, 43(3)61–64, March 1983.

Brown, M. A.: Adolescents and Abortions: A Theoretical Framework for Decision Making, *J. Obs., Gyn. & Neonatal Nurs.*, 241–247, July/Aug. 1983.

Clary, F.: Minor Women Obtaining Abortions: A Study of Parental Notification in a Metropolitan Area, *J. Pub. Hlth.*, 72(3), 283–285. March 1982.

Cohn, S. D.: The Living Will from the Nurse's Perspective, *Law, Med. & Health Care*, 11(3)121+, June 1983.

Creighton, H.: You and Your Will, *Nurs. Management*, 14:51–52, Sept. 1983.

Dean, K. A.: The Nurse as Witness: Deposition, *Focus Crit. Care*, 10(3)20–22, June 1983.

Eddy, J. M., et al.: Consumer Aspects of Death and Dying, *Health Educ.*, 11:10–12, Nov./Dec. 1980.

Facts to Know About Living Wills, *Nursinglife*, 4(1)26–27, Jan./Feb. 1984.

George, J. E.: Emergency Department Wills, *JEN*, 8:104, March/April 1982.

Gough, D.: The Hippocratic Oath, *Nurs. Mirror*, 153(21)15, Nov. 18, 1981.

Henshaw, S. K., and Wallisch, L. S.: The Medi-caid Cutoff and Abortion Services for the Poor, *Fam. Plan. Perspectives*, 16(4)170–180, July/Aug. 1984.

Hershberger, W. S.: Ins and Outs of Wills Require Expert Advice, *Nephrol. Nurse*, 4:43–44, Jan./Feb. 1982.

Kapp, M. B.: Legal Guardianship, *Geriatr. Nurs.*, 2:366–369, Sept./Oct. 1981.

Langslow, A.: The Test of "Wills," *Aust. Nurs. J.*, 13(6)29–31, Dec./Jan. 1984.

Londner, R. B.: The Importance of Naming a Guardian for Your Children, *Am. Baby*, 42:22+, Dec. 1980.

Living Will Raises Difficult Questions, *AORN J.*, 37(7)1422, June 1983.

Rea, K. M. J.: Appearing in Court, *Nursing* (Oxford) 1:1550–1551, April 1982.

Trandel-Korenchuk, D., and Trandel-Korenchuk, K.: Minor Consent in Birth Control and Abortion: Part 1, *Nurse Practitioner*, 47–54 (March/April 1980); Part 2, *Nurse Practitioner*, 48–54, May/June 1980.

WVNA Supports Living Will and Patient's Rights, *Weather Vane*, 52(6)4, 6–10, Dec./Jan. 1984.

Eleven
SOME CURRENT LEGAL AND ETHICAL PROBLEMS FACING NURSES

OVERVIEW

Today, nurses face many legal/ethical problems in their work. As Merton has explained, the social value of their profession is concerned with, first, the value placed upon systematic knowledge and intellect—*knowing*; second, the value placed upon technical skill and trained capacity—*doing*; and third, the value placed upon putting this conjoint knowledge and skill to work in the service of others—*helping*.[1] In order to help today's clients or patients, the nurse must know and understand the health problems that arise and confront such persons in a highly technological society.

Many new advances in medicine and surgery are rapidly outpacing our willingness to make difficult ethical and moral decisions about them. Several current issues are clamoring for answers, and the conflicting opinions surrounding them will not be easily resolved. The legal decisions may vary with the jurisdiction and reflect a range of ethical and moral opinions. The list of problems covered in this chapter is not inclusive, but some of the legal and ethical issues that nurses face in caring for clients or patients in their work will be discussed.

ETHICS

The public is aware that professions set standards of conduct for their members, and they expect professional people to be governed by such standards in their work. "Ethics" is concerned with the principles of right and wrong conduct as   253 they apply to professional problems. Ethics protect professionals and enable them to serve clients better. Violations of professional ethics mar the scene of today's world and re-emphasize the responsibility of each professional to abide by such ethics. When violations of professional ethics occur, the profession, through its association and legal boards, acts to discipline the practitioner.

Codes of ethics were adopted by ancient as well as modern people. The American Medical Association uses the modified Hippocratic oath. To guide the Allied Military Tribunal in its prosecution of Nazi physicians following World War II, the Nuremberg Code of Ethics in Medical Research was written. The Codes for Professional Nurses adopted by the American Nurses' Association and the International Council of Nurses, as well as the widespread use of the Nightingale pledge, evidence the concern of United States' nurses with the ethics of their work.

ABORTIONS

Inasmuch as nurses may encounter problems involving abortions among their patients, this topic warrants more detailed consideration. Prior to the decision in *Roe* v. *Wade*,[2] at common law, any person who, with the intention of prematurely ending a pregnancy, willfully and unlawfully does any act that causes a miscarriage is guilty of the crime of procuring an abortion. A similar wording is used in statutes defining the crime of abortion. In most of these statutes, there is a specific exemption of those abortions performed in good faith for the purpose of preserving the life of the mother. Such an abortion is commonly referred to as a therapeutic abortion. It has been said that there is a presumption that the physician acts in good faith.[3] In a widely discussed English case, a prominent English physician was tried on an abortion charge when he induced an abortion on a 15-year-old girl who had been raped.[4] The physician was acquitted. The judge said:

> There remain three further cases in which the arguments in favour of procuring abortion might be very strong. These are:
> (a) where the woman is pregnant as the result of rape;
> (b) where the woman is insane and becomes pregnant while insane;
> (c) where the woman is under the age of consent

The 1973 Abortion Ruling

In *Roe* v. *Wade*,[5] the U.S. Supreme Court ruled that a Texas statute banning all abortions unnecessary to save a mother's life violates her right to privacy to make the abortion decision, which is included within the fundamental personal liberty protected by the Fourteenth Amendment due process clause of the U.S. Constitution. During the first three months of pregnancy, any licensed physician may decide with the consent of the woman patient when, where and how to terminate the pregnancy. The court's guidelines concerning the second trimester of pregnancy require that the state base its regulation solely on "the preservation and protection of maternal health." In this period, due to "compelling state interest," the states, if they so desire, may regulate abortion with respect to licensure of the health care professionals and facilities involved. During the final trimester of pregnancy, when the viability of the child is generally recognized, the regulation of abortion may be geared to the protection of the baby's life, but this is limited by the requirement that the mother's life and health may not be endangered.[6] In addition, the court indicates that its standard for the last trimester is limited to "meaningful life outside the mother's womb."

In a second decision, *Doe v. Bolton*,[7] the Supreme Court decided that a comparatively liberal Georgia statute violated fundamental constitutional rights of the pregnant woman desiring abortion. Under this ruling, medical-moral committees, abortion committees and so forth violate the Fourteenth Amendment. Also, JCAH accreditation cannot be mandatory since it violates the equal protection clauses of the Fourteenth Amendment. It is worth noting that in this decision the Court said: "Under the Georgia statute the hospital is free not to admit a patient for an abortion. Further, a physician or any other employee has a right to refrain for moral or religious reasons from participating in the abortion."

In May 1972, the Nurses Association of the American College of Obstetricians and Gynecologists issued a statement of principles and guidelines on abortion. This specifies that nurses have the right to refuse to assist in the performance of abortions or sterilization procedures in keeping with their moral, ethical or religious beliefs, except in an emergency when a patient's life is clearly endangered, in which case the questioned moral issue should be disregaded. Moreover, this refusal should not jeopardize the nurses' employment, nor should they be subjected to harasssment or embarrassment because of their refusal.[9]

In *Doe v. Bellin Memorial Hospital* in 1973, a judge in the First District Court for the Eastern District of Wisconsin ordered a hospital affiliated with the Methodist Church to permit the performance of an abortion on demand and to provide the necessary supportive staff.[10] Shortly thereafter, the Seventh Circuit Court of Appeals issued a stay order.[11] The court ruled in effect that a private hospital does not forfeit its right to determine whether it would accept abortion patients because it receives Hill-Burton funds. Constitutionally, such a hospital may refuse to permit its facilities to be used for abortions. However, in passing, the court said that a woman's right to an abortion is protected and that a statute that makes performance of an abortion a crime or that requires the medical profession to observe unnecessary abortion-restricting rules is invalid. The U.S. Supreme Court refused further intervention. In Texas in 1974, the Attorney General citing this case upheld the right of a private hospital to refuse the use of its facilities for doing an abortion.[12]

The Court has had to deal with the interpretation of public morality or religion conflicting with First Amendment freedoms. In *Wisconsin v. Yoder*,[13] the rights of the Amish people for school education in accordance with their religious views were upheld, and in *Braunfield v. Brown*,[14] the blue laws restricting public and commercial activities on Sunday in accordance with the religious views of some were struck down. In *Reynolds v. United States*,[15] and, more recently, in the *Church of Latter-day Saints v. United States*,[16] the Court denied the right to practice polygamy even though it was a religious belief at that time.

In *Natale v. Sisters of Mercy*,[17] the court stated that the fact that a private hospital received a government donation to enable it to carry on its work or funds from the city or state to care for sick, disabled or indigent persons, as well as the fact that the hospital was granted exemption from taxation, does not make a private hospital a public corporation.

As Schulte says in a discussion of many of the same cases, the courts must weigh the newly defined right of the pregnant female against other individuals' rights to practice their religion in the health apostolate.[18]

Under the law, hospitals are private institutions recognized as separate persons. In a denominational hospital, the right of individual members of the hospital to practice their religion is basic. Such a hospital is a part of the practice of moral teaching, not merely a business.

Nurses who wish to retain their employment but do not wish to participate in abortion procedures and who work in a hospital or institution where abortions are performed should make their moral or ethical reservations known to the Nursing Service Office, so that appropriate arrangements can be made for substitute coverage.

When a hospital is owned or operated by a governmental body, it may be required to allow abortions that are not illegal under valid state laws. In *Hathaway* v. *Worcester City Hospital*,[19] the appellate court sustained a lower court and ordered the performance of elective, induced abortions in a hospital owned and operated by the City of Haverhill because such activities are considered a state action. At the same time, this would not mean that physicians or hospital personnel, such as nurses, would be required to participate in the performance of abortion procedures. In *Roe* v. *Ferguson*,[20] a Federal District Court judge held that the Ohio State auditor could not constitutionally refuse to pay for elective abortions under the state's Medicaid program.

The court has further decided that a husband's consent is not necessary for sterilization. Hence when a woman had a sterilization operation without her husband's consent, the Oklahoma Court of Appeals dismissed the litigation, holding that the natural right of a woman to her health is not qualified by requiring her husband's prior approval for surgery.[21]

In a Florida case, a nurse at an ambulatory center in Miami sought reinstatement for lost wages, compensatory and punitive damages, court costs and attorney's fees where she had been demoted to part-time, on-call status for refusing to assist with abortions. She alleged that her demotion violated her right to be free from religious discrimination. The appellate court found that the evidence did not establish that additional accommodation efforts would have caused the center undue hardship since the nurse was able to assist in approximately 84 per cent of the procedures performed. There was no evidence that schedules could not have been arranged to accommodate the nurse's religious beliefs. There was an order reinstating the nurse in her former position and determining the amount of damages. Nurses faced with discrimination for refusal to participate in an abortion should check to see if their state has a protection statute similar to Florida's.

An important related point concerns the consideration to be given to nursing students in relation to their views, beliefs and moral standards on abortion or related matters of contraception and sterilization. Do instructors know, respect and protect such rights, or are the grade and status of students jeopardized if they disagree with the instructor? Furthermore, are nurse students permitted without penalty to refuse to prepare a woman for an abortion, or to refuse to counsel a patient wanting contraceptive or sterilization assistance?[23] If people are to enjoy "the equal protection of the law," then nursing students who refuse to assist in keeping with their moral, ethical and/or religious beliefs must receive adequate protection from instructors who have an opposite point of view on such matters. The fact that both the scholastic standings of nursing students and the employment of professional nurses are jeopardized in numerous circumstances, in violation of their basic rights, is apparent from situations presented in seminars and workshops conducted by the author in the various sections of the United States.

The problem of abortion in an unmarried minor is a thorny one with many ramifications for the individual, her family and health personnel who administer care to her. The California Civil Code, Section 34.5 (1953) states: "Nothwithstanding any other provision of the law, an unmarried, pregnant minor may give consent to the furnishing of hospital, medical, and surgical care related to her pregnancy, and such consent shall not be subject to disaffirmance because of minority. The consent of the parent or parents of an unmarried, pregnant minor shall not be necessary in order to authorize hospital, medical, and surgical care related to her pregnancy."[24]

In a case in which a woman who was pregnant with an illegitimate child refused to have an abortion, even though the father agreed to pay for it, the court found that the father was not denied equal protection of the laws in being required to provide for the child although he had been denied any decision as to its birth. The court held that the decision not to have an abortion was that of the mother alone. In the judgment of the Alabama Supreme Court, a man who was adjudged to be the father of the illegitimate child was liable for the child's care, maintenance and education, and for all penalties for failure to perform these obligations.[25]

A Missouri statute, requiring a woman seeking an abortion to certify in writing that she has been informed of the termination of parental rights if the child is born alive, is constitutional.[26]

A Florida court upheld the conviction of a registered nurse for unlawful termination of a pregnancy. It also upheld the constitutionality of the statute that provides that only a physician may perform an abortion. However, it held to be invalid the requirement of the statute making it unlawful to terminate a pregnancy unless the termination is effected in an approved facility by a physician who submits written certification stating certain reasons for termination. Because the statute was not limited to abortions performed after the first trimester of pregnancy, the court also held that the statute was invalid.[27]

By reason of *Bigelow* v. *Virginia*, the state may not restrict the advertising of abortion services—not even the advertising of out-of-state abortion clinics.[28] As a consequence of *Planned Parenthood* v. *Danforth*, the consent of the father is unnecessary for the abortion of his baby, and the consent of either the father or the mother is unnecessary for a minor girl who desires an abortion.[29] Also by reason of *Planned Parenthood* v. *Danforth*, it is unconstitutional for the state to require the physician to give the same care to the unborn child destined for abortion as to a child intended to be brought forth alive.[30]

Roman Catholic View

On this topic, it is important to know the point of view of the Roman Catholic Church: In all pregnancies, it is forbidden to kill the mother in order to save the child, or to kill the child in order to save the mother.* However, providing a physician does what he can to save both lives, the indirect loss of one life resulting from an attempt to save the other is morally justifiable.[31]

After a criminal abortion, if a woman dies and it can be proved that the person responsible knew that the act was likely to cause serious bodily harm or death, he or she can be charged with murder. When the responsible person does

---

*Canon 2350 states: "Those who procure abortion, not excepting the mother, incur, if the effect is produced, an excommunciation latae sententiae reserved to the Ordinary; and if they be clerics they are moreover to be deposed."

the act without such knowledge, he or she is charged with manslaughter. A wrongful unsuccessful effort to secure an abortion is called "attempting to procure an abortion," which is a crime. Before the Supreme Court ruling, anyone who induced an abortion in a woman, unless it was necessary to preserve her life, was criminally liable.

In the latter part of 1984, some Roman Catholics have publicly opposed the church's traditional viewpoint on abortion.

IN VITRO FERTILIZATION*

Today, health professionals are frequently called upon to help people make decisions about responsible parenthood. At the outset, one has to accept the fact that the Judeo-Christian community is profoundly divided over a number of such issues.

The original intention of in vitro fertilization was as a method to help a couple have a child of their own where the woman had fallopian tubes that were absent, blocked or somewhat damaged. Now a wider application includes remedying infertility "that arises through hostile cervical mucus, immunity to spermatozoa in either partner, unexplained infertility, and that from other causes."[32] As Wells describes it, an ovum is removed from the prospective mother's ovary and placed in a culture dish to be fertilized by the prospective father's sperm.[33] When the attempted fertilization is successful, cell division begins. As soon as the resulting embryo is at the four-cell stage of development, it is transferred to the mother's uterus.[34]

A detailed description of the program carried out at the University of Pennsylvania Hospital (HUP) is given in Wells's article. A surgeon, financial counselor, clinical social worker and nurse coordinator are utilized. The surgeon who specializes in the treatment of infertility explains the steps of the in vitro process. The financial counselor explains the billing procedure (cost at HUP in 1983 is $3500 for each attempt). Emotional counseling and testing services are provided by a clinical social worker. For each couple, a nurse coordinator organizes the professional team and provides support, counseling and education. The nurse schedules the screening laparoscopy, starts the woman on hormone therapy, draws blood for estradiol levels and pregnancy tests, schedules sonograms and surgeries and teaches the husband how to administer progesterone to his wife. All test results are obtained by the nurse coordinator, who reports them to the physicians and patients. The preoperative assessment and preparation of necessary instrumentation are the work of the perioperative nurse. The retrieval of the ovum is done by the surgeon. The postoperative care of the woman is given by the nurse. The perioperative nurse makes a postoperative evaluation by telephone the next day. When fertilization occurs, the couple returns to day surgery for the woman to undergo the embryo transfer procedure, in which the nurse assists the surgeon.[35] Afterward, a series of progesterone injections is given by the husband to his wife to help the process of implantation.

Controversy concerning in vitro fertilization began some 10 years before Louise Brown's birth in July 1978. The initial publication in the scientific journal *Nature* brought a wave of criticism, opinions and condemnations from a variety of church leaders, reporters and scientists. Schukraft reports that a recent public

---

*This section first appeared as an article in *Nursing Management*, 16:12–14, April 1985.

opinion poll clearly showed that most Australians were in favor of a continuation and expansion of the in vitro fertilization program.[36] At the personal level, the intervention to give couples the opportunity to have children has found a fairly wide acceptance regardless of religious belief. However, many feel disquiet regarding the possibilities and consequences within the scientists' grasp as a result of the technique.

> Concerning the Roman Catholic view, Pius XII (1951) said: "To consider unworthily the cohabitation of husband and wife, and the marital act as a simple organic function for the transmission of seed, would be the same as to convert the domestic hearth, which is the family sanctuary, into a mere biological laboratory . . . . The marital act, in its natural setting, is a personal action. It is the simultaneous and direct cooperation of husband and wife, which is the expression of the mutual giving which, in the words of Scripture, results in the union "in one flesh.""[37]

Pius XII in 1957 condemned the practice as illicit for Roman Catholics. Generally, to obtain the husband's sperm, masturbation is required, and in the absence of married love at the time of conception, this practice is forbidden. As O'Donnell said, it is undoubtedly legitimate to use medical art to find remedies for sterility and even to intervene in the marital act itself to promote its fertility, for example, by techniques such as the use of a syringe or cervical spoon, or methods of concentrating the sperm density of semen emitted in intercourse. In all these cases, the child is begotten as the fruit of an actual expression of unitive love.[38]

A split in Catholic writers is evidenced by Daniel, Principal of the Jesuit Theological College in Melbourne, Australia, who states in the book *Test Tube Babies*: "In the context of in vitro fertilization, it may be argued that masturbation has a meaning and a purpose, and that this is one of the meanings of our sexuality overall. It is not the act of one turned in on himself; it is, in the circumstances, an other-directed act." He argues that taking part in an in vitro fertilization program may portray a much deeper commitment of a couple to one another, as it requires an enormous amount of cooperation between husband and wife.

Also, in the book *Test Tube Babies*, Fletcher, a Christian ethicist, claims that laboratory-assisted reproduction is "radically human compared to conception by ordinary human intercourse. It is willed, chosen, purposed and controlled, and surely these are amongst the traits that distinguish *Homo sapiens* from others in the animal genus."

Professor Paul Ramsey of Princeton University argues that in vitro fertilization followed by implantation is an immoral experiment upon a possible future life, since researchers cannot exclude the possibility that they will do irreparable damage to the possible offspring. He says: "We ought not to choose for another the hazards he must bear, while choosing at the same time to give him life in which to bear them and to suffer our chosen experimentations."[41]

With respect to the Jewish point of view, in vitro fertilization with the husband's sperm and the reimplantation of the tiny embryo into the same woman's womb with the subsequent birth of a healthy baby has received qualified approval by the Sephardic Chief Rabbi of Israel, Ovadiah Yosef.[42] Shlomo Green, the Ashkenazic Chief Rabbi, has asserted that, although conception in this manner is morally repugnant, it is unobjectionable according to the Halakah.[43] Since the husband's sperm is used, in vitro fertilization is not considered adultery. Because the aim is to fulfill the biblical commandment, sperm and egg procurement for this procedure is permissible. The offspring is legitimate and the parents fulfill their obligation of having children.[44]

Bleech says, however, that despite the happy initial success in the case of the Brown infant, it will require the birth and maturation through adolescence and into adulthood of a significant number of healthy and normal test-tube babies before the technique of in vitro fertilization may be viewed as morally acceptable.[45] Bleech also stresses that, even in the absence of moral or Halakic objections, no woman is required to submit to in vitro fertilization.

The technique of in vitro fertilization fills many people with foreboding and grave concern. The development of genetic engineering could lead to selective breeding, cloning (duplicating the person by asexual means), the production of hybrids and so on. In agriculture and horticulture, scientific intervention is being used to produce desirable strains, and human beings could be similarly manipulated. The possible outcomes are thought-provoking, and nurses must study morals, ethics and the law to find correct answers. As this article points out, the clergy are among those who should be consulted.

Aproximately 1000 babies have been born after in vitro fertilization and implantation in the women from whom the eggs were taken.[46] These issues are here to stay and to confront nurses, who will have to make moral decisions, as will clients or patients. If you deprive patients of the responsibility for making a moral decision about their health care, this is a violation of their rights.

Next, nurses have to consider the "tolerance ethic" in the thinking and actions of contemporary society. As Fletcher says, this discourages the imposition of one's own moral opinions on anyone else. It defends individuals' rights to be free to decide for themselves what is right.[47] As Hawks points out, the tolerance ethic distorts our moral thinking because it fails to consider what is right and concentrates on who decides what is right.[48] As a result, moral and ethic decision making becomes individualistic, and there remains no basis to criticize anyone's behavior. Consequently, to suggest that an individual's behavior is wrong becomes an act of moral intolerance. Hawks is correct in stating that the tolerance ethic does society a great disservice by implying that actions and their consequences are morally irrelevant.

Ashley and O'Rourke[49] state that the consequences of an individual's actions should be of primary concern. Individuals must examine critically the consequences of their actions and accept responsibility for them.

If nurses offer moral advice to their patients, they have to be prepared with a knowledge of those ethical and legal issues relevant to patients and their families. To this end, the foregoing material is offered as a beginning on the in vitro fertilization problem.

ARTIFICIAL INSEMINATION*

Artificial insemination presents a number of legal and ethical problems. Generally, a couple requests artificial insemination because of infertility, which has been defined as the "inability to conceive after one year of regular intercourse or the inability to deliver a live infant after three conceptions."[50] Since some 10 to 15 percent of marriages are estimated to be infertile, the problem of infertility is a common one.[51] As a means of remedying this infertility, artificial insemina-

---

*This section first appeared as an article in *Nursing Management*, 16:18–20, May 1985.

tion presents two types of problems: (1) the permissibility of the procedure itself; (2) afterward, questions which arise with regard to paternity, such as consanguinity and rights of inheritance.[52]

As Ashley and O'Rourke state, artificial insemination is any process by which fecundation of an ovum takes place not as the result of sexual intercourse, but as the result of the sperm being introduced into the vagina by artificial means.[53] When the semen used is that of the husband of the woman who wishes to conceive, it is called homologous insemination or artificial insemination by the husband (AIH). When the semen used is that of a man other than the husband, it is called heterologous insemination or artificial insemination by a donor (AID).

While the theoretical possibility of conception without intercourse was recognized by the sages of the Talmud, the problem was not common until the 1930s and later. Today, most physicians refuse to inseminate single women. Many physicians require a series of psychological tests to determine whether the couple will be able to handle the strains and stresses that may result in married life as a result of this procedure. Where AID is utilized, a genetic screening, a health examination that includes a test for venereal diseases and a semen analysis are done.

The process of artificial insemination is simple. The semen is collected in a sterilized container. It may be frozen and used at a later date, but frequently it is used within a few hours. As close as possible to the day of ovulation, the semen is introduced into the vagina by means of a syringe or plastic cap placed at the cervix. In 1967, McFadden commented:

> There is surely no knowledge or skill proper to the medical profession which is involved in the procedure. Members of a dozen walks of life—such as veterinarians, biochemists, biologists—would be equally capable of executing the action.[54]

Research reveals no state that prohibits AIH—artificial insemination by the husband. The child born of such procedure is legitimate, and there is no inheritance problem. The wife is not guilty of adultery, and no legal problems ensue.

The legal problems arise with AID. According to D'Andrea, only 14 states (Arkansas, California, Colorado, Connecticut, Georgia, Hawaii, Kansas, Montana, North Carolina, North Dakota, Oklahoma, Texas, Washington and Wyoming) have specific laws dealing with artificial insemination by donor.[55] If there is no law, it is not illegal or a crime for the couple, the nurse and the physician to participate in the AID procedure. However, the problem arises as to whether the child can inherit from his or her nonbiological father. As D'Andrea points out, this can be solved in three ways: (1) The child may be adopted after birth; (2) the husband may name the child as heir in his will without stating the nature of the father:child relationship; and (3) if no one knows that the child is the result of AID, the question of legitimacy may never be raised. If both the husband and the wife sign the consent form, this is a further protection from legal problems.[56] The consent form should also list the risks involved, the possible complications of any pregnancy, any agreement to match the characteristics of one member of the couple and an agreement that the couple will not attempt to identify the donor.

In 1967, Oklahoma, by statute, authorized artificial insemination and stated that a child born as a consequence is legitimate. In 1968, California decided the issues of heterologous insemination. After 15 years of married life without children, a husband and wife both consented to artificial insemination and signed a statement on a physician's letterhead in which they requested the procedure. The physician selected the semen, and the name of the donor remained unknown to the couple. Following artificial insemination, a boy was born to the wife, and the husband was named as the father on the birth certificate. Four years later the couple separated and divorced, the mother kept the child and asked for no support. Several years later, the mother was obliged to seek public assistance following an illness, and a support order against the husband was secured. The court held that the woman's former husband was the lawful father, and refused to rule that the artificial insemination was adulterous.[57] In New York, following a divorce, a father was given the right to visit a child who resulted from the heterologous insemination of the wife to which the husband had consented.[58] On the other hand, an Illinois trial court held that a wife who had received heterologous insemination with or without her husband's consent was guilty of adultery and such a child was illegitimate.[59]

As Ashley and O'Rourke state, most Catholic theologians reject AID as a method of solving the problem of childless couples. They quote George Lobo, who wrote:

> The bond of mutual and exclusive human sexual love between parents is violated if the sperm of another man is introduced into the woman's vagina. If conception occurs, the child has no relation to the love that binds man and wife together.[60]

This is in accordance with the teaching of Pius XII (1949), who said:

> Artificial insemination in marriage, with the use of an active element from a third person, is equally immoral and as such to be rejected summarily. Only marriage partners have mutual rights over their bodies for the procreation of new life, and these rights are exclusive, nontransferable, and inalienable. . . .[61]

When it is possible to use the husband's semen (AIH), some Catholic theologians believe that it can be permitted. They argue that in AIH, the artificial procreative process remains *remotely* ordered to the unitive act of love. The partners express their love regularly by intercourse which they would render fertile if they could, but since they cannot, they use an artificial process to achieve this legitimate purpose.[62] The theologians who have written on the question of licit methods of obtaining semen admit the licity of prostatic massage or aspiration from the epididymis or testicles but reject masturbation.[63]

In Jewish law, AIH poses no problem insofar as the act of insemination is concerned.[64] The means of obtaining the husband's semen is the main question, and the preferred method is retrieval of the semen from the vagina following intercourse or use of a condom. In moderate infertility due to low sperm count, the problem may be corrected by combining sperm obtained in several ejaculations.

According to Rosner, using the semen of a donor other than the husband to artificially inseminate a wife is considered by most rabbinic opinions to be an abomination and is strictly prohibited.[65] Among the reasons are the possibility of incest, the lack of genealogy and the problems of inheritance. As he says, some authorities regard such insemination as adultery and require that the husband divorce his wife and that the wife forfeit her marriage settlement. Other rabbinical opinions hold that if there is no sexual act involved, the woman is not guilty of adultery.[66]

Fletcher, a Christian ethicist, in the book *Test Tube Babies*, claims that laboratory-assisted reproduction is "radically human compared to conception by ordinary human intercourse. It is willed, chosen, purposed and controlled, and surely these are among the traits that distinguish *Homo sapiens* from others in the animal genus."[67]

The problem of artificial insemination relates to nurses and nursing, since it may be discussed in planned parenthood sessions or in an artificial insemination program in which nurses participate. D'Andrea describes in detail the work of the nurse practitioner in an artificial insemination program at the University of Massachusetts Medical Center (UMMC).[68] According to her, nurse practitioners provide comprehensive care to the couple by combining their abilities as a teacher, counselor and technician. Initially, artificial insemination candidates are interviewed by a gynecologist who specializes in infertility and microsurgery and who assesses the couple's reasons for requesting AID, the history of their infertility, their knowledge of other alernatives to parenthood and their understanding of the procedure. Afterward, the woman undergoes a complete history and physical examination. Following this, the couple goes to the interview office, where the insemination procedure is explained, including the timing of the inseminations during the menstrual cycle. The donor program is explained including the screening process, the need for anonymity, the need for a legal permit signed by both partners and the cost of insemination. The couple is then seen by a nurse who works with the physician. The nurse explains any necessary tests, teaches basal body temperature charting, provides support and provides a card with the nurse practitioner and R.N. phone numbers and directs the couple to call for a nurse practitioner interview.

At the nurse practitioner interview, the nurse assesses emotional status in light of the diagnosis of infertility and a marital history. When the decision for AID is made, she or he reviews and teaches the insemination procedure and donor program, gets a signed consent form and provides necessary legal material relating to artificial insemination in the state. At UMMC, the secretary of the gynecology department is the coordinator between the donor and the couple. As D'Andrea points out, the ability of nurse practitioners to perform the insemination procedure gives them access to patients that enables them to monitor their emotional responses and to intervene when appropriate.[69]

With this review of the nurse and nurse practitioner's role, nurses must consider whether in accordance with their moral and ethical values they can, in good conscience, perform such duties. In the previous section on in vitro fertilization, the tolerance ethic was discussed. Both patients and nurses must examine critically the consequences of their actions and be responsible for them. One way of expressing concern for the consequence is by voicing an opinion about the morality of an action. According to Hawks, usually nurses should honor a patient's or client's request for advice.[70] Thus, moral advice can become a valuable role in total patient care.

SURROGATE MOTHERS

Abram's wife, Sarai, was unable to bear him a child for their marriage, so she arranged for her handmaiden, Hagar, to bear a child for them. Abram consummated this arrangement by going in unto Hagar and she bore him a son.[71] As surrogate motherhood is practiced today, it differs only in insemination technique.

A couple who is childless because of the wife's infertility may seek a surrogate mother, who has proven to be fertile and who is willing to be inseminated artificially by the husband of the childless couple, to bear an infant and then to give complete custody of the child to the biological father. An unmarried man without children may also endeavor to secure a child through the services of a surrogate mother. Generally, a surrogate mother receives a fee of up to $10,000 and medical expenses from the biological father for the delivery of a healthy child.[72]

A survey of the women applying for the surrogate mother program reveals that the average education of these women is slightly above the high school level, that they have relatively normal personalities and their reasons for entering such a program are an interesting mixture of financial and altruistic factors.[73] Markoutsas, in the *Chicago Tribune*, reported a story in which the surrogate mother performed her service out of love and friendship, and the participants later appeared on Phil Donahue's nationally syndicated talk show.[44] In another survey,[75] the applicants averaged 25 years of age; half were Roman Catholic and half Protestant. Among the 60 percent who were employed or who had a spouse with a job, annual incomes ranged from $6000 to $55,000. Again, most had a high school diploma, and a quarter of the group had gone for courses at a college, business college or nursing school. Altruistic factors and money were motives. One woman gave as her reason having killed a baby (abortion); she could make up for it by giving an infant to a childless, loving couple.

The legal problems of surrogate motherhood are several—including the contract. The responsibilities of the contracting couple are the promise they make to the surrogate mother to pay for the financial costs of pregnancy and the surrogate's fee and to accept the child after birth. Whether a contract for surrogate motherhood is valid and legal is uncertain today; the practice is ahead of the legal and ethical establishment. Such a contract may be found invalid if it violates public policy or state adoption laws. If valid, then according to contract law, there is considerable freedom in its terms. The parties who enter into such contracts should specify in detail the rights and responsibilities of each party to clarify their intent and to provide guidance to a court in determining appropriate remedies in cases of a breach.[76, 77]

In *Doe v. Kelley*, a Michigan court held "baby bartering" to be against the state's public policy.[78] In *Syrkowski v. Appleyard*, a childless couple made an agreement with a married woman who had two children, and she was artificially inseminated with the plaintiff husband's semen. Upon the birth of the child, the couple would have custody, and the defendant would receive $10,000 in addition to her medical expenses. Although the Michigan Appellate Court did not want to decide whether surrogate-mother contracts are against public policy, it did conclude that the Paternity Act's purpose of providing support for children born out of wedlock did not encompass the monetary transaction proposed.[79]

Because they violate the Oklahoma Trafficking in Children statute, the Oklahoma attorney general issued an opinion that surrogate parenthood contracts are illegal. According to that opinion, the statute does not apply except in cases where compensation above medical expenses is paid and adoption is planned or takes place.[80] The attorney general of Kentucky in an opinion said that surrogate parenthood violated at least three Kentucky state laws as well as a strong public policy against buying and selling children.[81] In early 1983, a similar opinion was issued by the Ohio attorney general.[82]

Like other people, children cannot be bought and sold. The Thirteenth Amendment of the United States Constitution prohibits slavery, sale of one person by another. This seems pertinent whether the surrogate mother is paid before the woman is inseminated or after the baby is born, since the intention of the parties to the contract is to pay money in exchange for a baby.[83] On the other hand, a surrogate motherhood could be legalized by state legislation as an exception to the rule that children cannot be bought and sold. If the same is done, the law would have to make some provision for children who are born defective or where a mother chooses to terminate her pregnancy. As Gerez points out, state legislatures and courts may give great weight to statutory and case law of artificial insemination because of its close analogy to surrogate motherhood.[84] He also notes that the application of the antibarter statutes may be offset by the United States recognition of the right of personal privacy, which includes the interest in independently making certain kinds of important decisions such as procreation.[85]

From the Roman Catholic point of view, Ashley and O'Rourke state that, although artificial fecundation is illicit, it would seem that artificial gestation might be licit, provided there would be sufficient reason for so extraordinary a procedure. For example, if a child were conceived in the natural way and if, for one reason or another, the woman would not be able to carry the child to viable term, artificial gestation would assist the natural process, rather than subvert it. Transferring the child to an artificial womb would thus protect its life.[86]

Rosenfeld concludes that if fetal transplantation is performed 40 or more days after conception, the child is considered to be the legal offspring of its biological parents since the child became "completed" while still in the biological mother's body.[87] However, Jewish law views differently a situation of a fetal transplant occuring within 40 days after conception. Even if the donor was married, the recipient is not considered an adulteress. The recipient of an ovarian transplant must be considered the legal mother of any child conceived and born. Bleich states that the host mother nurtures the embryo and sustains gestation and, perhaps, should be considered the legal mother of the offspring. Other authorities view the host mother as the mother in the eyes of Jewish law since the prohibition against feticide is applicable from the moment of conception. Others consider the possibility that two maternal relationships may exist simultaneously. The question remains unresolved.[88]

According to Britain's Chief Rabbi, Immanuel Jakobovits, to remove a mother's naturally fertilized egg and to reimplant it in a host mother for reasons of "convenience for women who seek the gift of a child without the encumbrance and disfigurement of pregnancy is offensive to moral susceptibilities."[89] Also, Jakobovits says, "To use another person as an "incubator' and then take from her the child she has carried and delivered for a fee is revolting degradation of maternity and an affront to human dignity."

Paul Ramsey, a Protestant moralist, believes such procedures as artificial insemination from a donor, artificial inovulation and cloning or other forms of asexual reproduction are wrong—wrong because morally licit reproduction must be done heterosexually by human intercourse within the context of marriage and the family.[90] Joseph Fletcher, on the other hand, states:

> To be men we must be in control. That is the first and last ethical word. For when there is no choice there is no possibility of ethical action. Whatever we are compelled to do is amoral.[91]

It seems doubtful that the surrogate mother arrangements can be effectively prevented. Nurses will become involved, since they assist the physicians who perform most of these services. Nurses must consider: (1) Should they engage in such activities? and (2) When their advice is sought by patients or clients, what will their response be? This problem is another illustration of where our medical and surgical know-how has outdistanced our moral and ethical thinking.

There is an abundance of legal material relating to the problems of surrogate motherhood but relatively few documented moral, ethical or religious articles discussing the same. There will be a call for government intervention to stop what some people regard as undesirable changes in traditional conceptions of human beings, families and society. We must think again about responsible parenthood and develop sensible social policies. Capron makes five suggestions: (1) A multidisciplinary public committee should be charged with investigating new reproductive procedures; (2) the National Conference of Commissioners of Uniform State Laws should empanel a committee to go beyond the Uniform Parentage Act and draw upon the conclusions of the multidisciplinary committee; (3) any law should have the prime objective of protecting the well-being of the children involved, including genetic and medical screening of all donors, confidential records, limitation on number of offspring from a single donor, restrictions on use of frozen germinal material after death of person from whom material was derived and explicit rules about financial and other obligations; (4) the commercialization of reproductive techniques should be discouraged; and (5) the status of in vitro fertilization and other forms of extracorporeal manipulation of germinal material should be clarified at state and Federal levels.

Nurses must read and study these new developments, such as surrogate motherhood. Not only must they work with patients or clients seeking this alternative but also with physicians engaged in this treatment. As nurses, also, we must participate on ethics committees considering this and related matters. To assist nurses with such work, this material is offered as a beginning.

WRONGFUL BIRTH*

Impaired children's claims may involve the failure of the physician, the testing laboratory or the genetic counselor to properly obtain relevant information and thus to give potential parents incorrect or insufficient information upon which to make their reproductive decisions. Other claims involve unsuccessful sterilizations or abortions where the physician fails to effectuate the patients' informed choice to avoid the birth of an impaired child. It is the duty of the physician to facilitate the parents' decision based upon the best available knowledge.

Nurses must work closely with the couple who desire to have a child. To this end they must secure a complete health history, assess the readiness of the couple for the undertaking and, along with the physician, counsel them so that the best possible health will follow for mother and baby. When the pregnancy results in the birth of an impaired child, the nurse as a patient listener must hear the reactions of the couple, assess both parents and baby and help them cope with the problems they face.

The body of developing law indicates four different positions on wrongful birth.

1. *Nonrecognition of any Damages Resulting in the Birth of a Child.* The physician was negligent in failing to warn the mother, who had German measles

---

*Material in this section first appeared in an article in *Nursing Management*, 14:41–42, July 1983.

early in pregnancy, that there were risks of defects in the fetus. The parents in a wrongful birth action failed to recover damages where the child was born with birth defects.[93]

2. *Complete Recovery for the Costs of Child Rearing.* Where a mother of eight children was unsuccessfully sterilized and had a healthy ninth baby, the court held that she could recover damages. The family exchequer was ordered replenished so that the new arrival would not deprive other family members of what was planned as their share of the family income.[94]

3. *Child Rearing Benefits Offset by the Benefits of Parenthood.* Where parents with eight children decided to limit the size of their family, the physician prescribed an oral contraceptive. The licensed pharmacist negligently supplied a mild tranquilizer and the woman delivered a ninth normal, healthy child. The plaintiffs alleged mother's lost wages, medical and hospital expenses, the pain and anxiety of pregnancy and childbirth and the economic cost of rearing a child as damages. The assessment of damages was within the competence of the trier of fact and not unduly speculative.[95]

4. *Exclusion of Child Rearing Costs as Damages.* The patient brought an action against a physician who negligently failed to perform a proper abortion and a normal child was born to the plaintiff. The patient was precluded from recovering damages for costs in rearing and educating the child, but she was not precluded from recovering hospital and medical costs of her unwanted pregnancy.[96]

WRONGFUL LIFE

Does a child or his parents have a good cause of action for wrongful life? The abundance of material on the highly inflammatory subjects of abortion and contraception, which have raised questions involving rights of privacy and basic social morals, evidences the level of public concern.[97]

In *Bonbrest* v. *Kotz*,[98] a fetus viable at the time of injury could recover for injuries. According to *Sylvia* v. *Gobeille*[99] viability means that the fetus is capable of living outside the womb. More recent cases, such as *Labree* v. *Major*,[100] have not stressed viability.

An accompanying movement toward expansion of the right of privacy to include a woman's right to control her own bodily functions, including the right to terminate her pregnancy, is illustrated by *Doe* v. *Bolton*,[101] where a Georgia criminal abortion statute was held unconstitutional. In *Roe* v. *Wade*,[102] a Texas criminal abortion was held unconstitutional as violating a woman's fundamental right to decide whether or not to terminate her pregnancy. In this case, abortions in the first trimester of pregnancy were held beyond the scope of state regulation. Abortions in the second trimester may be regulated in the interest of the mother's health. Abortions in the third trimester may be regulated.

As a result of these opposing developments, the legal status of the fetus has become a present-day dilemma. To date, actions for wrongful life have been litigated under tort, contract and warranty.

In *Stewart* v. *Long Island College Hospital*,[103] a parent's suit for damages due to the defendant's failure to abort a rubella-stricken fetus was dismissed. The New York court held:

> [T]here is no remedy for having been born under a handicap, whether physical or psychological, when the alternative to being born in a handicapped condition

is not to have been born at all. To put it another way, a plaintiff has no remedy against a defendant whose offense is that he failed to consign the plaintiff to oblivion. Such a cause of action is alien to our system of jurisprudence.[104]

In *Dumer v. St. Michael's Hospital*,[105] a mother and child sued in tort for the defendant physician's and hospital's failure to diagnose rubella, so the fetus could be aborted. The child's claim was denied and the mother's allowed.

In *Ball v. Mudge*,[106] in an unsuccessful action for wrongful life of a child, the husband and wife alleged breach of warranty in failure to render the husband sterile. In warranty and contract actions, the plaintiff must prove the existence of a contract to achieve a special medical result. If this contract is absent, the physician does not warrant the success of the operation.[107] Also, the courts, as in *Rogala v. Silva*,[108] may require that the warranty be expressed, that the plaintiff prove his reliance on the warranty and that a separate consideration be paid. In *Stills v. Gratton*,[109] a child who was born after an unsuccessful abortion had no cause of action for his wrongful life, but his mother could recover the usual damages for negligence, a California appellate court ruled.

When plaintiffs allege that their own birth was wrongful, in effect they ask the court to make a determination that they should not have been allowed to live. However, when the parent claims that the infant should not have been born, the parent does not seek to destroy the infant's present existence but seeks damages related to the fact of birth, not for birth iself.[110]

In *Custodio v. Bauer*,[111] the parents of nine children prior to a sterilization operation sought to recover damages after the birth of a tenth child. The action was brought, following the unsuccessful sterilization operation, for the medical expenses incident to the operation, for physical pain and mental anguish incident to the pregnancy and for economic loss occasioned by the unwanted child. The California Court of Appeals allowed recovery for the provable economic loss and recognized that the birth of a child might be less than a "blessed event." Since this case, other courts have awarded damages to parents for the birth of a normal child. In the Troppi[112] case, the defendant druggist negligently failed to provide the birth control drug prescribed for the plaintiff mother. Reasonable measures to mitigate damages are required, and the best interests of the child must be considered.

In *Jacobs v. Theimer*,[113] the court was faced with a demand for the cost of raising a child afflicted with defects resulting from rubella; the child would have been aborted except for alleged negligence. The court allowed recovery for costs reasonably related to the the child's physical defects but excluded expenses to be incurred in raising the child. It followed another Texas case, *Terrell v. Garcia*.[114] Similarly, in *Coleman v. Garrison*,[115] recoveries by parents of a healthy child born of a failed sterilization operation were limited to the actual expenses and anxieties attending the unexpected pregnancy.

In another group of cases, the court recognizes the parents' cause of action and gives damages according to normal tort principles. For example, in *Ziemba v. Sternberg*,[116] the court said:

> [T]he person responsible must respond for all damages resulting directly from and as a natural consequence of the wrongful act according to common experience and in the usual course of events, whether the damages could or could not have been foreseen by him.

Where an infant brought a wrongful life action because his father caused him to be born illegitimate, he was denied recovery.[117] The plaintiff's mentally deficient mother was raped while in a state mental institution, causing him to be born illegitimately, but he had no cause of action for wrongful life.[118] Where a child brought a malpractice action because he was born with serious impairments resulting from his mother's contracting rubella during the first trimester of pregnancy and she was not made aware of the potentially harmful consequences, recovery was barred.[119] A mother of advanced age who had not been warned of the dangers of childbirth or informed of amniocentesis sought damages on behalf of her mongoloid infant. However, the suit was unsuccessful because of the inability of the law to make a comparison between human existence with handicaps and no life at all.[120] Where a child was born with neurofibromatosis already evidenced in the child's siblings, a Pennsylvania court recognized the parents' cause of action but not the infant's.[121]

In *Curlender v. Bio-Science Laboratories*, a child with Tay-Sachs disease sought recovery for personal injury and wrongful life against a medical testing laboratory and a physician. The California Court said that the child could recover damages for the pain and suffering endured during the limited life span available to such a child and any special pecuniary loss resulting from the impaired condition including the costs of medical care that were not recoverable by the child's parents.[122] In *Turpin v. Sortini*, in a suit brought by parents of a deaf child seeking damages for defendant's failure to advise parents of the possibility of hereditary deafness, the court did not recognize the wrongful life action. It said that although the child could not recover general damages, the child could recover special damages for extraordinary expenses, which were necessary to treat the hereditary ailment.[123]

A patient's mother contracted rubella during the first trimester of pregnancy, and the physician did not inform her of the condition and thereby give her the option of terminating the pregnancy. The child was born with severe birth defects, but he could not recover damages from the physicians in a wrongful life suit. The court said that it could not view the patient's economic losses apart from the incalculable benefit of life.[124]

The Kentucky Supreme Court stated that establishment of a cause of action for wrongful life or wrongful birth was a matter for the legislature, not the courts.[125]

Confusion is rampant in the area of recovery for wrongful birth. Two classes of suits contain elements of wrongful birth actions but should be distinguished by the courts: suits for prenatal injuries, and suits by parents to recover the costs of raising a normal child born as the result of negligent or ineffective sterilization. In prenatal injury suits, the plaintiff seeks damages for an injury that is attributable to a cause other than mere birth. The child, as he or she exists, can be compared with the normal child he or she would have been. In suits where a normal child is born after unsuccessful sterilization, the parents sought a particular surgical procedure to accomplish a desired result. Where an operation performed for a designated purpose fails to achieve that purpose, liability is properly placed upon the physician who failed to meet reasonable medical standard. The only suits that should be included in wrongful life are those by illegitimate children and those by children who claim that they should have been aborted. When the first wrongful life suits were initiated, the question of conflict in public policy did not arise. In recent years, however, family planning, population control, and the mother's right of privacy have achieved the status of public policy.[126] Since the preservation of life is also an accepted public policy, the conflict is obvious. Thus far, actions for wrongful life have been poorly received.

BABY DOE CASES*

The media attention of the Baby Jane Doe case has raised several questions: If a baby is born with some severe physical defect(s) so that he can survive, if at all, with a very limited possibility of being more than a living vegetable, what shall we do about his nursing care? Shall we do our best to keep the child alive regardless of family desire or should we do as little as possible on the theory it is the ultimate kindness to let the child die naturally?

The same question has been faced for years by physicians, obstetricians and pediatricians. The problem is that our medical and surgical advances, i.e., our ability to keep people alive, have far exceeded our legal, moral and ethical progress in handling the problems.

Since the publicity associated with the celebrated "John Hopkins case"[127] some years ago, discussion on the matter has increased. In that case the baby was born with Down's syndrome (mongolism) and duodenal atresia, which is readily correctable by non-difficult surgery. After talking with spiritual advisors, the parents refused this surgery for their child. As a result, the baby died from starvation some 15 days later. The resulting case comment on the decision has been overwhelmingly unfavorable.[128]

In the *New England Journal of Medicine*, Doctors Duff and Campbell[129] reported on a study of 299 deaths among 2171 children treated in a special-care nursery at the Yale–New Haven Hospital over a 2½-year-period. In this group, 43 of the infants died after parents and physicians jointly agreed to discontinue treatment because of multiple anomalies, meningomyelocele, cardiopulmonary crippling or other central nervous system defects. The remaining 256, who received the best treatment modern medicine and nursing could provide, lived little, if any, longer than those who received no special treatment. For each of the 43 babies who received no further treatment, the physicians and parents made a decision that the prognosis was very poor or hopeless for "meaningful life." Doctors Duff and Campbell write:

> The awesome finality of these decisions, combined with a potential for error in prognosis, made the choice agonizing for families and health professionals. Nevertheless, the issue has to be faced, for not to decide is an arbitrary and potentially devastating decision of default. It may constitute a victimizing abandonment of patients and their families in time of greatest need.[130]

In his article "To Save or Let Die" McCormick concludes:

> It [life] is a value to be preserved precisely as a condition for other values, and therefore insofar as these other values remain attainable. Since these other values cluster around and are rooted in human relationships, it seems to follow that life is a value to be preserved only insofar as it contains some potentiality for human relationships.

To this he adds four caveats:

> First, this guideline is not a detailed rule that pre-empts decisions; for relational capacity is not subject to mathematical analysis but to human judgment .... It is the task of physicians to provide some more concrete categories or presumptive biological symptoms for human judgment.
> Secondly, ... mistakes will be made.

---

*This section first appeared as an article in *Nursing Management*, 15:16–18, Aug. 1984.

Third . . . the only point is whether this undoubted value has any potential at all, in continuing physical survival, for attaining a share, even if reduced, in the "higher, more important good."

Fourth, this whole matter is further complicated by the fact that this decision is being made for someone else . . . those decisions must be made in terms of the child's good, this alone.[131]

All physicians do not agree on what should be done in these cases. A goodly number state that the Hippocratic oath commits them to do all that they can to preserve life. The surgeon-in-chief at Children's Hospital Medical Center in Boston says: "No matter how expert we are, we can't predict outcome."[132]

In the case of Baby Boy Houle[133] the Maine Superior Court ordered emergency surgery at the Maine Medical Center to provide the baby with an opportunity to live. There, the baby was born with multiple malformations on the left side of his body, including the absence of a left eye, almost no left ear, a deformed left hand, some vertebrae not fused and tracheal esophageal fistula (allowing some air into his stomach instead of the lungs and fluid from the stomach going into the lungs). Although a tracheal esophageal fistula is readily corrected by surgery, the baby's condition was deteriorating without it and he contracted pneumonia. The parents refused their consent to surgery. Believing the baby needed surgery, several doctors took the case to court. The judge ordered the surgery to be performed, saying: "At the moment of birth there does exist a human being entitled to the fullest protection of the law. The most basic right enjoyed by every human being is the right to life itself."

The court said that the parents had no right to withhold treatment and that to do so constituted neglect in the legal sense. The court ordered the child's legal representative to consent to corrective surgery and other normal life-supportive measures. It also enjoined the parents from directing the physician or hospital to do anything that would injure the child. Following surgery, Baby Boy Houle did die on the fifteenth day of life.

In a much publicized case, Baby Jane Doe was born in Port Jefferson, New York, on October 11, 1983, with spina bifida and hydrocephalus. Today, surgery is available to mitigate the effects of these conditions. When her parents declined to authorize life-prolonging surgery, a local pro-life attorney went to court to attempt to protect the child. The New York courts ruled that the parents were within their rights, and the U.S. Supreme Cout declined to review the case. The Federal Department of Health and Human Services (HHS) requested Baby Doe's medical records from the hospital in which she resided, to determine whether she was being denied surgery in violation of the Rehabilitation Act and Baby Doe Rule. The hospital said it did not have to provide the records, and the Federal district court agreed. HHS appealed the decision, leading to 2 to 1 decision of the U.S. Court of Appeals for the Second Circuit in Manhattan, which ruled that Federal Civil Rights Law (Section 504) of the Rehabilitation Act of 1972 was never intended to "apply to treatment decisions involving defective newborn infants."[134] The court said:

To accept the position of the guardian would have far-reaching implications. As the guardian conceded in oral argument, acceptance of the proposition he espouses would be to recognize the right of any person, without recourse to the strictures of the Family Court Act, to institute judical proceedings which would catapult him into the very heart of a family circle, there to challenge the most private and most precious responsibility vested in parents for the care and nurture of their children—and at the very least to force the parents to incur the not inconsiderable expenses of extended litigation.[135]

According to published reports in April 1984, Baby Jane Doe is in stable condition, and her parents have consented to the surgery for the hydrocephalus.

With respect to spina bifida, an article in *Pediatrics*[136] reports that a team of doctors and other clinicians, using a quality of life formula, recommended that 24 out of 69 babies born with spina bifida between 1977 and 1982 not be aggressively treated. The 24 untreated babies died at an average of 37 days. Of those who were recommended for aggressive treatment, all lived except one killed in a car accident. Of those not recommended for treatment, six of the eight babies whose parents went ahead with treatment lived. The treatment recommendations was based in part on the child's expected "quality of life." This was formulated by multiplying the child's natural endowment with the sum of the financial and emotional contributions expected from the child's home and society:

$$QL = NE \times (H + S)$$

The formula was created by Dr. Anthony Shaw. This article has caused considerable controversy.

In the Medicine section of *Newsweek* a decade ago, there was reported a new and "merciful" policy of putting to death the "living vegetables" together with pro-euthanasia material including the article at Yale–New Haven Hospital's intensive care nursery.[137] *Newsweek* assured its readers: "Every effort was made to spare the babies from pain as they died, and every decision about their fate was made by parents and physicians acting in concert." The article quoted Dr. Duff: "The public has got to decide what to do with vegetated individuals who have no human potential."

As Ellen McCormack has pointed out, this material drew this moving response from Sondra Diamond of Philadelphia in a later issue of *Newsweek*:

> I'll wager my entire root system and as much fertilizer as it would take to fill Yale University that you have never received a letter from a vegetable before this one, but, much as I resent the term, I must confess that I fit the description of a "vegetable" as defined in the article. "Shall This Child Die?" (Medicine, November 12).
>
> Due to severe brain damage incurred at birth, I am unable to dress myself, toilet myself, or write; my secretary is typing this letter. Many thousands of dollars had to be spent on my rehabilitation and education in order for me to reach my present professional status as a consulting psychologist. My parents were also told, 35 years ago, that there was little or no hope of achieving meaningful "humanhood" for their daughter. Have I reached "humanhood?" Compared with Drs. Duff and Campbell, I believe I have surpassed it. Instead of changing the law to make it legal to weed out us "vegetables," let us change the laws so that we may receive medical care, education and freedom to live as full and productive lives as our potential will allow.[138]

The Supreme Court of Georgia ordered a cesarean section to save the life of a fetus where there was a 99 percent chance the fetus would not survive natural childbirth.[139] Where another couple applied for a limited guardianship to enable them to consent to surgery to correct a life-shortening heart defect in Phillip Becker, who had Down's syndrome and whose natural parents refused to consent to the surgery, the California Superior Court granted the request.[140]

Nurses should realize that, under most medical and nursing practice acts, diagnosis and prescription of corrective surgery and medical treatent are within the province of the physician. The response of patients to treatments as well as preventative nursing is within the realm of nursing. How competently, skillfully and conscientiously we practice our art and science of nursing depends on ourselves and is judged by our peers and superiors in nursing as well as by other health professinal colleagues and the consuming public. As Lewis has said, generally nurses constitute a group of employed personnel, not individually accountable to clients they serve but to the institution that employs them.[141]

However, as Horner currently says, whether and to what extent infants and children are treated can be influenced by physicians and nurses. For example, if the staff tells the parents:

> It is possible to operate on your baby and close his back, but his legs will still be paralyzed and deformed. Most likely he will never have bowel or bladder control and will probably develop hydrocephalus, which may require many operations with possible complications. Or, we can do nothing and allow him to die.

Would you be surprised if the parents opted for death?[142] As she points out, on the other hand, a positive attitude can go a long way in persuading parents to accept their baby. This has been the stance of the nursing staff at Shriner's Burn Institute in Boston. The nurses encourage the parents to touch, hold, feel, talk to and play with their infant. They tell them to bring in music boxes, toys and, later, even clothes. As Horner says, by focusing on the normal things the baby does, they foster a positive image of the child. Examples include, "Look how strongly he sucks," and "See how tightly she holds your finger," emphasize that their baby does things that all babies do.[143]

According to the International Council of Nurses Code, the fundamental responsibility of the nurse is fivefold: to promote health, to prevent illness, to restore health, to alleviate suffering and to promote the patient's spiritual environment.[144] The ANA Code for Professional Nurses as revised in 1983 simply states:

> The nurse provides services with respect for human dignity and the uniqueness of the client unrestricted by considerations of social or economic status, personal attributes, or the nature of health problems.[145]

Nurses should choose to preserve life and render the best nursing care of which they are capable in order to assist the baby to achieve his or her most basic right to life itself. Only in this way will we maintain our heritage of caring and of nurturing patients and be worthy of the trust reposed in us, who are the eyes of those who cannot see, the ears of those who cannot hear, the feet of those who cannot walk, the voice of those who cannot talk and who do for people the things they would do for themselves if they were able. Regardless of our expertise, we cannot predict the outcome. Therefore, we should strive, as those physicians who obey the Hippocratic oath, to preserve life.

WHAT IS DEATH AND WHO DETERMINES IT?*

Many years ago Benjamin Franklin said, "In the world nothing is certain but death and taxes." Two hundred years later, with modern heart-lung machines, dialysis machines, respirators, feeding tubes and organ transplants prolonging the lives of persons who otherwise would have died, defining death is more difficult than it once was.[146]

---

*This section first appeared as an article in *Supervisor Nurse*, 10:17–18, 74–75, Sept. 1979.

Traditionally, death was regarded as the "cessation of all vital functions of the human body"[147] or the combined cessation of heartbeat and respiration. In that era of medical opinion, cardiac arrest was synonymous with the cessation of life.[148] While the cardiac pacemaker and ventilatory equipment may artificially restore cardiac and pulmonary function, they have no curative powers for the brain. The concept of brain death merely makes alternative criteria available for establishing death in cases where the traditional standards are no longer adequate. Dr. S. Olinger states that human life is the sum of the phenomena directed by the cerebrum, that is, consciousness, awareness, memory, emotion and anticipation, without which the personal identifiable life of an individual cannot exist.[149] When he focuses on cerebral death as the determinant of human demise, he focuses on the quality of life, not simply its biological functioning.

The most attention to date has been given the criteria for irreversible coma established by the 1968 Ad Hoc Committee of the Harvard Medical School to Examine the Definition of Brain Death:

A. Unreceptivity and Unresponsivity:
There is total unawareness to externally applied stimuli and inner need and complete unresponsiveness. . . . Even the most intensely painful stimuli evoke no vocal or other response. . . .

B. No Movements or Breathing:
Observations by physicians covering a period of at least one hour are adequate to satisfy the criteria of no spontaneous muscular movements or spontaneous respiration or response to stimuli such as pain, touch, sound, or light. After a patient is on a mechanical respirator the total absence of spontaneous breathing may be established by turning off the respirator for three minutes and observing whether there is any effort on the part of the subject to breathe spontaneously.

C. No Reflexes:
Irreversible coma with abolition of central nervous system activity is evidenced in part by the absence of elicitable reflexes.

D. Flat Electroencephalogram:
Of great confirmatory value is the flat or isoelectric EEG . . . at least ten full minutes of recordings are desirable but twice that would be better.

E. All these tests must be repeated in 24 hours with no change.

F. There must be no evidence of *hypothermia or central nervous system depressants.*[150]

Reference is also made to the Duquesne University Law School criteria[151] and the World Medical Association criteria.[152]

In 1970, the Kansas legislature adopted the "alternative definitions" approach to defining death:

A person will be considered medically and legally dead if in the opinion of a physician, based on ordinary standards of medical practice, there is the absence of spontaneous respiratory and cardiac function and, because of the disease or condition which caused, directly or indirectly, these functions to cease, or because of the passage of time since these functions ceased, attempts at resuscitation are considered hopeless; and, in this event, death will have occurred at the time these functions ceased; or

A person will be considered medically and legally dead if in the opinion of a physician, based on ordinary standards of medical practice, there is the absence of spontaneous brain function; and if based on ordinary standards of medical practice, during reasonable attempts to either maintain or restore spontaneous circulatory or respiratory function in the absence of the aforesaid brain function, it appears that further attempts at resuscitation or supportive maintenance will not succeed, death will have occurred at the time when these conditions first coincide. Death is to be pronounced before artificial means of supporting respiratory and circulatory function are terminated and before any vital organ is removed for purposes of transplantation.

These alternative definitions of death are to be utilized for all purposes in this state, including trials of civil and criminal cases, any laws to the contrary notwithstanding.[153]

The Maryland statute[154] is modeled on the Kansas statute with small differences in the wording. The 1973 New Mexico statute[155] is quite similar to the Kansas and Maryland statutes, adding only that the law defining death does not affect the law of presumptive decedents in that state. However, the Virginia statute[156] defining death, modeled on the Kansas statute, includes several innovations. It makes clear that for death to have occurred in accordance with the brain-death definition, spontaneous respiration also must have ceased. Also, the Virginia statute requires that a consulting physician who is a specialist in neurology, neurosurgery or electroencephalography make the determination of brain death.[157]

As Hoffman and Van Cura point out in their discussion of a definition of death, there are three quanta of proof: (1) by a preponderance of the evidence; (2) by clear and convincing evidence, the degree of proof that will produce in the mind of the court or jury a firm conviction or belief; and (3) beyond a reasonable doubt to a moral certainty. In determining brain death, it is apparent that law, medicine and religion mandate a quantum of proof that may surpass beyond a reasonable doubt and to a moral certainty.[158]

Turning to the cases that involved the murder of unborn fetuses, the court said in *Evans* v. *New York*:

Death is the opposite of life; it is the termination of life; and death cannot be caused where there is no life. There must be a living child before its death can be produced.[159]

In another case, *Douglas* v. *Southwestern Life Insurance Company*, which involved accidental death benefits payable if death occurred within 90 days after an injury, the court said:

Death is not an ambiguous term, and there is no room for construction. Death has been defined as the termination of life and as the state or condition of being dead.[160]

In *Tucker's Administrator* v. *Lower*,[161] a transplant case in which a wrongful death action was brought against four doctors, the court permitted the jury (the trier of fact) to consider expert testimony concerning the decedent's isoelectric EEG among other factors in determining the time of death. The decedent was brought to the Medical College of Virginia Hospital after suffering a fall that caused massive head injuries. The next day at 11:30 A.M., he was placed on an artificial respirator. At 11:45 A.M., it was noted that his brain was irreparably damaged. At 3:30 P.M., support was withdrawn, and it was decided he was dead. At 3:35 P.M., he was reconnected to the respirator. At 4:32 P.M., his heart and kidneys were removed. The decedent's brother brought the action claiming decedent was not dead at the time his organs were removed. The jury decided that the removal of the decedent's heart was not the cause of his death.

In commenting on its own model Anatomical Gift Act, in a draft approved by the House of Delegates of both the American Medical Association and the American Bar Association, the National Conference of Commissioners on Uniform State Laws stated:

Subsection (a) leaves the determination of time of death to the attending or certifying physician. No attempt is made to define the uncertain point in time when life terminates. The real question is when irreversible changes have taken place that preclude return to normal brain activity and self-sustaining bodily functions. No reasonable statutory definition is possible. The answer depends upon many variables, differing from case to case. Reliance must be placed upon the judgment of the physician in attendance.[162]

In *Speight* v. *Sander*,[163] the 1950 New Hampshire case in which the defendant physician admitted injecting 40 cc of air into the blood stream of a suffering, hopelessly ill cancer patient, death resulted in less than ten minutes after the injection. Despite rather clear evidence, the jury acquitted the doctor. Fairey says there has never been a single indictment of a physician for mercy killing by omission.[164]

On the question of death, reference is made to articles by Crawford,[165] Wassmer[166] and the Twenty-Second World Medical Assembly.[167]

The question of whether the nurse should pronounce the patient dead arises because many nurses are being asked or expected to carry out this and other tasks at times and places that physicians find inconvenient. The review of the literature reveals that pronouncing a person dead is not always an easy matter, and it is the legal responsibility of the physician. When faced by the problem and the refusal of the physician to come and examine the patient, the nurse should chart the time and the signs and symptoms and actions taken, such as:

2:15 A.M. Respirations ceased, no carotid or apical pulse.

2:30 A.M. Pupils dilated, no reflexes present. Dr. John Doe notified.

Nurses should read current literature and think about their future as nurses before they all too willingly take on additional delegated medical tasks.

TERMINATING LIFE SUPPORT

"No Code" Orders

Lawsuits involving terminating life support began with the Karen Quinlan case, where the father of a young adult hospital patient who had been in a coma for a year and kept alive by a respirator sought judicial authority to remove the respirator so that she might die "with grace and dignity." The New Jersey Supreme Court, in a unanimous decision based on the patient's right to privacy, permitted the father to seek physicians and hospital officials who would agree to remove the respirator. The court said that if the responsible attending physicians conclude that there is no reasonable possibility of Karen Quinlan's return to cognitive and sapient life and that the life support apparatus be discontinued, they shall consult the hospital's ethics committee or similar group at the institution where she is hospitalized. If that consultative body agrees, the life support system may be withdrawn and the action shall be without any civil or criminal liability on the part of any participant, whether guardian, hospital, physician or others. Quinlan was removed from the respirator, and her heart and lungs continued to function.[168] On June 12, 1985, she finally died without regaining consciousness after more than 10 years in a nursing home.

In 1974 and 1980, The American Medical Association proposed that decisions not to resuscitate be formally entered in the patient's progress notes and communicated to all staff:

ORDERS NOT TO RESUSCITATE

The purpose of cardiopulmonary resuscitation is the prevention of sudden, unexpected death. Cardiopulmonary resuscitation is not indicated in certain situations, such as in cases of terminal irreversible illness where death is not unexpected or where prolonged cardiac arrest dictates the futility of resuscitation efforts. Resuscitation in these circumstances may represent a positive violation of an individual's right to die with dignity. When CPR is considered to be contraindicated for hospital patients, it is appropriate to indicate this on the physician's order sheet for the benefit of nurses and other personnel who may be called upon to initiate or participate in cardiopulmonary resuscitation.[169]

Many hospitals have published policies about withdrawal or nonapplication of life-prolonging measures. Examples are the Massachusetts General Hospital, Boston's Beth Israel Hospital and the Presbyterian-University Hospital in Pittsburgh.

In the case of *Superintendent of Belchertown State School* v. *Joseph Saikewicz*,[170] the initiation of life-prolonging chemotherapy for acute myeloblastic monocytic leukemia in a very retarded person was considered unnecessary. Joseph Saikewicz, who had an IQ of 10 and a mental age of two years, eight months, was 69 years old and had been in a state institution since the age of 14. After the Saikewicz case, some doctors, instead of writing no code orders, have written positive orders such as "comfort nursing measures only" or "routine nursing care only," which would unofficially mean that nurses were not to code the patient.[171]

In the case of Shirley Dinnerstein, a 67-year-old nursing home patient suffering from Alzheimer's disease sustained a severe stroke and was at high risk for cardiac or respiratory arrest. The petition by a son and daughter that a physician could enter a no code order without court adjudication was allowed. In the Dinnerstein case, the court said that the decision was one to be made by the primary physician, compatible with the wishes of the family and in compliance with medical practice standards.[172]

In re Storar and Eichner v. *Dillion*, the court said that statutory and decisional law consistently support the right of the competent adult to make his or her own decision to accept or reject treatment, although the treatment may be beneficial or even necessary to preserve the patient's life. While the patient Brother Fox was incompetent at the time the particular extraordinary means were applied to his body, the court found that statements had been made by him prior to his admission to the hospital as to his desire not to be subjected to extraordinary means of treatment. Hence the court said that Brother Fox had made the decision for himself before he became incompetent.[173]

In another case, Peter Cinque was an unmarried, 41-year-old former teacher who was blind and a double amputee as a result of diabetes. He also suffered from end-stage renal disease that required dialysis three times a week for four hours at a time, and he was wracked with pain from severe peripheral neuropathy. He discussed with his family his desire to discontinue treatment and secured their support. When Cinque refused dialysis, the hospital sought a court order compelling him to be treated. Two court-appointed psychiatrists found him coherent, relevant and clear in his purpose to stop dialysis and aware that it would result in his death. Cinque inquired of the pastor of his church and found that his decision to discontinue dialysis treatment did not violate the canons of the Catholic Church, since dialysis is an "extraordinary" rather than an "ordinary" means of treatment. Cinque's request to forego treatment was honored and he died.[174]

The basis for continuation of treatment as well as a "no code" must always begin with an evaluation of the patient's current condition or prognosis. Informed consent or refusal recognizes patients' increasingly active role in decisions related to their own health care. See *Schloendorff* v. *New York Hospital*[175] and Cushing's article on no code orders.[176]

Decisions on Food and Fluid in Life-Sustaining Measures

In the case of *In re Conroy*,[177] the guardian filed a complaint to obtain a judicial declaration that he had the right to have the nasogastric tube removed from the 84-year-old Conroy. Conroy was unable to swallow sufficient quantities of food and water to live without the help of the nasogastric tube. Her doctor testified that she was not brain dead, not comatose and not in a chronic vegetative state. Although she did not respond to verbal stimuli, she followed movements with her eyes, used her hands to scratch herself, and was able to move her head, neck, arms and hands voluntarily. An administrator-nurse testified that Conroy smiled when she was massaged or when her hair was combed, and moaned when she was fed. After a hearing at which the nephew-guardian, nurse-administrator, two doctors and a clergyman testified, the court ordered the nasogastric tube removed. The decision was made even though the removal almost certainly would lead to death by starvation and dehydration within a few days, and even though the death might be a painful one for the patient. During appeal, the nasogastric tube remained in place. The Superior Court of New Jersey reversed the decision. (Miss Conroy died of natural causes during the appeal.) Points for the nurse include: (1) If an institution where the nurse works does not have an ethics committee to consider such cases, the nurse should request the service of a person who can serve as a resource. Nurses, physicians, attorneys and members of the clergy are appropriate persons to serve on ethics committees to study treatment decisions. (2) Assessment of the patient and its recording on the chart are very important. Nurse Rittel's assessment of Conroy's conscious reactions are most important in concluding that Conroy was not in a chronic vegetative state, and is the key in the outcome of the case. (3) Nurse Rittel's willingness to testify on behalf of the patient is commendable. This nurse was a patient advocate.

In the Barber[178] case, a patient who underwent surgery for the closure of an ileostomy suffered a cardiorespiratory arrest and was placed on life-support equipment while in the recovery room. Three days later, the physicians decided he had suffered severe brain damage, leaving him in a vegetative state that was probably permanent, and so informed the family. Then, the family requested the hospital to remove the patient from all machines that were sustaining life, and this was done. The patient continued to breathe without equipment but showed no signs of improvement. Two days later, the doctors, after consulting with the family, ordered removal of the intravenous (IV) tubes that provided hydration and nourishment. The patient received nursing comfort measures but died. The patient's two attending physicians were charged with murder. The appellate court of California reversed the superior court and said that the omission to continue treatment under the circumstances was not an unlawful failure to perform a legal duty. In the Barber case, assessment by doctor and nurse showed that the patient made no conscious response to outside stimuli. Nurses should support the patient and family through continued nursing care to provide cleanliness and comfort and to preserve the dignity of the person who is dying.

In a much publicized case, the court ruled that a 12-year-old child suffering from Ewing's sarcoma was to get cancer treatment over the father's religious objections. Without treatment, the child would have died in six to nine months. The Director of the Offices of Human Services was designated to act on behalf of the child in consenting to necessary treatment.[179]

One State's Procedures for Terminating Life Support

The Florida court set forth procedures to be followed for terminal patients who do not want life-sustaining procedures:

1. Patient must be certified by two physicians as being terminal.
2. Patient must have previously indicated an intention not to be placed on life support systems.
3. His guardian may apply to the probate court for authority to instruct any health care provider to remove or not to furnish life-sustaining procedures.
   a. Application should be expedited.
   b. Standard of proof should be clear and convincing evidence.
4. Any person acting in good faith under a court order would not be liable in a civil or criminal action.[180]

Living Will

The California legislature became the first in the nation to approve a "right-to-die" bill, which was later signed by Governor Brown. The measure enables terminally ill patients to sign a so-called living will, a document instructing their doctors to withdraw or withhold life-sustaining procedures when those efforts "serve no purpose except to artificially delay the moment of death." Such a will or instruction, concerning what is to be done if the patient is terminally ill and near death, may be written by a person at any time. Under the new law, at least two physicians must state in writing that the patient is terminally ill. The bill requires all living wills to be signed by two witnesses, neither of whom can be a relative or a doctor. The attending doctor could not be liable for the death, and insurance companies could not construe such deaths as suicides in order to withhold life insurance payments.

The first two paragraphs of the Living Will are:

Death is as much a reality as birth, growth, maturity and old age—it is the one certainty of life. If the time comes when I, _____, can no longer take part in decisions for my own future, let this statement stand as an expression of my wishes, while I am still of sound mind.

If the situation should arise in which there is no reasonable expectation of my recovery from physical or mental disability, I request that I be allowed to die and not to be kept alive by artificial means or "heroic measures." I do not fear death itself as much as the indignities of deterioration, dependence and hopeless pain. I, therefore, ask that medication be mercifully administered to me to alleviate suffering even though this may hasten the moment of death.[181]

Although this will has the merit of brevity and simplicity, it is, as Bok[182] has pointed out, vague in such a way that real risks of misinterpretation arise. Precisely what do we mean by "physical" or "mental disability?" What happens if physicians, nurses or close relatives disagree with the intent of the will? Who will resolve the differences in interpretation of the key terms of the will? Further, there are many matters at the close of life in which people differ considerably, such as accurate knowledge of one's condition, amount of medicine one wants to receive, and various disabling conditions that some find acceptable and others find intolerable. The will makes no provision for such individual differences. Anyone who is interested in the matter should compare this document with "A Christian Affirmation of Life,"[183] "A Will to Live,"[184] "If I Become Ill and Unable to Manage My Own Affairs"[185] and "Directions for My Care."[186] Such a comparative study of documents is the least a person owes himself. The vague terminology of the Living Will, subject as it is to a variety of interpretations, should raise a flag of caution.

As pointed out previously, the decision in the Quinlan case is controversial, and the Quinlan case could set a dangerous precedent. The terms "cognitive" and "sapient" in the future must be uniformly understood and minimally susceptible to subjective interpretation, or we face trouble, as pointed out in a previous article, "Choose Life or Let Die."[187]

Legislation for terminating life-support systems in the form of "right-to-die" laws has been enacted in a large number of states: Alabama, Alaska, Arkansas, California, Delaware, Florida, Georgia, Idaho, Illinois, Kansas, Mississippi, North Carolina, Nevada, New Mexico, Oregon, Tennessee, Texas, Vermont, Virginia, Washington, West Virginia and Wisconsin as well as the District of Columbia.

ORGAN TRANSPLANTATION*

From the first kidney transplant in 1962 and Dr. Bernard's pioneering work with heart transplantation in 1967 to the recent experimental baboon heart transplant and artificial heart replacements, nurses, doctors and society have been fascinated with organ transplantation. In the Uniform Anatomical Gift Act, adopted in all 50 states, provision was made for organ donation, and the matter of organ procurement thus considered. According to law, persons who have filed a donor card can donate their organs after declaration of death, yet almost no physician or hospital will in fact remove organs without permission of next of kin. Although such permission is not legally required, it is apparently sought for personal, psychological or public relations reasons. However, relatives are more likely to agree to the donation if there is a signed donor card.[188] A vigorous campaign to educate the public and health professionals, including doctors and nurses, would be very helpful. The media could increase awareness about the need for public cooperation and the benefits to society of an active donor program. Informative documentaries and public service announcements would seem preferable to the publicizing of isolated, dramatic cases.

Across the United States, brain death has been recognized by the courts and legislatures.[189] Where doctors and nurses are unclear about this, education is needed. A new level of awareness was reached in 1984 with the proclamation by President Reagan of National Organ Donation Awareness Week, April 22–28. With such activities, the giving of organs is gaining public acceptance.

Legal Development

On October 19, 1984, President Reagan signed into law the National Organ Procurement Act.[190] This Act makes it illegal to buy or sell organs and sets up a 25-member task force to identify ways to increase organ supply. It also allocates $25 million over three years to provide:

---

*This section first appeared as an article in Nursing Management (in press).

○ Financial assistance for organ procurement organizations.
○ Prerequisites for such organizations.
○ The development of a computerized network for procurement and transplantation.
○ A scientific registry for patients and transplant procedures.

At the Federal level, the concern has been with increasing the supply of transplantable organs by making the organ procurement system more efficient.

At the state level, the Illinois Transplant Society has issued a free pamphlet, "Organ Donation: The Present for the Future."[191] Designed to promote organ donations, it is written for the lay person in clear, easy-to-understand language. In October 1984, the *Report of the Massachusetts Task Force on Organ Transplantation*, of which George J. Annas was chairman, was published by the Department of Public Health of Massachusetts.[192] As the report points out, the major public policy issue at the state level has been how to move simultaneously toward three goals: (1) quality of services, (2) equality of access to services and (3) cost containment.[193]

Need Versus Availability

A growing problem is the shortage of available organs for transplant operations.[194] There are 7000 patients on waiting lists for a kidney transplant. At any one time, there are 50 to 75 patients awaiting a heart transplant. Some 200 patients are reported waiting for a liver transplant, and doctors estimate that between 2000 and 5000 liver-disease patients are candidates for this operation. This does not take into account the many other patients waiting for cornea, pancreas and combined heart-and-lung transplants.

The success of transplant operations within the past several years is quite remarkable. In a 1983 study, 86 percent of recipients of kidneys from unrelated donors survived one year, and 78 percent survived to three years. Of those receiving kidneys from related donors, 95 percent survived one year, and 91 percent survived three years.[195] In the most recent phase of heart transplantation, December 1980 through May 1983, survival rates have improved to 82 percent at one year, and 78 percent at two years and an estimated 65 percent at five years.[196] For 23 heart-and-lung transplants performed at Stanford, 11 out of 17 patients are alive, including the first patient operated on in March 1981.[197] For liver transplants, one year survival has increased from approximately 30 percent in 1979 to about 60 percent in 1982, according to Starzl.[198] This dramatic improvement in survival rates appears to be the result of at least three medical factors: improved clinical and operative management, improved immunosuppression (including the introduction of cyclosporin A) and improved patient selection.

Kidney Transplants

Transplantation of kidneys differs from that in other terminal organ-specific diseases in two ways: (1) Since a person has two kidneys and can live comfortably with one, it is possible to obtain a healthy, well-matched kidney from a living donor as well as from one recently deceased. (2) Dialysis is an alternative life-sustaining measure. Therefore, patients with kidney failure can be treated by dialysis or a transplant, if available.

Kidney transplantation has raised the question of public financing of costly high-technology procedures. In 1982, more than 5300 kidney transplants were performed.[199] Except for the end-stage renal disease (ESRD) program of Medicare, there is no Federal policy of organ transplantation.[200] Several commentators have pointed out the disproportionate share of Medicare funds spent for ESRD recipients. For example, in 1980, ESRD beneficiaries were less than half of 1 percent of the total beneficiaries for Supplementary Medical Insurance, but ESRD costs represented 5 percent of the total medical budget for these services. Also, the United States provides dialysis for patients at a rate that far exceeds that of Europe and Israel.[201]

Determination of Priorities

Organ transplants are extremely expensive: the fully allocated average one-year cost is $230,000 to $340,000 for liver transplants and $170,000 to $200,000 for heart transplants. This is about 4 to 10 times the cost of other expensive medical technologies.[202] The Massachusetts Task Force on Organ Transplantation stated that, in the determination of need (DON), all currently available health care services should be presumed to have a higher priority than transplantation.[203] In addition, the applicant should have the burden of demonstrating that transplantation has a higher priority than any other currently available health care service from which organ transplantation diverts funds or support systems. Transplants of livers and hearts, the task force stated, should be permitted only if access to this technology can be made independent of the individual's ability to pay for it and if the transplantation does not adversely affect the provision of other public health care services with a higher priority.

The Massachusetts Task Force made six recommendations:

1. Liver and heart transplants should be introduced in a controlled manner that provides opportunity for effective evaluation and review of its clinical, social and economic aspects by a public accountable body after an initial phase of 2–3 years of limited transplantation.

2. The decision of where extreme and expensive medical technologies, like heart and liver transplantation, should be generally available should be made only after the clinical, social, and economic consequences of introducing the procedure . . . are studied and reviewed by a publicly accountable body.

3. In making a . . . DON for heart and liver transplantation, the Public Health Council should attempt to minimize and track the total incremental cost of adding [them] to the health care system.

4. Until . . . end of Phase 1, hospitals proposing to do these procedures . . . should not be given a certificate of need (CON) unless they agree to 1) support the operating expenses for [them] within current reimbursements set by the hospital's maximum allowable cost under Ch. 372, Acts of 1982 provided an exception . . . for the cost of cyclosporine; 2) collect evaluative data on the costs, outcomes, and displacements caused by transplant candidates . . . ; and 3) have the protocols reviewed, approved and monitored by the Institutional Review Board (IRB). . . .

5. Patient selection criteria should be public, fair, and equitable. Primary screening should be based on medical suitability . . . [for] those who can benefit the most from it in terms of probability of living for a significant period of time with a reasonable prospect for rehabilitation. If there are insufficient resources . . . selection from the medically suitable group should be based primarily on a first-come, first-served basis. . . .

6. If more than one hospital is granted a CON to do heart or liver transplantation, all hospitals so involved should be required to coordinate services in a way that comes as close as possible to a single, integrated medical service. . . . "[204]

Selection of Transplant Candidates

For the rationing of scarce medical resources, there are four major approaches: (1) the market approach, (2) the selection committee approach, (3) the lottery approach and (4) the "customary" approach.[205]

One of several approaches to organ transplantation, the market approach, would provide an organ to everyone who could pay for it. A presidential commission studying health care access has said: "Society has a moral obligation to ensure adequate care for all."[206]

An example of the screening committee approach is the Seattle Selection Committee. One of its lay members is quoted as saying:

> The choices were hard. . . . I remember voting against a young woman who was a known prostitute. I found I couldn't vote for her, rather than another candidate, a young wife and mother. I also voted against a young man who, until he learned he had renal failure, had been a ne'er-do-well, a real playboy. He promised he would reform his character, go back to school, and soon, if only he were selected for treatment. But I felt I'd lived long enough to know that a person like that won't really do what he was promising at the time.[207]

There was a general negative reaction against this type of arbitrary device when the bases of the selection committee were known.

The ultimate equalizer is the lottery approach, which puts equality ahead of every other value. It makes no distinctions about a candidate's potential for survival or quality of life and, in a sense, is a "mindless" method.[208] A first-come, first-served system is a type of lottery because referrals to a transplant program are generally done randomly in time.

The "customary" approach in the United States permits individual physicians to select their patients on the basis of "medical criteria" or "clinical suitability." This might contain much of what we would consider "social worth" criteria if it were explicitly stated.[209] In most cases, a combination approach is used. Any approach, to be socially acceptable, must be fair, efficient and reflective of important social values. The medical screening criteria should be uniform in the state, reviewed and approved by an ethics committee with significant public representation, filed with a public agency and made readily available to the public for comment.[210] To the extent that organs are specifically tissue- and size-matched and are made available to the most appropriate candidate, the organ distribution system itself will be a natural random allocation system.

Religious Considerations

With respect to the Roman Catholic view, the transplant of an organ (such as a kidney) from a living person would seem to be covered by the following directive from the United States bishops:

> The transplantation of organs from living donors is morally permissible when the anticipated benefit to the recipient is proportionate to the harm done to the donor, provided that the loss of such organ(s) does not deprive the donor of life itself nor of the functional integrity of his body.[211]

According to the *Massachusetts Task Force Report*, Pius XII held that, once death was established, organs could morally be removed for use by another provided two conditions were met: (1) the cadaver be treated with respect and (2) that consent be obtained from the deceased before his death or from those having a right to act for him after his death.[212]

While both rich and poor are entitled to have their delicate human feelings for the bodies of their deceased relatives considered, the papal teachings state:

> On the other hand, the public must be educated. It must be explained with intelligence and respect that to consent explicitly or tacitly to serious damage to the integrity of the corpse in the interest of those who are suffering is no violation of the reverence due the dead since it is justified by valid reasons.[213]

Moreover, the Roman Catholic Church's notion of distributive justice would call on the government to apportion fairly the benefits and burdens or organ transplants among its citizens.[214]

With regard to Protestant Christianity, no one can write for it as a whole because of the multiple denominations and traditions and because there is no single teaching authority. However, as Professor J. Robert Nelson of the Boston University School of Theology points out, there are four Biblical doctrines relevant to organ transplantation:

> 1. Each human being is created by God as an integrated unity of body, soul, mind and spirit. . . . One's body is a "temple of the Holy Spirit" and a "member of Christ" wrote St. Paul . . . (I Corinthians 6:15, 19, 20).
> 2. Jesus himself was best known as a divinely empowered healer of all manner of diseases. . . . (Luke 6:9).
> 3. Since the divine power of life was at Jesus' disposal, he willed . . . life in all its fullness for all people. . . .
> 4. And yet, in the last analysis, said Jesus, it is one's righteousness—the good, obedient, purposeful, loving will—which is more important than physical, bodily well-being. . . .[215]

Professor Nelson states that neither living organ donations nor cadaver donation is proscribed by Protestant Christianity and that each person's integrity and free decision must be respected. Concerning the perplexing social and economic problems created by transplants, Protestant Christians would urge that resolutions be sought only on the firm platform of opportunity and equitable treatment for as many persons as available resources allow.[216]

With respect to Jewish attitudes the task force report says:

> The infinite value of all human beings is a central and unequivocable principle in Judaism. To save a single life is regarded as if one has saved the entire world. Almost all ritual requirements may be suspended in the face of any danger to life. The duty to heal the sick is seen as a religious imperative.[217]

In accordance with this view, most rabbinic authorities state that organ transplants that serve to perpetuate life are permitted.[218] Where an organ is taken from a dead donor, transplant procedures must follow these guidelines:

1. Nothing shall be done to prepare the critically ill donor for transplant surgery if this procedure hastens death in any way.

2. Under Jewish law, death is determined by cessation of all spontaneous respiratory and circulatory activities for a sufficiently long period of time to make resuscitation medically impossible.[219] Conservative and reform rabbinic authorities will more readily accept "brain death" criteria.[220]

3. It is recommended to assign such judgements as "time of death" to a team of physicians not involved in the transplantation procedures.

4. Consent of the patient or next of kin.

5. "While . . . the use of an organ . . . permits the suspension of laws regarding desecration of the dead, every measure should be maintained to respect the dignity of the body and its burial in accordance with Jewish Law and practice."[221]

It is also permitted, but not obligatory, for a donor to endanger his or her life or health to supply an organ to a recipient whose life would be saved by this act.[222]

Concerning the allocation of limited resources, the *Jewish Compendium on Medical Ethics* states that the inclusion or exclusion of the patient's social value is unacceptable. It is also unacceptable to distinguish among patients with real therapeutic hope on the basis of their varying potential for recovery. The practice of triage, for example, is fundamentally incompatible with Jewish values and law.[223]

Transplantation represents a high-technology example of medical and nursing care that can be of real benefit to patients.[224] The Massachusetts Task Force Report and its recommendations will likely become a model for other states, and nurses should be familiar with them. Because there are insufficient organs available for everyone who would benefit from a transplant, some form of rationing seems likely. Nurses should be familiar with the various schemes of selecting transplantation candidates. Moreover, nurses, if they are to be co-professionals with other health professionals, must take the time to serve on committees and task forces dealing with organ transplantation.

LEGAL ASPECTS OF END-STAGE RENAL DISEASE AS IT AFFECTS PATIENT CARE*

In caring for the patient with end-stage renal disease, doctors and nurses are faced with legal problems. For example, do patients, weary with treatment, have the right to terminate their treatment and thereby to terminate their lives?

In a New York case, Justice Cardoza, then on the Supreme Court of New York, stated: "Every human being of adult years and sound mind has a right to determine what shall be done with his own body, and a surgeon who performs an operation without the patient's consent commits an assault for which he is liable in damages."[225]

In this case, a patient had surgery for a malignancy and was referred to a radiologist who administered cobalt treatments in which the patient was seriously burned. Where the patient had not been told about the risks of radiation, the court held that the radiologist has a positive duty to disclose such risks as a matter of law.

In *Salgo* v. *Leland Stanford Board of Trustees*, where the patient signed a consent for aortography without understanding the risk of permanent paralysis, the court said:

> A physician violates his duty to his patient and subjects himself to liability if he withholds any facts which are necessary to form the basis of an intelligent consent by the patient to the proposed treatment. Likewise, the physician must not minimize the known danger of a procedure or operation in order to induce his patient's consent.[226]

The intervention of the courts to secure lifesaving medical treatment at times involves minors whose parents express religious objections to blood transfusions and operations. Here, resort to the state's traditional *parens patriae* authority has uniformly upheld state interference with parents' control in order to safeguard the children.[227]

---

*This section originally appeared as an article in *Supervisor Nurse*, 10:39–40, 45, December 1979.

Several questions arise, such as: Does refusal to intervene entail acceptance of a right to die in the context of suicide and euthanasia? Or does it matter that the patient has dependents who will be disadvantaged by his or her death?[228] Cantor states that if the patient demonstrates the requisite state of mind and persists in refusal of treatment, that decision should be respected, though tantamount to suicide.[229] That a patient wishing to die should be permitted to decline treatment, as in continued renal dialysis, has distinct implications for legal approaches to suicide generally. If the person whose decision to die is clearly competent, deliberate and firm, he or she should be permitted to die. The form of self-destruction should not matter.

The deliberate killing of a person suffering from a painful and terminal illness by a physician or other person is a general definition of euthanasia or mercy killing. The withholding of medical treatment or therapy may be considered a form of euthanasia. Although in criminal law an affirmative act of euthanasia constitutes homicide, the legal status of the physician who merely withholds treatment at the patient's request is in great dispute with authorities, such as Glanville Williams and Yale Kamisar.[230] It is worth noting that all sources agree that no physician has ever been convicted for any such crime.

As Cantor suggests, a point is inevitably reached in the demise of the terminally ill patient when medical treatment no longer preserves life, but rather prolongs the act of dying. This last situation is met by authorities who state that extraordinary measures need not be used to keep the patient alive. This would permit disconnecting extraordinary equipment. However, no one has yet defined precisely the term "extraordinary." Blood transfusions and intravenous feeding are probably considered ordinary, whereas heart-lung machines, artificial respirators, and renal dialysis are not.[231] Cantor states that a patient's request to terminate further therapy should be honored, but affirmative acts, such as injections to terminate patients' lives, should not be condoned.[232] Since it is not currently criminal for a physician to defer to a patient's decision to refuse medical treatment, no statutory changes are needed to sustain refusals of treatment.[233] Inasmuch as the patient declining treatment normally remains alive for a period of time, she or he has some opportunity to express any change of mind.

When the patient declining care is the parent of a minor child, the courts have been likely to appoint a guardian to authorize treatment, as in the celebrated case of *Application of the President and Directors of Georgetown College*.[234] There, a 25-year-old woman, the mother of a 7-month-old child, had lost one third of her body's blood supply as a result of a ruptured ulcer. She refused on religious grounds, as did her husband, to authorize a blood transfusion. A circuit judge did authorize the transfusion and she lived; his main ground for so doing was an extension of the *parens patriae* doctrine, contending that the authorization would entail only minor infringement of the patient's religious beliefs.

In *John F. Kennedy Memorial Hospital* v. *Heston*,[235] court intervention was sought even in the absence of minor children. A single 22-year-old woman was severely injured in an automobile accident, and the court authorized a blood transfusion over the objection of the woman and her mother rather than subject the professional staff to the task of assessing the patient's competency or the validity of a release.

A strong case opposing interference with a patient's decision is *In re Brooks' Estate*.[236] In that case, a woman who was a Jehovah's Witness refused a transfusion necessary to the treatment of a peptic ulcer, and her spouse and adult children did not oppose her refusal. The unanimous decision of the Supreme Court of Illinois upheld the patient's right to determine her own fate. The court said:

> Even though we may consider [Brooks'] beliefs unwise, foolish or ridiculous, in the absence of an overriding danger to society we may not permit interference therewith . . . for the sole purpose of compelling her to accept medical treatment forbidden by her religious principles, and previously refused by her with full knowledge of the probable consequences.[237]

In the case of In re Raasch,[238] an unreported 1972 Milwaukee case, a judge refused to appoint a temporary guardian for a 77-year-old woman who refused to permit amputation of a gangrenous leg. Although the patient was physically weak, the court noted her clear determination to avoid the surgical procedure and ruled that competent adults have the prerogative of making life-and-death medical decisions about their own bodies. The court said: "I believe we should have [the patient] depart in God's own peace."[239] Several weeks after the decision, the patient died.

Since people afflicted with terminal illness, such as end-stage renal disease, rarely die at home, the success of medicine has shifted the place of dying to public and private care institutions, thus transferring control over treatment away from patients and their families to the health care provider and the state. However, the terminally ill patient may wish to forego treatment and suffering, for a variety of reasons. If courts take informed consent seriously, they must recognize the right of a competent terminal patient, such as those in end-stage renal disease, to forego treatment. Proper tests and measures to assure sufficient comprehension of relevant material for competency will meet society's interest in minimizing incorrect decisions.[240] The better view is that the patient, whether terminal or not, has a right to refuse treatment.

REFUSAL OF BLOOD TRANSFUSION

When patients refuse treatment and thus invite their own death, physicians, nurses and other health personnel are confronted by legal and moral problems. For years, there was the legal maxim to the effect that any competent individual has the right to refuse treatment and thus to die, and the law does not compel her or him to accept available help. In recent years, the courts have made many exceptions to this rule.

Much of the problem revolves around patients who have religious convictions against blood transfusions. These patients belong to two groups: (1) believers in healing by faith who oppose all forms of customary medical therapy, including blood transfusions; and (2) Jehovah's Witnesses, who accept customary medical therapy except for blood transfusions. The widow and children of an employee were not allowed to recover benefits under the Workmen's Compensation Act when he refused a needed blood transfusion following a serious injury on the job.[241] When medical science prescribes a blood transfusion for a child, the child has a right to live, and the court will protect him and will not permit him to be deprived of life because his parents' religious views oppose blood transfusion.[242] The court has held that temporarily depriving parents of a minor child for the purpose of giving him a blood transfusion is not depriving them of religious freedom and of their parental rights.[243] A mother's custody of her children had as a condition the elimination of the need for her consent to necessary blood transfusions.[244]

The rule with respect to competent adults is less clear. The court may uphold the right of an adult patient to refuse a blood transfusion even at the risk of life.[245] A release of liability form, signed by the patient, protects the hospital. In a case in which a patient was alert and competent while considering his decision, and no minors were involved, the court did not overrule his decision, and held that refusal of a needed transfusion was not the equivalent of suicide, which was a violation of state law.[246] However, when a patient had a massive hemorrhage from an ulcer, and the precariousness of her condition made a blood transfusion necessary, which both she and her husband refused, the court ordered a transfusion.[247] In a similar case, a Connecticut court ordered a blood transfusion for a Jehovah's Witness who refused permission for it.[248]

A court has also ordered a life-saving operation on a comatose patient whose wife refused consent.[249]

Serum hepatitis is a risk assumed by patients who received blood transfusion, and no damages are awarded.[250]

LEGAL IMPLICATIONS OF THE DRGs*

Diagnostic Related Groups (DRGs) came into existence as a result of the assumption that a large amount of expensive, acute medical care was being given wastefully and expensively. Beginning with the acute care hospitals and their medical staffs, DRGs were supposed to offer sufficient financial incentives to eliminate the waste and inefficiency without markedly limiting the patients' necessary access to high-quality care. The elderly under Medicare were singled out for this cost-control plan.

There are legal, ethical and economic reasons for physicians, nurses and hospital administrators to practice high-quality medical care.[251] Peer Review Organizations (PROs), created by the Social Security Amendments of 1983, are a major quality-assurance mechanism.[252] The respective codes of ethics commit health providers to high-quality care, and the threat of malpractice lawsuits provides an extra stimulus.

On the negative side of DRGs, two problems loom: (1) some form of rationing of health care and (2) decreased access to health care. DRGs will force some hospitals to close, others to specialize in certain types of care and still others to limit the number of patients—especially Medicare patients, who are costly to care for. Both factors have implications for malpractice.[253] The question arises as to whether physicians and hospitals are the most appropriate rationers of health care. Next, if they are, what are the risks for them?

The report of the President's Commission for the Study of Ethical Problems in Medicine and Biomedicine and Behavioral Research: Securing Access to Health Care acknowledges the difficulties and societal responsibilities in securing access to health care.[254] Traditionally, the patient has looked to the physician and caregiver to act only in her or his best interest. In the United States, the caregiver has seldom been constrained by economic factors when deciding what is best for the patient. Now, under the DRGs, the health care provider must consider the pursestrings, and this will limit the patient's trust in the caregiver to put her or his interests ahead of money.

---

*This section first appeared as an article in *Nursing Management* (in press).

On the other hand, today's health givers have expanded responsibilities—one of which may be the allocation of scarce resources. No one has a more comprehensive assessment of the patient's physical, psychological, economic and spiritual resources. Already we find that the number of patients needing kidneys, livers, and hearts exceeds the number of organs available for transplantation. Some priorities and guidelines must be established to determine who gets the needed operations.

The British National Health Service has established limits on resource availability, and individual caregivers must make choices within the overall constraints. As Aaron and Schwartz point out, it is not always easy to say that not all patients who can benefit by it can undergo dialysis.[255] As Mariner states, Great Britain has already circumscribed the range of choices, and the physician is free to act within that range in the patient's best interest.[256] If health caregivers in the United States are responsible for rationing, they may have to balance patient welfare and health care costs, which is a more difficult position.

While Professor Kapp suggests that the informed consent process may mitigate the physician-patient problem under the DRGs and may allow patients to make intelligent decisions in view of costs and available treatments, Mariner cites three reasons why this is not necessarily true.[257] First, all patients are not capable of making an informed consent about their personal treatment with respect to social and economic objectives. Second, all patients are not able to pay for treatments and services that they wish to receive but that are not financed under the DRGs. Third, the DRG system provides little, if any, financial incentive to the physician to spend extra time with his or her patients concerning the economic considerations that influence their judgment.

With the prospects for diminished quality in health care, patient dissatisfaction and lawsuits may increase. Patients or their families who are unhappy with their health care rendered under the DRGs may sue the physician, nurse, hospital or all three parties together.

What are some of the possible causes of such lawsuits? As Kapp points out, first, the patient may claim she or he received less diagnostic or therapeutic health care while in the hospital and that her or his injury was the result of the health caregivers' negligent omission.[258]

The DRGs put a premium on getting the patient out of the hospital as soon as possible. Reimbursement is based on the diagnosis and the average stay. If the hospital keeps the patient more days, it loses money. If the hospital keeps the patient fewer days, it makes money.

Both the PROs, which the government relies on for quality assurance, and hospitals' internal review mechanisms have incentives to limit the amount of in-hospital care. Nursing staffs are being reduced by layoffs and attrition, and the nurses who remain have increased workloads. As more patients are covered by fewer staff, quality care suffers. All nurses make more errors of omission or commission when overworked and tired. The hospital's public relations also suffers in such situations. As the Medical Malpractice Commission pointed out 10 years ago, public relations is the leading cause of malpractice actions.

Older patients, the ones with whom the DRGs currently deal, move more slowly, perhaps think and react less rapidly and are often confused or irritated by quick, "efficient" care—whatever the cause. In the name of efficiency (because it's quicker), nursing staff are tempted to do many things for older patients that, given time, they could do for themselves. This is counterproductive to rehabilitation efforts and fosters a loss of independence in the long run. The more intelligent patients will recognize the situation's negative impact on quality care and may be tempted to even the score by a malpractice suit.

Premature hospital discharge is a second DRG-related legal issue, as Kapp has pointed out.[259] Discharge planning, which should begin with the patient's admission, will probably receive more emphasis under the DRGs, because it is a way to lessen or avoid discharge-related patient injuries. Nevertheless, teaching and counseling components may be regarded by physicians and hospital administrators as an area where economy comes first. This problem is compounded by a shortage of home health care facilities (although they are rapidly increasing in many areas) and nursing homes equipped to care for the acutely ill older patient. Make no mistake about it, patients are being discharged "quicker and sicker" under the DRGs.[260] Nurses will have to make time to do adequate discharge planning. However, they may be faced with endeavoring to teach a patient who is still too ill to properly understand the material being "taught." Hence, health caregivers helping patients after hospital discharge will face an increased need for patient teaching.

As Kapp points out, the patient may also be injured by excessive care under the DRGs.[261] This is true because physicians, in an effort to qualify for a DRG paying a higher sum of money, may order an unnecessary test or surgical procedure. Whether or not this is an example of defensive medicine, it defeats the purpose of the DRGs.

However, there may not be as many malpractice lawsuits under the DRGs as one might anticipate at first. This is because of the way lawyers are paid in most instances. For the most part, U.S. lawyers in malpractice lawsuits are paid on a contingency-fee basis. This means that if the lawyer wins, she or he gets one third or more of the award—but nothing if she or he loses. The vast majority of elderly patients cannot afford to retain or pay a lawyer on an hourly basis.

Under the United States legal system, awards to older clients are usually less than to younger clients. One way of computing the size of the award is by multiplying the number of years of working life expectancy times annual earnings and adding the cost of medical and nursing care. Accordingly, if a client is a 64-year-old photographer (as in a recent Florida case where a toxic preservative was accidentally injected into the patient's spine leaving him comatose with little hope of recovery), the chances are that the sum recovered would be less than if he were 40 years old. Consequently, the elderly patient who can sue for negligence under the DRGs may have more difficulty securing good legal services, because the case may be worth less.[262, 263] However, there will be a number of lawsuits under the DRG, because the American public expects the highest standards of health care. To the extent they are disappointed with the quality of health care under the DRGs, they will bring lawsuits.

What are some of the implications of the DRGs for nurses as health caregivers?[264] First, we must accept the fact that some kind of cost controls have to be applied to health care. As Pastor Niemoller said in World War II, we need "the courage to change the things that can be changed, the serenity to accept the things that cannot be changed and the wisdom to know the difference." Second, nurses, physicians and other health caregivers must cooperate with each other and seriously strive to achieve cost reduction. Hospital administrators must recognize the ethical and professional responsibilities of nurses, physicians and other caregivers to their patients or clients. Third, nurses, physicians and other health caregivers must work together with hospital administrators in sharing scarce technical equipment and resources. Under the DRGs, it will no longer be feasible to duplicate resources wastefully. Fourth, there must be more and better communication with patients in the area of informed consent. As Light points out, we are moving from a professional concept of the best care at any price to good care at the best price, and patients must be informed sufficiently to decide whether they want to pay for health care that the regulations disallow.[265] Fifth, nurses, physicians and other health caregivers will have to do better documentation: what was done and when, why it was done and what was the decision based upon. Procedures that we do must have a basis in scientific evidence, not merely because "we have always done them this way." Nursing procedure manuals need thorough documentation.[266] Sixth, nurses, physicians and other health caregivers will need to supervise students and staff more closely to prevent errors—in medical care or in documentation—that could lead to lack of reimbursement or to lawsuits.

As DRG-influenced lawsuits are settled in the courts, nurses, physicians, hospitals and other health caregivers will learn the impact of this new factor in health care and nursing. One thing is certain, and that is we must keep up-to-date with legal developments and their ethical implications.

References

1. Merton, R. K.: Some Thoughts on Professions in American Society (address), Brown University, 1960, p. 9.
2. Roe v. Wade, U.S. Sup. Ct. No. 17–18, 410 U.S. 113 (U.S. St. Ct., 1973). See also Regan, W. A., Jr.: The Abortion Ruling, Commentary, Hosp. Prog., 54–90, March 1973.
3. State v. Shoemaker, 157 Iowa 176, 138 N.W. 381 (1912).
4. Rex v. Bourne, 3 A11 E.R. 615, 186 L.T. 87 (1938), (1939) 1 K.B. 687; Br. Med. J., 1938, 2, 199; 6 Univ. Chi. L. Rev. 107 (1939).
5. Supra, note 2.
6. Cf. Shaffer, T. L.: The Abortion Ruling, Commentary, Hosp. Prog., 54–84, March 1973.
7. Doe v. Bolton, U.S. Sup. Ct. No. 70–40, 1973.
8. Supra, note 4, Regan, W. A., Jr., p. 95.
9. OB/GYN Nurse Group Takes Stand on Abortion, Am. J. Nurs., 72:1311, July 1972.
10. Doe v. Bellin Memorial Hospital, U.S. Dist. Ct. E.D. Wis. No. 73-C-230 (1973).
11. Doe v. Bellin Memorial Hospital, 479 F. 2d 756 (U.S.C.A. 7th Cir., 1973).
12. Texas Attorney General Opinion, No. 4–369, Aug. 1974.
13. Wisconsin v. Yoder, 92 S. Ct. 1526 (1972).
14. Braunfield v. Brown, 366 U.S. 599 (1961).
15. Reynolds v. United States, 98 U.S. 145 (1878).
16. Church of Latter-day Saints v. United States, 136 U. S.i (1980).
17. Natale v. Sisters of Mercy, 52 N.W. 2d 701 (Iowa, 1952).
18. Schulte, E. J.: Abortion Decision May Set Precedent to Resolve 1st Amendment Conflicts, Hosp. Prog., 54:85, Sept. 1973.
19. Hathaway v. Worcester City Hospital, 475 F. 2d 701 (S. Ct. C.C.A. Mass., 1973).
20. Roe v. Ferguson, No. 74–315 (D. Ohio, Southern Dist., Sept., 1974).

21. Murray v. Vandevander, 522 P. 2d 302 (Okla., 1974); See also Schulte, E. J.: Law News, Hosp. Prog., 55:20, Nov. 1974.
22. Kenny v. Ambulatory Centre of Miami, Fla., 400 S. 2d 1262 (Fla. App. 1981).
23. Cf. Uzdawinis, R. M.: What Consideration Has Been Given to Students in Relation to Abortion Issue? Am. J. Nurs., 73:41, Jan. 1973.
24. California Health and Safety Code, sect. 25950 (1967).
25. Harris v. State of Alabama, 356 So. 2d 623 (Ala. Sup. Ct., 1978).
26. Frieman v. Ashcroft, 440 F. Supp. 1193 (U.S. Dist. Ct. E.D. Missouri, 1977); Pub. Health Ct. Dig., 24:6, Oct. 1978.
27. Wright v. State, 351 S. 2d 708 (Florida S. Ct., 1977); Pub. Health Ct. Dig., 24:1, Nov. 1978.
28. Noonan, J. T., Jr.: A Closer Look at the Court's Ruling, Life Cycle, p. 5, Nov. 1979.
29. Ibid.
30. Ibid.
31. Kelly, G., S.J.: Therapeutic Abortion, Hosp. Prog., 31:342, Nov. 1950: 370 (Dec., 1950). See also O'Donnell, T. J., S.J.: Morals in Medicine, Westminster, Md., Newman Press, 1956, pp. 121 ff.
32. Edwards, R. G., et al.: The Growth of Human Pre-Implantation Embryos in Vitro, Am. J. Obstet., Gynec., 408–416, Oct. 15, 1981.
33. Wells, M. P.: In Vitro Fertilization: Hope for Childless Couples, AORN J., 38:591–596, Oct. 1983.
34. Ibid.
35. Op. cit., note 33, p. 592–596.
36. Schukraft, R.: "To Be or Not to Be?" The Ethics of In Vitro Fertilization, Midwives Chron. & Nurs. Notes, 378–381, Nov. 1983.
37. Ashley, B., and O'Rourke, K.: Health Care Ethics. St. Louis: Catholic Hospital Assn., 1978, p. 290. See Chapter 10, pp. 266–307.
38. Ibid., p. 291.
39. Op. cit., note 36, p. 379.

40. *Ibid.*

41. Ramsey, P.: Shall We Produce? *JAMA,* 220(10)1346–1350, June 5, 1972; *JAMA,* 220(11)1480–1485, June 12, 1972. *The Ethics of Fetal Research.* New Haven, Yale Univ. Press, 1975.

42. Rosner, F.: Test Tube Babies, Host Mothers and Genetic Engineering in Judaism, *Tradition: a Journal of Orthodox Thought,* 19(2)141–148, 1981.

43. *JTA Daily News Bulletin,* July 28, 1978.

44. *Op. cit.,* note 42, p. 143.

45. Bleech, D.: *Judaism and Healing: Halakhic Perspective.* Ktav Pub. House, Inc., 1981, p. 88.

46. Capron, A. M.: The New Reproductive Possibilities: Seeking a Moral Basis for Concerted Action in a Pluralistic Society, *Law, Med. & Health Care,* 12:192–198, Oct. 1984.

47. Fletcher, J.: *Humanhood: Essays in Biomedical Ethics.* Buffalo, Prometheus Books, 1979.

48. Hawks, J. H.: Should Nurse Give Moral Advice? *Image: The Journal of Nursing Scholarship,* 16(1)14–16, Winter 1984.

49. *Op. cit.,* note 37.

50. NAACOG OGN Nursing Practice Resource. Infertility: an Overview, *NAACOG,* 7:2, 1982.

51. Mishell, D. R., Jr., and Darajan, V.: *Reproductive Endocrinology: Infertility and Contraception.* Philadelphia, F. A. Davis Co., 1979, p. 313–315.

52. *Op. cit.,* note 45, p. 80.

53. Ashley, B., and O'Rourke, K.: *Health Care Ethics.* St. Louis, Catholic Hospital Assoc., 1981, p. 288.

54. *Ibid.* p. 289.

55. D'Andrea, K. G.: The Role of the Nurse Practitioner in Artificial Insemination, *JOGN, Nursing,* 13(2)75–78, 1983.

56. *Ibid.*

57. People v. Sorensen, 66 Cal. Rptr. 7, 437 P. 2d 495 (1968).

58. Strnad V. Strnad, 190 Misc. 786, 78 N.Y.S. 2d 390 (1948).

59. Doornbos v. Doornbos, 12 Ill. App. 2d 473, 139 N.E. 2d 844 (1956). *See also* Creighton, H.: *Law Every Nurse Should Know.* 4th ed. Philadelphia, W. B. Saunders Co., 1981, p. 252–253.

60. *Op. cit.,* note 53, pp. 290–291.

61. *Op. cit.,* note 53, p. 291.

62. *Ibid.*

63. *Op. cit.,* note 53, p. 292.

64. *Op. cit.,* note 45, pp. 82–83.

65. *Op. cit.,* note 43, p. 142.

66. *Ibid.*

67. *Op. cit.,* note 36.

68. *Op. cit.,* note 55, pp. 75–78.

69. *Ibid.,* p. 78.

70. *Op. cit.,* note 48.

71. Genesis 16:1–6.

72. Franks, D. D.: Psychiatric Evaluation of Women in a Surrogate Mother Program, *Am. J. Psychiatry,* 138(10)1378, Oct. 1981.

73. *Ibid.,* p. 1379.

74. Markoutsas, E.: Parenting by Proxy—a Story of Love and Friendship, *Chicago Tribune,* Sec. 2, Jan. 14, 1980.

75. Sobel, D.: Surrogate Mothers: Why Women Volunteer, *The New York Times,* June 29, 1981.

76. Gerez, S. R.: The Contract in Surrogate Motherhood: A Review of the Issues, *Law, Med. & Health Care,* 12:107–114, June 1984.

77. Holder, A. R.: Surrogate Motherhood: Babies for Fun and Profit, *Law, Med. & Health Care,* 12:115–117, June 1984.

78. Doe v. Kelley (1979–1981). Reporter in Human Reproduction and the Law (Legal-Medical Studies, Inc.) II-B-15 (Wayne County Cir. Ct. Mich., Jan., 1980), Aff'm sub nom. Doe v. Attorney General, 307 N.W. 2d 438 (Mich. App. Ct., 1981), IV denied, 414 Mich. 875 (1982), Cert. denied 103 S. Ct. 834 (S. Ct., 1983).

79. Syrkowski v. Appleyard, 122 Mich. App. 506 (Ct. App. Mich., 1983).

80. Attorney General of Oklahoma, Opinion No. 83–162 (Sept. 29, 1983); *Citation,* 48:84, Jan. 15, 1984.

81. Op. Atty. Gen. 81–18 (Ky., 1981); Surrogate Mother Contracts Declared Illegal by Kentucky Attorney General, *Family Law Reporter,* 7:2247 (Feb. 17, 1981).

82. Op. Atty. Gen. 83–001 (Ohio, 1983).

83. *Cf.,* note 77, p. 117.

84. *Op. cit.,* note 76, p. 108.

85. *Ibid.,* p. 109. See Carey v. Population Serv. Int'l. 431 U.S. 678, 684 (1977); Skinner v. Oklahoma, 316 U.S. 535, 541 (1942); Griswold v. Connecticut, 381 U.S. 479, 495 (1965).

86. *Op. cit.,* note 53, p. 292.

87. *Op. cit.,* note 42, pp. 143–144.

88. *Ibid.*

89. Jakobovits, I.: Eugenics, *Jewish Medical Ethics.* N.Y., Bloch, 1975, pp. 261–266.

90. Ramsey, P.: *Moral and Religious Implications of Genetic Control, Genetics and the Future of Man,* J. D. Roslansky, ed. Amsterdam, North Holland Publ. Co., 1966, pp. 107–169.

91. Fletcher, J.: Ethical Aspects of Genetic Controls: Designed Genetic Changes in Man, *N. Engl. J. Med.,* 285:776–783, Sept. 30, 1971.

92. *Op. cit.,* note 46, p. 198.

93. Gleitman v. Cosgrove, 227 A. 2d 689 (N.J., 1967).

94. Custodio v. Bauer, 251 Cal. App. 2d 303, 59 Cal. Rptr. 463, 27 A.L.R. 3rd 824 (Cal. App. Ct., 1967).

95. Troppi v. Scarf, 187 N.W. 2d 511 (Ct. App. Mich., 1971).

96. Wilczynski v. Goodman, 73 Ill. App. 3d 51, 391 N.E. 2d 479 (Ill. App. 1st Dist., 1979).

97. Witherspoon: The New Pro-Life Legislation: Patterns and Recommendations, 7 St. Mary's L. J. 637 (1976); Coburn: Sterilization Regulations: Debate Not Quelled by HEW Document, *Science* 183. 935, 1974 (possible government coercion in connection with welfare regulations). Degnan: Law, Morals, and Abortion, 100, *Commonweal,* 305 (1974) (inconsistency between right to life

before and after birth). Larned: The Green-
ing of the Womb, *New Times*, Dec. 27, 1974,
p. 35 (use of hysterectomy as a means of
family planning). Furor over the Abortion
Issue—Hotter than Ever, *U.S. News and
World Report*, March 4, 1974, p. 43 (steep
rise in abortions). Second Thoughts About
Abortions, *U.S. News and World Report*,
March 3, 1975 (implications of conviction
of Boston physician for murdering a fetus
by doing an abortion).

98. Bonbrest v. Kotz, 65 F. Supp. 138 (D.D.C.,
    1946).
99. Sylvia v. Gobeille, 220 A. 2d 808 (R.I.,
    1973).
100. Labree v. Major, 306 A. 2d 808 (R.I., 1973).
101. Doe v. Bolton, 410 U.S. 179 (1973).
102. Roe v. Wade, 410 U.S. 113 (1973).
103. Stewart v. Long Island College Hospital,
    313 N.Y.S. 2d 502 (S. Ct. App. Div., 1970).
104. Id., p. 46.
105. Dumer v. St. Michael's Hospital, 233 N.W.
    2d 372 (Wis., 1975); *Regan Rep. on Nurs.
    Law*, 16:3, Dec. 1975.
106. Ball v. Mudge, 391 P. 2d 201, 203 (Wash.,
    1964).
107. Bishop v. Byrne, 265 F. Supp. 460, 463
    (S.D. W. Va., 1967).
108. Rogala v. Silva, 305 N.E. 2d 571, 573 (Ill.
    Ct. App., 1973).
109. Stills v. Gratton, 127 Cal. Rptr. 652 (Cal. Ct.
    of App., 1976); *Citation*, 33:39, 1976.
110. Brantley, J. R.: Wrongful Birth: The Emerg-
    ing Status of a New Tort. 8 *St. Mary's L. J.*
    140, 145, 1976.
111. Custodio v. Bauer, 59 Cal. Rptr. 463 (Ct.
    App., 1967).
112. Troppo v. Scarf, 187 N.W. 2d 511 (Mich.
    Ct. App., 1971); Betancourt v. Gaylor, 344
    A. 2d 336 (N.J. Super. Ct., 1971); Jackson v.
    Anderson, 230 So. 2nd 503 (Fla. Ct. App.,
    1970).
113. Jacobs v. Theimer, 519 S.W. 2d 846 (Tex.,
    1975).
114. Terrell v. Garcia (Tex. Civ. App. 1973) 496
    S.W. 2d 124, Cert. denied, 415 U.S. 927
    (1973).
115. Coleman v. Garrison, 327 A. 2d 757 (Del.
    Super., 1974).
116. Ziemba v. Sternberg, 45 A.D. 2d 230, 357
    N.Y.S. 2d 265 (1974).
117. Zepada v. Zepada, 41 Ill. App. 2d 240, 190
    N.E. 2d 849, cert. denied, 379 U.S. 945, 85
    S. Ct. 444, 13 L. Ed. 2d 245 (Ill. Ct. App.,
    1963).
118. Williams v. State, 18 N.Y. 2d 381, 276
    N.Y.S. 2d 885, 223 N.E. 2d 343 (S. Ct. N.Y.,
    1966).
119. Gleitman v. Cosgrove, 49 N.J. 22, 227 A. 2d
    689 (S. Ct., N.J., 1967).
120. Becker v. Schwartz, 46 N.Y. 2d 401, 413
    N.Y.S. 2d 895, 386 N.E. 2d 807 (N.Y. App.
    Ct., 1978).
121. Speck v. Finegold, 408 A. 2d 496 (Pa. Super.
    Ct., 1979).
122. Curlender v. Bio-Science Laboratories, 106
    Cal. App. 3rd 811, 165 Cal. Rptr. 477 (Cal.

Ct. App., 1980), 119 Cal. App. 3d 690, 174
Cal. Rptr. 128 (1981).
123. Turpin v. Sortini, 31 Cal. 3d 220, 643 P. 2d
    954, 182 Cal. Rptr. 337 (S. Ct. Cal., 1982).
124. Strohmaier v. Associates in Obstetrics &
    Gynecology, P. C., 332 N.W. 2d 432 (Mich.
    Ct. of App., 1982); *Citation*, 48:26, Nov. 15,
    1983.
125. Schork v. Huber, 648 S.W. 2d 861 (Ky. St.
    Ct., 1983); *Citation*, 48:25, Nov. 15, 1983.
126. Coleman: Family Planning, Population
    Control and the Law. *In Legal Medicine
    Annual* 401, 410 (Wecht, C., ed. 1973).
127. Gustafson, J. M.: Mongolism, Parental De-
    sires and the Right to Life. *Perspect. Biol.
    Med.*, 16:529, 599, 1973.
128. McCormick, R. A., S. J., To Save or Let Die,
    JAMA, 229:172, 1974.
129. Duff, R. S., and Campbell, A. G. M.: Moral
    and Ethical Dilemmas in the Special Care
    Nursery, *N. Engl. J. Med.*, 289:890–894,
    1973. The Hardest Choice. *Time*, p. 64,
    March 24, 1974.
130. *Ibid.*
131. *Op. cit.*, note 128, pp. 175–176.
132. The Hardest Choice, *Time*, p. 64, March 24,
    1974.
133. Maine Medical Center v. Houle, Me. Super.
    Ct. Docket No. 74445, February 14, 1974;
    Citation, 29:49, June 1, 1974.
134. "HHS Not Entitled to Infant's Records."
    Citation, 48:97–98, February 16, 1984, U.S.
    v. University Hospital of New York at Stony
    Brook, Docket No. CV 83 4818 (D.C.N.Y.,
    Nov. 17, 1983).
135. "No Court Order for Surgery That Sick
    Child's Parents Have Rejected." *Citation*,
    48:97–98, 15, 1984.
136. Gross, R. H.: Early Management and Deci-
    sion Making for Treatment of Myelomen-
    ingocele, *Pediatrics*, 72:450–458, Oct. 1983.
137. Shall This Child Die? *Newsweek*, Nov. 12,
    1973, p. 70. *See also* McCormack, E.: A
    Living Vegetable? Choose Life, No. 26, July
    1974, p. 1.
138. *Ibid.*
139. Jefferson v. Griffin Spalding County Medi-
    cal Authority, 274 S.E. 2d 457 (S. Ct. Ga.,
    1981).
140. *In re* Guardianship of Phillip B., 50
    U.S.L.W. 2133 (Sept. 8, 1981).
141. Lewis, E. P.: Identity Crisis, *Nursing Out-
    look*, 21:633, Oct. 1973.
142. Horner, M. B.: Dilemmas in Practice: Selec-
    tive Treatment. *Amer. Jour. of Nurs.*,
    84:309–312, March 1984.
143. *Ibid.*, p. 310.
144. New Code for Nurses Approved, *ICN Bull.*,
    3:4, May 16, 1973.
145. *The Code for Professional Nurses*, Rev.
    1983. Kansas City, American Nurses' As-
    sociation, 1976.
146. Hoffman, A. C., and Van Cura, M. X.:
    Death—The Five Brain Criteria, *Med. Tr.
    Tech.*, 224:377–407, 1978.
147. Arnet, W. F.: The Criteria for Determining
    Death in Vital Organ Transplants—A Med-

ico-Legal Dilemma, 38 *Missouri L. Rev.*, 220–221 (1973).

148. Conway, D. J.: Medical and Legal Views of Death: Confrontation and Reconciliation, 19 *St. Louis Univ. L. J.*, 172 (1974).

149. Olinger, S. D.: Medical Death, 27 *Baylor L. Rev.*, 22, 23 (1975).

150. A Definition of Irreversible Coma. Report of the Ad Hoc Committee of the Harvard Medical School to Examine the Definition of Death, *JAMA*, 205:337, 1968.

151. Kushnir, L.: Bridging the Gap: The Discrepancy Between the Medical and Legal Definitions of Death. 34 *Univ. Toronto Fac. L. Rev.*, 199, 204, Summer (1976).

152. *Id.*

153. Kan. Stat. Ann. Sec. 77–202 (Supp., 1975).

154. Md. Ann. Code, Art. 43, Sec. 54F (Supp., 1975).

155. N. Mex. Stat. Ann. 1–2–2.2 (Supp., 1975).

156. Va. Code, Sec. 32–364.3:1 (Supp., 1975).

157. Charron, W. C.: Death: A Philosophical Perspective on Legal Definitions, 54 *Washington Univ. L. Q.*, 979, 993 (1975).

158. *Op. cit.*, note 146, p. 394.

159. Evans v. New York, 49 N.Y. 86 (N.Y., 1972).

160. Douglas v. Southwestern Life Insurance Company, 374 S.W. 2d 78, 793 (Tex., 1964); Ct. note 132.

161. Tucker's Administrator v. Lower, No. 2831 (Ct. Law and Eq. Richmond, Va., 1972).

162. Jeddcloh, N. P.: The Uniform Anatomical Gift Act and a Statutory Definition of Death, *Transplant. Proc.*, VIII, No. 2, Supp. 1, p. 246, June 1976.

163. Fairey, W. F.: A Definition of Death, *J. N. Carolina Med. Assn.*, 73:7, Jan. 1977.

164. *Ibid.*, p. 5.

165. Crawford, J. M. B.: The Question of Brain Death. 128 *N. L. J.*, 224, 227, March 9, 1978.

166. Wassmer, T. A.: Between Life and Death: Ethical and Moral Issues Involved in Recent Medical Advances. 13 *Villanova L. Rev.*, 776 (1968).

167. Declaration of Sydney, *JAMA*, 206:657, 1968.

168. *In re* Karen Quinlan, 355 A. 2d 647 (N.J. S. Ct. 1976) reversing 348 A. 2d 80 (N.J. S. Ct. 1976). Creighton, H.: Terminating Life Support, *Superv. Nurse*, 9:68–69, 72–75, Oct. 1978.

169. Standards for Cardiopulmonary Resuscitation (CPR) and Emergency Cardiac Care (ECC); V. Medicolegal Considerations and Recommendations. *JAMA*, 227, Supp. 864–866, 1974; Standards for Cardiopulmonary Resuscitation (CPR) and Emergency Cardiac Care (ECC), *JAMA*, 244(5) 453–509, 1980.

170. Superintendent of Belchertown State School v. Saikewicz, 370 N.E. 2d 417 (S. Ct. Mass., 1977).

171. Schram, R., *et al.*: No Code Orders: Clarification in the aftermath of Saikewicz, *N. Engl. J. Med.*, 299:875–878, 1978.

172. *In re* Shirley Dinnerstein, 380 N.E. 2d 134 (Mass. App., 1978).

173. *In re* Storar and Eichner v. Dillion, 52 N.Y.S. 2d 363, 438 N.Y.S. 2d 266, 420 N.E. 2d 64 (S. Ct. N.Y., 1981).

174. Lydia E. Hall Hospital v. Peter Cinque, 455 N.Y.S. 2d 706 (N.Y.S. Ct., 1982). Creighton, H.: Termination of Life Sustaining Treatment, *Nurs. Management*, 14:14–15, Aug. 1983.

175. Schloendorff v. New York Hospital, 211 N.Y. 125, 105 N.E. 92 (S. Ct. N.Y., 1914).

176. Cushing, M.: "No Code" Orders: Current Developments and Nursing Director's Role, *J. Nurs. Admin.*, 11:22:9, April 1981.

177. *In re* Clair C. Conroy, 188 N.J. Super. 523, 457 A. 2d 1232. Reversed 190 N.J. Super. 453, 464 A. 2d 303 (N.J. Super. App. Div., 1983). Creighton, H.: Decisions on Food and Fluid in Life-Sustaining Measures, Part I, *Nurs. Management*, 15:47–49, June 1984.

178. Barber v. Superior Court of the State of California for the County of Los Angeles, 195 Cal. Rptr. 484 (Cal. Ct. App. 1983). Creighton, H.: Decisions on Food and Fluid in Life Sustaining Measures, Part II, *Nurs. Management*, 15:54–56, July 1984.

179. *In re* Hamilton, 657 S.W. 2d 425 (Tenn. Ct. of App. 1983); Appeal denied (Tenn. S. Ct. 1983); *Citation*, 48:104, Feb. 15, 1984.

180. John F. Kennedy Memorial Hospital v. Bludworth, 432 So. 2d 611 (Fla. Dist. Ct. of App. 1983); *Citation*, 48:18, Nov. 1, 1983.

181. A Living Will, Euthanasia Council, 250 West 57th Street, New York, n.d.

182. Bok, S.: Personal Directions for Care at the End of Life, *N. Engl. J. Med.*, 295:367–369, Aug. 12, 1976.

183. *A Christian Affirmation of Life.* St. Louis, Catholic Hospital Association of America, 1974.

184. Modell, W.: A Will to Live, *N. Engl. J. Med.*, 290:907–908, 1974.

185. Stead, E. A., Jr.: If I Become Ill and Unable to Manage My Own Affairs, *Med. Times*, 98:191–192, 1970.

186. *Op. cit.*, note 182.

187. Creighton, H.: Shall We Choose Life or Let Die? *Nurs. Management*, 15:16–18, Aug. 1984.

188. *Report of the Massachusetts Task Force on Organ Transplantation.* Boston, Dept. of Public Health of Massachusetts, 1984, p. 36.

189. Commonwealth v. Golston, 373 Mass. 249, 366 N.E. 2d 744 (1977), cert. denied, 434 U.S. 1039 (1978). *See* President's Comm. for the Study of Ethical Problems in Medicine and Biomedical and Behavioral Research, *Defining Death.* Washington, D.C., U.S. Government Printing Office, 1981, p. 136–138.

190. National Organ Transplant Law Enacted, *Law, Med. 8 Health Care*, 13:40, Feb. 1985.

191. *Organ Donation: The Present for the Future* is available from the Organ Transplant Society, Inc., 222 West Adams St., Suite 316, Chicago, Ill. 60606, phone: (312)732–9253.

192. Complete copies of the report may be obtained from the Department of Public Health, Commonwealth of Massachusetts,

150 Tremont St., Boston, Mass. 02111, phone: (617)227-7023.

193. *Op. cit.* note 188, p. 9.

194. Findlay, S., and Elias, M.: New Law May Increase Human Organ Donations, *USA Today*, Nov. 14, 1984.

195. Krakauer, H., et al.: The Recent U.S. Experience in the Treatment of End-Stage Renal Disease by Dialysis and Transplantation, *N. Eng. J. Med.* 308:1558–1563, June 20, 1983.

196. Shumway, N. E.: Recent Advances in Cardiac Transplantation, *Transplantation Proceedings*, XV: 1221–1224, 1983.

197. Reitz, B. A.: Heart-Lung Transplantation: A Review Heart Transplantation, *Heart Transplantation*, 1:8, 1982.

198. Starzl, T., et al.: Evaluation of Liver Transplantation, *Hepatology*, 2:614–636, 1982.

199. *Op. cit.*, note 188, p. 22.

200. *Ibid.* p. 105.

201. *Ibid.* p. 108.

202. *Ibid.* p. 9.

203. *Ibid.*

204. *Ibid.* pp. 10–20.

205. *Ibid.* pp. 73–74. *Also* Calabresi, G., and Bobbitt, R.: *Tragic Choices.* New York, Norton, 1978; and Fletcher, J.: Our Shameful Waste of Human Tissues. In Cutler, D. R. (ed.), *The Religious Situation*, Boston, Beacon Press, 1978, pp. 223–252.

206. President's Commission for the Study of Ethical Problems in Medicine and Biomedical and Behavioral Research, *Securing Access to Health Care.* Washington, D.C., U.S. Government Printing Office, 1983, p. 25.

207. Quoted in Fox, R., and Swazey, J.: *The Courage to Fail.* Chicago, University of Chicago Press, 1974, p. 232.

208. *Op. cit.*, note 188, p. 76.

209. *Ibid.*, p. 77.

210. *Ibid.*, pp. 78–83.

211. United States Catholic Conference, Ethical and Religious Directives for Catholic Health Facilities, Washington, D.C., 1971.

212. *Op. cit.*, note 1, pp. 100–101.

213. *Papal Teachings: The Human Body.* Boston, 1960, p. 382.

214. *Op. cit.*, note 188, p. 101.

215. *Ibid.*, pp. 97–99.

216. *Ibid.*, p. 99.

217. *Ibid.*, p. 102.

218. *Ibid.*

219. Feldman, Rabbi D. M., and Rosner, F. (eds.): *Compendium on Medical Ethics.* New York, Federation of Jewish Philanthropies of New York, 1984, p. 84.

220. Goldman, A. J.: *Judaism Confronts Contemporary Issues.* New York, Shengold Publishers, Inc., 1978, p. 238.

221. *Op. cit.*, note 188, pp. 102–103.

222. *Ibid.*, p. 103.

223. *Op. cit.*, note 32, pp. 104–106. *Cf.* note 1, p. 104.

224. The entire issue of *Law, Medicine and Health Care*, Vol. 13, No. 1, Feb. 1985, is devoted to organ transplantation.

225. Schloendorf v. Society of New York Hospital, 105 N.E. 92 (N.Y., 1914).

226. Salgo v. Leland Stanford Board of Trustees, 317 P. 2d 170 (Cal., 1957).

227. People ex rel. Wallace v. Labrenze, 411 Ill. 618, 104 N.E. 2d 769 cert. denied, 344 U.S. 824 (1952): Morrison v. State, 252 S.W. 2d 97 (K.C. Ct. App., 1952).

228. *Cf.* Cantor, Norman L.: A Patient's Decision to Decline Life-Saving Medical Treatment: Bodily Integrity versus the Preservation of Life, 26 *Rutgers L. Rev.*, 228, 229 (1972).

229. *Ibid.*, p. 258.

230. *Supra*, note 228, p. 259.

231. *Ibid.*, p. 260.

232. *Ibid.*, p. 261.

233. *Ibid.*

234. Application of the President and Directors of Georgetown College, 331 F. 2d 1000 (D.C. Cir.) cert. denied, 377 U.S. 978 (1964).

235. John F. Kennedy Memorial Hospital v. Heston, 58 N.J. 576, 279 A. 2d 670 (1970).

236. In re Brooks' Estate. 32 Ill. 2d 361, 205 N.E. 2d 435 (1965).

237. *Ibid.*, p. 442.

238. In re Raasch, No. 455, 996 (Prob. Div Milwaukee County Ct., Jan. 21, 1972). *Cf.*, *supra*, note 161, p. 235.

239. *Idem.*

240. *Cf.* Informed Consent and the Dying Patient, 83 *Yale L. J.* 1632 (1974).

241. Martin V. Industrial Accident Co., 304 P. 2d 828 (Cal., 1957).

242. Battaglia v. Battaglia, 172 N.Y.S. 2d 361 (1958). See also State v. Perricone, 37 N.J. 463 (1962) in which the court gave the superintendent of a hospital custody of a child whose parents refused a blood transfusion; and Morrison v. State, 252 S.W. 2d 97 (Mo., 1952) to the same effect.

243. People ex rel. Wallace v. Lawrenz, 104 N.E. 2d 769 (Ill., 1958).

244. Levitsky v. Levitsky, 190 A. 2d 601 (Md., 1963).

245. Brooks Estate v. Brooks, 205 N.E. 2d 435 (Ill., 1965).

246. Erickson v. Dilgard, 252 N.Y.S. 2d 705 (1962).

247. Jessie E. Jones v. President and Directors of Georgetown College Inc., 331 Fed. 2d 1000 (1964).

248. United States v. George 33LW2518 (Conn., 1965).

249. Collins v. Davis, 254 N.Y.S. 2nd 666 (1964).

250. Sloneker v. St. Joseph's Hospital, 233 F. Suppl. 105 (Colo., 1964).

251. Holsinger, J. W.: Cost Versus Quality. In Pena, J. J., et al. (eds.), *Hospital Quality Assurance: Risk Management and Program Evaluation.* Rockville, Md., Aspen Systems, 1984, pp. 89ff.

252. 49 *Fed. Reg.* 282ff., Jan. 3, 1984.

253. Johnson, R. L.: Shooting Oneself in the Foot: Congress May Re-Create Two Tier Care, *Hosp. Progress*, 64:32ff, Dec. 1983.

254. President's Commission for the Study of Ethical Problems in Medicine and Biomedical and Behavioral Research: *Securing Access to Health Care: The Ethical Implictions of Differences in Availability of Health*

Service. Washington, D.C., Government Printing Office, 1982, pp. 22ff.

255. Aaron, H. J., and Schwartz, W. B.: *The Painful Prescription.* Washington, D.C., Brookings Institute, 1984, pp. 100ff.

256. Mariner, W. K.: Diagnostic Related Groups: Evading Social Responsibility? *Law, Med. and Health Care,* 12:243–244, Dec. 1984.

257. *Ibid.,* p. 244.

258. Kapp, M. S.: Legal and Ethical Implications of Health Care Reimbursement by Diagnostic Related Groups, *Law, Med. and Health Care,* 12:245, 248, Dec. 1984.

259. *Ibid.*

260. Nemore, P.: Medicare Prospective Payment for Hospitals: Implications for Nursing Home Residents, *Clearinghouse Rev.,* 17:1308ff., 1984.

261. Op. cit., note 258, p. 248.

262. *Cf., ibid.,* pp. 249–250.

263. Nathanson, P.: Future Trends in Aging and the Law, *Geriatrics,* 8(3) 7–9 (Spring 1984).

264. *See,* note 8, pp. 251–252.

265. Light, D. W.: Is Competition Bad? *N. Engl. J. Med.* 309(21) 1315ff., Nov. 24, 1983.

266. Rubenstein, H. S., et al.: Standards of Medical Care Based Upon Consensus Rather Than Evidence: The Case of Routine Bedrail Use for the Elderly, *Law, Med. & Health Care,* 11(6)271ff., Dec. 1983.

General References

Am. Coll. of Ob. & Gyn., Ethical Issues in Surrogate Motherhood (statement of policy from Exec. Bd.), May 1983.

Annas, G. J.: Surrogate Embryo Transfer and the Perils of Parenting, Hastings Center Rep. 14(3)25–26, June 1984.

Baron, C. H.: If You Prick Us Do We Not Bleed? Of Shylock, Fetuses, and the Concept of the Person in Law, *Law, Med. & Health Care,* 11:52–63, April 1983.

Carson, R.: Ethics and the Law of Dying, *Death Educ.,* 8(1)70–76, 1984.

Contracts to Bear a Child, *Calif. L. Rev.,* 66(3)611 ff., May 1978.

Cranford, R. E., and Doudera, A. E.: The Emergency of Institutional Ethics Committees, *Law, Med. & Health Care,* 12:13–20, Feb. 1984.

Creighton, H.: Wrongful Birth, *Nurs. Management,* 14:41–42, July 1983.

Creighton, H.: Terminally Ill Patient's Right to Refuse Treatment, *Superv. Nurse,* 11:74, 77, Oct. 1980.

Creighton, H.: Withdrawal of Life Support Systems, *Superv. Nurse,* 11:52–54, Dec. 1980.

Creighton, H.: Nursing Assessment, *Nurs. Management,* 12:65–69, Nov. 1981.

Creighton, H.: Refusing to Participate in Abortions, *Nurs. Management,* 13:27–28, April 1982.

Creighton, H.: Wrongful Life, *Nurs. Management,* 14:54–56, April 1983.

Creighton, H.: Nursing Judgment, *Nurs. Management,* 15:60–63, May 1984.

Creighton, H.: Decisions on Food and Fluid in Life Sustaining Measures, Part I, *Nurs. Management,* 15:48–49, June 1984; Part II, *Nurs. Management,* 15:54–56, July 1984.

Creighton, H.: Shall We Choose Life or Let Die? *Nurs. Management,* 15:16–18, Aug. 1984.

Curtin, L.: Should We Feed Baby Doe? *Nurs. Management,* 15:22, Aug. 1984.

Cushing, M.: "Do Not Feed . . ." Withholding Treatment from Severely Defective Newborns, *Am. J. Nursing,* 83:602–604, 1983.

Donovan, P.: Wrongful Birth and Wrongful Conception: The Legal and Moral Issues, *Fam. Plann. Perspect.,* 16(2)64–69, March/April 1984.

Drane, J. F.: The Defective Child: Ethical Guidelines for Painful Dilemmas, *JOGN Nursing,* 13(1)42–48, Jan./Feb. 1984.

Flannery, D. M., et al.: Test Tube Babies: Legal Issues Raised by In Vitro Fertilization. 67 *Georgetown L. J.,* 1295ff., Aug., 1979.

Furrow, B. R.: Impaired Children and Tort Remedies: The Emergence of a Consensus . . . Wrongful Life Suits, *Law, Med. & Health Care,* 11(4)148–154, Sept. 1983.

Horsley, J. E.: Pulling the Plug Isn't Easy—Explaining it Is Even Harder, *RN,* 43:69–70+, Dec. 1980.

Keane, N.: Legal Problems of Surrogate Motherhood, 2 *So. Ill. Univ. L. J.,* 147ff., (1980).

Lyon, J.: New Treatments, New Choices, *Nurs. Life,* 4(3)48–52, 1984.

Macnaughton, C.: Artificial Insemination: Aiding and Abetting . . . Medical, Ethical, Moral, and Legal Difficulties, *Nurs. Mirror,* 152:30–31, Jan. 22, 1981.

Surrogate Motherhood: The Outer Limits of Protected Conduct, 1981 *Detroit Coll. of L. Rev.* 1131ff.

Paris, J. J.: Terminating Treatment for Newborns: A Theological Perspective, *Law, Med. & Health Care,* 10:120–124+, June 1982.

Philpott, M.: *Legal Liability and the Nursing Process.* Toronto: W. B. Saunders Company Canada Ltd., 1985.

Regan, W. A.: Doctor's Orders and Nursing Judgment, *Regan Rep. Nurs. Law,* 20(10)1, May 1980.

Regan, W. A.: Nursing Assessment and Nursing Judgment, *Regan Rep. Nurs. Law,* 20(12)4, May 1980.

Robertson, J. A.: Procreative Liberty and the Control of Conception, Pregnancy and Childbirth, 69 *Va. L. Rev.,* 405–465, April 1983.

Should "No Code" Become "All But . . . ?" *Am. J. Nursing,* 84:975–976, Aug. 1984.

Sandorff: Is it Right? *RN,* 43:24, Dec. 1980.

Smith, L.: Zero-Intake: The Lingering Death of Clarence LeRoy Hebert—and How One Nurse Blew the Whistle, *Nursinglife,* 3(6):18–25, Nov./Dec. 1983.

Strong, C.: Defective Infants and Their Impact on Families: Ethical and Legal Considerations, *Law, Med. & Health Care,* 11(4)173, Sept. 1983.

Taub, S.: Withholding Treatment from Defective Newborns, *Law, Med. & Health Care,* 10:4–10, Feb. 1982.

Weber, L. J.: Infant Treatment Decisions: Ethics and Costs, *Health Prog.,* 65:28–31, Dec. 1984.

AFTERWORD

In conclusion to this brief account of law that every nurse should know, I would like to call to the nurse's attention one other well-known and helpful rule of living:

Give thought to this day, for each day well-lived, gives hope for tomorrow.

APPENDIX

NURSING ASSESSMENT*

Both the JCAH Standards on Nursing and the American Nurses' Association Standards on Nursing state that the nursing assessment is the work of the professional nurse.

The decision in a California case hinged on the matter of nursing assessment and judgment. In *Sanchez v. Bay General Hospital*,[1] Sanchez sustained minor injuries in a 1973 automobile accident and filed a suit against the owners and operators of the other automobile. As a result of minor physical problems persisting after the accident, Sanchez was admitted to the hospital for a diagnostic procedure, a cervical myelogram. Following the myelogram, an elective surgery (laminectomy) was suggested, and Sanchez consented.

The surgery was successfully performed. On the morning of the surgery, a doctor placed an atrial catheter in Sanchez by inserting a plastic tube with a needle on the end into the vein of her left arm and advancing it up the vein until it entered the upper right mid-atrium of her heart. The purpose of the catheter was to drain off any air embolism that might develop. With the catheter in place, Sanchez was transferred to the recovery room at about 12:35 P.M. in satisfactory condition. She vomited slightly, a common postoperative event, while in the recovery room.

Her vital signs were checked every 15 minutes and appeared stable. At the time that her last vital signs were taken in the recovery room, her blood pressure was 120/80. Sanchez appeared comfortable, and at 3:00 P.M. she was asleep. While in the recovery room, Sanchez appeared to be recovering satisfactorily.[2]

At 3:15 P.M. Sanchez was transferred to the postoperative ward, where a series of complications arose in her condition. The atrial catheter was left in place and apparently used and regarded by the nursing staff as a peripheral IV. Although she left the recovery room apparently in satisfactory condition, her vital signs were not taken at that time. Sanchez arrived at the postoperative ward at about 3:30 P.M. Again, no vital signs were taken by the nursing staff at that time, and no examination was made of the medical chart from the recovery room. None of the nursing personnel of the postoperative ward was aware that Sanchez had an atrial catheter implanted.

On Sanchez's arrival in the postoperative ward, the nursing staff conducted no examination of her pupils, and they did not order any suctioning equipment, despite the fact that she had vomited in the recovery room. At 3.30 P.M., Sanchez's vital signs were taken by a nurse's aide. They showed a substantial decrease in blood pressure, pulse and respiration (96/60, 80, 18). The nurse's aide made no comparison with the recovery room vital signs, and the vital signs were not taken any more frequently thereafter. At that time, no check of medication was made, and no neurological examination, no test for responsiveness, and no examination of the pupils were done. The nursing staff were unaware of the existence of the atrial catheter in Sanchez's heart, and there was no notification of a supervisory nurse or a physician of the deteriorating vital signs.[4]

Requests by friends for medication and assistance were ignored. A friend visiting Sanchez reported to the nursing station that Sanchez was vomiting and in pain, and he requested medication and water to revive her. The hospital nursing staff did not leave the station to verify her condition but told him "everything has been taken care of" and

---

 *This material first appeared as an article in *Nursing Management*, 12:65–69, Nov. 1981.

told him he could get Sanchez water, although the operating surgeon had directed that no water be given.[5]

At 3:45 P.M. another nurse's aide took Sanchez's vital signs, which had decreased (90/50, 58, 16). No comparison of these vital signs was made with the ones taken at 3:30 P.M. or in the recovery room, and there was no direction that the vital signs be taken at more frequent intervals because they were deteriorating. Again, no neurological examinations or tests for responsiveness or examination of the pupils were done, and no physician or supervisory nurse was notified.

Sanchez vomited, so the nurse's aide reported this to the nurse who was team leader, and she came and checked the vital signs.[6] Sanchez continued vomiting, and she jerked violently, her pupils dilated and she became cyanotic before her heart arrested at 3:55 P.M. Her friend ran for assistance. Upon entering the room and seeing Sanchez, the nurse's aide ran out in panic. Thereafter and in response to the nurse aide's cries, the nurse entered the room, checked the pupils, pulse and blood pressure, and then she also panicked and did nothing to assist Sanchez. Sanchez's airway was not checked and no CPR was attempted.[7]

After a few moments, the emergency room physician came and attempted to treat Sanchez. Since he was not told that what appeared to be a peripheral IV was in fact an atrial catheter, all medications that he ordered were administered through the catheter directly into Sanchez's heart. By 5:00 P.M. Sanchez was "brain dead" and was transferred to an intensive care unit in critical condition. There she existed in a vegetative state for almost two months before she died.[8]

Added to this, the nursing staff in intensive care failed to properly inflate and care for a balloon cushion on the cuff of the tracheostomy tube. The nurse's note states: "No nursing personnel on floor will take responsibility for giving tube feeding due to inability to inflate trach cuff completely and knowingly."[9] As a result of this failure, the cuff of the tracheostomy tube gradually worked its way through the posterior of the trachea, eroded part of the thoracic vertebrae and the right innominate artery, and Sanchez bled to death.

A trial court granted a directed verdict on res ipsa loquitur grounds and awarded her survivors $400,000. The appellate court affirmed the decision.[10] The operating room doctor said:

> I think the important factor to me is that a grave event was going on and there was virtual paralysis in response to it. Nothing went on. There were people running back and forth but nothing was done and nobody informed until it was apparent that she had no pulse and no blood pressure, then Dr. Ochs came on the scene, then the RN came on the scene, and then people started calling people.[11]

The court further observed: "The record does not indicate a complete assessment and observation of her, and that appropriate actions were taken during this period of time."[12]

Owing to lack of a complete assessment, this patient was allowed to progress to the point of cardiac arrest. Then treatment based on inadequate assessment was inappropriate because it was based on lack of knowledge of the atrial catheter, which apparently was regarded and used by the nursing staff as a peripheral IV. Again, lack of assessment and care of the cuff of the tracheostomy tube allowed it to erode the right innominate artery, as a result of which she bled to death. In many states, nurse practice acts speak of nursing assessment and nursing judgment. As Regan points out, these are functions that involve the application of intelligence, understanding and experience.[13]

In the JCAH Standards of Nursing Services, Standard III states that:

> In striving to assure optimal achievable quality nursing care and a safe patient environment, nursing personnel staffing and assignment shall be based at least on the following:
> A registered nurse plans, supervises, and evaluates the nursing care of each patient;
> To the extent possible, a registered nurse makes a patient assessment before delegating appropriate aspects of nursing care to ancillary nursing personnel. . . .[14]

In the JCAH Standards of Nursing Services, Standard IV states:

> The nursing process (assessment, planning, intervention, evaluation) shall be documented for each hospitalized patient from admission through discharge. Each patient's nursing needs shall be assessed by a registered nurse at the time of admission or within the period established by nursing department/service policy. This assessment data shall be consistent with the medical plan of care and shall be available to all nursing personnel involved in the care of the patient.[15]

In the JCAH Standards of Nursing Services, Standard VI states:

> Written policies and procedures that reflect optimal standards of nursing practice shall guide the provision of nursing care. . . . Nursing department/service policies and procedures shall relate at least to:
>> assignment of nursing care consistent with patient needs, as determined by the nursing process; (assessment, planning, intervention, evaluation). . . .[16]

In the American Nurses' Association's *Standards of Nursing Practice*, Standard I states:

> The collection of data about the health status of the client/patient is systematic and continuous. The data are accessible, communicated and recorded.[17]

Nursing assessment is the responsibility of the registered, professional nurse as set forth by the Standards of Nursing Practice of the American Nurses' Association and the Joint Commission on Accreditation of Hospitals. The unfortunate results of not doing a complete nursing assessment are illustrated by *Sanchez v. Bay General Hospital*, where it cost a patient her life and the hospital $400,000 in a malpractice suit. In state after state, nurse practice acts speak of nursing assessments and nursing judgment.

References

1. Sanchez v. Bay General Hospital, 172 Cal. Rptr. 342 (Ct. of App. 4 Dist. Div. 1, 1981).
2. *Id.*, p. 344
3. *Id.*, p. 345
4. *Id.*
5. *Id.*
6. *Id.*
7. *Id.*
8. *Id.*
9. *Supra*, note 1, p. 346.
10. *Citation*, 43:62, July 1, 1981.
11. *Supra*, note 1, p. 347
12. *Id.*
13. Regan, W. A.: Liberated Nurses: Assessment/Judgment. *Regan Rep. Nurs. Law*, 22:1, June 1981.
14. Nursing services, *JCAH Standards*. Chicago, American Hospital Association, 1980.
15. *Ibid.*
16. *Ibid.*
17. American Nurses' Association: Standards of Nursing Practice. Kansas City, American Nurses' Association, 1973.

NURSING JUDGMENT*

The question arises concerning the legal responsibility of the nurse for nursing judgment. The essence of professional nursing lies not in its environment or the use of specialized equipment, but in its decision making on the part of the nurse. The well-being and, in some instances, the life of the patient depends on nursing judgment, and necessary action based thereon.

In *Utter* v. *United Hospital Center, Inc. et al.*,[1] the Supreme Court of Appeals of West Virginia held that whether the hospital was negligent in caring for a patient was a question for the jury. In that case, a patient sustained serious injuries of his right wrist, elbow and back. His arm was placed in a cast, and there was no complaint about the nursing care for two days.[2] Then, several nurses testified that the injured arm was swollen, black and very edematous and that there was a foul-smelling drainage emitting therefrom. The nurse on the day shift observed the serious condition of the patient and called the treating physician. She reported that, among other symptoms, the patient could not retain oral antibiotics. She did not report delirium. When the doctor did nothing further, the nurse did not call the departmental chairman or any other doctor as required by the pertinent provision of the nursing manual.[3] A day later, the patient was removed to another hospital where he received seven hyperbaric oxygen treatments, and then his right arm was amputated at the shoulder joint. The Circuit Court, after entering a judgment against both the doctor and the hospital, sustained the hospital's motion to set aside the verdict and enter a judgment for the hospital. The West Virginia Supreme Court reversed this and reinstated the jury verdict. The court said:

> Nurses are specialists in hospital care who, in the final analysis, hold the well-being, in fact in some instances, the very lives of patients in their hands. . . . If that patient, helpless and wholly dependent, shows signs of worsening, the nurse is charged with the obligation of taking some positive action. . . . The manual provides that if the practitioner in charge

*This material first appeared as an article in *Nursing Management* 15:60–63, May 1984.

does nothing or acts ineffectively, the nurse "shall call this to the attention of the Department Chairman." Evidence that such procedure was not followed in this case was adduced for jury consideration.[4]

In other words, there was a failure of nursing judgment, i.e., to see whether the attending physician provided needed care or to call this to the attention of the Department Chairman.

In another case, *Darling v. Charleston Community Memorial Hospital*,[5] a college football player sustained a broken leg. It was placed in a cast at a community hospital. The foot became cold two days later, and there was a foul smell in the room for two weeks. Eventually, the leg had to be amputated at a medical center to which the patient was transferred. Not long after the cast was applied, the patient complained of pain, and his toes were swollen and became dark. The cast was cut several times, and, in so doing, the leg was cut. After two weeks, the patient was transferred to a medical center.

The community hospital was held liable under *respondeat superior* because the nurses either did not observe, or at least failed to report, patient problems that were overlooked or not thought to be significant by the doctor. The physician himself settled out of court; he had no specialty training and had not secured consultation. The court said: "Thus, if a nurse or other hospital employee fails to report changes in a patient's condition and/or to question a doctor's orders when they are not in accord with standard medical practice and the omission results in injury to the patient, the hospital will be liable for its employee's negligence."[6]

Again, the nurses failed to use proper judgment in reporting the situation to their supervisor and up through channels when the doctor delayed in taking action on their reports of a patient's worsening condition.

In *Poor Sisters of St. Francis Seraph of the Perpetual Adoration, et al. v. Catron*,[7] a comatose patient was brought into the emergency room, where an endotracheal tube to aid the patient's breathing was inserted. The patient (Catron) was then admitted into the intensive care unit of the hospital under the care of her family physician, Dr. Weller. Weller kept the tube in place in Catron's throat because she was still comatose and unable to breathe on her own. Five days later, Weller ordered a nurse to remove the tube. When the nurse reported she was unable to do so, Weller removed the tube. When Catron, later that day, had difficulty breathing, Weller ordered a tracheostomy. About six days later, her condition improved, and she was discharged. After her release from the hospital, Catron experienced further breathing difficulties and had to return for another tracheostomy. As she experienced difficulty speaking, she underwent several operations to remove scar tissue and to open her voice box. These operations were unsuccessful. Catron sued the emergency room doctor and the hospital, and the jury rendered a verdict for $150,000 against the hospital. The judgment was affirmed by the Court of Appeals.[8]

The hospital owed a duty to Catron. Instruction No. 7 given by the trial court read as follows:

> Skilled hospital personnel have a duty to exercise reasonable care in administering services to patients in the hospital. If such personnel know that a licensed attending physician, without consultation, either by his failure to treat a patient or by treating a patient in a manner which is a substantial departure from accepted medical standards is endangering the health and life of said patient, then the hospital personnel have a duty to perform such acts as are within their authority to protect the health and life of said patient.[9]

A hospital is liable for exployees' negligent acts that are done within the scope of their employment. Therefore, a breach of that duty described in the instruction will result in liability.

The record contains testimony by an expert witness that inhalation therapists and nurses who work in intensive care units are specially trained to handle patients who have endotracheal tubes inserted. There was testimony by several witnesses that endotracheal tubes should not be left in a patient longer than three or four days. The head nurse in the ICU admitted she knew that the rule of thumb for leaving endotracheal tubes in place was no longer than three days. The inhalation therapist at the hospital who handled Catron's respirator knew the recommended guideline for leaving in endotracheal tubes was 48 to 72 hours. It is the nurse's duty to report any critical condition to the doctor in charge and, if nothing is done, then to report the condition to the supervisor.[10] Neither the nurses in the ICU nor the inhalation therapists reported Dr. Weller's care of Catron to their supervisors. The nurses did not bring to Dr. Weller's attention the fact that the tube was being left in longer than usual.[11]

In *Czubinsky v. Doctors Hospital*,[12] Czubinsky was coming out of anesthesia, after a routine and uneventful surgical procedure to remove an ovarian cyst, when she went into cardiac arrest and suffered a severe loss of oxygen to her brain resulting in total and permanent paralysis. She was awarded $982,000 damages against Doctors Hospital. When Czubinsky suffered these damages, only the anesthesiologist, Dr. Kushner, and the operating room technician, Harman, were present. The circulating nurse, Werner, left the room in answer to a call from Dr. Rand.[13]

Werner defended her leaving because she was "being yelled at." Werner concedes Czubinsky was at a critical postoperative period because she was undergoing the transition from anesthetized air to room air.[14] The hospital's own manual provides specific duties for the circulating nurse. It says: "He/she is also the member of the team who will be on hand to assist the Anesthesiologist during the entire procedure."[15]

The anesthesiologist, Dr. Kushner, testified that after Czubinsky's problem was discovered, he needed assistance with resuscitation. Because he was alone, he had to run back and forth around the operating room table alternating between CPR and ventilating her. Kushner further testified he needed help during this critical period of time because seconds count in a cardiac arrest such as this one.[16]

The registered nurse assigned to Czubinsky's OR had a duty to remain with her until she was transferred to the recovery room. The jury could properly conclude that it was a breach of duty, i.e., negligence, for the nurse to leave the unconscious patient's side. The court said:

> The nurse's absence from the OR was a patent, proximate, efficient cause of Czubinsky's injuries. She was the second most skilled person present. Her presence and skill would have led to a prompt observation of the preliminary warning signs of vital function failure.
>
> Had Nurse Werner been present, she could have assisted the anesthesiologist with CPR while the OR technician went for help. Instead the anesthesiologist was left alone, in a hopeless, ineffective attempt to resuscitate a patient in a rapidly deteriorating condition.[17]

From these cases, it is apparent that the courts seem to be increasingly inclined to hold nurses responsible for their nursing judgment.[18] In the emergency department, carefully developed guidelines will enhance the nurse's exercise of judgment.[19]

References

1. Utter v. United Hospital Center, Inc. et al., 236 S.E. 2d 213 (S. Ct. App. W. Va. 1977).
2. *Id.*, p. 214.
3. *Id.*, p. 215.
4. *Id.*, p. 216.
5. Darling v. Charleston Community Memorial Hospital, 33 Ill. 2d 326, 211 N.E. 253 (W. Va. 1965). Creighton, H.: *Law Every Nurse Should Know*, 4th ed. Philadelphia, W. B. Saunders Co., 1981, p. 163.
6. *Id.*, p. 333.
7. Poor Sisters of St. Francis Seraph of the Perpetual Adoration et al. v. Catron, 435 N.E. 2d 305 (Ct. App. Ind. 1982).
8. *Id.*, p. 306.
9. *Id.*, p. 307.
10. *Id.*, p. 308.
11. *Id.*
12. Czubinsky v. Doctors Hospital, 139 Cal. App. 3rd 361, 188 Cal. Rptr. 685 (Ct. App. 1983).
13. *Id.*, p. 686.
14. *Id.*, p. 687.
15. *Id.*
16. *Id.*
17. *Supra,* note 12, p. 688. Also *Cf.* Regan, W. A.: Nurse Specialists: Prime Legal Targets, *Regan Report on Nursing Law*, 23:1, April 1983.
18. *Cf.* Cushing, M.: Expanding the Meaning of Accountability, *Am. J. Nurs.*, 83:1202–1203, Aug. 1983.
19. Greenlaw, J.: Nursing Negligence in Hospital Emergency Department, *Law, Med. and Health Care*, 12:118–121, 32, June 1984.

PATIENT TEACHING*

With the advent of Diagnostic Related Groups (DRGs) and with the nurse practitioner increasingly becoming the role model, there is increased emphasis on the nurse's obligation and function to do patient teaching. For the prevention of accidents and disease, for the optimal maintenance of the chronically ill and for the optimal restoration of the injured and those with disabling conditions such as strokes, patient teaching by nurses is most necessary. Occupational health nurses, public health nurses and nurses in clinics are spending a major portion of their time in patient teaching. Increasingly, too, the hospital nurse and those in nursing extended-care facilities and homes are devoting

---

*This material first appeared as an article in *Nursing Management*, 16:12–18, Jan. 1985.

significant time to patient teaching. Where once patients depended upon their physicians for teaching them about health problems, this has been transferred largely into the nursing area. As early as 1928, the court held that it is well settled that one who assumes a responsibility to avoid the spreading of a contagious disease is liable for failing to adopt such means as will prevent the spread of that disease.[1]

Bernard v. Gravois[2] is the earliest case, perhaps, where the court accepted the premise that instruction and education are a nursing function. There, the nurse was absolved of liability where it was alleged that she was negligent in instructing the mother and aunt how to administer an electric heating pad to a child's neck in order to localize pus. For three days, the mother and aunt successfully administered the treatment per the nurse's instructions, and only when they became negligent on the fourth day was the child burned. It was established that the nurse had given proper instructions, and the injury was caused by the negligent manner in which the mother and aunt carried out those instructions.

The ANA Statement of Functions identifies teaching as one of the seven areas of professional nursing activity.[3] Lesnik and Anderson, in 1962, stated that the sixth area of professional nursing was, "the direction and the education to secure physical and mental care."[4] As they point out, the inherent difficulty of remaining within the legal limits of nursing practice and avoiding the invasion of the medical practice area is to resolve adequate direction and education without prescription of therapeutic or remedial measures.[5] They recognized that this is an area in which professional nursing is destined to contribute greatly to the public's health and welfare.

In a 1965 Washington case, a passenger on a Suburban Transportation System bus sued to recover damages for injuries sustained when the bus driver lost consciousness and the bus struck a telephone pole. The lapse in consciousness was attributed to the side-effects of the drug Pyribenzamine, which had been prescribed by his doctor for treatment of a nasal condition. At the trial, the bus driver testified that neither the doctor nor his nurse gave him any warning concerning possible side-effects of the drug. The trial court directed a verdict against the bus company and the driver and awarded damages. On appeal, the court reversed the trial court action in dismissing the doctor and Group Health as defendants and ordered a new trial.[6]

Four doctors testified at the trial that a warning should be given when the drug is prescribed because of its known side-effects. The Washington Supreme Court found that there was evidence in the record that the doctor failed to warn his patient of the dangerous side-effects of drowsiness and lassitude that may be caused by taking this drug, and this evidence was sufficient to submit the issue of the doctor's negligence to the jury. The court said that the doctor would be liable if the jury found that he failed to give a warning on the side-effects of the drug. Since the harm resulting to the plaintiff was in the general field of danger, the consequences reasonably should have been foreseen by the doctor when he administered the drug.

In a related Texas case, the plaintiffs appealed from a summary judgment in favor of a physician in the plaintiffs' negligence action arising from personal injuries sustained by one plaintiff when he was struck by a car driven by a patient of the physician. The case was reversed and remanded. The plaintiffs' petition alleged that the physician was negligent in prescribing the drug Quaalude for his patient and in failing to warn her not to drive an automobile while under the influence of such drug. The Court of Appeals held that such negligence was a proximate cause of the personal injuries sustained by the one plaintiff when he was struck by a car driven by the patient and that it was sufficient to state a cause of action against the physician.[7]

The factual similarities between these two cases are readily apparent. In both, doctors prescribed a drug for their patient that they knew could have detrimental effects on the patient's ability to drive a motor vehicle. In both cases, the harm, which was injury to a third party as a result of a patient's impaired driving ability caused by a prescribed drug, was reasonably foreseeable by the doctors when the drug was prescribed. In both cases, the doctors failed to warn or to teach their patients not to drive a motor vehicle while under the influence of the drug. Also, in both cases, the reasonably foreseeable harm did, in fact, result.

A Missouri case illustrates the increased responsibility of nurses in expanded roles for discharge instructions and for same-day surgery units.[8] There, the plaintiff brought an action for the wrongful death of his wife, who underwent a tonsillectomy. The cause was submitted to the jury on the theory that the defendant physician had performed an operation on the patient and sent her "home under inadequate nursing supervision." The verdict and judgment were for the plaintiff in the sum of $50,000, and it was reaffirmed on appeal.

The 48-year-old patient underwent a tonsillectomy in the morning in the office of a physician and surgeon in general practice who used a Sluder instrument, which tends to cause more bleeding than other methods. The patient was taken to another room to recover and await the arrival of her neighbor to take her home at about 4:00 P.M. The defendant doctor or his office assistant, who had no nursing training, looked in on the patient throughout the day. Around 2:00 P.M., the defendant found the patient with her fingers in her mouth. There was blood on her fingernails, and she was smoking. The doctor told her not to smoke. When the neighbor arrived, the patient was lying on the bed face-down. There was blood in her hair, and the bed was full of blood. The neighbor wiped the blood from the patient's face and took her to the bathroom, where she threw up a glassful of blood. The doctor released the patient to the neighbor without ascertaining whether the neighbor was adequately instructed about positioning the patient to avoid the swallowing of blood and strangulation. The neighbor, according to plans, was to stay with the patient until her husband came home from work. About 2½ hours later, her husband arrived and found her unresponsive, and she was pronounced dead. The cause of death was determined to be asphyxia or strangulation due to blood in the bronchial tree and edema of the glottis.

The court held that if the doctor was unable to personally attend the patient after surgery, it was incumbent upon him either to see that those persons who were to be in nursing attendance upon the patient were competent to perform those services or to give them such instruction as would enable them to competently care for the patient. The doctor testified that he had given the neighbor instructions to position the patient on her side or stomach with her head to the side. The neighbor testified that the doctor did not instruct her with respect to positioning the patient. Whether the defendant gave these instructions was for the jury to determine. There was no record of documentation of the discharge instructions. In this case, the failure to teach a person how to properly position a tonsillectomy patient within the first 24 hours after surgery, when there is the greatest danger of bleeding, resulted in the patient's death. The doctor was liable for failure to establish a standard of acceptable practice of adequate nursing supervision.

In a Louisiana case where the plaintiff sued for damages for wrongful death of her son, the Court of Appeals affirmed a judgment for the defendants.[9] There, the son was involved in an incident in which he was hit on the head with a baseball bat and stabbed in the shoulder. After being examined in the emergency room of the hospital, the emergency doctor told a nurse to telephone the son's home and have someone pick him up and take him home. The mother came to the hospital, took her son home and went to bed. The next morning, the son was found dead.

At issue in this case was whether or not it was an acceptable medical practice to give oral or written instructions for the home treatment of head injury patients, and whether instructions in either form were actually given in this case.

The testimony indicated that when, as here, certain objective symptoms are not present in head injury cases, it is proper to release the patient to his home under the supervision of family members or friends. The home treatment program requires that the injured person be awakened at regular intervals, questioned to determine whether or not comprehension is adequate and examined to determine if his pupils are the same size. Expert testimony established that, in 1975, the common practice was to give these instructions orally to the person responsible for the patient's care at home. It was also established that oral instructions may be more effective than written ones, depending on the person to whom the instructions are given. (A footnote in the opinion states that the testimony indicates that currently the home care instructions for head injury patients are almost always given in writing. However, this practice had come into being more as a protective measure for hospitals and their staffs than as a preferable form of instruction for persons offering such home care treatment.)

The plaintiff alleged she was given no such instructions. The nurse testified that she specifically recalled giving the instructions orally to the plaintiff and, for this reason, insisted that the plaintiff come to the hospital to get her son rather than sending him home in a taxi as the plaintiff had requested. The court gave considerable weight to the latter aspect of the nurse's testimony.

Where instructions are detailed or involved, written instructions may be necessary. When an emergency room or outpatient department cares for similar patients, written instructions, which are periodically reviewed, should be used to serve the best interests of patients, staff and hospitals. Such written instructions should be supplemented by oral explanations and discussions.[10]

In *Kyslinger v. United States*, a Federal trial court ruled that a widow failed to prove that she and her deceased veteran husband, who had polycystic kidney disease, were given inadequate instruction on a home dialysis unit. Both the patient and the wife were instructed on the operation, maintenance and supervision of treatment during the 10 months in which he underwent biweekly hemodialysis in the hospital. Two years later, after home dialysis, he died of renal failure. At the end of a full trial, the court concluded that there was no inadequacy in training.[11]

The question of whether an R.N. in patient teaching may suggest alternative procedures for the treatment of cancer arose in the Tuma case. Jolene Tuma, R.N., was employed as a clinical instructor of nursing by the College of Southern Idaho. Her work included performing nursing services while supervising student nurses at the Twin Falls Clinic and Hospital. A hospital patient was informed by her doctor that she was dying of leukemia, that chemotherapy was her only hope for survival and that this procedure was life-threatening and had undesirable side-effects. Nurse Tuma, who was interested in the special needs of dying patients and aware of the patient's condition, asked to be assigned to her. She told the patient about the use of Laetrile at the hospital in Salt Lake City and later discussed the alternative treatment with the patient's family. After a family member called the doctor and informed him of Nurse Tuma's discussions with the patient, the doctor ordered the chemotherapy stopped because of a change in the patient's attitude. Later, after a discussion, the chemotherapy was restarted, and the patient died in two weeks.

The Board of Nursing received a complaint from the hospital that Nurse Tuma had interfered with the the physician-patient relationship. The Director of the Board of Nursing prepared a petition for the suspension or revocation of her license, and a hearing was set. It was concluded by the hearing officer that Nurse Tuma had violated the Idaho Professional Code by interfering with the physician-patient relationship and thereby engaging in unprofessional conduct. The findings were approved by the board, which suspended Nurse Tuma's license for six months. When she appealed the decision to the district court, it affirmed the decision of the hearing officer and the order of the board suspending her license. Nurse Tuma then appealed to the Supreme Court of Idaho, which held that, because the Board of Nursing had no rules and regulations adequately indicating that the actions complained of were prohibited, the state statute allowing for the suspension of her nursing license could not be invoked simply because she engaged in discussions with patients relative to alternative treatments.[12]

As these cases indicate, the nurse's professional duty to provide patient teaching does develop into a legal duty. Ambulatory care services and same day surgery affect the who, when and where of patients and their caregivers. At NIH, a new course on patient teaching includes a demonstration of the computerized assessment of patient learning needs, ongoing documentation of care planning during hospitalization and elements of patient discharge care plans.[13]

References

1. Jones v. Stanko, 160 N.E. 456 (S. Ct. Ohio 1928).
2. Bernard v. Gravois, 20 So. 2d 181 (Ct. App. La. 1944).
3. Functions of Nursing, *Am. J. Nursing*, 54:868–871, 994–996, 1130, 1954.
4. Lesnik, J., and Anderson, B. E.: *Nursing Practice and the Law*, 2d ed. Philadelphia, J. B. Lippincott Co., 1962, p. 260.
5. *Ibid.*, p. 276.
6. Kaiser v. Suburban Transportation System, 398 P. 2d 14, Amended 401 P. 2d 350 (Wash. S. Ct. 1965).
7. Gooden et al. v. Tips, M. D., 651 S.W. 2d 364, (Ct. App. Tex. 1983).
8. Bateman v. Rosenberg, 525 S.W. 2d 753 (Mo. Ct. App. 1975).
9. Crawford v. Earl K. Long Hospital, et al., 431 So. 2d 40 (Ct. App. La. 1983).
10. *Cf.* Cushing, M.: Legal Lessons on Patient Teaching, *Am. J. Nursing*, 84:721–722, June 1984.
11. Kyslinger v. United States, 406 F. Supp. 800 (D.C. Pa. 1975).
12. Tuma v. Board of Nursing, 593 P. 2d 711 (S. Ct. Idaho 1979).
13. Carlsen, R. H.: Educating Nurses for the Hospital Computer Age: The NIH Experience, in *2d National Conference, Computer Technology and Nursing.* Bethesda, Md., NIH Pub. No. 84–2623, Sept. 1984.

R.N. ADVOCATE AND THE LAW*

While there is much literature on the nurse as a patient advocate, until recently there have been few decided cases. In the opinion of Christy, "The great nursing challenge of the 1970s is that of advocacy, to be the patient's sponsor, supporter, and counselor."[1]

Both Leah Curtin, in "The Nurse as Advocate: A Philosophical Foundation for Nursing,"[2] and Sally Gadow, in "Existential Advocacy: Philosophical Foundation of Nursing,"[3] distinguish the concept of advocacy associated with the patient rights movement. Many of their colleagues either have failed to appreciate the distinction or have rejected it. As Patricia Donahue has pointed out, only through the attainment of nurses' rights will we be able to act on behalf of others, have the power base and be able to deliver quality nursing care.[4] For a discussion of nurses' rights, the reader is referred to Fagin's article, in which she says that the highest order of responsibility in our priority system should be the responsibility of seeing, through unified action, that our rights are obtained.[5]

Rather than being loyal soldiers, as the old metaphor of nurses described us, George Annas has offered a replacement—the nurse as a courageous advocate.[6] This new image is essentially legal. According to Annas, the patient needs the right to adequate information about proposed medical procedures, the right to refuse any and all procedures, the right to full information about prognosis and diagnosis, the right to leave the hospital and so on. All these concepts are incorporated in the *Patient's Bill of Rights.*[7] The assumption in these discussions is that the patients' rights were often threatened, and Annas hoped that nurses would take up the fight on their behalf.

A volume of literature on the nurse as a patient advocate has followed. Among the articles are Payne's "The Nurse as a Patient Advocate in the Rehab Setting,"[8] Sklar's "Patient's Advocate—A New Role for the Nurse?"[9] Flaherty's "The Nurse *Is* a Patient Advocate,"[10] Namerow's "Integrating Advocacy into the Gerontological Nursing Major"[11] and Kohnke's "The Nurse as Advocate."[12]

The usual definition of advocacy is the act of defending or pleading the case of another. Kohnke offers a parallel definition as "the act of informing and supporting a person so that he can make the best decisions possible for himself."[13] As she says, the actions of the advocate are twofold: first, to inform the patients of what their rights are in a particular situation and then to make sure they have all the necessary information to make an informed decision and, second, to support clients in the decisions they make.[14]

The late 1970s and the 1980s have witnessed some legal decisions in regard to the nurse's role as a patient advocate. The first case was that of *Tuma v. Board of Nursing.*[15] In that case, Jolene Tuma was employed as a clinical instructor of nursing by the College of Southern Idaho. Her work included performing nursing services while supervising student nurses at the Twin Falls Clinic and Hospital. A hospital patient was informed by her doctor that she was dying of leukemia, that chemotherapy was her only hope of survival and that this procedure was life-threatening and had undesirable side-effects. Nurse Tuma, who was interested in the special needs of dying patients and aware of the patient's condition, asked to be assigned to the case. She told the patient about the use of Laetrile at the hospital in Salt Lake City and later discussed the alternative treatment with the patient and the family. After a family member called the doctor and informed him of Nurse Tuma's discussions with the patient, the doctor ordered the chemotherapy stopped because of a change in the patient's attitude. Later, after a discussion, the chemotherapy was restarted and the patient died in two weeks.

The Board of Nursing received a complaint from the hospital and doctor that Nurse Tuma had interfered with the physician-patient relationship. The director of the Board of Nursing prepared a petition for the suspension or revocation of Nurse Tuma's license, and a hearing was set. It was concluded by the hearing officer that Nurse Tuma had violated the Idaho Professional Code by interfering with the physician-patient relationship and had thereby engaged in unprofessional conduct. The findings were approved by the board, which suspended Nurse Tuma's license for six months. When she appealed the decision to the district court, it affirmed the decision of the hearing officer and the order of the board suspending her license. Nurse Tuma then appealed to the Supreme Court of Idaho, which held that, because the Board of Nursing had no rules and regulations adequately indicating that the actions complained of were prohibited, the state statute

---

*This material first appeared as an article in *Nursing Management*, 15:14–17, Dec. 1984.

allowing for the suspension of her nursing license could not be invoked simply because she engaged in discussion with patients relative to alternative treatment. In conclusion, the court said:

> Given no written guidelines as to what conduct might possibly result in a suspension of her license for unprofessionalism, Nurse Tuma may very well have surmised that she was on thin ice with the particular doctor, or the medical profession in general, in suggesting to a patient alternative procedures for the treatment of cancer. But she could not know, having not ever been forewarned against so doing, that this constituted unprofessional conduct.[16]

While the litigation was underway, Nurse Tuma wrote to the editor of *Nursing Outlook* and described her situation:

> Does the nurse have the right to assist the patient toward full and informed consent? Litigation against nurses already shows us we have the responsibility when we do not properly inform the patient. But do we have the authority to go along with this responsibility as the patient's advocate?[17]

Reactions to the Tuma case was mixed. According to Purtilo and Cassel, Tuma believes that her actions were justified and that her personal hardships were repaid by the fact that the patient's rights were defended and that public attention has been directed to the nurse's role as a patient advocate.[18] In a survey by *RN* magazine of 12,500 nurses, over 80 percent of the respondents agreed that a nurse who acted as Tuma did would be doing the right thing.[19] On the other hand, Tuma did not regain her teaching position, she had to face three years of legal appeals, and it was too late to change the results for the patient. Both the physician and some members of the patient's family were unhappy with the nurse's actions. In order to avoid the consequences that Nurse Tuma faced, it would seem to be the better part of discretion for a nurse to discuss *in advance* with the doctor any teaching she proposed to do.

The more recent case of R.N. advocacy of the patient is the case of *Wrighten v. Metropolitan Hospitals*.[20] In that case, the court's ruling came on behalf of a nurse who was discharged when she complained at a news conference about the treatment of black patients at the hospital where she worked. In the legal action, the hospital alleged that she was terminated for insubordination. The nurse had met with the hospital's Affirmative Action officer and president on several occasions before going public with her complaints. She neither impeded the hospital's operation nor abused her duties as a nurse. In his opinion, Circuit Judge Goodwin states: "By advocating the proper care of her patients, however, Wrighten was fulfilling her duty as a nurse. Patient advocacy by a nurse is not insubordination."[21]

According to the court ruling, the nurse was protected by the antiretaliation provision of Tital VII of the Civil Rights Act of 1964. The court points out that 42 U.S. Section 2000 e-3 provides that an employer cannot discriminate against an employee "because he has opposed any practice, made an unlawful practice by this subchapter," or "because he has made a charge, testified, assisted or participated in any manner in an investigation proceeding, or hearing under this subchapter."[22]

The court found that the nurse's complaints were justified. It concluded that the evidence indicated that the hospital, by discharging the nurse, retaliated against her for involvement in a protected activity.

Gerald Winslow, in an article "From Loyalty to Advocacy: A New Metaphor for Nursing," says that the season for the nurse as an advocate has arrived and that the language of advocacy provides a new way to express a growing sense of professional responsibility and power.[23] As he points out, the ethic of advocacy, with a concern for rights and the virtue of courage at its center, is an important change in the moving away from a heteronomous morality of constraint toward a more autonomous morality of cooperation.

However, Winslow does mention five ambiguities and potential criticisms of the advocacy role: (1) The meaning of advocacy needs clarification; (2) the states' nurse practice acts need revision; (3) patients (or their families) are often unprepared to accept the nurse as an advocate—there must be appropriate public education; (4) advocacy is frequently associated with controversy; nursing educators who share the ethic of advocacy must ask how well the nursing curriculum prepares nurses to cope with the potential conflicts; and (5) as advocate, the nurse is bound to be torn, at times, by conflicting interests and loyalties. An article by Natalie Abrams supports these views.[24]

Nurses are moving toward the role of advocacy. The cases upholding this trend are beginning to appear in law reports. The 1976 revision of the ANA Code requires nurses to protect the client from "incompetent, unethical, or illegal practice of any person." And in the interpretive statements, the code uses the language of advocacy: "In the role of client advocate, the nurse must be alert to and take appropriate action regarding any instances of incompetent, unethical, or illegal practice(s) by any member of the health team or health care system itself, or any action on the part of others that is prejudicial to the client's best interests."[25]

In its 1973 revision, the International Council of Nurses omitted all mention of loyal obedience to the physician's orders and said that the "nurse's primary responsibility is to those people who require nursing care" and that the "nurse takes appropriate action to safeguard the individual when his care is endangered by a co-worker or any other person."[26]

The controversy over patient advocacy continues. Nurses by a sizable margin favor the nurse's role as a patient advocate. However, since most nurses are employees, they face very real problems in pursuing the role.[27]

References

1. Christy, T. E.: New Privileges . . . New Challenges . . . New Responsibilities, Nursing '73, 3:8, Nov. 1973.
2. Curtin, L. L.: The Nurse as Advocate: A Philosophical Foundation for Nursing, Advances in Nursing Science, 1:1–10, April 1979.
3. Gadow, S.: Existential Advocacy: Philosophical Foundation of Nursing, Nursing Images and Ideals, pp. 79–101, 1974.
4. Donahue, M. P.: The Nurse–A Patient Advocate? Nursing Forum, 27:143, 147, No. 2, 1978.
5. Fagin, C.: Nurses' Rights. Am. J. Nurs., 75:85, Jan. 1975.
6. Annas, G.: The Patient Rights Advocate: Can Nurses Effectively Fill the Role? Superv. Nurse, 5:21–25, July 1974. Also Annas, G., and Healey, J.: The Patient Rights Advocate, Jour. Nurs. Admn., 4:25–31, May/June 1974.
7. Patient's Bill of Rights. Chicago, American Hospital Association, 1972.
8. Payne, M. E.: The Nurse as a Patient Advocate in the Rehab Setting, ARN, 4:8–11, Sept./Oct. 1979.
9. Sklar, C.: Patient's Advocate–A New Role for the Nurse? Canadian Nurse, 74:39–41, June 1979.
10. Flaherty, M. J.: The Nurse Is a Patient Advocate, Nurs. Management, 12:12–13, Sept. 1981.
11. Namerow, M. J.: Integrating Advocacy into the Gerontological Nursing Major, Jour. of Geron. Nurs., 8:149–151, March 1982.
12. Kohnke, M.: The Nurse as Advocate, Am. J. Nurs., 80:2038–2040, Nov. 1980.
13. Ibid., p. 2038.
14. Ibid., p. 2039.
15. Tuma v. Board of Nursing, 593 P. 2d 711 (S. Ct. Idaho, 1979). Creighton, H.: Law Every Nurse Should Know, 4th ed. Philadelphia, W. B. Saunders, 1981, p. 25–26.
16. Id.
17. Tuma, J.: Letter to the Editor, Nursing Outlook, 25:846, Sept. 1977.
18. Purtilo, R., and Cassel, C.: Professionalism and Advocacy, Ethical Dimensions in the Health Professions. Philadelphia, W. B. Saunders Co., 1981, p. 136.
19. Sandroff, R.: Protecting the M.D. or the Patient: Nursing's Unequivocal Answer, RN, 44:28–33, Feb. 1981.
20. Wrighten v. Metropolitan Hospitals, 33 FEP Cases 1714 (U.S. Ct. of App., 9th Cir.) (San Francisco) 1984. See also RN Advocacy of Patient Upheld by Appeals Court, Texas Nursing, 58:7, May 1984.
21. Id., p. 1722.
22. Id., p. 1719.
23. Winslow, G. R.: From Loyalty to Advocacy: A New Metaphor for Nursing, The Hastings Center Report, 14:32, 38, June 1984.
24. Abrams, N.: A Contrary View of the Nurse as Patient Advocate, Nursing Forum, 17:258–267, 1978.
25. American Nurses' Association, Code for Nurses with Interpretive Statements. Kansas City: American Nurses' Association, 1976, p. 8.
26. Davis, A. J., and Aroskar, M. A.: Ethical Dilemmas and Nursing Practice. New York: Appleton-Century-Crofts, 1978, p. 13–14.
27. Smith, C. S.: Outrageous or Outraged: A Nurse Advocate Story, Nursing Outlook, 28:624–625, Oct. 1980.

COLLECTIVE BARGAINING*

Beginning in 1937, ANA has recommended that nurses use their professional organization to "improve every phase of their working lives."[1] In 1946, the ANA convention adopted an economic security program and called for collective action on such items as a 40-hour

---

*This material first appeared as an article in Nursing Management, 11:61–62, Sept. 1980.

work week, higher minimum salaries, improved fringe benefits and nurses' planning and administration of nursing services.

The National Labor Relations Act states that:

> To bargain collectively is the performance of the mutual obligation of the employer and the representatives of the employees to meet at reasonable times and confer in good faith with respect to wages, hours, and other terms and conditions of employment, or the negotiation of an agreement, or any question arising thereunder, and the execution of a written contract incorporating any agreement reached if requested by either party; but such an obligation does not compel either party to agree to a proposal or require the making of a concession.[2]

Such collective bargaining can provide nurses with leverage in negotiating the terms of their employment contract. Many state nurses' associations provide the service of negotiating employment contracts for nurses, but nurses must elect and invite their professional association to serve as the bargaining agent.[3] When the NLRA was amended to include nonprofit hospitals, management in many hospitals and other agencies convinced nurses that collective bargaining is not desirable or needed. As a practical matter, it is useful in obtaining salary increases and fringe benefits, which are poor in nursing, particularly if one looks at pensions.

According to Metzger and Pointer, irritants that drive employees into collective bargaining are:

> The presence of a larger group of minority workers; a difference in fringe benefits between departments and across job classification; inconsistent and indefensible scheduling; wage and fringe benefits which are not competitive; depersonalization and routinization of jobs; gains in negotiated wages and fringe benefits in blue-collar and unionized white-collar situations.[4, 5]

The NLRA sets forth procedures whereby employees may select a labor organization as their collective bargaining agent to negotiate with the health care institution over employment matters. The health care institution includes any hospital, health maintenance organization, health clinic, nursing home, extended care facility or other institution devoted to the care of sick, infirm or aged persons.[6] Without recourse to the formal NLRA procedure, a health care institution may recognize the collective bargaining agent or union. When the formal process is used, the employees vote on union representation in an election held under the supervision of the NLRB. If the union is successful, the NLRB certifies it as the employees' bargaining representative.[7] Whatever representative is selected by the majority of employees is the exclusive bargaining agent for all employees in the unit.

In *Wing Memorial Hospital Association and Massachusetts Nurses' Association* v. *NLRB*,[8] all registered nurses employed by the employer at its hospital in Palmer, Massachusetts, including the diabetic teaching nurse, the admissions coordinator, the nurse anesthetist, charge nurses and head nurses, but excluding all other employees, the director of nursing, (shift) supervisors, operating room supervisor, community health center department head and all other supervisors, constituted a unit appropriate for the purpose of collective bargaining within the meaning of Section 9 (b) of the Act. "The term 'supervisor' means any individual having authority, in the interest of the employer, to hire, transfer, suspend, lay off, recall, promote, discharge, assign, reward, or discipline other employees, or responsibly to direct them, or to adjust their grievances, or effectively to recommend such action, if in connection with the foregoing the exercise of such authority is not of a merely routine or clerical nature, but requires the use of independent judgment."[9]

In *St. Catherine's Hospital of Dominican Sisters of Kenosha, Wisconsin, Inc.* v. *NLRB*, the board found that an appropriate bargaining unit consists of all the employer's technical employees, including licensed practical nurses, but excluding office clerical employees, service and maintenance employees, professional employees, members of a religious order, guards and supervisors as defined by the Act.[10] In *Nathan and Miriam Barnert Memorial Hospital Association* v. *NLRB*, the board found the L.P.N.'s to be technical employees and included the L.P.N.'s in the technical unit they found to be appropriate.[11] In *NLRB* v. *Evangelical Lutheran Good Samaritan Soc.*, licensed practical nurses were held not to be supervisors.[12] On the other hand, a licensed practical nurse in a nursing home is a supervisor where on one shift he or she is in charge of a portion of the nursing home, supervises nurse's aides and orderlies, reviews patients' charts as to proper medication and diet and observes and reports patients' symptoms to the head registered nurse.[13]

Neither registered nurses nor licensed practical nurses were supervisors where they lacked authority to affect employment status of aides and orderlies working under their direction, had no disciplinary role except making reports to the director of nursing and gave work assignments and directions only in accord with previous scheduling or as dictated by patients' needs.[14]

Although licensed practical nurses occasionally directed and assigned work to nurse's aides, they were not supervisors where such directions and assignments did not require exercise of independent judgment but were made pursuant to established procedures and as dictated by patients' needs, and where they did not hire, discharge, promote, reward or discipline aides or effectively recommend such action.[15]

In *Presbyterian Medical Center and Colorado Nurses' Association v. NLRB*, the board refused to allow the L.P.N.'s to join the R.N.'s in a bargaining unit, stating that, based on the entire record, they are satisfied that the evidence does not support the petitioner's contention that L.P.N.'s are professional employees within the meaning of the Act. Thus, their inclusion in the same bargaining unit with R.N.'s is prohibited, unless the latter are given a separate vote as to whether they wish to be *included* with nonprofessional employees.[16]

The NLRA says that the denial by some employers of employees' right to organize and the refusal by some employers to accept the procedure of collective bargaining lead to strikes and other forms of industrial strife and unrest, which have the intent or necessary effect of burdening or obstructing commerce. The inequality of bargaining power between employees who do not possess full freedom of association or actual liberty of contract and employers who are organized in a corporate or other form of ownership association substantially burdens and affects the flow of commerce. This tends to aggravate recurrent business depressions by depressing wage rates and the purchasing power of wage earners in industry and by preventing the stabilization of competitive wage rates and working conditions within and between industries.

Experience has proved that protection by law of the right of employees to organize and bargain collectively safeguards commerce from injury, impairment or interruption. It also promotes the flow of commerce by removing certain recognized sources of industrial strife and unrest, by encouraging practices fundamental to the friendly adjustment of industrial disputes arising out of differences as to wages, hours or other working conditions and by restoring equality of bargaining power between employers and employees. It is the policy of the United States to encourage the practice and procedure of collective bargaining, by protecting the exercise by workers of full freedom of association, self-organization and designation of representatives of their own choosing, for the purpose of negotiating the terms and conditions of their employment or other mutual aid or protection.[17]

Except for the NLRA protection, health care institutions are under no obligation to negotiate with their employees on any issue and have the absolute right to set wages, hours, working conditions, fringe benefits and so on, subject only to certain basic Federal and state laws that apply to all employees and the nondiscrimination legislation. Possible subjects for collective bargaining under NLRB include prohibited subjects that are already regulated by Federal or state law. The mandatory subjects include terms and conditions of employment whereas voluntary subjects include all other possible subjects.[18]

Effective use of collective bargaining could enable professional nurses to speak with one voice—something they have not done through the years. In the struggle for control of nursing, some nurses have also used collective bargaining for increased involvement at the decision making levels regarding patient care and changes in the health delivery system and in operating and staffing health care institutions. In the Seattle and San Francisco strikes, nurses won the right to participate in decisions affecting staffing and patient care.

As Katz[19] points out, a collective bargaining agreement could incorporate a nurse committee with power to consider professional practices and patient care issues and to make recommendations for those improvements that it considers advisable. She further states that some common objectives for such a committee are:

1. To consider the professional practice of nurses.
2. To work constructively for the improvement of patient care and nursing practice.

3. To recommend to the hospital ways and means to improve patient care.

A profession has the right, the ability and the responsibility to control its own practice. Nurses have increasingly realized that collective bargaining is an effective input into the health care system. Nurses must unite and support their organizations in meaningful numbers. While Hopping and others argue that collective bargaining reduces professionalism, Katz and others regard it as a means to achieve true professional status.

References

1. Metzger, N., and Pointer, D. D.: *Labor-Management Relations in the Health Services Industry: Theory and Practice.* Washington, D.C., Science and Health Publications, Inc., 1972, pp. 34–35.
2. U.S.C.A. Title 29 Sec. 158 d. p. 718.
3. Lawrence, J. C.: Confronting Nurses' Political Apathy, *Nurse Forum,* 15:(4) 363, 368, 1976.
4. *Op. cit.,* note 1, pp. 152, 120, 124–125, 168, 195, 203.
5. Hopping, B.: Professionalism and Unionism Conflicting, *Nurse Forum,* 15:(4) 372, 374, 1976.
6. U.S.C.A. Title 19, Sec. 152 (14).
7. Katz, B. F.: Why Nurses Form Unions, *Nurs. Law & Ethics,* 1(2)1, 2, 6, Feb. 1980.
8. Wing Memorial Hospital Association and Massachusetts Nurses' Association v. NLRB, 217 NLRB 172 (1975).
9. NLRB Title 29, Sec. 152 (11.)
10. St. Catherine's Hospital of Dominican Sisters of Kenosha, Wisconsin, Inc., v. NLRB, 217 NLRB 133 (1975).
11. Nathan and Miriam Barnert Memorial Hospital Association v. NLRB, 217 NLRB 132 (1975).
12. NLRB v. Evangelical Lutheran Good Samaritan Soc., 477 F. 2d 297 (CCA9, 1973).
13. University Nursing Home, Inc., v. NLRB, 168 NLRB 263, (1967).
14. Madeira Nursing Center, Inc. v. NLRB, 203 NLRB 42, 1973 CCH NLRB Para. 25311.
15. Leisure Hills Health Centers, Inc. v. NLRB, 203 NLRB 46 (1973), CCH NLRB, Para. 25312.
16. The Presbyterian Medical Center and Colorado Nurses' Association v. NLRB, 218 NLRB 192 (1975).
17. U.S.C.A. Title 29, Sec. 151.
18. *Op. cit.,* note 7, p. 2.
19. *Ibid.,* p. 6.

GIVING REFERENCES*

When a nurse is discharged, the question arises as to whether you have the legal right to make a disclosure regarding the cause for termination. What is a privileged communication and what is not? The problems of theft, alcohol and drugs arise. If a former employer did not disclose the truth to you, what would be your reaction?

According to Wigmore, generally regarded as an outstanding authority on evidence, four fundamental conditions are recognized as necessary to the establishment of privilege against disclosures of communications:

    1. The communication must originate in a *confidence* that they will not be disclosed.

    2. This element of *confidentiality must be essential* to the full and satisfactory maintenance of the relation between the parties.

    3. The *relation* must be one which in the opinion of the community ought to be sedulously *fostered.*

    4. The injury that would inure to the relationship by the disclosure of the communications must be *greater than the benefit* thereby gained for the correct disposal of litigation.[1]

A 1978 case[2] deals with many of the problems. The case involved a slander action against the plaintiff's former employer where the Circuit Court, Wayne County, entered judgment for the defendant, and the state Court of Appeals affirmed the judgment.

The plaintiff worked as a ward clerk for the defendant hospital from 1969 until 1973. In the spring of 1973, she was injured in an automobile accident and was treated by her family physician, who prescribed a muscle relaxant, a pain killer and other drugs for her. When the plaintiff returned to work in the summer, her supervisor told her to report for her annual physical examination. The plaintiff furnished blood and urine samples as part of that examination. Some days later, the plaintiff attended a meeting with the director of personnel of the hospital, the executive director of personnel, the plaintiff's supervisor and a person representing the American Federation of State, County and Municipal Employees (AFSCME). The executive director of personnel told the plaintiff that there was a problem regarding the urine sample and asked her to obtain from her doctor a list of all medications prescribed for her during the previous six months. The employee complied with this request. At another meeting attended by the executive director of

---

*This material first appeared as an article in *Supervisor Nurse,* 10:68–69, Jan. 1979.

personnel, the director of personnel at defendant hospital, the same AFSCME representative and the plaintiff, the executive director of personnel told the plaintiff that the urinalysis revealed morphine sulphate. Within a short period, the employee received a letter from the director of personnel at the defendant hospital terminating her employment for the stated reason that the plaintiff had violated a work rule forbidding "any activities regarding personal use or abuse of drugs." Soon thereafter, the plaintiff employee filed a lawsuit charging defamation.

In this case, the court said that an employer has a qualified privilege to defame an employee by publishing statements to other employees whose duties interest them in the subject. Here, the employees were supervisors, personnel department representatives and company officials and, as such, were those employees to whom the defendant's qualified privilege extends.[3]

However, in *Silas v. General Motors Corp.*, a former employer called in former fellow employees and "explained" that a former employee had been released for misappropriation or conspiring to misappropriate the former employer's property. It was held that the employer had published a slanderous statement and that publication was not protected by a qualified privilege because fellow employees were not supervisors, personnel department representatives or the employer's officials.[4] Nurses are advised to give honest references, but in so doing one must be careful to adhere closely to the rules of qualified privilege.

References

1. Wigmore, J. H.: *Evidence in Trials at Common Law*, McNaughton Rev. Boston, Little, Brown and Co., 1961, 8:sect. 2285.
2. Merritt v. Detroit Memorial Hospital, 81 Mich. App. 279, 265 N.W. 124 (1978).
3. See also Personnel Problem: Suits by Former Employers. *Regan Rep. Hosp. Law*, 19:4, June 1978.
4. Silas v. General Motors Corp. 372 Mich. 542, 127 N.W. 357 (S. Ct. Mich., 1964).

OCCUPATIONAL HEALTH NURSE'S LIABILITY*

In recent years, the expanded responsibility, accountability and autonomy of specialized professional nurses have been recognized. Today, occupational health nurses are working in Employee Occupational Health Units in hospitals as well as in industry. Because of the independent setting in which occupational health nurses work and laws with respect to employers and employees, occupational health nurses have been involved in a number of lawsuits.

According to a decision of a U.S. District Court, Rose Marie Meierer, a professional nurse who was discharged from her job as an occupational safety nurse (at the Cooper River plant of E. I. du Pont de Nemours & Co.), won a $1 million dollar damage suit. However, payment of damages has been delayed to allow Du Pont time to appeal.

In December 1980, the nurse informed the company's executives that there were possible chemical hazards in the plant because of the recurring incidents of dermatitis, ulcers of the mouth and nose, eye burning, and irritations and, among other things, finger nail and toenail cyanosis among the employees. Meierer stated that the Du Pont officials told her those alleged health problems were not her concern and that she should refrain from reporting incidents of dermatitis and other chemical-related illnesses because they might gain the attention of the Federal Occupational Safety and Health Administration. The nurse got the same reaction from the plant officials when she requested a list of all chemicals used in the plant, particularly formaldehyde, which was extensively used at the plant as a finishing agent and which had been listed by the United States as a pre-carcinogenic chemical.[1] This decision substantiates the nurse's role in protecting the health of clients. Article Three of the ANA *Code for Nurses* states:

> The nurse acts to safeguard the client and the public when health care and safety are affected by the incompetent, unethical, or illegal practice of anyone.[2]

To minimize problems, the occupational nurse must rely on company policies and procedures, and have and use written protocols for care that involves medical treatment based on nursing diagnoses. Where the nurse's practice in an independent setting depends

---

*This material first appeared as an article in *Nursing Management*, 16:49, 52–53, Feb. 1985.

on standing orders, they should be written, dated and signed. The occupational health nurse must act within the limits of each state's nurse practice act. All nurses, physicians and employers should know the workers' compensation and OSHA (Occupational Health and Safety Act) regulations.

The occupational health nurse, as is true of other nurse practitioners, is held to the standard of the reasonably prudent professional practitioner in the same or similar circumstance.[3] Her duties and responsibilities and her negligence through commission or omission of acts are judged by general principles of malpractice laws.

According to Brown, four sets of activities are comprised in the work of the occupational health nurse.[4] These include pre-employment physicals and periodic health assessment of workers, and their follow-up care which includes teaching and education to ensure the worker's continued well-being. In addition, nurses as part of a multidisciplinary team (physicians, nurses, industrial hygienists, health physicists and safety professionals) work with management and employee representatives in planning and conducting activities to ensure medical care, sanitation, healthfulness and safety of the work environment as well as education of workers in personal hygiene, health protection, safe work practices and accident prevention.[5]

Negligent acts constitute the largest area of legal problems for most occupational nurses. They may be acts of either commission or omission. As a primary care giver, the occupational health nurse's assessment and nursing diagnosis are most important to determine care required.[6] In *Cooper v. National Motor Bearing Co., Inc.*,[7] an employee brought a lawsuit for damages against a company and an occupational health nurse for malpractice in the treatment of a wound received in an industrial accident. While working, an employee was struck by a small piece of metal. At the time of the accident, the employee went to the dispensary, and the nurse swabbed and bandaged the wound but did not probe it for possible foreign matter. Eventually, the wound healed but a small red area remained, and it began to spread and to become puffy. After 10 months' treatment, the employee requested the nurse to send him to the doctor, where a laboratory examination showed a malignant growth that was removed by surgery. The nurse and her employer were both held liable in damages. In her progressive assessment of the worker's wound, the nurse erred in not referring the patient to the doctor at a much earlier date since any sore that does not heal is one of the seven danger signals of cancer. As the court said:

> A nurse in order to administer first aid properly and effectively must make a sufficient diagnosis to enable her to apply the appropriate remedy. Usually she receives some history of the patient's accident or illness from the patient, inspects a wound, and bases her choice of treatment on the deductions thus made. She has been trained but to a lesser degree than a physician, in the recognition of symptoms of diseases and injuries. She should be able to diagnose. . .sufficiently to know whether it is a condition within her authority to treat as a first aid case or whether it bears danger signs that should warn her to send the patient to a physician.[8]

Where the diagnosis is uncertain or the employee is not responding to treatment as expected, the nurse should make appropriate referrals.

Since most occupational health nurses work pursuant to standing orders or protocols, the latter are of concern to the nurses. All standing orders or protocols should be dated and signed by a physician and kept up-to-date. The occupational health nurses make a nursing diagnosis, but they cannot make a medical diagnosis. Their interventions are based on protocols. These protocols should be developed by the nurse and physician working together. If a nurse practices without a protocol, she would be liable for practicing medicine without a license.[9] The occupational health nurse should note that the physician cannot delegate duties to her that are not authorized by the state nurse practice act or are beyond her education and experience. As the scope of nursing practice expands, there are a number of gray areas as to what is nursing and what is medicine. Nurses must remember, too, that theory concerning a nurse's new responsibilities develops considerably faster than its acceptance into everyday nursing practice.

Negligence has been defined as the omission to do something that a reasonable person, guided by those considerations that ordinarily regulate human affairs, would do, or as doing something that a reasonable and prudent person would not do.[10] Every nurse is responsible for his or her own omissions that occur within the scope of his or her employment. Through the doctrine of *respondeat superior*, this responsibility may also apply to the employer.[11] At law, an employer is one who has the right to control what the employee does, whether or not he exercises this right of control. If the nurse is subject to the control of another merely as to the result of the work, and not the means by which the result is reached, he or she may be an independent contractor.[12] The occupational health nurse should know the different types of employment and, specifically, how he or she is employed.

Occupational health nurses should be familiar with Workmen's Compensation Laws, which, with some exceptions, provide for a fixed schedule of benefits and medical benefits to employees or their dependents in case of industrial accidents or disease.[13, 14] "Workmen" has the same meaning as "employees." Hence, nurses are interested in determining whether they qualify under such legislation. First, they have to know whether they are employees and whether their employers come within the coverage of the compensation law. The Workmen's Compensation Laws do away with the requirement of proof that the employer was negligent or that the employee was free from contributory negligence. Usually, when an injury or illness of an employee, which occurs within the scope of employment, is covered by a workmen's compensation law, the statutory compensation is the only remedy. Only in a few states (Alabama, Arizona, Minnesota, Nebraska, Rhode Island, South Dakota, Vermont and Wisconsin), and under the Federal Employees Compensation Act, is the employer immune.[15]

As Brown states, all information about a person's state of health should be considered confidential and it should not be revealed to an employer without the employee's permission.[16] In *Horne* v. *Patton*,[17] the Supreme Court of Alabama held that there was a confidential relationship between the doctor and his patient that imposed a duty upon the doctor not to disclose information concerning his patient obtained in the course of treatment, that the physician's release of the information to the patient's employer constituted an invasion of the patient's privacy and that by entering into the patient-physician relationship the physician implicitly contracted to keep confidential all personal information given him by the patient. In general, the complaint charged that the doctor wrongfully disclosed to the patient's employer that the patient suffered from a longstanding nervous condition with feelings of anxiety and insecurity and that the proximate result of the release of the information was the patient's dismissal from his employment. In reversing a lower court's decision to dismiss the charges, the court ruled that a physician had a general duty not to disclose confidential patient information, which was an invasion of his privacy, and that the physician may be liable in damages to the patient for breach of an implied contract if unauthorized disclosure of such information is made. Although the nurse-patient relationship is different from the physician-patient relationship, nurses have a similar duty to respect the employee's privacy and risk being sued when confidential information is released without the employee's consent.[18]

In *Betesh* v. *United States*,[19] the widow-executrix and parents of a decedent brought a medical malpractice action against the United States under the Maryland survival statute and the Maryland wrongful death statute. Government doctors found an abnormality in a chest x-ray taken as part of the decedent's pre-induction physical, but failed to notify the examinee of the abnormality until they called him for re-examination some six months later. During that time, the examinee reasonably believed that his rejection from induction was due to a knee problem. The six months' delay in notifying the examinee resulted in a tumor progressing from a highly curable stage to a terminal state, and the district court held that the United States was liable for the examinee's death. It held that there was breach of a government regulation requiring such examining physicians to notify rejected examinees who need medical attention to seek advice from a doctor and a breach of common law duties under Maryland laws. The wife was entitled to damages of $25,000 under the wrongful death statute. She was also entitled as executrix to $75,000 damages under the survival statute. Whether there is a physician-patient or nurse-patient relationship, whoever provides health care has a "duty to act carefully."

In *Coffee* v. *McDonnell-Douglas Corporation*,[20] the Supreme Court of California affirmed a judgment for a pilot who brought an action for damages resulting from failure to discover disease in the course of a pre-employment physical examination where the plaintiff was examined by the defendant employer to determine the plaintiff's physical fitness to serve as a pilot. The employer decided it was essential to analyze a blood sample, but the blood test report indicating an inflammatory condition was never seen by the defendant's medical employees because of corporate procedure allowing the report to be filed without evaluation. The Supreme Court of California affirmed that a jury could find that failure to discover the inflammatory condition was a consequence of the employer's own negligence. The pilot collapsed after a long flight some months later and was found to have multiple myeloma, which required extensive treatment. The employer generally owes no duty to prospective employees to ascertain whether they are physically fit for the job they seek, but where he assumes such duty, he is liable if he performs it negligently.

Occupational health nurses, in addition to the institution's policies and procedures, must use standing orders and written protocols for care of employees that involves medical treatment based on nursing diagnoses. Nurses must work within the limits of the state's nurse practice act as well as their own education and experience. OSHA (Occupational Health and Safety Act) regulations and workmen's compensation regulations govern occupational health programs, and the nurse must be familiar with the same. Since the work of the occupational health nurse is a rapidly expanding area, he or she must (as is true of all nurses) keep his or her education up-to-date. It is desirable for such nurse to carry his or her own professional liability insurance even though most occupational health nurses are employees.[21]

References

1. *Rose Marie Meierer v. E. I. du Pont de Nemours & Co.*, Civil Action No. 82-2050-B (U.S. Dist. Ct., Charleston Div. S.C., 1984). Trail complaint, brief and verdict courtesy of A.D. Toporek, Esq.
2. RN Fired for Reporting Hazards Wins 1 Million in Damage Suit, *American Nurse*, 16:16, Sept. 1984.
3. Prosser, W.: *Handbook of the Law of Torts*, 4th ed. St. Paul, West Publishing Co., 1971, Sec. 151–161.
4. Brown, M. L.: *Occupational Health Nursing*. New York, Springer Publishing Co., 1981, p. 28.
5. *Ibid.*, p. 27.
6. *Ibid.*, p. 71 ff.
7. *Cooper v. National Motor Bearing Co., Inc.*, 288 P. 2d 581 (Cal. Dist. Ct. App. 1955).
8. *Ibid.*, p. 587.
9. Bruce, J. A., and Snyder, M. E.: The Right and Responsibility to Diagnose, *American Journal of Nursing*, 82:645, April, 1982.
10. Creighton, H.: *Law Every Nurse Should Know*, 4th ed. Philadelphia, W.B. Saunders Co., 1981, p. 154.
11. *Op. cit.* note 3, sec. 458.
12. *Op. cit.*, note 10, p. 78.
13. *Ibid.*, p. 76.
14. Larson, A.: *Workmen's Compensation for Occupational Injuries and Death*. New York, Matthew Bender & Co., 1983, Sec. 100 and 72.
15. *Ibid.*, Sec. 72.10, 72.21.
16. *Op. cit.*, note 4, p. 83.
17. *Horne v. Patton*, 287 So. 2d 824, 825, 826, 830, 832 (S. Ct. Ala. 1973); rehearing denied, 1974.
18. *Op. cit.*, note 4, p. 82.
19. *Betesh v. United States*, 400 F. Supp. 238 (U.S. D.C. 1974).
20. *Coffee v. McDonnell-Douglas Corp.*, 105 Cal Rptr. 358, 503 P. 2d 1366 (S. Ct. Cal. 1972).
21. Bowyer, E. A.: *See also* The Liability of the Occupational Nurse, *Law, Med. & Health Care*, 14:224–226, 238, Oct. 1983; Bruce, J. A., and Snyder, M. E.: The Right and Responsibility to Diagnose, *American Journal of Nursing*, 82:645–6, April 1982; Cushing, M.: The Occupational Nurse's Liability, *American Journal of Nursing*, 81:2207–2208, Dec. 1981; Manicini, M.: The Law and the Occupational Health Nurse, *American Journal of Nursing*, 79:1628–1630, Sept. 1979.

CASE INDEX

SUBJECT INDEX

325